October 1973
New Haven, Conn.

COMPARATIVE METHODS IN SOCIOLOGY
ESSAYS ON TRENDS AND APPLICATIONS

CONTRIBUTORS

David E. Apter
Heinz Professor of Comparative Political and Social Development, Yale University

Susan Bettelheim Garfin
Assistant Professor of Sociology, Sonoma State College

Talcott Parsons
Professor of Sociology, Harvard University

Guenther Roth
Professor of Sociology, University of Washington

Neil J. Smelser
Professor of Sociology, University of California, Berkeley

Robert H. Somers
Research Sociologist, Institute for Research in Social Behavior and
Wright Institute, Berkeley, California

Guy E. Swanson
Professor of Sociology, University of California, Berkeley

Ivan Vallier
Professor of Sociology, University of California, Santa Cruz

Sidney Verba
Professor of Political Science, University of Chicago

R. Stephen Warner
Lecturer in Sociology, Yale University

Morris Zelditch, Jr.
Professor of Sociology, Stanford University

COMPARATIVE METHODS IN SOCIOLOGY

ESSAYS ON TRENDS AND APPLICATIONS

EDITED BY

IVAN VALLIER

Published under the auspices of the
Institute of International Studies,
University of California (Berkeley)

UNIVERSITY OF CALIFORNIA PRESS

BERKELEY, LOS ANGELES, LONDON

1971

UNIVERSITY OF CALIFORNIA PRESS
BERKELEY AND LOS ANGELES, CALIFORNIA
UNIVERSITY OF CALIFORNIA PRESS, LTD.
LONDON, ENGLAND
COPYRIGHT © 1971
BY THE REGENTS OF THE UNIVERSITY OF CALIFORNIA
ISBN 0-520-01743-9
LCCC NO. 76-121194
PRINTED IN THE UNITED STATES OF AMERICA
DESIGNED BY DAVE COMSTOCK

PREFACE

The essays in this volume are intended to help social scientists do better comparative research and thereby to improve our possibilities for creating more satisfactory explanations or theories. These broad aims are advanced throughout the book in several ways: (1) by an identification and assessment of the methodological strategies of exceptionally important comparativists, past and present; (2) by an explication and refinement of logics of procedure that are central to many types of comparative research; (3) by a presentation of new research models that link or bridge heretofore separate lines of comparative inquiry; and (4) by the definition of methodological criteria by which theories and conceptual frameworks can be more fruitfully related to and qualified by comparative studies. Specific problems such as comparability, causal inference, conceptualization, measurement, and sampling are addressed in various sections of particular essays.

Unlike many volumes of a collaborative nature, this one did not spring full-blown from a special conference or research seminar, but has grown incrementally from the interests of individual authors working within their own fields of study. Each author was asked to focus on methodological issues or problems that he considered important for comparative research. Some authors have chosen to concentrate attention on particular men and their works. Others follow a general format by examining problems that cut across many lines of thought and investigation. There are also essays that give primary attention to issues that have emerged on the interfaces between established approaches. For these reasons the aggregate intellectual configuration is more like a group of independent outcroppings in a geological series than a single, ten-story building. We have emphasized methodologies rather than a method, strategies rather than a strategy, and procedural alternatives rather than single solutions.

My job as editor has been lightened considerably by both the cooperation of the authors and by the contributions of members of the Research Scholars group at Berkeley who read the essays as they came in and made valuable suggestions for their improvement. My thanks go to Robert N. Bellah, William H. Geoghagen, Charles Y. Glock, Ernst B. Haas, Eugene A. Hammel, Martin E. Malia, Nelson W. Polsby, Thomas C. Smith, Arthur

L. Stinchcombe, and Frederic E. Wakeman, Jr. Two other members of this group have been especially helpful to me: David E. Apter and Neil J. Smelser. They helped to work out the original plans for the volume and assisted me in convincing prospective authors that the enterprise was worthwhile. As Chairman of the Research Scholars group, Smelser organized the sessions that were given to editorial discussions and frequently helped me distill those discussions into meaningful reports to the authors. For seeing some of the manuscripts through several typings and for the final preparation of all of them, I very much appreciate the contributions of Cleo Stoker and Bojana Ristich.

Ivan Vallier

Santa Cruz, California

CONTENTS

INTRODUCTION

COMPARATIVE STUDIES: A REVIEW WITH SOME PROJECTIONS

DAVID E. APTER

It is a bit out of the ordinary to write a critical introduction. I intend to do so in this case because in its range of concerns, the present volume represents a summing up or review of several main themes which scholars interested in comparative analysis have considered both important and intellectually attractive. Precisely because it includes so much it will perhaps be of interest to consider what has been left out, for it is in a new round of studies that present lacunae will disappear and new concerns move to the center of the analytical stage.

To look beyond the essays is worthwhile too because these speak for themselves extraordinarily well. To review their specific contributions would be a gratuitous exercise. Nevertheless, there may be some virtue in discussing some of the issues raised in them not only in the light of recent developments in the field of comparative analysis but in a more "projective" manner. This, in turn, will require us to comment briefly about the wider character of the "field," if that is truly what it is.

Before doing so, and as an aside, we want to remark on the curious quality of the word "comparison." To have substance, its emphasis must first of all be a methodological one. But as surely as there is no one comparative method or even a good set of rules to which we can all subscribe, such an emphasis is insufficient. Theoretical models and general scientific paradigms must also be considered for their influences on comparative research. Nor is it a matter of one theory, or of one scientific logic. The contemporary situation, after all, is one distinguished by methodological pluralism, with many open-minded initiatives and a corresponding diversity of priorities concerning research goals and techniques of analysis. But this state of affairs is not an end in itself. Pluralism is good but it does leave us with some peculiar questions. To what extent is open-endedness a snare for the unsuspecting? Hints rather than answers are provided by these essays. I would like to discuss this matter more directly.

Perhaps a most useful (and astringent) evaluation of the state of the arts in comparative studies generally is one recently ascribed to the field of comparative politics:

> Methodologically speaking, comparative politics knows much of the best and some of the worst of it. We emphasize the former for a straightforward reason. Despite the continuing dominance of inelegant research and of even less sophisticated writing, the field of comparative politics has experienced important advances toward the construction of broad-gauged empirical models. Foremost among the signposts of a better research tomorrow are: (1) a recognition of the often-dominant significance of "informal" political processes; (2) a blending of institutional studies with functional approaches; (3) more systematic utilization of existing historical studies, particularly by conceptually relating discrete case studies through the drawing of analogies at higher levels of generalization; (4) identification of political concepts with significance in all political systems; (5) more vigorous concern with the process of change, as opposed to purely static description; and (6) great and growing interest in quantification and/or mathematization designed to facilitate the comparability of comparative studies.[1]

Remove the word political in the above quotation and it will apply perfectly to the field of comparative analysis. A glance at the comparative studies bibliography in this volume provides a good illustration of that. Moreover, the growing interest in quantification, including the use of what Duverger has called "qualitative mathematics," has pushed aside earlier functional and behavioral models. Substantive theories about motivation, learning, perception, and other "personality" matters are almost as old hat as is the search for latter-day equivalents of the Protestant ethic.

All this can be put into better perspective by examining some of the methodological and theoretical issues that were most salient among comparativists during the recent past. The first of these was how best to treat many different types of empirical units or societies within a single set of analytical categories in order to obtain categorical universals, perhaps the central analytical contribution of functional anthropologists in the 1930's (and Aberle, Levy, and their associates in the 1940's and 1950's). The language of functionalism, crude though it was, had as a broad aim the location of universal categories of human (social) purpose which in the hands of a Radcliffe-Brown or a Malinowski could reveal the meaning of unique empirical practices.

If the first methodological problem of comparative analysis was how

---

1. See Robert T. Golembiewsky, William A. Welsh, and William J. Crotty, *A Methodological Primer for Political Scientists* (Chicago: Rand McNally, 1969), p. 229.

best to obtain such universals, the second was to determine whether these constituted a static or stable set. One kind of method was supplied by analogy or even (in the hands of a Lévi-Strauss) metaphor. In the contextual examination of kinship or the conceptual exegesis of religious beliefs, a map or "constitution" was articulated which revealed certain constant themes, control or manipulation of the universe, the relation of taboo to the formation of kinship, the relation between instrumentalism and magic, and so on, all these being extensions of organized functional activities like making a living, adjudicating disputes, and the like. These are what Geertz has elsewhere called a "template." A second was by experiments in the mind, i.e., fancying what effects the presence or absence of a kind of activity might have on the collectivity as a whole. The problem here is fundamental validity. Such experiments, in order to be useful, required a logical-deductive method in the absence of good experimental techniques.

Whatever its defects, early functionalism had the advantage of being closely related to field work, particularly of the sort entailing "participant observation" or some approximation of it. The observer used his experiences to transcend his own cultural limitations and project himself into the situations and roles of more exotic others. But research requirements in the fields of sociology and political science, where a similar concern with functionalism manifested itself, went beyond this. The methods of observation applying universals took the more systematic and theoretical "requisite analysis" form. This marks the transition from naive functionalism to its more sophisticated forms. Parsons' work, *The Structure of Social Action,* constituted the point of transition. Universals were obtained by identifying certain confluences in theory in terms of a "means-ends" schema; the abstracted contributions of Marx, Marshall, Durkheim, Weber, and others were employed as validated insights which had become fundamental knowledge. This represented a major step forward in the search for suitable deductive applications. To a large extent both the strengths and weaknesses of modern functionalism derive from precisely the originating difficulties of this procedure. First of all, consensus does not serve as a good basis for validation any more than a hunch, even when shared by the experience of others, and it is not a good basis for deductive theories. The principal inductive job still needs to be done and with more precise experimental tests. Moreover, a functional approach, useful though it might be for making insights into systematic categories, fails nevertheless to establish independent variables. The latter question alone is critical. Without independent variables there can be no theory, only a method.

Even for a method there are difficulties. At its worst, functionalism has resulted in innumerable typologies, only a few of which have been offered with some charity and in the spirit of universality. Historical sociologists like Marx and Weber provided a rich source of typological variables since they were able to discover dichotomous variables in the precarious discontinuities of real life, especially in those remaining sectors of pre-industrial as compared with industrial life in their times. It was these accumulating findings on which Parsons capitalized. As discontinuous variables and with the addition of a behavioral dimension the so-called pattern variables represented a basis for basic comparisons of whole systems, particularly around broad themes of transition from pre-industrial to industrial society. History became an important source of knowledge to be plundered for more than coincidences and periodized roles (and their relationships) for correlations. Whatever the deficiencies of method, the advantages of functionalism were clear. Using a macro-systemic approach, it became possible to examine many cases in terms of boundary-maintaining relationships, or a single case through time while employing analytically defined core functional problems. Specific problem emphases could vary widely (from the role of school superintendents to the total phenomenon of collective behavior). The range of substantive concerns is too well known for recapitulation here. Yet it is also remarkable how diverse were the interests of comparativists of the post-Parsons' generation, both methodologically and theoretically. Some like Levy and Merton pursued the methodological implications of theory around broad themes of societal transformation. Others like Bellah and Geertz worked at the intersection of culture and social systems with emphasis on the former and comparative religion as the primary concern. Moore and Smelser worked more directly on social structure using industrialization as a specific focus. More specialized functional studies included the work of Fallers on African bureaucracy, Southall on urbanization and tribal social structure, Almond and Apter on political development. All these scholars whose work connected to and derived from functional methods traced at least a part of their intellectual pedigrees from Weber, Durkheim, and other historical sociologists.

In terms of sheer output, type of studies, and range of concerns, the result was remarkable. Considering the varied treatments of process variables like development, or modernization, or industrialization, and the use of diverse units (including exotic cultures and societies) allowed by functionalism, one could argue that the cumulative effect of functionally based comparative studies on contemporary comparative theory has been immense. Yet it may come as a surprise to recall that in spite of its influence at no time has it dominated the field of comparative studies *per se*. The reasons for this have already been suggested. For one thing, despite the systemic character of functional models, these lend themselves better to broad macro-comparison in history or between empirical systems, than to detailed and close observation. The resulting methodological gap is more than the usual argument over deduction versus induction. Functional methods dealing with "macro-problems" failed to generate good deductive theories, which is one reason for their being so often referred to as "exploratory" or "conceptual" in character. Another reason why functionalism did (2) not gain wider currency was that other systemic approaches, more directly quantitative in method, underwent rapid development and asserted themselves as instruments of basic research. Consensual validation was replaced with replication and experiment, especially in the area of attitude formation, socialization, public opinion, and the like. If the functional method was a strategy for research, the application of statistical methods of inference became synonymous with research itself. The difference is more than emphasis. As we suggested it is a question of the validity of results. In the first instance validity is a matter of analogy, agreements, or disagreements. In the second, it is the definition and measurement of error.

A third reason why functionalism did not achieve dominance in competition with other approaches was that its value varied directly with the (3) size of the units, the duration of time, and the degree of discontinuity in the process. That is, the larger the empirical unit (such as "society"), the greater the time span (historical periods) and the sharper the discontinuity (pre-industrial vs. industrial), the easier it was to work with. For "smaller" units, like government, bureaucracies, kinship structures, and so on, insofar as these were not mere exhibition cages for larger societal level processes, the use of functional variables was less illuminating and less flexible (less powerful) than others. New models gained importance accordingly. Communications and cybernetics approaches, emphasizing the filtering and screening of messages and catalogued responses, allow for the exploration of alternative mechanisms of feedback. Information theory represents a solid alternative to functionalism. Others are "conflict theory" and "neo-Marxism," both of which relate specific historical phenomena in terms of independent variables based on the productive process. Barrington Moore has provided a useful alternative on the macro-level to functionalism in history. If these newer approaches run into the same problems as functionalism in terms of dangers of overgeneralization and inadequate quantification, they at least build process directly into their models and not as the result of a sequence of static or equilibrium situations.

Despite these weaknesses, as these essays show very well, functionalism has been an important bridge between older and more institutional methods of working and contemporary theoretical ideas. It made more heterodox the concerns which formerly separated various disciplines like anthropology, sociology, political science, and psychology. It served an historical intellectual function just at the time when work on exotic areas and unfamiliar peoples required the employment of universals. Now it is being pushed aside as the exploration of micro-units by means of positive techniques preoccupies scholars. No doubt a marriage between some revised form of functionalism and computer programming will be possible. The use of discontinuous variables lend themselves to that. The capacities of computers to handle variables that are discontinuous, to create causal-feedback systems, and to use qualitative data, make them indispensable. Their utilization would also allow comparison of many kinds of units and a virtual infinity of cases. So far, however, no such program has been written. In the meantime, the shift to the use of multiple regression analysis using more *ad hoc* theoretical notions, time series aggregate data, and causal modeling all have opened up quite different emphases in research. They have also required a very different training.

It is precisely to explore such issues which provides the rationale for the present volume. Both Zelditch and Vallier go into the competing criteria which form a rationale for a style or method of comparative research. Reliance on simple formulae like the method of differences or concomitant variations—Mill's famous canons—are not sufficient to make valid deductions. Vallier in particular discusses the overemphasis on macro-structures and society as the unit and points out the need for alternative emphases. If the use of "historically saturated" cases is an improvement over "mental experiments" (particularly of the requisite analysis variety), one may ask whether the empirical advantage of the first is at the expense of the abstract emphasis of the second. Nor does the one necessarily lead to the other. Smelser's analysis of Tocqueville leads after all to the derivation of a descriptive model, not an analytical one. Verba, in effect following the moving finger of descriptive emphasis, turns our attention away from the historical into the practical problems of cross-national research. His is not a concern with abstract theory but rather the effects of specific research designs and the need to improve comparability.

The difficulty is, as indicated above, that one cannot return to the general theory suggested by Parsons and others in *Towards a General Theory of Action* in order to offset the trend. As Parsons' essay in this volume reveals very well, the nature and focus of his core ideas, although far richer in content than say Easton's adaptation of general systems theory to political systems, nevertheless fail to rekindle the imagination and insight necessary for formal theorizing which at one time might have been hoped for. Quite the contrary, what Verba and Somers may touch off, better than Parsons, is a renewed search for highly formalized abstract models in which both empirical descriptiveness, organized in quantitative form, and broad organismic or functional theory, can be subsumed.

Indeed, what is suggested by this ensemble of articles is not merely a series of ideal typical shifts in comparative study, i.e., from macro to micro, from qualitative to quantitative, from historical sequences to time series, and so on, but rather what the ingredients of a general comparative theory might be. Much of the general wriggling about by social theorists is an attempt to establish a good set. The criteria are certainly sufficiently clear. What a general comparative theory ought to contain is a set of formal and logical categories in the form of statements of relationship in which the variation of any one variable leads to "regulated" alteration in the others. Such categories could be contentless (symbolic notation) and definitional. Providing them with content, however, should make regulated alteration "sociologically" predictable. This requires that behind the formal language should lie a descriptive one, the content of which needs to make both logical and empirical sense. Operationalism in this sense would mean that for each descriptive category there would be specific surrogates or indication variables, preferably quantitative in nature, capable of manipulation by statistical and other methods of data gathering. Such criteria for comparative analysis are in this sense no different from those of the pure sciences. There formal or mathematical models, translated into empirical events, are also capable of being categorized by descriptive surrogates whose indicators are programmed.

If that is a goal it is still not the whole story. Let us for a moment turn away from science in its more strict or empirical sense to its more philosophical connections. Consideration of general theory requires us to pay attention to two important questions. One is the matter of how research problems are defined. Should such definition arise out of the professional needs of research, the refinement of tests for validity, experimentation, and the like? In one sense the answer must be yes. But this can hardly be the whole purpose, goal, or interest of comparative social analyses. Today's scholars increasingly share the view that in the search for theories, general or partial, the originating source, i.e., intellectual discourse itself, which to some extent relates to "experiments in the mind" or anticipations of outcomes in moral terms, have been pushed aside. Professional emphases can serve to "kill off" genuine inquiry. In its more extreme form, preoccupation with method is napalm against the living green of intellectual discourse. It is perhaps a remarkable omission here that such matters as the relation of professional to intellectual life, assuming that there are broad differences in emphasis and discretion implied in each, have not been discussed.

A second question, related to the first, is how much new knowledge has been accumulated in comparative studies of an analytical sort? Do we have anything approaching "laws," "themes," or even durable and anticipated probabilities? The answer is not as comforting as it might be. At present we seem to be rearranging known theories and generalizations (sometimes in highly ingenious ways and with growing sophistication). The fund of new theoretical knowledge does not seem to grow very much. This does not mean to suggest that Aristotle, or Marx, or Weber said it all before and better or that, in effect, we remain their research assistants. But there is not nearly as much new under the theoretical sun as there is under the technological. That is to say that the technology of research has far outstripped the speed of theoretical innovation. This leads some to hope that method will create theory rather than the other way around, the reason being what might be called the lack of that special intellectual resonance among professionals, which can render a quick but constant interest in the moral measure of events into systematic theory. This being so, it becomes a sad irony that we will need to rely on the computer to adjudicate morality.

But rhetoric aside there is no chance of that. And this is precisely where the present volume is reassuring. What a rich harvest of specific concerns we do find discussed! A quick review indicates more than ordinary food for thought. Somers and Smelser raise the question of how to strengthen the conclusions which derive from comparisons using many variables but few cases. On the other hand, Swanson, Vallier, and Zelditch suggest research designs capable of combining structural variables, large numbers of cases, and statistical methods of inference. Swanson distinguishes some of the differences between the comparative studies of the 1920's and 1930's and the present time. Somers raises the matter of unit boundaries and what conventions should prevail if replicative studies are to be a goal and experimentation is to be added to comparison. Smelser deals with the comparison of units within a system as between systems, or cross-unit comparison. Parsons, Somers, and Smelser discuss the procedures for combining diachronic and synchronic comparisons. Verba deals with the ways in which configurational-institutional studies can be made more relevant for cross-national review. Types of comparative studies are noted and discussed in several essays. Zelditch, for example, distinguishes between "matched" and "statistical" comparisons, indicating the advantages and deficiencies of each. Somers, coming in from a quite different angle, indicates how the logic of sample survey research can be advantageously applied to historical-comparative studies of institutions. The ways in which theoretical frameworks, investigative paradigms, and comparative research are subtly connected are made explicit by Zelditch and Swanson, with the latter giving extended attention to the constraints and blocks that major theories impose on empirical studies.

Swanson raises the question of goals for comparative studies in terms of various levels, societies in general, particular types of societies, and individual cases. Zelditch asks whether comparative research generates controversies which arise from conflicting paradigms or methodological procedures. Roth concerns himself with a review of Weber's research aims and methods and their relevance for modernization studies. Rules that form the logical foundations of comparative analysis are formulated and evaluated by Zelditch; procedural problems central to measurement and comparability in cross-national surveys hold a special place in the essay by Verba. Programmatic statements on research training, the communications of research results, and designs for relating intra-societal and cross-societal variables are provided by Vallier, Somers, and Verba. Finally, Parsons deals with the most important question of all; namely, the difference between comparisons based on systems theory and those based on the strategy of "similarities and differences." This last is perhaps one way of throwing the comparative cat among the analytical pigeons. For it is in the context of these contrasting forms of research method that debates of a theoretical and methodological nature will wax and wane.

This does not nevertheless come to grips with the problem of "intellectual resonance," the lack of which is in part responsible for our present predicament. Indeed, from a sociology knowledge point of view, what some of the neo-Marxists and other groups of the new left are saying is that much of what we take for granted professionally as data, as the informational base, is precisely that given ensemble of organizations and instrumentalities by means of which known roles are formed and regulated. From bureaucracies to political parties, from families to other kinship units; from the organization of work to the organization of play the *given* institutions become the *only* institutions. They point to the need to interpret the moral consequences of activities which follow from such organizations and instrumentalities, their sinister as well as their problematical consequences, so that we might consider new ways in which they might be refashioned and reshaped. No professional scholar really addresses the question of what new sets of roles might be created and which might not merely improve upon the old ones, but create quite new patterns of relationship in society.

Is it a matter of professional modesty which makes us hesitate to pursue such concerns or something more basic? Whatever the reason, most "experiments" in roles are not an accepted part of social theorizing. Role creativity in its moral form is left to those who by rejecting the present ensemble of roles opt for different and perhaps more bizarre forms of living. Such changes in life styles represent a dramatistic rather than a thought-out challenge to the status quo. Perhaps as a result of such posturing, this is how real change, in the end, will occur, but I doubt it. (Aside from some modifications in fashions, taste, and style and to some slight extent alteration in basic values and personal options, the student confrontations, communes, various anarchist or other movements will leave little more than a deposit.) Certainly it is an open question how changes in life style will affect the deep structures of our society. But whether they do or not, does change always need to occur without benefit of thought? Any belief in rationalism would suggest that the answer is no.

In my view, along with his more usual work, a contemporary theorist needs to engage in a review of what alternate options are open in the arrangements in modern and especially industrial society. For example, if it is true, as many have charged, that the utilitarian emphasis of values characteristic of our society has lead to the emergence of the meritocracy (a system of continuous screening in which equal access validates unequal "fallout" generating an aristocracy of the mind, and in descending order, a "marginalization" of the rest) with resulting problems of self-hatred, loss of efficacy, and indeed individual powerlessness, what alternative forms of social strategy can be generated to prevent this? What forms of participation, what alternative valuations of the human predicament are required to fit together a modified social order? These are "real" and utopian questions simultaneously and they are not likely to disappear.

In short, the two questions we have raised center about the relative stagnation of social theory itself in the face of (1) the need for societal reform of a rather fundamental character; and (2) dramatic changes in the "technology" of information processing. The second point suggests two emergent possibilities. Either the social theory we have known since Marx and Weber, as adumbrated and systematized by generations of scholars (some of whom are well represented in this volume), needs to be transformed directly from its present emphasis on qualitative variables into quantitative ones, or theories of information mechanics, i.e., general systems translated into discrete variables such as cybernetic, ecological, and transactional ones (where cause and flow can be charted and correlated), will take over. To put it another way, if our present analytical theories are to survive and prosper, I suggest that they need to be pushed into two directions simultaneously, the one toward greater abstraction in the form of formalization and the other more empirical and descriptive. Formalization would allow translation into computer languages so that the "mindlessness" of the computer can be compensated for by the power of the theory programmed into it. This is very difficult to do. For such purposes not only do the formal terms of a model need to be absolutely unambiguous but the categories employed must be able to locate empirically the explicit variables which they identify. At the moment there are gaps between formal theory, the location of strategic variables, and the explicit empirical categories of data. The present substitutibility of data is a flaw because when the body of data has a transitive character it can illustrate but not prove.[2]

But with regard to our first point, i.e. the concern with theoretically planned social change and innovation, failures to project new solutions and the weakness of contemporary analytical theory are related. The problem can be restated as follows: when based simply on the manipulation of concrete data, theories take the larger universe as descriptively given. Previously understood imperfections can be demonstrated such as those arising in the relationship between types of electoral methods, or systems of representation and "democratic government." But if these previously understood "givens" are themselves subject to question, then method and theory open up a very wide arena of discourse indeed. Specifically, what if the concept of representation itself is the fundamental problem? Insofar as few contemporary theorists address themselves to such fundamental matters as ecological studies, or transactional or aggregate analysis based on given demographic and related variables, or indicator analysis in which a general proposition is suggested in the light of simple comparative indices, all take too much for granted. The main questions have been decided in advance. This is why it comes as a surprise to contempory theorists when suddenly the fundamentals are "up for grabs" in the hands of a new generation.

But we need to go further. Asking the main questions themselves will remain an empty exercise, and this is the point, unless they inform hypotheses and suggest projections about fundamentals which delineate new strategies and outcomes. It is here that the combination of formal-empirical theory using all the techniques of contemporary manipulation becomes important. This was perhaps the monumental achievement of Marx, to serve not as a folk hero for the new left but as a standard of projective general theory. Nor will the computer be a form of salvation. It is the discipline of theory which after all defines strategies for identifying what is important while theory as a discipline defines how what is important will be examined. We have been a good deal more preoccupied with the second than the first. It is time to bring them together. More formalization—that is one need.

2. The most useful introduction to these matters is Arthur L. Stinchcombe, *Constructing Social Theories* (New York: Harcourt, Brace & World, 1968). See also Gideon Sjoberg and R. Nett, *A Methodology for Social Research* (New York: Harper & Row, 1969).

More descriptive precision with formal categories—that is the second. More projective and imagined solutions—that is the third. The links between each of these need to be explicit, the results quantifiable and capable of programming, and the projections capable of intellectual resonance, or, in other terms, a more precise form of imagination.

If the points raised so far are valid ones then their implications ought to be clear. It is not only a better social science that we are after in the sense that its theories give greater predictability and therefore more control over the environment, but also a better philosophy. There is an unacknowledged obligation running through our disciplines and it refers to philosophical concerns. All the papers here (like virtually all such work) skirt philosophical issues. Indeed, one of the problems of modern political and sociological theories is that having rightly cut themselves off from past metaphysics they continue to avoid precisely those synthetic efforts necessary to create powerful analytical systems. If this is correct then one can predict that the next step will be the rediscovery—or at least the rejuvenation—of philosophical systems in the context of modern social science research. That is the effect of questioning first principles and even more is a consequence of the effort to combine formalization with empirical work.

What kind of philosophical systems? The old categories, materialism-idealism, nominalism-realism may come back, but they lack the conviction of their historical times. One possibility is a form of neo-Hegelianism in which the formal is the rational, the rational the real, and the real the empirical. Moreover such an emphasis has the added advantage of identifying purposes, if not in some ultimate unfolding sense, at least in terms of the growth of precisely that theoretical awareness which can lead to changing priorities that define improvement. If we seem to have-lost the capacity for improvement (and there are many in the social sciences today who mourn its loss) neo-Hegelianism is one possibly persuasive cry for relevance.

If these are some of the reasons favoring a neo-Hegelianism (and I use the term very loosely) there are many reasons against it, most of which are connected to the stuff of these essays. The analytical "spirit" of this book is architectural but away from any forms of political or social predestination. The neo-Hegelian ideal is a universalized tendency, the positivist one is open. A new philosophy must be thoroughly compatible with rules and uses of empirical evidence, stripped of all mysticism, historicism, and obfuscations in which projective theorizing and social change remain continuously unorthodox. One might wonder if, under such circumstances, the reference to Hegel is even useful? It is, but as a warning that insofar as the subject matter of the empirical world and the concepts and relationships it suggests are continuous, linked by experience all of which is comprehensible, then there will be a continuous desire for a philosophical integument. This brings us back to our opening comment. The precise philosophical forms will emerge in the practice of linking formalism with practice, mathematical and logical relations with events, categories and classes of events. Formal closure and philosophical openness, that is the goal. This book has) a special value in such endeavors. It marks a necessary transition from the more prolonged amateur but brilliant efforts of professional social scientists to avoid philosophy while doing science, in favor of a more complete control over matters of consciousness and perception in their larger sense. Science is after all how the mind creates ideas out of experience. And that is the fundamental question of philosophy.

These concerns and others make this volume perhaps unique in the current literature. Many of the issues raised and examined in the essays were discussed in the context of the Research Scholars' Group of the Institute of International Studies at Berkeley, whose primary concern has been with matters of theoretical and comparative analysis as these related to area and cross-national research in social sciences. The group, which I as Director of the Institute of International Studies helped organize in 1966, carried on its deliberations under the chairmanship of Professor Neil Smelser. The editor, Professor Ivan Vallier, then Associate Director of the Institute, took on the major task of organizing this volume. The group as a whole discussed various manuscripts and served as an editorial advisory body.

PART ONE
EARLY STRATEGIES OF COMPARISON

ALEXIS DE TOCQUEVILLE
AS COMPARATIVE ANALYST*

NEIL J. SMELSER

Alexis de Tocqueville (1805-1859) has been widely hailed and extensively analyzed as a perceptive and brilliant commentator on American society;[1] as a profound prophet;[2] as a theorist of mass society;[3] as an original thinker on the history and sociology of revolutions,[4] and, to a lesser extent, as a political figure involved in and around the Revolution of 1848 in France.[5] However, his work has not been extensively analyzed from the standpoint of comparative sociological analysis,[6] even though his comparative emphasis is widely appreciated. My objective in this essay is to undertake such an analysis.

More specifically, I intend to treat Tocqueville's two classic works—*Democracy in America* and *The Old Regime and the French Revolution*—as a single study in comparative sociological explanation. At first glance this may seem unjustified, because the publication of the two works was separated by more than 20 years, and because the former is primarily an attempt to describe, account for, and examine the consequences of the

---

*I owe a debt to Barclay Johnson, who read an earlier draft of this essay and pointed out a number of important ambiguities in my interpretations.

1. Alexis de Tocqueville, *Democracy in America*, vol. 1 first published in 1835, vol. 2 in 1840. All references in this essay are to the Vintage Book edition by Alfred A. Knopf and Random House, 1945.

2. Especially for his prediction of the emergence of the United States and Russia in *Democracy in America*, vol. 1, p. 452. See also his predictions of continued social stability in Great Britain, written in September, 1833, in J. P. Mayer (ed.), *Alexis de Tocqueville: Journeys to England and Ireland* (Garden City, N.Y.: Doubleday, 1968), pp. 51–59.

3. See, for example, William Kornhauser's interpretation of this aspect of Tocqueville's work in *The Politics of Mass Society* (Glencoe, Ill.: Free Press, 1959).

4. Alexis de Tocqueville, *The Old Regime and the French Revolution*, originally published in 1856. References in this essay are to the Doubleday Anchor Edition (Garden City, N.Y.: 1955), and *The Recollections of Alexis de Tocqueville*, edited and introduced by J. P. Mayer (Cleveland and New York: World Publishing Company, 1965).

5. See *The Recollections of Alexis de Tocqueville*.

6. An exception is Melvin Richter, "Comparative Political Analysis in Montesquieu and Tocqueville," *Comparative Politics*, 1 (1969): 129–160.

conditions of social equality in an entire nation, and the latter is an attempt
to account for the rise, development, and consequences of a monumental
historical event. Study of the works reveals, however, that in both of them
Tocqueville was preoccupied with a single set of intellectual issues concerning equality and inequality, freedom and despotism, and political stability and instability. Furthermore, the works constitute something of a
double-mirror; Tocqueville's analysis of the condition of America is continually informed by his diagnosis of French society, and vice versa.[7] And
finally, as I hope to demonstrate in this essay, a single perspective on social
structure and social change informs his insights about each nation and
renders the two nations comparable.

The essay will be divided into three sections. In the first I shall outline
Tocqueville's view of Western social structure—with special reference to
equality—and its historical evolution. In the second I shall outline his account of the most important causes of this evolution, his account of the
consequences of different conditions of equality, and his account of the
differences between the United States and France. And in the third section,
I shall identify his comparative strategies—the kinds of empirical data and
logical argumentation he used to buttress his case.

TOCQUEVILLE'S GENERAL PERSPECTIVE
ON SOCIETY AND CHANGE

It is possible to discern in Tocqueville's work an overriding preoccupation with a single idea, without reference to which many of his observations
or insights cannot be properly appreciated. This idea is social equality.

In considering this concept, moreover, Tocqueville tended always to
think of two extreme ways of structuring equality in society—the aristocratic, in which equality was minimized, and the democratic, in which it
was maximized. And though Tocqueville did not develop anything like a
methodology of the "ideal type," his use of the notions of aristocracy and
democracy throughout his work suggests that they are, indeed, abstract
concepts to which no empirical instance perfectly corresponds, but to
which different degrees of historical approximation may be found.

Tocqueville looked back to 11th-century France to identify one close

7. Tocqueville revealed his comparative perspective on the first page of his
"Author's Introduction" to *Democracy in America,* when he observed that the
quality that most distinguishes the United States—"the general equality of condition
among the people"—is furthest developed in that country, and is in the process of
unfolding in Europe. Later in the Introduction, he noted that "as the generating
cause of laws and manners in the two countries is the same [i.e., equality of condi-
tion], it is of immense interest for us to know what it has produced in each of them"
(*The Recollections of Alexis de Tocqueville,* vol. 1, p. 14). See also George Pierson,
Tocqueville in America (Garden City, N.Y.: Doubleday, 1959), vol. 1, pp. 53–54.

approximation to the pure case of a society organized according to aristocratic values: "the territory was divided among a small number of families, who were the owners of the soil and the rulers of the inhabitants; the right of governing descended with the family inheritance from generation to generation; force was the only means by which man could act on man; and landed property was the sole source of power." [8] While unequal from the standpoint of distribution of wealth and power, France and other societies in medieval Europe were nonetheless regulated by a web of customs and understandings that encouraged freedom and social stability and inhibited the development of despotism.

> There was a time in Europe when the laws and the consent of the people had invested princes with almost unlimited authority, but they scarcely ever availed themselves of it. I do not speak of the prerogatives of the nobility, of the authority of high courts of justice, of corporations and their chartered rights, or of provincial privileges, which served to break the blows of sovereign authority and to keep up a spirit of resistance in the nation. Independently of these political institutions, which, however opposed they might be to personal liberty, served to keep alive the love of freedom in the mind and which may be esteemed useful in this respect, the manners and opinions of the nation confined the royal authority within barriers that were not less powerful because less conspicuous. Religion, the affections of the people, the benevolence of the prince, the sense of honor, family pride, provincial prejudices, custom, and public opinion limited the power of kings and restrained their authority within an invisible circle. The constitution of nations was despotic at that time, but their customs were free. Princes had the right, but they had neither the means nor the desire of doing whatever they pleased.[9]

For an approximation to the pure case of democratic society, Tocqueville looked toward the United States of America. Writing in 1835, he saw America as the nation where the great social evolution toward equality "seems to have nearly reached its natural limits." [10] In direct contrast to the aristocratic society, its laws of inheritance call for equal partition of property, which makes for a "constant tendency [for property] to diminish and . . . in the end be completely dispersed." [11] Tocqueville commented on Americans' love of money, but added that "wealth circulates with inconceivable rapidity, and experience shows that it is rare to find two succeeding generations in the full enjoyment of it." [12]

Tocqueville argued that democratic societies are likely to become

8. *Democracy in America*, vol. 1, p. 4.
9. *Ibid.*, pp. 338–339.
10. *Ibid.*, p. 14.
11. *Ibid.*, p. 51.
12. *Ibid.*, p. 53.

despotic as men turn away from public affairs, as government becomes more centralized, and as public opinion develops into a tyranny of the majority. Yet Tocqueville found in America a number of social forces that "allow a democratic people to remain free." [13] He singled out various "accidental" factors contributing to this effect, such as the absence of hostile neighboring powers,[14] but he emphasized certain laws and customs as the most important forces. Among the laws, he identified the principle of federal union, the institutionalization of townships, and the judicial system; and among the customs he found the presence of a common religion that encourages liberty, the separation of church and state, a common language, and a high level of education.[15] Comparing the impact of laws and customs, he found the latter more decisive.[16] He also regarded the freedom of the press and the presence of voluntary political associations as important mechanisms to forestall the development of despotism.[17]

Nothing stands out more clearly in Tocqueville's work than his conviction of the inexorability of the Western historical transition from aristocracy to democracy, from inequality to equality. In 1832 he wrote that the development of the principle of equality is "a providential fact. It has all the chief characteristics of such a fact: it is universal, it is lasting, it constantly eludes all human interference, and all events as well as all men contribute to its progress." [18] Writing in 1848, he professed not to be surprised at the events of the recent revolution in France, because of his long awareness of the universality and irresistibility of the advance of the principle of equality.[19] And in 1856 he wrote that "all our contemporaries are driven on by a force that we may hope to regulate or curb, but cannot overcome, and it is a force impelling them, sometimes gently, sometimes at headlong speed, to the destruction of aristocracy." [20]

Furthermore, Tocqueville found many of the roots of despotism, tyranny, and instability in the transition between aristocracy and democracy. If any single proposition dominates Tocqueville's interpretation of the cause of the French Revolution and its excesses, it is this: France had historical origins similar to many other European—and indeed American—societies. But in the 18th-century France had experienced certain social

13. *Ibid.*, p. 342.
14. *Ibid.*, p. 299.
15. *Ibid.*, ch. XVII.
16. *Ibid.*, pp. 330–334.
17. *Ibid.*, chs. XI and XII.
18. *Ibid.*, p. 6.
19. *Ibid.*, p. ix.
20. *The Old Regime and the French Revolution*, p. xii.

changes that had *partially* destroyed aristocratic society and *partially* advanced the principle of equality. It was this unstable mixture of the two principles that made for the dissatisfaction, selfishness and self-seeking, conflict, despotism, and diminished national morale that culminated in the revolutionary convulsion late in the century.[21] One of the advantages that America possessed, moreover, was that it was able to start afresh, to establish a democracy without having to go through the pains of destroying an aristocracy. "[America] is reaping the fruits of the democratic revolution which we are undergoing, without having had the revolution itself." [22]

Two fundamental distinctions thus inform Tocqueville's comparative work. The first is the distinction between aristocracy and democracy. The second is the distinction between either of these conditions, institutionalized consistently, and the social condition built on a mixture of both. Between 18th-century France and 19th-century America the comparison then becomes one of a society that had proceeded part way along the transition from aristocratic to democratic, with one that had been born democratic, as it were, and manifested in relatively pure form the characteristics of a democratic system. With this perspective, furthermore, a number of specific comparative questions emerge: Through what historical process is aristocratic society eroded by the principles of equality? How does this contrast with the historical development of the principle of equality *de novo*? [23] What consequences for ideas and social outlook are generated by these two conditions of society? [24] What are the political consequences that follow from these ideas, particularly with respect to political revolution and the development of despotism? [25]

Having framed the basic comparative problems that guided Tocqueville's research, let us now turn to his answers.

21. *Ibid.*, pp. xiii-xiv.
22. *Democracy in America*, vol. 1, p. 14.
23. Tocqueville devoted most of Part II of *The Old Regime and the French Revolution* to the first question. He characterized this part as an effort to specify the "circumstances remote in time and of a general order which prepared the way for the great revolution" (p. 138). Most of the first volume of *Democracy in America* was devoted to the second question.
24. Tocqueville's analysis of the characteristics of the revolutionary ideology in *The Old Regime and the French Revolution* addressed itself to these questions, as do the first three books of vol. 2 of *Democracy in America*.
25. Tocqueville addressed this question in his discussion of the political impact of the French Revolution in *The Old Regime and The French Revolution*. He discussed the same set of issues in the fourth book of vol. 2 of *Democracy in America*, which is entitled, "Influence of Democratic Ideas and Feeling on Political Society."

TOCQUEVILLE'S EXPLANATION OF THE DIFFERENCES
BETWEEN FRANCE AND AMERICA

France vs. America: Equality obtained at the cost of aristocracy vs. "pure" equality. Two historical trends were especially powerful in undermining the principle of aristocracy in eighteenth-century France, according to Tocqueville: the centralization and paternalization of government and the partial advance of certain social classes in French society toward the principle of equality.

Tocqueville devoted much of the early part of his work on the *ancien régime* to describing the extensive centralization of powers in the government in Paris:

> We find a single central power located at the heart of the kingdom and controlling public administration throughout the country; a single Minister of State in charge of almost all the internal affairs of the country; in each province a single representative of government supervising every detail of the administration; no secondary administrative bodies authorized to take action on their own initiative; and, finally, "exceptional" courts for the trial of cases involving the administration or any of its officers.[26]

Why had this centralization taken place? Tocqueville notes simply that the government "merely yielded to the instinctive desire of every government to gather all the reins of power into its own hands."[27]

Far as these tendencies had proceeded, they had not gone all the way. Local assemblies still existed, but they had no real power;[28] those who had been previously in the ruling classes still possessed their ranks and titles, "but all effective authority was gradually withdrawn from them."[29] The old aristocratic order was in a state of partial eclipse.

Other groups had also experienced changes in their social condition, but unlike the aristocracy—which was being edged out of its former position of influence—they had enjoyed partial advances. The bourgeois class had improved its situation with respect to wealth, education, and style of life, but it had failed to gain access to various feudal rights.[30] The peasants owned more land than in times past and had been freed from the harshness of government and landlords, but were still subjected to certain traditional duties and taxes. And, in addition, "in an age of industrial progress they

26. *The Old Regime and the French Revolution*, p. 57.
27. *Ibid.*, p. 58.
28. *Ibid.*, p. 50.
29. *Ibid.*, p. 51.
30. *Ibid.*, pp. 80–81.

had no share in it; in a social order famed for its enlightenment they remained backward and uneducated." [31]

Why should these changes have been unsettling to all these groups? To answer this question Tocqueville invoked—though only implicitly—a version of the psychological principle that we now refer to as "relative deprivation." The social changes experienced in 18th-century France yielded a number of groups which were losing in some respects while retaining or gaining in others. For Tocqueville these inconsistencies were psychologically more unsettling than the social arrangements of aristocratic feudalism, for under that system men might have been worse off in some absolute sense, but their access to the good things in life was organized according to a consistent principle. On the basis of this kind of assumption Tocqueville argued that the various groups—noblemen, middle classes, and peasants—were more dissatisfied with the state of affairs in France than they had been in the past.

This complicated system of social inequities had the consequence of isolating these groups and setting them at odds with one another. Each group tried to clutch those privileges that it had, to gain those it did not, and to rid itself of burdens not shared by other groups. Relative deprivation appeared to foster a peculiar form of social aloofness and antagonism:

> . . . while the bourgeois and the nobleman were becoming more and more alike in many ways, the gap between them was steadily widening, and these two tendencies, far from counteracting each other, often had the opposite effect . . . the bourgeois was almost as aloof from the "common people" as the noble from the bourgeois. [32]

The central government itself welcomed this social divisiveness, since no single group could muster the strength to challenge its power. [33] The cumulative effect of all these conditions was to leave 18th-century France in a very precarious state of integration:

> . . . once the bourgeois had been completely severed from the noble, and the peasant from both alike, and when a similar differentiation had taken place within each of these three classes, with the result that each was split up into a number of small groups almost completely shut off from each other, the inevitable consequence was that, though the nation came to seem a homogenous whole, its parts no longer held together. Nothing had been left that could obstruct the central government, but, by the same token, nothing could shore it up. This is why the grandiose edifice

31. *Ibid.*, p. 133.
32. *Ibid.*, pp. 84, 89.
33. *Ibid.*, p. 106.

built up by our Kings was doomed to collapse like a card castle once disturbances arose within the social order on which it was based.[34]

By contrast, Tocqueville saw in America a multitude of factors making for a general equality of condition, and inhibiting the development of either aristocracy or centralization. Many factors inherited from the colonial tradition contributed to this: the unifying effect of a common language; the common social origins of most of the immigrants; land in plenty; an emphasis on education; and a religious tradition that nourished a spirit of liberty.[35] He identified the township as a particularly important corrective to centralization. The township was "the nucleus around which the local interests, passions, rights, and duties collected and clung. It gave scope to the activity of a real political life, thoroughly democratic and republican."[36] The township was able to resist the incursion of the states and the federal government; and it was, in fact, the generalization of the loyalty to the small township at the national level that gave American patriotism its distinctive character.[37] Interestingly, Tocqueville found a point of common origin to the French parish and the North American township—the medieval rural parish. In America, however, the parish had been "free to develop a total independence" into the township, whereas in Europe it had become "controlled at every turn by an all-powerful government." The French and American systems of local government thus "resembled each other—in so far as a dead creature can be said to resemble one that is very much alive." [38]

Out of their colonial origins the Americans had created a federal constitution, electoral and party systems, and a free press, all of which contributed to the political liberty of the people. Tocqueville repeatedly stressed that the Americans were a people dominated by uniform customs and by the sway of public opinion; but politically America contrasted with many of the European countries in that relatively little control over the lives of the people was exercised by a centralized government.

What are the implications of these conditions of equality and liberty for feelings of relative deprivation, and the relations among groups and classes in society? Tocqueville certainly saw the Americans as an ambitious, restless, and chronically dissatisfied people. And these characteristics arose from the condition of equality. When ranks are intermingled and men are forever rising or sinking in the social scale, there always exists a class of

34. *Ibid.*, pp. 136–137.
35. *Democracy in America*, vol. 1, ch. II.
36. *Ibid.*, p. 42.
37. *Ibid.*, pp. 62, 68, 170.
38. *The Old Regime and the French Revolution*, p. 48.

citizens "whose fortunes are decreasing" and a class of citizens "whose fortune is on the increase, but whose desires grow much faster than their fortunes." [39] Under conditions of equality the slightest inequalities are likely to become the object of envy.

> Among democratic nations, men easily attain a certain equality of condition, but they can never attain as much as they desire. It perpetually retires from before them, yet without hiding itself from their sight, and in retiring draws them on. At every moment they think they are about to grasp it; it escapes at every moment from their hold. They are near enough to see its charms, but too far off to enjoy them; and before they have fully tasted its delights, they die.[40]

The spiritual life of a democratic nation, then, reveals a kind of haunting melancholy in the midst of abundance.

Having acknowledged this great restlessness, however, Tocqueville proceeded to argue that its consequences for social instability were not significant. And in doing so he once again appealed to his distinction between aristocracy and democracy, citing 18th-century France as the mixture of the two. In aristocracies, great inequalities prevail, but dissatisfaction is low because "the people . . . get as much accustomed to poverty as the rich to their opulence. The latter bestow no anxiety on their physical comforts because they enjoy them without an effort; the former do not think of things which they despair of obtaining, and which they hardly know enough of to desire." [41]

When ranks and privileges erode, however, and when the principle of equality begins to advance, ambition runs rampant:

> . . . the desire of acquiring the comforts of the world haunts the imagination of the poor, and the dread of losing that of the rich. Many scanty fortunes spring up; those who possess them have a sufficient share of physical gratifications to conceive a taste for these pleasures, not enough to satisfy it. They never procure them without exertion, and they never indulge in them without apprehension. They are therefore always straining to pursue or to retain gratifications so delightful, so imperfect, so fugitive.[42]

The people inherit the standards of opulence of the old society, and combine them with the ambitiousness of the new. The result is a great gulf between expectations and reality.

39. *Democracy in America*, vol. 2, pp. 51–52.
40. *Ibid.*, p. 147.
41. *Ibid.*, p. 137.
42. *Ibid.*, p. 137.

As indicated, democratic societies are also characterized by great ambition and envy. But because social differences are less extreme, because the rich were once themselves poor, because they do not hold themselves aloof from the poor, social distinctions are not so invidious. People are ambitious, but their ambitions are limited to modest expectations. "Rich men who live amid democratic nations are . . . more intent on providing for their smallest wants than for their extraordinary enjoyments . . . thus they are more apt to become enervated than debauched." [43]

Furthermore, democracies tend to individualize ambitions, and to throw men back upon themselves. Because no group is powerful enough to sway the fortunes of the nation, people "acquire the habit of always considering themselves as standing alone. . . ." [44] The principle of aristocracy, by contrast, links men into an organized system of estates. And once again, Tocqueville saw the transitional period of democratic revolution as combining both aristocratic and democratic principles. Such a revolution creates "democratic confusion," in which ambition reigns, but in which it has not yet become completely individualized. Relative deprivation is still collectivized, and as a result "implacable animosities are kindled between the different classes of society." [45] Whereas democracy encourages men to draw apart from one another, "democratic revolutions lead them to shun each other and perpetuate in a state of equality the animosities that the state of inequality created." [46] In democracies, collective action and collective conflict tend to be based less on class and more on the formation of voluntary associations, which Tocqueville interpreted as a corrective both to extreme individualism and isolation and to the tyranny of the majority that endangers democracies. [47]

France vs. America: Revolutionary ideals vs. pragmatism. Given these contrasts in social conditions, it is not surprising that Tocqueville also found great differences in national ideas and outlook between France and America. Basically he found Frenchmen more speculative and revolutionary in outlook, Americans more pragmatic and conservative. It is possible to find in Tocqueville's work three basic kinds of explanation for these differences.

(1) The condition of equality itself accounts for the differences. As we have seen, Tocqueville viewed all classes in France as having moved part

43. *Ibid.*, p. 140. Elsewhere Tocqueville noted that "among democratic nations, ambition is ardent and continual, but its aim is not habitually lofty; and life is generally spent in eagerly coveting small objects that are within reach" (*ibid.*, p. 258).

44. *Ibid.*, pp. 105–106.

45. *Ibid.*, p. 107.

46. *Ibid.*, p. 108.

47. *Ibid.*, vol. 1, ch. XII, and vol. 2, chs. V-VI.

way toward the principle of equality, and all classes were rankling under the burden of institutional inconsistencies. These circumstances go far toward explaining why a "total" revolutionary ideology developed in 18th-century France. The irregular decay of France's aristocracy had left a confused social system. All classes were experiencing inequities, but these took different forms in each class. The kind of ideology that was most likely to have widespread appeal was that which created "an imaginary ideal society in which all was simple, uniform, coherent, equitable, and rational in the full sense of the term."[48] The particularities of each class's outlook could be subsumed only under a generalized belief that reconstructed everything in society rather than tinkered with some of its parts. Frenchmen believed that everything feudal had to be destroyed, and "all [classes] were quite ready to sink their differences and to be integrated into a homogeneous whole, provided no one was given a privileged position and rose above the common level."[49] Such were some of the pressures to revolutionize and universalize ideas about man and society in 18th-century France.

In democratic America Tocqueville found a great deal of frantic activity, which took the form of "a small, distressing motion, a sort of incessant jostling of men, which annoys and disturbs the mind without exciting or elevating it."[50] Yet great revolutionary ideas were rare. Tocqueville attributed this to the existence of equality. Democratic societies have some very wealthy and some very poor men, but between these two groups stands "an innumerable multitude of men, who without being exactly either rich or poor, possess sufficient property to desire the maintenance of order, yet not enough to excite envy."[51] Revolutions are not attractive to this middle class, because revolutions invariably threaten the property system. The majority of people in the United States, being commercial, displayed little inclination for ideas that threatened to modify the laws of property. Because of these differences in equality in America and Europe, Tocqueville concluded that "in America men have the opinions and passions of democracy; in Europe we have still the passions and opinions of revolution."[52] For the same reasons, he saw the only serious possibility of revolution in America to lie in "the presence of the black race on the soil of the United States," a race which continues to experience inequities in a system dedicated to equality.[53]

48. *The Old Regime and the French Revolution*, p. 146.
49. *Ibid.*, p. 96.
50. *Democracy in America*, vol. 2, p. 44.
51. *Ibid.*, p. 266.
52. *Ibid.*, p. 270.
53. *Ibid.*, vol. 2, p. 270. Future historians, viewing the turbulences of the 1860's and the 1960's, may view this passage as yet another of Tocqueville's great prophecies.

(2) The level of political participation creates differences in political outlook. Tocqueville did perceive a penchant for generalizations among the Americans that was greater than that of the British. He also attributed this to the existence of equality in America: "He . . . who inhabits a democratic country sees around him on every hand men differing but little from one another; he cannot turn his mind to any one portion of mankind without expanding and dilating his thought till it embraces the whole."[54] Yet he found eagerness for general political ideas to be greater in France than in America, which seems paradoxical, since he viewed democracy as generally less advanced in France than in America. He explained the difference, however, not in terms of equality of condition but in terms of the level of political participation. In America, in which the institutions compel all citizens to take part in government, the "excessive taste for general theories in politics which the principle of equality suggests" is diminished.[55] In France, by contrast, social conditions "led them to conceive very general ideas on the subject of government, while their political constitution prevented them from correcting those ideas by experiment and from gradually detecting their insufficiency."[56] Because Frenchmen could not make their voices heard in any meaningful political way, they tended to be drawn to the more abstract principles generated by the philosophers.[57] In noting these differences Tocqueville was enunciating two ideas of what has become almost a sociological axiom: political exclusion and frustration generates generalized disaffection and utopian thinking, whereas political participation generates moderation and a preoccupation with particulars.

(3) The place of religion in society creates differences in political outlook. Tocqueville noted that in America religion was not only separated from politics, but itself encouraged the principles of democracy.[58] One consequence of this is that religious controversy was separated from political controversy, and the ideologies associated with each were also separated. As a result, these ideologies were more limited in their generality. In Europe, however, where the breakdown of the feudal order was incomplete, and where the church was intimately associated with the political life of the nation, "unbelievers . . . attack the Christians as their political opponents rather than as their religious adversaries."[59] This fusion of religion and politics meant that protest became both more extreme and more generalized:

54. *Ibid.*, p. 16.
55. *Ibid.*, p. 20.
56. *Ibid.*, p. 19.
57. *The Old Regime and the French Revolution*, p. 205.
58. *Democracy in America*, vol. 1, pp. 45–46; vol. 2, ch. V.
59. *Ibid.*, vol. 1, p. 325.

. . . both religious institutions and the whole system of government were thrown into the melting pot, with the result that men's minds were in a state of utter confusion; they knew neither what to hold on to, nor where to stop. Revolutionaries of a hitherto unknown breed came on the scene: men who carried audacity to the point of sheer insanity; who balked at no innovation, and, unchecked by any scruples, acted with an unprecedented ruthlessness.[60]

France vs. America: Revolution and increased centralization vs. stability and inhibited centralization. Everything so far indicates that Tocqueville viewed the institutions of France as predisposing her to great social revolutions and the institutions of America as predisposing her to a social stability combined with frenetic individual activity. However, most of the conditions described—the level of centralization of government, the level of collectivized relative deprivation, and so on—are rather indeterminate in their character, and, of themselves, they do not really explain the occurrence or lack of occurrence of a single historical event such as a revolution but, rather, increase or decrease the probabilities of the occurrence of such events.

Tocqueville was aware of the different levels of generality of the factors he used to explain the occurrence of the French Revolution. He devoted Part 2 of *The Old Regime and the French Revolution* to specifying the "circumstances remote in time and of a general order which prepared the way for the great revolution."[61] Most of the factors we have reviewed thus far fall in this category. Most of his explicit comparisons between France and America, moreover, were made at this level. But in order to gain a more precise explanation of the Revolution, Tocqueville also examined—in Part 3—the "particular, more recent events which finally determined [the revolution's] place of origin, its outbreak, and the form it took."[62] These include events such as the increasing relative deprivation of various classes in the decades before the revolution;[63] various repressive measures, such as the abolition of the *parlements* in 1771;[64] hasty and ill-conceived reforms, some of which were reversed;[65] and a variety of unjust practices against the poor.[66]

Thus a kind of general historical model of historical causation emerges —a model of general, indeterminate causes, within the scope of which more

60. *The Old Regime and the French Revolution*, p. 157.
61. *Ibid.*, p. 138.
62. *Ibid.*
63. This took various forms, such as increasing prosperity (*ibid.*, pp. 174–176), the increasing institutional uncertainty of the workers (*ibid.*, p. 193), and the increasing concern for the welfare of the poor (*ibid.*, p. 186).
64. *Ibid.*, p. 166.
65. *Ibid.*, pp. 188, 194–198.
66. *Ibid.*, pp. 190–191.

particular and determinate causes are identified. On the basis of the combination of these predisposing and precipitating conditions, Tocqueville regarded the French Revolution as "a foregone conclusion."[67] The effect of the combined factors "was cumulative and overwhelming."[68]

On the last two pages of his book on the French Revolution he had recourse to yet another explanatory factor—French national character—which made the Revolution "more drastic" than it was elsewhere:

> Ordinarily the French are the most routine-bound of men, but once they are forced out of the rut and leave their homes, they travel to the ends of the earth and engage in the most reckless ventures. Undisciplined by temperament, the Frenchman is always more ready to put up with the arbitrary rule, however harsh, of an autocrat than with a free, well-ordered government by his fellow citizens, however worthy of respect they be. . . . He is more prone to heroism than to humdrum virtue, apter for genius than for good sense, more inclined to think up grandiose schemes than to carry through great enterprises. Thus the French are at once the most brilliant and the most dangerous of all European nations, and the best qualified to become in the eyes of other peoples, an object of admiration, of hatred, of compassion, or alarm—never of indifference.[69]

This "all-or-nothing" feature of the French temperament suggests that French revolutions would tend to be more extreme than others. Add to this Tocqueville's earlier argument that the inequities among the several classes in 18th-century France made for a total onslaught on all the archaic institutions, and the inevitable conclusion unfolds: The extreme destructiveness of the French Revolution created the setting for an even more centralized government to enforce order in its wake:

> Since the object of the Revolution was not merely to change an old form of government but to abolish the entire social structure of pre-revolutionary France, it was obliged to declare war simultaneously on all established powers, to destroy all recognized prerogatives, to make short work of all traditions, and to institute new ways of living, new conventions. . . . But beneath the seemingly chaotic surface there was developing a vast, highly centralized power. . . . This new power was created by the Revolution, or rather, grew up almost automatically out of the havoc wrought by it. True, the governments it set up were less stable than any of those it overthrew; yet, paradoxically, they were infinitely more powerful.[70]

The effect of French political ideas and actions, then, was to set in motion

67. *Ibid.*, p. 203.
68. *Ibid.*, p. 211.
69. *Ibid.*, pp. 210–211.
70. *Ibid.*, pp. 8–9.

a circle of revolutionary instability and increasing centralization and despotism.

As we have seen, Tocqueville regarded the main forces of American democracy as inhibiting great revolutions and making for a generally stable social order. Yet in cases of pure democracy he saw many forces that increased the probability of despotism. In the Fourth Book of Volume II of *Democracy in America* he set out to trace the political influence of democratic ideas, and in this effort he enunciated the following principle: "That the opinions of democratic nations about government are naturally favorable to the concentration of power."[71] Since democracy minimizes the vesting of power and privileges in social groups, the possibility of strict uniformity of laws, emanating from a central source, arises.[72] Furthermore, because democracies foster individualistic sentiments, they encourage attention to private affairs, and abandonment of public business to the state.[73] Equality breeds conditions of individual independence and powerlessness, and the tendency to rely on the state to protect the individual against others.[74] In these ways democracy and centralization may become involved in a spiral of mutual reinforcement:

> [The] never dying, ever kindling hatred which sets a democratic people against the smallest privileges is peculiarly favorable to the gradual concentration of all political rights in the hands of the representative of the state alone. . . . Every central power, which follows its natural tendencies, courts and encourages the principle of equality; for equality singularly facilitates, extends, and secures the influence of a central power.[75]

Tocqueville found this spiral more pronounced in some democracies than others, and once again, he found the absence of aristocratic traditions in America to be important in diminishing the tendencies to centralization. In America, freedom was a characteristic of the people from their birth, whereas in Europe, "equality, introduced by absolute power and under the rule of kings, was already infused into the habits of nations long before freedom had entered into their thoughts."[76] When the old regime was swept away by the storm, there remained a "confused mass," which was ready to turn powers over to the central state. Thus Tocqueville invoked his explanatory principle of the transition between aristocracy and democracy once again:

71. *Democracy in America*, vol. 2, p. 306.
72. *Ibid.*, p. 307.
73. *Ibid.*, p. 310.
74. *Ibid.*, p. 311.
75. *Ibid.*, p. 312.
76. *Ibid.*, p. 315.

. . . the supreme power is always stronger, and private individuals weaker, among a democratic people that has passed through a long and arduous struggle to reach a state of equality than among a democratic community in which the citizens have been equal from the first. The example of the Americans completely demonstrates the fact. The inhabitants of the United States were never divided by any privileges; they have never known the mutual relation of master and inferior; and as they neither dread nor hate each other, they have never known the necessity of calling in the supreme power to manage their affairs. The lot of the Americans is singular: they have derived from the aristocracy of England the notion of private rights and the taste for local freedom; and they have been able to retain both because they have had no aristocracy to combat.[77]

TOCQUEVILLE'S COMPARATIVE METHODS

Thus far I have been concerned mainly with the *substance* of Tocqueville's comparisons between France and America—the general perspective that informed these comparisons, the specific explanatory problems he posed, and his explanatory account of the contrasting histories of the two nations. Now we turn to the *methods* by which he attempted to demonstrate his case. What kind of comparative arguments did he use? To what kinds of comparative data did he refer? What, in short, were his comparative strategies?

In approaching Tocqueville's methods, it must be remembered that his national comparisons and contrasts were made in the context of a partially formulated "model" of the complex interaction of historical forces. I have attempted to outline the guiding assumptions and the central propositions of this "model" in the foregoing pages. To facilitate the discussion of Tocqueville's comparisons, I have represented schematically, in Figure 1, some of the "circumstances remote in time and of a general order" that predisposed France to revolutionary turmoil.

Several comments on Figure 1 are in order. (1) I have entered as "variables" the historical forces identified by Tocqueville in *The Old Regime and The French Revolution*. The arrows indicate causal direction, as inferred from his analysis. Factors not in parentheses refer to features of French society identified by Tocqueville as critical to his analysis, whereas factors in parentheses indicate psychological assumptions and assertions employed by him to round out his analysis. (2) The chart is only a partial and illustrative representation of Tocqueville's theory. In particular, I have

---

77. *Ibid.*, p. 316. Tocqueville cited a number of other circumstances—level of education, infrequency of wars, and strategies of the sovereign—that influence the level of centralization. His discussion implied comparisons between America and Europe, but he did not make them explicit (*ibid.*, vol. 2, pp. 316–320).

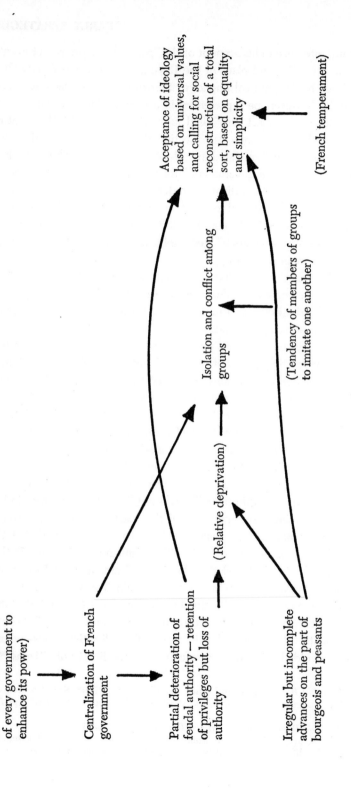

Figure 1

Tocqueville's model of "circumstances remote in time and of a general order"

omitted any reference to his account of the "particular, more recent events" that affected the time and place of the Revolution's occurrence, as well as any reference to the political impact of the revolutionary ideology. These factors could, however, be represented in a way similar to Figure 1. (3) The variables in the chart are "filled in" with reference to 18th-century France. It could be redrawn, substituting different values for the same variables as they were manifested in 19th-century America. The variable of "centralization of French government," for example, would be replaced by a variable such as "decentralization and the autonomy of the American township"; the "isolation and conflict among groups" would be less in America than in France; and so on. In addition, the American "map" would incorporate certain "accidental" geographical and historical factors that conditioned the main variables.

Given Tocqueville's guiding conceptual framework, it is not surprising that most of his comparative illustrations focused on the *differences* rather than the *similarities* between France and America (as well as other countries), because he wanted to account for the divergent historical courses taken by these two countries. In pursuing this method of difference, moreover, Tocqueville used a number of related but distinguishable strategies.

(1) *Two-nation comparisons: Different Causes Associated with Different Effects.*—Tocqueville's most common strategy was to identify two sets of different characteristics of two nations with the explicit or implicit claim that the differences on one set of characteristics (effects) are to be explained with reference to the other (causes). In discussing the causes of intensive group conflict in France, for example, Tocqueville noted that in Britain the social classes are less isolated from one another than they were in France, implying that group conflict was not likely to be so bitter in England.[78] In discussing the importance of the "partial advance" of French peasants toward proprietorship and freedom, Tocqueville noted that this process had not gone nearly so far in either England or Germany,[79] thus implying that the level of "relative deprivation" among both British and German peasants was less than in France. Or again, Tocqueville contrasted the centralization of France with the local autonomy of the United States, claiming that the former encroached on the powers and responsibilities of traditional aristocratic classes—thus increasing their dissatisfactions—whereas the latter avoided this effect by safeguarding the liberty of citizens.[80]

78. *The Old Regime and the French Revolution*, pp. 97–98. See also his comments on the "openness" of the British aristocracy in *Journeys to England and Ireland*.

79. *The Old Regime and the French Revolution*, pp. 24–25.

80. Above, pp. 31–32. In a footnote in *Democracy in America*, Tocqueville made explicit the different impact of the two systems of administration: "when I see

By dozens of such contrasts Tocqueville sought to strengthen each of the causal links in his complicated explanatory account. The common element in all these illustrations is that Tocqueville was asserting that different outcomes in two nations (e.g., revolutionary turmoil vs. relative political stability) can be traced to a variety of historical causes. Furthermore the fact that nations differing with respect to the outcomes also differ with respect to the causes lends greater plausibility to his case than the example of one nation alone.

(2) *Within-nation Comparisons: Different Causes Associated with Different Effects.*—To further bolster his causal arguments, Tocqueville attempted to replicate between-nation differences by showing that the same relations obtained within nations. After pointing out that peasants in England and Germany had advanced less than those in France, for example, Tocqueville turned to the German situation:

> It was chiefly along the Rhine that at the close of the eighteenth-century German farmers owned the land they worked and enjoyed almost as much freedom as the French small proprietor; and it was there, too, that the revolutionary zeal of the French found its earliest adepts and took most permanent effect. On the other hand, the parts of Germany which held out longest against the current of new ideas were those where the peasants did not as yet enjoy such privileges. . . .[81]

Within-Germany comparison thus yielded the same results as the France-Germany comparison. Noting that the general increase in prosperity in the second half of the 18th-century aggravated the French social situation, Tocqueville observed that "it was precisely in those parts of France where there had been most improvement that popular discontent ran highest."[82] And on a number of occasions he pointed to the internal differences within the United States—particularly between New England and the South—to show that variations in the equality of social conditions produced different results.[83]

The logic of within-unit contrasts is identical to that of between-unit contrasts: to associate different effects with different causes. The objective of the within-unit comparisons, moreover, is to lend greater plausibility to

---

the communes of France, with their excellent system of accounts, plunged into the grossest ignorance of their true interests, and abandoned to so incorrigible an apathy that they seem to vegetate rather than to live; when, on the other hand, I observe the activity, the information, and the spirit of enterprise in those American townships whose budgets are neither methodical nor uniform, I see that society is always at work" vol. 1, p. 95.

81. *The Old Regime and the French Revolution*, p. 25.
82. *Ibid.*, p. 176.
83. *Democracy in America*, vol. 1, pp. 211, 343 ff.

the causal assertion by observing the association in which it is presumably manifested in several different kinds of social units.[84]

(3) *Within-unit Comparisons Over Time: Different Causes Associated with Different Effects.*—Tocqueville employed still another minor refinement on the method of difference. Arguing that the burst of prosperity just before the French Revolution was of great importance in precipitating the turbulence, he noted that "a study of comparative statistics makes it clear that in none of the decades immediately following the Revolution did our national prosperity make such rapid forward strides as in the two preceding it.[85] In another passage he contrasted the severity of the 1789 revolution with the mildness of subsequent revolutions by pointing to the greater stability of the administrative system in the first half of the 19th-century.[86] Once again, the logic of contrast is the same as in the previous two illustrations; the difference is that time, rather than national unit or region, is the basis of variation.

(4) *Addition of a Third, Varying Case to Bolster a Two-nation Comparison.*—Most of Tocqueville's national analysis involved two-nation references that highlighted differences relevant to his causal framework. On occasion, however, he supplemented this basic strategy by developing a contrast among three cases. I have already illustrated this strategy on a general level: both "pure" democracies and "pure" aristocracies differ from the transitional mixture of the two principles. The two extremes stand on opposite sides of the mixture.[87] Let me now turn to a more specific illustration. In the third book of the second volume of *Democracy in America*, Tocqueville set out to trace the influence of equality on manners and customs. Among the objects of his attention were the relations between masters and servants. He began by noting that these relations were most distant in England, least distant in France, with America occupying a middle position.[88] On first reading, this assertion struck me as anomalous, since in many respects Tocqueville regarded Britain as most aristocratic of the three, America as most democratic, and France as intermediate. He accounted for the differences, however, by relating them not only to the degree of equality in general, but also to the now-familiar fact that aristocracy was in the process of breaking down in France. In England both masters and servants still constituted "small communities in the heart of the nation, and certain

84. For a brief elaboration on the importance of within-unit comparisons, cf. Neil J. Smelser, *Essays in Sociological Explanation* (Englewood Cliffs, N.J.: Prentice-Hall, 1968), pp. 72–73.
85. *The Old Regime and the French Revolution*, p. 174.
86. *Ibid.*, pp. 202–203.
87. Above, pp. 22–23.
88. Vol. 2, p. 187.

permanent notions of right and wrong are ultimately established among them." As a result, masters and servants agreed on the nature of "fame, virtue, honesty, and honor," and servants maintained themselves in a position of "servile honor."[89] In America, by contrast, the relations between masters and servants were organized in a way which made the two classes only temporarily unequal. The servant was willing to assume a subordinate role, because he knew it is organized on a contractually reciprocal and functionally specific basis.[90] England and America differed, then, on the kind of rules on which the master-servant relationship was legitimized.

In France, however, it was a matter of the breakdown of aristocratic rules by the partial intrusion of democracy. In such "sad and troubled times," Tocqueville saw

> . . . a confused and imperfect phantom of equality [haunting] the minds of servants; they do not at once perceive whether the equality to which they are entitled is to be found within or without the pale of domestic service, and they rebel in their hearts against a subordination to which they have subjected themselves and from which they derive actual profit. They consent to serve and they blush to obey; they like the advantages of service, but not the master; or, rather, they are not sure that they ought not themselves to be masters, and they are inclined to consider him who orders them as an unjust usurper of their own rights.[91]

Given the nature of the contrast Tocqueville was attempting to make—between two "pure" types and one mixed type—the selection of one comparative case to represent each type strengthened his argument more than any two-way comparison might have done.

(5) *Identification of Common Characteristics of Different Nations to Strengthen a Preferred Explanation.*—One of the consequences of democracy, Tocqueville argued, was to make the daily intercourse between people relatively simple and easy. To bolster this argument he cited the differences in the behavior of Americans and Englishmen traveling abroad. Americans are at once friends because they conceive of themselves as equal. Englishmen, however, are still and remote unless they happen to be of the same social rank. To convince his readers that differences in equality of condition were responsible for these differences in behavior, Tocqueville pointed to the fact that "Americans are connected with England by their origin, their religion, their language, and partially by their customs; they differ only in their social condition. It may therefore be inferred that the reserve of the English proceeds from the constitution of their country much more than

89. *Democracy in America,* vol. 2, p. 188.
90. *Ibid.,* pp. 191–193.
91. *Ibid.,* pp. 194–195.

from that of its inhabitants."[92] The logic of this argument complements the methods of difference: If it can be demonstrated that different outcomes (differences in daily comportment between Americans and English) are associated with similarities between the countries, this constitutes a *prima facie* case that the similarities cannot be operative as causes. Or, to put it more succinctly, a common cause cannot have different effects, and causes which vary between the two nations must be sought.

(6) *Comparative Statements with Unknown Comparative References.* —On most occasions Tocqueville was quite explicit in identifying the units which manifested the differences he wished to explain—units such as specific nations, specific regions, or specific periods in time. On occasion, however, the comparative reference was left implicit at best. The clearest illustration of this is his characterization of the importance of the French temperament as an important conditioning feature of the French revolution.[93] After describing this temperament, he concluded that "France alone could have given birth to revolution so sudden, so frantic, and so thoroughgoing, yet so full of unexpected changes of direction, of anomalies and inconsistencies."[94] In this case no other temperaments were identified, and Tocqueville left it to the reader to fill in one or more "other" temperaments that would not have caused or permitted such turbulent effects. The argument is one variant of the method of difference commonly found in Tocqueville's work, but in this instance the differing cases were not specified.

Assessment of Tocqueville's comparative strategies.—Having reviewed Tocqueville's array of comparative arguments, I turn now to what might be called a "methodological critique" of his comparative procedures. I venture this critique in a very restricted sense. I do not intend to imply that Tocqueville should have proceeded differently in executing his studies, or that he ignored important concepts or sources of data. My intention is, rather, to discuss certain problems of inference which arise in his procedures and which bear on the validity of his conclusions.

I mention only in passing one large and obvious problem connected with his studies—the qualitative and impressionistic nature of much of the data on which he based his conclusions. Tocqueville was a thorough and indefatigable scholar, who attempted to maintain maximum objectivity in his research.[95] Despite such qualities, much of the archival material available to him was necessarily limited. Furthermore, many of his comparisons

---

92. *Ibid.*, p. 180.
93. Above, p. 32.
94. *The Old Regime and the French Revolution*, p. 211.
95. In *Democracy in America* Tocqueville remarked: "This book is written to favor no particular views, and in composing it I have entertained no design of serving or attacking any party" vol. 1, p. 17.

were based on his impressions gained as a traveler, which, however penetrating, were of limited reliability.[96] As a result, appropriate qualification must be exercised in accepting his comparative observations.

Having recorded the problem of the inadequacy of his data, however, I feel it would be very tedious and not very helpful to follow it out in detail and examine each of his conclusions according to the quality of data on which it was based. Instead, I shall focus on a number of more general aspects of his comparative interpretations. I group these problems under three headings: (1) The use of indirect indicators for comparative variables. (2) The selection of comparative cases. (3) The imputation of causal relations to comparative associations.

(1) *The Use of Indirect Indicators for Important Comparative Variables.*—From time to time Tocqueville examined some of the methodological difficulties that arose in making national comparisons. At one point in *Democracy in America* he was led to inquire whether public expenditure was greater in France than in the United States. And in a remarkably detailed argument, he concluded that this could not be ascertained, both because the total wealth of neither country could be accurately known, and because the administrative and budgetary figures of the two countries were both incomplete and incomparable.[97] Furthermore, he warned that even to attempt an approximate statistical comparison would be misleading, adding wryly that "the mind is easily imposed upon by the affectation of exactitude which marks even the misstatements of statistics; and it adopts with confidence the errors which are appareled in the forms of mathematical truth."[98] Rather than adopt a direct measure, however approximate, Tocqueville turned to his impressions of how prosperous American citizens seemed, "after having paid the dues of the state," and concluded that anyone who viewed the external appearance of Americans would "undoubtedly be led to the conclusion that the American of the United States contributes a much smaller portion of his income to the state than the citizen of France."[99] Such a measure suffers not only from being impressionistic but also from the fact—acknowledged by Tocqueville—that the total wealth of the respective nations was not known. Tocqueville should perhaps not be criticized since he affirmed in principle the desirability of a direct measure. Yet the indirect measure he proposed appeared to pose all the methodolog-

96. For example, his "facts" on the differences between master-servant relations in France and England were based on an observation made by an American traveler, which Tocqueville believed confirmed his own impressions. *Democracy in America*, vol. 2, p. 187.

97. Vol. 1, pp. 228–231.

98. *Democracy in America*, vol. 1, p. 232.

99. *Ibid.*

ical problems posed by the direct measure, plus a few additional ones because it was indirect.

The example just cited is a minor one, and inconsequential, on the whole, for Tocqueville's general analysis. A more serious problem arises in connection with his reliance on what I have referred to as "relative deprivation." As we have seen, Tocqueville regarded this psychological condition as an important intervening causal factor in his explanation of social stability and instability.[100] In particular, he argued that the incongruity of the social condition of the population of 18th-century France—in which all the major classes were experiencing discrepancies between their expectations and their experiences—made for a higher level of social dissatisfaction than existed in societies that were organized on consistently aristocratic or consistently democratic principles. This dissatisfaction, moreover, generated group conflict and ultimately revolutionary overthrow in France, phenomena which were less in evidence in the other types of societies.

Most of the evidence that Tocqueville adduced to demonstrate the different levels of experienced deprivation in different societies is of two sorts: (1) data referring to the presumed social causes of the dissatisfaction —for example, that the French middle classes were advancing on some fronts and not others; and (2) data referring to the presumed social effects of the dissatisfaction—for example, group conflict, attraction to revolutionary beliefs. In most cases, that is, the evidence for deprivation is indirect; and refers either to its causes or its effects. To be sure, direct information on psychological states of groups was scarcely available in Tocqueville's day, and the indirect measures were no doubt better than none. But with respect to the explanatory force of his argument, it is clear that without direct measures of deprivation Tocqueville's argument had to rest on the two unverified psychological generalizations: that discrepancies in status privileges are the source of greater dissatisfaction than absolute deprivations with respect to these privileges; and that these dissatisfactions manifest themselves in group conflict and revolutionary activity. Only with some direct measure of deprivation could the validity of these two generalizations— which are very critical links in the chain of Tocqueville's reasoning—be established.

(2) *The Selection of Comparative Cases.*—The main comparative preoccupation in Tocqueville's work lay in the systematic exploration of the similarities and differences between the United States and France. Sometimes, however, he cited other cases to underscore a point he was arguing— England, Germany, Mexico, for example. I have already noted a number

100. Above, pp. 25, 28.

of these ancillary comparisons. In general, it is methodologically desirable to add more cases as a way of increasing the plausibility of comparative statements. Unless the investigator specifies the criteria by which additional cases are selected, however, he is likely to run two sorts of risks. First, he is likely to skip around illustratively, citing only a case or two that might support a point and ignoring other cases that might not be so clearly supportive. Second, to extract apparently similar (or different) phenomena from a variety of societies, without comparing also the socio-cultural context within which these phenomena occur, may lead to misinterpretations. As Tocqueville's work repeatedly illustrates, what appear to be surface similarities between countries often turn out to be manifestations of very opposed principles of social organization—for example, his characterization of rural parishes in France and the local townships in America.[101] By and large, moreover, Tocqueville seemed to have a keen intuitive sense for the socio-cultural context of any given social item. Nevertheless, unless the criteria by which different cases are selected are made explicit—that is, unless the respective contexts are specified—the danger of comparing phenomena which are in fact not comparable is raised.

Tocqueville's comparative references are selective in a second sense. As we have seen, all his specific comparisons must be read in connection with the elaborate causal framework that informs his work. Most of his comparative illustrations were meant to demonstrate the validity of a single causal link in this framework, usually by pointing to salient differences between two cases. But comparative data were not brought to bear equally on all the links in the framework, and, as a result, some of the causal links are not "proved"—in so far as Tocqueville's comparative method offers limited proof—by comparative reference.

In particular, Tocqueville's most extensive comparative illustrations were made with reference to the "circumstances remote in time and of a general order," that is, to the general institutional characteristics of 18th-century France and their contrasting counterparts in America. The same cannot be said of the "particular, more recent events" preceding the French revolution. In Part 3 of *The Old Regime and the French Revolution*—where he examined these events—very few comparative references to America (or to any other country, for that matter) are to be found. The reason for this is not difficult to ascertain. When general, predisposing characteristics of a nation's culture and social structure are being compared, broad classes of events can be subsumed under general comparative categories—categories such as the structuring of equality or inequality, the

101. Above, p. 26.

centralization of government, and so on. But when it comes to the comparative analysis of discrete historical events—a legislative act, a governmental decree, a strike, for example—these are most difficult to compare directly *because they derive their meaning and significance from the context established by the general, predisposing characteristics*. It would have been difficult, for example, to compare the impact of specific changes in welfare policy in late 18th-century France and England, without at the same time reading continuously back to the structural and cultural contexts which loaded these policies with meaning. Only when a common socio-cultural context can be reasonably assumed is the direct comparative analysis of specific historical events possible.[102]

(3) *The Imputation of Causal Relations on the Basis of Comparative Associations.*—Because Tocqueville was dealing with historical material, the experimental method—one of the most powerful tools for establishing causal relations—was not available to him. In addition, because the number of comparative cases (countries) was very small, his ability to prove that the causes he posited were actually operative was correspondingly restricted. The number of variables in his causal network vastly exceeded the number of societies he studied. As a result, the procedures of multivariate analysis to rule out spurious causes and to increase confidence in suspected causes could not have been used, even if these procedures had been available to him. (These limitations, incidentally, are not peculiar to Tocqueville's work. They apply to all attempts to study multi-variable systems when only a few cases are available.)[103] Even so, by his ingenious and extensive use of the method of difference, Tocqueville moved a certain distance toward ruling out certain historical factors and creating a presumption in favor of others.

A more subtle and complicated issue concerning causal imputation arises from the relations between Tocqueville's conceptual framework and his comparative empirical illustrations. As I attempted to demonstrate in the first part of this essay, Tocqueville's analysis rested on a "model" of interacting historical causes. A partial representation of this model is given in Figure 1. Furthermore, since he was utilizing a nascent theoretical system, it may be assumed that the modification of one causal relation in the system would reverberate throughout the system and affect the other causal rela-

102. Similarly, in the comparative analysis of individual persons, it is easier to compare people on the basis of various predisposing characteristics—attitudes, character, traits, defense mechanisms—than on the basis of specific acts, unless it can be assumed that a given act is general in meaning (i.e., has a common significance for all actors).

103. I have discussed this problem in more general terms elsewhere. *Essays in Sociological Explanation*, pp. 18–19 (see footnote 84).

tions. For example, if the middle classes in France had been advancing steadily on all fronts in the 18th century, and had remained tranquil, this circumstance would have affected the impact of governmental centralization, reduced the level of group conflict, diminished the appeal of revolutionary ideas, and so on; in short, it would have affected a whole range of causes. The logic of Tocqueville's "model," therefore, rests on the assumption that a whole cluster or pattern of causal links obtained, not simply a number of discrete pairs of causal links. Furthermore, any one causal link does not contribute to the explanation unless the others do at the same time. For example, the unhappiness of the French bourgeoisie would not have had the same impact on French society unless all the other causal relations in the model also held.

Such an explanatory "model" calls for a certain strategy of comparative empirical analysis. Instead of seeking for discrete *pairs* of causal connections between two different societies—which is mainly what Tocqueville did—it becomes essential to try to establish *clusters* of causal empirical relations, because only the simultaneous establishment of all the interactive causes could be said to demonstrate the workability of a model. To establish only one or two causal links would not do so, because these can be operative only in the context of the operation of the other causal links.

It might be argued that Tocqueville's study of the United States and France, considered *in toto,* does add up to something like the comparison of a whole cluster of causal links, because with respect to almost every causal link shown in Figure 1, he attempted to point out a consistent line of contrast between the two societies. With respect to his more *ad hoc* comparisons with other societies, however, his comparative strategies are more vulnerable to criticism, because he tended to contrast France (or the United States) with another society with respect to only one causal link. Even if he could have definitively established the contrast with respect to this link, however, the comparison would have been very limited in value, because all the other necessary links could not have been considered to be simultaneously established.

This line of reasoning raises a dilemma for the comparative investigator.[104] On the one hand it is theoretically realistic to conceive of historical processes as complicated networks of interacting causes. To do so, however, calls for more than establishing a number of pairs of empirical associations comparatively; it calls for a strategy of establishing a whole pattern of causal regularities. To do only the former would create a discrepancy between the logic of the "model" employed as explanatory device and the

104. I am grateful to R. Stephen Warner for making explicit this dilemma. Personal communication, November 1, 1968.

logic of comparative empirical investigation. To attempt to pursue the latter strategy, however, creates additional problems. Not only does the investigator have to investigate the operation of a large number of variables—which is difficult enough with a small number of comparative cases—but he must operate under the further constraint that these variables have to be associated in a definite causal *pattern* in order to verify the model. This further aggravates the "many variables, small *N*" problem that hinders comparative analysis in any case. The student of comparative analysis, in short, must continually attempt to strike a compromise between: (*a*) constructing complex and realistic models of the historical process which, however, cannot be verified comparatively because of the limited number of cases, and (*b*) positing simplified and comparatively verifiable causal relations, the causal significance of which, however, may differ among the societies in which they obtain.

Two rhetorical "strategies:" the elimination of apparently plausible ideas and the resolution of paradoxes.—All the strategies considered up to this point have involved the explicit or implicit comparison of different data as between two different social units, usually societies. In addition to these strategies, however, Tocqueville occasionally made his case more convincing by using a number of conceptual and stylistic devices, which I shall note in concluding this essay. These devices are not "comparative strategies" in the sense discussed above, to be sure, but are rather attempts to establish a point of view by a particular style of persuasion.

On occasion Tocqueville began an argument with a statement of what was a plausible or widely held view. Then he proceeded to assert and then demonstrate that the truth was the opposite, or at least more complex than on the surface. Consider the following: "How the chief and ultimate aim of the Revolution was not, as used to be thought, to overthrow religious and to weaken political authority in France."[105] Or, after describing the differences among master-servant relations in England, France, and America: "Such is the fact as it appears upon the surface of things; to discover the causes of that fact, it is necessary to search the matter thoroughly."[106] Or again: "A first glance at the administration of France under the old order gives the impression of a vast diversity of laws and authorities, a bewildering confusion of powers."[107] Going beyond this first glance, Tocqueville argued that, on the contrary, France had "a single central power located at the heart of the kingdom and controlling public administration throughout

---

105. *The Old Regime and the French Revolution*, p. 51.
106. *Democracy in America*, vol. 2, p. 187.
107. *The Old Regime and the French Revolution*, p. 33.

the country. . . ."[108] He then proceeded to account for this fact by one of his favorite notions: "Whenever a nation destroys its aristocracy, it almost automatically tends toward a centralization of power."[109]

Closely related to this strategy of "going behind the scenes" is Tocqueville's occasional practice of stating an apparent paradox, then resolving it by making recourse to a new way of looking at the phenomenon. In discussing the differential spread of revolutionary fervor in European countries, Tocqueville first whetted the reader's appetite with a paradox:

> At first sight it may appear surprising that the Revolution, whose primary aim . . . was to destroy every vestige of the institutions of the Middle Ages, should not have broken out in countries where those institutions had the greatest hold and bore most heavily on the people instead of those in which their yoke was relatively light.[110]

He then "resolved" this paradox by substituting a new assumption for the one that was implicit in the paradox. The new assumption was the notion of relative deprivation—that a half-decayed social system is more burdensome than a consistently organized system, even though the latter may be oppressive.

The essence of Tocqueville's method of argument is as follows: First, he identified a historical phenomenon that, given "common sense" causal assumptions, appeared to be surprising or unexpected. Then, by a gradually unfolding argument, he pointed to another set of causes that made the effect "expected" after all. In this operation he was not uncovering any new data; rather he was modifying the intervening causal link and thus "making sense" of existing data.

The arguments of "eliminating apparent causes" and "resolving paradoxes" are persuasive ones. The persuasiveness, moreover, seems to me to rest on both cognitive and emotional grounds. On the one hand, they are persuasive in that they involve the creation of new hypotheses that are more consistent with known data than other hypotheses. But there is a subtle emotional impact as well. By using these arguments Tocqueville led the reader to a world of new causes that other observers had either been unable to discern or had interpreted only superficially. Tocqueville's style often conveys the impression that he is sharing secret discoveries with the reader. He thereby capitalizes on the considerable psychological impact that is experienced when the apparently surprising and mysterious is converted into the expected and understandable.

108. *Ibid.*, p. 57.
109. *Ibid.*, p. 60.
110. *Ibid.*, p. 22.

THE METHODOLOGY OF MARX'S COMPARATIVE ANALYSIS OF MODES OF PRODUCTION *

R. STEPHEN WARNER

The contemporary scholarly community is witnessing a renaissance of interest in what are called "comparative studies" and in one of the major social theories relevant to such studies, Marxism. This paper on Marx's comparative studies combines these two interests. Our purpose is to analyze Marx's studies comparing capitalist and pre-capitalist economic formations and especially to make explicit his comparative methodology.

The task is neither idle nor facile. All over the world political leaders are pursuing or proposing policies of development in Marx's name, just as there are their adversaries whose programs declare Marx's irrelevance.[1] Moreover controversies about Marx's own theories among scholars who are Marxists or sympathetic students of Marx remain as deep as those between Marxists and anti-Marxists, and many of these controversies bear directly on problems of development: Can stages of development be "skipped"?[2] How does the history of China fit into Marx's scheme?[3] What aspects of any society are indispensable to its proper understanding? Which process—

*This paper results from research undertaken in collaboration with Professor Neil J. Smelser while the author was Research Assistant at the Institute of Industrial Relations, University of California, Berkeley. Many of the issues discussed herein were first raised in consultation by Professor Smelser, and the author gratefully acknowledges this stimulating advice. He is also grateful to Professor Reinhard Bendix for a number of helpful suggestions and criticisms and to Mrs. Janet W. Salaff for several crucial bibliographical references. Finally, he wishes to express his appreciation to the staff of the Institute of Industrial Relations and of the Social Science Division, Sonoma State College, for clerical and typing assistance.

1. E.g., Walt W. Rostow, *The Stages of Economic Growth: A Non-Communist Manifesto* (London: Cambridge University Press, 1960).

2. This is the famous problem which for so long divided the Russian radical movement.

3. See, for an analysis of this controversy, Benjamin Schwartz, "A Marxist Controversy on China," *Far Eastern Quarterly*, 13 (February 1954): 143–153.

internal development or external contact—should be more heavily stressed?[4] Is Marxian analysis relevant only to the West?

We shall here attempt to resolve some of these controversies by investigating the way in which Marx himself compared capitalist and pre-capitalist societies. In so doing, we shall draw out and codify his methodology for such cross-social comparisons. It is not our purpose here to criticize his empirical assertions, for that is beyond our competence and might also cloud the main task, which is to understand Marx's analytical method of dealing with the social world. The questions we shall deal with are the following: For what purposes did Marx engage in the study of pre-capitalist[5] societies? What kind of special interpretation did he give to them? What conceptual dimensions did he regard as important for comparing societies? How did he use these concepts? In what ways is Marx's approach to be distinguished from that of evolutionism? Finally we shall draw out a few implications for the strategy of comparative analysis today.

Two important limitations are placed on the scope of our analysis of Marx's works. First of all, we shall work with the writings of Marx himself (or those done as co-author with Engels) and therefore not with the other writings of Engels or later Marxists. It makes more sense to extract a systematic method of analysis from the work of a man than that of a movement. Moreover, the important and, in the Soviet Union today, decisive "scientific" and "dialectical materialist" spirit of Marxism beginning with the leadership of Engels is foreign to Marx's view that man and nature are fundamentally discontinuous.[6] We shall see later how Marx's theories are in essence sociological rather than materialistic. Secondly, we shall deal primarily with Marx's comparisons of capitalist with pre-capitalist societies and not with his social histories of contemporary Europe (e.g., the work on French classes). There is some question concerning the relation of these latter works to Marx's general social theory. As Aron remarks, ". . . on several points, his insight as an observer prevailed over his dogmatism as a

4. For an outstanding attempt to deal with an instance of this problem from a Marxian perspective, see E. Herbert Norman, *Japan's Emergence as a Modern State* (New York: Institute of Pacific Relations, 1940). For a brief critique of the immanence theory of history, see Otto Hintze, "Roschers politische Entwicklungstheorie," *Soziologie und Geschichte* (Göttingen: Vandenhoeck und Ruprecht, 1964), pp. 11–14, 20–40.

5. We shall use this term throughout in spite of its evolutionary implications, since the more neutral "non-capitalist" would include socialist societies as well. Marx's own expression "Formen die der kapitalischen Produktion vorhergehen."

6. See George Lichtheim, *Marxism: An Historical and Critical Study* (New York: Praeger, 1961), pp. 59–60, 237–240; Karl Korsch, *Karl Marx* (London: Chapman and Hall, 1938) pt. III, ch. IV; and Solomon F. Bloom, *The World of Nations: A Study of the National Implications in the Work of Karl Marx* (New York: Columbia University Press, 1941), p. 4.

theorist,"[7] particularly in his attention to day-to-day events of politics. He occasionally seems more concerned with demolishing bourgeois pretensions than with testing his theory. His studies in what used to be called political economy are more clearly intended to develop and support his general social theory. Thus it is with these studies that we shall deal.[8]

MARX'S INTEREST IN "PRE-CAPITALIST" SOCIETIES

Marx's studies of societies other than the modern bourgeois society that was the primary object of his attention fall roughly into three chrono-logical periods. In the first period, marked at the beginning by *The German Ideology* (1845–1846) and at the end by *The Communist Manifesto* (1847–1848), Marx drew on his liberal and classical education to rewrite European history in the light of his newly developed conception of history. In these writings Marx presents the familiar ancient–medieval–modern sequence in terms first of the advancing division of labor (*The German Ideology*) and then of class struggles (*The Communist Manifesto*).

The second period begins about 1852, after the revolutionary move-ments of 1848 had subsided. For the next six or seven years in conjunction with his studies of political economy, Marx deepened his knowledge of non-Western societies (particularly India and China) as well as of social relations in the late European feudal period. These studies were partly oc-casioned by "the imperative necessity of working for a living,"[9] since Marx was, from 1851 to 1862, European correspondent for the *New York Daily Tribune*. In that capacity he wrote about European economics and politics, British Imperial affairs in India and China, the American Civil War, and other subjects. For our purposes, the most important aspect of these studies is that Marx for the first time had to confront in depth a historical tradition outside the familiar European one. (His brief reference to tribal society in *The German Ideology* had been more a construct in the "state of nature" tradition than an exercise in historical analysis.) Hence, when once again, in 1859, he presented his scheme of economic progress, in what was perhaps one of the most influential sentences ever written, he had added a fourth

7. Raymond Aron, *Main Currents in Sociological Thought,* tr. Richard How-ard and Helen Weaver (New York: Basic Books, 1965), I: 258.

8. We reject, however, any allegation of an antinomy between history and theory. If Marx had trouble relating his theory to the events in France, then the substance of that theory and not historical theory as an enterprise comes into ques-tion.

For some detailed analyses of the works we here disregard, see Bloom, *op. cit.,* and Leonard Krieger, "Marx and Engels as Historians," *Journal of the History of Ideas,* 14 (June 1953), 381–403.

9. Marx, *A Contribution to the Critique of Political Economy* (Chicago: C. H. Kerr, 1904), p. 15. Hereafter cited as *Critique.*

epoch: the "Asiatic mode of production."[10] Although Marx published only this one sentence as an explicit summary of this second period of his studies, he had written a series of notes (*Grundrisse der Kritik der Politischen Oekonomie*), parts of which have recently become available in English as *Pre-Capitalist Economic Formations*.[11] The studies of the years 1852–1859 are the basis of what Marx (and Engels as editor) later worked into the three volumes of *Capital*.

For about a decade thereafter, Marx did little comparative research. He was preoccupied with the rewriting of *Capital*, with organizing and leading the First International, and was plagued with ill health and financial worries. But he took up a genuine comparative research interest again toward the end of the 1860's when he learned Russian in order to contribute to the current debate concerning Russia's prospects of avoiding the evils of capitalism. Little, however, was to come of these studies. Perhaps for personal reasons, certainly for political reasons, Marx was reluctant to commit himself on either side of the issue. He wrote a few letters to Russian partisans, pleading finally in a letter to Vera Zasulich in 1881 that his analysis in *Capital* had to do with Western European history, and hence implying, but only implying, that Russia might not have to undergo capitalism. Beyond that he was unwilling to go.[12]

If the *geographic focus* of Marx's studies varied from an exclusively European interest to an inclusion of non-Western societies, so also did the *purpose* of his comparative studies shift. *The German Ideology*, as Marx's first statement of theoretical history, was directed polemically at idealistic history writing. Marx warned against the tendency of German philosophy to be misled by the illusions that historical actors make up about themselves. He directed the concern of the historian toward the necessity of production and away from an exclusive concern with politics and ideology, such as the chronicling of the deeds of princes, armies, and ecclesiastics. He argued that the history of a period can only be understood by beginning with an analysis of the way in which men of that period enter into social relations with one another in order to produce their means of existence. The concern of Marx during this stage of his studies was above all to establish

10. "In broad outlines we can designate the Asiatic, the ancient, the feudal, and the modern bourgeois methods of production as so many epochs in the progress of the economic formation of society," *ibid.*, p. 13.

11. Marx, *Pre-Capitalist Economic Formations*, tr. Jack Cohen; ed. with an Introduction by E. J. Hobsbawm (New York: International Publishers, 1965). Hereafter cited as *PEF*.

12. For details, see Marx and Engels, *The Russian Menace to Europe*, P. W. Blackstock and B. F. Hoselitz, ed. (Glencoe, Ill.: Free Press, 1952), selections 18–20, and notes.

and explicate what later came to be called the "materialist conception of history."

When Marx turned to his thorough study of classical political economy, his polemical target shifted from the idealist notions of German philosophy to the smugness of Victorian economics. Whereas he had before wanted to refute idealism as a social theory, a refutation which would have been wasted on the English, he now wanted to demonstrate that bourgeois society and the principles of its economy were products of a particular historical period.[13] Thus in *Pre-Capitalist Economic Formations* and in *Capital* he addressed himself to the questions, "How has capitalism come to be?" and "What are the requisites of its development?" Insisting that the laws of bourgeois political economy are not timeless, he wanted to explain the conditions under which they hold true and, by implication, the conditions under which they could be superseded.[14]

By dividing Marx's studies in these ways, according to geographical and theoretical focus, we do not intend merely to restate the oft-heard distinction of the early, middle, and late Marx. We are not here concerned primarily with biographical questions. (However, our own view that Marx throughout his life maintained a remarkable theoretical consistency is demonstrated by our use in this paper of both the writings of 1845–1848 and of 1852–1867 as sources of a single Marxian theory.) What we do intend to say is that the immediate purpose of Marx's comparative studies shifted from a demonstration of the materialist conception of history to a specification of the historical conditions of modern bourgeois society.

THE HISTORICAL "EPOCHS" OR MODES OF PRODUCTION

When Marx writes that all history is the story of class struggles or that Asiatic, ancient, feudal, and modern societies are progressive epochs in the economic formation of society, he is interested not so much in the implications of these remarks for the theory of historical development as in their implications for the theory of any society.[15] What Marx wants to show in

13. It is often forgotten by American critics of Marx that the "materialism" of his political economy was very much that of the British theorists from whom he borrowed. Indeed, he criticized Malthus for being uncritically materialistic. What shocked the Victorian world was Marx's insistence that its days were numbered, not his materialism.

A recent symposium on Marx's economics held under the auspices of the American Economic Association (San Francisco, December 29, 1966), ignored this very heart of Marx's economic *weltanschauung*—the historical specificity of bourgeois political economy.

14. See *PEF*, pp. 86–87; also Marx, *Capital* (New York: Modern Library, n.d.), I: 833–834.

15. To what extent Marx was an "evolutionist" remains an object of controversy. We shall return to this issue below.

the first place is not how history works (that task comes later) but how society is founded. Thus in identifying, in *The German Ideology* and the *Communist Manifesto*, three historical epochs of society and in adding a fourth in the *Critique of Political Economy* he is simply saying to the educated opinion of his time that the kinds of society it recognized were all subject to his materialistic theory. Marx, then, merely borrowed the *designations* for his four "epochs"; his contribution is his *reinterpretation* of these epochs.

The basis of his reinterpretation was, of course, the materialist conception of history. Each society, said Marx, can best be characterized by the way in which its members relate to each other and to nature as they go about making a living. This "mode of production" is no mere addition of men at work here and at leisure there; it is a unity in itself:

> The way in which men produce their means of subsistence depends first of all on the nature of the actual means they find in existence and have to reproduce. This mode of production must not be considered simply as being the reproduction of the physical existence of the individuals. Rather it is a definite form of activity of these individuals, a definite form of expressing their life, a definite mode of life on their part.[16]

The system or unity which Marx calls a mode of production is basically composed of the forces of production available and the relations of production men enter into in order to make use of these forces.[17] (By this, Marx undoubtedly has in mind the differences in social relations among men occasioned by the differences between, say, a technology of subsistence agriculture and a technology of industrial factories. However, here as elsewhere in his historical-comparative writings, as distinguished from his writings in theoretical economics, Marx does not give formal definitions of his concepts. Thus one must define Marx's concepts in the light of the way he used them.) Forces of production include technology, communications, skills, population, and generally those implements and that knowledge by means of which we can keep ourselves alive. "Relations of production" is Marx's way of expressing the have vs. have-not issue, with the specification that Marx is interested in who owns the means of production (this being more basic than ownership of the means of subsistence).

So much for the theoretical statement. From it we might expect that

16. Marx and Engels, *The German Ideology* (pts. I and III), R. Pascal, ed. (New York: International Publishers, 1947), p. 7. See, however, the caveat in Marx, *Capital* (Chicago: C. H. Kerr, 1909), III: 919.

17. *German Ideology*, pp. 28, 36. See also Oscar Lange, *Political Economy, I: General Problems*, tr. A. H. Walker (New York: Macmillan, 1963), ch. II.

Marx will base his typology of societies at least in part upon the different "actual means" their members "find in existence." However, one looks in vain in Marx's comparative analyses for a sustained comparison of technologies in the different epochs. There are, Marx submits, good reasons for this lack, one of them being that technological potential cannot be measured if under the fetters of antagonistic property relations.[18] Yet whatever these reasons, the fact remains that Marx's comparative analyses deal with social relations and not with material technology. Let us proceed, then, to a consideration of the pictures Marx drew of the various "modes of production." A careful reading of the relevant works (especially *The German Ideology, The Communist Manifesto, Pre-Capitalist Economic Formations, Capital,* and the articles for the *New York Daily Tribune*) yields the following characterizations.

Asiatic.—When Marx spoke of the Asiatic mode of production he had in mind the picture of a despotic empire suspended above a mass of small, isolated, identical village communes. This of all Marx's modes of production is static, since there are no classes, no private ownership of land. The monarch, as head of the state, in effect owns the land; the village-based producers work the land and pay their surplus production to and do their forced labor for the state in such a way that rent and taxes coincide. Within the village, production is carried out communally with each taking a share of the produce of the whole; any division of labor that appears is a static one, hallowed by long tradition.[19] If the population of the village grows beyond a certain point a new village is set up exactly like the old. Hence there is no intercourse between villages. The village boundary is the horizon. (In Russian, as Marx pointed out, *mir* means both "world" and "commune".) The unity of society is secured only by the despotic state, which rested on the economic necessity to provide irrigation for the villages in the arid Asiatic climate.[20]

Marx emphasized that "the absence of private property in land" is the "key" to the Asiatic mode. There is no basis for antagonism, no individualization, within Asiatic society. The individual is the property of the community;[21] the community is constituted according to a set pattern.

18. See *Critique,* p. 271; Korsch, *op. cit.,* p. 209; Hobsbawm, "Introduction," to *PEF,* p. 13.
19. An example is the village-based Indian caste system. Marx did not regard the caste system as a class system; see *German Ideology,* p. 30. Marx's notions about the Indian village and caste system are put to the test in Lloyd I. Rudolph, "The Modernity of Tradition: The Democratic Incarnation of Caste in India," *American Political Science Review,* 59 (December 1965): 975–989.
20. However, the "Asiatic Mode" also appears in Java, the Aztec and Inca empires, and even in Russia.
21. *PEF,* p. 83.

The simplicity of the organisation for production in these self-sufficient communities that constantly reproduce themselves in the same form, and when accidentally destroyed, spring up again on the spot and with the same name—this simplicity supplies the key to the secret of the unchange-ableness in such striking contrast with the constant dissolution and re-founding of Asiatic States, and the never-ceasing changes of dynasty. The structure of the economical elements of society remains untouched by the storm-clouds of the political sky.[22]

Change occurs only when political rule accomplishes economic revolution, as was the case when British industry under the protection of the Raj under-sold the Indian village industry and thus destroyed the self-sufficiency of the village.

Ancient.—Unlike Asiatic society, the ancient city and the forms of society succeeding it in the West are dynamic societies, since the antago-nisms of private property and class relations appear within them. This fact has the consequence that the description of these forms must deal with change.

Fundamentally, the ancient city is a community of individual land-owners organized together for the purposes of protecting their holdings—land and slaves. The fundamental condition of ownership is that one must be a member of the community (a citizen) and provide tribute to it pri-marily in the form of war service. For unity against a hostile social environ-ment (alien territories and domestic slaves) is the *raison d'être* of the ancient city. This "unity," however, is not as thorough as in Asiatic society, because the community and the individual exist side by side, as is evidenced by the coexistence of individual property and public land (*ager publicus*). Yet individualization has not proceeded to the extent it does under capital-ism: "Among the ancients we discover no single enquiry as to which form of land property, etc., is the most productive, which creates maximum wealth. . . . The enquiry is always about what kind of property creates the best citizens."[23]

Yet the ancient city does not remain in that idyllic state. Originally merely a settlement of agriculturalists, it develops a division of labor of crafts. Although unsanctioned by official opinion, a few crafts and com-

22. *Capital*, I: 393–394. See also *PEF*, pp. 69–70, 83; "The British Rule in India," *in* Marx and Engels, *The First Indian War of Independence*, 1857–1859 (Moscow: Foreign Languages Publishing House, 1959), pp. 14–21; letter from Marx to Engels dated June 2, 1853, in *Basic Writings in Politics and Philosophy*, Lewis S. Feuer, ed. (Garden City, N. Y.: Doubleday Anchor, 1959), pp. 454–456; and George Lichtheim, "Marx and the 'Asiatic Mode of Production,' " *St. Anthony's Papers*, no. 14 (1963), pp. 86–112, also in Lichtheim, *The Concept of Ideology and Other Essays* (New York: Vintage Books, 1967), pp. 62–93.
23. *PEF*, p. 84.

merce develop, and landownership becomes concentrated.[24] However, because of slavery (and perhaps because of the prejudice against acquisitiveness, although Marx does not commit himself on this) these developments have "no further industrial and commercial consequences." Slavery is inimical to the development of technology and to the polarization of class relations.[25]

Feudal.—Marx does not deal adequately with the transition from ancient to feudal society. He does, however, insist that conquest is not the determining factor, since the transition to a country landed estate system had already been accomplished by the Romans.[26] Indeed his picture of feudal society as a whole excludes the military and political aspects with which we are all familiar. For Marx, the history of feudal society is the history of the changing relations of town and country.

Feudal society is based upon the self-sufficient household of the peasant or serf, who produces by means of small-scale agriculture and household crafts what he needs to subsist. His surplus labor he pays to the owner of his land either as rent in kind or labor rent. These owners—the feudal lords—together make up the state as an association, not (as in Asiatic society) as the alien owner of the land, nor (as in ancient society) as a unity. Feudal society is more individualized than previous ones.

Yet feudal society is not yet free of those "motley feudal ties" and "numberless indefeasible chartered freedoms" that capitalism was to do away with. Relationships were not yet, as we now say, "rationalized."[27] The peasant or serf, while not owner of his land nor personally free, is the possessor of his land; he is, as occupant and producer, organically tied to it. Even for the owner of the land, his property is not freely alienable. The craftsman at first is similarly hedged in (or protected) by such traditions: His home, his tools, and even his customers are passed down from father to son.[28]

24. *German Ideology*, p. 11. This is an example of Marx's frequent use of legal stipulations as sociological data.

25. *Ibid.*, p. 60. On class relations in a slave-based system, see *ibid.*, p. 11; Marx, *The Eighteenth Brumaire of Louis Bonaparte* (New York: International Publishers, n.d.), p. 8; and Marx and Engels, *The Civil War in the United States* (New York: International Publishers, 1961), pp. 68–69. On technology in a slave economy, see the statement of Marx's argument in Lange, *op.cit.*, p. 21.

26. *German Ideology*, pp. 10–11, 62–63; *Critique*, p. 288.

27. Marx and Engels, *The Communist Manifesto* (New York: International Publishers, 1948), p. 11. See also Bert F. Hoselitz, "Karl Marx on Secular and Social Development: A Study in the Sociology of Nineteenth Century Social Science," *Comparative Studies in Society and History*, 6 (January 1964): 142–163, and 151–152.

28. *German Ideology*, p. 47; *Capital*, III: 918–919; *PEF*, p. 78–79; Marx, *Letters to Dr. Kugelmann* (New York: International Publishers, 1934), pp. 98–99; and Lichtheim, "Marx and the 'Asiatic Mode of Production,'" *op. cit.*, pp. 104–105.

This country-based, idyllic society is undermined by the growth of the city or, more generally, by the division of agricultural from industrial and commercial labor and the resulting exchange between them.[29] With this exchange, too, comes the development of commerce as a separate enterprise with the resulting concentration of free mobile resources, i.e., moneyed wealth. As money becomes more important to the feudal lord for his trade, he begins to require money rent of his peasants and they, in turn, must begin to produce crops and crafts for the market. In this way the self-sufficiency of the peasant household is eroded. Thus "the Middle Ages . . . starts with the countryside as the locus of history, whose further development then proceeds through the opposition of town and country."[30]

Modern Bourgeois.—We come to the type of social organization whose economic aspect is known as capitalism. Marx's picture of bourgeois society is too well known to require and too rich to admit the kind of capsule summaries we have presented of his other types of society. However, some aspects of bourgeois society, especially where they stand in contrast to aspects of the earlier types, deserve special attention.

Unlike the "bourgeois political economist," Marx does not deal with "capital" as a factor of production in an abstract way without regard for specific social relations. Capital is a product of historical development; it appears only when means of production are *concentrated* in private hands as free *resources*. It does not typically appear in early modes of production: "The scattered means of production that serve the producers themselves as means of employment and subsistence, without expanding their own value by the incorporation of the labour of others are no more capital than a product consumed by its own producer is a commodity."[31] To Marx it is only a fetishism to presume capital to be anything other than a product of man's historical development.

As for capital, so also for free labor. Economists and economic sociologists have recently come to consider problems of "labor mobility" and "labor commitment" in developing economies. They have come to agree with Marx's insistence that one could not assume that the presence of an absolute level of population guaranteed that one had a labor market. India was heavily populated but had not the other requisites of capitalism, especially a wide-scale division of labor and a concentration in private hands of the means of production. The United States, despite heavy immigration, suffered a labor shortage because of the availability of frontier land. These

29. It is not clear, when we begin to consider the city, just where feudalism leaves off and capitalism begins. Quite obviously, they overlap, but Marx never makes clear what his pure picture of feudal society is.

30. *PEF,* p. 78; *Capital,* III: 842, 930.

31. *Capital,* I: 733.

factors also restricted the growth of a domestic market for consumer commodities.[32] Ireland *lost* population, yet capitalism became more dominant
there because the loss of population did not keep pace with the concentration of land.[33]

Therefore, what is distinctive about capitalism (as well as any other
mode of production) is not its technology or even its more general forces
of production. In comparative perspective, capitalism requires the nega-
tion of previous relations of production:[34] (1) property in land, characteristic of the feudal and ancient modes of production; (2) property in the
instruments of production, including tools and special skills, characteristic
of the craftsmen of the feudal mode; (3) property in the means of subsistence as directly appropriated by the laborer, characteristic of the feudal
serf and the "Asiatic" peasant.[35] In these two respects, then—capital and
free labor—the modern bourgeois mode of production is most crucially
distinguished, i.e., in terms of property relations.

To these distinctive social relations of modern bourgeois society must
be added two other aspects in which capitalism differs significantly from
previous modes: the division of labor and the predominance of exchange
value. Marx undoubtedly goes too far when he says that "the various stages
of development in the division of labor *are* just so many different forms of
ownership,"[36] for his analysis makes clear that the division of labor *conditions* or, perhaps in the long run, *determines* the form of ownership. The
transition from feudalism to capitalism demonstrates that the separation of
city and country, then of commerce and industry, and then of craft trade
from craft trade, *lead to* a rise of commerce, of money, and the concentration of moneyed wealth. This development breaks up the self-sufficiency
of the peasant household economy and makes possible the expropriation
from his land of the peasant, now dependent on an impersonal market and
hence on powerful merchants and usurers.[37] The changing division of labor
thus leads to changing property relations. The two concepts are conceptually independent and the analyst must characterize an epoch (as Marx does)
on both of them.

32. *Ibid.*, p. 842. See also Bloom, *op. cit.*, pp. 170–175.
33. *Capital*, I, ch. XXV, sec. 5 f.
34. This requirement presumably applies to an unspecified portion or segment of the population.
35. *PEF*, pp. 99–105.
36. *German Ideology*, p. 9, emphasis added. Robert C. Tucker is misled by
statements of this sort into identifying the two concepts; hence he misses the dynamic and progressive aspects of the division of labor; see "The Marxian Revolutionary Idea," in *Nomos VIII: Revolution*, C. J. Friedrich, ed. (New York: Atherton
Press, 1966), pp. 224–229. See also David Braybrooke's response, "Marx on Revolu-
tionizing the Mode of Production," *ibid.*, pp. 245 ff.
37. *Capital*, III, ch. XX; *German Ideology*, pp. 43–56.

The advancing division of labor also, however, leads to a new relationship to work, the production of commodities. However Marx might like to emphasize the unity of these socio-economic processes, he recognized that property relations and commodity production as consequences of the division of labor are different matters. Previous modes of production, according to Marx, had been characterized predominantly by production for direct use, either of the producer, his lord or master, or his immediate customers. However, the division of labor and exchange introduced by capitalism brings with it a new emphasis on production in the abstract, and this is true whether or not the worker is involved in a capitalist enterprise—whether or not, that is, he is a "free laborer" confronting capital concentrated in private hands:

> It is . . . clear that in any given economic formation of society, where not the exchange value but the use value of the product predominates, surplus labour will be limited by a given set of wants which may be greater or less, and that here no boundless thirst for surplus labour arises from the nature of the production itself. . . . But as soon as people, whose production still moves within the lower forms of slave-labour, corvée-labour, etc., are drawn into the whirlpool of an international market dominated by the capitalistic mode of production, the sale of their products for export becoming their principal interest, the civilized horrors of over-work are grafted on the barbaric horrors of slavery, serfdom, etc.[38]

Property relations, division of labor, commodity production—these, then, are the crucial aspects in which capitalism differs from previous formations.

Yet Marx insists that a capitalistic economic formation is not a mere congeries of such elements; it is a *system* which, once set going, has a development all its own. It was, of course, the purpose of *Capital* to "lay bare the economic law of motion of modern society."[39] (The problems this methodological approach raises for Marx are discussed below.) How capitalism comes to be such a unitary working system, however, has yet to be explained; its explanation involves the fourth aspect of our comparison, the role of the state:

> It is not enough that the conditions of labour are concentrated in a mass, in the shape of capital, at the one pole of society, while at the other are grouped the masses of men, who have nothing to sell but their labour-power. Neither is it enough that they are compelled to sell it voluntarily. The advance of capitalist production develops a working-class, which by education, tradition, habit, looks upon the conditions of that mode of pro-

38. *Capital*, I: 260.
39. *Ibid.*, p. 14.

duction as self-evident laws of nature. The organization of the capitalist process of production, once fully developed, breaks down all resistance. The constant generation of a relative surplus-population keeps the law of supply and demand of labour, and therefore keeps wages, in a rut that corresponds with the wants of capital. The dull compulsion of economic relations completes the subjection of the labourer to the capitalist. Direct force, outside economic conditions, is of course still used, but only exceptionally. *In the ordinary run of things, the labourer can be left to the "natural laws of production,"* i.e., to his dependence on capital, a dependence springing from, and guaranteed in perpetuity by, the conditions of production themselves. *It is otherwise during the historic genesis of capitalist production.* The bourgeoisie, at its rise, wants and uses the power of the state to "regulate" wages, i.e., to force them within the limits suitable for surplus-value making, to lengthen the working day and to keep the labourer himself in the normal degree of dependence. This is an essential element of the so-called primitive accumulation.[40]

In fully developed bourgeois society the state takes a subordinate role, acting only in exceptional cases. In this sense, the modern state differs from the state in previous societies, not in the sense of being the tool of one class for the oppression of others—that is true of all political power—but in the sense that economic power is differentiated from political power. In previous societies surplus labor was extracted by political force, e.g., by the feudal lord who was simultaneously landowner and holder of political authority or by the Asiatic state whose income was simultaneously rent and taxes. In bourgeois society the "natural laws of production," as bourgeois and limited as these may be, can assert themselves, under ordinary circumstances, autonomously.

Although these brief summaries of Marx's historical "epochs" necessarily omit much of the richness and charm of Marx's more complete statements,[41] they do illustrate for us the two purposes Marx pursued in his comparative studies. We have seen that Marx interpreted each type of society as a "mode" or "form" of production (i.e., in accordance with the "materialist conception of history") and that he was particularly interested in illuminating what he thought were the crucial respects in which the earlier forms differed from his own bourgeois society.[42] We shall now turn

40. *Ibid.,* p. 809, emphases added.
41. See Lichtheim, "Marx and the 'Asiatic Mode of Production,'" for a more complete appreciation. See also the cited articles by Hobsbawm and Schwartz for discussions of periodization.
42. Not that this characterization is eccentric. It differs only in minor detail from that of Max Weber, who indeed borrowed it largely from him. See *The Protestant Ethic and the Spirit of Capitalism,* tr. Talcott Parsons (New York: Scribner's, 1958), p. 22 for the decisiveness of the element of free labor; p. 53 for the dominance of exchange values; and pp. 54–55, 62, 68, 72, and 181 on the crucial

to a systematic consideration of these comparative dimensions. We shall inquire of Marx what aspects of a society he believed to be indispensable for its analysis in comparison with other societies.

COMPARATIVE DIMENSIONS

To look first at the analyses Marx actually made of pre-capitalist societies rather than at his more generalized theoretical propositions means that the concepts there emphasized may not be the ones ordinarily thought of as distinctive to Marxian theory. Though the reader familiar with Marx may not have found anything unexpected in the previous discussion, he may have missed a discussion of *classes* and of *technology*. Those discussions are simply not taken up in Marx's comparative analysis of pre-capitalist societies.[43] Marx does not live up to his implied promise of interpreting history as the progressive conflict of the *material* forces of production with the *social* relations of production. His analysis throughout is a social one as opposed to a more narrowly technological or even a mixed social-technological one. As for classes, Marx does, of course, mention classes as groups defined by differential relations to the means of production; but classes, in these analyses, do not play the historical role of revolutionary action assigned by Marx to the proletariat in bourgeois society.[44] There are no classes in Asiatic society; class action in ancient society is precluded by the three-way class structure of patricians, plebs, and slaves. The force that fundamentally revolutionizes feudal society is the division of labor (and individuals in roles conceptualized by "division of labor") rather than a self-conscious bourgeoisie. However important the French Revolution may have been as a model for Marx's programmed socialist revolution, it has little place as a model for his comparative analyses. In-

---

difference between capitalism nascent and dominant. Even the difference between Marx and Weber on the rise of capitalism has been exaggerated, due perhaps to the widespread unfamiliarity with their comparative writings and to Weber's own stereotyped image of Marx. See Hobsbawm, *op. cit.*, p. 17; Lichtheim, "Marx and the 'Asiatic Mode of Production,'" *op. cit.*, p. 106; and Karl Löwith, "Max Weber und Karl Marx," in *Gesammelte Abhandlungen: Zur Kritik der geschichtlichen Existenz* (Stuttgart: W. Kohlhammer, 1960), pp. 62–63.

43. As opposed to his studies of class relations in the various Western capitalist countries; see pp. 53–55 above and the references cited in notes 7 and 8.

44. On the tension between the definition of class and class as historical actor (klasse an sich vs. klasse für sich), see Reinhard Bendix and Seymour Martin Lipset, "Karl Marx' Theory of Social Classes," in their *Class, Status and Power* (Glencoe, Ill.: Free Press, 1953), pp. 26–35; and Ralf Dahrendorf, *Class and Class Conflict in Industrial Society* (Stanford, Calif.: Stanford University Press, 1959), ch. I. On the process by which Marx arrived at the prescription for a revolutionary role for the proletariat, see Leonard Krieger, "The Uses of Marx for History," *Political Science Quarterly*, 75 (September 1960), 355–378, and 373–374.

deed, the most mature statement of Marx's theory of history—the 1859 "Preface"—makes no mention of classes.[45]

Let us then proceed to a consideration of those comparative dimensions Marx did in fact use consistently. There are, as we shall see, four: property, division of labor, state and society, and the purpose of production. These may be found as the threads running through the characterizations we have just summarized of the various modes of production. Two of them—property and division of labor—have an explicit and prominent role in Marx's theoretical statements. The latter two he often spoke of as epiphenomenal and hence, by implication, as having no history. Yet he finds that he cannot adequately analyze different forms of society without their mention.

Property Relations.—At first glance, this seems a simple matter to deal with. A man either owns something or he does not; the bourgeois "has" and the proletarian "has not." Marx found, however, partly through his studies of non-capitalist societies, that the matter is not so simple. First of all Marx is interested in the ownership of the means of production (not, e.g., of a hoard of consumer goods), for it is his problem to understand how it comes to be that a mass of propertyless men confront *and become dependent upon* the few property owners in order to pursue a livelihood. Secondly, however, property has two important aspects, for which Marx uses various terms but most consistently, "ownership" and "possession." *Ownership* is legally recognized control over the means of production; it is the expression of the fact that in any historical society some individuals (or the state as a whole) have legal title to the surplus-product of producing individuals. *Possession*, on the other hand, is occupation by the producer of his means of production recognized as a customary right.[46] The feudal peasant or serf *possesses* his land whereas the lord *owns* it.

Capitalism is possible only when *ownership* is concentrated in private hands and when the mass of individuals are not so much propertyless as *dispossessed*.[47] It is not enough that mere moneyed wealth exists in a few hands; this is a fact of all historical societies.

Division of Labor.—"Division of labor" is mentioned by Marx in many contexts, but not all of them are important for his comparative analyses. Marx discussed the sexual division of labor as well as the detailed division

---

45. *Critique,* pp. 11–13.

46. For this distinction under various terminologies, see *PEF*, pp. 67, 72, 77, 79, 82; *Capital,* III: 699, 918–919, 926; *German Ideology,* pp. 58–59. A further distinction, the separation of ownership and management, is discussed by Marx only as an aspect of the increasing division of labor in the workshop; see *Capital,* III: 449, 459, 516–522. This phenomenon as a change in power relations is analyzed extensively by Dahrendorf, *op. cit.,* ch. II and *passim.*

47. *PEF*, pp. 99–105.

of labor, and his discussions were moralistic as much as analytical. But we are not here concerned with Marx's indictment of "that all engrossing system of specializing and sorting men, that development in man of one single faculty at the expense of all other faculties,"[48] but rather with his comparison of societies according to their *social division of labor*. Now Marx, as we have seen, uses "division of labor" to label many different phenomena: the separation of agriculture and manufacture, the separation of making and selling, and so on. The common theme that runs through these discussions, however, is the division of labor as leading to *exchange, communication*, and the introduction of new techniques, practices, and ideas. All of the historical societies discussed by Marx have a division of labor, even the primitive Indian village. What Marx is interested in for purposes of comparison, however, is not a division of labor within a family, a village, or a workship, but a *society-wide* division of labor. It is the lack of such a society-wide division of labor that is the key to the stagnation of Indian society, as we have seen above. This, too, is what distinguishes the "wide-awake factory operative of modern manufacturing Babylons" from "the bashful journeyman tailor or cabinet maker of a small country town."[49] And it explains the backwardness of the French peasant:

> Their field of production, the small holding, admits of no division of labour in its cultivation, no application of science and, therefore, no multiplicity of development, no diversity of talents, no wealth of social relationships. Each individual peasant family is almost self-sufficient; it itself directly produces the major part of its consumption and thus acquires its means of life more through exchange with nature than in intercourse with society. The small holding, the peasant and his family; alongside them another small holding, another peasant and another family. A few score of these make up a village, and a few score of villages makes up a Department. In this way, the great mass of the French nation is formed by simple addition of homologous magnitudes, much as potatoes in a sack form a sackful of potatoes.[50]

An advanced social division of labor leads to exchange, to the separation of use and exchange value and thus to the possibility of expropriating

---

48. *Capital*, I: 389. See also Marx, *The Poverty of Philosophy* (New York: International Publishers, 1963), p. 136. Tucker (*op. cit.*, p. 229) concentrates on this negative aspect to the detriment of his analysis.

49. Quoted in Bloom, *op. cit.*, p. 136.

50. *Eighteenth Brumaire*, p. 109. The similarity to Durkheim's idea of mechanical solidarity is striking and is probably due to Marx and Durkheim's common intellectual ancestry in Rousseau. But where for Durkheim the advancing division of labor provides the basis for a new kind of solidarity, with Marx it is profoundly subversive.

the erstwhile self-sufficient producer, to a multiplicity of social relationships, and to the growth of class consciousness.

State and Society.—The concepts of division of labor and property relations take an explicit and prominent part in Marx's comparative analyses, and this we expect. However, two other concepts—not identified as such— have a prominent part in his analyses, the state-society relations and the purpose of production. One does not have to take a position on Marx's distinction of substructure and superstructure to insist that these aspects of society do have histories and that therefore the characterization of any society is much the poorer without their mention.

Marx's view, that the state is an epiphenomenon of the class struggle, that it is the apparatus used by the owning classes for the suppression of the producing classes, is well known if oversimplified. The corollaries of this view are that if no one class is dominant (as in mid-19th century France) the state machinery may have relative autonomy (as under Louis Bonaparte), and that under more general circumstances, the state has a revolutionary and then a conservative role. The state is used as a revolutionary force when a new class has just become dominant and needs force to destroy the remnants of the old society. Once the new society is established the state is merely used to enforce existing relations.[51] These phenomena are an historical constant the demonstration of which is much of the burden of *The German Ideology*, which argues that the state is but the political aspect of ownership.

But Marx also found that there was a difference between the relation of state and society in the various historical epochs of which he spoke. The state in Asiatic society is the owner of the land and hence of the surplus value. The Asiatic state is the expression of the identity of the scattered individual villages. Since, because of lack of intercourse and a lack of individualization, the individuals in these communities do not develop separate interests and thus cannot combine on the basis of those interests, "the despot here appears as the father of all the numerous lesser communities, thus realizing the common unity of all."[52] The state of ancient society, however, exists side by side with society as a network of individual landowners; both the state and the individual are owners of land, although the individual is subordinated to the state in his role as citizen. The all-encompassing existence of the state is further reduced in feudal society, where the state is only an association of landowners, no longer a union.[53] However political

51. See above, pp. 60–61; see also Marx, "Critique of the Gotha Program," in *Basic Writings in Politics and Philosophy*, p. 127; *Capital*, I: pp. 813–814, 823–824; III, 809, 918–921; Lichtheim, *Marxism, op. cit.*, pt. VI, chs. II-III.
52. *PEF*, p. 84.
53. *Ibid.*, p. 78.

control is still confounded with economic control. The feudal lord is both owner and political authority in his domain. His relation to his peasants is not one of naked exploitation but is still "veiled by religious and political illusions."[54] "Under such conditions the surplus labor for the nominal owner of the land cannot be filched from them (the peasant producers) by any economic measures, but must be forced from them by other measures, whatever may be the form assumed by them."

Political force is still used in the day-to-day operation of the feudal economy. But this becomes no longer true in bourgeois society, when state and society become abstracted from one another.[55] True, the state remains as the tool of the owning classes, but also it has become the mere adjunct to the activity of developing the economic forces of society. In bourgeois society the bourgeois "natural laws of production" can assert themselves freely once the capitalistic framework has been established. But this process is completed only under communism when society, reorganized as community, will be free of the state altogether.

The Purpose of Production.—The foregoing brings us to the last of the important comparative dimensions used by Marx. Of course, he used many a residual category: historically active social groups which, like the "lumpenproletariat," cannot be defined as classes; military-political force as an "economic power"; nationality and race; and "accidents".[56] Some of these references are sophistries, others are the observations of a sensitive historian, but none has a consistent role either in his theory or in his comparative analysis.

One other dimension, however, is used consistently by Marx in his comparison of societies; it is somewhat related to the state-society distinction. This last dimension is the institutional purpose for which production is undertaken. This distinction has, Marx seems to feel, a decisive importance for the characterization of societies. In previous historical societies material production was undertaken in order to reproduce the existing social relations. In ancient society specifically, landownership and agriculture were lauded as the training grounds of the military virtues. Precapitalist economic activity had been limited by the specific needs of the community, producer, lord, or customer; goods were produced for direct use. Capitalism, however, because of its highly developed division of labor,

54. *Communist Manifesto*, p. 11. The following quotation is taken from *Capital*, III: 918.

55. See Karl Löwith, *From Hegel to Nietzsche*, trans. David E. Green (Garden City, N. Y.: Doubleday Anchor, 1967), pp. 242–244.

56. The references are, respectively, to *Eighteenth Brumaire*, pp. 65–68; *Capital*, I: 823–824; *Letters to Dr. Kugelmann*, pp. 67–68, 96, 107–108, 115; and *ibid.*, p. 125.

produces commodities for exchange. It institutionalizes productivity in the abstract:

> The historical destiny of capital is fulfilled when, on the one hand, needs have become so highly developed that surplus labor above what is essential has become a general requirement, and on the other general industriousness . . . has become developed as a general characteristic of the new generation.[57]

Here economic activity is separated from and dominant over all other concerns. No longer is man a citizen; now he is only a producer. And while Marx may, with Rousseau, see the limits of this new conception, he can also see its revolutionary possibilities:

> Thus the ancient conception, in which man always appears (in however narrowly national, religious or political a definition) as the aim of production, seems very much more exalted than the modern world, in which production is the aim of man and wealth the aim of production. In fact, however, when the narrow bourgeois form has been peeled away, what is wealth if not the universality of needs, capacities, enjoyments, productive powers, etc., of individuals, produced in universal exchange? What, if not the full development of human control over the forces of nature—those of his own nature as well as those of so-called "nature"? What, if not the absolute elaboration of his creative dispositions, without any preconditions other than antecedent historical evolution which makes the totality of this evolution—i.e. the evolution of all human powers as such, unmeasured by any *previously established* yardstick—an end in itself? What is this, if not a situation where man does not reproduce himself in any determined form, but produces his totality? Where he does not seek to remain something formed by the past, but is in the absolute movement of becoming? In bourgeois political economy—and in the epoch of production to which it corresponds—this complete elaboration of what lies within man, appears as the total alienation, and the destruction of all fixed, one-sided purposes as the sacrifice of the end in itself to a wholly external compulsion. Hence in one way the childlike world of the ancients appears to be superior; and this is so, in so far as we seek for closed shape, form and established limitation. The ancients provide a narrow satisfaction, whereas the modern world leaves us unsatisfied, or, where it appears to be satisfied with itself, is *vulgar*, and *mean*.[58]

There is, then, a revolutionary (i.e., qualitative) difference in the institutionalized purpose of production between capitalist and pre-capitalist so-

---

57. Translated and quoted by Hoselitz, *op. cit.*, p. 156. This should not prejudice the argument whether or not "industriousness" is a requirement of the *genesis* of capitalism, as Weber suggests.

58. *PEF*, pp. 84–85.

ciety: the change from use-value to exchange-value. This difference is interpreted by Marx in *causal connection* with changes in the other three aspects; yet it is *not the same* conceptually and hence must be expressed as a separate dimension.

SOME METHODOLOGICAL ISSUES

With this study of Marx's actual comparative analyses and of the concepts he employed in them behind us, we are in a position to comment on two additional issues, especially as they relate to his use of concepts: his theory of history as it relates to evolutionism and his use of data.

Theory of History.—Marx designates "the Asiatic, the ancient, the feudal, and the modern bourgeois methods of production" as "so many epochs in the progress of the economic formation of society."[59] What does this mean? We have seen that Marx concerned himself with at least four elements of each of these epochs. Each of these elements demonstrates, in succeeding epochs, a movement closer to the pattern apparent in modern bourgeois society. Property is increasingly individualized and freed of traditional restraints, on the one hand, and the mass of individuals are dispossessed, on the other. The division of labor becomes more widespread, leading to a greater wealth of social relationships. Civil society is increasingly freed from narrow political or religious conceptions. And production, from being subordinate to immediate use, becomes an end in itself. Each succeeding epoch is closer to the individualized, rationalized, secularized, bourgeois society of Marx's day. Each epoch develops more of the historical conditions for the appearance of that society:

> . . . man is only individualized through the process of history. He originally appears as a *generic being, a tribal being, a herd animal*—though by no means as a "political animal" in the political sense. Exchange itself is a major agent of this individualisation. It makes the herd animal superfluous and dissolves it.[60]

Marx, then, has an unambiguous notion of what "progress" is; the movement of the history of civil society in the West (as opposed to the history of regimes, which is a matter of "clouds" in the "sky," or of philosophy and religion, which, strictly speaking, have no history) has by and large been in that progressive direction. Certainly the historical section of the *Communist Manifesto*, where Marx and Engels most succinctly state this view of history, reads like a success story.

59. See footnote 10 above.
60. *PEF*, p. 96. See also the articles by Hobsbawm, Hoselitz, and Lichtheim cited above.

Is this not evolutionism? Many would reject out of hand any suggestion that Marx is an evolutionist because of his insistence that *revolution* is the motor of history and that history is a matter of qualitative change. But this objection is superficial: many of the defining characteristics of evolution can be found in Marx's theory, such as a unilinear conception of history, an emphasis on change as immanent in the thing changing, and a single factor as the dynamic of change.[61] In some respects, perhaps, the label of "evolutionist" may be made to fit a simplified picture of Marx. Yet in one crucial respect Marx does not fit the mold, and that respect is most important for anyone today engaging in a Marxian comparative analysis. Put simply, *Marx regarded capitalism as a world-historical occurrence.* Once fully developed capitalism comes on the scene, the long, painful process of its coming-to-be no longer has to be repeated. Put in evolutionist terms, the stages prior to capitalism may be skipped. One need not, moreover, go to Marxism esoterica to find this crucial idea; it is there in the *Manifesto*:

> The bourgeoisie, by the rapid improvement of all instruments of production, by the immensely facilitated means of communication, draws all nations, even the most barbarian, into civilization. . . . It compels all nations, on pain of extinction, to adopt the bourgeois mode of production; it compels them to introduce what it calls civilization into their midst, i.e., to become bourgeois themselves. In a word, it creates a world after its own image.[62]

Marx himself analyzed this process with respect to India and Russia, and whatever he might have said about the problem of skipping the stage of capitalism, he never suggested that India or Russia might have to go through the "ancient" or "feudal" stages.

If, therefore, latter-day Marxists concern themselves with sterile controversies on historical periodization in the modern world,[63] they do not take their lead from their putative master. They would be truer to his spirit,

61. See Kenneth E. Bock, "Evolution, Function, and Change," *American Sociological Review*, 28 (1963), 229–237; and Pierre L. van den Berghe, "Dialectic and Functionalism: Toward A Theoretical Synthesis," *ibid.*, pp. 695–705.

62. *Communist Manifesto*, p. 13. Among innumerable other references, see *German Ideology*, p. 49; "The British Rule in India," pp. 14–21; *The Russian Menace to Europe*, pp. 216–218; and Hobsbawm, *op. cit.* For a differing view, see T. B. Bottomore, *Classes in Modern Society* (New York: Pantheon, 1966), pp. 15–16. The problem of moving directly into socialism without undergoing capitalism is too vast to be considered here. Yet at least two of Marx's reasons for assuming the necessity of capitalism do not rest on a theory of "immanent change": (1) that capitalism was in fact creating a world revolution; (2) that only capitalism could develop the material conditions (i.e. economic abundance) necessary for the realization of socialist society.

63. For a discussion of such a controversy, see Schwartz, *op. cit.*

as well as methodologically better advised, to analyze social development in terms of Marx's leading concepts, which we have discussed above as "comparative dimensions."

Marx is, to be sure, a "historicist" in Popper's sense,[64] but it is important to understand in what ways this label holds true. It applies to his view of Western European history as a determinate process, but it does not apply to his view that there may be other roads to capitalism. It applies to his view that the "laws of political economy" are specific to the bourgeois era, but this is hardly damaging. Where Marx's historicism is most troublesome, however, is in his view of fully developed capitalism: Marx insists that the model of bourgeois economy he has constructed has captured the "essence" of modern society and that the future of that society can be inferred from the model. Once the decision (or compulsion) has been made to enter into the modern bourgeois mode, Marx says, the future is determined by that decision.[65] To the smug German who pities poor England as he reads *Capital*, Marx says, "De te fabula narratur!"[66]

This is only another way of saying that Marx has two types of concepts which are in an uneasy tension with each other. One type consists of the "comparative dimensions"—those aspects of any society seen as relevant for comparative analysis—which we have identified above. Another type, which we might call "cluster concepts," includes the unitary characterizations of the "epochs" or "modes of production." Capitalism is seen as a unity, a cluster of attributes identified by comparative analysis, the cluster moving as a whole. Other analysts have employed "cluster concepts," notably Max Weber in his "ideal types." But the latter conceptualizations of dynamic processes are, in contrast to Marx's, conceptualizations of *aspects of society* rather than of *social wholes*. Marx, too, employs concepts of aspects of society—the "comparative dimensions"—but he seems to disregard their possible conceptual independence when once he begins to analyze fully developed capitalism. Then he sacrifices the analytic method of his comparative studies to his unitary model of capitalism. Weber, on the other hand, though he has a conception of the overall movement of modern society ("rationalization"), maintains a more varied array of conceptually independent, ideal-typical concepts for its empirical analysis.[67]

64. Karl R. Popper, *The Open Society and Its Enemies* (rev. ed. New York: Harper Torchbooks, 1963), II, chs. 13-21; and Popper, *The Poverty of Historicism* (Boston: Beacon Press, 1957), pt. III.

65. *The Russian Menace to Europe*, pp. 216-218.

66. *Capital*, I: 13.

67. For related criticisms of unitary notions of development, see Reinhard Bendix, *Nation-Building and Citizenship* (New York: Wiley, 1964), pp. 8-15; and Randall Collins, "Two Approaches to Comparative Politics," in Reinhard Bendix,

Use of Data.—Since Marx did not provide definitions of his comparative concepts, we cannot assess the way in which he made operational definitions on a cross-cultural basis. In fact the four basic concepts we have here discussed were refined in our analysis by the opposite process, i.e., by inferring the concept from the way in which Marx seems to use it.

Moreover, Marx has little help for us in his use of historical data. To be sure, he set for himself this scientific task: "Empirical observation must in each separate instance bring out empirically, and without mystification and speculation, the connection of the social and political structure with production."[68] He does not, however, engage in this kind of observation himself in his comparative studies. What he does is to use the observations made by others, sometimes in a fairly thorough manner (as in the chapter on "The Working-Day" in *Capital*), but more often by way of illustration. Even then, the form of the illustration is often "as, for example, in Rome," with or without a citation. The fact is that Marx was *uncritical of empirical sources*, trusting to a remarkable extent in the reliability of the observer who presented them. For England, he relied largely on the reports of factory inspectors (praising them, at the time, for their objectivity); for India, on parliamentary reports; for Rome, on Mommsen's history.[69]

It was, in fact, his favorite scholarly gambit to quote the "bourgeois ideologists" to their own disadvantage. That he was able to do so is an index of the extent to which he shared in the intellectual perspective of his time. Most of his key sociological concepts—the three-class model of bourgeois society, the division of labor, the state-society distinction, the labor theory of value—are drawn from the bourgeois social theory of the 18th and 19th centuries: Ricardo, Adam Smith, Adam Ferguson, Locke, Rousseau, Hegel, Saint-Simon, and even apologists such as Andrew Ure. The empirical weaknesses of these theories thus contribute to the empirical weaknesses of Marx himself.

The *critical* aspect of Marx's approach was, then, not so much in his empirical analyses but in the kinds of inferences he drew. Marx is Marx not as "empirical observer" but in the way he "brings out connections." More

---

et al., eds., *State and Society: A Reader in Comparative Political Sociology* (Boston: Little, Brown, 1968).

68. *German Ideology*, p. 13.

69. In this respect he differs little from Weber, who complained at the necessary reliance of the non-specialist comparative analyst on a scholarly literature that was itself controversial; see *Protestant Ethic*, p. 28. Weber, like Marx, was often wrong because of errors made by his sources and often begged crucial empirical questions with expressions such as "everyone knows" and "beyond doubt"; *ibid.*, pp. 51, 233, 244, 277–278, 280, 283. See also C. K. Yang's Introduction to Weber's *The Religion of China*, trans. H. H. Gerth (New York: Macmillan, 1964), pp. xxxviii-xl.

often than not he agrees with his ideological opponents on the facts, but he disagrees on the implications (theoretical as well as moral) to be drawn from them. The following passage is typical in its criticism of idealistic historiography: "When the crude form in which the division of labour appears with the Indians and Egyptians calls forth the caste-system in their state and religion, the historian believes that the caste system is the power which has produced this crude social form." [70] Marx and his idealistic historian agree on the factual conjunction of caste and a "crude" division of labor; they disagree on what is to be made of the connection. Marx's "critical" approach is also to be seen in his insistence that bourgeois economy was a science limited in its applicability to a society in which concentrated capital was confronted by the free wage laborer who had been disciplined into habits of dependence. He insisted that this system had to be created by human action; but his picture of the creation was not far from that of Ricardo. [71]

CONCLUSION

The foregoing analysis might be seen to require a revision of commonly held views on the nature of Marx's theory; it might even require a rewriting of his own theoretical position itself in view of his consistent use of some implicitly developed concepts. This, however, would be a task far exceeding the limitations of this paper. [72] Yet this much about Marx's method is clear from this analysis of his comparative work: Marx was an acute analyst of *comparative institutions*.

He analyzes societies according to their legal (i.e., property), economic (i.e., division of labor and exchange), and political institutions. True to his theoretical perspective (as stated, for instance, in the "Preface" of 1859), he disregards religion and philosophy as comparative dimensions. Somewhat more surprisingly, but understandably, as we have seen above, he also disregards technology and classes as social actors in these comparative analyses. But perhaps most striking of all is his emphasis on *legal relations (i.e., property) as constitutive of society*. Whatever may be the temporal relation of the division of labor and property, these two aspects of Marx's interpretation stand out: (1) A society cannot be adequately characterized without reference to these legal data (perhaps because they

70. *German Ideology*, p. 30.

71. The originality and insight of *interpretation* rather than of empirical investigation also characterizes Weber's comparative analyses; see Yang (note 69 above).

72. See, however, the above-cited work of Dahrendorf (note 44) and Lichtheim (notes 6 and 22).

are static and differ in forms by qualitative or discontinuous steps whereas economic processes are more dynamic);[73] and (2) that which most decisively distinguishes East and West is the presence or absence of certain property relations.

What, finally, are the implications to be drawn for comparative analysts today? Marx's work illustrates for us three uses of comparative analysis, three reasons, that is, for which we might want to take into consideration data drawn from more than one society. The first is the evolutionist's construction of "stages": theological-metaphysical-positive, with Comte; military-industrial, with Spencer; mechanical-organic with Durkheim; and the four epochs with Marx. Insofar as this "comparative method" merely places snapshot pictures of various societies on a scale of pre-modern to modern, it is not comparative; it is merely another way of describing societies.[74] Unfortunately, much that has been called Marxian analysis has interpreted Marx's approach to consist solely in this concern for periodization. After all, Marx's characterization of the "epochs" was unoriginal; he borrowed the names from the thought of his time. Since then the world has changed, and the old epochs may no longer be the most relevant. Moreover, as we have seen, he felt that the old "forms" were rapidly disappearing in the face of the capitalist onslaught.

His interpretations of the epochs, of course, are another matter. They illustrate a second use of comparative studies: the reinterpretations of various societies as exemplifying a principle or principles of a social theory. Marx wanted to show that any society could be best understood if one brought to bear upon it his "materialist conception of history." A more recent example of this kind of approach is the functional interpretation of comparative politics, wherein each political system (usually a nation-state) is reinterpreted in the light of an input-output or capabilities model of the polity.[75] These studies have the merit of identifying processes according to a coherent theory and then of analyzing their interrelations in the social context. Thus Marx's discussion of the dynamics of population and property relations [76] according to the principles of his theory is an important contribution. Yet Marx's method here can stand modification. Insofar as he insists that "modes of production" are unitary phenomena to be explained by reference to a single "law," his approach is not as flexible for

73. See Krieger, "The Uses of Marx for History" (note 44).

74. See Kenneth E. Bock, "The Comparative Method" (Ph.D. diss., Department of Sociology, University of California, Berkeley, 1948).

75. See, for example, Gabriel A. Almond and G. Bingham Powell, Jr., *Comparative Politics: A Developmental Approach* (Boston: Little, Brown, 1966).

76. See above, p. 54.

comparative purposes as is, say, Weber's method of "ideal types."[77] We have seen that he tended to disregard this insistence in his treatment of pre-capitalist societies; perhaps we can learn to do the same for capitalist societies. Perhaps, that is, we can focus on the conceivably independently variable concepts we have identified as comparative dimensions, modifying them when necessary.[78]

A third approach,[79] however, was most fruitfully used by Marx in his comparative analyses. This approach, which we might call "the method of specification by comparison," attempts to understand the conditions for the appearance of a particular historical configuration or to highlight the characteristics of that configuration. By this method—which Marx practiced but did not himself emphasize—he came to the conclusions which have so illuminated our understanding of modern society. He has shown us in what ways that society is new and requiring of a new interpretation. To compare conceptual elements across societies was useful to him, therefore, but he did not spend much effort in recommending this procedure to us. Perhaps in this respect we ought to take the example of his deed.

77. See Collins, *op. cit.*

78. For instance, the role of the state. Marx justifiably minimized this role in his analysis of nineteenth-century bourgeois society (i.e., England). Such a minimization today, however, is less justifiable, as Lenin certainly recognized.

79. For further note on the uses of comparative studies, see the "Introduction" to Reinhard Bendix and others, eds., *State and Society.*

MAX WEBER'S COMPARATIVE
APPROACH AND
HISTORICAL TYPOLOGY *

GUENTHER ROTH

WEBER IN THE DEVELOPMENT LITERATURE

Much of the development literature has been concerned with two issues: the preservation or creation of an innovative spirit and of effective political authority. One set of studies has searched for "functional equivalents" to the Protestant Ethic and the spirit of capitalism, ranging from traditionalist religious incentives to sectarian Communist party discipline. Another set has dealt with legitimation and authority, particularly with regard to bureaucratic and charismatic organization. In addition, the neo-evolutionist literature has attempted to place contemporary "developed" and "underdeveloped" countries within a world-historical scheme of developmental stages.

In all three lines of inquiry the importance of Weber's work has been acknowledged by many scholars with purposes divergent from his.[1] Changing historical situations and shifting theoretical interests require the modification, in varying degrees, of older approaches. In many instances it may be neither necessary nor feasible to follow Weber's path, but whatever strategy a scholar may want to adopt, it should be informed by a clear

*This essay combines ch. VI, sec. 1 and 3, and ch. XIII, sec. 1 and 2 from Reinhard Bendix and Guenther Roth, *Scholarship and Partisanship: Essays on Max Weber* (Berkeley and Los Angeles: University of California Press, 1971).

1. No survey of the literature is attempted here. Representative of the first line of inquiry is Robert N. Bellah's work. For an overview see his "Reflections on the Protestant Ethic Analogy in Asia," *Journal of Social Issues*, 19 (Jan. 1963), 52–60, reprinted in S. N. Eisenstadt, ed., *The Protestant Ethic and Modernization* (New York: Basic Books, 1968), pp. 243–251; representative of the inquiries into legitimation and authority is David Apter's work, especially on *Ghana in Transition* (New York: Atheneum, 1966); for his own reassessment, see "Nkrumah, Charisma, and the Coup," *Daedalus*, 97 (Summer 1968), 757–792; the neo-evolutionary approach has been most prominently espoused in Talcott Parsons, *Societies. Evolutionary and Comparative Perspectives* (Englewood Cliffs, N.J.: Prentice-Hall, 1966).

understanding of what Weber and others have tried to accomplish in the past. This may be useful for the clarification of his own purposes.

I shall first comment on the difference between Weber's studies in the sociology of religion and the current search for "functional equivalents." In the second section I will deal with Weber's critique of evolutionism and the genesis of his typological approach. In the third section I will sketch the model character of his types in relation to his long-range historical explanations.

Weber's studies on the world religions endeavored to explain the rise of Western rationalism. But what was a specific historical question for him has become a general issue of "development" and "modernization." The analytical focus has shifted from a unique course of events to the conditions under which cultural borrowing, combined with indigenous mobilization, can lead to similar results. This shift has often involved a reinterpretation, sometimes subtle and sometimes blatant, of Weber's purposes. A subtle example is Neil Smelser's remark that "one of Weber's enduring preoccupations was with the conditions under which industrial capitalism of the modern Western type would arise and flourish. . . . The 'Weber thesis' has stimulated much analysis of the economic implications of religious systems other than those Weber himself studied. Other analysts have argued that secular beliefs, especially nationalism, exert an even more direct force on economic development."[2] Strictly speaking, however, Weber attempted to explain the *absence* of these conditions outside of western Europe and the United States. His purpose was not the positive identification of optimal conditions for industrialization. And in his work on India he referred to the modern nationalist intelligentsia only to indicate that it did not belong into the historical context of his research.[3] Weber did not address himself to the issue of industrializing and modernizing "underdeveloped" countries. In his time Japan had already demonstrated that an Asian country could copy Western institutions and technology. He did not doubt that other countries would follow suit, although he recognized the much greater obstacles in India. But his study of Hinduism and Buddhism dealt with the purely historical question of the absence of the "spirit of capitalism." Only in passing did he touch on the modern development problem:

> Obviously it was unthinkable that a community dominated by such spiritual forces could have created on its own what we call here the "spirit of

2. Neil J. Smelser, *The Sociology of Economic Life* (Englewood Cliffs, N.J.: Prentice-Hall, 1963), pp. 15 and 41.

3. Weber, *Hinduismus and Buddhismus*, vol. II of *Gesammelte Aufsätze zur Religionssoziologie* (Tübingen: Mohr, 1920), pp. 362 f.; cf. Hans H. Gerth and Don Martindale, tr. and eds., *The Religion of India* (New York: Free Press, 1958), p. 328.

capitalism." Even the reception, in the Japanese manner, of the economically and technically ready-made artifact has here met, understandably enough, with very serious, and apparently greater, difficulties, in spite of the English domination. Today the penetration of Indian society by capitalist interests is so thorough that it can probably not be eradicated, but only a few decades ago very knowledgeable Englishmen could remain convinced that . . . the old feudal robber romanticism of the Indian Middle Ages would erupt again with undiminished force if the thin stratum of European masters and the Pax Britannica enforced by it should disappear.[4]

There is, then, a considerable hiatus between Weber's studies in the sociology of religion and the bulk of the development literature. The fact is that they deal with bygone days, not with present and future development. Still, the historical content of these writings is far from irrelevant to the new concerns since each country labors under persistent age-old legacies. It appears to me that the hiatus is less significant in the case of *Economy and Society*. True, it too deals with the events of many centuries, but its historically saturated typologies may be more readily adaptable to the study of present-day development than the "mental experiments" in the sociology of religion. These experiments were the last, if very precarious, step in a long series of comparisons in which similarities were identified for the sake of narrowing down crucial differences. Without claiming any misplaced "scientific" precision, Weber tried to hold political, social, and economic factors relatively constant on a world-historical scale in order to suggest explanations for the differential impact of the ethical prescriptions of the world religions. His familiar conclusion was that, within a long chain of historical causation involving many non-religious phenomena, only Puritanism had the effect of furthering economic capitalism (in contrast to political capitalism). Yet the sweep of these mental experiments was so vast that the "results" (as Weber called them) were not meant to be more than rough hypotheses. In fact, Weber advanced a very modest claim for the essays in the sociology of religion: "They are perhaps useful, in some way, for supplementing the formulation of questions in the sociology of religion and here and there probably in economic sociology."[5] That may have been a deliberate understatement. As a self-confident scholar, he believed that he had divined tenable answers and taken some steps toward their empirical support. But the "results" were indeed not sufficient in guiding new research

4. *Op. cit.*, p. 359; for a different wording see *The Religion of India*, p. 325.
5. Introduction, *Gesammelte Aufsätze* . . . , I, p. 237. Weber took up the first of these studies—on Confucianism and Taoism—in 1913, without having finished *Economy and Society*, especially the chapters on religion and charisma. When he first published the studies in 1915, he called them merely "Sketches in the Sociology of Religion," later—in 1920—"Essays (*Versuche*) in the Comparative Sociology of Religion" (p. 237).

in various fields. Feasible answers—as will be shown in the section dealing with historical models—remained dependent on the typologies employed prior to the historical theses.

Since the "results" of the essays concerned religious beliefs, much of the subsequent functionalist literature could easily integrate them into its own theoretical framework, in which values appear crucial. The essays on China and India, however, also drew on the typologies of organization and domination in *Economy and Society,* in which the social structural level predominates.[6] When Weber prepared the first volume of his collected essays on the sociology of religion in 1919–1920—the only one readied before his death—he reminded the reader that "only a systematic presentation could demonstrate how far the [typological] distinctions and terminology chosen here are expedient."[7] Since the systematic exposition is contained in *Economy and Society*—then unpublished—the typologies and generalizations will be explored on the basis of the earlier opus (1909–1913).

First, however, I shall briefly describe Weber's critique of evolutionism and the emergence of his typological approach.

THE CRITIQUE OF EVOLUTIONISM AND THE GENESIS OF THE TYPOLOGICAL APPROACH

In Weber's student days unilinear evolutionism and monocausal theories were widely held. Herbert Spencer exerted considerable influence on the generation of Weber's teachers. Although the unilinear conception was gradually abandoned, schemes of developmental stages or theories of cycles

---

6. In fact, Weber dealt with both the level of values and that of organization as early as his two works on the Protestant ethic (1904) and the Protestant sects (1906). Stephen Berger has recently pointed out that "if people understood the relationship between the Protestant sect essay and the Protestant Ethic thesis, they would be more sensitive to questions like: What kinds of groups become autonomous and separate in a given society and what makes this possible? They would also be somewhat more suspicious about the possibilities of using pre-modern values and social structures to generate modern ones. But they have not been so suspicious in the past, and their attempts to find analogies to the Protestant Ethic have been largely searches for similarities in values, not in social structures. Hence my plea to become more sophisticated users of Max Weber's ideas." See Stephen D. Berger, "The Sects and the Breakthrough into the Modern World," paper presented at the April, 1970 meetings of the Midwest Sociological Society, p. 8 (mimeo).

7. *From Max Weber,* Hans Gerth and C. W. Mills, tr. and eds. (New York: Oxford University Press, 1946), p. 299. In an untranslated explanatory note on the essays in the sociology of religion Weber pointed to their close connection with *Economy and Society:* "The essays were intended . . . to be published together with the treatise on *Economy and Society* . . . and to interpret and supplement the section on the sociology of religion (but also to be interpreted by it in many ways). Even in their present state they can probably serve this purpose, albeit in a more incomplete manner. Whatever the present essays lack because of their sketchiness and unevenness, the work of other men will certainly accomplish much better than I could do

remained popular throughout his lifetime. Osward Spengler fascinated many of the young students in the last years of Weber's life. As against general theories of social change, Weber became increasingly concerned with the actual changes and vicissitudes of Occidental history. He did not think that the ranking of economic, political, legal, and religious factors in a general scheme of development was possible. Therefore, historical inquiry had to decide their relative impact in a given case.

HISTORICAL LAWS AND THE USES OF ANALOGY

As a young scholar, Weber too had been under the sway of evolutionary thought. In his *Roman Agrarian History* (1891) he employed August Meitzen's categories of Indo-Germanic development. At the time he still considered it "scientifically correct to say that if a trend dominant in the metropolitan center is not yet prevalent in the outlying areas it is because for the time being other tendencies oppose it. It is possible to construe the general developmental law in terms of mere tendencies that can be hindered by stronger local ones. Hence I considered it methodologically correct to proceed for the time being from an agrarian development inside the most advanced provinces of the Empire without further detailed investigation [of the outlying areas]." [8] When Weber wrote his second major study of Antiquity in 1908, he declared that he had erred in his attempt to apply Meitzen's evolutionary categories to heterogeneous conditions.[9] By that time he had presented his critique of evolutionary assumptions, historical laws, and analogical reasoning, but he was only just beginning to work out his own typologies as an alternative.

His first critique of historical laws of development appeared in 1903, when he returned to writing after his prolonged illness. This was a critical examination of Wilhelm Roscher, whose works he had first read in his Heidelberg student days.[10] Roscher had formulated his views in the 1840's and taught until the 1890's. Searching for historical laws (*Entwicklungsgesetze*) of state and economy, he believed in their divine origin and, therefore, in their ultimate inscrutability. In perceiving universal laws he dif-

---

it here. Even if the essays had been finished, they could never have claimed 'definiteness,' since the author had to rely on translated sources." *Gesammelte Aufsätze* . . . , I, p. 237.

8. Weber, *Die römische Agrargeschichte in ihrer Bedeutung für das Staats- und Privatrecht* (Stuttgart: Enke, 1891), p. 4.

9. Weber, "Agrarverhältnisse im Altertum," *Gesammelte Aufsätze zur Sozial- und Wirtschaftsgeschichte* (Tübingen: Mohr, 1924), p. 287; abbr. GAzSW.

10. Weber, "Roscher und Knies und die logischen Probleme der historischen Nationalökonomie" (1903–6), *Gesammelte Aufsätze zur Wissenschaftslehre* (Tübingen: Mohr, 1951).

fered from the Historical School in jurisprudence, but he shared its belief
in peoples as historical "individuals" and embodiments of the folk spirit.
He advocated especially the study of Antiquity, because its peoples had
passed through their natural stages. He urged that ancient literature be
compared with Romanic and Germanic liturature for the sake of discovering the developmental patterns of all literature. In Weber's view, such a
search for historical constants and repetitions missed the vocation of history
—to find the reasons for, and the meaning of, historical changes. Roscher's
approach appeared unable to achieve any "causal transparency," because
parallels and regularities are not self-explanatory but constitute merely the
beginning of research.

> If we strive for intellectual understanding of the reality about us, of the
> way in which it was by needs individually determined in a necessarily
> individual context, then the analyses of those *parallels* must be under-
> taken solely from the viewpoint of elucidating the specific meaning of
> concrete culture elements with regard to concrete, intelligible causes and
> consequences. In this case the parallels would merely be a means of
> comparing several historical phenomena in their full individuality for the
> sake of identifying their specific character.[11]

Instead of using parallels for the ultimate purpose of arriving at laws,
subsuming lower under higher regularities, Weber stressed their utility for
the formation of historical concepts. Of course, this utility depended on the
given case; parallels could be illuminating as well as misleading. At any
rate, they were meant to serve causal analysis, not to represent explanations
in their own right. In his "Critical Studies in the Logic of the Cultural
Sciences" (1906) Weber pointed to the widespread confusion in the literature, from Roscher to Karl Bücher and Eduard Meyer, between explanations in terms of cause and of law, a confusion made worse by the linguistic
habit of speaking of the "causal law" (*Kausalgesetz*). He advocated "mere"
causal analysis: "The historian's problem of causality . . . is oriented toward
the attribution of concrete causes, not toward the establishment of abstract
'uniformities' (*Gesetzlichkeiten*)."[12]

After his critique of Eduard Meyer (in the first part of the "Critical
Studies") Weber clarified the categories of objective possibility and ad-

11. *Ibid.*, p. 14.
12. Weber, "Critical Studies in the Logic of the Cultural Sciences," in *The
Methodology of the Social Sciences*, Edward Shils and Henry Finch, tr. and eds.
(New York: Free Press, 1949), p. 168. Shils and Finch translate *Zurechnung* as
"correlation," but the term is easily confused with the statistical notion; hence, I
prefer to speak of "attribution." Weber did not have in mind the correlation approach
which today is often used as an alternative to a causal approach.

equate causation, which involve an inherently comparative mental experiment. He wanted to demonstrate that every historian, whether he knows it or not, undertakes some kind of mental experiment in assessing a given case, in fact, that he is forced to be explicit about it when his interpretation is challenged.[13] The historian's mental experiment is, however, not yet a systematic undertaking using parallels and analogies for the construction of ideal types and generalizations. Weber emphasized that "the comparison of 'analogous' events is to be considered as *one* means of this imputation of causal agency, and indeed, in my view, one of the most important means and one which is not used to anywhere near the proper extent."[14]

Weber's essay on the controversies about ancient Germanic social structure—still untranslated, although it was intended for presentation at the St. Louis Congress of 1904—shows clearer than the critique of Eduard Meyer how he took a step closer to historical typology.[15] At issue was the historical significance of manorial domination, broadly speaking, of large-scale land ownership. For a time the predominant view held that most of the political and economic history of Germany could be explained monocausally from this institution. In view of the dearth and ambiguity of historical sources, some scholars attempted to buttress their view of the historical primacy of manorial domination in Europe by drawing on analogies with contemporary primitive peoples or tribes. This implied universal stages of development, an assumption for which Weber saw no empirical justification. He insisted that it was the business of cultural history to explain change from the viewpoint of current concerns—how the major institutions and values of the present had come about; this was a problem-oriented, "subjectivist" rather than a law-oriented, "objectivist" endeavor. The search for analogies and the comparison of developmental stages were just heuristic devices.

Weber's own use of analogy was twofold: (*a*) illustrative, helping the reader visualize a phenomenon by reference to something with which he was familiar; (*b*) typological, drawing on similar phenomena for the sake of formulating typologies. Weber considered unfeasible the kind of analogy that relied too much on a single trait without taking into account other internal or environmental features. As an example he cited an analogy used by Richard Hildebrand and Werner Wittich: If contemporary nomads such as Bedouins and Kirghiz look down upon agricultural labor, the Germanic tribes of Caesar's time, presumably also nomads or semi-nomads, must have

13. Cf. *ibid.*, pp. 177, 183.
14. *Ibid.*, p. 130.
15. "Der Streit um den Charakter der altgermanischen Sozialverfassung in der deutschen Literatur des letzten Jahrzehnts" (1904), *GAzSW*, pp. 508–556.

done likewise. As against this kind of analogy, Weber offered, albeit illustratively, a more adequate one:

> If one wants to search at all for such distant analogies as the Kirghiz and Bedouins, the traits of an "autarkous state" [an allusion to Fichte's collectivist utopia] found among the Suevi will remind one much more of the robber communism that existed in Antiquity on the Liparian islands or—if the expression be permitted—the "officers' mess communism" of the ancient Spartans—or the grand booty communism of the Caliph Omar. In one phrase, these traits are the outcome of "warrior communism." They can easily be explained as of purely military interest. . . . They would scarcely be in tune with the living conditions of a tribe stagnant at the nomadic stage and ruled by large-scale cattle owners in a patriarchal manner.[16]

The reference to "officers' mess communism" was an illustrative analogy drawn from the clubhouse life of the officers corps in Imperial Germany and meant to be familiar as well as ironically alienative; in a manner similar to Thorstein Veblen, Weber liked to point out historical residuals. The three other cases more closely resembled one another than the more "distant" analogies criticized, although in each case there was likely to be some ground for scholarly disagreement. Important for Weber's comparative approach was that the examples made up a type (warrior communism).

CLEAR TYPES AND RULES OF EXPERIENCE

If there are no "whole societies," unilinear developments, universal stages, or causal master keys, the varieties of historical structures must be conceptualized in a different way. Weber's alternative was the ideal-typical approach, which appeared more static only in comparison with the long-range evolutionary schemes or the mono-causal theories. Instead of searching for a basic causal agent throughout the ages, he tried to rank factors according to their explanatory significance for a given historical case. He believed that this could be accomplished only with the help of clear concepts and rules of experience. Causal explanation

> requires as an indispensable preparation the isolation (that means, abstraction) of the individual components of the course of events, and for each component the orientation toward *rules of experience* and the formulation of *clear concepts*. This should be taken into account especially in the economic field in which inadequate conceptual precision can produce the most distorted evaluations.[17]

16. *Ibid.*, p. 523.
17. "Agrarverhältnisse," *op. cit.*, p. 288.

By "clear concepts" Weber meant not just carefully defined general concepts but historically derived ideal types. Problematical for historical investigation was not the abstractness and selectiveness of the types; in this regard the evolutionary stages and Marxist concepts, too, were ideal-typical. Rather, the challenge lay in the empirical adequacy of the concepts. Weber granted that "all qualitative contrasts in reality, in the last resort, can somehow be comprehended as purely quantitative differences in the combination of individual factors."[18] However, after formulating an analytical problem, the researcher's task consists in discerning significant historical differences, although "historical reality always appears in mixed forms."[19] As Weber put it in a methodological aside on the construction of religious types: "Those features *peculiar* to the individual religions . . . but which at the same time are important for *our interest*, must be brought out strongly."[20] Thus, even though Weber agreed with the epistemological view of the world as an infinite manifold—"the continuous stream of actual phenomena"[21]—his approach was based on the assumption that it was fruitful to reduce social reality to intelligible typological proportions. This was a nominalist position, distinguishing Weber from men like Hegel and Marx, who believed that concepts and objects were intrinsically related.

The construction of typologies presupposed certain historical judgments. Weber gave so much attention to political typology because of his conviction that the form of rulership affected both social stratification and the economy. In "The Protestant Ethic and the Spirit of Capitalism" Weber made it plain that he did not propose to pit an idealist interpretation against a materialist one, but in the essay on Germanic social structure he stated his judgment about the historical primary of the political factor unambiguously:

> The oldest social differentiation of Germanic and mediterranean prehistory is, as far as we can see, determined *primarily politically, in part religiously,* not, however, primarily economically. Economic differentiation must be considered more as a consequence and epiphenomenon or, if you want it in the most fashionable terms, as a "function" of the former, rather than vice versa. . . . It means a reversal of the usual causal relationship to view the later manorial constitution not as a consequence but as the original basis of the privileged position of the high-ranking families. The

18. From the introduction to the essays in the sociology of religion, in *From Max Weber,* Hans Gerth and C. Wright Mills, tr. and eds. (New York: Oxford University Press, 1946), p. 292.
19. Weber, *Economy and Society,* G. Roth and C. Wittich, eds. (New York: Bedminster Press, 1968), p. 1002.
20. *From Max Weber,* p. 292.
21. *Economy and Society,* p. 945.

historical primacy of manorial domination appears highly unlikely, first
of all, because in an age of land surplus mere land ownership could not
very well be the basis of economic power.[22]

In addition to such a specific historical judgment, Weber took into
account certain "rules of experience" for the formulation of clear historical
types. Before setting up his types of authority, he drew upon the following
historical rules: (1) Legitimation is important because "simple observation
shows that . . . he who is more favored feels the never ceasing need to look
upon his position as in some way 'legitimate,' upon his advantage as 'de-
served,' and the other's disadvantage as being brought about by the latter's
'fault' "; (2) "The sociological character of domination will differ according
to the basic differences in the major modes of legitimation"; (3) Rulers use
coercion in addition to legitimation; hence, the typology must deal with
domination "insofar as it is combined with administration"; (4) "It is a fact,
after all, that only a limited variety of different administrative techniques
is available" to rulers and their staffs.[23]

These rules were complemented by another rule which Weber considered empirically undeniable: The state was "the most important constitutive element of every civilization (*Kulturleben*)," just as law was for a
civilization "the most important form of normative regulation."[24] This statement had nothing to do with Hegelian state metaphysics; it was meant as
a plain observation about the major civilizations, and indeed did not necessarily conflict with the Marxian view of the state as the executive committee
of the ruling class. Weber pointed merely to the *structural* importance of
the state among other organizations; he distinguished this "rule" from the
prevailing legal definition of the state, which postulated its sovereign
powers, by stressing empirical variation: In society as an arena of contending associations, the state was not necessarily more powerful than
religious groups or economic interest groups.

Weber elaborated his political typology, still without the label "sociology," first in the "Agrarian Conditions of Antiquity" (1908–1909). This
book-length study for the *Handwörterbuch der Staatswissenschaft* (where
it first appeared under this narrow rubric) presented a substantive theory
of ancient capitalism and related it to what Weber considered the crucial

22. "Der Streit . . ." *GAzSW*, pp. 554 f.
23. *Economy and Society*, pp. 953, 947, 948, 1309.
24. *The Methodology* . . . , *op. cit.*, p. 67. In the English text the sentence:
"The most important constitutive element of every civilization (*Kulturleben*) is the
state, and the most important form of its [i.e., civilization's] normative regulation is
law" was telescoped and reads erroneously: "The state is the most important form
of the normative regulation of cultural life."

variable: the political structures. For this reason he constructed a politico-military typology of the ancient polities with a limited and open developmental scheme.[25] His next step, in *Economy and Society* (1909–1913) was a typology broad enough to encompass the last two and a half millennia. This time he also included law and religion, the latter partly because of its inherent importance, partly because of the controversies about "The Protestant Ethic." *Economy and Society,* the real title of which, significantly, is *The Economy and the Arena of Normative and De Facto Powers,* was intended to bring into one analytical orbit political and administrative organization, religious, ethical and legal prescription, and the economic resources of the historical actors.

HISTORICAL MODELS AND SECULAR THEORIES

In *Economy and Society* Weber addressed himself to some of the big historical issues and to the construction of historical types, which are a logical prerequisite for their elucidation. His strategy was to elaborate historical summaries of similar cases, which will here be called *historical models,* in order to suggest specific historical explanations, here called *secular theories.* I want to speak of Weber's ideal types as "historical models" in order to make the point that they involve historical dynamics and are not just "static" descriptions of structural properties. In his first exposition of the ideal type in 1904 Weber did not deal explicitly with its model character; rather, he took it for granted, as is demonstrated by the fact that the "laws" and developmental constructs of academic and Marxian economic theory appeared to him as outstanding examples of the ideal type.[26] At that time Weber was polemically concerned with the difference between scientific laws proper and ideal types, arguing that only the latter could reveal the cultural significance of a phenomenon.

Historical models specify how empirically similar, typologically identical cases function under certain conditions, such as absence or presence of a money economy, newly conquered territory, or outside military pressure. They spell out a range of variation, incorporating the tendencies toward greater stability as well as toward decline or transformation. Yet the models remain primarily tools for *ex post facto* analysis; in view of the limited number of cases they do not permit prediction or quantification, and in this sense, they are not "scientific." There are, after all, only five world

25. For a summary of the typology, see my introduction to *Economy and Society,* pp. xlvii-li.
26. Cf. Weber, "Objectivity in Social Science and Social Policy," in Edward Shils and Henry Finch, tr. and eds., *The Methodology of the Social Sciences* (New York: Free Press, 1949), pp. 90 f. and 103.

religions, or six if Judaism is added—as Weber did—because of its great significance for Western rationalism. There are only about half a dozen major examples in European history for the alliance of political and hierocratic powers. For certain features of a model there are sometimes only one or two illustrations, if not just some logical possibilities. Moreover, the transition to secular theories is fluid. Generally, a statement is part of a model if it refers to more than one historical case. The models are meant to facilitate the construction of secular theories, but they must in turn be built from historical explanations proper. Thus, the level of religious rationalization, an historical ("secular") theory, becomes part of the model of hierocracy and Caesaro-papism (cf. below).

The static and dynamic aspects of the models are fused in the major body of *Economy and Society* (Part Two), but this has been obscured by Weber's very attempt at simplification. When he found out that the discursive treatment of a large number of concepts within a massive body of historical data made reception and retention difficult for the reader, he resorted to an enumerative exposition (Part One) in a catalogue form. The "crystallizing" effect of the categorization was so strong that it tempted the reader to overlook his cautionary remarks and his cross-references to the subsequent presentation of the workings of a given type of domination— he spoke of the "detailed description" (*Einzeldarstellung*) in contrast to the summary enumeration of the type cases *(Kasuistik)*.[27]

I shall briefly review bureaucracy, patrimonialism, hierocracy, and Caesaro-papism to illustrate the nature of the models.[28] I am concerned with their formal side, but some descriptiveness is inevitable in view of the concrete historical content.

MODERN BUREAUCRACY

Weber constructed a model by beginning with closely similar phenomena before moving along a declining line of comparability to other historical and contemporary cases. "Modern bureaucracy" was built largely from the French and German cases—historically and geographically proximate—and to a lesser extent from the older bureaucracy of the absolutist state and from the modern large-scale enterprise. Since profit or

27. This was a particular handicap for English readers, since Part One of *Economy and Society* appeared under a somewhat misleading title in 1947, whereas Part Two was not published in its entirety until two decades later. See Talcott Parsons, ed. and tr. (with A. M. Henderson), *The Theory of Social and Economic Organization* (New York: Oxford University Press, 1947).

28. The following is a very condensed treatment. For a general exposition of Weber's Sociology of Domination, see my introduction to his *Economy and Society* (New York: Bedminster Press, 1968), pp. lxxxii-xciv.

revenue was a precondition of continuous bureaucratic administration, the prevalence of a natural economy made the other "historical bureaucracies" inherently unstable and largely patrimonial—Egypt since the New Kingdom; the Roman principate, especially from the Diocletian monarchy to the Byzantine polity; China from Emperor Shih (third century, B.C.); the Roman Catholic Church since the end of the thirteenth century.

Although modern bureaucracy has greater stability on purely technical grounds, its predominance is by no means inevitable. It is true—and has often been quoted—that Weber wrote: "Once *fully established,* bureaucracy is among those social structures which are hardest to destroy. . . . Where administration has been *completely bureaucratized,* the resulting form of domination is practically indestructible." [29] But this was a conditional proposition. In the same context Weber pointed out that the advance of bureaucracy may be slowed down or deflected if older administrative forms remain technically adequate to the tasks at hand, as was the case in England.

Moreover, the dynamics of bureaucracy are related to those of mass democracy: "Bureaucracy inevitably accompanies modern mass democracy." [30] There is typically a tension between the two forces, as there is between both and charismatic rulership. All of them may reinforce as well as conflict with one another. The democratic value of equality before the law is also a bureaucratic norm; the same is true of the preference for examinations as against selection on the basis of ascriptive status. Bureaucrats and democrats alike fight the notables of the nobility, but bureaucrats will resist the development of direct democracy. Both uphold the right to office and tenure as a protection against arbitrary intervention from above. However, the right to office tends to weaken not only the ruler's arbitrariness but also to create a new status group inimical to democratic tendencies. In turn, if the democratic demand for equality changes into a demand for substantive or material justice (equity), it becomes as detrimental to rational (bureaucratic) justice as the star chamber of an absolutist ruler; both forms of justice make an arbitrary will—the people's or the ruler's—the ultimate yardstick. Because of the play of these diverse forces, Weber concluded that "it must remain an open question whether the power of bureaucracy is increasing in the modern states in which it is spreading. . . . Hence, one must *in every historical case* analyze in which particular direction bureaucratization has developed." [31] Thus, Weber first constructed a model of bureaucracy and of the potential directions of bureaucratization.

29. *Ibid.,* p. 987.
30. *Ibid.,* p. 983.
31. *Ibid.,* p. 991.

The explanation of the course of bureaucratization in a given country and during a given period was the subsequent task of secular theory.

Literature on organization in America has not taken sufficient note of the fact that Weber's enumeration of the formal characteristics of modern bureaucracy is part of an historical model of bureaucracy and mass democracy. Instead a truncated type has frequently been employed as a blueprint to be compared with the "natural system" or the "informal structure" of private and public organizations. Ironically, the famed, if not fabled, "classic Weberian type," comprising mainly the first few pages of the chapter on bureaucracy, is the least original of Weber's contributions, because the formal characteristics were part and parcel of the academic teaching of public administration in his time. Weber did not deal systematically with the distinction between formal and informal structure, because he was not interested in a general theory of organization. Instead, he was concerned, on the one hand, with the formal aspects of modern bureaucracy in relation to other historical forms of organization, and on the other with the politics of bureaucrats and other office-holders. His systematic focus, then, was on the power struggle between ruler, staff and subjects. Bureaucracies develop their own vested interests. Whereas modern bureaucracy is technically superior to older forms of administrations, a given bureaucracy can obstruct, in its own self-interest, the intentions of the ruler as well as the subjects.

PATRIMONIALISM

In the case of patrimonialism, a traditionalist form of domination, Weber built its dynamics right into his definitions. Patrimonialism was "*domestic* authority *decentralized* through assignment of land and sometimes of equipment." [32] Because the traditionalist obedience of the patriarchal household remained the pattern of patrimonial legitimacy, decentralization of such personalized relationships was likely to weaken the ruler's grip unless it could be buttressed by other means. The conflict potential was even stronger under *political* patrimonialism, Weber's primary concern. In the patrimonial state "the prince organizes his political power over extrapatrimonial areas and political subjects just like the exercise of his patriarchal power"—if he is strong enough.[33] The range of conflict is circumscribed in these terms:

(1) The benefice is a universal phenomenon under patrimonalism.
(2) There is an inherent tendency on the part of the benefice-holders and their heirs to appropriate the benefices.

32. *Ibid.*, p. 1011.
33. *Ibid.*, p. 1013.

(3) If the ruler can maximize his power, he will usurp contempt powers and turn political subjects into patrimonial dependents.
(4) There is a continuous struggle between the ruler and the local notables.

The outcome of this struggle obviously turns on the distribution of power, which again depends partly on the technical nature of the administration, partly on economic development. Therefore, Weber goes to great lengths to identify the military and civilian modes of administration, on the one hand, and the relationship of trading and capitalist operations to the political struggle on the other. In each case he endeavors to draw up a ledger sheet of the advantages and disadvantages from the viewpoint of ruler and staff, an implicitly functionalist procedure. Although the individual ruler could rise and fall rapidly, patrimonialism tended toward a political stalemate, which might last for generations. Here ends the historical model. Weber moves on to the secular level when he shows how the patrimonial stalemate was broken in two ways: In the Orient military conquerors periodically upset the pattern of appropriation and typification in their favor; in the Occident the expanding money economy at first facilitated the appropriation and commercialization of benefices, but in the end permitted the absolutist ruler to reorganize his administration along bureaucratic lines. This resulted in such a different kind of organization that another model had to be applied—modern bureaucracy.

HIEROCRACY AND CAESARO-PAPISM

Just as Weber linked the dynamics of bureaucracy and mass democracy, so did he encompass hierocracy and Caesaro-papism in one historical model. Hierocracy, which in its bureaucratic form is called a church, means the political dominance of the priests; in turn, Caesaro-papism denotes the secular ruler's control over the priesthood. These contrasting types were important both with regard to legitimation and administration. Weber showed the range within which religious and political forces would clash or cooperate with one another. The primeval antagonism between political and magical charisma was reenforced in time by organizational and power interests. Since it was very rare for either side to gain a full victory, the patterns of antagonistic cooperation were more important than the extreme ("pure") forms. Each side had something to offer to the other. For political rulers, hierocracy served two "functions": (a) It provided legitimation for rulers who had some personal or institutionalized charisma but needed further legitimation, a frequent historical case; (b) hierocracy was the "incomparable means of domesticating the subjects in things great and

little" [34] and thus particularly suitable to conquerors. For hierocracy, the
political ruler was useful because he could (a) suppress opponents of the
hierocracy and annihilate heretics and (b) extract taxation in its favor.

The power balance depended on several conditions: (1) The constellation of status groups—this involved an indirect economic co-determinant.
The petty bourgeoisie was the typical ally of hierocracy; the secular nobility was its typical opponent. (2) The state of religious rationalization. The
political ruler tended to gain the upper hand as long as priestly charisma
was of a personal magical nature. Quite similarly to his phrasing of the in-
vincibility of bureaucracy, Weber stated that "a *fully developed* ecclesias-
tic hierarchy, with an established body of dogmas and particularly well-
organized educational system, cannot be uprooted at all." [35] (This has
proved true of the Catholic Church up until now.) (3) The specific character of the religion. Only the Catholic Church and Calvinism had a notion
of a divinely ordained ecclesia, in contrast to Lutheranism, the Eastern
church, and Buddhism. (4) The importance of military force. If the religion
was established by force, the secular ruler tended to retain control over the
priests; witness the caliphs.

After listing the conditions, Weber turned to the consequences.
Caesaro-papist regimes encouraged stereotyped forms of religion and ritual-
ist manipulations of supernatural powers. Hierocracy had more consequences: regulation of conduct by way of unlimited ethical claims, institutionalization of magic, control over secular education, promotion of
transcendental speculation, defense of the "weak," opposition to innovation, including new social groups. These consequences obtained in spite of
the diverse origins of the religions. Among the economic consequences of
hierocracy were land accumulation, usually resisted by the secular nobility,
competition with bourgeois trading and craft interests, and opposition to
inherently non-ethical capitalism. However, the policies of a hierocracy had
a greater impact than its own economic operations.

After spelling out the consequences of hierocracy in general, Weber
turned to the secular theory of Western hierocracy. He considered it impossible to reduce the parallel development of urban trades and religious
rationalization to an "unambiguous relation of cause and effect: Religious
rationalization had its own dynamics, which economic conditions merely
channel; above all, it is linked to the emergence of priestly education." [36]
The main channel was the urban setting, but rationalization was also very
much affected by hierocracy's gravest problem: the irrepressible conflict

34. *Ibid.*, p. 1176.
35. *Ibid.*, p. 1175.
36. *Ibid.*, p. 1179.

between institutional and personal charisma, the clergy and the monks. Therefore, Weber turned his attention to the monastic movements, which required a typology of their own.

Monasticism was charismatic, anti-rational and anti-economic, but this very fact made for great rational achievements. The double nature of monasticism meant that it could be an adversary or ally of hierocracy and Caesaro-papism. For the latter it reinforced the uses of hierocracy, legitimation, and domestication; in addition, it proved the cheapest kind of clerical and teaching personnel. Most importantly, it could be used as an instrument of patrimonial or bureaucratic rationalization against the nobility. However, this cheap methodical work force had a high price: In matters religious, monks were more intransigent than regular clergy, and once monasticism gained strength, it was bound to clash sooner or later with Caesaro-papist claims. For hierocracy the uses of monasticism were "far more problematical" in view of the ineradicable tension between institutional and personal charisma.[37] However, there were several advantages: Monks served as the troops of the monocratic head of the church; they helped control the urban masses through missionary activities; and in a natural economy they provided, through their communal living, the only defense against feudalization.

Weber envisaged three overlapping uses for his models: comparisons of (1) models with one another, leading to "clear concepts"; (2) one model or submodel with cases within its range; and (3) batteries of models with a given case. The latter two comparisons led to the construction of secular theories.

(1) Weber made the first kind of comparison hundreds of times, until he almost exhausted the similarities and differences. For instance, bureaucracy and patrimonialism contrasted sharply with regard to legitimacy and rational division of labor, but both were relatively normative, stable, and routine forms of administration; their armies were centrally supplied and functioned best under a money economy, thus contrasting with popular levies and militias. Weber dealt with similarities between two models in order *(a)* to call attention to structural correspondence, *(b)* to bring out the contrast to still another model, or *(c)* to point to gradual long-range transitions. Example: "In the course of financial rationalization, patrimonialism moves *imperceptibly* toward a rational bureaucratic administration, which resorts to systematic taxation." [38] In this instance, the model shades off into secular theory.

37. *Ibid.*, p. 1171.
38. *Ibid.*, p. 1014.

(2) The second application is the blueprint method. A model is compared with a case ("natural system"), occasionally a hypothetical one. The model serves as a set of bench marks: "By the terminology suggested here, we do not wish to force schematically the infinite and multifarious historical life, but simply to create, for specific purposes, *useful concepts of orientation.*" [39] With the help of refinements (subtypes) Weber fixed the typological location of a case as well as its historical drift. Thus, in England domination by the justices of the peace was "a combination of patrimonialism of the estate type with a pure type of autonomous administration by notables, and it tended much more toward the latter than toward the former." [40] Such specifications prepared the secular theory of English history, which explicated its leading role in industrialization and democratization. Weber's great interest in the rise of industrial capitalism accounts for the ubiquity of the English case in the various models. China was a negative test case. Here Weber applied the model of bureaucracy in order to establish both *formal* fit and *functional* difference. "From a formal viewpoint [the qualifying examinations and official certificates of conduct] constitute the most radical application of bureaucratic objectivity possible and therefore an equally radical break with typical patrimonial office-holding." This statement on the model level is then followed by historical explanation proper: "Nevertheless, Chinese officialdom did not develop into modern bureaucracy, for the functional differentiation of spheres of jurisdiction was carried through only to a very limited extent in view of the country's huge size. . . . The specifically modern concept of the functional association and of specialized officialdom, a concept which was so important in the course of the gradual modernization of the English administration, would have run counter to everything characteristically Chinese and to all the status trends of Chinese officialdom." [41]

(3) The battery approach is an extension of the simple blueprint method and facilitates case studies proper. After working out the three models of domination as well as the mixed forms of hierocracy, Caesaropapism, and urban polity, Weber applied them to his study of Confucianism and Taoism. This explains why this first study on the "economic ethics of the world religions" reads at the outset like a continuation of the Sociology of Domination in *Economy and Society,* for it begins not with religion but the Chinese city, patrimonial administration, the emperor's charisma and the country's economic features. The application of models to a given

---

39. *From Max Weber,* p. 300; translation slightly changed.
40. *Economy and Society,* p. 1063.
41. *Ibid.,* p. 1048 f.

case makes it necessary to devise hyphenated constructs: "We shall be compelled again and again to form expressions like 'patrimonial bureaucracy' in order to make the point that the characteristic traits of the respective phenomenon belong in part to the rational form of domination, whereas other traits belong to a traditionalist form of domination, in this case to that of status groups." [42]

In principle, most models are applicable to tribes no less than modern states. Caesaro-papism and hierocracy, for instance, apply backward and forward from their type cases, the Byzantine and Carolingian empire. The Holy Roman Empire was the "exemplary case" [43] for the rivalry between political and religious power. Weber began the construction of these models with familiar medieval examples and ultimately came back to the uniqueness of Europe in the secular theories, which take up the larger part of his analysis. Sometimes he speedily shifted back and forth between model and secular theory. Since his time, some of his contemporary cases have become merely illustrative of a model. But irrespective of whether Vatican II, for instance, has attenuated the doctrine *extra ecclesiam nulla salus*, the phrase remains valid as "the motto of all churches." [44]

Weber was extremely insistent on the limits of his generalizations. On issues such as the economic co-determinants of religious phenomena "no meaningful generalization can be made." Time and again he pointed to historical imponderables: "Fateful events play a tremendous role." [45] Both Pope and emperor could have triumphed over one another, with incalculable consequences for European culture, if certain historical "accidents" had not happened. Likewise, if the Irish monks had prevailed, the church could have become monastic rather than bureaucratic. Instead the monks' integration into the bureaucratic church became a major step toward modern rationalism. Weber concluded that the uniqueness of Occidental culture resulted, among other reasons, from the tension and balance between office charisma and monasticism, on the one hand, and between the contractual feudal state and the autonomous bureaucratic hierocracy on the other.[46] Thus, although historical accidents and the plurality of historical factors make it impossible to predict the actual course of events, the construction of types (or models) is necessary, for the historical conclusions are couched in typological language. This is the ultimate methodological rationale of their indispensability.

42. *From Max Weber*, p. 300.
43. *Economy and Society*, p. 1159
44. *Ibid.*, p. 1167.
45. *Ibid.*, pp. 1174 and 1176.
46. Cf. *Ibid.*, p. 1192.

PART TWO

GENERAL THEORY AND COMPARATIVE RESEARCH

COMPARATIVE STUDIES
AND EVOLUTIONARY
CHANGE

TALCOTT PARSONS

Professor Vallier has suggested that in this chapter I attempt to sum up some of the principal ideas about comparative studies which have emerged as significant to me out of my rather long experience with them.

I was really introduced to such studies in my first year of graduate work in London in 1924-1925. The dominant figure in the field there was L. T. Hobhouse, who was very much an evolutionist. I of course read his work, but my first systematic introduction was through Morris Ginsberg who, in Hobhouse's absence on account of illness, gave the course of lectures of *Comparative Institutions*. A year later at Heidelberg I began my acquaintance with a rather different orientation to these problems—that of Max Weber—which has been of central significance to me ever since.

Another significant early experience lay in the fact that, with the establishment of a Department of Sociology at Harvard in 1931, I was asked, as a very junior member, to serve as "coordinator" of an omnibus collaborative course called Comparative Social Institutions in which a rather distinguished group of faculty members in historical fields and disciplines related to sociology participated. These included, for example, Charles H. McIlwain, William S. Ferguson, Walter E. Clark, Arthur D. Nock, A. M. Tozzer, Edwin F. Gay, and Arthur M. Schlesinger, Sr. Though it proved not to be feasible to hold such a team together for many years, Comparative Social Institutions has been a continuous teaching venture for me ever since, the title of the course having been pared down eventually to simply *Institutional Structure*.

A major antecedent influence on me was my exposure, as an undergraduate (at Amherst College), to biological thinking. Since the conception of evolution has been so very central in that field, I started with a predisposition in favor of it, for the socio-cultural field as well as the organic. At the same time, my early intellectual maturity coincided with a major wave of reaction against evolutionary thinking in favor of the idea of cultural relativity. This response was especially strong among anthropologists, but also appeared among sociologists. The Hobhouse-Ginsberg type of evolutionary thinking was one of the most widely attacked and, in large measure, I tended to "go along with" the attack. Nevertheless, I was never convinced that the anti-evolutionists had in any way seriously damaged the evolutionary components of Weber's historical-sociological analyses, nor those of Durkheim as I came to appreciate their nature better.[1]

Seen in the framework of the sociology of knowledge, it is clear that the anti-evolutionist wave was a partial manifestation of the social sciences' need to assert their independence from the biological. The original anthropological meaning of the word "culture" was thus that class of determinants and/or products of human action which were not "reducible" to terms of biological heredity. By and large, however, this "independence" movement in the social sciences has now long since succeeded, making it possible to acknowledge kinship—a little like the rebellious adolescent who, after having established his independence, can again acknowledge some genuine kinship with his parents in more than a biological sense.

It was in that frame of mind that I found myself, a number of years later, more and more positively concerned with evolutionary ideas. This interest led me back to biological reference points and to an attempt to understand some of the newer developments in biological science. Out of this I emerged strongly convinced about the basic continuity of the evolutionary development of all classes of living systems, including a continuity between the organic level and the socio-cultural.[2]

One particularly important point regarding the biological and socio-cultural levels may be noted immediately, though others will be developed as we go along. This is the "analogy" or functional similarity between the role of the genetic constitution in the organic world and that of the cultural system in the world of human action systems, an insight I owe especially to the biologist Alfred Emerson, who spoke of the parallel between "gene" and "symbol." This idea linked up in a special way with the "four-function paradigm" with which I have worked since 1953. Among the four functional categories, namely, those of adaptation, system goal-attainment, integration, and pattern maintenance, the last occupied a special place as relatively invariant, i.e., changing by something like "evolutionary" processes on a long-time scale, rather than by short-run "adjustive" processes.

During about the same period it also became clear that the fourfold

1. Robert Bellah, "Durkheim and History," *American Sociological Review*, 24 (August 1959), 447–461.

2. The more autobiographical aspect of this development has been recounted in my article, "On Building Social System Theory: A Personal Account," in *Daedalus* (Fall 1970), and need not be repeated here.

paradigm could be used at the "general action" level as distinguished from that of the social system, with which I had worked most intensively. At this level the four "primary subsystems of action" were clearly the "behavioral organism," the psychological or personality system, the social system, and the cultural system. The special position of the pattern-maintenance system was the primary key to another major insight, namely, that the fourfold scheme fitted the economic classification of the factors of production and the shares of income, and that within that "land" clearly belonged in the pattern-maintenance position.[3]

Soon after that I became aware of certain developments outside my own field which went far to give a deeper theoretical rationale to Emerson's "equation" between the gene and the symbol. One of these was the development of linguistics in ways which connected it with cybernetic and information theory, treating language as organized about "symbolic *codes,*" and the emergence in the new "microgenetics" of essentially the same conception, most dramatically set forth in the discovery of the chemical structure of DNA and the subsequent development of the conception of the "genetic code." [4] One might say, if language, the status of which as a central aspect of culture was scarcely in doubt, and the biochemistry of the genetic process were organized in terms of "codes" the main structure of which was resistant to short-run change, why should not the aspects of culture with which sociologists had been more concerned fit broadly into the same conception?

SOME RELEVANT SOCIOLOGICAL THEORY

I do not mean to suggest that all of this perspective was borrowed from models of biological theory. There has been, over the years, on my own part and based on an impressive growth of the social science literature, a considerable accumulation of knowledge and insight at social science levels, the digesting and organizing of which, for me, revolved above all about two foci. One was my continuing concern with Max Weber's pattern of comparative and historical analysis of societies and their cultural traditions. The other was the "pattern-variable" scheme, which had "fathered" the four-function paradigm of which I have spoken. Perhaps this is sufficiently familiar to most readers so it is not necessary to outline it here, especially as it was used as the main organizing conceptual framework of my book, *The Social System* (1951).

3. Talcott Parsons and Neil Smelser, *Economy and Society* (New York: Free Press, 1956).

4. Gunther S. Stent, "DNA,"*Daedalus* (Fall 1969).

Another very important leading conception does, however, link directly with biology, namely that of *differentiation*. This conception and its complement, that of integration, have of course figured very prominently in social as well as biological science—perhaps most notably in Herbert Spencer. Among its various aspects, it seems appropriate first to emphasize that differentiation is a *directional* process, it has a starting point, namely an "un" or "less" differentiated state of a system and, at a later time, a differentiated or a more differentiated state.

An important point about differentiation as a process is that in living systems it follows, very generally indeed, the *binary* principle. What begins as one unit or subsystem divides into two. Perhaps the best known case in the organic world is the process of cell division. If there is at least a presumption in favor of the binary principle, this fact introduces among other things a very welcome element of both simplification and symmetry. It has been particularly congenial to me through its connection with the logic of certain aspects of the theoretical scheme with which I have worked, such as the dichotomous character of pattern-variable pairs and the conception of four primary system functions. Furthermore, in tracing developmental processes this presumption may be a very useful guide in any attempt to identify stages.

The concept of differentiation is a basic unifier of the evolutionary and the comparative perspectives. A process of differentiation proceeds in a temporal sequence of "from—to." In the process it brings about *differences* among parts of the system which did not previously exist. Furthermore, since these differences are conceived to have emerged by a process of change *in* a system, which I interpret to mean in some sense within the "framework *of* the system," the presumption is that the differentiated parts are comparable in the sense of being *systematically* related to each other, both because they still belong within the same system and, through their interrelations, to their antecedents.[5]

The term "systematically related" as used above of course needs to be defined. Here my assumption is that *function* is the master concept for analysis of the organization of living systems.[6] As such it is superordinate to both "structure" and "process." That structures and processes should be differentiated along functional lines within the same system implies their *comparability*. If they were in principle incomparable, first the nature of

    5. Talcott Parsons, "Pattern-Variables Revisited," *Sociological Theory and Modern Society* (New York: Free Press, 1951, 1967).
    6. Talcott Parsons, "Some Problems of General Theory in Sociology," in John McKinney and Edward Tiryakian (eds.), *Theoretical Sociology and Perspectives and Developments* (New York: Appleton-Century-Crofts, 1970).

the system could not be rationally understood and, second, it would not be possible to account for its integration as a system. Integration is an essential concept for living systems, even though in another sense and at another level a parallelogram of forces may be treated as a system without any assumption of integration, at least as the concept of integration is being used here.

This approach poses the question of comparability in a somewhat unusual way. The more usual way is to seek out "similars" which resemble each other in that they can be subsumed under the same logical "class" but are also significantly variant. From this starting point one could proceed to the building up of a "taxonomic" scheme in terms of the definition of more general classes, and various orders of subclasses, without reference to the question of whether the instances are or are not included in the same system.

If we are to take the "system" approach, rather than that of "similarity and difference," two dimensions become relevant to comparative studies which are not found at the taxonomic level. These are the nature and implications of the belongingness of compared items within the same system and, second, the genetic dimension of relatedness, namely, with respect to differentiation in what respects from what common origin. In this connection it is also essential to recognize the importance of the pluralism of systems. In the organic world the individual organism looms particularly large especially at the higher evolutionary levels. But the main genetic heritage is "carried" at another level, namely, that of the species, which is the primary system of reference for the subscience of genetics and for evolutionary theory. There is a variety of other system references at the organic level, such as that of "ecosystems."

At the human level, organism and personality are especially intimately linked system levels. An older generation of anthropologists tended to set both of these, more especially personality, over against "culture," as the other crucial reference, which is in some ways comparable to the species. Here, however, in a rather special way a fourth system reference, the social, i.e., the system constituted by the interaction of a plurality of organism-personality units within a cultural framework, becomes very central. This is true in a way which does not probably apply directly to subhuman species, even to the famous "social insects." The salient difference, of course, lies in the mediation of human social interaction by cultural level communication, which is unique to the human world, even though it has some antecedents.

At first glance the approach to comparability through common system-belongingness may seem to be a very limited one. This would indeed be the case if we were to accept the extreme "cultural relativity" view, com-

plete with its German "historistic" antecedents, and maintain that meaningfulness of characterization of a structural unit or process could be defined
only within *one* very specific system. If human "history" consisted of a
population of essentially unique "cultures," as has been alleged, this consideration would indeed virtually eliminate the relevance of "comparative
method." But empirically, this simply is not the case; history consists rather,
like the system of organic species, of an immensely ramified "inverted
branching tree" of forms at many levels of system reference.

What ties the "branches," forms, and levels together into a macro-
system, is in the first instance common genetic origin. This is to say that
differences among subsystems have, by and large, arisen through processes
of differentiation from what in some sense have been "more primitive"
forms. The human socio-cultural universe is by no means so variegated as,
at least superficially considered, the organic seems to be, but it is by no
means narrowly constricted.

SOCIO-CULTURAL DEVELOPMENT FROM A SINGLE ORIGIN

A particularly important point here concerns a dual thesis. The first is
that the organic development of man as species must have been essentially
coincident with that of what we know as society and culture. The second is
that the evidence seems to point to a *single* evolutionary origin of man. If
this dual thesis is correct, the problem of comparability can in principle be
held within the framework of differentiation and continuing inclusion within the same system. Furthermore, differences can be referred back to those
emerging through processes of differentiation from a common origin.

If these two propositions are correct, then Durkheim's search, in forming the plan for his last major work, for the "most primitive" type of society
and its religion, was sensible. However difficult it is to define and to find
specific empirical evidence of such primitiveness, and however unsatis-
factory Durkheim's attempt may appear in the light of both empirical and
theoretical evidence which has become available in the sixty years since he
wrote, this proposition concerning the importance of primitiveness remains
valid. Moreover two major things can be said about such a primitive "society." At the action system level it must be the least differentiated which
can be found. Secondly it must comprise all of the essential components of
a scoring system of action, not in "rudimentary" form but in an important
sense as "fully evolved." That the organic basis capable of "carrying" a
cultural system must be present, goes without saying. We know something
about the organic prerequisites involved, notably the capacity to "process
information" through a special kind of central nervous system, to "deal

with" the physical environment especially through hands and arms, and to form trans-organism solidarities, the latter emerging in the first instance, I suggest, through the potentialities of the erotic component of motivation.

"Culture" must be involved, first of all, through language as a genuinely symbolic medium of communication and expression, and also through what Durkheim, in a deliberately undifferentiated sense, called "religion." This latter must include a system of "constitutive symbols," which Durkheim, perhaps in an overly rationalistic way, called "beliefs," and a set of "practices" which above all are "symbolically significant" acts. These latter are generally called "rituals" and are performed for the most part by groups in organized social settings. Religion serves above all, at this level, to give cultural "meaning," both to the "society" and its principal substructures, seen collectively, and to the individual personality and organism as they bear on acting in social relations and in the context of cultural symbolization.

If religion is the primary cultural "glue" which integrates such an action system, it is kinship—a set of relations of social solidarity organized about the two foci of "blood"—which integrates action at the social system level. That these two foci of kinship organization are related to each other in complex ways is attested by the fact, which should be theoretically derivable, of the universal existance of an "incest taboo," i.e., the limitation of sexual unions, especially those legitimized by prospective parenthood, to certain subgroups of the membership of the society. These relations are defined both positively and negatively, i.e., by rules of endogamy and of exogamy.

Finally, society, personality, and organism are related, in ways always also involving culture, by two complexes concerned with human relations to the physical environment. The first of these is primarily economic, concerning man's relation to the environment as the location of resources necessary to meet his needs for food, shelter, clothing, and the like. The other is the organization of social relations with respect to the territorial location of behavior, which concerns place of "residence" but also concerns the territory within which groups may carry out their activities. This territorial focus may also regulate the involvements between society's members and nonmembers. The functional complex referred to as territoriality includes control of the use of physical force. In this and other respects it can be thought of mainly as a "political" complex.

I may now consider the question of what may reasonably be meant by the concept "undifferentiated" in this context. It clearly must be defined relative to system reference and not equated with simplicity in some vaguely general sense. Thus the kinship systems of the Australian aborigines are notoriously complex. Similar things can be said about primitive languages, and the length at which Durkheim found it necessary to discuss Australian totemism could certainly suffice as the basis for an adequate analytical treatise on a major branch of Christianity, which is certainly a more highly differentiated religion.

One major point is that differentiation is not only internal complicatedness, but differentiation *from*. The word "from" then must be defined as meaning differentiated from other components of what is treated as the same system. Thus even though Australian kinship is highly complex, it is not highly differentiated from structural components with primarily economic, political, religious, and other functions. This is very unlike kinship in modern societies which in one sense is much "simpler" but in another is much more highly differentiated from other structures with different functions. In a society like the Australian the *whole society* is a single nexus of kinship relations which then constitutes a structure which, in the nature of the case, is to a high degree "functionally diffuse."

If function is, as I suggested above, the master-concept for the analysis of living systems, then the criterion of high vs. low levels of differentiatedness must be differentiation with respect to kinds of functional importance or "contribution" to the functioning of the specific system, or class of systems, of reference. By this criterion, kinship, religion, economic, and political organization are far more highly differentiated from each other in modern than in any less "evolved" type of society.

MODES OF SOCIAL DIFFERENTIATION

Two problems open out from here. One concerns the axes on which differentiation may be expected to occur or, conversely, can retrospectively be interpreted. If we work with a very simple basic scheme, in this case one involving only four functions, then the cases that are too complex to fit directly into such a scheme must be dealt with in terms of plural system-references, which is in the nature of the case a difficult enterprise. The second problem concerns the delineation of some scheme of evolutionary stages in the realm of human action systems.

With respect to the first problem, a "landmark" insight occurred which was nearly contemporaneous with the emergence of the four-function paradigm and had much to do with it, namely that of the highly generalized significance of the lines of differentiation of the nuclear family on the axes of generation and sex roles. The nuclear family is, of course, a social grouping which is in a special sense "biologically based" and hence may have special significance for the problem of continuity and articulation between the organic and the action level of living systems. It became evident that these two axes of generation and sex were, on a general theoretical level, essentially the same as those which Bales and his associates had found in the experimental study of small groups, whose members were essentially uniform by sex and age, and were without the "diffuse enduring solidarity" which ideally characterizes families. These two axes constitute what is, in some sense, an hierarchical status-difference: in the familial case as between the parental and the filial generations, and in the case of the experimental groups, a leadership-followership differentiation. The other axis is that of a differentiation between qualitative "types" of function in the system: in the family case, the sex-role; in that of the experimental groups, the distinction formulated as that between primarily "instrumental" and primarily "expressive" functions.

The first or generational axis, which I would postulate as not characteristic of the most primitive societies, is that on which systems of stratification are built. As I have noted in Societies,[7] stratification entails the rupture of the "seamless" nexus of kinship relations, so that the emerging "classes" become exogamous to each other. At both ends, however, the principal kinship units, notably lineages, remain to a high degree functionally diffuse, not only with respect to the "personality-focused" functions of the modern family, but economic, political, and religious functions as well.

However this rupture of the kinship nexus cannot occur without segmentation of the former society into at least two, unless there is a basis of solidarity which is not fused with kinship ties and which crosses the class line. It would, I think, be very generally agreed that such solidarity in the early stages is political and religious. It very generally involves the emergence of "centers" in Shils' sense[8] and frequently the kind of chieftainship which merges into monarchy. Military functions, oriented both toward effectiveness in relation to other societies and toward maintaining order and control within the population and area of the society, are likely to be prominent, just as they are in more complex societies. However, religion, with the development of genuine cults and with them more or less definitely specialized priesthoods, tends also to be very prominent. Any very considerable differentiation of economic institutions tends to come later.

The analytical interpretation of these generally accepted facts raises certain questions. Clearly the second, "horizontal" or "instrumental-

---

7. *Societies: Evolutionary and Comparative Perspectives* (Englewood Cliffs, N. J.: Prentice-Hall, 1966), ch. 2.

8. Edward Shils, "Centre and Periphery," *The Logic of Personal Knowledge: Essays Presented to Michael Polanyi* (London: Routledge and Kegan Paul, 1961), 117–131.

expressive," axis is involved. In spite of there being stratification, central-ization, and an "elite," there is a pronounced tendency at the very top for the political and religious components to be combined, most strikingly in the institutions of a "God-King," even though lower down political function-aries, like the military and civil "administrators," will be differentiated from predominantly religious personnel, usually called "priesthoods." The prin-ciple of the heredity of status through kinship, however, remains very strong for both political and religious groups. Such social mobility as there is operates either through such mechanisms as favoritism—e.g., "adoption" into kinship status, and merging into "patrimonialism"—or through the consequences of political overturns, conquests, and coups.

It seems most reasonable to treat this massive set of phenomena, within the simple four-function paradigm, as the differentiation of the system along one "diagonal," namely that of pattern-maintenance and goal-attainment as distinguished from adaptation and integration. The function-al reasons for this asymmetry seem to concern the strains incident to the combination of major new steps toward collective effectiveness—in the "po-litical" context—and at the same time from the problem of maintaining the kind of solidarity which would at least contain centripetal tendencies, es-pecially as between elite and "common people." Here Weber's very fun-damental analysis of the *legitimation* of political authority is central. This legitimation must at some level be conceived and institutionalized in re-ligious terms.

It will be evident to many readers that this is the axis which Durkheim classically formulated as that of "mechanical solidarity." He did not, how-ever, I think, sufficiently emphasize its connection, at least in early societal evolution, with the emergence of stratification and the simultaneous func-tional imperative of promoting collective effectiveness and legitimizing the agencies of that effectiveness in ways which asserted solidarity *across* the lines of stratification.

The suggestion then is that stable differentiation on the more or less "pure" instrumental-expressive axis depends on some kind of prior "solu-tion" of the problem of legitimizing politically oriented stratification and its relation to a cultural base. Here a fundamental point concerns the differ-entiation of the legitimation of inequalities from that of qualitative function-al contributions. There are innumerable concrete contexts in which this problem has arisen, but one which has been perennial right down to the present is that of the roles of the sexes, which, as I suggested, seems to be in some sense "prototypical" of this instrumental-expressive axis. In spite of the nearly obvious qualitative basis of the differentiation of role-function, there has been a very persistent tendency at the same time to define it as a superiority-inferiority relationship. In an important sense a new phase of strain over this problem has very recently arisen in modern societies.

Durkheim again suggested a line of analysis which seems to be of central importance here. This is, if I may interpret freely, the development of "organic solidarity" as the essential condition of institutionalizing the *combination* of instrumental-expressive differentiation and equality of status. Put in analytical terms, this means that the egalitarian component must be not only a "value" pattern, but that it must also be rather firmly institutionalized in the integrative sector of the social system if it is to be capable of resisting the pressures toward inequality that stem both from the urges toward collective political effectiveness and from the recognition of competent achievement. This institutionalization must be reinforced by autonomous control of adequate economic resources.

Only in the broadest sense can an ultra-simple fourfold scheme like that with which I have been working deal with such problems as the delineation of the main structural outline of the earlier phases of socio-cultural evolution. Even if the exceedingly schematic pattern just outlined is in any sense acceptable, there are immense complications and difficulties in dealing with the details of internal structuring of particular societies and the ranges of variation among them, even at what, by analytical judgment, may seem to be "about the same level of differentiation."

SYSTEMS OF SOCIETIES

Perhaps, in view of the limitations of this discussion, I may be permitted to bypass these many complications and "cut through" to a consideration which I think has by and large not received sufficient attention among comparative sociologists. For understandable reasons we have tended to assume the system-reference of a "society" to be the relevant one, and to speak of differentiation, integration, and the other functions in this context. The concept of *a* society, is by no means a simple and obvious one, and I have found myself forced to attempt to clarify and refine it considerably.[9] One of the important outcomes of these attempts has been the emergence of the conception of a *system of societies*, precisely as a social system, with all its cultural, psychological, and environmental concomitants.

Perhaps the most obviously tangible criterion of a society here is that it is a relatively autonomous territorially organized unit, the members of which on the whole display a relative solidarity and sense of identity—i.e., constitute a "societal community"—though of course this solidarity need not be exclusive. Relative "autonomy" in these senses is, however, by no means

9. Parsons, *Societies*, ch. 2.

incompatible with, not only interdependence of various sorts with other societies, but also systematic differentiatedness relative to certain of the societies with which the one of reference stands in relations of interdependence. Here a highly important consideration is that there should be evidence that the system of societies had, in the course of its history, undergone a process of differentiation, the main steps of which can be traced. Of course other processes of change are also implied, some of which will be discussed presently.

At the present writing I have in press a small book—the sequel to the one entitled *Societies: Comparative and Evolutionary Perspectives*—with the title *The System of Modern Societies*.[10] The use of the plural form of the word "society" in the title is quite deliberate and centrally important. We can of course meaningfully speak of "modern society" as a type, but I do not think it would be useful for sociologists to speak of the Soviet Union, Britain, France, the Scandinavian countries, and the United States—to name a few of the most important—as constituting *one society*. But if they are many, it does not follow that their differences from each other follow a pattern of random variation, explained in each case by unique "histories."

The broad pattern of analysis which I have followed for modern societies first crystallized for me in reading Marc Bloch's *Feudal Society*, particularly his characterization of differences in the extent and characteristics of "feudalism" in the high Middle Ages among Italy, France, England, and Germany. The variations he outlined seemed definitely to fit into a four-function pattern.[11]

When, however, from these clearly "premodern" background considerations, I came to try to characterize the first main emergence of the modern system, this type of functional classification became even more important as a framework for systematization. It became clear that the first "truly modern" phase should not be placed, as so many have, in the late 18th century signalized by the industrial revolution, but in the 17th. It was also clear that, with respect to the centrally important institutional developments like the legal system, governmental organization, parliamentarism, religion, secular culture, and economic innovation, there was clearly a "lead sector" of the European system in that period, namely, the "Northwest Corner" including England, Holland, and France, even though France was quite different in certain respects from the other two.

The same period saw the emergence of Prussia as a major political unit

10. *The System of Modern Societies* (Englewood Cliffs, N. J.: Prentice-Hall 1971.

11. Marc Bloch, *Feudal Society*, trans. by L. A. Manyon (Chicago: University of Chicago Press, 1964), 2 vols.

on the Northeastern Corner of the system, as well as a good deal of political and military ferment involving above all Poland and Sweden. Then the "Southern tier," comprising the two "great powers" of Austria and Spain, united for a time under the House of Hapsburg, and a changing post-Renaissance Italy, all on the background of the Counter-Reformation, could be regarded as constituting the more ascriptive, pattern-maintenance and integrative base of the system. For special reasons, which I cannot enter into here, I assigned the goal-attaining role to the Northwest corner, the adaptive role, to the Northeast.[12]

At a much later phase, that of the present century, the same paradigm seemed to be usable again, but in terms of an expanded and northward-moving central system. The "lead sector," I have contended, had become North America, especially of course the United States, and the Northeast frontier role had come to be played by the Soviet Union, while the center of gravity of the pattern-maintenance base had moved clearly to continental Europe north of the Alps, including I thought both France and Germany, with England and the smaller northern countries assuming primarily the integrative role.

There is a further very essential aspect of this paradigm of a modern system of societies. This is the insight—I think it is more than a "contention" —that the modern type of society has had a *single* evolutionary origin. This is a crucial fact parallel to that of the unitary origin of the human species, and with that, of human culture, society, and personality. The older social evolutionists in one sense held this view, but they were not at all clear about the line between modern and premodern. My own appreciation of it came above all from Max Weber, most succinctly stated in his Introduction to the general series on the Sociology of Religion, the first volume of which he himself prepared for press in the last year of his life.[13]

What I have just said about 17th-century Western society implies that by that time the system was already differentiated to the point of involving at least four distinguishable types of society, with perhaps certain further complications such as the status at about that time of the "city-state belt" rather closely following the Rhine river, and the still somewhat peripheral Northern sector.

As part, then, of the task of comparative systematization, these primary societal types acquire, in their differentiatedness from each other and from

12. See *The System of Modern Societies*, ch. 4.
13. As early as 1930 I was sufficiently impressed with the importance of this statement to translate it and include it with the essay on the *Protestant Ethic*, though it was not part of that study, having been written more than fifteen years later. It was, however, not many years later that the full significance of social and cultural developments in the "west," as he called it, gradually became clear to me.

their place in the system, a certain level of sociological meaningfulness. This, however, can be considerably reinforced by following the problem of comparability and comparison back in the developmental sequences. In the same third chapter of the forthcoming small book I have attempted to outline what seem to be the most important considerations. My reference to Bloch makes clear that I think a major structural differentiation of what at least were partially subsocieties had already begun by the high Middle Ages. They existed, however, still within the framework of a formally common religious culture, namely Roman Catholic Christianity, and one which at the political level had not yet clearly broken up into "national states," even though the Holy Roman Empire was very loosely organized. The fact that England and France were at best only equivocally incorporated into the Empire was of course one of the starting points for their lead position at the decisive period.

The Reformation period clearly involved the breaking up of what was the previous Mediaeval unity, both through the split in formal religious organization and through the relation of this to national political organization. It is particularly important that the two themes cross-cut each other. Thus England, Holland, and Prussia became Protestant powers, whereas France, after a near-miss of Protestant ascendancy, became a Catholic power, but one which allied itself with Protestant powers against the Hapsburgs and others. Of course the cultural ferment of the Renaissance was very important in the background.

The development of the European system seems to me to have depended heavily on the inheritance of certain elements of common culture and institutions from the ancient world. These were both religious and secular in the usual senses. The Church, however, not only incorporated certain crucial elements of the Jewish religious tradition, and the Christian innovation itself, but certain structural patterns which derived from the Greek polis and from Rome, especially at the legal level. Similarly Roman law was so widely influential that through its incorporation into Canon Law, the broad ideal of a "roman" state never died, and the institutional traditions of the polis survived in the traditions of "municipal" organization, including the Italian and Rhenish "city-states." Clearly, as the recent "Ecumenical" movement makes clear, the Reformation was a process of differentiation *within* Western Christianity, not the introduction of a "foreign" element into it, nor a total "segmentation" of the religious system.

These combined cultural and institutional commonalities, however, were clearly, in the European case, related to an underlying "variegatedness" of subsocieties and cultures, varying most broadly on a regional basis. This was substantially less variegated than the Roman empire, but of the same general character. The crucial early "segmentation" was the split between the Eastern and Western territories, reflected above all in the usage of the Greek as distinguished from the Latin language, and the "orthodox" as distinguished from the "Catholic" church. Only in the later modern phase did the question of the inclusion of the "East" in this sense arise seriously again, focusing of course on Russia, since the "Middle East" was for long Islamic, then socio-politically quite chaotic.

This regional difference then had to do with such factors as, first, the old locus of culture and political authority (Italy) and the movement of the center of gravity of both economic and political interests north of the Alps —starting with the definition of the Holy Roman Empire as the "German Nation." Then the difference between the currently opening sea frontier, ranging from the Iberian Peninsula to England, as distinguished from the land frontiers, of which Austria and Prussia were the prototypical guardians, became another major focus of differentiation. The integrative role of France was very directly associated with its location at the intersection of the processes of religious and political differentiation.

It is my view that these foci of variation have come gradually to be built into the structure of the modern system. The fact that these foci represent a very broad pattern of internal functional differentiation may be taken as one of the principal conditions of the development of the modern system. This broader, more variegated set of components is a condition that the Roman Empire even at its height could not, I think, have satisfied. That it was satisfied in later times set the stage for a process which I should treat as being probably as important as that of differentiation, namely, what I have been calling *inclusion*.

THE PROCESS OF INCLUSION

I think of inclusion as the process by which structural components which have been either peripheral to a social system, or on its boundaries but "outside," are brought into a status of fuller integration *in* the system and hence *with* its other components. This integration can be defined either with respect to the dimension of stratification, i.e., in some sense the hierarchical dimension, or that of qualitative functional differentiation, or of course some "diagonal" combination of the two. Inclusion may also refer to continuing retention in the system of elements which have become separated from others by segmentation or differentiation, as distinguished from their "extrusion."

The process of inclusion stands in a kind of "dialectical" relation to that of differentiation. Thus, in the temporal perspective I am emphasizing, the line along which inclusion processes have taken place in a previous time period may become, at a later stage, an axis of differentiation. Thus perhaps the most massive inclusion process underlying the European system of modern societies was that of the "Germanic" world which was sufficiently broad to comprise not only "Germany" but the Anglo-Saxon and Scandinavian complex, i.e., in a very broad sense those peoples speaking languages not of Latin derivation, nor of Slavic, nor the residual Celtic, or Finnish, or Hungarian enclaves.

In the Roman imperial period, the Roman "colonization" of these areas that did take place consisted mainly of establishing frontier outposts, such as the line along the Rhine, and Vindobonum near Vienna. Britain was far more fully "colonized" than other areas, and there is a highly significant relation between its early Roman occupation and the "conquest" by the Normans nearly a millenium later. Hence, there is a sense in which it can be said that France—"Gaul"—was predominantly "Latin" with a non-Latin substratum, and that Britain was predominantly "Germanic" with a Latin substratum. This balance seems to me clearly to relate to their capacities to assume "lead" functions in the modern system.

However, when the basic processes of differentiation that destroyed the "Mediaeval" system crystallized, the great religious division broadly followed the earlier ethnic-regional lines. The Reformation was clearly a predominantly "Germanic" movement, whereas the Catholic Church, especially in the Counter-Reformation, was predominantly Latin. Indeed, as I have suggested, this differentiation goes back to the Middle Ages, in that the Church at that time was mainly Latin in orientation, while the Empire was of the "German Nation." With the migration of political power and economic development north of the Alps, a "material" underpinning of the Reformation was clearly present.

These lines of differentiation are still important in the political party alignments of European countries.[14] This ethnic-regional inclusion process was predominantly "lateral" in terms of our main functional paradigm, and helps to explain the nature of East-West differentiation within the modern system. Since a major development of the early modern period was also that of territorially independent political units, the process of inclusion on the vertical or stratification axis was not so visible as a phenomenon of the system as a whole. That the main structure of European society inherited a "class" axis of differentiation goes almost without saying. As Bloch noted, the crucial phenomenon was the institution of aristocracy, which became

14. Seymour Lipset and Stein Rokkan, "Cleavage Structures, Party Systems and Voter Alignments: An Introduction," *in* Lipset and Rokkan (eds.), *Party Systems and Voter Alignments* (New York: Free Press, 1967).

the main focus of European "feudalism" even in the sense in which Marx, rather vaguely, formulated its characteristics.

It can then be said that the "core" of the emerging modern system consisted in the combination of "church and state" but with the church focused in the *first* instance on the religious orders, and the "state" on the aristocracies, with monarchs in the position above all of *primus inter pares*—after all the heads of aristocratic lineages were very generally called "peers," not only of each other but of royalty itself. From this reference point on, we can speak of a grand scale process of inclusion of the "common people" into statuses of "full" membership in their respective societies. There have been a number of aspects of this process, too complex to follow here. However, let me mention that, in English development, the concept "common" emerged at two particularly strategic points.

The first of these is in the conception of the *Common Law,* which was, as distinguished from "manorial" law, common to the whole realm, but also defined the rights of "Englishmen" whether they were aristocrats or not, i.e., it was law for "commoners." This development was clearly one in the direction of institutionalization of a "societal community" which was not confined to aristocrats. The second development was the conception of the British Parliament as consisting of two "houses," a House of Lords (Peers), and very significantly, a *House of Commons.* It is of course true that in the early periods most of the members of the latter House were members of the "gentry" rather than of the "common people" in the more radically democratic sense, but its composition was open-ended in the downward direction of the social status scale, and it was capable of evolving into a legislative assembly representative of the "people" as a whole.

In a more dramatic way the "democratic revolution" came to focus in France with an abrupt shift from a monarchical-aristocratic regime to one which represented the "people" as *citizens—Citoyen* was the central symbol of the French Revolution. In those aspects of the process of inclusion which have come to be called the "democratic revolution," England and France performed one of their most important "lead" functions in the earlier phases of the modern system of societies, England, significantly, coming first since the two basic developments just noted occurred pre-emiently in the 17th century.

Two other modes of inclusion, which have figured prominently in the modern development, but also elsewhere, should be briefly discussed. The first is the process of reintegration that occurs after a process of differentiation which, in the nature of the case, generates such high tensions that the system seems to be undergoing destruction. The Reformation was such a development and seemed to many for a long time to have created two

quite independent "civilizations" that, among other things, engaged in bit-
terly destructive wars with each other. Even the truce under the formula
cuius regio, eius religio, seemed to confirm this. As early as the 17th century,
however, England and Holland introduced limited *internal* religious toleration. A major step was taken with the separation of church and state—as
distinguished from their differentiation—in the American Constitution.
From negative toleration of the right of religious dissent, then, there has
been a gradual process in the direction of what today is usually called "ecumenicism": the positive inclusion of plural religious groups in a single
"moral community" (in Durkheim's sense) which comprises the societal
communities of most of the societies which are members of the modern
system.[15] This inclusion has led widely to a process of differentiation whereby "church" religion has become differentiated from what Robert Bellah,[16]
in his very illuminating conception, calls "civil" religion. The latter can, of
course, be shared by members of plural denominational groups.

The second type of inclusion process has been intimately associated
with the reintegration just discussed, but is in certain respects different. In
the case of the inclusion of the "Germanic" world discussed above, whole
societies were "brought into" the European system by processes which
comprised both military conquest and political consolidation, as well as
religious proselytization. The case in which this has occurred on the largest
scale is the United States, wherein mostly unorganized population elements
with differing religious and ethnic heritages have immigrated into a host
society. Then, provided they are not to be temporary visitors, the question
naturally arises as to what their status and that of their descendants is to be
in the host society.

In the American case it seems to be clear that there has been an important interactive process involved. Though most immigrants, starting with
Negro slaves, have entered the society in relatively low status positions, the
presence of very large immigrant groups and the fact of the society's relative openness to social mobility have encourged a general trend to pluralization of the social structure. Religious ecumenicism is one of the main
outcomes; indeed it is at least probable that the American example has
accelerated this process for Western society as a whole. There has also been
ethnic pluralism which is related to religious ecumenicism in complex ways.
Thus the predominant elements in the U.S. Roman Catholic religion are
highly diverse ethnically and these groups, e.g., of Irish, Italian, Polish,

15. A qualification must be made for the societies under the control of Communist parties which, with varying degrees of rigor, recognize the moral legitimacy
only of the "political religion" of Marxism-Leninism.

16. "Civil Religion in America," *Daedalus* (Winter 1967). 1–22.

French-Canadian, Latin American origin, have been juxtaposed with each other in a way quite different from the European situation involving the same ethnic groups. The "pull" of this ethnic ecumenicism has at last begun powerfully to put pressure for the enhanced inclusion of the Negro minority.

Such pressures toward pluralistic inclusion could not, however, have operated as effectively as they have, had the more general social structure not, in certain respects, favored such inclusion. Not only did the United States have a very liberal immigration policy in the decisive period, but it did not exert the strongest conceivable pressure toward full "assimilation"—though many have asserted ideologically that it did. Not only was there relative religious freedom, but also freedom for private educational programs and other organizational initiatives based on ethnic lines.[17] However this may be, the American societal community which has emerged is, though uniformly English-speaking, no longer a WASP (white, Anglo-Saxon, Protestant) community, but an ethnically and religiously pluralistic community, however important the remaining "discriminations," notably by race, may be.

Dealing with certain phases of the problem of analyzing the processes of inclusion has led us to shift attention from the level of the system of societies to that of the internal processes of particular societies. Before taking up the important question of the more general relation between the two levels, however, it is well to discuss briefly the other two categories of the paradigm of a phase of progressive developmental social change with which I have been working in recent years, namely what I call "adaptive upgrading" and "value-generalization."

ADAPTIVE UPGRADING IN RELATION TO INTEGRATION

By adaptive upgrading, I mean enhancement of the capacity of an action system—in this case a social system—to maintain and generate resources which can serve to improve the system's level of adaptation to the environments in which it is situated. Relative to the attainment of system-*goals* the adaptive function is generalized; it involves resources which are relevant to the attainment of plural and alternative goals. At the social system level economic resources are prototypical in this sense, as fluidly available through the use of money and the market mechanism.

In the above characterization of the adaptive function I have deliber-

---

17. It is interesting to note that the policy of requiring almost all Catholic parochial schools to use the English language was not enforced by government, but by the Church itself, which was dominated in *its* government by English-speaking Irish bishops.

ately used the word environment in the plural. The common sense of social science is still deeply imbued with the conception that there is one environment and it is "obviously" the physical environment. As human beings, however, we are very much involved in interaction, not only with the physical world in the narrower sense, but with the nonhuman part of the organic world. At the action level, then, the *social* system must treat human behavioral organisms, including those of its own members, as environmental objects. The same kind of reasoning leads us to treat the personalities of individuals, including societal members, as environmental to the social system, and finally also the cultural systems with which it is involved. Of course a social system must also include other social systems in the environmental category of the society, especially other societies.

Certain imperatives of the human relation to the physical and non-human organic environments have clearly given a certain premium to the economic aspects of adaptation, which has a special relation to these environments. However, the prominence, on occasion, of the health complex should warn us that the adaptive function in relation to our own organisms is far from negligible, and the prominence of education has emphasized even more the importance of personalities. Such considerations suggest that the very special prominence of economic considerations which has characterized the period of the industrial revolution, extending in some respects into our own time, is a function of a special combination of circumstances rather than of a universally "inherent" relation between man and his physical-organic environment. Such a point of view relativizes the "economic interpretation of history" in a double sense: First, it challenges the generalized predominance of "economic factors" in the determination of human action and, second, it suggests that such predominance as economic factors have varies as a function of a complex constellation of circumstances, many of which are predominantly noneconomic in character.

Indeed I suggest that Western society has been to a high degree adaptively oriented. This means above all two things. First, it has been oriented toward the management of its relations to its environments, i.e., their "control," if this concept is properly understood. One aspect of this is the concern for active adaptation as distinguished from passive adjustment, the latter being that which was very prominent in the earlier discussions of organic evolution. Secondly, however, as between the two basic functions involving stress on orientation to the external, environmental world, priority has tended to run in favor of the adaptive as distinguished from the system-goal attainment complex—of A over G in our functional shorthand. Thus my suggestion has been that the "lead" has been taken by the relatively "decentralized" societies—England and Holland at one period, North America on the other—rather than the highly centralized, hierarchical ones, e.g., Prussia and the Soviet Union.

Within this framework there has been not one but a series of environmental foci of adaptive processes, with corresponding variations in the structures and processes of the internal system. The process which is here called "upgrading" includes a trend toward the salience of environments progressively higher in the cybernetic scale. It is apparent, however, that this trend has not been fully uniform because it has been intertwined with nonadaptive functional exigencies, notably the integrative.

Within the cultural framework of which Roman Catholicism and the recently differentiated Protestantism were the main features, the first major adaptive process which belongs to the complex of modern societies seems to have been "political" in a special sense, namely the emergence of the territorial states from the matrix of the Empire. This placed a heavy adaptive-goal attainment stress on foreign affairs which has in certain respects persisted ever since, though just what the continuities and changes have been raise complex questions.

It seems that this political focus brought the functional problems of societies sufficiently "down to earth" so that, at a societal rather than only a local level, a much more differentiated concern with strictly *economic* exigencies could develop. This development, again very broadly, may be said to have occurred in the two main stages of the "commercial revolution" which was part of the efflorescence of the 17th century and came to be centered in the Northwest corner after initial developments during the Renaissance in Italy and the Rhineland. The great "issue" at this stage was that of "mercantilism," namely the role of government in the control of economic interests and processes.

These adaptive processes soon came to be balanced by somewhat corresponding ones in the integrative sector. The developing symbolization of statehood, including palaces, the trappings of courts and the like, certainly belong in this category. But probably the most important process in the early modern era was the development of legal systems, mainly a modernized Roman law on the Continent of Europe, but a more distinctive system in the English Common Law which, however, developed continuously from Roman Law origins. These developments laid the foundations of what T. H. Marshall called the "civil" component of the modern institution of citizenship which he particularly exemplified by the "rights of Englishmen."[18]

The second main stage of economic upgrading was the "industrial revolution," gathering force in the later 18th century and penetrating much

18. *Class, Citizenship and Social Development* (New York: Doubleday Anchor, 1965), esp. ch. 4.

more deeply into the social structure, especially through the enormous spread of what we now call "occupational" roles and the organizations in which they function.

I think that what is ordinarily called the "democratic revolution" should be considered to be in the first instance a new set of repercussions centering in the integrative sectors of modern societies, following the immense changes in the relations of these societies both to the other societies that impinged on them and to their physical-organic environments. The latter relational changes took place primarily through technological and economic mechanisms. The relation of the "democratic revolution" to the process of inclusion as discussed above is nearly obvious. Characteristically the English version involved a rather gradual movement of the inclusion process downward in the social scale from the aristocracy—T. H. Marshall's account of the British growth of the citizenship complex admirably exemplifies this.[19] By contrast the French development was much more oriented to foreign relations and hence "patriotism"—thus the *Marseillaise* remains to this day as the symbolic song both of the Revolution and of French nationalism. This is not true in the same sense of "God Save the King."

The democratic and the industrial revolutions, taken together, raised acute problems about the integration of modern societies, the first centering almost directly on the question of what constituted a "member" of such a society, i.e., a citizen; the second centering more indirectly around the question as to what the allocation of *human* resources to economic production meant for the other aspects of the status of the "labor force." These two functional problem complexes clearly dominated societal "concern" through most of the 19th century and into the present one.

Another integrative thrust, connected especially to the adaptive developments of the industrial revolution and surely importantly related to political democracy, is that which Marshall has called the development of the "social" component of citizenship, eventuating in what is often called the "welfare state."[20] This is essentially the public guarantee of minimum standards of access to the conditions of "welfare" for the whole population of a modern society, especially protection against destitution through unemployment and through the social and organic disabilities of old age. However, access to health services and to educational opportunity, which will be discussed presently, have also figured prominently.

These integrative strains operating in modern societies clearly have had something to do with the emergence of three new adaptive concerns relative to three of the social system's environments. These are respectively the

19. *Ibid.*, esp. ch. 4.
20. *Ibid.*, esp. ch. 4.

"human-organic," the cultural, and the psychological or the level of the personality.

It is surely significant that the second half of the 19th century saw an altogether new level of concern with problems of health, mostly at the level of the organism. This of course was bound up with the new potentialities which grew out of the extension of the science and technology, which had "worked" in relation to the physical environment, to the emergence of the "life sciences" and with them new technologies for dealing with the somatic problems of health. The most sensational development in this connection was Pasteur's discovery of the role of bacterial infection and the opening up of major possibilities of its control.

THE EDUCATIONAL REVOLUTION

By this time, however, the "educational revolution" was well under way. This can be considered to be a dual process. One side of it, taking root a little before mid-century, was the process of universalization of formal education, beginning with simple literacy and gradually moving up the educational ladder. It is of course well known that early in this century in most of the modern societal world, elementary education had been nearly completely universalized. Russia of course lagged but has caught up rapidly. In the middle third of the present century, especially in the United States, a relatively analogous pattern in the universalization of secondary education has gone far, and starting near the middle of the century we have seen the beginning of mass higher education which seems to point in the direction of universalization.

It does not seem necessary to elaborate further on this much-discussed development. From the present, formally analytic point of view, it may be interpreted to be a highly active process of adaptation between the social system and the personalities of individuals; in that sense it is part of the "socialization" process about which much has been said in recent years. It is thus by no means simply a process of "adaptation to" personalities on the part of social systems, but first, of modification of them in directions of functional significance to the social system of reference. This involves a process analogous to the "mastery" of the physical environment by technology and the "conquest" of disease by modern medicine and public health measures at the somatic level.

There is, however, another and subtler aspect of the process, and one in which the concept of "mental illness" provides a better model than does that of somatic illness as indicated in the classical meaning of "scientific medicine." Indeed the mental illness case is actually intermediate. This has to do with the fact that the process of modification of personalities involves the *interpenetration* of social and personality systems through the "internalization" of the normative structures and symbols of culture and of "social objects," both collective and individual. Of the many complex consequences of such a development, a particularly salient one concerns the undermining of many of the traditionalistic and ascriptive components of social status and "security" in such statuses. These processes occasion still another complex of integrative problems, about which something will be said presently.

Before entering into that, however, I want to emphasize that the educational revolution, if I may call it that, has not been an isolated phenomenon but has developed, especially at the levels of higher education, in very close relation to a "cultural revolution" which has centered in the area of *cognitive rationality*, namely, the growth and other forms of development of philosophy and science. It seems to be significant that the two great phases of the development of the system of modern societies, the 17th century and the 19th to 20th, have been integrally connected with major developments in both philosophy and science, perhaps particularly the latter. In the case of the second of these main phases there have been, of course, major new developments in the area of physical science, but also for the first time a high peak of development of the biological sciences with their medical and other applications, and a not yet so impressive, but still far from negligible development of the action, behavioral, or social sciences as they are variously called.

In a sense including empirical validation, theoretical sophistication, and differentiatedness, we can speak of a modern system of the *intellectual disciplines* which, however impressive its antecedents may have been, is a *new* phenomenon of the cultural world. This of course has become basically "international" and is not bound to any particular national unit of the system of societies, nor is it bound to any particular "ideological" position.

Elementary, and for the most part secondary, education should still utilize essentially the received cultural bases. There was a process of societal adaptation going on in that these "given" cultural factors came to play a new role in the personal orientations and societal concerns of modern societies. At the level of higher education, however, the educational process as such came to be involved most intimately with major processes of cultural innovation, especially those usually categorized under the rubric of "research."

We might, in a certain sense, suggest that these circumstances established a special kind of society-environment relationship. It is generally true that, from both the perspective of the social system and that of the personality, the cultural environment is a "man-made" environment, and becomes problematical to the degree that those aspects which center on the intellectual disciplines constitute a "special" kind of societal-environment relationship. Thus under the heading of "charisma" there has been much discussion of the process of change at both the levels of constitutive symbolism and moral-evaluative symbolization.[21] Here perhaps Weber's comparative studies in the sociology of religion constitute the prototypical analytical statement of the problem. Weber's "exemplary prophet" seems to typify the creator of new constitutive symbolism; his "ethical prophet," that of new moral imperatives. Distinct in important ways from both of these have been the concentration on what I have called "expressive symbolization" which in its most differentiated form concentrates in what we know as the "arts." It is perhaps significant that the term "creative"—which in our religious history was a special prerogative of the divinity—has settled more on the artist than any other order of cultural specialist, even the religious. Certainly there is far more resistance to characterizing a scientist as "creative" than an artist. The fact that the scientist is bound by obligations of fidelity to the "constraints" of environmental considerations—sometimes called "the facts"—while the artist is permitted to be much more freely "imaginative," may have something to do with this intriguing linguistic usage.

However this may be, what I count to be the fourth main category of content of the cultural system, namely that centering on "empirical cognition" and its products, has come to occupy a special place in both the cultural environment and the cultural constitution of modern societies. The sense in which this place is special may in the first instance be looked at in terms of the pattern of cultural differentiation. The most important single step in this differentiation has been the "secularization" of various branches of culture, among which the intellectual disciplines loom very large.

In the first instance it may be noted that empirical cognition is the adaptive subsystem of cultural functioning and that for this reason it can be expected to play a special part in processes of adaptive upgrading. Furthermore its focal position in the system of formal education generally suggests that there has been a kind of "spiral" of development from the commercial and industrial revolutions (the "counterpoint" in the integrative context being the democratic revolution and the rise of nationalism) to a new predominantly adaptive phase, in which a new level of empirical knowledge and its utilization by a highly educated population has assumed a central place.

For this reason the strong stress on adaptive function in the value

21. Talcott Parsons, "Culture and the Social System: Introduction," in Parsons and others (eds.), *Theories of Society* (New York: Free Press, 1961), 963–997.

systems of modern societies is clearly significant—and I have called this primary value pattern, with special reference to the American case, "instrumental activism." The combination of the development of science and of higher education has given rise to an immense new proliferation of technologies, very conspicuously in the physical-engineering fields, but also in fields of applied biological science and partially of behavioral science. It has also given rise to an immense increase in the numbers and the relative importance of the professions in the occupational structure, including of course the "academic" profession.

This complex within the professions has come to embody, although with structural variations in the different societies, the dual functions of teaching at levels of higher education and of "research" or institutionalized provision for the continuing advancement of knowledge. Even where a large proportion of relatively "basic" research is done in specialized institutes, this development has elevated the institutions of higher education, especially the universities, to an especially salient position in the most recent phase of the development of modern societies. This is perhaps particularly true of the United States where, on the one hand, the research and the teaching functions tend to be combined in the same groups and where, on the other hand, mass higher education has extended furthest.

The impact of the educational revolution has of course been spreading through sectors of the society other than the primary centers of innovations involved in it, as happened also with the industrial and democratic revolutions. The contributions of recent technology to the standard of living are clear as well as more recently in the context of the salience of the problem of environmental pollution. The growth in importance of the professions has also brought about a major change in the nature of instrumentally oriented collectivities, notably in industry and government, in such a way as to make obsolete, in important respects, not only Marx's picture of the "capitalistic" firm, but also Weber's of bureaucratic organization and its predominance in both business and government. Related to this of course is the general upgrading of the labor force, very conspicuously by the elimination of very large numbers of unskilled tasks through mechanization and automation.

Two further sets of repercussions, however, are of special interest here. The first concerns the relation of the educational revolution to the integrative function, while the second set of repercussions will serve as a transition to a brief discussion of the fourth of the central processes of structural change which I have been reviewing here, namely, value *generalization*.

Both the industrial and the democratic revolutions occasioned major social disturbances. The events in France in the Revolutionary period, from 1789 at least to the ascendancy of Napoleon, as well as those that occurred in many other countries for several decades are familiar.[22] In the case of the industrial revolution, various kinds of "labor" disturbances took place, the most important developing toward the middle of the 19th century.[23] These included not only "protests" and movements toward unionization, but also the political labor movements, including the socialist parties.

The reasoning and evidence which connect these two sets of disturbances with the democratic and industrial revolutions respectively would lead one to expect that the educational revolution, if its consequences are as important as we have suggested, should also be the storm center of comparably severe social disturbances which are mainly generated by it and, though linking up with other sources of strain in the society, center more in it than at any other point. These disturbances should also have a special relation to problems concerning integrative functions because of the specially important dynamic relations between adaptive and integrative processes.

Clearly the most likely parallel phenomenon is student disturbance. There are two especially interesting features of this parallel. In the educational system, students clearly constitute, relatively speaking, a low-status group, as compared to members of faculties and administrative officers. In this respect they have had positions in some ways analogous to those of commoners by contrast with aristocrats, and of workers by contrast with owners and managers. Secondly, however, it has become increasingly and widely recognized that the spearhead of such protest or radical movements has not come from the most disadvantaged groups. Thus in the democratic revolution it has been the "bourgeoisie" rather than the lower class which has been in the forefront. Even the Parisian "sansculottes" were predominantly what we would call "lower-middle-class" people rather than the "poor." Similarly in the labor movement it has been the relatively skilled workers that have led rather than the mass of the unskilled laborers. Two considerations then apply to the student disturbances. First, it is college and university students who are the focus of disturbances, not those in secondary schools, to say nothing of primary schools. Second, it is students in the institutions of higher standing rather than the more disadvantaged sectors of the system of higher education, who have been most disturbed.

There is, however, one particularly salient difference. While the "bourgeoisie," including the sansculottes, and the "proletariat" could be categorized as "classes," this designation is not appropriate for students, for the simple reason that, increasingly with the spread of mass higher education,

22. R. R. Palmer, *The Age of Democratic Revolutions* (Princeton: Princeton University Press, 1959).

23. Neil J. Smelser, *Social Change in the Industrial Revolution* (Chicago: University of Chicago Press, 1959).

they constitute a category of the stage-of-life course rather than one of as-cription to lifelong status. Clearly, there is a complex of "mobility prob-lems" for students, both with respect to access to higher education at var-ious levels, and with respect to propects following the educational process,[24] but in its primary "meaning" student status is not one of presumptively permanent inferiority. As a major focus of structurally conditioned disaffec-tion, hence, it may be regarded as essentially a new phenomenon in the developmental pattern of modern societies.

Erikson has made a particularly illuminating suggestion[25] about the symbolic meaning of student status. For the democratic revolution, the focal context of evil was subjection to arbitrary "authority," notably that of mo-narchical regimes which denied the legitimacy of citizen participation.[26] Secondarily, the focus was "privilege" with special reference to the status of aristocracies. In Marxism, and the socialist movement more generally, it was "exploitation," usually defined primarily in an economic sense but in-cluding the conception that economic advantage was reinforced by political power.

Erikson's suggestion is that the current focus is neither of these, but "dependency." Thus he says that the common theme which links dissident students with the groups which they seek as allies in the United States—notably the "blacks," the "poor," women, and the "third world" as putative victims of "colonialism"—is their perception of common dependency on presumptively illegitimate organs of control.

I suggest that the following are the main structural background de-velopments underlying these three dominant themes. The authority theme mainly concerned the process of differentiation between the polity and the societal community. The focal concern was that persons and groups ex-ercising authority, hence, using power, ostensibly in a collective interest, should be accountable to the membership of the societal community as a constituency—eventually on a "fully democratic" basis, though this took a long time to develop.[27] The theme of "exploitation," in turn, has concerned primarily the differentiation of economy from polity. Of course, there have been important complications connected with this process. In the earlier

24. Christopher Jencks and David Riesman, *The Academic Revolution* (Gar-den City: Doubleday, 1968).
25. Erik H. Erikson, "Reflections on the Dissent of Contemporary Youth," *Daedalus* (Winter 1970): 154–177.
26. Fred Weinstein and Gerald Platt, *The Wish to be Free* (Berkeley and Los Angeles: University of California Press, 1969).
27. Stein Rokkan, "Mass Suffrage, Secret Voting and Political Participation," *European Journal of Sociology*, 2 (1961): 132–152.

phase, that of the "commercial revolution," the "business" community felt constrained by the power of government. The classical statement of this feeling is perhaps Adam Smith's famous attack on mercantilism. In the later phase, the "workers" felt constrained by the economic and, I think, in a more analytical sense, by primarily the political power of the "capitalists."

In the current rhetoric, focusing around student disaffection, these themes of attack on allegedly illegitimate authority, exploitation, and combined power, continue to reverberate. At the same time I think that Erikson is correct that there is a new and different note sounded by the dependency theme. This concerns the process of differentiation in the first instance between the personality of the individual and the social system. By contrast with the authority context, students feel not so much "dominated" as "constrained," and by contrast with that of economic class, not so much "exploited" as "alienated."

Put in formal terms, this "disturbance" constitutes a new point on a "spiral" of societal community development which is parallel to that which shifted emphasis from the economic function to that of empirical cognition on the adaptive side. It constitutes a shift of focus from the level of the social system alone to that of the general system of action. Here the crucial medium is not authority-power, but the relation between performance capacity, and *affect*, i.e., the individual's attachment (cathexis and identification) in the social systems in which he participates. The primary trend, looking toward resolution of these severe conflicts, I should expect to lie in the direction of the conception of "institutionalized individualism" which leads to enhancement of the autonomy of the personality, but in the context of certain types of institutionalized structure. In relation to these problems, Durkheim has been the preeminent theoretical forerunner.

The knowledge side of the educational revolution derived from cultural developments, in the first instance in interaction with the social system in the areas of the social organization of education itself and of research. The developments of which we have just been speaking, on the other hand, derive mainly from developments in the system of personalities, in interplay with social system agencies of socialization, in the earlier phases primarily the family of orientation, but then with the system of formal education, and its closely associated peer group cultures, playing a prominent part.

However, we feel that the phase which has just been outlined is new in that a special set of processes, having to do with socialization as well as predominantly cognitive learning processes, have developed at the level of *higher* education. It has been customary for sociologists and personality psychologists to terminate the main process of socialization with the transition from adolescence. We feel, however,[28] that mass higher education and attendant structural changes have brought about a new process centering about the status we call "studentry." This has very much to do with socialization for universalistically evaluated achievement, of which performance of the professional type of function is prototypical, but also for responsible membership and leadership roles, especially in associational types of collectivity, which includes the acceptance of authority both on the "receiving" end and in psychological capacity to exercise leadership and authority.

THE PROCESS OF VALUE-GENERALIZATION

For a very long time I have treated institutionalized value-patterns as a primary, indeed in one special respect the most important single structural component of social systems. What is often called the "content" aspect of a value system would concern the balance among the broadest types of orientation alternatives, such as between instrumental and consummatory emphases and between religious and secular emphases. In these respects the broadest evidence seems to indicate that the most firmly institutionalized value systems have considerable stability transcending the shorter-run change in the structure of particular societies—meaning time periods up to several centuries. Thus I should argue that the system of modern societies has had a broadly stable pattern of value-orientation, which derives in the main from the "marriage" of Israelitic and Greek components in the Christian movement, notably as this became institutionalized in "western" society.[29]

The dimension of concern here, however, is a different one. It involves the primary point of articulation between the differentiatedness of a social system and its values. The basic proposition is this: The more differentiated the system, the higher the level of generality at which the value-pattern must be "couched" if it is to legitimate the more specified values of *all* of the differentiated parts of the social system. Thus in the background of modern societies the differentiation of church and state, whereby the "state" or secular society acquired religious legitimation, was fundamental, as was the Reformation and later, in the early modern period, the first phases of "secularization."[30]

28. Talcott Parsons and Gerald Platt, "Higher Education, Changing Socialization, and Contemporary Student Dissent," A *Sociology of Age Stratification*, Vol. 3 of *Aging and Society* (New York: Russell Sage Foundation, forthcoming, 1970).
29. Parsons, *The System of Modern Societies*, 1970.
30. Parsons, "Conference on the Culture of Unbelief: Commentary," in R. Caporale and A. Grumelli, eds., *The Culture of Unbelief* (Berkeley and Los Angeles: University of California Press, 1971).

Perhaps the crucial point here is the institutionalization, in Durkheim's sense, of a "moral community" which both cuts across "denominational" lines—in the more narrowly religious sense—and those of ethnic culture, but also includes legitimation of structures which are both "sacred" and "profane." Here I use "cutting across" to mean the inclusion, *under* a single legitimizing value-pattern, of components which are not only diverse and differentiated from each other, but many of which have, historically, claimed some sort of an "absolutistic" monopoly of moral legitimacy. Thus clearly at one stage only "good Catholics" could be full citizens of many Western societies; at the height of nationalism, e.g., only "good Frenchmen," understood in an ethnic-cultural sense, could be full citizens; or, more recently, only "good members of the working class," with a presumptive eligibility for membership in the Communist Party, could be full citizens. In this context value-generalization is of course intimately associated with the structural "pluralization" of modern societies. A major component of what Karl Mannheim called "utopias" may be considered to mark steps in value-generalization, such as the liberal-democratic and the socialist-communist utopias.[31]

What, then, can we say about the *process* of value-generalization? First it must be conceived as involving the zone of interpenetration between cultural and social systems—as well, especially, as personalities—in such a way that a significant change in the social structure must at the same time comprise cultural change. The stimulus for such change can come from a wide variety of sources, most of which can be categorized under the heading of "strain" in the social system, including for example the strain over the problem of "usury" in the period of the commercial revolution[32] and the strain over the problem of clerical celibacy in the Catholic church at present.

To state a framework within which further clarification can be sought, three primary stages of specification of value-institutionalization can be stated. The first is what may be said to precede secularization of any serious sort, namely where values are directly ascribed to specific religious commitments or orientations. This is the familiar case of either a predominantly "traditional" situation or one dominated by an established religion where subscription to its tenets at all levels provided the criteria of moral accept-

31. Karl Mannheim, *Ideology and Utopia*, tr. by Louis Wirth and Edward Shils (New York: Harcourt, Brace, and World, 1936), and Parsons, "The Sociology of Knowledge and the History of Ideas," *Dictionary of the History of Ideas* (New York: Scribners, forthcoming).

32. Benjamin Nelson, *The Idea of Usury*, 2d ed. (Chicago: University of Chicago Press, 1969).

ability as a member of the society. In the modern societal systems this position was under severe attack in the early phase and had already begun to
give way.

The second stage is the one outlined above where "denominational
pluralism" has become more or less fully established and religious particularism is transcended by a "moral" unity by virtue of which the society becomes a "moral community," in Durkheim's sense, and which is also characterized by an "ecumenical" civil religion. The third stage or level concerns
transcending this primacy of societal commitment in favor of a new kind of
"moral autonomy" of the societal unit—in the "last analysis" the individual
person, but within a framework of the sort referred to above as "institutionalized individualism." Here both of the other levels "survive" in the total
pattern of value-orientation, and above all imply the second level as the
term institutionalization has just been used. There is, however, a new element in that the individual or other unit comes to be "free" within ascertain-
able limits, to define his own value-commitments, independently either of
a received religious base or of the imperatives of societal moral authority.

What I have called the second level comprises the main pattern of
differentiated societal functions—such as economic production, contribution
to political effectiveness, or even to societal solidarity—but goes beyond this
to sanction spheres of autonomy and initiative whether or not they "contribute" in the above sense. The familiar strictures on mutual compatibility
of the modes of exercise of such autonomy of course apply, i.e., remaining
within the limits both of compatibility with the interests of the societal
system and not too greatly injuring the interests of other units of the system.

It is my view that a principal source of the turmoil in which modern
societies are involved in their current phase has to do with the initiation and
spread of this extension of legitimate value-commitments to a new level of
generality and hence inclusive tolerance of variation. If the "absolutizing"
of the societal moral community, which I take to be characteristic of the
Communist societies, is no longer legitimate, the question becomes urgent
of the basis of which a viable mode and level of societal community solidarity can work out. The current mood seems to be one of loudly asserting
claims to freedom *from* societal obligations, but these assertions, for which
there are many historical precedents, will not just make the problem "go
away." Perhaps the problem of violence, when and how it is justified, how
it shall be controlled, is in course of becoming the focal center of the *value*
problems involved in this transition.

Any such threefold classification of levels must of course, on a more
general theoretical basis, be considered to be relative. Thus one could, I

think, fairly argue that within small limits the third level was briefly attained in the male citizen body of the more advanced Greek *poleis* in their culminating period—only very marginally for a few women. The conditions of consolidating this institutionalization, however, were not present, to say nothing of its immediate extension, though some of the best features of Roman Imperial society may be said to have constituted a partial institutionalization of it on a broader basis than in any previous case. In the modern world it is unevenly institutionalized in particular "national" societies, and to a considerable extent in "international" contexts, but its current status is both highly incomplete and precarious. A major extension beyond particular societies seems to me to depend on the institutionalization of a firmer and broader system of societies than we have yet seen. Such a process would entail a repetition of the stage-process on a wider set of system-reference bases. The general conceptual structure of the series I conceive to be a "spiral," which is parallel to that involving the adaptive factors in the technological, economic, and scientific series, on the one hand, and the integrative factors in the field of the generalization of affect, on the other.

To return to the problem of process. A first point concerns what I have called "value-pressure." Assuming that a value-pattern has in fact become internalized and institutionalized to a significant degree, discrepancy between the valued "ideal state" and the actual state of affairs becomes a source of strain. The commitment to the ideal then constitutes a set of factors exerting pressure toward changing the actual state in the direction of conformity with normative standards. This pressure is likely to be stronger in proportion as the value-pattern is "activistic," i.e., calls for positive goal-attainment and active adaptation rather than more passive "adjustment" to the system's environments.

A value-pattern, no matter how firmly institutionalized, constitutes only one major factor in the determination of social process, though in cybernetic terms it is placed at the highest level. The factors of "interest," notably in the economic and political categories, are analytically independent as, when properly understood, are norms as distinguished from values. Moreover the value-*system* itself is not simple but complex. It consists not only of a "master pattern," but also of many levels of subvalues, specified both in terms of level of the functions in the system which they regulate, and of qualitative differentiation among such functions—e.g., the subvalues governing a business firm are different from those of a university. Nonvalue factors can, of course, operate in interdependence at every level and type of specification. This is one of the main reasons why maintenance of the "integrity" of the value-pattern, as I have called it, is empirically problematical.[33] This complicatedness of the value-system itself is clearly a function of the pluralism and differentiatedness of the social system of reference.

Very broadly we may say that the "pressure" of interests tends to be "centrifugal," with a built-in tendency to escape the "control" of values, whereas the tendency of the value-pattern's pressure is obversely "centripetal." Among action components and types other than values themselves, then, the effect of the value-pattern tends to be selective in the sense of creating various difficulties for the types of actions which do not fit, and advantages for the ones which do. This is a process which is in certain respects, though by no means all, analogous to the process of natural selection in the organic world. There is also, of course, collective action directly oriented to the implementation of values, most conspicuously shown in crisis situations, though not always. Hence both the selective and the directly implementive aspects of value-institutionalizations must aways be considered.

The maintenance of what I have called the integrity of a value-pattern can occur in more than one way. Besides "implementation" in the most direct sense, which is the "moral" equivalent of "law-enforcement," it can occur through two other primary processes, namely specification, as just referred to, and value-generalization. The two are, of course, concretely interdependent with each other, as well as with other factors in concrete social process.

I have suggested that differentiation is in part a consequence of value-pressure. At the same time it creates problems from the point of view of integrity, namely, will the value-pattern, as institutionally "conceived" in Kluckhohn's term, legitimize both parts of the newly differentiated complex, rather than only the one which existed prior to the step of differentiation? Thus in a classical example, when occupational roles came to be differentiated from those in kinship-based households, massively through the industrial revolution, a value-problem was created, which has reverberated for a long time, essentially around the question as to whether work outside the household is basically legitimate. The Marxian concept of the "alienation" of labor is clearly a negative answer to this question. Similarly when the societal community became differentiated from a religiously sanctioned collectivity, a process, often called "secularization," gave rise to the question of whether it did not constitute "simple" abandonment of religious commitments.

The pattern of specification constitutes a meaningful linkage between

33. Parsons, "On the Concept of Value Commitments," reprinted in my collection of essays, *Politics and Social Structure* (New York: Free Press, 1969).

more general and more particular levels of generality. Hence, it is nearly obvious that, in order to bring new particulars together with old under a common general rubric, the general rubric may be redefined at a higher level of generality than before. The problem of integrity here concerns the question of whether, in being generalized, the pattern does or does not maintain the same "orientational" character, i.e., whether the change is one of generalization to include new modes of implementation of the "essential" pattern or represents a step in the direction of "eclecticism," namely, willingness to tolerate types of action which are in fact incompatible with the value-pattern. The concept of value-generalization in my sense excludes the "eclectic" alternative.

The process of institutionalizing a new level of value-generality is very often fraught with conflict in concrete situations. Those genuinely committed to the old, and now inadequate, level are very likely to feel that *any* alteration of their concrete commitments is a surrender of integrity to illegitimate interests. This I have called the "fundamentalist" reaction. Along the lines of Smelser's analysis of collective behavior it may be said that strain tends, in proportion to its severity, to propagate defensive reactions upward in the cybernetic order, and that the appearance of conflict at what ostensibly is the level of values, is the "end of the road" at least within the social system as distinguished from other subsystems of action.

The tendency to "de-differentiation" among groups motivated to innovative social change is essentially another aspect of the same basic phenomenon. It is the attempt to legitimize the innovations by appeal to a more "primordial" level of values than can fit the newly possible structural manifold; it is also a resort which is very generally motivated in substantial part by an attempt to "discredit" the fundamentalists. The result tends to be a polarization of conflict at the value level, with both "poles" assuming a position of "value-absolutism." The conflicts attendant on the Reformation, the French Revolution, and the socialist opposition in the industrial revolution all exemplify this polarization. This pattern of polarization is also prominent in the conflicts of our own time.

In most cases it is intrinsically possible, though never inevitable, that such polarizations should be resolved by redefining the relevant value-patterns on a level of sufficient generality to include *both* sides of the previous polarity. Thus we now have an "ecumenical" conception of basically Christian religion which includes both Catholics and Protestants, to say nothing of others. We have a legitimation of "liberal democracy" which includes both "elite" classes and the common people—with all the difficulties of legitimizing "what elites?" On somewhat similar grounds I should argue that the old polarization between "capitalism" and "socialism" is in process of attenuation. If these historical interpretations are correct, a process of value-generalization has been occuring as an essential ingredient of these processes.

Most generally, I should say that without a process of generalization at the value level, the other processes of basic and potentially "progressive" social change which have been outlined here cannot eventuate in a stable new state of a social system. It is particularly important to distinguish between value-generalization and inclusion, which is the version of the more general imperative of integration which has figured in the present paradigm. Too low a level of value-generality tends to impede inclusion and to favor polarization over that issue. Thus many innovative trends, particularly in our own time, press for new inclusions. Fundamentalists, in the above sense, tend to resist, and the proponents of change reciprocally, tend to assert value-positions which cannot be generalized to include both. Indeed this combination of inadequately generalized value-commitments, with the "sponsoring" of or resistance to important new inclusions, is perhaps the most important formula for defining a "revolutionary situation." Such conflicts may be resolved without actual revolution; or they may lead to revolution, with an eventual resolution which both includes and legitimizes what originally were both "sides"; or, of course, they may not be resolved at all—one possibility in this category being segmentation: they simply go their separate ways. The realistic possibilities in this latter direction are, however, clearly limited.

PARTICULAR SOCIETIES AND SYSTEMS OF SOCIETIES

In the above discussion I have stressed the concept of system of societies rather than that of the particular society, because it is considerably less familiar than the latter and also because of its special relevance to the evolutionary perspective. Though I had intended, when I began the discussion, to devote more attention to premodern societies as systems, it seemed better to concentrate on the modern system as I got into the matter. Even so, within the limits of this paper, I have been able only to single out a few illustrative themes and problems rather than presenting a systematic survey.

In my own experience the emphasis I have used here is a product of a kind of three-stage, if you will in a rough sense, "dialectic" development of interest and theorizing. It began, as I stated, with exposure to the Ginsberg-Hobhouse version of comparative analysis. This was continued in the early Harvard course which, within a theoretical framework that was very loosely structured, attempted on the one hand to deal comparatively with functional complexes of "institutions" in terms of the then current classificatory rubrics such as economic, political, religious, kinship, and the like, and, on the other hand, to deal in a brief synthetic way with a series of "total" societies, e.g., European Feudalism, Greece, Rome, Ancient China, India. However rough and crude, this pattern of organization did contain the main axes of later, more sophisticated conceptualizations.

It was perhaps a not unusual experience for sociologists with macrosocial interests to become rather especially concerned with problems of the nature of their own society. In the very early 1940's, just as the crisis of Western society over Nazism was coming to the climax in the generalized Second World War, I introduced a course under the title "Social Structure of the United States," which, with a few interruptions, I have continued to teach ever since.[34]

I have very explicitly used my comparative interests as a means of trying to gain an improved perspective on the problems of American society— a task of particular difficulty for a student of it who is also directly involved in it at a time when its state has been one of rapid change and relative turbulence. Conversely, the relatively greater intensity and depth of study of American society has raised many problems and suggested interpretations which were relevant to a broader comparative perspective.

Over the years it has become increasingly clear that to achieve genuine perspective on more or less contemporary American society there had to be "historical depth" not only in the history of the United States, but of the wider "Western" system of which it was a part. To this may be added the consideration that America and other Western societies were coming into increasingly significant contact with other societies which were not, except remotely, genetically derived from the same sources, notably of course those of Asia. Considerations such as these have led me to attempt, increasingly, to generalize from the more usual kinds of "historical" concerns to those which can be called evolutionary. This trend of thought coincided with a set of developments within biological theory and in general science— notably the "new genetics" and cybernetic theory—which indicated a far greater continuity between human socio-cultural evolution and that of the organic world than had been at all widely appreciated, especially after the social science revolt against evolutionary ideas to which I referred earlier.

My own specific work within this framework has involved two phases or foci, exemplified by the two small volumes referred to in the *Foundations of Modern Sociology* series. The first of these is the very sketchy attempted

---

34. The two fields, "Comparative Institutions" and the course of American society, have for thirty years now been the mainstay of my teaching of substantive sociology, excluding courses in theory as such and in certain topical fields, such as sociology of religion or the professions.

codification of comparative-evolutionary ideas for premodern societies, including those outside the "western orbit" which have remained premodern, in the theoretical sense, well into the modern age.

I may perhaps single out two interpretive conceptions which have been central to that work, not for careful development, but illustrative mention in the present context. Some years ago I concurred with Robert Bellah in trying to work with a very tentative five-stage paradigm of societal evolution, as presented by him in his notable paper "Religious Evolution."[35] This scheme has constituted an important part of the analytical framework used in the two small volumes referred to. Apart from the kind of concerns with the structure of the modern system which have been discussed above, there were two especially important theoretical pay-offs for me which clustered about Bellah's conception of the stage of "historic" religion.

The first concerns a remarkable historical situation in which apparently the main outline of the process of differentiation between the great civilizations of the Orient and of the Western world, in the broadest sense, took shape. Considering the primitive character of communications at the time, it is remarkable that near the middle of the first millennium B.C. there developed nearly simultaneously four very major cultural movements: Confucianism–Taoism in China, Brahmanism in India, the Prophetic movement in Israel, and the emergence of "philosophy" in Greece. What seems to be common to them is a much sharper level of differentiation between cultural and social systems—and somewhat less directly between both and personalities and organisms—than had been the case for "archaic" levels. The theme of rejection of the world appeared, something which Weber analyzed in his well-known essay and to which Bellah brings a new sense of interpretation. This theme was most pronounced in Brahmanism, but also prominent in the Taoist countercurrent to Confucianism, in the "Dionysian" countercurrent to the main Greek trends, and in the mystical undercurrents which became prominent in post-Prophetic Judaism.

Weber never attempted to systematize the pattern of differentiation of these four main cultural movements, all of which were either very specifically religious or included a major religious aspect. If, however, as Weber did not do, the four mid-millennium movements are treated together and separated from Christianity, it seems that they can at least plausibly be fitted into the four-function paradigm, namely, Brahmanism in the Pattern-maintenance cell, Confucianism in the Integrative, Greek classical in the Adaptive, and Prophetic Judaism in that of Goal-attainment. The system-

35. *American Sociological Review*, 29 (June 1964): 358–374.

reference here must be societal-cultural as a whole, though the movements were clearly associated with the process of differentiation on the social-cultural axis also. All four, taken together, constituted a cultural-social *system* at the most general level.

The two Oriental systems were clearly concerned with the emphasis on "immanence" of principles of divinity and related themes, as compared with the theme of "transcendence" in the Western cases. There is, however, another interesting difference. Both the Indian and the Chinese cultural developments arose within what were probably in their day the most "advanced" large-scale societies, and did not establish clearly differentiated subcollectivities with religious primacy within them. This is to say there was no structural situation at all closely analogous to the Mediaeval differentiation between Church and State which underlay the modern development. The largely, though not wholly, "traditional" order—in Weber's sense—was "sacralized" by Brahmanic and Confucian constitutive symbols: the conceptions of transmigration and Karma and their relation to ritual purity on the one hand, and those of Tao, Yang, and Yin and their relation to "propriety" on the other.

In addition to this "sacralization" of traditional social orders—a phenomenon which was quite new compared to cases like ancient Egypt—there was in both cases a more or less "monastic" safety valve for persons who were more radically committed to new religious patterns: the Taoists in China; the Brahmanistic "mystics" and the Buddhists in India. However for many centuries in both cases the sacralized traditional order prevailed, though this seems to have come into flux in the most recent period.

In the West, however, the two main culturally innovative movements arose, not in the principal large-scale societies, notably those of Egypt or Mesopotamia, but in small "marginal" societies, or, as in the case of the Greek Poleis, systems of societies, namely Israel and Greece. Partly because these societal systems were small in scale and marginal[36] to the "big"

---

36. When I say "marginal," I would like that to be interpreted to mean that they were both "member societies" in a system of societies, or possibly more than one. This seems to be true in a sense of which I was not fully aware at the time of writing *Societies*. Probably the correct statement is that both belonged in the same system of which the political center was the Empire of Mesopotamia. There was clearly a time when Israel was in the Egyptian orbit, but the whole story leading up to the Exodus and the prophetic role of Moses seems to constitute a basic breakaway from that orbit. The later conquest by the Babylonians and the "exile" in Babylon does not contradict the suggestion of Israel being a "satellite" society in the Babylonian system, and later of course part of the Hellenistic and Roman successors of Babylonia.

It is quite clear that there were important structural continuities, in some-

political systems, the *whole* socio-cultural system in each case could come to be differentiated from its neighbors in line with the cultural innovation. Thus Israel became, as "People," the societal institutionalization of a distinctive "historic" religious orientation—the "religion of Jahwe"—in a sense that had not occurred in any archaic society. In parallel, the system of Greek Poleis could become the institutionalized embodiment of the new culture of the "corporate rationality of a citizen body in accord with Nature," to put it in a very awkward and complex phrase.

As it happened, neither of these radical cases of institutionalization of a new cultural orientation turned out to be politically viable, in the sense of any realistic prospect of maintaining their independence relative to the "great powers" of the time. Indeed, both came to be absorbed into the growing Roman Empire. In the process of this absorption, however, the main cultural component came to be differentiated from the structure of the host society and, I think, largely *because* there had been a societal carrier in the background, i.e., the "people" of Israel and the Greek "polis." Thus it was possible for a basis to develop in social structure which could exert societal and not only cultural "leverage" for future development. The maintenance of precisely the *societal* integrity of the Jewish communities in the Diaspora is the outstanding "interim" example, but considerations of this sort underlay the crucial significance of the Christian *Church*.

As I put it in *Societies*,[37] Israel and Greece constituted "seedbed" societies, from the point of view of their impact on the future. Precisely because they became differentiated so far "out of line" with the main societal system of the time, they could not maintain their independence. But their cultural innovations survived. The Christian "breakthrough" was clearly a major cultural innovation beyond either the Judaic or the Greek. Part of its distinctiveness consisted in the cultural "marriage" between these two patterns. At the same time, however, both seedbed societies offered models of societal organization which could be synthesized within the conception of the Church as an entity set over against the Roman Empire of the time,

---

what different directions, between the society of Mesopotamia and that of the Northeast corner of the Mediterranean. (Compare chs. 4 and 6 of *Societies*.) In particular a "city-state" component was common to both. From the Greek point of view the Mesopotamians were not quite complete "barbarians" in the sense in which the "Scythians" were.

Both of these seedbed societies, however, enjoyed for a critical but brief period a special order of independence relative to the political center of the Mesopotamian system and, though the societal aspect of the independence was lost in both cases, the cultural innovation was not reabsorbed along with much of the political and social structure.

37. Parsons, *Societies*, ch. 6.

involving a special combination of a "people" in the Judaic sense and of a "citizen body" in the Greek sense.[38]

The "syncretism" which constituted this crucial cultural "marriage" was part of a very broad welter of syncretisms occurring decisively about this time, which notably included Egyptian and Persian themes—e.g., the cult of Isis and Osiris and Mythraism.[39] It thus seems reasonable to suggest that a decisive advantage of the Christian synthesis lay in the fact that it carried with it the Value and, even in part, the Norm basis for a pattern of firm collective organization, independent of the society within which it developed. It is of course quite clear that without the individualism and universalistic cosmopolitanism of Imperial Roman society, it could not have survived, to say nothing of being able to proselytize. Equally essential was the break with the Israelitic ethnic community since even a restructured "Judaism" could not have become the official religion of the Roman Empire.

Subject to conditions such as these, however, the makings of the social institution which became the Christian Church constituted a set of decisive factors in making not only the survival and spread of early Christianity within Roman society possible, but in making it possible, at a much later time, for Christianity to become the main cultural base of the unique development of modern society.[40] The above very sketchy discussion of the differentiation among the "historic" religions, in Bellah's sense, and the special circumstances in which two of them in combination laid the cultural foundations of modern society will illustrate, I hope, the utility of the particular version of comparative and evolutionary conceptualization for the analysis of certain crucial features of premodern socio-cultural development which has been discussed here. In this connection, again, the conception of a system of societies (and cultures) has been of critical importance.

In conclusion I should like to sketch out one more illustration, this time with reference to modern, up to very recent, developments. This con-

---

38. This duality seems to be symbolized in the Eucharist, the basic ritual of the Church. The wine, as symbolizing the "blood" of Christ, seems to connect with the Judaic background, the "people," whereas the bread, symbolizing the "body" of Christ, seems to derive from the conception of the polis as a collective body in which the individual participates as a "member." There is a very striking parallel here to David Schneider's analysis of modern kinship, with his categories of the importance on the one hand of "blood" relationships, and of those involving "law" as prescribing relatedness through observance of a "code of conduct." Schneider, *American Kinship* (Englewood Cliffs, N. J.: Prentice-Hall, 1968).

39. Franz Cumont, *Mysteries of Mithra*, tr. from 2d rev. French ed. by Thomas J. McCormack (New York: Dover Press, 1956), and A. D. Nock, *Conversion* (London: Oxford University Press, 1933).

40. For my views on these matters see my article "Christianity" in David Sills, ed., *International Encyclopedia of the Social Sciences*, vol. 2 (New York: Macmillan, 1968).

cerns the problem, noted above, of perspective on the development of American society. It may be pertinent first to remark that my earlier predilections were, in line with the main intellectual currents at the time, first to emphasize the decisive importance of economic emphases, not only in the descriptive characterization of modern and especially American society as "capitalistic," but to carry through to the conception that this was not only a characterization but an explanation. Max Weber cast considerable doubt on the latter set of inferences, but introduced still another note, namely, that of the prevalence of "bureaucracy," not only in government but in the field of economic organization.

In the sense in which Weber's essay on the *Protestant Ethic* proved decisive for me in beginning to question the adequacy of the prevalent "economic interpretation" of social processes, if not of "history" as a whole, my beginning concern with the significance of the professions in modern society contained the seeds of a questioning of the thesis of the all-pervasive "dominance" of bureaucracy,[41] a thesis which has received massive ideological reinforcement in recent years from the "New Left."

By that time I was thoroughly acquainted with Durkheim's work. Moreover, a fact that was particularly significant was that within the framework of the convergence of theory between him and Weber, which was so important to me, Durkheim was giving an emphasis in his interpretation of some of the main trends of modern society that was different from Weber's emphasis on bureaucratization. It gradually became clearer that this pattern identified by Durkheim was closely associated with that of the professions and, up to a point, also with that of the economic market, precisely in contrast with the predominantly hierarchical stress of bureaucracy.

The conception, however, of a system of modern societies, which has been discussed at some length in the present paper, helped greatly to focus and crystallize views on this issue, with special reference to the "diagnosis" of American society in its recent phases of change. A certain pattern of continuity, as discussed above, was particularly clear, beginning with the case of England and Holland in the 17th-century phase of modern development, in contrast both with Prussia in particular, and with the older Counter-Reformation powers, notably Austria and Spain.

In this respect, then, the "hierarchical" aspect of British society, centering above all on the institution of aristocracy, could be seen as relative; and in the system as a whole, one giving way gradually to a new level of "egalitarianism" in America, especially perhaps in the phase described by

41. James L. Peacock and A. Thomas Kirsch, *The Human Direction* (New York: Appleton-Century-Crofts, 1970).

Tocqueville. This theme, however, not only connects with democracy in a political and a perhaps vague "social" sense, but also with the implications of the new levels of development of education and of the professions, as again broadly outlined above.

It has become my view that a highly bureaucratized social system, like that of the Soviet Union, can borrow and utilize such cultural and social components often, from certain points of view, more effectively than the societies which favored their original creation, but that, since the Middle Ages at least, the more creative centers of structural innovation of modern society have remained and are likely to remain in the future in the less "tightly" and hierarchically organized subsocieties of the system. The very fact that the United States has recently become a center of conspicuous turmoil, which many interpret as heralding its early decline, may on the contrary be a sign that it continues to harbor the seeds of major socio-cultural innovations which will be decisive for the future. The analogy to the turbulence of the 17th century in the European Northwest Corner is evident.

However this may be, I think it is correct that American society is in many respects the most individualistic, the most "collegial," and the most universalistically oriented of the major units of the modern system, and that the accusations that it is uniquely "repressive," far from being true, constitute simply a case of a familiar ideological "reversal." The best previous case perhaps is that of the "liberation" of productive capacity through the industrial revolution which was, in the socialist movement, interpreted to be mainly a process of "exploitation" of the workers.

Whatever the merits or demerits of such perspectives, I think I can say that without the evolutionary and comparative frame of reference, I could not have remotely approached satisfying my intellectual conscience with respect to a sociological view of my own society. To me the intellectual need to understand what is going on in one's own social milieu and how it fits in a broad spectrum of antecedent structures and processes, and of similarities and differences with other currently extant social systems, are correlative and mutually imply one another. I do not think one can be a first-rate interpreter of any current social situation without comparative and evolutionary perspective nor, vice versa, that one can be a good comparativist or evolutionist without the deepest concern for one's own society and the "meaning" of its characteristics and trends of change.

FRAMEWORKS FOR COMPARATIVE RESEARCH: STRUCTURAL ANTHROPOLOGY AND THE THEORY OF ACTION

GUY E. SWANSON

Robert Marsh's position is of the sort that no one can ever totally deny.[1] "Both sociology and social anthropology," he tells us, "have been distinguished by intensive analysis of particular societies and by discussions of general concepts rather than by extensive cross-societal research into comparative problems." That is how he opens his informative book *Comparative Sociology*. Three hundred and twenty-seven pages later, he concludes: "The unifying goal . . . [of comparative studies] is that of social science itself: the continuing reassessment of which theories and propositions hold for all societies, which only for certain types of societies, and which only for individual societies." That conclusion misleads. Scientists, not science, have goals and, although most scientists want to establish propositions valid for some universe of events, there is often good reason for them to come late, or never, to the kind of reassessment March proposes. A man's scientific lifetime, the resources he has available, and the scope of the questions that command his attention, all of these are limited. It is efficient for him and his science that he not expressly estimate the universality of his findings until there is serious reason to question it. That is a parsimony inevitable in the practice of empirical research.

I begin with this point because we often mistake the purpose of comparative research. We then err in estimating the value for it of particular bodies of theory.

We may, for example, perpetuate the mistake contained in the very words "comparative studies." Those words erroneously imply that some research is not comparative. That is an error because all behavior and, consequently, all research entails comparisons: comparisons with what was,

1. Robert M. Marsh, *Comparative Sociology, A Codification of Cross-Societal Analysis* (New York: Harcourt, Brace & World, 1967), p. 5.

with what might be, and with what might have been; comparisons among practical alternatives; comparisons between what is practical and what meets some more general standard. Marsh does not perpetuate that mistake. He rightly says that comparative studies are often undertaken to determine the validity of an explanation across some range of circumstances.

A second mistake is to believe that comparative research is something new in social science. Merton begins to rectify this error in his foreword to Marsh's book:

> From the time sociology crystallized as a distinct discipline, it has been committed to the comparative study of societies, cultures, and their institutions. So much was this the case that the founding fathers of to-day's sociology—Marx, Weber, Durkheim, and, in their own ways, Spencer and Pareto—employed comparative analysis as the self-evident way of going about the business of sociological inquiry. After these substantial beginnings, however, serious work in comparative sociology dwindled for several decades. But after World War II it reemerged on a scale greater than ever before. . . . More and more sociologists the world over have been devoting themselves to detailed, systematic comparisons of social stratification, political and kinship structures, economic organization, and the complex interrelations of the three.[2]

I read our history somewhat differently. Explicitly comparative research has at all periods been common. Attention to comparisons relevant for the truth of a particular theory has been standard in sociology from the beginning. (Since the introduction of sampling in the 1930's, most sociologists have felt hard pressed to justify any study that was not expressly comparative.) For an indication of the incidence of comparative research, consider only the period between the "fathers" and 1950, a period of roughly forty years, and recall only a few of the leading names and investigations in sociology:

°Howard Becker, *German Youth, Bond or Free*, 1946.
°Ernest W. Burgess and Harvey J. Locke, *The Family, From Institution to Companionship*, 1945.
 Charles H. Cooley, *Social Organization*, 1909.
°Lyford P. Edwards, *The Sociology of Revolution*, 1927.
°Franklin H. Giddings, *Civilization and Society*, 1932.
°Everett C. Hughes, *French Canada in Transition*, 1946.
°Harold D. Lasswell, *World Politics and Personal Insecurity*, 1934.
 Robert and Helen Lynd, *Middletown*, 1929.
 Robert and Helen Lynd, *Middletown in Transition*, 1937.
 Roderick D. McKenzie, *The Metropolitan Community*, 1933.

2. *Ibid.*, p. v.

*John M. Mecklin, *The Passing of the Saint,* 1941.

Howard W. Odum, *Southern Regions of the United States,* 1936.

*William F. Ogburn, *Social Change,* 1922.

*Robert E. Park and Herbert A. Miller, *Old World Traits Transplanted,* 1921.

*Robert E. Park and Ernest W. Burgess, *Introduction to the Science of Sociology,* 1924.

*Edward A. Ross, *The Changing Chinese,* 1911.

Clifford R. Shaw and Henry D. McKay, *Delinquency and Urban Areas,* 1942.

*Albion W. Small, *The Cameralists,* 1909.

*Pitirim A. Sorokin, *Social Mobility,* 1927.

*Pitirim A. Sorokin, *Social and Cultural Dynamics,* 1937–41.

*William G. Sumner, *Folkways,* 1906.

*Walter A. Terpenning, *Village and Open-Country Neighborhoods,* 1931.

*Dorothy S. Thomas, *Social Aspects of the Business Cycle,* 1925.

*William I. Thomas and Florian Znaniecki, *The Polish Peasant in Europe and America,* 1918–20.

*Pauline V. Young, *Pilgrims of Russian-town,* 1932.

These few references will do. They remind us that sociologists in this period were determinedly comparing communities, classes, types of family, subcultures, historical periods, regions, generations, social types, and so on and on. Nor was it unusual to compare whole societies or whole cultures. I have placed an asterisk before works in which that was undertaken on some sizable scale.

This list corrects a third possible error. A detailed study of a single organization or culture can be comparative or not depending on the theoretical framework in which it is interpreted. I think, for example, of the monograph by Young on Russian immigrants, by Hughes on French Canada, by the Lynds on Middletown, and by Becker on the German wanderers. Each focuses on one case, but interprets that case in a comparative framework. A clear and recent example is Henry Elsner's investigation of Technocracy.[3] Elsner chose to study this social movement exactly because it seemed to fit into the corpus of modern extremist movements but to be importantly unlike the others.[4] One outcome of his work was an expansion and refinement of a scheme that Lipset had earlier presented for interpreting such movements.[5]

But there is a fourth error beside which the first three are merely venial.

3. Henry Elsner, Jr., *Technocrats, Prophets of Automation* (Syracuse: Syracuse University Press, 1967).

4. Edward A. Shils, "Seeing It Whole," *The Times (London) Literary Supplement* (28 July 1966), pp. 647–648.

5. Seymour M. Lipset, *Political Man* (Garden City, N.Y.: Doubleday, 1960).

It is the error of assuming that comparative studies always arise in order to determine whether some existing proposition is valid in *all* organizations, or, at any rate, in *all* societies or cultures. Immediately when one thinks of putting this prescription into practice its futility becomes apparent. My point is not to show that such a goal is inoperable nor do I counsel perfection; rather I want to note other purposes that generate comparative research. Max Weber, for example, surveyed the great world religions to explicate not the universality of Calvinism but its uniqueness. Kroeber and Toynbee compared the world's civilizations not so much to test hypotheses as to generate explanations. It is my impression that in sociology the banner of comparative research is newly hung to rally those who want to discover what about social organization is important to explain.

These differences in purpose are not trivial. Theory helps us reach our objectives. The theories of Parsons and Lévi-Strauss will be important for the new comparativist movement in sociology if they serve its purposes. Merton's observations direct us toward a better understanding of those purposes.

The total volume of sociological research increased markedly in the period after World War I. I think that what Merton sees as a decline in the *incidence* of comparative studies was instead an increase between 1920 and 1945 in the *proportion* of all investigations that made comparisons other than those between whole societies or whole cultures. These new varieties of study were in part undertaken because sociologists developed reliable techniques for their research that was not based upon historical archives: techniques such as the interview, content analysis, tests, questionnaires, and participant observation. The newer types of study permitted an expansion of the questions that sociologists were competent to investigate. The rise of the newer methods was not accompanied, however, by a decline in the volume of research that compared societies or cultures.

There was, nevertheless, one feature of the new techniques that threatened not comparative studies but sociology itself. The new methods made it easy to obtain information on individuals, not on organizations or cultures. When the use of these methods came to be a mark of rigorous, scientifically advanced work, the study of organizations, including societies, and the study of cultures came to be considered a second-class enterprise. At the crest of this period, problems in social psychology became the focus for sociologists' research.

As I understand what happened immediately after World War II, it was that many sociologists, especially younger sociologists, reasserted the importance of the problems and phenomena at the heart of their field and committed themselves to use whatever methods were suited for work on

those problems.[6] Marsh documents the vigor of this new and current movement. By tabulating only those studies published between 1950 and 1963
in which two or more societies were "systematically and empirically compared." he obtains a list of 952 titles.

This movement was consonant with great public issues of the 1950's
and 1960's. We find in the first subjects to be studied in this new fashion—
extremist politics in Europe and America and the problems of bureaucratic
organizations—a focus on social developments that were salient just after
World War II, that could not easily be interpreted through the use of social
psychological theories, and that could be studied in only limited ways by
relying upon methods that obtained information from and about individuals. The Cold War, the rise of the new nations, the modernization of traditional economies, the swiftly changing character of complex organizations
and of their internal problems, the continuing differentiation and secularization of advanced societies: all of these and other social developments
have riveted sociologists' attention upon comparative studies of organizations, especially large organizations and societies. It is understandable that
in these circumstances there is renewed attention to older works having a
similar emphasis, such as the monographs of Durkheim, Weber, Tocqueville, Marx, Michels, Mosca, Tawney, and Marshall. Just as this return to
comparative sociology reached its first crest, Talcott Parsons published *The
Social System*. And at this time, although not immediately known to sociologists, there appeared the first of Claude Lévi-Strauss' broadly comparative investigations *Les Structures élémentaires de la Parenté*.[7]

Thinking without comparisons is unthinkable. And, in the absence of
comparisons, so is all scientific thought and all scientific research. No one
should be surprised that comparisons, implicit and explicit, pervade the
work of social scientists and have done so from the beginning: comparisons
among roles, organizations, communities, institutions, societies, and cultures. The novelty in the social sciences today is not comparative research
but the primary reasons for undertaking it.

Contemporary lines of work arose in the 1950's as part of an effort in
sociology and anthropology to study social organizations as organizations,
and not as aggregations of individuals; to study properties of organizations

6. Few developments in sociology are more striking than the aggressive rejection by many leading investigators of the most elaborate and best rationalized
technologies for research. This rejection is of special interest because most of the
men involved had as students mastered a working knowledge of those technologies
and many had employed them in earlier research.

7. Talcott Parsons, *The Social System* (Glencoe, Ill.: Free Press, 1951);
Claude Lévi-Strauss, *Les Structures élémentaires de la Parenté* (Paris: Presses Universitaires de France, 1949).

and not to confuse them with properties of personalities; to study whole organizations, major components of organizations, major institutional systems, and complex patterns of culture; to obtain a sample of cases in which the covariance of essential components of these phenomena could be compared. These efforts reflected the judgment that core problems had been slighted in the period before and immediately following the end of the Second World War, a period in which social psychological interests had predominated.

I believe, however, that this sketch omits what is even more distinctive and important about the current wave of comparative investigations, especially those in sociology. I believe that the present great attraction of comparative studies is that they embody that union of sociological theory and research so often advocated and so seldom achieved. The new comparativists seem principally distinguished by their programmatic commitment to that union and by one procedure for effecting it. Lévi-Strauss makes the main point about procedure: "The comparative method consists precisely in integrating a particular phenomenon into a larger whole, which the progress of the comparison makes more and more general. . . ."[8] Notice that this procedure consists of more than the making of comparisons and more than the use of general theory. It specifies that comparisons be made in such a fashion that they bear upon theory and force the progressive elaboration and generalization of theory. It requires that theory be at once general enough to subsume the phenomena being compared and responsive enough to differences among phenomena to describe and account for those differences. By Lévi-Strauss' prescription, research is so conducted that theory is at every point in touch with observations, and observations are so selected that they insure the further growth of theory. This, we shall find, is exemplified in his own work.

At minimum, the new comparativism reinstates morphological studies as an essential part of the sociological enterprise, making of them a source and a standard for all other work. Explanation, not morphology, is still seen as the desirable end of scientific work, but there is a new appreciation of the uses and necessity of good morphology in determining what it is that is important to explain and how adequate one's explanations really are. Begin, for example, with the polities of ancient empires. Compare them with one another, with the empires of primitive peoples, and with the empires of 19th-century Europe. Through these comparisons isolate abstract

8. Claude Lévi-Strauss, *Totemism*, Rodney Needham, tr. (Boston: Beacon Press, 1963), p. 85. Copyright © 1963 by Beacon Press, first published in France in 1962 by Presses Universitaires de France under the title *Le Totemisme aujourd'hui*, Copyright © 1962.

features of polities that will enable one to classify all of these cases without obliterating their salient differences. Now add to the comparison a direct democracy of some complexity—Athens, for example. A host of fresh differences appear, requiring that one rework the features of polities already identified. Can we now see some principle by which some of these features can properly be construed as transformations of others? Do some combinations occur with disproportionate frequency? Others not at all? Can we move beyond morphological considerations to account for the incidence of particular combinations? And so on. Whether purely morphological or something more, the new and minimum *scientific* objective—held self-consciously and programmatically—is the development of a *progressively* more general and complete apparatus of concepts and classification. In this respect, morphology moves beyond the uses made of it in history or in natural history and beyond the uses made of it by earlier sociologists.

The new legitimation of morphological work adds merit to meticulous empirical studies of social organization. There again is scientific value in a lively interest in the substance of social life and in a deep and concrete knowledge of its variations. All comparisons among organizations become of possible importance in the advance of theory. They will be worthwhile to the extent they are accurate. A full, careful report of the "facts" is once more to be treasured. The more imaginative, speculative accounts are still of value, but not to the detriment of studies of which the chief merits are completeness and craftsmanship. What is undertaken is not merely descriptive ethnography. It is guided by theory and promotive of theoretical advance.

Once accepted as a mode of procedure, this form of comparative research also offers the scientist a personal advantage. Provided only that he execute a competent study of a theoretically salient case, he is assured of making a contribution to his field. If his work provides evidence concerning some hypothesis, well and good. But if not it will still be a worthy candidate for inclusion among those paradigmatic cases that force some further distinctions in theoretical classifications or explanations. Insight, inspiration, good luck in research—none of these can be acquired by formal education. All are subject to personal and professional vicissitudes. By contrast, most investigators can expect through formal education to prepare themselves to make worthwhile contributions to comparative research as it is now envisioned.

But how does one select a theoretically salient case—not one of startling importance, but one that is worth a man's attention? In the procedure that involves least risk, one does this by immersing himself in some sector of existing theory and of comparative investigations, and finding there those points at which the theory fails to classify, let alone to explain, the variations observed.

And in any such endeavor, sustained if not focal interest in whole societies and whole cultures plays a critical role. In the absence of other leads, these most embracive social units can serve an investigator as that "larger whole" into which Lévi-Strauss suggests we integrate particular phenomena. In any case, they constitute an object into which it should someday be possible to integrate more circumscribed phenomena. Thus they serve as empirical surrogates for the complete theoretical structure that is never attained. They are available in its absence to guide all special investigations, and they extend the assurance that all social phenomena are empirically united however disparate they may at present appear.

It is in stimulating theory and in providing a systematic framework for observations that the current attention to formal organizations and to the most advanced of societies and cultures has its special theoretical force. Sociologists hope through studying the entire system of an organization to force themselves to take into account a myriad of analytic distinctions and interrelations, seeking by successive approximation to generalize from these toward a theory applicable to all organizations. The most complex of organizations, of societies, and of cultures come under special scrutiny because they contain the greatest variety of internal components and because, in them, more of those components are sufficiently differentiated—and hence are more readily observable. A theory constructed through the generalization of these systems of components, it is often argued, should suffice for the simpler, smaller organizations as well.

I have stressed that the new comparativism will restore to sociology respect for observation, for a wide scholarship, and for craftsmanship, that it entails an especially close union of theory with research, and that it makes possible numerous and worthwhile investigations for which the graduate schools can equip most of their students. I noted that the movement gives added value to knowledge of whole societies and cultures, especially those that are most complex. It will of course not insure that sociologists work on general or profound problems of their field. It may even promote a regression, by encouraging more investigators to be satisfied to perform descriptive studies rather than trying to gather evidence or to develop explanations. It may, by virtue of the role in theoretical interpretations that it gives to whole societies, produce a falsely complete, symmetrical, and unified picture of the organizational structures within a population. But all approaches have their dangers.

My purpose here is not to celebrate the new comparativism but to understand it and, from the perspective of its thrust and style, to examine the meaning for it of the two most comprehensive sociological theories recently to emerge—those of Parsons and Lévi-Strauss. In evaluating their works I adopt as a standard the objective each sets for himself. Both men seek to provide a general and comprehensive theoretical apparatus for the analysis of social events. They have in mind not a system of explanation—that is, a deductive system from which all or many social phenomena are known to be logical consequences—but a system of concepts from which explanations can be developed and can be interrelated. What they want is a theoretical orientation. In their judgment, and in mine, comprehensive explanatory systems are always an unreachable ideal. Lacking such a system, the working scientist operates with partial explanations that may be generated and unified by a theoretical orientation.

In the ideal case, a theoretical orientation provides a scientist with a definition of the elementary units of which all subject matter in his field will consist, a conceptualization of the general character of the effects that those units have upon one another, and a characterization of the processes through which those effects are attained. Thus, in certain theoretical orientations to legal analysis—Hofeld's, for example—the units are actors, individual or collective, in the status as participants in a legal order; the effects are changes in the rights or obligations held by actors within that order, and the process is the adjudication of complaints. We are all familiar with economic analyses in which the units again are actors, individual or collective, in their status as sources of demands or supplies within a market relationship, the effects are the exchange and subsequent use by those actors of goods and services, and the process is conceived as one of bargaining. These illustrations are simplified, but the orientations themselves tend to be spare and general. They provide an investigator with concepts that help him to place his problems in the context of existing explanations and then to formulate new explanations that can be tied by bonds of concept and inference to work already completed. Systematic progress in science comes through building upon an orientation, through assessing its power to formulate mutually coherent explanations for diverse observations, and, most dramatically if less frequently, through revisions of the orientation itself.

If we are to think in a general way about comparative studies of organizations and cultures, and to judge the promise for them of ideas found in Parsons and Lévi-Strauss, our interest is not in specific explanations devised by these men for specific phenomena. It is in the theoretical orientation contained in their work, in the main directions in which they have elaborated that orientation, and in the powers and limitations for comparative work that seem inherent in their general approach.

The kind of assessment we need is unlike certain others. An orientation is to be judged more for the generality and comprehensiveness of its conceptualization than for its empirically verified validity. We either can or cannot use its ingredients, and the derivatives from those ingredients, to explain the phenomena we have in mind. Few questions of logical structure arise because the logical structure of an orientation is usually very simple, however complex the implications drawn from it. The primary need is for a precise delineation of the essential components of the orientation and, from that delineation, a judgment of what can and cannot be conceptualized by means of those components. That is what I shall try to provide concerning the theoretical work of Lévi-Strauss and Parsons.

In reviewing each man's work, I ask what "larger whole" it provides into which particular phenomena may be fitted. I also ask about the means that each man makes available to effect that "fit" (e.g., classification, explanation, or both). I review problems of comparative method of which the theorists themselves are aware. I examine one instance of each man's comparative work with the objective of seeing how he operates and what problems remain unsolved. I restrict myself to the most central features of each scheme. Because Lévi-Strauss' work is less familiar to American readers than is Parsons', I treat it at greater length.

STRUCTURAL ANTHROPOLOGY

To provide orientation, here is a one-paragraph overview of the present state of Lévi-Strauss' work: As I understand it, his programmatic objective is to construct a general theory of culture. He requires that this theory be consistent with Marx's view of culture as superstructure. His procedure is both inductive and synthetic. He begins with a general notion of the place of culture in human affairs. He then addresses himself to a specification of the components and internal structure of culture, doing this by examining one large complex of culture after another in each of many societies. Because he is a Marxist and therefore, derivatively, a Hegelian, and because he is a French social anthropologist trained in the tradition of Durkheim and Mauss, he always chooses to study a complex of culture that subsists as a bounded, empirical system within each of several societies. In this way he tries to insure that he will have a coherent, empirical system of phenomena for study and that these phenomena will be integrated with an empirical social organization—with the organization of a particular society. This practice is sometimes obscured by a neo-Kantian language. (A description of his thought as Kantian has been admitted by him as accurate.) He writes of wanting to understand the "mind of man," and desiring to develop a characterization of humanity and of human nature. Nonetheless, his style of analysis is more immediately Durkheimian and Hegelian and Marxian. He always works from holistic depictions of some one of the cultural systems of particular societies rather than from human nature; he focuses upon the properties of collective rather than of individual thought and action; and he analyzes only those cultural events that are interrelated, not merely by his having classified them together, but by their joint mediation of the empirically bounded social relations that constitute their substructure. He wants to derive from these specific investigations the essential components of all culture and of its principal varieties, and to learn the "grammar" by which all are systematized. To that end, he must first uncover the components of an appropriate theoretical orientation. His progress toward that first goal, and the methods he employs, will be my chief concern.

I begin with his root conception, culture, and with its relation to nature. I then discuss the grounds on which he identifies certain features of culture as being more fundamental than others and discuss the principles by which he distinguishes among the major varieties of culture. I review his treatment of totemism in order to discuss his procedures for uncovering the "grammar" of culture. In that connection, I examine his own prescriptions for comparative research. I evaluate specifics of his work as I go along, reserving a more general appraisal of its import for comparative studies until I have also described the framework of Talcott Parsons. Now to Lévi-Strauss on culture and nature.

The idea seems to have been there all along, a guide for the whole course of Lévi-Strauss' work.[9] Its full importance may first have crystallized while he was writing his monograph on totemism: "Rousseau," he wrote, "poses the central problem of anthropology, *viz.*, the passage from nature to culture."[10] And he noted approvingly that, in Rousseau, this passage is understood from an "extraordinarily modern view" and one "based . . . on the emergence of a logic operating by means of binary oppositions and coinciding with the first manifestations of symbolism."[11] And, again, "The advent of culture thus coincides with the birth of the intellect."[12] Only a short time before, in 1960, he asked in his first lecture as Professor of Social Anthropology in the Collège de France, "What . . . is social anthropology?" and replied:

9. Lévi-Strauss, *Structures,* chs. 1 and 2.
10. Lévi-Strauss, *Totemism,* p. 99.
11. *Ibid.,* p. 101.
12. *Ibid.,* p. 100.

. . . No one . . . was closer to defining it . . . than Ferdinand de Saussure, when, introducing linguistics as part of a science yet to be born, he reserved for this science the name semiology and attributed to it as its object of study the life of signs at the heart of social life. Did he not, furthermore, anticipate our adherence when he compared language to "writing, to the alphabet of deaf-mutes, to symbolic rites, to forms of politeness, to military signals, etc.?" No one would deny that anthropology numbers within its own field at least some of these systems of signs, along with many others: mythical language, the oral and gestural signs of which ritual is composed, marriage rules, kinship systems, customary laws, and certain terms and conditions of economic exchange.

I conceive . . . of anthropology as the bona-fide occupant of that domain of semiology which linguistics has not already claimed for its own, pending the time when for at least certain sections of this domain, special sciences are established within anthropology.[13]

Lévi-Strauss granted, in that lecture, that some special disciplines, economics, law, political science among them, already focus on certain areas of semiology. What anthropology offers is an apprehension of these and other areas:

. . . in their most distant manifestations, or from the angle of their most general expression. . . . the particular social sciences . . . would not know how to aspire to generality were it not for the cooperation of anthropology, which alone is capable of bringing them the accounts and the inventories which it seeks to render complete.[14]

The passages just cited contain in capsule form all but one of the major themes that characterize Lévi-Strauss' work. Why, it remains to be asked, should one study primitive peoples? In answering, Lévi-Strauss further specifies what distinguishes nature from culture.

It at first seems that Lévi-Strauss is making a banal point in method: Primitives provide us with experiences far removed from our familiar round and thereby force us to re-examine our assumptions about human society; they force us, if we live with primitives, to be socially born anew, to learn once more to speak and understand the simplest of ideas and habits. His actual point is more subtle and is known to the ethno-methodologists among us.[15] It derives from the emphasis, traditional among French sociol-

13. Claude Lévi-Strauss, *The Scope of Anthropology*, Sherry O. Paul and Robert A. Paul, tr. (London: Jonathan Cape, Ltd., 1967), pp. 16–17. The quotations are taken from Ferdinand de Saussure, *General Course in Linguistics*, Wade Baskin, tr. (New York: Philosophical Library, 1959), p. 16.

14. Lévi-Strauss, *op. cit.*, pp. 17–18.

15. Harold Garfinkel, *Studies in Ethnomethodology* (Englewood Cliffs, N.J.: Prentice-Hall, 1967).

ogists, upon first interpreting the action of specific individuals and groups according to their role in the whole of the society in which they arise. This interpretation can be effected by emphasizing either of two procedures. First, one can begin with the values ultimate in a society and with the organizations that are most concerned to define and conserve those values, and one can then display the relations of individuals and of less comprehensive groups to those ultimate values and organizations. One thus begins with the goals normatively ultimate in a population and works downward.

The second procedure is to seek the rudimentary principles in a population by which any action becomes normative and by which normative links are constantly created and dissolved between individuals and among groups. As Lévi-Strauss sees it, the first approach was primarily that of Durkheim, the second, that of Mauss. It is as a former student of Mauss that he then generalizes his and his teacher's position:

> . . . it seems to me that in the theory of the "total social fact" . . . the notion of totality is less important than the very special way in which Mauss conceived of it: foliated as it were and made up of a multitude of distinct yet connected planes. Instead of appearing as a postulate, the totality of the social is manifested in experience. . . . this totality does not suppress the specific character of phenomena, which remain "at once juridical, economic, religious, and even aesthetic or morphological," so that totality consists finally in the network of functional interrelations among all these planes.
> . . . "What counts," said Mauss, "is the Melanesian of such-and-such an island . . ." . . . behind the rationalized interpretations of the native—who often makes himself into an observer and even theoretician of his own society—one will look for the "unconscious categories" which, Mauss wrote . . . are determinants "in magic, as in religion, as in linguistics." [16]

It is those "unconscious categories"—those hidden, but ever-potent, meta-norms that embody the logic of all social life—that will be the most basic subject matter of the semiological science Lévi-Strauss seeks to advance, and he extols the study of primitive peoples because it is through that study, and especially through living with primitives, that one is most dramatically forced to become aware of this logic.

> . . . It is to the extent that so-called primitive societies are very distant from our own, that we can discover in them those "facts of general func-

16 Lévi-Strauss, *op. cit.,* pp. 11–12. For another comparison of Durkheim and Mauss, see Claude Lévi-Strauss, "French Sociology," *in* Georges Gurvitch and Wilbert E. Moore, eds., *Twentieth Century Sociology* (New York: Philosophical Library, 1945), pp. 503–537.

tioning" of which Mauss spoke, which stand a chance of being "more universal" and "more real." In these societies . . . "one grasps individuals, groups—and behavior . . . one sees them driven as in a piece of machinery . . . one sees agglomerations and systems. . . ."[17]

It is Lévi-Strauss' faith that the "unconscious categories" and the "facts of general functioning" are universal to mankind, rooted in a frame of experience and contingency common to all societies, however humble, and common to all men, however educated. The essential processes, mental and social, are one for all men of all times and places.[18]

It is, however, man's tragedy that society and culture were at the beginning insufficiently differentiated. From the Neolithic revolution, and through the early stages of the industrial revolution, populations advancing in the exploitation of the environment did so primarily by "calling on that driving force of collective life which takes advantage of the contrast between power and opposition, a majority and minority, exploiter and exploited"—in short, by the differentiation of society into castes or classes and by enslavement.[19] But the industrial revolution made possible an end to injustice as a necessary cost of social advance: "It made possible the transfer to *culture* of that dynamic function which the proto-historic revolution had advanced to society."[20] The growth of culture—of ideas and machines—can now occur without concomitantly making at least many men into things:

> . . . Then, culture having entirely taken over the burden of manufacturing progress, society would be freed from the millennial curse which has compelled it to enslave men in order that there be progress. Henceforth, history would make itself by itself. Society, placed outside and above history, would be able to exhibit once again that regular and, as it were, crystalline structure which the best-preserved of primitive societies teach us is not antagonistic to the human condition. In this perspective, . . . social anthropology would find its highest justification, since the forms of life and thought which it studies . . . would correspond to a permanent hope for mankind over which social anthropology, particularly in the most troubled times, would have a mission to watch.[21]

This sounds like a kind of Marxism, and Lévi-Strauss so intends it. How can this be reconciled with his career in developing a theory of culture, of "super-structure"? Perhaps it can on the grounds that his career produced

17. Lévi-Strauss, *Scope of Anthropology*, p. 46.
18. For a qualification, see Claude Lévi-Strauss, *The Savage Mind* (London: Weidenfeld and Nicolson, 1966), pp. 268–269.
19. Lévi-Strauss, *Scope of Anthropology*, p. 47.
20. *Ibid.*, p. 48.
21. *Ibid.*, p. 49.

a first analysis of the dawning era of true communism when culture takes from men the burden of subordination. Lévi-Strauss himself prefers a related justification:

> . . . Marxism, if not Marx himself, has too commonly reasoned as though practices followed directly from *praxis* . . . Without questioning the undoubted primacy of infrastructures, I believe that there is always a mediator between *praxis* and practices, namely the conceptual scheme by the operation of which matter and form, neither with any independent existence, are realized as structures, that is as entities which are both empirical and intelligible. It is to this theory of superstructures, scarcely touched on by Marx, that I hope to make a contribution. The development of the study of infrastructures proper is a task which must be left to history—with the aid of demography, technology, historical geography and ethnography. It is not principally the ethnologist's concern, for ethnology is first of all psychology.[22]

The connection of ethnology with psychology is not accidental. It also appears in Saussure's treatise on linguistics which Lévi-Strauss has on several occasions identified as a formative source of his own ideas. I begin again with the quotation from Saussure cited in Lévi-Strauss' inaugural lecture, quoting it more fully than he chose to do:

> *A science that studies the life of signs within society* is conceivable; it would be a part of social psychology and consequently of general psychology; I shall call it semiology. . . . Semiology would show what constitutes signs, what laws govern them. . . .
>
> To determine the exact place of semiology is the task of the psychologist. The task of the linguist is to find out what makes language a special system within the mass of semiological data. [Semiology should not be confused with semantics, which studies changes in meaning.] . . .
>
> .   .   .   .
>
> . . . If we are to discover the true nature of language we must learn what it has in common with all other semiological systems. . . . By studying rites, customs, etc. as signs, I believe that we shall throw new light on the facts and point up the need for including them in a science of semiology and explaining them by its laws.[23]

With this quotation we come again to the central problem that occupies Lévi-Strauss and to his solutions. The transition from nature to culture seems to mean many things to him, depending on the referent of nature.[24]

22. Lévi-Strauss, *Savage Mind*, pp. 130–131.
23. Saussure, *General Course*, pp. 16–17.
24. But he has recently written (*op. cit.*, p. 247); "The opposition between nature and culture to which I attached much importance at one time . . . now seems to me of primarily methodological importance."

In discussing totemism he seems to see the natural species as nature and he tells us that they provide for men a likely foundation for systems of classification, hence a foundation for culture. On other occasions he has written of rules of marriage as cultural facts that are rooted in the natural distinction between the sexes and that effectuate, through the exchange of women, a union of families and of partners in procreation. Similarly, he writes of both economic and technological relations as aspects of culture and portrays them as uniting men with one another as biological systems and as also uniting men with the environment from which sustenance must be gained. But it is to linguistics and semiology that he has turned most frequently. In that context, nature is man as biological organism. Linguistics "makes it possible to pass from" the domain of the organism to culture and back

> and . . . in two different ways: first, because it is possible to show that phonemes have a physical basis. . . . Second . . . is the theory of communication [which] shows us that there is a direct relationship between what we may know of the structure of the brain and the way in which communication processes operate. . . . And, of course, communication is not only a field for linguistics, but it can be said that society is, by itself and as a whole, a very large machine for establishing communication on many different levels between human beings.[25]

What we find in semiology—in the science of signs and of the laws that govern them—is the general class of which linguistics is an instance. Working out from general psychology, it conceives man not simply as organism but primarily as behaving—as a behaver—and it shows that the systematics of signs are rooted in the very nature of the human mind. And that is not all. The character of the mind is such that the formal properties of its operations correspond in wondrous fashion to those of the extra-human environment: "The human mind is working unconsciously along lines similar to nature's."[26] The passage from nature to culture therefore occurs in every human act. We can never recover its first occurrence in the faded past, but we can at every moment see it occur afresh in the life of every man.

SOCIAL STRUCTURE

By his own account, Lévi-Strauss was making structural analyses before he knew what social structure was, before he first self-consciously

---

25. Sol Tax and others, eds., *An Appraisal of Anthropology Today* (Chicago: University of Chicago Press, 1953), p. 321.
    26. *Ibid.*, p. 62.

sought the criteria by which his own analyses had been ordered.[27] The results of his search appeared in 1953 in his paper "Social Structure."[28]

When we look at anything social, Lévi-Strauss tells us, we see regularities of relationship among persons or collectivities. These regularities are *social relations*. How can they be explained? The participants themselves often advance an explanation. Sometimes it is very close to the truth. Quite often, however, it is inadequate. In no instance will participants fully know why it is that they relate to one another as they do. They are in some important degree unaware, unconscious, of the conditions that actually determine their joint enterprise. There is thus a difference between the rationales they advance and the conditions that are really important, and people must make an effort to avoid seeing that gap. They must deceive themselves lest, through skepticism or uncertainty, they lose the capacity for collective action.[29]

When Lévi-Strauss asks whether a social relationship can be explained, he is not usually asking a question about its historical origin. What he wants, rather, is the system of criteria that participants share and that they jointly employ to interpret and guide their behavior toward one another. Grammar provides an example of such systematized criteria. We observe, let us say, Americans striking up a conversation. Their use of language embodies great regularities and they find one another intelligible. Here, then, are people engaged in a social relationship and, although the participants probably do not know it, they employ, in grammar, certain systematized criteria by which regularities in their relationship are formulated.

But, as Lévi-Strauss reminds us, the grammar of language is only one possible example of what he has in mind. He wrote his first major theoretical treatise in order to explicate the system of criteria underlying the exchange of women in marriage. Those criteria are the rules of marriage. Similarly there are criteria governing the exchange of goods and services, the exchange of worship and spiritual powers, the relations among the components of a myth or a ritual, the conduct of politics, fashions in clothing, and so on. These systems of criteria are what he means by *social structure*.[30] Structural anthropology is distinguished by a search for these systems and

27. *Ibid.*, p. 116.
28. Claude Lévi-Strauss, "Social Structure" *in* Alfred L. Kroeber and others, *Anthropology Today, an Encyclopedic Inventory* (Chicago: University of Chicago Press, 1953), pp. 524–553.
29. *Ibid.*, p. 534; Claude Lévi-Strauss, *Structural Anthropology*, Claire Jacobson and Brooke G. Schoepf, tr. (New York: Basic Books, 1963), pp. 131–163.
30. He regards the family as an instance of social relations and a society as a social structure. See Claude Lévi-Strauss, "The Family," *in* Harry L. Shapiro, ed., *Man, Culture, and Society* (New York: Oxford University Press, 1956), p. 284.

by an effort to test the adequacy of systems that the anthropologist believes to be at work in particular situations.[31]

Several things are evident. (1) Lévi-Strauss means by social structure a part of what modern sociologists refer to as culture. (2) The criteria he seeks, and their systematic relations, are products of social relations and serve to guide those relations. (3) Although he prefers to restrict the term "norms" to the rationales that participants themselves offer for regularities in their relations, the systems of criteria that he has in mind are nonetheless normative—that is, they are socially required as well as socially generated and there are social sanctions that encourage conformity to them and that punish deviance from them. (4) It is also evident that the systematic relations among these criteria do not consist in effects of causes or derivations from premises. Rather they consist in the differing but complementary relevance of these criteria for collective action: their relevance as subjects, objects, or objectives in action, as means and ends, as phases preparatory for action or phases entailed in the recovery of integration following action. (5) At least some of these systems of criteria—certainly those to which Lévi-Strauss has given most attention—are more than prescriptions or proscriptions. They are formulae, as grammar is a formula, available to be used as needed for the formulation of ongoing social relations or of new social relations. The method of science is such a grammar. So are general ethical principles. So are rules of art or law or musical composition or mathematical logic. So are endless others. Lévi-Strauss often refers to all such systems of criteria as grammars. Sometimes he writes of them as homologous with the rules of a game.

Now there are very many languages, each with its own grammar, and there are very many games, each having its own rules, and there are many social structures, each distinct. But grammars have been shown to be amenable to formal mathematical treatment. So, in the theory of games, have crucial components of games. So, in Lévi-Strauss' own treatment of kinship, have some aspects of rules of marriage.[32] So, he believes, will other social structures. And he holds out the special hope, a hope exemplified in his analyses of myths, that, when mathematized, many of the special struc-

31. For a contrast between social structure and social process, consult Claude Lévi-Strauss, "Les limites de la notion de structure en ethnologie," in Roger Bastide, ed., Sens et usages du terme structure dans les sciences humaine et sociales (The Hague: Mouton, 1962), pp. 40–45.

32. André Weil, "On the Algebraic Study of Certain Types of Marriage Laws (Murngin's System)," Cynthia White, tr., in Harrison C. White, An Anatomy of Kinship, Mathematical Models for Structures of Cumulated Roles (Englewood Cliffs, N.J.: Prentice-Hall, 1963), pp. 151–157.

tures will prove to be only special cases or logical transformations of others. Thus there will emerge what may be called—depending on one's rhetorical preferences—hyper-structures or deep-structures or meta-structures. In a discussion to which we shall return, Lévi-Strauss links these most basic structures to myth and to religion.[33]

I must now confess that I have taken some liberties in sketching Lévi-Strauss' ideas of social structure. My excuse is his. Neither of us quite knows what Lévi-Strauss intends and both of us are trying to discover the structure of his thought, even as he suggests we should seek to discover social structure itself: that is, by making trial models and testing their ability to order all the observations. I should therefore note that certain observations are not well ordered by his own explicit statements or by mine: He writes in his paper "Social Structure" that the term has nothing to do with empirical reality but with models which are built up after it, and he quotes with approval von Neumann's statement that models must be similar to the reality they represent.[34] On the same page he says that social structure "cannot claim a field of its own among others in the social studies" and declares that it is "a method to be applied to any kind of social studies." But, after these words were published, he said:

> In my mind, models are reality, and I would even say that they are the only reality. They are certainly not abstractions . . . but they do not correspond to the concrete reality of empirical observation. . . . It is necessary, in order to reach the model which is the true reality, to transcend this concrete-appearing reality.[35]

Moreover, he terms "social structure" the "unconscious" reality that Durkheim and Mauss sought as the ground of native categories of thought, and he states that the goal of the structural method is to "derive constants . . . from an empirical richness and diversity."[36] These and many similar comments suggest that, for Lévi-Strauss, as for Durkheim and Mauss, social structure is a social fact.

Perhaps what has happened is that Lévi-Strauss sees social structure as a method—as the "talking about" social facts, the analytic scheme representing certain social facts—and that he also sees structure as the facts appropriately subjected to such an analysis. This seems to me probable and, since it both expedites my discussion and seems not to distort his meaning,

33. Lévi-Strauss, "Social Structure," p. 548.
34. *Ibid.*, p. 525.
35. Tax and others, *An Appraisal*, p. 115.
36. Lévi-Strauss, *Structural Anthropology*, p. 82.

I shall work as if it were true. I plan to focus on structure as a social fact rather than on structure as a method.

EMPIRICAL SOCIAL STRUCTURES

The paper on social structure describes two main types of empirical structures, static and dynamic. "A society," says Lévi-Strauss, "consists of individuals and groups which communicate with one another." Social statics concerns structures of communication.

> In any society, communication operates on three different levels: communication of women, communication of goods and services, communication of messages. Therefore, kinship studies, economics, and linguistics approach the same kinds of problems on different strategic levels and really pertain to the same field. . . .[37]

All are shown to be parts of "one great field, that of communication" and to "consist exclusively of the study of *rules* and to have little concern with the nature of the partners (either individuals or groups) whose play is being patterned after these rules."[38]

Social dynamics refers to subordination structures. These are of two varieties. The first, the order of elements (that is, of individuals or groups) in the social structure, concerns all relations of domination or dependency. The second, the order of orders, consists of transcendent structures through which structures at lower levels are interrelated.

> It is the most abstract expression of the interrelationships between the levels to which structural analysis can be applied, general enough to account for the fact that the models must sometimes be the same for societies which are historically and geographically disparate. . . . By *order of orders*, then, I mean the formal properties of the whole made up of subwholes, each of which corresponds to a given structural level.[39]

Law, art, myth, and religion are apparently among these orders of orders. At least two of them, myth and religion, are sharply different from the structures of communication and of subordination in a further respect. They are "thought-of" orders:

> . . . they correspond to mechanisms which can be studied from the outside as a part of objective reality. But no systematic studies of these orders can be undertaken without acknowledging the fact that social groups, to achieve their mutual ordering, need to call upon orders of different types,

37. Lévi-Strauss, "Social Structure," p. 536.
38. *Ibid.*, p. 538.
39. Lévi-Strauss, *Structural Anthropology*, p. 333.

corresponding to a field external to objective reality and which we call the "supernatural." These "thought-of" orders cannot be checked against the experience to which they refer, since they are one and the same thing as this experience. Therefore, we are in the position of studying them only in their relationships with the other types of "lived-in" orders. The "thought-of" orders are those of myth and religion. The question may be raised whether, in our own society, political ideology does not belong to the same category.[40]

How do the transcendent orders relate to other social structures?

> I do not postulate a kind of pre-existent harmony between the different levels of structure. They may be—and often are—completely contradictory, but the modes of contradiction all belong to the same type. Indeed, according to dialectic materialism it should always be possible to proceed, by transformation, from economic or social structure to the structure of law, art, or religion. But Marx never claimed that there was only one type of transformation—for example, that ideology was simply a "mirror image" of social relations. In his view, these transformations were dialectic, and in some cases he went to great lengths to discover the crucial transformation which at first sight seemed to defy analysis.
>
> . . . it becomes possible—in the final analysis, and on the condition that we disregard content—to characterize different types of societies in terms of the types of transformations which occur within them. . . .[41]

Why are the communication structures called static and the subordination structures "dynamic"? Because, says Lévi-Strauss (illustrating from studies of kinship) the function of kinship systems, of marriage rules, and descent groups is that of a coordinated ensemble by means of which women are pumped out of their consanguineous families and redistributed in affinal groups with the result that new consanguineal groups are constantly created. Were no external factor affecting this mechanism, it would work indefinitely and the social structure would remain static. But "this is not the case, . . . hence the need to introduce into the theoretical model new elements to account for the diachronic changes of the structure, on the one hand, and, on the other, for the fact that kinship structure does not exhaust social structure."[42]

LÉVI-STRAUSS ON TOTEMISM: AN ILLUSTRATION OF THE ANALYSIS OF SOCIAL STRUCTURE

In *The Savage Mind,* the author concisely reviews his own accomplishment:

40. Lévi-Strauss, "Social Structure," p. 548.
41. Lévi-Strauss, *Structural Anthropology,* pp. 333–334.
42. Lévi-Strauss, "Social Structure," p. 546.

All that I claim to have shown so far is . . . that the dialectic of superstructures, like that of language, consists in setting up *constitutive units* (which, for this purpose, have to be defined unequivocally, that is by contrasting them in pairs) so as to be able by means of them to elaborate a system which plays the part of a synthesizing operator between ideas and facts, thereby turning the latter into *signs*. The mind thus passes from empirical diversity to conceptual simplicity and then from conceptual simplicity to meaningful synthesis.[43]

The monographs on *Totemism* and *The Savage Mind*, the two being one work in two parts, appeared after his study of kinship and before his first principal investigation of mythic thought. It was between the completion of his work on kinship and the publication of this pair of treatises that he became self-consciously explicit about the meaning of social structure and the methods appropriate for studies of culture. *Totemism* and *The Savage Mind* serve, therefore, as a bridge from his earlier work to his most recent. They do so not only because they were produced in the period that intervened but because they link the contents and theory of the old and new. A totemic belief contains a systematic nomenclature for designating kin-based groups, typically clans or moieties, and their interrelations. It also contains myths describing the origin of that nomenclature and of those interrelations. It thus provides a structure that links a communication structure with an order of orders. But totemism contains more, and that is the subject discussed in *The Savage Mind*. It embodies with unusual clarity certain features essential to all culture, they being a part of the meta-dialectic of superstructure: classification, systems of transformation, categories, elements, species, numbers, universalization and particularization, the conceptualization of individuals, and time and timelessness. In *Totemism* there thus appear all of the essential analytic considerations Lévi-Strauss has developed for the study of social structure. These are there embraced within an application of the comparative method.

THE COMPARATIVE METHOD

To repeat an earlier quotation: "The comparative method consists precisely in integrating a particular phenomenon into a larger whole, which the progress of the comparison makes more and more general. . . ."[44] If that is the method, to what problem is it applied? ". . . we are confronted with the following problem: how may it be explained that social groups, or segments of society, should be distinguished from each other by the as-

43. Lévi-Strauss, *Savage Mind*, p. 131.
44. Lévi-Strauss, *Totemism*, p. 85.

sociation of each with a particular natural species? This . . . is the very problem of totemism. . . ."[45]

Why should we think that the larger whole into which totemism may be integrated is a social structure? Putting the question differently, how do we know that the totemic associations between social groups and natural species are cultural?

"Because," says Lévi-Strauss, "they are conceived and not experienced." He documents this with such examples as the following:

> In the Trobriand Islands, native clans are arranged in a status hierarchy. This arrangement is said to correspond to, and to follow from, the hierarchy that long ago came to exist among a fabulous dog, the pig, the iguana, the crocodile, the snake, and the opossum. No one, says Lévi-Strauss, has actually seen that hierarchy among the animals and one animal, the dog, is a purely mythical creature. Likewise, no one actually saw the sacred events through which the Trobriand clans were aligned with the hierarchy among the beasts.

> In Australia, some native groups perform ceremonies to increase the number of flies and mosquitos even though they suffer as do other men from the bites of these insects. The ceremonies, says Lévi-Strauss, are held to bring rainfall. Flies and mosquitoes are associated, as signs, with the rainy season that men so greatly desire. The important point, he notes, is that these insects serve here as concepts, not as stimuli.

> Contrary to some of the earlier ethnographers, totemic creatures are often of no visible importance to men except as signs: they often have no economic importance, they do not constitute a zoological or magical class, they may not be physically dangerous, they may have no special role in folklore. He cites several examples from the totemic scheme of the Tallensi.[46]

How do we integrate totemism into a larger structural whole? The first step is to select the class of events of which totemism is an instance. If totemism is a type of sign, we distinguish it from other types by defining "objectively and in its most general aspects the semantic field within which are found the phenomena commonly grouped under the name of totemism."[47] Note that an analysis of the grammatical and syntactic features of totemism waits upon this first, semantic, placement. What then?

> The method we adopt, in this case as in others, consists in the following operations:

45. *Ibid.*
46. *Ibid.*, pp. 62–64, 72–73.
47. *Ibid.*, p. 16.

(1) define the phenomenon under study as a relation between two or more terms, real or supposed;

(2) construct a table of possible permutations between these terms;

(3) take this table as the general object of analysis which, at this level only, can yield necessary connections, the empirical phenomenon considered at the beginning being only one possible combination among others, the complete system of which must be reconstructed beforehand.

The term totemism covers relations . . . between two series, one natural, the other cultural. The natural series comprises on the one hand categories, on the other particulars; the cultural series comprises groups and persons. . . .

There are four ways of associating the terms, two by two, belonging to the different series, i.e., of satisfying with the fewest conditions the initial hypothesis that there exists a relation between the two sets.

	1	2	3	4
NATURE	Category	Category	Particular	Particular
CULTURE	Group	Person	Person	Group

Figure 1

To each of these four combinations there correspond observable phenomena among one or more peoples. Australian totemism . . . postulates a relation between a natural category (animal or vegetable species, or class of objects or phenomena) and a cultural group (moiety, section, sub-section, cult-group, or the collectivity of members of the same sex). The second combination corresponds to the "individual" totemism of the North American Indians, among whom an individual seeks by means of physical trials to reconcile himself with a natural category. . . .

Logically speaking, the four combinations are equivalent, since they are all the results of the same operation. But only the first two have been included in the sphere of totemism. . . .[48]

To generalize, totemism is a social structure generated by a still larger structure, the latter constituted by the rule that either a class or an individual of a natural series can be symbolically associated with either a class or an individual of a cultural series. The more generalized table that this entails is as follows:

	Class	Individual
Nature	Category	Particular
Culture	Group	Person

Figure 2

48. *Ibid.*, pp. 16–17.

When I first read Lévi-Strauss' three rules, I found them surprising. I had expected him to identify the appropriate semantic field by comparing totemism with, say, ritual or with a group's development of an emblem. His rules instead limit us to the two series involved in totemism itself: a natural series and a cultural series. The common meaning of "totemism" that he inherited from the literature already specified the association of the categories of a natural series with either a set of social groups or a set of persons. This received meaning produces three of the cells in Figure 2. It then remains to fill in the fourth cell and to identify the marginal headings for the resultant columns. Following this procedure Lévi-Strauss obtains a "larger whole" within which to integrate totemism.

This integration being achieved, he immediately derives one conclusion from it: Totemism (as defined by columns 1 and 2 of Figure 1) is in no way strange or bizarre; it involves no mental processes peculiar to primitive men. Contrary to Lucien Lévy-Bruhl and to other writers, totemism entails only procedures for classification and combination used by all mankind. The singularity of totemism is declared an illusion:

> The totemic illusion is . . . the result, in the first place, of a distortion of a semantic field to which belong phenomena of the same type. Certain aspects of this field have been singled out at the expense of others, giving them an originality and a strangeness which they do not really possess; for they are made to appear mysterious by the very fact of abstracting them from the system of which, as transformations, they formed an integral part. . . .[49]

There are, of course, curious features in this argument: (1) Were we to accept his reasoning, we would conclude that to analyze any phenomenon is to show that it is an illusion. This follows from the fact that an analytic scheme must be more general than the phenomena to which it is applied. It therefore treats each such phenomenon only insofar as the latter is an instance of a more general class, disregarding whatever may be peculiar to it. (2) Lévi-Strauss has removed the mysteries from totemism as a result of the context in which he chose to treat it: as a principle of classification of individuals and classes into a natural and cultural series. Perhaps the mystery would have been greater had he retained in his classification the distinction between magical and other principles of relationship or had he asked why plants and animals rather than, say, supernatural beings or cultural artifacts were aligned with clans or lineages.

But the argument illustrates a more basic point: the manner in which he determines what in a family of signs is formally elementary. He would

49. *Ibid.,* pp. 17–18.

have us believe that the marginals and the combination rule embodied in Figure 2 are more elementary than the four combinations generated from them. They are for him a deeper reality than those combinations. They are formative, and the four combinations express their formative power. Make no mistake. For Lévi-Strauss, the marginals and combination rule are veridical conditions in the empirical world—in the mind of man—and not merely logical properties of a table in a book. I shall return to this point after completing my review of his interpretation of totemism.

Lévi-Strauss does move our understanding of totemism beyond the point attained by the discussions traditional in anthropology. His conclusion: Totemism, itself defined by a process of classification, is in turn distinguished only by the basis for classification that it contains. He reached that conclusion by unexceptional means: by reviewing the interpretations of others, by re-examining a large part of the relevant ethnography, and by determining which elements of which interpretations seem most plausible. Here are some samples of Lévi-Strauss at work:

> Ethnographic reports: The items in the natural series employed in some societies are nonsensical or bizarre. Conclusion: It is possible that people's interest in these items is a product of attitudes that ritual engenders toward those items rather than an interest in the items themselves.

> Ethnographic report: Three clans among the Marquesans express their relationship to the natural species through ritual; the fourth clan through prohibitions and prescriptions. Conclusion: There may be some level of events of which ritual on the one hand, and prohibitions and prescriptions on the other, are merely instances, the level in question being more general than either.

> Ethnographic reports: The exact character of the association in totemism between the natural series and the cultural series varies greatly from one society to another. For some peoples, the categories or individuals in the natural series are the ancestors of those in the cultural series. For others, the natural series is the spiritual essence of the cultural or is its emblem. Conclusion: One must look to a form of association more general than any of these for what is common to all instances of totemism.[50]

His own solution to the problem of totemism originates in the last of these ethnographic reports.

> . . . we shall never get to the bottom of the alleged problem of totemism . . . by thinking up a solution having only a limited field of application and then manipulating recalcitrant cases until the facts give way, but by reach-

50. *Ibid.*, pp. 25, 76.

ing directly a level so general that all observed cases may figure in it as particular modes.[51]

The decisive idea he finds in Radcliffe-Brown's second theory of totemism: Why, asked Radcliffe-Brown, does a people select one species rather than another? And he answered: The individual species are not important. What people seek is to symbolize relations found in human society by means of a similar pattern of relations among species or other natural events. Thus in Western Australia the moieties of the dual tribal division are sometimes represented by eaglehawk and crow:

> . . . The Australian aborigine thinks of himself as a "meat-eater," and the eaglehawk and crow, which are carnivorous birds, are his main rivals. When the natives go hunting by lighting bush-fires, the eaglehawks quickly appear and join in the hunt: they also are hunters. Perching not far from the camp fires, the crows await their chance to steal from the feast.

> . . . The resemblances and differences of animal species are translated into terms of friendship and conflict, solidarity and opposition. In other words the world of animal life is represented in terms of social relations similar to those of human society.[52]

Lévi-Strauss' summation differs from Radcliffe-Brown's more in its certainty than in its content:

> . . . alleged totemism is no more than a particular expression by means of a special nomenclature formed of animal and plant names (in a certain code, as we should say today), which is its sole distinctive characteristic, of correlations and oppositions which may be formalized in other ways, e.g., . . . sky/earth, war/peace, upstream/downstream, red/white, etc. . . .

> . . . their perceptible reality permits the embodiment of ideas and relations conceived by speculative thought on the basis of empirical observations. . . . natural species are chosen not because they are "good to eat" but because they are "good to think." [53]

PROGRAMMATIC IMPLICATIONS

H. S. Hughes:

> The overriding aim of his career as a social scientist was to dig below every theoretical level yet discovered and to come at last to a basic structure of

51. *Ibid.*, p. 77.
52. *Ibid.*, p. 87.
53. *Ibid.*, p. 89.

the human mind which would at once cancel out and reconcile the countless explanations of their behavior that men had offered through all ages and all types of savagery or civilization.

. . . .

He brought to his labors a characteristic French conviction that cultural phenomena obeyed an immanent law. . . .[54]

Claude Lévi-Strauss:

If, as we believe . . . the unconscious activity of the mind consists in imposing forms upon content, and if these forms are fundamentally the same for all minds—ancient and modern, primitive and civilized (as the study of the symbolic function, expressed in language, so strikingly indicates)—it is necessary and sufficient to grasp the unconscious structure underlying each institution and each custom in order to obtain a principle of interpretation valid for other institutions and other customs, provided of course that the analysis is carried far enough.[55]

H. S. Hughes:

Lévi-Strauss' own method of coping with the emotions was to intellectualize them. He reduced subjectivity to its "intellectual laws," proposing a "sequence of constantly narrower definitions of the unconscious." The result, as the philosopher Paul Ricoeur complained, was an unconscious that was "rather . . . Kantian than Freudian," an unconscious that dealt in categories and combinations—a formulation of his own thought to which Lévi-Strauss in the end was quite willing to assent.[56]

It will not do to take Lévi-Strauss' dictum on totemism as itself his conclusion from this work. The principal conclusion is only provisional and is as follows: Men everywhere seek to objectify social relations and hence more effectively to relate to them. This is in part accomplished by symbolizing those relations. When the relations concerned are those among corporate groups that are differentiated from one another, and when those groups form a system, then an appropriate symbolization must represent that system and the orderly differentiations it contains. Totemism is one symbolization that meets those requirements.

54. H. Stuart Hughes, *The Obstructed Path, French Social Thought in the Years of Desperation, 1930–1960* (New York: Harper and Row, 1966), pp. 267, 269. On this theme, see also Clifford Geertz, "The Cerebral Savage," *Encounter,* 28 (April 1967); 25–32; "Healing Words, Dr. Lancan's Structuralism," *The Times (London) Literary Supplement,* 67 (25 January 1968), pp. 73–75.

55. Lévi-Strauss, *Structural Anthropology,* p. 21.

56. Hughes, *Obstructed Path,* p. 282.

How does it happen that a "natural" series is chosen to represent relations among kin groups? Lévi-Strauss answers that all men behave much of the time as do primitives. They employ as symbols whatever is appropriate and ready at hand. The choice of a natural series is made in the same manner as a handyman or jack-of-all-trades (a *bricoleur*) chooses materials for his work.[57] He rummages through a midden of remains from former projects; ruminates about his earlier enterprises; determines that a board here or a gear there or a switch, or a coil of wire, can be assembled in such a way as to serve his present purpose. He thus depends for his work upon whatever is on hand, imposing upon these otherwise unrelated ideas and materials the form of his purpose, making them into means for his ends. Among these materials that are ready to be "found" are the natural series and, for some purposes, they are especially appropriate.

It is outside our purpose to criticize systematically Lévi-Strauss' conclusion concerning totemism or his formulation of the problem. Nonetheless a few observations are in order. (1) He never does explain why a series of animals or of plants, rather than some other, is adopted to symbolize relations among social groups. He merely shows how such a series can serve that purpose. (2) His general conclusion follows neither from the logic of his argument nor from any prepossessing evidence. But that is too obvious to require discussion. (3) In its final form, his conclusion is impossible to test. (What could we with confidence conclude should we observe a case of totemism and not discover a metaphorical association between the natural series and the cultural series?) (4) In his search for generality he has dropped from the problem of totemism exactly those observations that so tantalized his predecessors: the prevalence of belief in the magical potency of plants and animals, and the role in thought of metaphor, metonymy, and synecdoche. He frequently mentions all of these things, but it cannot be said that he brings serious evidence to bear upon his interpretations. (5) What he has to offer us is, rather, a vision of the comparative study of superstructure, of culture, and a sketch of some basic substantive questions that such research should address, and certain proposals concerning methods of work. These essentials are embodied in his treatment of totemism. It remains to make them explicit.

STRUCTURAL ANALYSIS: PROGRAM, POINTS OF METHOD

Consider again the course of Lévi-Strauss' career. First there was a period of field research on Brazilian tribes, then the study of marriage, now mythic thought, and, between marriage and myth, the two-part study

57. Lévi-Strauss, *Savage Mind*, ch. 1.

Totemism and *The Savage Mind*. It is this two-part study that most explicitly contains his program, a program derived from main trends in his earlier work and self-consciously pursued in his current endeavors. To appreciate and appraise his comparative studies, we may judge them against the standard of his programmatic aims.

His great aim, we have seen, is to explicate the main principles of human thought. As we look more closely, however, we discover that this is not a program like that of Wundt or Dewey or Bruner or Piaget, but is aimed at the principles of order internal to collective thought—collective representations—and not the thought of individuals. Lévi-Strauss sometimes says that what he wants is to understand the human mind, but his work is always on the essentials of the collective conscious and the collective unconscious. Even that is not quite accurate. However often or interestingly he writes of collective processes, unconscious or otherwise, they are not what he systematizes. Rather he focuses upon the systems of criteria—culture itself—according to which collective choices are made and in which past choices are retained for later use. To say, as he does, that he is interested in "thought" misleads the reader. Words like "mind" or "thinking" lead us to expect a systematic analysis of processes of selecting, deciding, implementing, searching, exploring, recognizing, integrating, attending, and the like. These have their sociological homologues in the study of collective behavior. But they are not what Lévi-Strauss takes as his analytic problem. Rather he looks at culture as linguists examine language. In Lounsbury's words:

> Linguistics is concerned with the structure of the verbal response. Only within relatively narrow limits is it concerned with the stimulus conditions under which a verbal response is produced or with the nature of the stimulus-response connection and its establishment in the individual. It is primarily descriptive and formulative, rather than interpretive. . . .

> . . . .

> The linguist's special concern is with the "structure" of language in its grammatical, phonological, and—somewhat less frequently—semantic aspects. Many of the problems of special concern to psychologists are of secondary concern to the linguist. Some of these are the acquisition of language, concept formation, the instrumental use of language, the study of individual differences in various specific verbal skills, the measurement of these, their relation to problem solving, second-language learning, etc., the relation of verbal patterns to various types of nonverbal behavior and to personality, the study of the statistical properties of language, or word

associations, response latencies, symbolism, phenomena of interference, speech pathology, etc., and even perception. . . .[58]

In a passage that many reviewers quoted from *The Savage Mind,* Lévi-Strauss declares that the "ultimate goal of the human sciences is not to constitute man but to dissolve him." He means by this the dissection of any sector of culture as linguists dissect language, locating certain irreducible units and depicting all else as combinations of those units by means of invariant rules.[59] To the extent this can be accomplished, the novelty and indeterminism with which some idealist and romantic thinkers endowed the collective mind will be drastically narrowed—in Lévi-Strauss' opinion, extirpated.

Because meta-culture is never encountered directly, it must always be separated from the specific contents that hide its presence. All his talk about formal linguistics and the theory of games and systems of logic is an effort to identify procedures that may, when applied to culture, reveal its more general structure.

His strategy is to choose first one and then another great sector of culture, seeking in each the general structure peculiar to it and progressively identifying the structure common to all sectors. Here is the place at which his sketch of a society comes into play. He distinguishes among the structures of any society, noting, for example, structures of communication and structures of domination. These notions in no way constitute a comprehensive and consistent analytic scheme. Rather they point to sectors of social relations that presumably differ in the nature and functions of the culture that each bears. Each of Lévi-Strauss' larger works takes up some one of these sectors not previously explored. His first synthetic study, *The Elementary Structures of Kinship,* described the systematics of one of the three basic structures of communication: the rules of marriage. His continuing investigation of mythic thought centers upon the culture involved in an "order of orders": the sacred history recounted in any myth. *Totemism* and *The Savage Mind* are, as we have seen, concerned with aspects of culture common to two or more of these special sectors.

And we can further specify how he works. He selects within a sector of a society some problem of interpretation already classic among anthropologists. He then shows that the problematic phenomena are cultural in character. By dissecting out the broad regularities embedded in those phenomena, he resolves the problems of interpretation, showing that all the

58. F. G. Lounsbury, "Linguistics and Psychology," *in* Sigmund Koch, ed., *Psychology: A Study of a Science* (New York: McGraw-Hill, 1963), 6:552–553.
59. Lévi-Strauss, *op. cit.,* p. 247.

conundrums are only transformations of relations among some stable units of culture according to one or a small set of rules of combination. (Executed with brilliance, the results unfailingly impress. There is the careful, dispassionate review of the whole literature on a problem that everyone judges to be important. There is the meticulous comprehensive return to the observations originally cited by disputants in support or refutative of interpretations. There is the separating out of the observations and interpretations that still merit attention. There is the final, elegant resolution of all antitheses.) We have already seen these steps in his work on totemism.

It is from his judgment that culture consists of systematized signs that Lévi-Strauss reaches two further conclusions about method: first, that the models he seeks are mechanical, not statistical, and, second, that because he is making experiments he need not concern himself with sampling. It is his employment in research of topics already the center of major controversies in anthropology that enables him successfully to act upon these dicta. Let me explain.

It is by definition the case that the meaning of any sign becomes determinate only as that sign can be located in a system of signs—as it can be compared with other signs in terms of identities and differences. It is also the case that the possible meaning of any sign within a given system of signs is fixed by the number of distinctive comparisons in which it can in principle be included. It is considerations like these that lead to Lévi-Strauss' confidence that any cultural item—any sign—will prove to be embedded in a system of signs and that there will be present in that system meta-criteria identifying the identities and differences to which people are to attend, thereby specifying the meaning of each sign and the transformations permissible among all signs in the collection. Thus, when, as in discussing totemism, he constructs Column 1 in Figure 1, he assumes that its presence in a society is attended by the marginals of Figure 2, they being the meta-criteria from which Column 1, Figure 1 gains its specific meaning. In other words, for people to have the norm of symbolizing social groups according to the system of categories provided by some natural series, they must distinguish classes of objects from the peculiarities of singular objects and must distinguish nature from culture. To generalize his point: To the extent that anything is a sign it is part of a system of signs, the system being at least sufficient in size and in its rules of combination to specify the meaning of the sign in question. In any such system, a meaning can be specified only because some comparisons are prescribed and all others proscribed; some combinations are permitted and required and others are excluded. It is this combination of features that Lévi-Strauss describes as comprising a mechanical model of analysis. He says that mechanical models are the ones appropriate for ethnology—for the study of culture.[60] He contrasts them with statistical models. Statistical models are those systems of normative criteria that do not prescribe or proscribe all alternatives.[61]

> The laws of marriage provide the best illustration of this difference. In primitive societies these laws can be expressed in models calling for actual grouping of the individuals according to kin or clan; these are mechanical models. No such distribution exists in our own society, where types of marriage are determined by the size of the primary and secondary groups to which prospective mates belong, social fluidity, amount of information, and the like. A satisfactory . . . attempt to formulate the invariants of our marriage system would therefore have to determine average values— thresholds: it would be a statistical model.[62]

When he later wrote for undergraduates, he gave the same illustration and sharpened it.

> In order to insure that families will not become closed and that they will not constitute progressively as many self-sufficient units, we satisfy ourselves with forbidding marriage between near relatives. The amount of social contracts which any given individual is likely to maintain outside his or her own restricted family is great enough to afford a good probability that, on the average, the hundreds of thousands of families constituting at any given moment a modern society will not be permitted to "freeze" if one may say so. On the contrary, the greatest possible freedom for the choice of a mate (submitted to the only condition that the choice has to be made outside the restricted family) insures that these families will be kept in a continuous flow and that a satisfactory process of continuous "mix up" through intermarriage will prevail. . . .
>
> Conditions are quite different in the so-called primitive societies: there the global figure of the population is a small one. . . . Besides, social fluidity is low. . . .
>
> Given such conditions, it is still possible to insure the blending of families into a well-united society by using procedures similar to our own, i.e., a mere prohibition of marriage between relatives without any kind of positive prescriptions as to where and whom one should correctly marry. Experience shows, however, that this is only possible in small societies under the condition that the diminutive size of the group and the lack of social mobility be compensated by widening to a considerable extent the range of prohibited degrees. . . .

60. Lévi-Strauss, "Social Structure," p. 529.
61. Lévi-Strauss has been needlessly vague in presenting his case. See Hugo G. Nutini, "Some Considerations on the Nature of Social Structure and Model Building: A Critique of Claude Lévi-Strauss and Edmund Leach," *American Anthropologist*, 67 (June 1965): 707–731.
62. Lévi-Strauss, *op. cit.*, p. 528.

However, the great majority of primitive peoples have devised another method to solve the problem. Instead of confining themselves to a statistical process, relying on the probability that certain interdictions being set up a satisfactory equilibrium of exchanges between the biological families will spontaneously result, they have preferred to invent rules which every individual and family should follow carefully, and from which a given form of blending, experimentally conceived as satisfactory, is bound to arise.[63]

But how does Lévi-Strauss decide what signs will prove to be parts of a single, coherent system—thus making appropriate the use of a mechanical model—and how does he determine the exact boundaries of that system? His answer to those questions may help us to understand how Figures 1 and 2 were actually constructed. Certainly his three rules of procedure do not suffice to produce them. He has on grounds not included in those rules decided that totemism can be explained only if we keep in mind that the social groups involved are *systematically* related and only if we focus on the *relations* among the natural categories—and not the individual categories themselves. He has decided that it is fruitful to contrast a category with a particular and a group with an individual person. He has decided that the fruitful question to ask is how either a series of categories or a series of particulars can be linked with either groups or persons. Of equal importance, he has decided that "the four combinations are equivalent, since they are all the results of the same operation." Had he made other choices, the table and the problems posed would be quite different. For example, had he not determined that the groups were serially related, he might have used the word aggregate rather than group. Had he no basis to the contrary, he might have contrasted group with aggregate rather than with person and might have contrasted category with disorder or chance rather than with particular. Were there no special assumptions guiding his work, he might have decided to consider the differences between category and particular or group and person to be continuous rather than discontinuous and he might have left open to investigation the possibility of no relationship over certain sectors of the two series.

But there are special assumptions. Lévi-Strauss knows and is immersed in the long-standing discussions of totemism. The second and third and fourth combinations in Figure 1 do not appear by accident. As he says, Frazer considered the third to be a preliminary form of totemism and the fourth a vestige. The second category has been salient for anthropologists at least since Ruth Benedict published her description of the guardian spirit in North America. What surely has happened is that Lévi-Strauss

63. Lévi-Strauss, "The Family," pp. 278–280.

considered the debates and confusions in this tradition and so devised his
table as to bring all the important alternatives within a holistic framework.
His classification is as much a product of his profession as of the data.

The assumption that a determinate system of signs is required to specify the meaning of any given sign seems also to undergird Lévi-Strauss'
rejection of all complaints that he ignores problems of sampling. His re-
joinders vary according to the nature of the complaint. In the simplest case,
he agrees that sampling is required for studies where statistical models are
appropriate. Because those models are not appropriate for his work, neither
is this sampling. But this rejoinder will not handle all complaints. The more
difficult cases can be found in his work on totemism but are even more
evident in his work on myths.

A first problem in studying myth is to decide on which myths to focus.
Lévi-Strauss has made a choice without giving any particular reason for
it. He has chosen to deal primarily with myths of origin: the origin of mankind or society, or a particular array of clans, or cooking, or the natural
species, or some array of social roles, or of the earth, or whatever. As
Ricoeur, Douglas, Leach, and others have noted, his " 'examples of mythic
thought have been taken from the geographical areas of totemism and never
from Semitic, pre-Hellenic, or Indo-European areas.' "[64] It has further
been observed that virtually the only myths which he considers "are those
in which some or all of the characters in the story are animals endowed with
human attributes. This delimitation makes it particularly easy for Lévi-
Strauss to support Rousseau's thesis that a distinction between . . . Culture
and Nature . . . is one of the primary preoccupations of primitive human
thought."[65]

Lévi-Strauss is less troubled by the possible atypicality of his materials
than are his readers. His reasons are substantive and methodological. On
the substantive side, he argues that he wants to study what he believes in
principle to be a human universal: the working of the mind of man. Mythic
thought, not myths, is his subject matter, and mythic thought is as "rigorous
as that of modern science, and . . . the difference lies, not in the quality of
the intellectual process, but in the nature of the things to which it is applied."[66] Again, "man has always been thinking equally well; the improvement lies, not in an alleged progress of man's mind, but in the discovery of new areas to which it may apply its unchanged and unchanging
powers."[67]

64. Edmund Leach, ed., *The Structural Study of Myth and Totemism* (London: Tavistock Publications, 1967), p. ix; Paul Ricoeur, "Structure et hermeneu-
tique," *Esprit*, no. 322 (November 1963), pp. 596–627.
65. Leach, *op. cit.*
66. Lévi-Strauss, *Structural Anthropology*, p. 230.
67. Lévi-Strauss, *Savage Mind*, p. 13.

With respect to method, he says that his work is experimental in nature and that any well-performed experiment is sufficient to demonstrate a principle in science. He introduces this argument by reminding us that structural studies are intensive and time-consuming. To get at the grammar of a myth one must reflect upon that myth and one must see it in the whole context of other myths in the same society and in the matrix of the social arrangements of that society. Only a small number of cases can be studied with such intensity. He then quotes Durkheim and Kurt Goldstein as they address themselves to comparable problems. The first passage is from Durkheim's *Elementary Forms of the Religious Life* where the author anticipates critics who contend that he has illegitimately generalized from Australian totemism to all of religion:

> It may be objected that one single religion, whatever its field of extension may be, is too narrow a base for such an induction. We have not dreamed for a moment of ignoring the fact that an extended verification may add to the authority of a theory, but it is equally true that when a law has been proven by one well-made experiment, this proof is valid universally. If in one single case a scientist succeeded in finding out the secret of the life of even the most protoplasmic creature that can be imagined, the truths thus obtained would be applicable to all living beings, even the most advanced. . . .[68]

Goldstein makes a similar point in defending his derivation of general laws "of organismic life" from observations on a few persons with brain injuries:

> First: The accumulation of even a myriad of imperfectly investigated cases can in no way guide us toward recognition of the true facts. There is no alternative to carrying the examination of each case to the extent we have indicated.
> Second: Important though it may be to seek repeated confirmation of our findings through new case material, such confirmation adds nothing essential to our knowledge. Those patients must be subjected to investigation who offer a guarantee of unequivocal statements of fact, as well as of theoretical interpretation. Under such conditions, the conclusions drawn from one case will likewise have validity for others. . . . True, a new observation may induce us to modify somewhat our original assumptions; but if the analysis of the first observation was sufficient, this modification can be made without conflict.[69]

What Durkheim says is that, if anything is an *x* (e.g., a living form), and if one performs a "well-made experiment" on it, then the result of that

---

68. Joseph W. Swain, tr. (Glencoe, Ill.: Free Press, n.d.), p. 415.
69. "The Organism," *A Holistic Approach to Biology Derived from Pathological Data in Man* (New York: American Book Co., 1939), p. 27.

experiment will hold for anything else to the extent it is an x. Goldstein's point is similar. But these statements will scarcely help Lévi-Strauss—or any other working scientist. Every experiment is one of a prospective sample of replications of that experiment, and experience has shown that the findings of many experiments cannot be replicated. That discouraging result is itself the product of the sampling entailed in replication. Similarly, the extent to which an object of study has a certain property, call it x, is always a matter of degree. Therefore some sampling of a population of that type of object is required to separate out what they have in common.[70] Certainly in any field as unexplored as the study of myth, these and other problems of sampling will need special attention. Lévi-Strauss' dismissal of sampling is premature.

What would be more defensible, and what Lévi-Strauss might want to say, would be this: "Each myth consists of signs and is itself a sign. Its meaning and the meaning of its components are determinate only within a larger system of signs. My effort is to identify the essentials of that system. This enterprise would not be advanced except indirectly by my examining a sample of myths from the same or other societies. Moreover, my work is like a well-performed experiment in the sense that I devise a set of meta-criteria and then see whether they are truly adequate to specify the full meaning of the myth under study. I judge their adequacy according to their potentiality for specifying the meanings of variant versions of the myth, whether in this society or in neighboring societies, and for revealing the whole set to be but transformations of the meta-criteria I employ."

Given this strategy, his choice of topics that are controversial among anthropologists again proves helpful. He will usually need to have his attention called to deviant cases. They may be quite uncommon. The most likely way to find them is to work with subjects for which there is an excellent descriptive literature that contains many anomalies, these being the focus of many professional debates concerning interpretation. This procedure, not sampling, will most efficiently lead him to the cases he needs.

But sampling is not the only question he must face. How can we know when reports of myths or totemic systems are full and accurate? If they are, how do we know that we correctly catch their meaning? As Evans-Pritchard has said of Lévy-Bruhl, his work was ever clouded by the possibility that no modern mind can understand what primitives really mean.[71]

---

70. This point did not escape Durkheim. See *The Rules of Sociological Method*, Sarah A. Solovay and John H. Mueller, tr. (Chicago: University of Chicago Press, 1938), pp. 138–139.

71. In Lucien Lévy-Bruhl, *Soul of the Primitive*, L. A. Clare, (New York: Praeger, 1966).

What Lévi-Strauss replies to such questions is that regularities are regularities, and if a modern mind discovers them in some sector of a primitive society's culture they are at least among the things that are truly there, whatever else may be missed. Furthermore, there may, in specific investigations, be opportunities to supplement one's evidence by using other sources. He found these opportunities in his work on myth and in his study of marriage. They deserve our attention.

Myths are redundant. Redundancy is a characteristic of individual myths and of bodies of myth taken from given societies and across societies. Even within a particular myth, the same themes appear again and again. This may be a dramatic device of the teller of a myth to underscore the main points. It may occur because myths are oral communications. Alfred Lord has shown that the situation in which myths are told is often one in which the audience drifts in and out of the circle around the teller, and he from time to time provides a précis of earlier portions of the story for listeners who have recently joined the circle.[72] In any event, mythic themes are made easy to identify because they recur in single myths and in collections of myths.

Occasionally, Lévi-Strauss finds further assistance. This is the reason for his delight in discovering in a neighboring society a version of a myth in which all the characters and events are present but reversed. Such a direct but inverted transformation is strong evidence that he has correctly coded the themes crucial to this mythic plot. It also tests the adequacy of his rules of transformation. Will they provide for an inversion?

Finally, in his study of rules of marriage, he encountered in some societies internal contradictions in the norms stated by the natives themselves. In disentangling these contradictions, he sharpened his own understanding of the actual situation. For example, the Sherente Indians of Brazil have norms concerning spatial configuration and a moiety system. From each moiety depend four clans, the clans being differentiated by ceremonial functions and privileges. Marriage is regulated exclusively by the moiety system, or so the Sherente say. But an inspection of their rules of marriage shows otherwise. There are missing "the usual corollaries of dual organization, namely distinction between parallel-cousins and cross-cousins; merging of patrilateral and matrilateral cross-cousins; and preferential marriage between bilateral and cross-cousins."[73] "Neither the terminology nor the rules of marriage coincide with an exogamous dual organizations."[74] From

72. Albert B. Lord, *The Singer of Tales* (Cambridge, Mass.: Harvard University Press, 1960); Eric Havelock, *Preface to Plato* (Cambridge: Harvard University Press, 1963).

73. Lévi-Strauss, *Structural Anthropology*, p. 121.

74. *Ibid.*, p. 123.

an inspection of that terminology and those rules, Lévi-Strauss derives a genuinely appropriate model.[75]

LÉVI-STRAUSS: AN AFTER-VIEW

To say that Lévi-Strauss' analyses are brilliant is true but irrelevant. What matters in science is whether they are correct or whether they are at least more valid than others'. This is a principal stumbling block. We can say that his work on totemism is a shade more general than that of Radcliffe-Brown and that he has integrated the phenomenon into a wider set of categories than did his predecessors. We find that his approach overcomes some objections to the older interpretations of myth and primitive classification. His interpretation of rules of marriage is more comprehensive than is that of others. But all his work is being debated. Unsettled questions of fact pervade the disputations. It will take a very long time to know how well he has done.

We can, however, make a few points about what has been accomplished, whether it proves true or false:

1. Lévi-Strauss has given us a programmatic objective but not yet a substantial product. He has revived the work of the Durkheimian school, getting out with fresh clarity and with more precise tools to study the structure of collective representations. In several areas he has greatly clarified the issues and has proposed new analytic schemes. It must also be said that he has produced little toward a systematic treatment of the ultimate subject of his work: the structure, not of this or that normative subsystem, but of culture itself. For all his writing on the classifications of primitives or on marriage or myth, it is difficult to discover within it more than four or five principles or procedures, and these are all so vague that even those other scholars who are favorably inclined have found them impossible to apply in replicating his work.[76]

2. The few principles of structure that Lévi-Strauss has proposed fall short of the conditions of adequacy that he himself has advocated. For example, we could not, by using them, reconstitute the rich variability of the social world from which they were derived.[77]

3. He has done all of his own coding. This is inevitable in the early

___

75. He then discusses the question of why societies having one social structure should mystify themselves by claiming they have another. For his answers, see *ibid.*, pp. 131, 333–334, 344.

76. See, for example, Edmund Leach, "Lévi-Strauss in the Garden of Eden: An Examination of Some Recent Developments in the Analysis of Myth," *in* William A. Lessa and Evon Z. Vogt, eds., *Reader in Comparative Religion, an Anthropological Approach* (New York: Harper and Row, 1965), pp. 574–581.

77. Lévi-Strauss, *Savage Mind,* p. 247.

stages of research and, in some studies, the amount of material to be read may preclude any other practice. But this is a major deficiency in his evidence. Would another investigator trained in his techniques interpret the same myths as has Lévi-Strauss? Would he readily see that all myths in a collection are but transformations of certain meta-criteria? And what would happen were both he and Lévi-Strauss to apply Lévi-Strauss' procedures to a body of myths neither had previously considered? From what is known about these procedures and about the difficulties of coding reports like those with which he has worked, we could expect only low reliability between raters.

4. Much thought needs to be given to the relation between culture, on the one hand, and organizations and individual behavior on the other. It is well established that norms and behavior will often diverge and in some situations they diverge more often than not. Yet our only knowledge of the existence of norms is through the observation of behavior. If we find diverse or contradictory norms, which ones shall we regard as authentic? Lévi-Strauss provides no theoretical solution for this problem.

5. Lévi-Strauss has depended on happy fortuities to establish the validity of his interpretations. Can he find some routine procedures for the same purpose? Is there, for mythology, the equivalent of the linguist's informant —the "adult, informed, native speaker" whose utterances are observed and who can be presented with hypothetical utterances and asked to judge their correctness? A further advantage in this procedure is that the phenomena of interest are produced at will and not merely observed after the fact.

PROLEGOMENA TO THE THEORY OF ACTION

In 1945 there appeared a collection of papers, *Twentieth Century Sociology*, edited by Georges Gurvitch and Wilbert E. Moore. It contained what can now be seen as prophecies of their own work by Claude Lévi-Strauss and Talcott Parsons.[78] At that time, Lévi-Strauss was well along toward developing a structural analysis of kinship but had yet to articulate even for himself the general approach that he was employing. Parsons had, for at least 15 years, conceptualized both individual and collective behavior as action but had yet to discover a method for applying that insight to the interpretation of complex variations in any large body of data.

As Parsons saw the problem in 1945, sociology consisted of scattered observations and concepts and theories. But this would change: "The most important single index of the state of maturity of a science is the state of

78. Gurvitch and Moore, pp. 42–69, 503–537.

its systematic theory. . . . Sociology is just in the process of emerging into the status of a mature science."[79] He stated his own program so well that his main points deserve to be quoted as they first appeared:

> A theoretical system in the present sense is a body of logically inter-dependent generalized concepts of empirical reference. . . .
> The two most general functions of theory are the facilitation of description and analysis. . . . It is only when the essential facts about a phenomenon have been described in a carefully systematic and orderly manner that accurate analysis becomes possible at all. Adequacy in description is secured in so far as determinate and verifiable answers can be given to all the scientifically *important* questions involved. What questions are important is largely determined by the logical structure of the generalized conceptual scheme which, implicitly or explicitly, is employed.
>
> .   .   .   .
>
> The functions of a generalized conceptual scheme on the descriptive level seem to be performed mainly in terms of two types of conceptual elements. The first consists in . . . the "frame of reference." This is the most general framework of categories in terms of which empirical scientific work "makes sense." Thus, in classical mechanics, three-dimensional rectilinear space, time, mass, location, motion are the essential elements of the frame of reference. Every descriptive statement, to be applicable to a mechanical system must be referable to one or more "particles" each with a given mass, capable of location in space, changing its location in time through motion, etc. Besides providing the specific categories in terms of which a system is described, the function of the frame of reference is above all to provide a test of the determinacy of the description of a system. It is a logical implication of the structure of the conceptual system that there is a limited number of essential categories, specific values for which must be obtained before the description can be determinate. . . .
> The second level is that of the structure of systems as such. Phenomena which are significantly interrelated, which constitute a system, are intrinsically interrelated on the structural level. . . . Structure is the "static" aspect of the descriptive mode of treatment of a system. From the structural point of view a system is composed of "units," of sub-systems which potentially exist independently, and their structural interrelations. Thus a system in mechanics is "made up" of particles as its units. The structure of the system consists in the number of particles, their properties, such as mass, and their interrelations such as relative locations, velocities and directions of motion.
> The functions of the frame of reference and of structural categories in their descriptive use are to state the necessary facts, and the setting for

79. *Ibid.*, p. 42.

solving problems of dynamic analysis, the ultimate goal of scientific investigation. . . .

.   .   .   .

The essential feature of dynamic analysis . . . is the treatment of a body of
interdependent phenomena simultaneously, in the mathematical sense. . . .

.   .   .   .

To be susceptible to this type of analytical manipulation a variable
. . . must vary only in numerically quantitative value on a continuum. . . .

The most essential condition of successful dynamic analysis is continual and systematic reference of every problem to the state of the system
as a whole. If it is not possible to provide for that by explicit inclusion of
every relevant fact as the value of a variable . . . there must be some
method of simplification. Logically, this is possible only through the removal of some generalized categories from the role of variables and their
treatment as constants. An analytical system of the type of mechanics does
just this for certain elements *outside* the system which are conditional to
it. But this is also logically feasible *within* the system. That is . . . what
happens when structural categories are used in the treatment of dynamic
problems.

Their function is to simplify the dynamic problems to the point where
they are manageable without the possibility of refined mathematical analysis. At the same time the loss, which is very great, is partly compensated by relating all problems explicitly and systematically to the total
system. For the structure of a system . . . ensures that nothing of vital importance is inadvertently overlooked, and ties in loose ends, giving determinacy to problems and solutions. . . .

.   .   .   .

Once resort is made to the structure of a system as positive constituent
of dynamic analysis there must be a way of linking these "static" structural
categories and their relevant particular statements of fact to the dynamically variable elements in the system. This link is supplied by the all-important concept of function. Its crucial role is to provide criteria of the
importance of dynamic factors and processes within the system. They are
important in so far as they have functional significance to the system . . .
in terms of . . . specific functional relations between the parts of the system
and between it and its environment.

.   .   .   .

It is . . . the functional reference of all particular conditions and processes
to the state of the total system as a going concern which provides the logical equivalent of simultaneous equations in a fully developed system of
analytical theory. . . .

The logical type of . . . theoretical system under discussion may thus be called a "structural-functional system" as distinguished from an analytical system.

.   .   .   .

This type of generalized system has been most fully developed in physiology and more recently . . . in psychology. . . . In recent psyhcology, it is . . . personality which plays the role analogous to that of anatomical structure in biology while "motives" in relation to situations are the dynamic elements.

It is the primary thesis of this paper that the structural-functional type of system is the one . . . most likely and suitable to play a dominant role in sociological theory. . . . [80]

Although many of the specific points in this paper will later prove important for our thought, I shall first comment on one connection between this paper and Parsons' earlier work, and on the practical steps by which Parsons then implemented the program of theory construction to which this paper points. Comparative studies of whole societies and cultures are a fulfillment of his earlier objectives and a necessary method for the construction of the theory he later envisioned.

Parsons began his career as an economist, having a primary initial focus on "what the 1920's called 'institutionalism.'" The institutional school in economics had its principal centers in the United States and Germany and it was at Heidelberg, after a year's study of anthropology at the London School of Economics, that Parsons earned his doctorate, writing a dissertation on the treatment of capitalism as an institutional system in German economic literature, concerning himself particularly with the writings of Marx, Sombart, and Max Weber.[81] The institutionalists in all countries were united by a perspective and an antipathy. In the economist Paul Homan's description of their position (published in 1931) we find enduring qualities in Parsons' thought:

The cardinal tenet of institutionalism is that contemporary society is a complex of institutions or habitual forms for organizing and regulating the behavior of individuals. Social institutions, including the economic, . . . are subject to change because of the impact of human nature, changes in technology and the general development of knowledge and ideas. In a certain sense the development of institutions is a competitive process, and its outcome determines what forms of behavior are acceptable and sanc-

---

80. *Ibid.*, pp. 43–49.
81. Talcott Parsons, "An Approach to Psychological Theory in Terms of the Theory of Action," *in* Sigmund Koch, ed., *Psychology: A Study of Science*, (New York: McGraw-Hill, 1959), 3:620.

tioned. At any given time the behavior of individuals or groups is restricted within limits set by such formal or informal sanctions. Since . . . "original
human nature" is remarkably stable, most overt behavior must be explained
by reference to the prevailing institutional structure, and this in its turn
is intelligible only if viewed as a result of cumulative change.

The bearing of this general ideology on economics is in the first
place critical. Institutionalism impugns the credibility of orthodox economic theory on the following counts: it asserts that orthodox economics
depends upon a discredited hedonic theory of human behavior; that its
basic institutional postulate of individualistic competition is inadequate
and inaccurate; and that its central problem of determining the conditions
of economic equilibrium rests on an untenable analogy to physical science
and implies a static view of economic organization at variance with the
actual processes of development. The institutionalists believe that while
the equilibrium concept and the marginal method may be found useful for
some subordinate purposes of analysis fundamentally correct explanations
of economic phenomena are possible only by reference to the nature and
prescriptive force of social institutions. [82]

Although certain premises of institutional economics, and its critical stance,
were clear-cut, the field lacked a coherent, positive content. The chief task
for an institutional economist was to construct the laws of economics as an
institution. Given their premises, the institutionalists required that this be
done by seeing the economy as only one institution in an embracive social
order, the properties of the whole order bearing in crucial ways upon the
activities of the parts. Parsons' work took form as an effort to supply that
positive content. Whereas other American sociologists and economists—
Thorstein Veblen, W. F. Ogburn, and C. H. Cooley, for example—derived
that content from studies of the impact of technology on society and also
from a view of society as a network of relations among individuals and
groups, Parsons took his departure from what he has since called the "collectivistic" and idealistic components prevalent in the thought of Continental Europe.[83] His great resource was the work of Max Weber, followed by
the writings of Durkheim and Pareto—with those of Marx being always in
the background. His first major book, *The Structure of Social Action*, compared the works of these and other important systematists of institutions,
seeking in them whatever general interpretation they might contain and
reporting the discovery by these men of a conception of social life as a

82. Paul T. Homan, "Institutional Economics," *Encyclopaedia of the Social
Sciences*, (New York: Macmillan, 1931), 5: 388–389.

83. Talcott Parsons, "The Point of View of the Author," *in* Max Black, ed.,
The Social Theories of Talcott Parsons (Englewood Cliffs, N.J.: Prentice-Hall,
1961), p. 313.

process of action.[84] To summarize their complex position: Human action is best conceived as a process of choice in which ends determine the identification of means and selections from among them. Human action, whether individual or collective, is a creative, exploratory process. Parsons subscribed to their essential conclusions.

Despite its origin in "collectivistic" thought, this view of human action construes it as a process of an individual, characterizing it without systematic reference to other people or to organizations. In the years between the publication of *The Structure of Social Action* (1937) and the first large work that he published after World War II (in 1950), he repeatedly brought the conception of social action to bear upon particular institutions and upon relations among institutions, trying always to elaborate the conception and to discover its power to describe institutions and their interrelations. He had in this way self-consciously moved with his problem from economics into sociology where, he has written, his "focus . . . was on the comparative treatment of institutions."[85] This was so, but, as we shall find, it was so in only one sense.

One autumn, while working on *The Structure of Social Action*, Parsons wrote an article for the *International Journal of Ethics*, titling it "The Place of Ultimate Values in Sociological Theory."[86] Everything it contains appears later in this book, but the article points more clearly than the book to the vital role that ultimate values would play in his solution for the great problem of the institutionalists.

"An end," he wrote, "is thought of as a logically formulated anticipation of certain elements in a future state of affairs, and the relation of means to end is thought of as based on knowledge of the inherent connections of things."[87] "Ultimate empirical ends are justified to the actor in terms, not of scientific, but of metaphysical theories. He may, however, by virtue of his metaphysical theories pursue not merely empirical but also transcendental ends."[88] Finally, ultimate ends must have orderly relations with one another in terms of a still wider system of principles, otherwise how could one explain the existence of rational choice?[89]

84. New York: McGraw-Hill, 1937.

85. Parsons, "Approach to Psychological Theory," p. 620.

86. Vol. 45 (1934–35), pp. 282–316. For a discussion of this article from another point of view, see John F. Scott, "The Changing Foundations of the Parsonian Action Scheme," *American Sociological Review*, 28 (October 1963): 716–735.

87. Parsons, "Ultimate Values," p. 286.

88. *Ibid.*, p. 291.

89. *Ibid.*, p. 294.

Ultimate ends do not occur in random fashion, but . . . both in the case of
the individual and of the social groups they must be thought of as to a
significant degree integrated into a single harmonious *system*. . . .

This common system may be thought of as related to the rest of
the . . . mean-end chain—above all, the intermediate sector. . . . The
actions in pursuit of non-ultimate immediate ends may be thought of as
governed by normative rules, institutions. Institutions may be classified as
technological, economic, and political, according to what elements of the
intermediate chain they govern.

The theory of institutions will . . . form one of the most important,
as well as difficult, branches of sociological theory. But in order to see its
role in perspective, it is necessary to place it in terms of a coherent scheme
of the elements of action, as we are attempting to do. It is this which has,
more than anything else, been lacking in previous attempts to formulate a
theory of institutions.[90]

Here is a root idea. Institutions are normative rules that govern the intermediate sectors of a normative chain, the chain itself consisting of criteria
that govern the identification of ends and the formulation of means. The
theory of institutions will be unified by working outward from the values
(ends) which are at its core, and institutions will be distinguished according
to the components of the intermediate sector that they govern. They will
be interrelated according to their role in the total pattern, more specifically,
according to their relation to the ultimate values.

Many theoretical experiments and "trial" applications (see his *Essays
in Sociological Theory, Pure and Applied*) intervene between this paper and
The Social System and *Working Papers in the Theory of Action*, but the
elements of his future work are already in place.[91] Structural-functionalism
as he described it in 1945 is a sketch of the formal properties of the theory
that he would produce. The collaborative work *Toward a General Theory
of Action* (1951) and *The Social System* (also dated 1951) herald a new effort
to construct the theory of institutional systems.[92] The culmination, however, is in the second chapter of *Working Papers in the Theory of Action*
(published in 1953).

THE ELEMENTARY SOCIAL SYSTEM

There are two places in *The Social System*, both near the end, where

90. *Ibid.*, pp. 299–300.
91. *Essays in Sociological Theory, Pure and Applied* (Glencoe: The Free
Press, 1949); *The Social System* (Glencoe, Ill.: Free Press, 1951); *Working Papers in the Theory of Action* (Glencoe, Ill.: Free Press, 1953).
92. *Toward a General Theory of Action* (Cambridge: Harvard University
Press, 1951).

Parsons describes the substance of sociology.[93] It consists, he says, in institutionalization. More exactly, it is

> *that aspect of the theory of social systems which is concerned with the phenomena of the institutionalization of patterns of value-orientation in the social system,* with the conditions of conformity with and deviance from a set of such patterns and with motivational processes in so far as they are involved in all of these. . . .

If sociology is defined late in his book, institutionalization is defined early, the core analysis of *The Social System* depending upon this conception. It could not be otherwise. In Parsons' view, a social system exists only to the degree that a plurality of actors are integrated with one another in relationship to some situation. Institutionalization *is* that kind of integration:

> The basic condition on which an interaction system can be stabilized is for the interests of the actors to be bound to conformity with a shared system of value-orientation standards. There is a two-fold structure of this "binding in." In the first place, by virtue of internalization of the standard, conformity with it tends to be of personal expressive and/or instrumental significance to ego. In the second place, the structuring of the reactions of alter to ego's action as sanctions is a function of his conformity with the standard. . . . In so far as, relative to the actions of a plurality of actors, conformity with a value-orientation standard meets *both* these criteria, that is from the point of view of any given actor in the system, it is both a mode of the fulfillment of his own need-dispositions and a condition of "optimizing" the reactions of other significant actors, that standard will be said to be "institutionalized."
>
> . . . .
>
> The polar antithesis of full institutionalization is . . . *anomie*, the absence of structured complementarity of the interaction process or, what is the same thing, the complete breakdown of normative order in both senses. . . .[94]

And that is saying a great deal. In any sense that Parsons plans here to analyze them, social systems are not merely instances of interaction. Nor are they merely instances of interaction that exhibit regularities, however persistent—nor merely instances that are in some fashion bounded. Rather they exist to the extent that participants—individuals or collectivities—are positively interdependent: drawn to one another under circumstances in which each is fulfilled only if, and as, he fulfills the others, and under circumstances in which each has some understanding of his situation and finds

93. Parsons, *Social System,* pp. 548–552.
94. *Ibid.,* pp. 38–39.

it, on balance, worthwhile. We can see at once that this eliminates large sectors of social life: social unions enforced by naked power or its equivalents; the rise and structuring of markets by the blind operation of the "hidden hand"; all behaviors through which people collectively search for a fruitful new norm of organization; all social relations that lie outside some "realm of right" or that occur in ignorance of objective interdependence.

Something else is eliminated even earlier in his treatise: the actors in their status as elements, that is, as entities that exist independently of any particular social system. This is a direct break with the prescription for social structure offered in 1945: "From a structural point of view a system is composed of 'units' . . . which potentially exist independently. . . ."[95] In *The Social System* and thereafter, the units of a system of interaction are called "status-roles," thus reflecting their absorption into a status as *parts* of the system. The units thereafter act as the system's agents or meet their obligation to perform contractually required services for other actors in the system, but they never act strongly or primarily in their own particular interest.[96]

One soon finds that, from the conception of a social system—especially if one has abandoned any systematic treatment of actors as *elements* in social life—there is just one way to locate units, to distinguish among them, and to classify their major relations or combinations. That is through differentiating them as parts from the whole. One likewise discovers that in the defining character of a social system appear inherent bases for differentiation. These steps are described in *The Social System*. They are elaborated with even greater subtlety in subsequent works, beginning with *Working Papers in the Theory of Action*. In those works is employed the fourfold analysis for which Parsons is now best known.

As finally rationalized, the fourfold analysis rests upon two observations, the first owing to Bales and to his laboratory studies of small groups.[97] Those studies show that the action of a group requires that participants

95. In Gurvitch and Moore, p. 45. But it is consistent with his recent definition of social structure: "The structure of a system is that set of properties of its component *parts* and their relations or combinations. . . ." (Emphasis supplied) For this quotation, see Talcott Parsons, "Some Considerations on the Theory of Social Change," *Rural Sociology*, 26 (September 1961): 219–239.

96. Parsons, *Social System*, pp. 25–26.

97. Talcott Parsons, "General Theory in Sociology," *in* Robert K. Merton and others, eds., *Sociology Today, Problems and Prospects* (New York: Basic Books, 1959), p. 7: "In the present analysis I do not use pattern-variable terms because I think the new scheme is a more generalized one from which the scheme of pattern variables can be derived." See also Talcott Parsons, "Pattern Variables Revisited: A Response to Robert Dubin," *American Sociological Review*, 25 (August 1960): 467–483.

attend to the outer environment from which resources are obtained and to the inner world of their own relations—for example, to the coordination and maintenance of those relations. In informal groups, leadership tends to be polarized around these two foci.

The second observation concerns the nature of action itself as a joining of means and ends. As action, the operation of a group entails both the generating of resources (means) that may be used for a variety of purposes and the selective expenditure of those resources to attain specific objectives.

All acts of all groups will take into simultaneous account the inner and outer worlds in which the group operates and also the production and allocation of resources. Some acts, or aspects of acts, will focus primarily on only certain of these features—on one of the cells in Figure 3 presented below.

	Instrumental		*Consummatory*	
External	A:	Adaptive Function	G:	Goal-Attainment Function
Internal	L:	Pattern-Maintenance and Tension-Management Function	I:	Integrative Function

Figure 3

Functions of a Social System

The two axes in this figure "must be considered, not as continua, but as qualitatively differentiated reference categories. . . ."[98] What is to be "differentiated?" Any social system. In what sense is it differentiated? In the sense that the collective acts of which the system consists will each take into simultaneous account all four of the marginal values in Figure 3, the distinguishing character of any *given* act being specified by the *combination* of those marginals with which it deals, e.g., Cell A or Cell G or Cell I or Cell L. The marginals in Figure 3 are socially embedded criteria for the formulation of given acts and are therefore as fully cultural in character as are the marginal values in the tables of Lévi-Strauss.

As Parsons conceives them, the simplest social systems are those in which only this degree of differentiation is present.[99] As we have seen, however, the leadership of even small, transient laboratory groups tends to polarize around the internal-external distinction. It does so to such an ex-

98. Parsons, "General Theory . . . ," p. 6.
99. *Ibid.*, pp. 7–11.

tent that different individuals tend to be primarily responsible for leadership in one or the other environment, but not both.[100] In organizations of somewhat greater size and durability, one or several people come to have primary and continuing responsibility for one or a few of the four system functions. As they do, further differentiation occurs.

Consider, for example, the Parent-Teacher association of an elementary school. Imagine that, in it, a few people are put in charge of raising funds and recruiting new members. Their activities are primarily instrumental and are oriented to the external environment. They therefore should be classified as serving the organization's Adaptive Function. But once this subgroup exists, it becomes an environment for the other members and they for it. Moreover, in their own newly specialized affairs, the members of this subgroup will now confront the same criteria that are embodied in the marginals of Figure 3. That is, a subgroup, having arisen to specialize in performing the adaptive function for the whole organization, will necessarily subdivide its adaptive activity into four parts corresponding to the four cells of Figure 3. This is represented in Figure 4.

	Instrumental	Consummatory
External	A	G
Internal	L	I

Figure 4

Functions of a Social System Showing Differentiated
Functions within Cell A

Should certain persons come to specialize in performing the adaptive function within this adaptive subgroup, they, in turn, will confront the necessity of performing all four system functions within their sub-subgroup. And so our tables become increasingly refined until specialization ends.

At some point, between the simplest and the most complex social systems, it becomes appropriate to use the term "institution" to refer to the elaborated cultural apparatus through which an organization as a whole performs any one of the four basic activities. In the quotation that follows, Parsons distinguishes this cultural apparatus from a group (he uses the word "collectivity") but he does not make clear that it is from the fact of the functional specialization of individuals and collectivities that additional cultural differentiations emerge.

100. Talcott Parsons and Robert F. Bales, eds., *Family, Socialization, and Interaction Process* (Glencoe, Ill.: Free Press, 1955), pp. 259–306.

> An *institution* will be said to be a complex of institutionalized role integrates which is of strategic significance in the social system in question. The institution . . . is made up of a plurality of interdependent role-patterns or components of them. . . . An institution in this sense should be clearly distinguished from a collectivity. A collectivity is a system of concretely interactive specific roles. An institution on the other hand is a complex of patterned elements in role-expectations which may apply to an indefinite number of collectivities.[101]

Thus it is that, with reference to whole societies, Parsons comes to speak of the subsystems that specialize in serving the four system functions as "institutions," and to write of them as, respectively: adaptive function, the economy; goal-attainment function, the polity; integrative function, the integrative system; pattern-maintenance function, the pattern-maintenance system.[102] In this fashion he resolves one of the problems with which his career began: He presents a systematic basis for classifying the economy together with other major institutions, for determining what those other institutions will be, and for describing in highly general and comparable terms the internal structures of each and the interrelations among them. Moreover, he has attained this objective by means of a unitary theory in which the "value-factor" is paramount, this being the case because all institutions are defined according to the service they provide for a collective task, according, that is, to the means they embody in the course of action toward a collective goal. (This breakthrough came only four or five years after he had deplored in a Presidential Address to the American Sociological Society the lack of "systematization of the bases for *comparative* analysis of social structures," and had said that, "in spite of the magnificence of Max Weber's attempt, the basic classificatory problem, the solution of which must underlie the achievement of high theoretical generality in much of our field, has remained basically unsolved.")[103]

STEPS TOWARD DIFFERENTIATION

Parsons has on several occasions stressed that differentiation does not just happen. As we have already seen it entails the emergence of systematic cultural distinctions and these in turn are products of the specialization of individuals or subgroups in the performance of some system function. In his own account of differentiation, Parsons points especially to the adjust-

---

101. Parsons, *Social System*, p. 39.
102. Talcott Parsons and Neil J. Smelser, *Economy and Society* (Glencoe, Ill.: Free Press, 1956), ch. 2.
103. Talcott Parsons, *Essays in Sociological Theory, Pure and Applied* (Glencoe, Ill.: Free Press, 1954), p. 361.

ments in cultural arrangements that are required. Thus, in discussing the modernization of family farms in the United States, and the differentiation of household functions from production functions, he writes:

> Some of the familiar things which must happen for the process to take place are (1) a loss of functions by the kinship unit, (2) a new pattern of organization of the functions which have come to be dissociated from the kinship unit, (3) a substitution of new ways of taking care of the needs of the kinship unit which are occasioned by this loss of service to it, (4) a way of organizing the terms of their relationships including the handling of the risks entailed in "cutting loose" from kinship in favor of employment in the new organization, and (5) a way of balancing the legitimation of both units at both the collectivity and the role levels so that the inevitable component of conflict of interest is "contained" within a pattern of mutual contribution to higher-order system functioning.[104]

And he generalizes this illustration as follows:

> Successful differentiation involves normative reorganization at four levels: (1) the provision of opportunity through the emancipation of facilities from ascriptive [i.e., from less differentiated] ties; (2) *inclusion* of differentiated units in higher level collectivity structures; (3) *upgrading* of norms to higher levels of generality; (4) *extension* of values to legitimize new functional units. . . .[105]

Because the emergence of these several activities takes time, and because an older order must gradually disappear as a new order becomes sufficiently crystallized to function, social changes in the form of differentiation—evolution is the prototype—will not be smooth and will exhibit discontinuities and "stages" or "levels."

LEVELS OF DIFFERENTIATION AND EVOLUTION

Evolution is the production through differentiation of a new type of functional unit. The production of such a unit requires, we have seen, certain important reorganizations of the social system in which it emerges. It is in his discussion of evolution that we come to what is currently the frontier of Parsons' theoretical work, and we come, for the first time, to a broad range of comparative observations that were not involved in the development of his scheme, yet bear upon its fruitfulness and even its validity.[106]

Parsons is a great classifier. His "theory" is a classificatory scheme. It

104. Parsons, "Some Considerations," pp. 227–228.
105. *Ibid.*, pp. 219, 235–239.
106. Talcott Parsons, "Evolutionary Universals in Society," *American Sociological Review*, 29 (June 1964): 339–357; Talcott Parsons, *Societies: Evolutionary and Comparative Perspectives* (Englewood Cliffs, N.J.: Prentice-Hall, 1966).

is, however, a scheme of great subtlety, having been so constructed as to avoid numerous errors that flawed the work of earlier theorists and having been planned so as systematically to incorporate large numbers of conceptual distinctions already existing in theories in psychology, economics, political science, sociology, and anthropology. At the conceptual level, it is a major accomplishment in synthesis. (I have already noted in discussing the nature of a social system that it is incomplete.)

One can properly ask of a classification—of a filing system—whether it is clear or comprehensive or helpful or suggestive and whether its categories are mutually exclusive. One cannot ask, as one must in the case of a scientific *theory*, whether its generalizations are empirically valid. A classification may be built upon generalizations, but itself advances none. In the study of evolution, there are empirical observations that test some generalizations underlying Parsons' classificatory work.

These same empirical observations are also of interest because they are almost the first that he has tried to order *prospectively* by means of his scheme. He has sometimes employed a loose conceptual approach to interpret a specific phenomenon—his scheme enabling him to perceive some order in the data but the data in no way validating or invalidating the scheme. At other times he has developed a conceptual apparatus from the review of large bodies of existing observations and theories, devising the apparatus to incorporate the distinctions evident within the data. Indeed he has for 40 years worked primarily and repeatedly on the same observations and theories sketched in *The Structure of Social Action*. But, as experienced investigators so well know, there is usually less than perfect reliability between a classification—a code—developed from one set of observations and its application to a new set of observations for which the code should be equally relevant. In the study of the evolution of societies, Parsons for the first time puts himself in the position of making such an application.

One desirable feature in a theory of evolution is that it provides a systematic basis for describing the major stages that are observed. This is equivalent to asking that it provide for major differences in level of differentiation. Parsons says something about those levels in several works.[107] Perhaps his single most important discussion appears in his paper "Some Ingredients of a General Theory of Formal Organization" as somewhat modified in his paper "General Theory in Sociology."[108] Social systems, we

107. Parsons and Bales, *Family* . . . , ch. 2; Parsons and Smelser, *Economy and Society*, ch. 3; Talcott Parsons, *Structure and Process in Modern Societies* (Glencoe, Ill.: Free Press, 1960), chs. 1 and 2; a related discussion appears in Neil Smelser, *Theory of Collective Behavior* (New York: Free Press, 1963), chs. 1 and 2.

108. Parsons, *Structure and Process*, ch. 2; "General Theory in Sociology," *in* Merton and others, *op. cit.*

are told, have four levels of organization, these ranging from the technical upward through the managerial, institutional, and societal. The ascending order is hierarchical, the higher orders controlling the lower by cybernetic mechanisms and the lower providing energy to the higher. The levels correspond, in ascending order, to four types of "reality," the higher realities affording coordinating and directing principles for relations among units at the next lower level.

> At the "bottom" of the structure the social system is rooted in the concrete human individual as a physical organism acting in a physical environment. This individual, as personality, participates in processes of social interaction through his various roles. Roles are organized and aggregated to form collectivities, and these in turn are regulated by higher and higher orders of generalized institutional norms. At the "top" of the system is the society as a total system, in the modern case organized as a single political collectivity, and institutionalizing a single more or less integrated system of values. . . .[109]

In sum, the types of reality are human organisms, human personalities (as they interrelate through roles and collectivities), social institutions, and societies. Each level contains the familiar AGIL components. From a cybernetic approach, it is the L cell of the societal level that exercises ultimate control.

Exactly because these four levels appear in *every* social system, they alone are of little help in describing historical differences in the evolutionary levels of societies. But the necessary augmentation is already in hand. Social systems, including societies, will vary in the extent to which the AGIL functions at each of the four levels are themselves differentiated. Indeed Parsons' approach allows in principle for an infinite number of such further differentiations.

Parsons' most elaborate treatment of evolution itself appears in his monograph *Societies: Evolutionary and Comparative Perspectives*, and he there describes four evolutionary levels (promising to add to the series in a later work): primitive societies, advanced primitive societies, archaic societies, and historic, intermediate empires. What are the critical defining criteria that distinguish these levels?

> Advanced primitive: strict status equivalence of intermarrying kinship groups breaks down and is complemented by "a generalization in the solidarity of the clan, so that common identities prevent the more advantaged lineages from asserting themselves as independent clans."

109. *Ibid.*, pp. 7–8.

What might precipitate such developments?

> Two primary sets of forces seem to support the emergence of differentiation among lineages. One . . . is the tendency to differential advantage, property in land being its most important vehicle. . . .
>
> The other basis arises from the growth in importance of the *societal* collectivity as such, including its tendency to become more definitely bounded. . . . Hence, there is pressure to symbolize the collective identity more . . . explicitly and also to develop more effective instrumentalities for its functioning as a system, especially in the contexts we consider governmental. . . . all advanced primitive societies are characterized by stratification and by some kind of central political organization based upon relatively secure territorial boundaries. . . .[110]

To continue with the remaining levels:

> Archaic societies: characterized by the literacy of one sector of the society's elites (probably the priesthood) and by a cosmological religion (i.e., a theology in which all things, divine and natural, have a place).[111]

> Historic, intermediate empires: characterized by the literacy of the entire upper class and by a historic religion, that is one that has broken through to philosophical levels of generalization and systematization.[112]

Parsons' discussion of differentiation and of levels of organization would hardly have prepared us for these definitions. Suddenly we find to be important whole ranges of criteria not touched upon before: stratified lineages; the growth, for whatever reason, of the relative importance of the society as a collectivity; the invention of writing and the diffusion of skill in reading. We have not been provided with concepts by means of which these events could with any confidence be described as differentiations. Moreover, some of them seem clearly unanticipated by any rationale built into Parsons' scheme. For example, I find nothing that hints that the "societal collectivity" might vary in importance relative to the other levels of organization. We are told that it, and the other levels, are present in every social system and that all are important—in fact, that all are inherent. Likewise, I find no differentiation envisioned in the scheme that might have sufficed to produce the invention of writing. Writing is, of course, an elaboration and

---

110. Parsons, *Societies*, pp. 43–44, 47.
111. See also: Robert N. Bellah, "Religious Evolution," *American Sociological Review*, 29 (June 1964): 364.
112. Parsons, *op. cit.*, p. 51.

differentiation within a society's culture, but so, by Parsons' definitions, is all differentiation. Stated a bit differently: Writing does not seem to be one of the varieties of differentiation for which he has provided. As for religion, cosmological or historic, there is considerable evidence that these arise in more complex societies and that they serve the function of pattern maintenance. But we have not been given a systematic basis in the four levels of organization and in the four system problems that would lead us ineluctably to forecast the defining properties of either type of faith.[113]

I come away with the impression that, whatever its utility in other contexts, Parsons' theoretical apparatus for identifying levels in evolution has proven of little use in his own work and that he has fallen back upon certain widely reported, but as yet unsystematized, criteria.

But there is a second feature desirable in any theory of evolution: It should define levels of complexity such that the more advanced have all the capacities of their predecessors and such that, to reach a more advanced level, a society must successively develop all of the capacities present at all lower levels. Even if we accept the defining criteria of evolutionary levels that Parsons finally invokes, there seem to be a great many exceptions to what one would expect on the basis of a sound evolutionary scheme. For example, the Nuer tribesmen of the Sudan have a weakly defined "society." They also have stratified lineages and a cosmological religion. They are illiterate. This case is important not merely because the picture is inconsistent with Parsons' levels of evolution but because it is inconsistent in one respect that is forbidden by his scheme: The cultural development in the L cell of the societal level of Nuers' social system (the cosmological religion) is wildly disparate from other aspects of their system's evolutionary level.

Consider next the matter of literacy. We are not told how to define a society's upper class, but, by common sense criteria, a large fraction of the elites of western Europe were illiterate well through the 16th and 17th centuries, this in societies having a historic religion. And literacy seems to have been far from universal in the elites of southern Asia, the Zorastrian regimes in Persia, the Mohammedan emirates in Africa and the Middle East; all these had a historic religion.

There is nothing in Parsons' scheme that says a society at a lower level of complexity will move to a higher level, but the scheme does prescribe necessary steps to be taken if that movement is to occur. Does it prescribe the right steps? From the historical record, it would seem that crucial steps are missing from his theory. The Nuer serve to document this, and so do his own observations that the societies that ultimately came to be most ad-

113. Bellah, *op. cit.*

vanced—the societies of Western Europe—were converted to a historic religion (Christianity) long before even a sector of their elites were literate and his observation that some of them then passed through the organizational "regression" entailed in the feudal dissolution of larger hegemonies before they once again established powerful "societal collectives." This last observation reminds us of other cases in which relatively primitive or barbaric societies have been those that suddenly leaped into the van of evolutionary advance.

There is no profit in belaboring these points. An evolutionary theory is difficult to construct. Because of the central place of differentiation in Parsons' theory of the social system, one would expect that theory to have a role in some final account of evolution. Whatever role it may have, it seems evident that it now is inadequate and that its creator has not been able by means of his theory to describe systematically or even explain the grossest differences in evolutionary level among societies.

I think that this failure is instructive for our appraisal of his theory as a whole. Near the beginning of my discussion, I pointed out the restricted range of social events that the theory is designed to handle. The difficulties encountered in conceiving and dealing with evolution remind us that those omitted aspects of social life are always present and important. The same difficulties remind us that the distinctions embodied in Parsons' work were devised in a *post-hoc* fashion to rationalize observations and certain prior theories, those theories, in turn, having been constructed to account for the rise of the modern West and for its internal social structure. Parsons has effected the conceptual synthesis he sought. But no synthesis will order what its author has not chosen to synthesize.

PARSONS: AN AFTER-VIEW

The development of AGIL enabled Parsons to do most of what, from the beginning, he had desired. It enabled him to compare institutions, this according to their function in the social system as a whole. It enabled him to relate institutions, this according to the definitional requirement that these functions be coordinated and that their service to the whole consist in their service to other parts. It enabled him to conceptualize the institutional materials already incorporated in economic theory, and in political science theory, to place them within his scheme, and thus to enrich his own analysis and to clarify and synthesize existing analyses in other social sciences. AGIL embodied more sharply than the conceptual scheme of Weber a break with historical analyses and the breaking through of social science.

Weber had cast his problem as that of understanding the social de-

velopment of the modern West. This led him to comparisons with the
Western situation in earlier times and to comparisons with non-Western
societies and cultures. But, in all of these comparisons, the persistent standard was constituted by the social structure judged specific to the modern
West—that standard being employed to clarify what was peculiar to the
West, and to determine especially those features of other societies and
periods that differed from the West in modern times. Parsons, by centering
attention on the whole complex of an advanced society's institutions, has
developed a scheme that provides ahistorical criteria for comparisons. This
is not to say that the scheme is not rooted in observations from history; it is.
It is not to say that Parsons' applications of the scheme are not colored by
problems important for modern America and by his views of those problems.[114] (As his critics have repeatedly shown, Parsons is unlike Hegel, that
other exponent of the power of values and of the importance of differentiation, in saying almost nothing about the competition and conflict inherent
in a differentiated institutional order—this struggle being perhaps subordinated under some higher integration but never resolved by it.) It is to
say that the scheme permits a comparison of institutions that considers each
in its own wholeness and not merely those features of a given institution that
contrast most obviously with features of some other institution. When applied to societies, the scheme enables—indeed it forces—attention to the
whole complex of institutions, not just those in which the societies concerned
most obviously differ.

In "The Place of Ultimate Values . . ." Parsons set himself the objective
of creating "a system of sociological theory embodying the value-factor."[115]
The theory of action is one such theory. Employed as an interpretation of
history, it takes a form reminiscent of the sacred histories that culminated in
the work of Hegel.[116] Like Hegel's interpretation, Parsons' is the work of
"a Protestant, with skeptical tendencies."[117] In his view, it is through a
differentiation in the timeless order of ultimate values that there is set in
motion a reorganization of that order and, through this change in values,
there occurs a reorganization in time—in history—of the careers of men and
organizations. And the differentiations successively strip away, from the
value that is "in truth" ultimate, all the "idols" that might be confused with
it, freeing it to be for men what in fact it is: displaying the infinite layers
between itself and history, layers across which it nonetheless exercises its

114. Some examples can be found in Parsons, "Evolutionary Universals,"
pp. 355–356.
115. P. 314.
116. Reviewed in Frank E. Manuel's *Shapes of Philosophical History* (Stanford: Stanford University Press, 1965).
117. Parsons, *op. cit.*, p. 309.

sovereignty. "The Reformation must continue," cried Schleiermacher.[118] In Parsons' view it will throughout all of history. And throughout a social system every differentiated unit is essential, revealing some necessary aspect of the order in which it exists. To omit from our analyses any functional unit is to mistake the character of the others and of the whole. Parsons' career is built upon the importance of developing a comprehensive analysis. His exhortation to social scientists is like Calvin's to sinners: The only sufficient word is the whole Word.

LÉVI-STRAUSS AND PARSONS

I have tried in the course of my exposition to indicate what each of these authors has systematized and what he has not, and, by that means, to describe the resources that his theories offer for comparative studies. I would like in closing to note certain points of similarity and difference between their schemes.

Both men have been inspired by problems that inherently required them to undertake comparative work. Although employing different materials, both have pursued that work primarily through a progressively elaborated classification, both men believing that, in the marginals required to order their tables, there was a deeper level of reality that could be found in the entries in the cells. Morphology was thus employed as a means of discovery—not of unsuspected cells—but of unforeseen marginals. (This is the procedure of Lévi-Strauss in revealing the structure of each major area of culture that he has examined. It is the procedure of Parsons in his classifications of existing theories and of the key observations upon which they are built.)

These writers differ in principles they use to generate a classification. Lévi-Strauss, we discovered, is looking for a set of universal principles by which the human mind formulates and solves all problems whatsoever. He is looking for a set of universal *means*. He begins with detailed but delimited empirical observations and tries to classify within a single scheme all the variance they contain. Parsons, like Durkheim, begins with *ends* universally ultimate in social systems, classifying phenomena according to the role they play in relation to those ends. Lévi-Strauss begins with signs, assuming that they are systematized through a grammatical structure; Parsons begins with social relations, assuming that they are one through their place in the life— the process of action—of a collective actor. Lévi-Strauss has opted for syn-

---

118. Quoted in James L. Adams, "Tillich's Concept of the Protestant Era," *in* Paul Tillich, *The Protestant Era*, James L. Adams, (Chicago: University of Chicago Press, 1948), p. 273.

chronic analyses—in part, he tells us— because ethnographic materials rarely afford us a historical picture. He seeks, however, to keep diachronic analysis in view, and, in his most extended discussion of analyses through time—his comments on dialectic in *The Savage Mind*—he makes it clear that he conceives social processes much as Parsons conceives "action." Parsons, by contrast, founds his sociological classification upon action as a process of a collective actor: upon a diachronic event. Then, by dealing primarily with the normative criteria that action entails, he converts his analysis into a synchronic picture of the culture—the normative criteria—that are employed in systematic relations among that actor's component parts. We may be misled by Parsons' often elaborate discussions of the inputs and outputs among the functional sectors of a social system. These inputs and outputs prove upon inspection to be merely statements of the relations among the sectors, the statements following from the definitions of the sectors as parts or phases of the whole.[119]

Both Parsons and Lévi-Strauss have been struck by the "binary" character of differentiation. This may be a profound insight or merely an artifact of their reliance upon classification. Classification proceeds, after all, through the location of similarities and, among things that are similar, through the location of differences. It is not difficult to show that this process, if carried out completely for any set of objects, will entail a binary expansion. Neither man has demonstrated that empirical cultures or social organizations actually differentiate in this fashion.

As we have already discovered, there are only limited points at which the empirical validity of the two schemes can be examined. Perhaps for that reason, among others, both men have put themselves under the discipline of comprehensiveness, the completeness of a classification being one test of its empirical relevance. Indeed, Lévi-Strauss' completeness has so impressed some anthropologists that they suggest he must be right. I do not know whether he or Parsons is right or wrong, but the social sciences have not been lacking in comprehensive schemes—schemes enabling the interpreta-

---

119. At least since 1945, Parsons has seen these functional relations as having the role in his analyses that systems of equations play in hypothetico-deductive analyses. Except as a strained analogy, this is untrue. The components of a system of equations have an unchanging meaning from one equation to another. The formal terms that indicate the relations of those components also have a stable meaning. In Parsons' scheme, however, the components have a particular meaning only in terms of their present relationship to other components, and the terms that relate the components, the inputs and outputs, for example, vary according to the functional sector from which they come and to which they are directed. (See Parsons and Smelser, *Economy and Society*, chs. 1 and 2.) We are again reminded of the restricted sphere of social science for which Parsons' scheme has relevance when we note that systems of equations are commonly and appropriately employed in much of economic analysis.

tion of circumscribed events—and all of these schemes have been shown to be less than fully comprehensive and many of them have later proven to be badly conceived. The names of Freud, Marx, Spencer, and Max Müller may suffice to recall the problems and limitations.

Morphological and classificatory work is more markedly advanced by the discovery of deviant cases than by random sampling. The cases that do not fit a classification are the ones that require a modification of existing concepts. We have seen that Lévi-Strauss has followed procedures that maximize his attention to these cases. So has Parsons. But both men are sometimes trapped into the error of supposing that, because certain characteristics are "close" to one another in their classifications-by-differentiation, those characteristics will appear together in nature. We saw this error in Parsons' treatment of evolutionary levels, the cases that do not fit his paradigm being at least as frequent as those which do. Lévi-Strauss' critics have found seeming instances of the same sort in his interpretations of myth, dual organizations, and kinship.

Near the beginning of this paper, I suggested that it is essential for wide-ranging comparative studies to have at least a theoretical orientation. Up to the present, Lévi-Strauss has neither developed nor employed such an orientation. His great effort is to build one. Up to the present, he has sought to isolate a phenomenon—culture with its internal systematics—for which such a framework is required. He has yet to specify the units that are appropriate for his purpose or the general nature of their interrelations. As a consequence, his theoretical apparatus is not presently in a form usable by other investigators. What is immediately useful is his procedure. He has repeatedly exemplified some steps by which successive comparisons can be made and exemplifies steps by which comparisons can be pointed toward the uncovering and elaboration of a more general theoretical structure. It is in his example, and in these methods of operation, that comparativists will find a contribution to their resources.

Parsons, by contrast, has taken parts of a theoretical orientation inherited from others—the theory of action—and has evolved a conceptual scheme suited to the functional relations consequent upon social interdependence. As I noted earlier, his treatment, although desirably general, omits important ranges of social phenomena. In particular, he does little to characterize social actors, whether individual or collective, in their status as elements—as entities having particularistic goals, and as forming, supporting, or discontinuing social relations according to the relevance of those relations for such goals. It is also evident that his units—actors in their status as roles—are defined from the beginning in terms of their interrelations, leaving no room for introducing principles according to which they might influence one another. On the other hand, Parsons has found systematic grounds for drawing distinctions among a large number of roles. This certainly facilitates the handling and comparing of diverse roles, and also the comparing of organizations in terms of their roles in the larger society—organizations in their status as institutions. This conceptual richness of Parsons' work may be contrasted with the trend in Lévi-Strauss' analyses in which a handful of universals tend to be derived from an originally diverse set of observations. Although it certainly is not inherent in Lévi-Strauss' procedures, he presently uses them in a way that curtails rather than systematically enlarges our ability to relate diverse phenomena. Parsons provides, within a broad but limited range, a set of theoretically interrelated discriminations by means of which comparative observations can be "placed" and their relations in some measure explicated. That, indeed, is the principal use that seems to have been made of Parsons' scheme by his students and admirers.

EMPIRICAL COMPARISONS
OF SOCIAL STRUCTURE:
LEADS AND LAGS

IVAN VALLIER

Fields of scientific inquiry are typically informed, in any given time period, by certain underlying methodological styles or truth-seeking strategies. Sociology in the United States since World War Two is no exception.

One such strategy has held unusual influence: macro-structural analysis. Although labels are always equivocal in both meaning and utility, there are common themes of intellectual activity which set this tradition off from other styles. Four such themes may be noted:

1. Macro-structuralists, whatever their particular theoretical inclinations or positions, are preoccupied with problems of structure and change in large-scale, complex units, e.g., societies, international systems, institutions, bureaucracies, or other wide-ranging organizations.[1]

2. Their styles of thinking and modes of addressing problems are characteristically guided by classical theories, abstract classificatory schemes, ideal-types, and systemic models which serve to reduce or order complex ranges of empirical phenomena into manageable units or clusters.

---

1. Although macro-structural analysis, as I use the phrase, includes structural-functional works, it is meant to be more inclusive. The thing that identifies functional inquiries is not that they are macro or comparative but that they are guided by a strict causal model, namely that items (such as the incest taboo, stratification systems, and political machines) carry direct, latent effects for other processes, relationships, or goal states. To verify such hypotheses, strict experimental designs are required. Merton pointed this out many years ago. Addressing the problems of validating statements about functional relationships, he writes as follows: "Throughout the paradigm, attention has been called repeatedly to the specific points at which assumptions, imputations and observations must be validated. This requires, above all, a rigorous statement of the sociological procedures of analysis which most nearly approximate the *logic* of experimentation. It requires a systematic review of the possibilities and limitations of *comparative* (cross-cultural and cross-group) *analysis*." Robert K. Merton, "Manifest and Latent Functions," in *Social Theory and Social Structures* (rev. ed., Glencoe, Ill.: Free Press, 1957), p. 54, italics in the original.

3. Macro-structuralists evidence a deep and pervasive interest in structural variations and socio-cultural universals, both of which stimulate them to make explicit and often bold applications of the "comparative method."[2]

4. Discourse and analysis are typically holistic and contextual, bringing attention to multiple levels of socio-cultural reality, part-part and part-whole relationships, and patterns of interdependence among major structural entities.

The controversies that cut across this broad enterprise are numerous, but at least three hold special importance: (1) the degree to which social action and structural patterns are determined by "ideal" as against "material" factors; (2) the relative merits of seeking far-reaching, "universal" generalizations as against showing the unique features of societies, cultures, and institutions; and (3) whether scientific development depends on a systematic, comprehensive, unified single theory or moves ahead more quickly when various limited perspectives compete in an eclectic, laissez-faire way. These controversies are played out on the wide screen of the whole world, historical and contemporary. Marx, Weber, and Tocqueville are the classical points of reference, though in any single encounter many other voices from the past can be heard.

The basic features of macro-structural analysis are displayed in many recent works, though in varying proportions and degrees of explicitness, e.g., Shmuel N. Eisenstadt, *The Political Systems of Empires*;[3] Joseph Ben-David and Randall Collins, "A Comparative Study of Academic Freedom

2. Several other attempts have been made recently to characterize the distinctive features of macro-sociology, typically with explicit attention to comparative analysis: Edward Shils, "On the Comparative Study of the New States," *in* Clifford Geertz, ed., *Old Societies and New States* (New York: Free Press, 1963), pp. 1–26; Yehudi A. Cohen, "Macroethnology: Large-Scale Comparative Studies," *in* James A. Clifton, ed., *Introduction to Cultural Anthropology* (Boston: Houghton Mifflin, 1968), pp. 403–448; S. N. Eisenstadt, "Problems in the Comparative Analysis of Total Societies," in *Transactions of the Sixth World Congress of Sociology* (Geneva, International Sociological Association, 1966), pp. 187–201; Lloyd A. Fallers, "Societal Analysis," *in* David L. Sills, ed., *International Encyclopedia of the Social Sciences* (New York: Free Press, 1968), 14: 562–572.

Fallers identifies at least six features of comparative macro-sociology: "(1) a holistic and contextual emphasis, (2) priority to clinical analysis rather than generalizations, (3) explicitly or implicitly comparative, (4) concern with the consequences or roles of particular institutions or patterns on broader systems, (5) the construction and application of "models" which are built up from historical knowledge and then applied to or tested against other societies, and (6) a continuing dialectic between comparative conceptualization and historical experience" *ibid.*, pp. 564–567.

3. New York: Free Press, 1963.

and Student Politics;"[4] Zbigniew Brzezinski, "Deviation Control: A Study in Doctrinal Conflict [Communist Party versus the Society of Jesus];"[5] Marion J. Levy, Jr., "Contrasting Factors in the Modernization of China and Japan;"[6] Stein Rokkan, "The Structuring of Mass Politics in the Smaller European Democracies: A Developmental Typology;"[7] Talcott Parsons, *Societies: Evolutionary and Comparative Perspectives*;[8] Barrington Moore, Jr., *Social Origins of Dictatorship and Democracy*;[9] Clifford Geertz, *Islam Observed*;[10] Irving Louis Horowitz, *Three Worlds of Development: The Theory and Practice of International Stratification*;[11] Norman Birnbaum, *The Crisis of Industrial Society*;[12] Robert N. Bellah, "Religious Aspects of Modernization in Turkey and Japan";[13] Samuel P. Huntington, *Political Order in Changing Societies*;[14] and Ivan Vallier, *Catholicism, Social Control, and Modernization in Latin America*.[15] These contributions are not "all alike," yet with regard to the scope of problems addressed, the types of units chosen for observation and analysis, the levels of generalizations reached, the explicit comparative emphases, and the overwhelming reliance on non-quantified data as bases of inference, they represent a recognizable genre of sociological investigation.

Graduate students who are inclined to take up with this macro-structural enterprise are rapidly immersed in, or tantalized with, such questions as these: What are the generic sociological processes that underlie patterns of transformation, stagnation, and evolution in large-scale societies, both historical and contemporary? Which factors—religious, economic, political—gave rise to the distinctive institutional systems of the Western world? What are the limits of variation between cultural systems and structural patterns? How do context and culture reshape, transform, or weaken certain systems of universal values? What are the ranges of variability in the development of non-Western societies, both those that have emerged from the great, high-cultures and those that rest on primitive or rudimentary sociological bases? Along with these kinds of questions, the student is en-

4. *Comparative Education Review*, 10 (June 1966): 220–249.
5. *American Political Science Review*, 56 (March 1962): 5–22.
6. *Economic Development and Cultural Change*, 2 (October 1953): 161–197.
7. *Comparative Studies in Society and History*, 10 (January 1968): 173–210.
8. Englewood Cliffs, N.J.: Prentice-Hall, 1966.
9. Boston: Beacon Press, 1966.
10. New Haven: Yale University Press, 1968.
11. New York: Oxford University Press, 1966.
12. New York: Oxford University Press, 1969.
13. *American Journal of Sociology*, 64 (July 1958): 1–5.
14. New Haven: Yale University Press, 1968.
15. Englewood Cliffs, N.J.: Prentice-Hall, 1970.

couraged to ponder the reasons for the universality of the incest taboo, to grapple with principles of evolutionary thought, and to probe as deeply as possible into the sociological factors that gave birth to modern, industrial society. In short, students are stimulated to think broadly, as well as deeply, about total societies, historical epochs, major processes of change, and the ways in which political struggles and charismatic movements have helped to modify and even replace human institutions.

Within the social sciences, macro-structural studies hold visible influence and prestige, and there is every reason to believe that the kinds of problems they address will continue to be regarded as central to the disciplines. In both our own society and other regions of the world, problems of institutional change, the growth of large-scale organizations, and the relations among major status groups and collectivities automatically assume significance. Nevertheless, many macro-structuralists are becoming increasingly uneasy about the state of their field.[16] They are beginning to recognize that something more than abstract generalizations should be attempted,

16. Bendix, for instance, identifies the macro-sociologists' reliance on universal concepts as a main difficulty, i.e., concepts that are deemed applicable to all social situations without qualification by time and space. He proposes that concepts such as the division of labor, stratification, urbanization, and universalism–particularism should be specified and disaggregated, or logically decomposed, and brought into touch with socio-historical configurations as means of showing ranges of variations and co-variations. Through such specifications and accompanying comparative studies, we will learn to select indicators that are valid for specific types of situations rather than making inferences on the basis of assumptions that are parochial and culturally biased. From Bendix's article we gain certain investigative guidelines, as follows:

Step 1: Identify a "universal" issue or sociological problem. He takes "the friction between private interest and public authority" as an example.
Step 2: Select societies as observational units and identify how this friction is solved in empirical circumstances, i.e., the ways in which private interest is subordinated to public authority.
Step 3: Use variations in types of subordination as a basis for distinguishing types of political communities.
Step 4: Compare and contrast types of political communities, first, in order to illuminate particular historical configurations, such as the 'medieval political community' and second, as a means of identifying corollaries to types of political communities, i.e., types of political protest.
Step 5: Examine the persistence and change of structural configurations through time: "Analyze the transformation a given structure undergoes without losing its distinguishing characteristics."

Reinhard Bendix, "Concepts and Generalizations in Comparative Sociological Studies," *American Sociological Review*, 28: 4 (August, 1963), 532–539.

Eisenstadt identifies four sets of methodological problems that deserve to be given attention in the comparative study of total societies:

1. The problem of delimiting "units of comparison within which the variables out of which types are being constructed can be meaningfully applied—whether these are 'total societies,' institutions, groups or cultural tracts [*sic*]

that many of their conceptual schemes do not lead to testable hypotheses, and that intuitive measures and idiosyncratic definitions of complex phenomena do not provide the basis for a strong, cumulative macro-science. Macro-structuralists may be viewed as caught in a distinct set of cross-pressures. On the one hand, their theoretical and substantive interests are centered on what we have come to refer to as "big-range" problems, macro-

---

—and of the range of time over which such units can be viewed as homogeneous."

2. The problem of "construction of indices through which some of the variables investigated can be compared—indices of cultural orientations, of societal complexity or of organizational structure."

3. The problem of "comparability of both of the units of comparison and of the indices—i.e., the extent to which these abstractions are still useful when taken out of their concrete cultural settings."

4. The problem of sampling which is "common to most comparative studies—and especially those focusing on institutional or organizational variablès."

S. N. Eisenstadt, "Problems in the Comparative Analysis of Total Societies," in *Transactions of the Sixth World Congress of Sociology*, Vol. I, Geneva, International Sociological Association, 1966, p. 191. In the context of discussing the problem of sampling, Eisenstadt takes up basic problems of research design, especially the constraints that the small number of total societies impose on scientific analysis. He suggests that these strictures may be partially overcome by constructing "special intensive comparisons" or trying to "approximate semi-experimental (albeit usually post-hoc) conditions."

A more pointed discussion of methodological problems attending macro-comparisons is provided by Smelser, with special attention to economic phenomena. Smelser's main focus is on concept-indicator relationships in studies that attempt to get at universals. Holding that the problem is not resolved either by choosing single indicators or by dealing with each economy as entirely unique, Smelser proposes that the units of comparison must be chosen with regard to value systems: ". . . in comparative analysis the question of wants as the ultimate defining basis for economic activity and measurement cannot be taken as a parametric given; it must be treated in relation to variable societal values and goals. . . . The investigator of comparative economic activity, then, must allow cultural values and meanings to intervene between his most general concept ('the economic') and its specific measurements." Neil J. Smelser, "Notes on the Methodology of Comparative Analysis of Economic Activity," in *Transactions of the Sixth World Congress of Sociology*, Vol. II, Geneva, International Sociological Association, 1967, pp. 107–108.

LaPalombara, a political scientist, feels very strongly that new approaches and stricter methodologies are needed to strengthen macro-structural studies. In a recent essay evaluating the trends in political science, LaPalombara pleads for a research strategy in comparative politics that combines theories of the middle range, the study of segments or partial systems, and rigorous methodologies. One of the priority substantive themes, in this judgment, is *decision-making* phenomena. Joseph LaPalombara, "Macrotheories and Microapplications in Comparative Politics: A Widening Chasm," *Comparative Politics*, 1, (October 1968): 52–78.

For earlier analyses of methodological problems in macro-comparative studies, see S. F. Nadel, *The Foundations of Social Anthropology* (Glencoe, Ill.: Free Press, 1951), especially ch. IX, "Experimental Anthropology," pp. 222–255; Gideon Sjoberg, "The Comparative Method in the Social Sciences," *Philosophy of Science*, 22 (April 1955): 106–117; Marion J. Levy, Jr., "Some Basic Methodological Difficulties in Social Science," *Philosophy of Science*, 17 (October, 1950): 291–294; and Fred Eggan, "Social Anthropology and the Method of Controlled Comparison," *American Anthropologist*, 56 (1954): 743–763.

ssytems (intra-societal and international), and complex structural relationships. But as social scientists they are also obligated to the standards of an
empirical discipline wherein systematic procedures of verification and testing (not just the formulation) of hypotheses are automatically honored. This
combination of involvements creates a professional role that is extremely
difficult to consolidate.

Men under cross-pressures seek equilibrium, stimulating some to stress
"pure theory," others to assume roles as social analysts and diagnosticians,
and still others simply to abandon macro-structural studies for more rigorous and manageable fields such as demography, small groups, and voting
studies. There is, I think, another alternative: namely, to identify, in increasingly specific ways, the work habits that impede verificational studies
and, as a corollary, to learn what we can from our more methodologically
inclined colleagues.

The aims of this essay are three: first, to identify several of the investigative habits or tendencies found in macro-structural analysis that I
consider inhibitive of cumulative empirical studies; second, to examine
directions that are being taken in structural studies that I find methodologically positive; and third, to draw implications from these materials concerning the problems of research collaboration and graduate training.

SOURCES OF LAG AND UNDERDEVELOPMENT IN MACRO-STRUCTURAL ANALYSES

It is unlikely that the further development of systematic methodologies
for macro-structural analysis will be achieved without an examination of
investigative assumptions and work habits that presently block growth. In
this section, four sources of lag are identified and discussed briefly.

AN OVER-CONCERN WITH SOCIETY AS THE UNIT OF OBSERVATION

Macro-structuralists are typically concerned with the study of societies,
or at least with relationships and changes that include societies as one major
point of reference. This preoccupation stems from an assumption that the
total society is the most significant of human collectivities. Societies not only
face the task of solving all the major functional problems but also generate,
in the course of their existence and development, emergent properties that
cannot be observed in subsocieties or single institutional sectors. The study
of total societies not only opens the way to identify singularly important
kinds of variables but also presents theoretical problems having to do with
integration, legitimacy, continuity, and order, that are not exhibited in
other types of collectivities.

There is, then, a special devotion to *society* as the unit of observation and analysis.[17] Attention is given to the properties of societies, to their dominant features and structures, and to their characteristic styles of action, e.g., flexibility or rigidity, mobility or stagnation, and so on. These inferences about the properties of *total societies* or the position a given society holds on a general dimension or continuum are, of course, observations about typicality and modality.[18] The statement that society X is "highly bureaucratized" *implies* that observations have been made on a "sample" or total universe of behavioral arenas and that, in comparison with other societies (which supposedly have also been observed in detail), society X shows a higher incidence of "bureaucratic" relationships and structures. But if this kind of study were actually done, would such a statement be possible? Probably not, for in making such a study it would be expected that no simple summary score could be fashioned. Instead we would expect to find that behavioral arenas vary both in extent of bureaucratization and in type of bureaucratization. Thus instead of a simple summary reading, we would find something like the following:

17. Of course, the ways in which society is conceptualized or broken down into sectors, institutional spheres, variables, or subsystems vary enormously. Marsh, for instance, defines comparative sociology as studies involving "explicit comparisons of data from two or more societies" but then goes on to indicate that the primary focus in his book is on "social systems, and within that category, upon three of the major subsystems of societies—(1) kinship, (2) polity and bureaucracy, and (3) stratification and mobility." Robert M. Marsh, *Comparative Sociology* (New York: Harcourt, Brace & World, 1967), pp. 16–17. Rose, on the other hand, focuses attention on "institutions"—"clusters, or groups of complex behavior patterns within the culture . . . [with] a high degree of specificity and internal cohesiveness. . . ." These institutions make up a "large part of the social structure of the society." Arnold M. Rose, ed., *The Institutions of Advanced Societies* (Minneapolis: University of Minnesota Press, 1958), p. 30. Hopkins and Wallerstein distinguish several kinds of societal-level properties. The first three are termed integral, compositional, and structural properties. Integral properties designate "states or conditions of the society per se;" compositional properties are constructed from the "characteristics of a society's *individual* members;" and structural properties as mainly the characteristics of networks and groups. Two other types of properties—contextual and positional (or relational)—pertain to the international settings of countries. Terence K. Hopkins and Immanuel Wallerstein, "The Comparative Study of National Societies," *Social Science Information;* 6 (October 1967): 50–51.

18. One of the chief drawbacks of characterizing societies in terms of general, typical, and modal patterns is that recourse, in explanation, must be given to "cultural" variables (dominant values, overarching beliefs, and so on) or to "external" variables. On the other hand, if intra-country variations in structural patterns are stressed, geographic, political, demographic, economic, religious, ethnic, and many other types of variables can be brought into this analysis. Even greater difficulties emerge, in my judgment, when investigators begin societal analyses with characterizations of total value systems and then proceed to isolate structural patterns that embody the dominant values. Values are assumed to be the key independent variables, thus closing off other possible explanatory levels.

Society X

Behavioral contexts or arenas

Elements of Bureaucratization	I	II	III	IV
Dimension A	high	high	med	low
Dimension B	high	low	low	high
Dimension C	low	low	low	low
Dimension D	med	low	high	high

It is to be expected that empirical research would show that intra-societal variation exists in "bureaucratic" patterns. How could this now be summarized as a single property of the whole society and then compared with simple scores on other societies? It probably shouldn't be; instead the focus of comparisons should be *behavioral arenas* (type I, II, III, IV) in several societies, so that if France, England, and Germany were being compared, we would focus on comparisons of *degrees* of bureaucratization in each behavioral arena, e.g., civil service organizations, welfare agencies, universities, etc.

There is no such thing as a macro-structure at the societal level, if by macro-structure we mean an identifiable, durable, and relatively stable sociological "shell" that is coincident with the total geographical territory of a sovereign nation. There are, of course, societal-wide laws, norms, and regulations, as well as basic beliefs, traditions, and the like, that are either applicable to all members and organized units and entities that fall within the limits of the territory or that are more or less shared by the members as individuals.[19] Moreover, there are structures with national or societal scope (in terms of tasks), e.g., those statuses and units that are specialized and designated to handle nationwide problems, to preserve and interpret the society's constitution, to guard the apertures where goods, people, and information flow across the borders from outside. But is there any single overall structure, in the sense of an overarching organizational arrangement? Does the whole population of a complex, contemporary society ever act as a single actor? No—instead total societies "act" through designated leaders and specialized agencies. In other words, the study of the structure of com-

19. That is, people who live within the boundaries of a politically sovereign nation typically fall under a general range of cultural, legal, and regulatory phenomena, but the existence of these nationwide norms and rules does not allow any inferences about conformity, nor about key features of social structure. While "dominant values," if described and validated empirically, may allow some general predictions about structural patterns, values are probably not as adequate as bases for structural predictions as are demographic, ecological, and economic variables. I am suggesting that macro-structuralists often talk as though structural patterns hold a 1:1 relation to value patterns, without allowing, sufficiently, for situational, historical, demographic, and economic variables as key sources of structural variation within national societies. The "cultural" fallacy in certain kinds of macro-structural studies is as prevalent, and perhaps as misleading, as the ecological fallacy in studies of behavior.

plex, contemporary societies boils down to research on specific organizations, structural fields or sectors, inter-level relationships, lines of specialized activity and leadership, and many decision-making and control centers.

From this perspective, the fashionable distinction between macro and micro disappears. If we keep attention focused on structural phenomena—role systems, status hierarchies, division of labor, decision-making procedures, etc.—then structures that are specialized vis-à-vis national-level tasks are no more macro than those that are anchored in a local school system. The difference is not macro or micro in terms of sociological essentials, but rather in terms of the system of reference that is built into the tasks of the particular structures. The structure of the National Security Council connected with the President's office of the United States is no more macro in terms of group or collective features than is the advisory board of a small college. The structural difference lies in the sociological scope or systems of reference that pertain to each of the units and the specific membership roles. Whereas the National Security Council's members are concerned with policies, trends, and problems pertaining to the *whole* nation, the members of the advisory board of the small college are focused on the special problems of finances, appointments, plant development, and certification that have to do with its particular goals. In fact, the structure of the advisory board may be more highly institutionalized than the structure of the National Security Council, but the concreteness of the two units, centering around membership roles and persons who fill those, are no different. They simply work with differing levels of responsibility and vis-à-vis different social systems of reference. Macro and micro are appropriate terms for descriptive purposes when attention is directed to the level of social scope that is particular to a given structure, but the distinction is not helpful in dealing wih the features of structural phenomena *per se*.

There are several other implications of taking the total society as the main focus of macro-structural studies. In the first place, societies are limited in number. Linz and Miguel see this as a major handicap:

> One of the greatest problems of macrosociology has been the limited number of cases available for systematic analysis, particularly when we are interested in the effect of changing and different social contexts—structural contexts—on relatively similar institutions, behaviors and attitudes. Using the whole nation, the number of cases that can be studied tends to be limited and consequently the range of variation considered is limited; . . . .[20]

20. Juan J. Linz and Amando de Miguel, "Within-Nation Differences and Comparisons: The Eight Spains," *in* Richard L. Merritt and Stein Rokkan, eds., *Comparing Nations: The Use of Quantitative Data in Cross-National Research* (New Haven: Yale University Press, 1966), p. 268.

If one adopts Murdock's conception of comparability, then there is no problem with the number of units since he estimates that there are approximately 5,000 distinct societies.[21] Of these, however, ethnographic documentation exists for only about 2,000.[22] Murdock's *Social Structure*, 1949, includes observations on a total of 250 societies and his subsequently developed World Ethnographic Sample contains 500. Marsh lists 581 societies in his Appendix reporting scores for an index of differentiation.[23] So long as all types of societies are included as potential for comparative work, the problem of sheer quantity is not severe; however, those of comparability and sampling are. Comparability problems are especially complex and it is now being appreciated that comparisons that range across such different units as the preliterate tribe and the modern, industrial society are quite weak, unless attention is limited to illustrative comparisons. The trend now is to move toward more bounded and subsocietal classes of units, e.g., regions, formal organizations, and communities.

A second problem concerns the relationship between "observations on societies" and inferences about societies, i.e., how are the structures and institutions of total societies studied? The most typical procedure of the qualitatively oriented macro-sociologist is to generalize from a series of data that are aggregated from a variety of sources, such as personal observations, extant empirical studies, macro-interpretative writings, and broad descriptions of institutions and historical trends.[24] Such broad generalizations are products of very complex and very subjective intellectual processes: selectivity, abstraction, and intuitive reasoning. Theoretical models are also used as diagnostic and interpretative bases. However, even when the investigator's focus is more restrained, as in instances where attention is limited to major status groups or particular sectors of societies, the problem of linking observations to macro-structural concepts remains central.

21. Robert M. Marsh, *Comparative Sociology. A Codification of Cross-Societal Analysis* (New York: Harcourt, Brace & World, 1967), p. 14.
22. *Ibid.*
23. *Ibid.*, p. 336 ff.
24. For differences in approaches to the definition, characterization, and analysis of major "societies," see the following contributions to the *International Encyclopedia of the Social Sciences*, David L. Sills, ed. (New York: Free Press, 1968): Franz Schurmann, "Chinese Society," 2: 408–425; Seymour M. Lipset, "Anglo-American Society," 1: 289–302; F. G. Bailey, "Asian Society: South Asia," 1: 412–423; W. F. Wertheim, "Asian Society: Southeast Asia," 1: 423–438; Richard N. Adams, "Middle American Society," 10: 272–285; Morroe Berger, "Near Eastern Society: The Islamic Countries," 11: 90–101; Dorothy Willner, "Near Eastern Society: Israel," 11: 101–116; Ivan Vallier and Vivian Vallier, "South American Society," 15: 64–77; Herbert Passin, "Japanese Society," 8: 236–249; Sidney W. Mintz, "Caribbean Society," 2: 306–319; Jacques Berque, "African Society: North Africa," 1: 125–137; Jacques Maquet, "African Society: Sub-Saharan Africa," 1: 137–155; and Douglas L. Oliver, "Oceanian Society," 11: 254–269.

We seem then to be in need of methodological strategies that yield systematic data on structural and institutional phenomena about societally relevant structures just as the sample survey experts have worked out procedures for tapping a variety of data from respondents in a given national population. But is this possible? Can lower-lovel (sub-societal) units be identified that are isomorphic with the level of the total society, so that data from the lower-level units can be validly used to make inferences about the total society? This is a problem that needs to be addressed.

The methodological importance of organizational studies for the analysis of total societies is pointed to by Turk: The main structural features of societies must necessarily be based on knowledge about organizations and organizational relationships. Not only are mass responses to societal issues "formulated and enacted" by organizations; in addition all important societal roles are organizationally anchored:

> It proves . . . difficult to conceive of roles at the societal level outside the context of national and international organizations. Power positions within larger cities and nations appear to rest heavily on organizational memberships; and organizations appear to absorb an ever-increasing number of occupational roles. Even diffuse orientations vis-a-vis the broader setting may be acquired and exercised through contacts with organizations of all kinds, and not only those specializing in the transmission of influence. Further, settings marked by *cleavage* might also be expected to include a *variety* of organizational proponents for each point of view and a variety of organizational means for its implementation.[25]

The problems that inhere in making the total society the primary observational unit emerged with special clarity when I began to plan a comparative study of structural change in the Roman Catholic Church. Three countries were selected for the study: France, Chile, and the United States. Then came the question: How are structural changes in these complex, Catholic systems to be researched? Several strategies were considered: (1) One plan would involve the depth study of a single Catholic community in each society, but this would hardly provide a basis for talking about each "national" Catholic Church. No local community—whether Lyons in France, Rockford, Illinois, or Talca, Chile—could be assumed to be typical or suitable as a basis for talking about the "whole." So the case study idea was rejected. (2) The second possibility had to do with a sample survey study of Catholics in the three countries, with attention to their attitudes toward institutional change, clergy-laity relations, perceptions of ecclesiastical lead-

25. Herman Turk, "Interorganizational Networks in Urban Society: Initial Perspectives and Comparative Research," *American Sociological Review,* 35 (February 1970): 2, italics in original.

ership and policy, ecumenical relations, and religious participation. However, the focus of the study was on the structural features of the Church and the kinds and degrees of changes that were occurring in decision-making structures, in communal activities, in the Church's relations with the wider society, and other factors. Sample survey techniques are unsuitable for these kinds of problems, since attitudes, reported behaviors, perceptions, and notions of priority are not equivalent to institutional structure and organizational patterns. (3) The third possibility that began to take shape involved a research design that promised to yield systematic information about Church structure and, simultaneously, opened the way for studies of variations at both the cross-societal and intra-societal levels. For each country, four dioceses were chosen with reference to demographic, geographic, and leadership factors. On the leadership factor, for example, we chose two dioceses in each country that were headed by conservative bishops and two under progressive bishops. Then for each country we carried out a four-tiered study. At the national level, we interviewed national officials, social scientists studying the Church, journalists in charge of major Catholic publications, and directors of special national programs. Then for each diocese, we carried out a field study at three levels of Church structure, through interviewing and observational methods: diocesan officials and elites, lay leaders at the level of associations and action organizations, and finally interviews with small samples of rank-and-file members.[26]

Through this comparative design, we were able not only to gain first-hand information on Church structures, organized initiatives, inter-strata patterns, and lines of institutional change, but also an ethnographic understanding of the social, economic, and political contexts within which the dioceses are imbedded. Instead, then, of trying to grasp the "essential" features of the French Church, or of the American Church, or of the Chilean Church, in order to make statements about the whole, we identified structural arenas and concrete settings within each nation that opened the way toward studying central variables and their interrelationships. This does not mean that we reject the idea that there is something that can be called the "structure of the American (or French or Chilean) Church." There may be, but an empirical study of the Church's macro-structure could not be satisfied by examining "national-level" organizations, such as the Assembly of Archbishops and Cardinals in France, the Chilean Episcopal Conference, and the National Catholic Welfare Council in Washington, D.C. Though in each country national-level organizations exist and operate

26. The basic features of the research design are reported in Ivan Vallier and Jean-Guy Vaillancourt, "Catholicism, Laity, and Industrial Society: A Cross-National Study of Religious Change," *Archives de Sociologie des Religions*, no. 23, 1967, 999–1020.

and programs of national scope are carried out, the properties of these units would not be acceptable to any macro-sociologist as exclusive indicators for the Church's macro-level features. What, then, do observers rely on when they make generalizations about the Church's structure at the societal level? They do just as they do with regard to statements about the "political system" or the "educational system"; namely, they aggregate various kinds of data (systematic, experiential, and impressionistic) into some kind of "modal measure" and then submit that as descriptions of the macro-structure. Small wonder that so much of our macro-sociology is taken with a grain of salt.

When we get right down to it, then, macro-structural inferences are actually subtle, intuitive aggregations about structural patterns in sub-societal contexts. There is not something "out there" which can be called the "overall structure" of American society, but only a diverse and specialized range of structural arrangements that involve concrete role systems, concrete sequences of problem-solving, and concrete collectivities and their environments.[27] If this is true, then the most appropriate observational units for the systematic study of the structural features of societies are not "societies" but various kinds of behavioral arenas and structural contexts that carry the everyday life of the nation. Some of these subnational structures are, of course, focused on local or regional problems and clienteles; others will be differentiated in terms of functions having to do with national or international systems. But at each level, the behavioral arenas and structural units can be identified concretely: 200 city banks, 300 colleges and universities, 500 law firms, 100 export companies, 250 political clubs, and so on. These collective concrete units that constitute the work points of society are the necessary focus for carrying out empirical studies of social structure.[28]

27. One of the issues that needs to be clarified with regard to studies of societies is whether they are taken as contextual units, *observational* units, or units of *analysis* and *inference*. Most macro-structural studies implicitly or explicitly take societies as observational units, yet this is probably the least productive of the three possibilities since it is somewhat difficult to "observe" a total contemporary, complex society. One might arrive at a summary score (e.g., based on aggregate data) or a description of modal relations (as in authority spheres), but it is simply misleading or grossly elliptical to say that one is observing the whole thing. On the other hand, if one makes clear that society is the contextual unit (or field site) or that it will be taken, at certain stages of research, as the unit of analysis and inference, then many of the basic problems would be avoided.

28. The tendency to adopt the total society as the unit of observation puts an investigator under pressure to search for distinct "essences" and comprehensive summations of typicality. These procedures, in turn, have the effect of presenting modern societies as homogeneous entities, e.g., the U.S.A. is a mobile, materialistic middle-class society. In fact, however, very important intra-societal variations in structure (family life, state political systems, economic arrangements, class structure, religious patterns) exist and constitute very important sources of the society's dynamic, including types of cleavages, forms of competition and conflict, and the strains that accrue from sectorial lags and imbalances. Intra-societal variations in structure are undoubtedly the frontier for future studies of cross-national scope.

The central problem is to work out procedural rules that will allow us to reach down into society to lower-level units as sources of data—thus allowing us to increase the N—and subsequently to move from those data to make inferences about the total society. This is essentially a problem of aggregation (not to be confused with aggregate data as a general category). It means constructing societal level indexes from units lower in the hierarchy of systems than the society. The problem of validity is extremely obvious, since an attempt is being made to treat lower-order units as a "sample" of societal phenomena. This is not the problem of part to whole. The idea of a part (as used in macro-structural studies) is quite different from a "sample" or a unit that is intended to bear an isomorphic relationship to a higher level of structure. Though it is quite appropriate to observe that economic system is a part of society X, it is quite another thing when we say that 100 subunits or contexts (e.g., having to do with relationships between the operation of the legal system, decision-making structures, and group solidarity, or with some such problem as particularism, corruption, moral trust, and the like) is a "sample" of the whole from which generalizations about the total society are made. Instead of a sample being part of the whole in the structural-functional sense, it is in fact a set of representative units of the macro-structure. This distinction between a part of a whole system and a sample of "representative units" of society's structure should not be lost on comparative sociologists.

A LOW VALUATION OF DESCRIPTIVE STUDIES

Macro-sociology tends to emphasize the activities of theorizing, analyzing, and interpreting over and above descriptive research on social structure. These habits may be due, in part, to a relatively high involvement with historical materials which typically supply the macro-sociologist's data. But I think the problem has other sources. An emphasis on total societies and other large-scale units inevitably involves processes of abstracting, synthesizing, and reorganizing enormously diverse materials in terms of some analytical framework or model. Through these highly personal operations, the "real" and the "heuristic" often become confounded, leading to imprecise conclusions, abstract generalizations, and a strong component of sheer argument. In many fields that fall within the macro-structuralists' range of view, description is underplayed and there is, to use the words of Merton, a "compelling urge to arrive directly at an explanatory idea."[29]

29. Robert K. Merton, "Notes on Problem-Finding in Sociology," *in* Robert K. Merton, Leonard Broom, and Leonard S. Cottrell, Jr., eds., *Sociology Today* (New York: Basic Books, 1959), p. xiv.

Few of us would find it possible to formulate a theory explaining variation in "political development" in the low-income countries if nothing is known about changes in political participation (not just voting), changes in the structure of decision-making, and changes in the effectiveness of governmental agencies to implement plans. In the field of contemporary Catholicism, with which I am somewhat familiar, a staggering "literature" on change in the Church has emerged over the past ten years, yet I have not found in any of these publications any basic facts or systematic descriptions about the actual change of "institutional patterns." Is the French Church undergoing change more rapidly than the Church in the United States? Who knows? Furthermore, we can't know until we begin to define the meaning of change, devise indicators of cross-national *applicability* for the concept of change, and then set to the task of describing (for representative spheres and over a given period of time) the "changes" that have taken place and are now occurring. Questions such as these can only be answered by collecting data—not, of course, without reference to either theoretical issues or key sociological concepts.

In matters of descriptive research, a great deal can be learned from specialists in sample surveys who recognize and assign special importance to descriptive studies. According to Hyman: "*The focus of* [descriptive surveys] . . . *is essentially precise measurement of one or more dependent variables in some defined population or sample of that population.*"[30] Obviously the unit in descriptive studies of social structure is not the individual, but the advantages of descriptive work in macro-sociology are just as clear at this level as in sample survey research. Descriptive studies not only supply knowledge about variabilities and regularities, but also stimulate investigators to define master terms unequivocally. A concern with description also turns attention to the kinds of facts that are being made available through official data collection procedures and thus indicates what kinds of new information may be needed. The current interest in defining social indicators for total societies is a case in point. By deciding what we need to know descriptively about contemporary societies, our chances are increased for instituting procedures for getting those data.

Types of Descriptive Research in Social Structure.—The typical view that all descriptive studies are alike is simply not true. An ethnography is one thing: "The descriptive approach in anthropology constitutes the field of *ethnography.*"[31] The construction of a descriptive or "representational"

30. Herbert Hyman, *Survey Design and Analysis* (Glencoe, Ill.: Free Press, 1955), p. 68, italics in original.
31. S. F. Nadel, *The Foundations of Social Anthropology* (Glencoe, Ill.: Free Press, 1951), p. 20, italics in original.

model is another. Berger and others define a representational model as one in which the aim is "to represent in as precise and formally simple a manner as possible a recurrent but specific instance of an observed social phenomenon."[32] A third type of description, that neither attempts to provide a complete substantive picture of a social unit nor tries to formalize the essential properties of a specific phenomenon, involves systematic observation of a range of variation in similar units on explicit dimensions, e.g., the degree to which authority relationships vary in prisons, the degree to which decentralization in decision-making structures varies in middle-sized cities, or the ways in which local governments vary in their relationships with national governments in federal republics. Vidich and Bensman's description of the stratification patterns in a small town approximates the ethnographic style;[33] Goffman's description of the "total institution" approximates the "representational" model style, though it is not formalized;[34] my own work on "levels of structural development" in the lay sphere of twelve Roman Catholic dioceses in three countries approximates the "range of variation" style.[35] Of course, particular studies may encompass all three in varying proportions. My only interest here is to suggest that the notion of descriptive studies of social structure needs to be clarified and made a more prominent focus of our total investigative efforts.

Descriptive comparative studies especially should be encouraged and rewarded. Instead of placing students under the heavy burden of "doing something theoretically significant," it might be advantageous to direct their attention to specific kinds of descriptive problems that involve multiple units or systems. In this connection I believe that the demographers, as well as the sample surveyors, have a great deal to teach us. Many of the research programs that Kingsley Davis has undertaken over the past fifteen years are essentially descriptive, always, of course, with a clear relation to general theoretical problems. From his efforts a growing body of reliable and systematic data on fertility, world metropolitan areas, and migration patterns is being made available.[36]

    32. Joseph Berger, Bernard P. Cohen, J. Laurie Snell, and Morris Zelditch, Jr., *Types of Formalization in Small-Group Research* (Boston: Houghton Mifflin, 1962), p. 7.
    33. Arthur J. Vidich and Joseph Bensman, *Small Town in Mass Society: Class, Power and Religion in a Rural Community* (Princeton: Princeton University Press, 1958).
    34. Erving Goffman, "On the Characteristics of Total Institutions" in *Asylums* (New York: Doubleday Anchor, 1961), esp. pp. 4–12.
    35. *The Erosion of Caste in the Church*, (tentative title), forthcoming.
    36. For one of his most recent descriptive monographs, see Kingsley Davis, *World Urbanization 1950–1970. Volume I: Basic Data for Cities, Countries, and Regions* (Berkeley: Institute of International Studies, 1969).

I judge that hypothesis-testing studies of social structure would enter a rapid phase of growth if macro-structuralists encouraged and even engaged in certain types of descriptive research.[37] The benefits of trying to roll analytical models, piecemeal descriptions of social structure, and abstract generalizations into one wad are dubious. It seems that the need to move from theoretical problems to basic descriptive studies as a preliminary to explanatory work has gone largely unrecognized by macro-structuralists.

A CONFOUNDING OF RESEARCH OBJECTIVES

We take it for granted that social scientists know what they are doing and that their intellectual goals are clearly in mind. Yet there are inherent problems of clarity of purpose when attention is being directed to complex, macroscopic phenomena. Theoretical and conceptual interests often get mixed up with substantive and empirical objectives, with the result that intellectual products are frequently ambiguous and non-cumulative.[38] When, as an instance, an investigator tells his readers that he is undertaking "a comparative analysis of institutional change," this may mean one of several things: It may mean that he aims to identify variations or similarities in the nature, rate, or sources of change; it may mean that the focus is on isolating the conditions (through historical-comparative study) of change in particular institutional spheres; or it may mean that he is concerned with aggregating indicators of various change patterns into types of change sequences. Each of these complex objectives is appropriate and, if carried out properly, significant for the work of social science, but all too frequently such broad charters lead to diffuse, incomplete, and often ambiguous results. It is not clear to the reader that the originally stated objectives have been gained or, more seriously, if the author shows that he thinks he has met them, how they were gained. In short, the stated conclusions do not always tally with the statement of objectives, or conversely, the conclusions reached are not fully congruent with the preceding analyses.

37. An encouragement of descriptive studies is not equivalent to the piling up of facts, but is very definitely directed to the problem of theoretical growth. In order to test, qualify, and improve general theories, systematic empirical data are needed on whole classes of units or samples thereof. These data will necessarily be collected in terms of theoretic variables.

38. Although it is unnecessary to single out any macro-structuralist as being more prone to waver in purpose than others (we are all culpable), some works strike me as especially good examples of what I have in mind: S. N. Eisenstadt, "Primitive Political Systems: A Preliminary Comparative Analysis," *American Anthropologist*, 61 (April 1959): 200–220; Stein Rokkan, "The Structuring of Mass Politics in the Smaller European Democracies: A Developmental Typology," *Comparative Studies in Society and History*, 10 (January 1968): 173–210; and Irving Louis Horowitz, *Three Worlds of Development* (New York: Oxford University Press, 1966).

The problem of defining and holding to clear research objectives is characteristically evident in studies of complex sociological phenomena. There are apparent difficulties in separating descriptive work from typological analysis. Explanatory and interpretative modes also get mixed. Some of this confusion is built into macro-sociology, i.e., societies and other large-scale systems are complex, canons of empirical procedure are relatively absent, and, as some investigators hold, "things are always undergoing change." But I hesitate to lay all the blame on the objects under study. Instead the problem stems from ingrained intellectual habits, including a rather arrogant disregard for committing oneself to a definite, steady course.

Particularly conspicuous meanderings and shifts, of course, come to light in studies that are labelled by their authors as "comparative." Some social scientists see comparative work as identifying the common properties of units that make up a set. Comparisons in these instances serve to highlight similarities and provide a basis on which abstract, ideal types can be constructed. Others do comparisons when they seek to establish broad-ranging empirical generalizations about variable interrelationships. The focus is not that of abstracting essential and common properties from a selected number of concrete cases, but on establishing concomitant variations among the characteristics of a set of units. Thus the logics of comparison, adopted by Murdock in his *Social Structure*, by Ben-David and Collins in their study of university systems,[39] and by Weber in his comparative studies of religion are quite different.

There are also those who employ comparative designs in order to approximate "experimental conditions." Variously termed paired-comparisons, controlled comparisons, or post facto experiments, these studies focus mainly on identifying heretofore undisclosed sources of variation in some dependent variable. Levy [40] began his inquiry with the question as to why Japan had achieved a rapid and stable level of industrialization, then turned to China as a basis of control. Nadel,[41] Eggan,[42] Ben-David,[43]

39. Joseph Ben-David and Randall Collins, "A Comparative Study of Academic Freedom and Student Politics," *Comparative Education Review*, 10 (June 1966): 220–249.

40. Marion J. Levy, Jr., "Contrasting Factors in the Modernization of China and Japan," *Economic Development and Cultural Change*, 2 (October 1953): 161–197.

41. S. F. Nadel, "Witchcraft in Four African Societies," *American Anthropologist*, 54 (1952): 18–29.

42. Fred Eggan, "Social Anthropology and the Method of Controlled Comparisons," *American Anthropologist*, 56 (1954): 743–763.

43. Joseph Ben-David, "Scientific Productivity and Academic Organization in Nineteenth-Century Medicine," *American Sociological Review*. 25 (1960), 828–843.

Vallier,[44] and others have also adopted essentially this same strategy, and in the service of research objectives logically similar to Levy's. The chief product of such inquiries is an explanatory hypothesis about a specified range of variation. No general test of the hypothesis is made; that would require another type of research design, since a different objective is at stake.

There are many special variations on these dominant patterns of choosing research objectives. But because we have tended to neglect making the definition of specific research goals an explicit focus of methodological concern, the notion of "doing comparative studies" has become synonymous with any inquiry that is pitched at problems of social structure and change. This is not a reflection of intellectual tolerance so much as a product of methodological confusion or procedural naïveté.

Gauging the Scope of the Study in Relation to the Problem Being Posed.—A great deal of waste occurs in research because the relationship between problem and scope of inquiry is not systematically decided. Thus a case study may prove to qualify or disprove a key assumption of a general theory, witness Malinowski's repudiation of Freud's Oedipal theory by research on the Trobiand Islanders, or Goode and Fowler's case study with regard to the generalizations of industrial sociologists.[45] Case studies can be powerful in terms of general theory and empirical generalizations, but only when they meet the criteria of an *experimentum crucis*.[46] On the other hand, if the aim is to identify the ways in which the structure of authority, professionalism, and the division of labor are interrelated in governmental bureaucracies of industrial societies, we can hardly claim special importance for the case study (unless by strict sampling criteria a single case constituted a representative sample—hardly likely). Instead a universe must be defined that covers all governmental bureaucracies and then either the total universe must be studied or a designated sample. If such a study were considered important, made feasible, and carried out properly, then the results could be taken as a basis for generalizing about the relationships among the variables for governmental bureaucracies in industrial societies.

To take another typical research objective: to analyze the "role of a given structural pattern or complex for some other variable or sub-system." Since this type of inquiry begins with an assumedly important independent

44. Ivan Vallier, "Church, Society, and Labor Resources: An Intra-denominational Comparison," *American Journal of Sociology*, 68 (1962): 21–33.

45. William J. Goode and Irving Fowler, "Incentive Factors in a Low-Morale Plant," *American Sociological Review*, 14 (1949): 618–624.

46. Samuel A. Stouffer, "Some Observations on Study Design," *American Journal of Sociology*, 55 (1950): 359.

variable and seeks to assess its impact or significance for a specified dependent variable, a systematic comparative design is called for; otherwise, the imputed effects of the independent variable cannot be validated. To study the role of religion on economic development in low-income countries, assuming that these broad terms are specified, means that (even for a given sub-set of such countries) cases must be chosen that show important differences in the independent variable—religion—as well as significant variations on the dependent variable—economic development—with all other theoretically important variables held constant. If, under these quasi-experimental conditions of control, the presence of religion (as defined) is positively correlated with economic growth, while the absence of religion is negatively associated with economic growth, we have some basis for talking about the "role of religion in economic development." But to attempt an inquiry of this type by resort to a global study of a single society is an exercise in futility. Case studies are not able to carry certain kinds of scientific freight.

The initial stage of formulating the objectives of a study involves much more than grasping a general topic and setting to work. Besides requiring a clear formulation of the problem and deciding about the type of study required, the investigator must also gauge the relevant scope of the study. To study six countries when one would be sufficient for the purposes at hand is waste; to study one country when six are implied in the definition of objectives is shortsightedness. Of course the criteria for making these decisions are not as clear as I imply, but that doesn't mean that the issues can be ignored.

In short, there is a relative absence of explicit research designs. One of the major weaknesses in most macro-structural research stems from an impatience with or complete disregard of a key procedural step, namely, the formulation of an explicit research design and its inclusion in the body of the work. Since a research design is a device for relating a designated range of empirical phenomena to intellectual objectives, it serves at least a threefold function: (1) a research design makes explicit the investigator's intellectual objectives or his scientific goals; (2) a research design forces the investigator to specify his major concepts or variables and their anticipated or hypothesized interrelationships; and (3) a research design brings to a focus the nature of the units to be observed, the kind of sociological scope that is deemed appropriate to the research objectives, and the techniques and procedures that are to be followed in data collection. Several other important aspects of research are facilitated by an explicit research design, including communicating to one's colleagues the thought processes that have gone into the development of the study and bringing into full view the decisions that have been made in selecting particular units for study. Of course, many of these issues are dealt with, at one place or another, in the published text, but there is too seldom a chapter or section that lays out the bare bones of the research design and makes explicit the rationales adopted for key decisions.

Concern with research designs may seem academic or even irrelevant, but these charges cannot be taken seriously. Any field that moves ahead, whether measured in terms of validated generalizations or fruitful explanatory theories, inevitably emphasizes the formulation of explicit research designs and their explicit communication to the professional community. It is not always a matter of just "better theory" or "better data," but how intellectual goals are harnessed and brought into consistent and systematic tensions with observations of the empirical world.[47]

RELUCTANCE TO SPECIFY AND MEASURE MASTER CONCEPTS

Research objectives may vary, but one of the basic requirements of any empirical study is the translation of master concepts into measurable variates or variables. Macro-structuralists are inclined to cast their analyses and conclusions in abstract, composite concepts. The products are typically ambiguous, partly because the master concepts have not received sufficient specification, by which I mean extricating the implied dimensions of the concept or indicating the sub-types of the phenomenon the concept is supposed to represent. These procedures may also be identified as disaggregating a concept or the exhausting of its analytical components.

The concept "modernization" suffers magnificently under this over-

47. Stouffer recognized the implications of inadequate attention to research designs twenty years ago. Speaking of "bad work habits" and "random ratlike movements," Stouffer suggests that all research endeavors will benefit by: (1) designing studies in advance, so that "the evidence is not capable of a dozen alternative interpretations"; (2) being clear in our own minds as to what constitutes proof; (3) stating our problems "so that they are in decent shape for fitting into an ideal design"; (4) undertaking each study as though it had the status of an *experimentum crucis*; (5) sharply defining the variables under consideration so that possibilities for scaling are gained; and (6) making explicit our criteria for deciding "whether a particular variable may be treated as a single dimension" or as a series of sub-dimensions. He brings these proposals together in the following statement: "I have tried to set forth the model of the controlled experiment as an ideal to keep in the forefront of our minds even when by necesity some cells are missing from our design. I have also tried to suggest that more economy and orderliness are made possible, even in designing the exploratory stages of a piece of research—by using theory in advance to help us decide whether a particular inquiry would be important if we made it; by narrowing down the number of variables; and by making sure that we can classify our data along a particular continuum, even if only provisionally. And a central, brooding hope is that we will have the modesty to recognize the difference between a promising idea and proof." Samuel A. Stouffer, "Some Observations on Study Design," *American Journal of Sociology*, 55 (1950): 356–360, above quote from p. 361.

load of definitional creativity but gains little clarity in its measurable structural dimensions. Levy, for instance, uses "modernization" in the title of his essay but shifts to a focus on "industrialization."

> A system for present purposes will be considered more or less industrialized to the extent that its system of allocation of goods and services (including in that allocation both consumption and production) involves tools that multiply or magnify in whatever complex way the effect of human energy involved in their use and to the extent that inanimate sources of power are applied.[48]

Bendix seeks to "avoid misunderstanding" by distinguishing modernization from industrialization and development:

> Modernization (sometimes called social and political development) refers to all those *social* and *political changes* that accompanied industrialization in many countries of Western civilization. Among these are urbanization, changes in occupational structure, social mobility, development of education—as well as political changes from absolutist institutions to responsible and representative governments, and from a laissez-faire to a modern welfare state.[49]

Fallers moves along other lines by drawing a distinction between the structural and cultural aspects of modernization. "Structural modernization" refers to a process that changes the bases of social stratification and increases the differentiation between occupational and non-occupational contexts, such as the family and ascriptive enclaves:

> What is specifically modern is not specialization as such—although of course the development of modern technologies has been accompanied by a much greater degree of differentiation among occupations roles—but rather the very widespread separation of occupational roles from domestic life and their location instead in specialized structures such as business firms and governmental bureaucracies.[50]

Cultural modernization, which is claimed to follow structural modernization, consists in the formation of ideologies and beliefs which help integrate the new roles and structures with meaning systems, including traditions.

Stinchcombe, in opposition to the concept of modernization set forth by Apter, states that

48. Marion J. Levy, Jr., *op. cit.*, 1953, p. 163.
49. Reinhard Bendix, *Nation-Building and Citizenship* (New York: John Wiley & Sons, 1964), p. 5, italics in original.
50. Lloyd A. Fallers, "Equality, Modernity, and Democracy in the New States," *in* Clifford Geertz, ed., *Old Societies and New States* (New York: Free Press, 1963), p. 181.

Modernization is a process of increasing the control of social activities by theories or doctrines about what will work for achieving human ends. . . . Thus, imposing the discipline of theories over human activities is the main political problem of modernization.[51]

Modernity for Geertz is achieved when the primordial, communal, and particularistic bonds that tie traditional men together are lifted "to the level of political supremacy" and when social integration is shifted from bases that involve primordial sentiments to a functioning, whole "civil order." He goes on to identify the specific aspects of political modernization which consist of "the political normalization of primordial discontent."

After reviewing the cases, he writes:

> . . . One common developmental tendency does not stand out: the aggregation of independently defined, specifically outlined traditional primordial groups into larger, more diffuse units whose implicit frame of reference is not the local scene but the 'nation'—in the sense of the whole society encompassed by the new civil state.[52]

The concept of modernization serves only to illustrate a much broader problem of terminological confusion in the field of social change:

1. The basic concepts perpetuate ambiguity by fusing processual imagery with notions of "states" of structural forms. "Modernization" implies a process; modern or modernized does not. By injecting both change and structure into a single term, the chances for delimiting specific variables are appreciably reduced.

2. Although many of the master concepts possess referents that are typically micro-sociological or even psychological—freedom of the individual, particular attitudes, or role relationships—the level of exposition and analysis remains tied to total societies or broad epochs, i.e., the macro-level. This duality or incongruity breeds confusion and makes it even more difficult to specify the basic variables.

3. Many specialized structural configurations and processes are aggregated into a simple concept—the umbrella syndrome.

4. Definitions are, by nature, descriptions of a phenomenon's essential, distinguishing characteristics, but they are not equivalent to conceptualization and specification which entail translating essential properties into variables, dimensions, or other "scaling" devices.

51. Arthur L. Stinchcombe, review of David E. Apter, *The Politics of Modernization* (Chicago: University of Chicago Press, 1965), in *American Sociological Review*, 31 (April 1966), 266.
52. Clifford Geertz, "The Integrative Revolution," *in* Clifford Geertz, ed., *Old Societies and New States* (New York: Free Press, 1963), p. 153.

Some of these problems can be reduced by classifying key variables into groups which can then be explicated and measured. As a preliminary step, I suggest that students of social structure work with four major types of variables: *relational* variables, having to do with the connectedness among structural or systemic units, e.g., differentiation, integration, autonomy, segmentation, and interdependence; *capacity* variables, such as productivity, effectiveness, outputs, and goal attainment; *compositional* variables, or the internal make-up (in terms of structural and "organic" patterns) of systems, institutional spheres, large-scale organizations, e.g., status density, number of specialized units, sanction and control structures, and the like; and fourth, *permanency* or continuity variables having to do with the processes of structural change, over-time continuity, transformation of structural patterns, the processes of institutionalization, development, retrogression, and decline. Despite the fact that in any concrete investigation these types of variables get bound up together and in some cases even overlap (as in the case of relational and compositional variables or with regard to capacity and permanency variables), it seems to me quite clear that the types are analytically distinguishable and lie at the core of most macro-structural endeavors.

The "problem of theory" also needs more attention in relation to the formulation and testing of hypotheses. It is clear that debates about the quality of theory, its relevance to research, and the ways to go about it are prominent in most social science disciplines. These are likely to continue, and they should. But there is another aspect to the theory question: the ambiguity of the term and the consequences this has for research on social structure. In some respects we have come to associate a "theoretical dimension" with macro-structural work for three reasons: many of the concepts employed are abstract in nature, the entities or problems dealt with are large-scale and complex, and many investigators frame their problems around explanatory questions, such as "Why variation?" Macro-problems and complex systems, by their very formidableness (they are like enigmatic giants), stimulate much of what we term theory simply because there seems to be so little one can do to conduct systematic, rigorous studies of these phenomena.

However, an overconcern for theory can be its own undoing simply because these exaggerated preoccupations can deflect attention away from rigorous, systematic research. Theory often stimulates the quick generalization, abstract typologizing, and all-or-none causal hypotheses. Abstracting from *ad hoc* observations and the fashioning of ideal-types are easier than defining researchable variables and measuring them. It is also less work to diagnose a complex system by reference to some "general model" than it is to test a "general hypothesis" (rendering it either more valid or more suspect). And it is easier to analyze several historical cases in analytical terms than to order multiple cases into a design that will allow for the disclosure of co-variations.

Our preoccupation with theory can be interpreted in part as an escape from difficult research. If this happens then both enterprises (if they can be separated at all) lose. In a field with which I have some preliminary acquaintance, the contemporary Latin American societies, this "theory syndrome" is readily apparent. Within the past ten years, we have been gorged on "stage theories of modernization," "theories of conflict and political instability," "typologies of cities, political parties, elites, and peasants," and broad "theoretical" constructs regarding patrimonialism, ethnic groupings, leadership styles, and religious systems.

All important, and all interesting. Yet I judge that if some of the best minds in current Latin American studies continue to work at these levels of "theory," both the development of our knowledge and the building of theory will suffer tremendously. This preoccupation of Latin Americanists with theoretical work is every bit as strong for students of Southeast Asia, the Middle East, and Africa. In fact, the past fifteen years of work on the new nations has left some astute observers rather pessimistic about the future of social science and particularly about the possibilities for "general theory." Though some are moving toward new styles of research, there still appears to be no deep awareness of the central problems (which I have identified as procedures for the definition, classification, measurement, and comparison of macro-structural phenomena).

SUMMARY STATEMENT

I have identified four broad methodological postures, or investigative habits, that lie beneath the surface of many macro-structural analyses: (1) ambiguity in dealing with society as a unit of study, (2) an impatience or disdain for systematic descriptive research, (3) a confounding of intellectual objectives, and (4) reluctance to specify and disaggregate master concepts. This is not intended as a complete inventory; many other sources of lag would need to be discussed, including a lack of consensus as to the nature of "social structure,"[53] the reliance on *ad hoc* criteria for the choice

53. Compare, for instance, the conceptions of "social structure" set forth by Talcott Parsons, *Essays in Sociological Theory*, rev. ed. (Glencoe, Ill.: Free Press, 1954), p. 230; Robert K. Merton, *Social Theory and Social Structure*, rev. and enl. ed. (Glencoe, Ill.: Free Press, 1957), pp. 133–135; 162–163; 284–285; Neil J. Smelser, "Processes of Social Change" *in* Neil J. Smelser, ed., *Sociology: An Introduction* (New York: John Wiley & Sons, 1967), p. 690; Erik Allardt, "Implications of Within-Nation Variations and Regional Imbalances for Cross-National Re-

of concrete units for comparison, an overemphasis on constructing abstract typologies instead of delimiting explicit variables as the basis of comparison, and a seemingly forthright disregard for describing the intellectual processes that have gone into reaching inferences and conclusions. These tendencies are not just problems of theory, nor do they pertain only to those works that some of my colleagues would characterize as "functional analysis." Instead, they are tendencies that have to do with procedures by which an investigator moves from the choice of a topic to the statement of conclusions. Nor do I intend these broad evaluations as an attack on any particular investigator or group of scholars. My main objective has been to formulate some of the problems that I think are worth discussing as attempts are made to combine more fruitfully our interests in both scope and rigor.

SOME PROMISING LEADS IN STRUCTURAL RESEARCH

Macro-structuralists are largely incapable of testing and verifying the hypotheses they formulate, this being especially evident when attention is directed to contemporary societies, international relations, and institutional interdependencies. This state of affairs opens the possibility for quasi-political interpretations and ideological assertions to play the role of setting the issues and determining conclusions. Although problems of politicization loom large in all scientific endeavors, they become particularly intense in fields that address core human problems but are unable to bring systematic evidence to bear on specific hypotheses. Ideological and political outlooks begin to claim more than their appropriate share of the intellectual stage. We can state this in a hypothesis: the lower the capacity of social scientists to test (reject, verify, qualify, and so on) hypotheses central to their special fields, the higher the likelihood that polarization and divisions within the field will be based on ideological positions. From this we would expect such fields as experimental small group studies, demography, and family studies to be much less politicized than macro-structural analysis. This does not imply that the more methodologically advanced fields are static, nor

---

search," in Richard L. Merritt and Stein Rokkan, eds., *Comparing Nations* (New Haven: Yale University Press, 1966), p. 339; Reinhard Bendix, "Concepts in Comparative Historical Analysis," in Stein Rokkan, ed., *Comparative Research Across Cultures and Nations* (Paris–The Hague: Mouton, 1968), p. 71; Marion J. Levy, Jr., *The Structure of Society* (Princeton: Princeton University Press, 1952), pp. 57–58; Peter M. Blau, "Objectives of Sociology," in Robert Bierstedt, ed., *A Design for Sociology: Scope, Objectives, and Methods* (Philadelphia: The American Academy of Political and Social Science, Monograph no. 9, 1969), pp. 58–63; and Stanley H. Udy, Jr., "Social Structure: Social Structural Analysis," in David L. Sills, ed., *International Encyclopedia of the Social Sciences* (New York: Free Press, 1968), 14: 489.

that there are no internal controversies and divisions; instead it means that the divisions that exist will more likely be centered on specific theoretical positions or investigative strategies, than on issues that are tied to international politics and interpretations of history.

There are other sound reasons for encouraging the development of rigorous structural methodologies. Theory, for instance, is one of the preoccupations of many macro-structuralists, yet theory cannot develop very far unless the propositions it yields are tested and strengthened through empirical studies of comparative scope. Macro-structural theory is frequently little more than abstract generalizations or the conceptual ordering of some topical field. Intellectual perspectives become substitutes for testable hypotheses. These patterns blunt the macro-structuralist's capacities for relating his work to problems of policy and planned change. In order for a theory to be useful for choosing among policy alternatives, it must be translatable into variables that are, first, measurable and, second, tractable (at least in part). A theory that deals with the problem of political centralization and decentralization in industrial societies, and purports to identify the consequences and corollaries of varying levels of centralization for educational development, economic growth, or societal integration, can be directly relevant to policy if it specifies these broad concepts, formulates their interrelationships in variable language, and indicates how changes in tractable or manipulable variables have "causal" connections with other variables. The theory becomes both a way of organizing variables into explicit propositions and of indicating which of those variables are strategic for institutional change. Theories that meet these criteria can be tested and qualified through research, because the elements of the theory (variables) and the propositions they generate are measurable in a variety of structural contexts. On the other hand, a "theory" that builds into its perspective various empirical generalizations about the phenomenon of political centralization and its consequences is not a theory but an abstract description of the situation. It is a general argument or conclusion rather than a source of hypotheses.

Thus on several counts—the problem of ideological polarization, the problem of theoretical development, and the problem of relating knowledge to policy needs—there is strong reason for encouraging methodological work that will provide macro-structuralists with capacities for testing relationships among structural and institutional variables. In this I think that it will be necessary to modify some of our notions about units of comparison, about theory, about field research, and about strategies of measurement and analysis. Fortunately, these trends are already under way in the work of some structuralists. The main focus of this section is to identify and discuss some of the work habits that, in my judgment, constitute the beginnings of a macro-structural methodology.

My starting point is the growing emphasis on the refinement of master concepts, i.e., decomposition or disaggregation. The disaggregation of concepts, which is basic to measurement procedures, involves explication and dimensionalization. Explication has to do with definition and meaning: "the process whereby an initially vague and imprecise concept may be attributed with a more exact meaning, thereby increasing the likelihood of its intersubjective certifiability."[54] Research objectives may vary, but one of the basic requirements of any investigation is the translation of master concepts into measurable variates or variables. Macro-structuralists typically work with a core cluster of master concepts: social structure, institutional interdependence, situational exigencies or threats, social integration, intergroup conflict, structural differentiation, modernization, development, institutional change, bureaucracy, and so on. Observations are made on complex units in terms of these concepts, leading to various types of hypotheses, clinical interpretations, and generalizations. However, investigators rarely agree on the definitions of these phenomena, reducing thereby the possibilities for the cumulative growth of empirical generalizations. On the other hand, when basic concepts are disaggregated and operationalized, discussion and disagreement can move to specific problems of measurement and concept-indicator validity.

As more attention is given to the disaggregation of master concepts, two gains are almost predictable: first, the growth of theory, because a disaggregation discloses new dimensions and typological possibilities; second, it will be recognized that we need not make false jumps in the direction of substituting data on individuals for data on collectivities because with greater explication and specification possibilities for the empirical measurement of central structural variables will be increased. In other words, dimensionalization and disaggregation of concepts helps to set the stage for measurement. As Tannenbaum and Bachman state it: "Structural variables should be chosen first on the basis of theoretical meaningfulness. Measurement is a second step, and tests of relationship between these variables and others a third."[55]

Nye correctly argues that the debates about the similarities and differences in processes of supranational integration can only be resolved through

54. Richard G. Dumont and William J. Wilson, "Aspects of Concept Formation, Explication, and Theory Construction in Sociology," *American Sociological Review,* 32 (December 1967): 990.

55. Arnold S. Tannenbaum and Jerald G. Bachman, "Structural versus Individual Effects," *American Journal of Sociology,* 69 (May 1964): 594.

"the formulation of precise hypotheses (with clearly stated limits) which are susceptible to falsification. . . . Yet efforts to formulate such hypotheses are hindered by the fuzziness of the general concept of integration." [56] From this departure point, Nye sets the aim of his article: "To formulate falsifiable hypotheses by disaggregating the concept of integration into different types and developing specific indices for the various subtypes." [57] The most fruitful next step is "to disaggregate the concept of integration, develop simple measurements for its component parts, and leave the relationship between them open for empirical verification." [58]

The first breakdown that Nye makes is to distinguish types of integration: economic integration, social integration, and political integration. He argues that these types of integration are more promising than "levels" of integration, because "the composite definitions tend to prevent us from noticing differential rates of change among different indicators and thus deprive us of useful information for causal analysis." [59] He then goes on to suggest that specific indicators be developed for each of the three types of integration, making it possible to show if political, economic, and social integration among the same units vary independently. Indicator variables are identified for the major types and sub-types of integration.

In many instances, disaggregation is facilitated through focusing on single structural patterns as a starting point for comparative research. This delineating of a dependent variable is one of the most effective procedures for shifting structural analyses away from thematic, discursive modes. A dependent variable, referred to by logicians as the *explandum*, is the empirically relevant dimension (or scale) on which observations are organized and toward which explanation is directed. According to Smelser: "Sociological analysis begins with a problem. Posing a problem means identifying some variation in human behavior and framing a 'why' question about this variation. Such variation becomes the dependent variable—that which is to be explained." [60] In strict experimental designs, the dependent variable is termed the "effect variable" as against the "stimulus variable," i.e., the independent variable.

Attempts to carry out empirical studies of complex units without making the dependent variable explicit typically produce confusion: The

56. Joseph S. Nye, "Comparative Regional Integration: Concept and Measurement," *International Organization*, BB (Autumn 1968): 855.

57. *Ibid.*, p. 856.

58. *Ibid.*, p. 858.

59. *Ibid.*

60. Neil J. Smelser, "Sociology and the Other Social Sciences," *in* Paul F. Lazarsfeld, William H. Sewell, and Harold L. Wilensky, eds., *The Uses of Sociology* (New York: Basic Books, 1967), p. 8.

focus of observation shifts unpredictably; research objectives are introduced in *ad hoc* ways and followed out inconsistently; statements tendered as explanations are not always addressed to a specific set of variations. All too often macro-structural analyses are unfocused with regard to which dimensions, patterns, or variables constitute the dependent variable. For this reason questions are legitimately raised about focus, consistency, and clarity.

One of the basic problems with the functional approach stems from an unwillingness on the part of its practitioners to make the dependent variable explicit. Survival is actually the key dependent variable; however, it is typically not defined nor dimensionalized so that goals states and survival levels can be studied for variation. So long as every society or unit under observation is assumed to be surviving with equal accomplishment, no crucial variations can possibly be identified. To shift the problem to structural variation, i.e., the ways in which different concrete systems work out institutional and collective solutions to the functional problems, is to beg the question and to diminish the probabilities of theoretical growth. The basic question is whether or not systems differ in their survival effectiveness; but in order to identify differences on this complex variable, it has to be made explicit and linked to empirical indicators.

Fortunately for macro-sociology, some investigators are defining explicit dependent variables as foci for comparative research. Here I report briefly on some attempts that I consider important:

1. Huntington's main dependent variable is political institutionalization. In a section entitled "criteria of political institutionalization," he defines the concept and then proceeds to disaggregate it into four subvariables or dimensions: "The level of institutionalization of any particular organization or procedure can be measured by its adaptability, complexity, autonomy, and coherence." [61] Each of these four components of the concept is defined and measurement procedures are suggested. Thus with regard to adaptability, the "age" of an organization is considered critical, because "success in adapting to one environmental challenge paves the way for successful adaptation to subsequent environmental challenges." [62] Three measures of age are discussed: chronological age, generational age (whether the first set of leaders has been replaced by a new generation), and functional age—whether or not an organization has survived one or more changes in its main functions. [63] Although Huntington does not base the key sections of his comparative discussions on these explicit refinements of the concept of political institutionalization, he has provided us with a clear example of

61. Samuel P. Huntington, *Political Order in Changing Societies* (New Haven: Yale University Press, 1968), p. 12.
    62. *Ibid.*, p. 13.
    63. *Ibid.*, p. 15.

how a key variable can be specified and rendered usable as a focus of empirical comparisons.

2. Ross and Hartman [64] are interested in variations in strike activity in fifteen countries. Six indicators are selected to measure strike activity, two of which prove to be particularly important: duration of strikes and the proportion of union members involved in strikes. They then classify the fifteen societies as either "high" or "low" on these two variables, resulting in four major configurations of strike activity. By beginning their study with a clear focus, making explicit the dependent variable (strike activity) and the devising of measures capable of determining variations across societies, they are able to address specific explanatory problems and, in addition, provide us with an exemplary mode of comparative work.

3. Ben-David, 1960:[65] One of the clearest examples of formulating, specifying, and measuring a dependent variable at the macro-structural level is found in Ben-David's comparative study of scientific productivity in France, Germany, England, and the United States. The author's purpose is "to describe and explain differences as well as fluctuations in the productivity of the medical sciences in Germany, France, Britain, and the United States, from 1800 to about the time of World War I." [66] Scientific productivity is defined with reference to two variables that are quantitative: (1) "the number of scientific discoveries (including scientifically important technical inventions), and (2) the numbers of people making such discoveries." [67] Ben-David proceeds to justify the relevance and applicability of these indicators and how scores will be computed. A rationale is also provided for limiting attention to the medical sciences.

With these important preliminaries out of the way, Ben-David turns immediately to a report on variations in numbers of discoveries in the four countries' medical sciences for the period 1800–1926. Noting variations in the number of discoveries both by time periods and countries, Ben-David brings his focus to a first explanatory problem: "What needs to be explained is the conspicuous change in the relative shares of the countries during this period (1800–1926)." [68] An index of countries' shares is developed and computed for ten-year periods.

He then turns to make observations on his second dependent variable—the number of discoveries. Here again variations are found that

64. Arthur M. Ross and Paul T. Hartman, *Changing Patterns of Industrial Conflict* (New York: John Wiley, 1960).

65. Joseph Ben-David, "Scientific Productivity and Academic Organization in Nineteenth Century Medicine," *American Sociological Review,* 25 (December 1960): 828–843.

66. *Ibid.,* p. 828.

67. *Ibid.*

68. *Ibid.,* p. 830.

correlate highly with his first measure of scientific productivity. Having established patterned variations by time periods and countries, Ben-David poses two major questions that will focus his explanatory analysis: "What explains the change of scientific leadership from France to Germany to the United States? And what explains the 'deviant' nature of the development in Germany during the middle and in the United States toward the end of the nineteenth century . . . ?" [69]

Ben-David's intellectual strategy for formulating and explaining these variations is not taken up here. Instead, I have introduced the procedures he followed in the first part of the paper to give focus to a complex topic, to delineate specific dimensions of the variable "scientific productivity," to measure the dimensions, and to demonstrate variations as a basis for undertaking an explanatory quest.

One of the most encouraging developments in structural studies involves the working out of empirical measures for structural variables. Through these efforts, possibilities are increased for combining the macrosociological level and hypothesis-testing.

In the more traditional forms of work, qualitative data are grouped into broad categories and then analyzed for distinctive themes, recurring patterns, and broad similarities and differences. Concrete cases of specific pieces of information are used to illustrate general arguments or abstract patterns. Other macro-sociologists develop general, qualitative categories that form a nominal scale. Murdock [70] developed a series of nominal scales for categorizing the properties of the societies he observed in his cross-cultural study of kinship structures. In a section on forms of inheritance, he divided the variations into three categories: patrilineal inheritance, matrilineal inheritance, and mixed inheritance. Nominal scales were also developed for rules of descent, rules of residence, and other items. Such categories, or classificatory schemes, represent mutually exclusive pigeonholes to which the units under observation are assigned. They are not additive among themselves, i.e., the investigator cannot speak in terms of a scale—higher-lower, more-less, etc.—but must confine his conclusions to simple summations of the number of cases that fall into a given category. Murdock can, however, report that of 159 societies under examination, 119 exhibit a patrilineal form of inheritance, 27 are characterized by the matrilineal form, and 13 possess mixed forms of inheritance. [71] Similarly Lipset's categories of types of governments or polities—stable democracies, unstable democracies, stable dictatorships, and unstable dictatorships—are used to

69. *Ibid.*, p. 832.
70. George Peter Murdock, *Social Structure* (New York: Macmillan, 1949).
71. *Ibid.*, pp. 37–39.

classify 50 American and Western European countries. [72] For the European and English-speaking nations, he makes a distinction between "stable democracies" and a combined category of "unstable democracies and dictatorships." For the Latin American nations, he makes a distinction between "democracies and unstable dictatorships" and "stable dictatorships." The 50 nations are then classified into these several categories. Aggregate data for composite indicators of industrialization are then correlated with separate types of polities.

In some cases the criteria used by an investigator for classificatory purposes are relatively clear, i.e., he defines the criteria and follows a systematic procedure in assigning cases to one or another category. Zelditch [73] provides his readers with a clear statement of his classificatory procedures, referring to these instructions as "Designation Rules for the Rating of the Cases." Zelditch is interested in determining how parental roles in the family systems of 56 societies are defined in terms of two major structural categories: instrumental leadership and expressive leadership. Since these concepts are very abstract and (as he notes) the data come from many different works and investigations, decisions regarding whether the male and female roles are primarily instrumental or expressive are problematic. He thereby finds it necessary to "specify the direct designation rules for instrumental and expressive leadership . . . in terms of the patterns of *action* of the role-incumbents."[74] These rules of designation must provide the investigator with a basis for classifying statements that validly represent his two analytical categories. We can draw from his formulation of one set of designation rules for classifying role action or performance as follows:

> Ego . . . will be considered instrumental leader of the nuclear family if the ethnographer's report offers statements of the form:
> 1. Ego is boss-manager of the farm; leader of the hunt, etc. Ego is the final court of appeals, final judge and executor of punishment, discipline, and control over the children of the family.
>
> Ego will be considered expressive leader of the nuclear family if the ethnographer's report offers statements of the form:
> 2. Ego is a mediator, conciliator of the family; ego smooths over disputes, resolves hostilities in the family. Ego is affectionate, solicitous, warm, emotional to the children of the family; ego is the 'comforter', is relatively indulgent, relatively unpunishing.[75]

72. Seymour M. Lipset, "Some Social Requisites of Democracy: Economic Development and Political Legitimacy," *American Political Science Review*, 53 (1959): 69–105.

73. Morris Zelditch, Jr., "Role Differentiation in the Nuclear Family: A Comparative Study," in Talcott Parsons and Robert F. Bales, *Family, Socialization and Interaction Process* (Glencoe, Ill.: The Free Press, 1955), pp. 317–320.

74. *Ibid.*

75. *Ibid.*, p. 318.

Zelditch then goes on to add a set of designation rules for classifying the attitudes of ego's associates so that additional data about role definition can be coded. By the time that Zelditch introduces the concrete materials of his cross-cultural study, the reader is very clear about how his data have been "measured," i.e., we know the rules that he has followed in assigning cases to the "instrumental" or "expressive" category.

Swanson's book, *The Birth of the Gods*,[76] provides an unusually detailed description of the procedures followed in measuring 39 variables for 50 societies. Here I think it sufficient to mention three types of coding arrangements:

1. Present-absent codes: On variables such as "primogeniture," "exuvial magic," "human sacrifice," and the like, a society is coded as either exhibiting that feature or practice or as not exhibiting it. Many aspects of societies can be handled in this way.

2. Nominal scales: For such variables as "principal source of food," "nature of sovereign organizations (territorial, kinship), and "non-sovereign organizations," a society is coded in one of six or more qualitative categories. Murdock has followed a similar procedure in his classification of the population size of political units and degrees of stratification in his World Ethnographic Sample of 565 societies.[77]

3. Frequency counts according to multiple criteria: In securing data for particular kinds of groups, structures, or patterns, Swanson developed an explicit list of qualitative criteria for a designated phenomenon and then coded the number of such units in each society. Sovereign groups, for example, "have original and independent jurisdiction over some sphere of social life. An organization has original jurisdiction if only that organization can legitimately originate a decision in some sphere of social life. It has independent jurisdiction if no other organization and no individual can legitimately abrogate its decisions." Having defined the minimal criteria for a sovereign organization, Swanson then sets forth eight additional criteria, often involving several specific indicators:[78]

(1) The group or its representatives must meet at least once a year;
(2) it must have customary procedures for making decisions;
(3) the group must be considered legitimate by its members;
(4) there must not be evidence which suggests that the group is perceived by its members as failing to persist into the indefinite future;
(5) the group must have three or more members;

76. Guy E. Swanson, *The Birth of the Gods* (Ann Arbor: University of Michigan Press, 1960).
77. George Peter Murdock, "World Ethnographic Sample," *American Anthropologist*, 59 (1957): 664–687.
78. Swanson, *op. cit.*, pp. 202–204.

(6) it must make decisions on actions which have a significant effect on its members (e.g., war and peace, the punishment of crimes, the distribution of food);

(7) it must not be an agency of another organization;

(8) it must be viewed as a distinctive organization by its members over whom it has jurisdiction.

Eisenstadt's comparative study of the political systems of empires[79] moves our attention into some very difficult measurement and coding problems. His methodological strategy deserves brief mention. In the "Appendix" the reader is supplied with classifications of the major variables, the scaling categories, and the ways in which numerical values were assigned to the categories.[80] Twenty-seven structural and systemic variables are defined for comparing the 32 societies. For each variable several ordinal scales are constructed as indicator variables. For example, under the variable "extent of differentiation of social structure," 16 indicator variables are defined, each of which has several sub-indicators.[81] The measurement process consisted in coding institutional and group configurations on a three-point scale, with each point embracing three degrees of variation. Thus for Table I, Variable III, the scale consisted of the following:[82]

Little or no differentiation:	1–3
Moderate differentiation:	4–6
High differentiation:	7–9

Taking only this one variable, we reproduce the pattern of scores for the Spanish–American Empire, with the Roman numerals at the top signifying the three major periods: I–1520 to 1580; II–1580 to 1759; III–1759 to 1820.[83]

Spanish-American Empire

Variable III. Differentiation of Social Structure by Time Periods

Structural Variables	Time Periods		
	I	II	III
A. Spheres—General	3	6	7
1. Economic	4	6	6
2. Political	3	6	7
3. Legal	3	6	7
4. Religious	6	7	7
5. Education & culture	2	6	7
6. Stratification	3	6	7

79. Shmuel N. Eisenstadt, *The Political Systems of Empires* (New York: Free Press, 1963).

80. *Ibid.*, pp. 375–471.

81. *Ibid.*, pp. 376–378.

82. *Ibid.*, p. 383.

83. *Ibid.*, p. 392.

B. Groups.—General

1. Peasantry	2	3	1
2. Gentry	—	4	4
3. Aristocracy	7	6	6
4. Urban groups	5	6	7
5. Legal profession	3	6	7
6. Military profession	1	1	1
7. Religious profession	5	6	7
8. Cultural-secular group	—	—	—

In his recent book on comparative studies of societies, Marsh developed a four-item scale of societal or structural differentiation. Two of the items—degree of political integration and degree of social stratification—were measured on the basis of ordinal scales to which scores were attached. These scales were used to measure the level of societal differentiation in the societies that are included in Murdock's Cross Cultural Sample. In order to gain a basis for showing differences in the extent of societal differentiation in contemporary, national societies, Marsh chose two other scales: "(1) the percentage of males in each society who are involved in nonagricultural occupations, and (2) the gross energy consumption of each society in megawatt-hours per capita for one year."[84] He then combined the two indicators into a single index of Societal Differentiation by converting the raw scores into standardized scores. Thus for each of the contemporary national societies, the score of societal differentiation consists "of its T-score for the nonagricultural labor force plus its T-score for per capita energy consumption."[85] Each of 581 societies is assigned to a specific category on one or another of the scales. Marsh proposes that his classifications be used as bases for selecting samples of societies in future comparative work.

The newer emphasis on structural measurement shows impressive gains in comparative studies of organizations. Udy's studies on structural variations in work organization[86] deserve special notice, as does the comparative study of small bureaucracies in North America by Peter Blau and his colleagues.[87] They focus on the interrelationships among structural attributes of more than 150 small bureaucracies: the division of labor, professionalization, the hierarchy of authority, and the administrative staff. Rules of measurement are devised for each structural variable. The division of labor, for example, is measured by "the number of distinct occupational titles per-

84. Robert M. Marsh, op. cit., p. 332.
85. Ibid., p. 335.
86. Stanley H. Udy, Jr., Organization of Work (New Haven: HRAF Press, 1959).
87. Peter M. Blau, Wolf V. Heydebrand, and Robert E. Stauffer, "The Structure of Small Bureaucracies," American Sociological Review, 31 (April 1966): 179–191.

taining to the non-clerical staff, not counting those indicative of status differences within a specialty rather than different specialties."[88] In turn, the variable is dichotomized "between three and four specialties."

Blau and others make clear that they are measuring the "structural characteristics of the bureaucracies . . . rather than merely attitudes or behaviors of individuals in these bureaucracies." [89] The role of comparative study is also made explicit:

> . . . the research design must involve the systematic comparison of a fairly large number of organizations, and not just a few cases assumed to be typical, in order to determine how variations in some characteristics affect variations in others. The important point is that such large-scale comparisons are required not only to test theoretical propositions once they have been formulated but also initially to formulate and refine the theory.[90]

Blau has made the problem of the measurement of structural phenomena a focus of attention more recently. In the context of identifying the basic differences in sociologists' definitions of core objectives, Blau writes:

> When one studies the characteristics of an organized collectivity, whether it be a bureaucratic organization or a community or a society, one may ask two quite different questions. One question that can be asked is how the characteristic conditions in this social structure affect human conduct. . . . But it is possible to ask an entirely different question about bureaucracy, or any other social structure, namely, how it came to develop these observed features. . . . The earlier social theorists were mostly interested in . . . accounting for the major institutions and other features of society, often in evolutionary or otherwise historical terms. Recent research, on the other hand, has centered attention on . . . how varying conditions in the social structure affect the attitudes and behaviors of individuals.[91]

Blau argues that the growing preponderance of this concern with the effects of structural conditions on individuals is largely due to "the extensive use of interviewing surveys in empirical studies. Interviewing surveys make the individual the unit of analysis particularly, though not only, if samples are used in which each respondent represents many other individuals with similar characteristics. With individuals as units . . . it is not possible to study variations in social structure and their determinants. To do the latter requires that the collectivities whose social structure is under examination be made the units of analysis in order to be able to compare structures with

88. *Ibid.*, p. 181.
89. *Ibid.*, p. 180, italics in original.
90. *Ibid.*, p. 190.
91. Peter M. Blau, "Objectives of Sociology," *in* Robert Bierstedt, ed., *A Design for Sociology: Scope, Objectives, and Methods* (Philadelphia: The American Academy of Political and Social Science, Monograph no. 9, 1969), p. 50.

different characteristics and search for related variations in antecedents that
may account for the differences."[92] Blau states further:

> The assumption that an understanding of the relations between collectivi-
> ties can be directly derived from a knowledge of the relations between
> individuals is surely as fallacious as the assumption that the self-interested
> pursuit of common goals by a collectivity can be explained by reference
> to the role of self-interest in individual behavior.[93]

The measurement procedures developed by Olsen[94] in his comparative
study of political development in 115 contemporary nations are also instructive. Olsen broke the concept "political development" into five dimensions:
(1) executive functioning, (2) legislative functioning, (3) party organization,
(4) power diversification, and (5) citizen influence. Each dimension was
translated into three empirical variables. As he describes the procedure:

> Each of the . . . five dimensions of political modernization was opera-
> tionalized with an index based on three empirical variables. . . . The
> source of data for all of these fifteen political variables was Banks and
> Textor, *A Cross Polity Survey* (1963). Each variable was subjectively
> coded by these authors into a three or four category ordinal scale using all
> of the available published materials plus frequent consultations with area
> specialists.[95]

Each qualitative category in the ordinal scale was assigned a numerical
value, making possible an overall score of political modernization for each
of the 115 independent nations.

Another scaling procedure is devised by Abrahamson[96] to measure
variations in the features of 38 pre-industrial societies. Six concepts are
selected as the framework of his study: political complexity, social differentiation, demographic complexity, socioeconomic development, pervasiveness of kinship organization, and external threat. His reasons for devising
scales, or indexes, are at least two: (1) whereas previous studies have restricted their measurements of political complexity in pre-industrial societies
to two qualitative categories—segmentary or stateless societies and centralized chiefdoms—Abrahamson wants to deal with political complexity as a
continuum or in terms of a more differentiated set of measurement categories; (2) in order to test his hypotheses about the relationships between
political complexity, structural differentiation, socioeconomic development,

92. *Ibid.*, p. 51.
93. *Ibid.*, p. 61.
94. Marvin E. Olsen, "Multivariate Analysis of National Political Development," *American Sociological Review*, 33 (October 1968): 699–711.
95. *Ibid.*, pp. 702–703.
96. Mark Abrahamson, "Correlates of Political Complexity," *American Sociological Review*, 35 (October 1969): 690–701.

demographic complexity, and level of external threat, Abrahamson found it necessary to translate qualitative materials into quantitative indexes so that statistical operations could be carried out. He writes: "Scales were constructed so that the degree of complexity in one institution could be systematically related to the degree of complexity in the others."[97]

For each of the concepts, except that of external threat (due to lack of data), Abrahamson constructs an index consisting of four dichotomized items which conformed to the requirements of a Guttman scale, i.e., a universe of items meets the criteria of a Guttman scale for a given class of units if it is possible to rank the units (societies, individuals, organizations, etc.) from high to low in such a way that a unit's total score alone can be used as a basis for reproducing its score on each of the items that make up the scale.

These examples, considered on their methodological relevance rather than in terms of the societies being examined or the specific hypotheses addressed, are important in at least three ways. First, they suggest that the problems of measuring (or classifying or categorizing) complex structural phenomena are not insuperable, although such undertakings do involve considerable clarification of the manifold features of the units being considered as well as explicit instructions regarding the bases for making decisions about inclusion-exclusion, "more" or "less," and similar items. Second, all such tasks connected with measurement, whether the procedures actually merit being called quantitative or not, nevertheless help the investigator clarify his own theoretical intentions, focus his attention on objectivity, and bring out new hypotheses and issues. Put another way, explicit procedures for coding complex phenomena not only open the possibilities for the application of certain statistical procedures, but perhaps more importantly assist the social scientist in his conceptual and substantive tasks. Third, a variety of measurement strategies and techniques can be followed in arranging observations in a systematic and comparative way.

It is my judgment that measurement is one of the most difficult tasks that students of structure and institutions face. This involves the construction of workable, relevant, valid, and comparatively equivalent indicators (and indexes) of patterned relationships. Although some important gains are being made, the practice of combining structural analysis with measurement has not yet taken hold strongly. But unless we move in that direction, the chances for achieving tests of general hypotheses, deriving adequate explanatory models, and realizing some bases for assigning priority to one or another independent variable (of special relevance to policy studies) are extremely slim, if not hopeless. Blalock rightly identifies mea-

97. *Ibid.,* p. 693.

surement as a central problem: "It seems to me that certain kinds of inadequacies in our measurement procedures may very well provide the major obstacle to overcome if sociology is to mature in the direction of becoming a 'hard' and disciplined social science."[98] "Progress in any scientific field ultimately depends on the adequacy of its measurement procedures."[99] Blalock then proceeds to call the reader's attention to some of the major sources of measurement error and how these may be overcome, in part, through sophisticated procedures of analysis. Yet he feels that progress at the macro-level will depend very much on the reliance on "our own resources with respect to measurement problems . . . where the unit of analysis is not the person but the group. . . ."[100] At the macro-level a particular set of problems arises which centers around "linking unmeasured with measured variables,"[101] and these problems have their source in the greater complexity of causal models that need to be constructed. Thus, in macro-level analysis "it becomes less plausible to assume a simple model in which all causal arrows run from the unmeasured to the measured variable or one of the unmeasured variables. . . . This greater complexity in linking up the two kinds of variables appears to be partly responsible for the gap between theory and research in macro-level analyses."[102] But Blalock also suggests that this continuing gap is partly the fault of the "verbal theorists" who overcomplicate the phenomena being considered: "Our basic ideas are not all that complex. In relation to the measurement problem, this obscurantism often takes the form of rather vague references to certain variables being 'indicators,' 'concomitants,' 'symptoms,' or 'aspects' of others, without telling the reader exactly what one is assuming about the causal connections between the measured indicators and the theoretical concepts."[103]

We need not search far to find instances of these ambiguities. I need to look no further than my own work. In an article published on religious development in five Latin American countries,[104] I defined four dimensions on which each of the five church systems were "measured." Each score consisted, typically, of a qualitative aggregation of many subjectively defined indicator variables. For the dimension "the degree to which the national church is autonomous or differentiated from the central operations

98. Hubert M. Blalock, Jr., "Comments on Coleman's Paper," in Robert Bierstedt, ed., A Design for Sociology: Scope, Objectives, and Methods (Philadelphia: The American Academy of Political and Social Science, Monograph no. 9, 1969), p. 115.

99. Ibid., p. 116.

100. Ibid., p. 117.

101. Ibid., p. 119.

102. Ibid.

103. Ibid.

104. Ivan Vallier, "Church 'Development' in Latin America: A Five-Country Comparison," Journal of Developing Areas, 1 (July 1967): 461–467.

of the secular political system," I took account of the following indicator variables: (1) legal status of the church vis-à-vis the government, (2) financial relationships, (3) status of the church in the civil courts, (4) types of political controls available to the government for restricting church activities and decisions, plus several other variables that figured into specific national settings. But none of these indicator variables was measured systematically, nor did I specify the causal model that I held in my mind about how these were related, nor the kinds of weights that needed to be assigned to this or that variable. In short, the study, despite its emphasis on constructing an index of religious development, remained essentially a subjective, rough-hewn, and qualitative comparative analysis. Equally significant problems of a measurement nature were glossed over at the point of relating the aggregated judgments together, because I gave each of the four dimensions equal weight, added up the scores for each church system, and took these to be "measures" of variation in overall religious development.

In short, processes of conceptualization only take us so far; then they begin to block and hamper rather than facilitate investigative efforts. To take one example, the concept of bureaucracy has been around for a long time. Its most famous characterization was provided by Weber, and we all know the elements he identified as an ideal-type. But Weber's definition or constructed type has figured as a continual focus of definitional disputes and refinements, i.e., Weber didn't include enough, or he covered too much; the type is not applicable to all cases; it lacks clear meaning, and on and on. Some sociologists, however, have stopped quibbling about the special meanings or "what Weber really had in mind" and turned, instead, to translating his basic concepts into measurable variables. Udy took some of the first steps.[105] He selected seven elements of Weber's ideal-type, translated them into variables, formulated objective indicators for each variable (limiting scalar complexity to "present" and "absent"), and then used data from 150 preliterate societies to examine patterns and relationships. Udy's conclusions have been criticized, as has his method, but that is not the reason for mentioning him in this context. Instead, Udy moved resolutely from a phase of conceptual haggling to comparative research, and his main avenue for accomplishing this qualitative jump was the dimensionalizing of concepts and devising procedures for measuring them.

In another article published in 1959,[106] Udy deals more explicitly with the concept of structural complexity. Three elements of variables are desig-

105. Stanley H. Udy, Jr., " 'Bureaucracy' and 'Rationality' in Weber's Organization Theory: An Empirical Study," *American Sociological Review*, 25 (December 1959): 791–795.
106. Stanley H. Udy, Jr., "The Structure of Authority in Non-Industrial Production Organizations," *American Journal of Sociology*, 64 (May 1959): 582–584.

nated to exhaust the concept: (1) the number of tasks performed, (2) the maximum number of specialized operations ever performed at the same time, and (3) the existence or non-existence of combined effort.

It is no longer true that macro-sociology and research on complex organizations are qualitative, intuitive, and couched in illustrations. With almost revolutionary speed, structural categories and macroscopic concepts are being transformed into quantifiable variables. Although these quantitative transformations do not always meet the strict assumptions that many statistical procedures require, current attempts at quantification carry many positive methodological benefits. Three may be noted.

First, the new emphasis on systematic measurement places investigators under burden to make their concepts clear, to formulate designation or classificatory rules, and to state their hypotheses in the form of quantitative relations. On this latter point one can easily recognize a difference between a hypothesis that states that one variable has an effect on another from one that emphasizes degree or level. In the first instance, a hypothesis of this form would emerge: Religion has positive consequences for social integration. The second type of hypothesis would take this form: The greater the emphasis in a religion on universalistic norms, the higher or greater its positive consequences for social integration.

A second gain from the newer measurement emphases pertains to the directions that social scientists can pursue in urging national and international agencies to collect needed types of data. Unless attempts are made to work out the quantitative implications of a given concept, it is impossible to instruct others how to go about collecting new data. One of the major implications of "social accounting" schemes, such as the one introduced by Gross,[107] is to draw attention to the kinds of data that are needed.

Finally, measurement emphases in macro-sociology bring us closer to the possibility of actually testing or verifying general hypotheses; this is exceptionally important in theoretical development. Unless we are able to eliminate incorrect hypotheses and substantiate correct ones, we do not know whether a theory is powerful or weak. Since most of the theories that relate to macro-sociological phenomena require quantitative tests as a means of verification and qualification, we have no way of knowing which one is good or bad until each has been placed against systematic, quantitative data.

I think that many cross-national measurement problems can be resolved through field studies that focus on the measurement of structural

107. Bertram Gross, "The State of the Nation: Social System Accounting," *in* Raymond Bauer, ed., *Social Indicators* (Cambridge, Mass.: MIT Press, 1966).

concepts through a variety of indicators: observational, records, informant reports, systematic interviews. These field studies would probably need to involve a double-exchange model of personnel arrangements, i.e., sociologists from countries A, B, C, and D would not only collaborate, as they do now, in completing a cross-national study but would do their field work in a foreign country. Thus in a study of the authority structure in bureaucracies in France, Chile, England, and the United States, sociologists from France would do field work in the United States, sociologists from England would work in Chile, sociologists from Chile would work in England, and sociologists from the United States would work in France. In other words, an integrated cross-national project would be designed around a common set of basic structural variables, samples of relevant concrete settings or units would be selected in each country, and then field work would be done through the double-exchange arrangement.

This would have several important by-products: (1) Since each field worker would have had experience in studying these variables in his own country and, now, the task of studying the same variables in another country, he would be in a particularly advantageous position to identify common indicators as well as country-specific indicators and to show their interrelationships and bearings on inferences and interpretations; and (2) "national" biases, or cultural biases, about the nature of centralization, bureaucratization, and "control" would be continually subjected to the test of field experience in another national setting, placing each investigator under burden to make clear his assumptions, his experiential biases, and the like.

There is probably no substitute for systematic and sustained field work (observation, participation, informant interviews, examination of concrete reports, and memoranda) when we undertake research on contemporary social structure. There is no substitute, in my judgment, for watching an organization or group pass through a major problem-solving sequence, i.e., of being there to see how decisions are made, resources mobilized, rules enforced, and tasks assigned. Though we may think that officially collected data, public reports, and the counting of formal status positions are both adequate and valid, there is a noticeable difference between conclusions about authority relations in French bureaucracy made by Crozier on the basis of first-hand field work and those that could be made on the basis of computing the ratio of managers to clerical workers or through sending mailed questionnaires to a sample of managers and workers. Crozier, for example, is able to identify the difference between the formal centralization of authority at the director level and the "content of authority": "Although his [the director's] authority may be considered absolute, he is in most cases helpless, and the amount of actual control he can exercise is extremely small."[108]

Similarly, through our field studies in twelve dioceses [109] we were able to identify the ways in which progressive bishops are developing diocesan-level lay programs to undercut the authority and control of traditional parish priests. In other words, some of the most important structural aspects of collective life are only inferable from field work activities that involve observations and interviews at many points in the total situation and from which a variety of data can be aggregated to bring out a specific relationship or pattern.

In broad outlines, the state of measurement on structural variables is still in its first stages of development. Many of the theoretically important concepts are only beginning to be disaggregated or dimensionalized. These more specific dimensions are being linked to bodies of official data, to counts of the incidence and arrangement of formal status positions, and to various kinds of extant monographic materials. From the side of the more quantitatively and individually oriented investigators, applications of sociometric devices and interview with purposively based samples of status occupants are adding new kinds of structurally relevant data.

It is quite likely that some of the most important advances in the measurement of structural variables will come from intra-societal comparisons of large samples of collectivities or structural arenas that share many broad features in common, i.e., that make up a class or species of units. Such studies, as I have tried to show, not only open the way toward a refinement of master concepts and allow for focusing explicitly on measurement problems, but also provide the basis on which the results of measurement can be analyzed to test general hypotheses. By increasing the size of the N, or the sample of units, investigators are able to deal with four, five, or six variables and apply statistical tests to the data as bases for inference. As these intra-societal bases are consolidated, the cross-national problems will be less difficult. Not only will we know a good deal more about intra-country variations for given classes of units, but we will have, as well, a background of measurement experience that will help give focus to the problems at the cross-national level.

Developments in structural measurement are being closely paralleled by efforts to designate classes (or universes) of social units from which samples can be drawn. In some instances, these social units are regions or formal administrative territories (cities, communes, provinces, counties); in

108. Michel Crozier, *The Bureaucratic Phenomenon* (Chicago: University of Chicago Press, 1964), p. 81.
109. *The Erosion of Caste in the Church*, (tentative title), forthcoming. ale, forthcoming.

other instances, the units are formal organizations (civil service agencies, business firms, hospitals, schools); still in other studies the units are more analytically defined—decision-making centers, elite networks, and the like. All of these explicit emphases on studying structural interrelationships across many similar units increase possibilties for testing general hypotheses. Merton recognized the significance of selecting samples of social units in his essay on "Manifest and Latent Functions." "To what extent," he wrote, "is functional analysis limited by the difficulty of locating adequate *samples of social systems* which can be subjected to comparative (quasi-experimental) study?"[110] Although this question was inserted as one of several queries related to strengthening inferences about functional relationships, it is clear that Merton saw the problem of sampling not so much as a matter of choice, but of necessity.

Murdock is, of course, one of the pioneers in the development of procedures for sampling social units. In 1937 he outlined his sampling method for studying the corollaries of patrilineal-matrilineal institutions as follows:

a. Tribes were chosen in approximately equal numbers from all the great regions of the world (with some inadequacy for South America because of low availability of ethnographic reports).

b. Within each great region, roughly the same number of tribes was selected from each smaller region or culture area, with care being taken to have them scattered in different parts of the area.

c. In order to give the study representativeness for "all known cultures, and not merely of the primitive peoples . . . a few samples were included from the higher civilizations of the Orient, of antiquity, and of the historical peoples of Europe."[111]

Since that time Murdock has proceeded to refine his sampling procedures for cross-cultural studies, as embodied in his World Ethnographic Sample. However, other studies carried out on cross-cultural materials have followed sampling plans specific to one or another of the research goals.

Naroll, who has given special attention to the problem of unit definition and comparability in cross-cultural studies, identifies several of the problems conventional procedures pose:

> To date all published cross-cultural surveys have depended on *purposive* sampling to choose the societies being studied. . . . By a purposive sample is . . . meant a judgmental sample in which the sampler

110. Robert K. Merton, *Social Theory and Social Structure*, rev. and enl. ed. (Glencoe, Ill.: Free Press, 1957), p. 54.
111. George Peter Murdock, ed., *Studies in the Science of Society* (New Haven: Yale University Press, 1937), p. 460.

tries to construct with his sample a model of the universe from which he is sampling. . . .[112]

The desired remedy, according to Naroll, is that of probability sampling wherein the sample is chosen "in such a way that the probability of choice of any member of the sampling universe is known."[113] Naroll stresses probability sampling, over and against simple random sampling, in order to avoid the problem of selecting clusters of geographically proximate units. To avoid Galton's problem, the sample should be made up of units widely scattered in space. Naroll has recently defined the "cultunit" as the focus of such sampling.[114]

Another field which has begun to follow "sampling" procedures in the study of complex units is that of community studies: Clark's study[115] of decision-making, budget expenditures, and urban renewal was carried out in 51 U.S. communities selected systematically "on the basis of region and population size." These 51 communities were situated in 22 states and their populations ranged from 50,000 to 750,000. Clark reports the mean as 250,786. "Cities in this range were selected in order to eliminate the somewhat unique metropolises and the smaller communities for which basic census-type statistics were not readily available."[116]

A number of more formal methodological attempts are being made to point up the advantages of conducting comparisons within designated classes of societies or among middle-level units. Heydebrand's programmatic essay, "The Study of Organizations," is an excellent example.[117] Three themes are emphasized: first, that current studies of organization tend to be ambiguous about "objects of analysis," the "relationships" selected for study, and their capacities to generalize from findings; second, studies that rely on data on individuals are inadequate for making inferences about organizational structure; and third, there is a need to identify the main methodological requisites for systematic, comparative studies of organizations. In terms of this latter theme, he gives attention to these requirements for the systematic study of organizations:

1. The whole organization is to be defined as the unit of analysis.

112. Raoul Naroll, "Some Thoughts on Comparative Method in Cultural Anthropology," in Hubert M. Blalock, Jr., and Ann B. Blalock, eds., Methodology in Social Research (New York: McGraw-Hill, 1968), p. 253.

113. Ibid., p. 255.

114. Ibid., pp. 248–253.

115. Terry N. Clark, "Community Structure, Decision-Making, Budget Expenditures, and Urban Renewal in 51 American Communities," American Sociological Review, 33 (August 1968): 576–593.

116. Ibid., p. 577.

117. Wolf V. Heydebrand, "The Study of Organizations," Social Science Information, 6 (October 1967): 59–86.

2. Large numbers of such units must be selected by sampling from more or less homogeneous universes of organizations.
3. Theoretically relevant variables for each unit are to be systematically measured.
4. Multivariate statistical analysis needs to be applied to these data for identifying significant relationships and developing explanations.

According to Heydebrand, "organizational research . . . [implies] the use of multivariate statistical analysis based on probability samples of organizations. Initially, this method entails the classification of a given sample of organizations into sub-groups and the use of partial correlation based on quantitative variables. . . . Essentially, this procedure amounts to the quantification of the comparative method (of social structure)." [118]

Hopkins and Wallerstein designate contemporary "national societies," as contrasted with pre-literate societies or extinct societies, as a proper focus of one type of comparative research—"pluri-national" studies.[119] They are skeptical about the usefulness of equating comparative sociology with the study of all societies, as emphasized by Marsh, Eisenstadt, and others. National societies are viewed as differing substantially from other kinds of societal units, "in their environmental patterns, in the causal processes responsible for the patterns, and in the research procedures appropriate to the empirical study of the patterns and processes. . . ."[120] Furthermore, national societies are linked historically and currently by the overriding theme of modernization or long-range processes of societal change. They also assert that "[A] national society exists always *within* the specific context of the *network* of nation-states."[121]

The importance of Hopkins and Wallerstein's essay for present purposes lies in their interest in identifying a class of societies for intensive comparative work. "Cross-national" research thus becomes the study of a particular type of society that, by definition, shares a number of common features, that possesses common types of relationships with wider international systems, and that is variously involved in a particular kind of long-range change—modernization.

In my comparative studies of Roman Catholicism, I recently developed a rationale for focusing on the diocese.[122] Since there are more than 2,000 diocesan units in the international Church, and because the diocese is both

118. *Ibid.*, p. 65.
119. Terence K. Hopkins and Immanuel Wallerstein, "The Comparative Study of National Societies," *Social Science Information*, 6 (October 1967): 25–58.
120. *Ibid.*, p. 34.
121. *Ibid.*, p. 39, italics in original.
122. Ivan Vallier, "Comparative Studies of Roman Catholicism: Dioceses as Strategic Units," *Social Compass*, 16 (1969): 147–184.

a major decision-making unit and a key linkage between the local, national, and international levels of organization, I consider it especially important to make it a focus in comparative work on the structure of the Church. In the article I conceptualize a series of dependent and independent variables related to the structure and operations of dioceses that I hope will become a focus of data collection and analysis. In the final section I propose a ten-year study involving 120 dioceses in 15 Western countries. Both cross-societal and intra-societal variations can be taken as foci of explanation.

These brief descriptions only touch the surface of the attempts that are being made to formulate criteria for systematic, empirical comparative studies of social structure. The shift from either "all societies" to particular types of societies or from the level of the total society to middle-level units is, I believe, one of the positive signs of resolving basic methodological problems that have tended to plague studies of social structure.

Although these newer emphases on comparisons *within* types of societies, intra-cultural comparisons, and comparisons focused on middle-level units are important, they also raise problems. By giving attention to intra-type or intra-species comparisons at the level of *total* societies, certain sacrifices have to be made. By reducing the N, there is less possibility for carrying through multivariate analysis (or the holding constant of certain independent variables in order to determine causal connections).

On the other hand, if attention is moved down from the societal level to middle-level units—elite systems, organizations, cities, or regions—it is possible to carry out tests of hypotheses using multivariate techniques. Large Ns for most such units can be gained, thus making various types of analyses possible. But in this strategy the problem of macro-inference arises: Can generalizations about society be made from studies of middle-range units, other than indicating that in societies X and Y certain relationships hold for these units? Such generalizations can be made, provided that the middle-range units are selected in such a way that the variables studied hold direct or indirect implications for the societal level. Thus in studying bureaucracies, one would select those that interpenetrate with societal variables, e.g., bureaucracies that encompass activities of key national elites or that carry some direct role vis-à-vis the total society. Data on the structure of these units would not only be data on the bureaucracies themselves but also on aspects of the society as a whole. *Thus the crucial criterion for selecting middle-level units for macro-inferences is the scope of the consequences of behaviors in the micro-context.*

The cumulative developments in empirical studies of structural variables in formal organizations over the past decade or so carry several important lessons for students of complex structures and institutional systems. First, these studies taken as a group suggest that theoretical propositions and empirical data enrich one another when, and only when, we begin to carry out high N comparative studies in terms of a limited number of measurable, structural variables. The points of this statement should not be lost from view. I am saying that it is not just a matter of selecting large samples of units, nor only that of focusing on organizational or structural variables, nor only that of formulating operational bases for scaling structural variables, but the combination of at least all three of these emphases: large samples, structural variables, and operational measuring procedures.

Second, it is suggested by the growing cumulation of studies in comparative organization that the way in which a unit is bounded carries important implications for systematic comparative research. Formal organizations are definite, identifiable, and bounded units relative to many other typical units that are given attention in structural comparisons, such as "institutional spheres," "communities," sectors, regions, and the like. Though no one would argue that formal organizations are insulated from their environments or that there are no significant interpenetrations between organizations and the wider society, it is still true that formal organizations have definite boundaries and that most of their relationships with environments are specialized and often carried out in terms of formal structures and specific goals. What this suggests is that comparative research in sociology is facilitated to the degree that we choose structural units that are not only encompassable and bounded, but also that they involve critical sociological variables for understanding basic processes and systemic patterns in many major spheres of a complex society's life. Organizations are pervasive in advanced societies as well as in many other types. The isomorphism between micro-units (intra-organization) and society is important.

Although any selection of cases from a wider cluster or "universe" of units requires some rationale and specifications of criteria, macro-structuralists have typically carried out these decisions in a rather loose way and without making their bases of choice systematic. These habits tend to create at least two kinds of ambiguities or limitations in the results: (1) Because the universe of the studied units is not specifically delimited, the findings cannot be generalized beyond the particular units; (2) the cases that are chosen, whether on the basis of convenience or because they are assumed to be *sui generis*, may not have been the most significant for the problem under consideration. The systematic definition of a universe, the selection of a sample, and attention to the relationship that the cases under study have to wider contexts help to clarify the objectives of a research inquiry. In short, concern with universes and samples increases the overall potentialities and strengths of any comparative study.

CONCLUSIONS AND IMPLICATIONS

This essay has focused attention on a broad, loosely-bounded enterprise which I have termed "macro-structural analysis." I identified several of the intellectual orientations and investigative styles that macro-structuralists share, and then proceeded to examine four of the methodological or meta-methodological postures that I consider inhibitive of cumulative growth in emprical studies of large-scale, complex structural phenomena. I argued that macro-structuralists are largely incapable of testing the hypotheses they formulate, not just because the topics they choose are complex, but mainly because the basic ingredients of a hypothesis-testing study are not emphasized. That is, research objectives tend to be stated in very general terms and may even undergo change in the course of exposition; master concepts are not disaggregated and dimensionalized, or systematically related to each other in propositional form; few attempts are made to work out meaningful indicators for conceptualized variables; and there is an overemphasis on societies as the units of observation. This overemphasis has several consequences: Each society's typical modal features are emphasized without attention to intra-societal variation; there is an insufficient number of cases to carry out multivariate analysis; and certain ambiguities arise regarding the ways by which observations are aggregated or how extensive multi-dimensional patterns are substructured.

Furthermore, descriptive studies are generally neglected, unless carried out selectively to buttress a particular theoretical position. Many works also begin by asserting the importance of some factor or variable (or the "role" of such and such a pattern) and then attempt to show that certain consequences or effects follow. In other words, an independent variable is selected and an attempt is made to trace out its effects—a verificational goal that can only be achieved adequately through a strict experimental design.

Those who read this essay may judge that I have overstated the case, that I have displayed the very habits that I criticize by attempting to characterize so large and heterogeneous a field of intellectual activities, and that macro-structuralists are making "tremendous contributions" to sociology despite the lack of an explicit emphasis on methodology. I readily grant that there is some truth to each of these prospective accusations, yet I think we must also face up to the record of the past twenty years. The 1950's opened with a rare enthusiasm for comparative studies of social structure. When Murdock's *Social Structure* [123] appeared in 1949, it was hailed as a major landmark and as a first step in what was expected to be a solid line of growth toward a general, empirical science of structural phenomena. However, Murdock's contribution helped consolidate some intellectual orientations that I think have worked against comparative studies. First of all, it helped direct attention to a search for "universals" (even though Murdock dealt much less with universals than with variations); it also helped reinforce the assumption that societies were the key unit of observation (even though some "societies" consisted of a single tribe, others were complex federations, and others national societies), and that major kinds of empirical work could be done by relying on extent monographs and other forms of available data without undertaking long-range, comparative-focused field studies. I am not saying that Murdock is responsible for these orientations, but his book helped to consolidate them. Had structuralists looked at Murdock's modes of conceptualizing structural phenomena, his explicit procedures for classifying and measuring variations, the ways in which he brought even rudimentary statistical procedures to bear on tests of general hypotheses, and had structuralists then taken these as methodological guidelines for addressing problems of structural variation in complex, contemporary societies, I think we would have been much further ahead than we are now.

Instead, a great deal of effort was given to formulating general conceptual schemes, undertaking historically based case studies of "total societies," and typologizing. These emphases were then transferred, almost *in toto*, to the new field of the developing countries. In reaction to these broad, clinical, and interpretative thrusts, several new strategies began to take shape in the late 1950's and early 1960's: (1) One of these is exhibited in the turn to "aggregate data" as a basis for macro-comparisons.[124] Aggregate data are quantitative materials that summarize (in terms of averages, percentages, and the like) one or another property of social life

123. George Peter Murdock, *Social Structure* (New York: Macmillan, 1949).

124. On developments in aggregate data analysis and the way basic methodological problems are being addressed, see Erwin K. Scheuch, "Cross-National Comparisons Using Aggregate Data: Some Substantive and Methodological Problems," in Richard L. Merritt and Stein Rokkan, eds., *Comparing Nations: The Use of Quantitative Data in Cross-National Research* (New Haven: Yale University Press, 1966), pp. 131–167; Hayward R. Alker, Jr., and Bruce M. Russett, "Indices for Comparing Inequality," in *ibid.*, pp. 349–372; Philippe C. Schmitter, "New Strategies for the Comparative Analysis of Latin American Politics," *Latin American Research Review* 4 (Summer 1969): 83–111; Ralph H. Retzlaff, "The Use of Aggregate Data in Comparative Political Analysis," *Journal of Politics,* 27 (November 1967): 797–817; and the essays *in* Mattei Dogan and Stein Rokkan, eds., *Quantitative Ecological Analysis in the Social Sciences* (Cambridge, Massachusetts: MIT Press, 1969), and C. L. Taylor, ed., *Aggregate Data Analysis: Political and Social Indicators in Cross-National Research* (Paris: Mouton, 1968).

in a territorial unit, e.g., average per capita income per year for the population of national societies, number of radios per 1,000 population, etc. This break towards macro-quantification looked, at first, to be the makings of a definite solution to the problem of combining scope, rigor, and hypothesis-testing. However, some disillusionment has set in, and rightly so. For the most part the aggregate data comparisons have been dominated by availability of data rather than theoretic variables. Census materials, governmental reports, and statistics gathered from all corners of the globe by international agencies have frequently dictated the choice of research problems.[125] Moreover, the measures of indices of macro-variables have been built up from empirical indicators that often hold little correspondence to the concepts. I think the aggregate data specialists are becoming aware that theory should be the point of departure and that theoretical variables require (in terms of empirical indicators) something other than the kinds of data that are conveniently arranged in reference works. To put it bluntly, the swing to macro-aggregate comparisons (cross-national) has not done much to further the enterprise of hypothesis-testing studies of social structure. (2) The other shift, emerging almost simultaneously with aggregate-data comparisons, involved the application of sample survey methods to cross-national topics. Daniel Lerner's *The Passing of Traditional Society* was published in 1958.[126] The next major work was that of Almond and Verba, *The Civic Culture*, published in 1963.[127] Here again, the prospects looked good and some decisive new steps were taken in trying to relate attitudinal and behavioral data to institutional systems. Yet sample surveys (even when systematic data are collected on sociometric patterns) do not reach major structural variables.[128] Even the much-published strategy of "contextual analysis" that is now being widely adopted by sample survey specialists only adds variables to the independent side of the equation. The dependent variables still remain the attitudes, per-

125. For critical evaluations of certain procedures in aggregate data analysis, consult Kingsley Davis, "Problems and Solutions in International Comparison for Social Science Purposes," Berkeley, University of California, Center for International Population and Urban Research, Population Reprint Series No. 273, 1966 (originally published as "La Comparición Internacional en las Ciencias Sociales: Problemas y Soluciones," *America Latina*, January–March, 1965, pp. 61–75); and Goran Ohlin, "Aggregate Comparisons: Problems and Prospects of Quantitative Analysis Based on National Accounts," *in* Stein Rokkan, ed., *Comparative Research Across Cultures and Nations* (Paris: Mouton, 1968), pp. 163–170.

126. Daniel Lerner, *The Passing of Traditional Society: Modernizing the Middle East* (Glencoe, Ill.: Free Press, 1958).

127. Gabriel A. Almond and Sidney Verba, *The Civic Culture: Political Attitudes and Democracy in Five Nations* (Princeton: Princeton University Press, 1963).

128. For specialized essays on the developments, procedures, and disciplinary contributions of sample survey studies, see Charles Y. Glock, ed., *Survey Research in the Social Sciences* (New York: Russell Sage Foundation, 1967).

ceptions, or reported behaviors [129] and involvements of individuals.[130] This is not to deprecate sample survey studies of either intra-national or cross-national scope, but it appears that they are not yet capable of handling key structural variables (structure of authority relations, decision-making structures, modes of structural integration, inter-organizational relations, or the structure of local-national political relations), as foci of explanation.[131]

The direction that I find most promising—a third way—consists of empirical studies of structural variables that allow the possibility for testing hypotheses. Moreover, the focus of these studies is gradually moving away from preliterate tribes and the "cross-cultural" method to structural variables that are central to complex, contemporary nations and international systems. In the previous section of the essay I attempted to identify several of the methodological procedures that are bound up with this new set of impulses, for example:

1. An unwillingness to abandon structural variables and sociological problems;

2. A greater self-consciousness about problem formulation and research design;

3. Attention to disaggregating concepts that have become the core elements of macro-system language in order to identify both subtypes and measurable dimensions;

4. A turn from the total society to lower-level contexts and configurations that, though less comprehensive, hold fundamental roles in national and international systems;

5. A concern with criteria and procedures for sampling social structure in ways that allow for intra-societal, cross-societal, and multiple-level comparisions;

6. A combining of attention to complex systems and social institutions

129. As Coleman puts it: "Most research techniques which analyze behavioral data take a short cut in data-collection, and base their methods on individuals' *reports* of their own behavior and, less frequently, on those of others. . . . Our study of both verbal and nonverbal behavior is often based on information obtained in settings outside the social frame under study . . . [and has thus] discouraged the development of techniques for studying behavior *in situ*. . . ." James S. Coleman, "The Methods of Sociology" *in* Robert Bierstedt, ed., *A Design for Sociology: Scope, Objectives, and Methods* (Philadelphia: The American Academy of Political and Social Science, Monograph no. 9, 1969), p. 109, italics in original.

130. For a critical discussion of methodological procedures in cross-national survey research, see Erwin K. Scheuch, "The Cross-Cultural Use fo Sample Surveys: Problems of Comparability," *in* Stein Rokkan, ed., *Comparative Research Across Cultures and Nations* (Paris: Mouton, 1968), pp. 176–209.

131. For one attempt to shift sample survey procedures to problems of social structure, consult Allen H. Barton, "Bringing Society Back In: Survey Research and Macro-Methodology," *American Behavioral Scientist*, November-December, 1968: 1–9.

with variables analysis, systematic measurement, and strict verificational procedures; and thus

7. An interest in the formulation, the testing, and thus the qualification
and/or elimination of hypotheses (theory building).

Of course, these developments are not tied to a single type of research
design, nor to a particular substantive field or geo-cultural area. There are
however two or three broad clusters of work that are beginning to take
shape:

1. High *N*, intra-national comparisons based on field data: In these
studies, many organizations, communities, or administrative units are examined in terms of selected structural variables. Woodward's study of
100 manufacturing firms in South Essex, England, focused on variations
in organizational patterns (dependent variable).[132] Attempts to explain
these variations with reference to management practices and variations in
corporate success were not fruitful. Attention was then turned to the production process as the independent variable. Eleven types of processes
were identified, reflecting a broad scale of technical complexity. Striking
"correlations" emerged; [133] firms that featured similar production systems
showed basically similar organizational structures. It should be noted that
Woodward and colleagues relied on several data collection procedures.
Depth surveys of the 100 firms were followed by extensive case studies of
20 firms and then intensive case studies of three firms.[134] The survey study
began in 1954, with field work continuing until the early part of 1958. The
book reporting the results of the study was published in 1965. I mention
the time span covered by the study to underline the idea that studies which
combined field study, many units, and structural variables require a project calendar of many years. Surely they cannot be done, as many attitudinal studies are, in a few months or one year. Several other studies exemplify the high *N*, intra-national comparisons format: William F. Whyte's
comparative study of Peruvian communities,[135] Gamson's study of conflict

132. Joan Woodward, *Industrial Organization: Theory and Practice* (London: Oxford University Press, 1965).

133. Some organizational variables showed very direct relationship with
technical complexity, e.g., the chief executive's span of control, the ratio of managers to total personnel, the ratio of clerical and administrative staff to manual
workers, the length of the line of command, the ratio of direct to indirect labor,
etc., *ibid.*, p. 51, ff.

134. The procedures followed in the extensive and intensive study of cases
are described in chapter 6, "The Case Study Approach," pp. 83–95.

135. Whyte and his collaborators are studying 26 communities located in five
areas of Peru. The first survey was conducted in 1964, followed by a second in
1969. The surveys are complemented by field work on "social structure, political
power, and social and economic processes." William F. Whyte and Lawrence K.
Williams, *Toward an Integrated Theory of Development: Economic and Non-*

in 18 Northeastern U.S. communities,[136] and Hall, Haas, and Johnson's study of 75 organizations.[137]

2. There is another cluster of studies that features emphases on many subsocietal units, structural variables, explicit measurement procedures, and multivariate analysis, but makes use of collected statistics, data archives, or published reference works of coded data on many social units. Field work, either in the form of face-to-face interviews or mailed questionnaires, is involved. Amos Hawley's study, "Community Power and Urban Renewal Success," [138] examines the relationships between a measure of community power and a measure of urban renewal success in 194 American cities with populations of 50,000 or more. A significant relationship between degree of power concentration and urban renewal success was found, even when controlling for such variables as region, educational level, type of industry, size of manufacturing plant, planning budget, age of housing, extent of dilapidation (in housing), type of city government, and median income. Hawley notes the exceptions, as follows: "The relationship is not dependable for cities with mayor-council governments, with a predominance of service industry, with small proportions of college graduates among their residents, and with locations in the northeast and the west." [139]

In a predictive study of interorganizational networks in urban settings, Turk [140] selected 130 U.S. cities with more than 100,000 inhabitants. From data on the number of headquarters organizations in each city, the incidence of community-wide organizations, per capita municipal revenue, per capita number of poverty dollars flowing into each city from federal agencies, the organizational arrangements developed (or used) for implementing anti-poverty programs, and figures on poverty rates, proportion of non-whites, and youth out of school, Turk developed measures for

economic Variables in Rural Development (Ithaca: New York State School of Industrial and Labor Relations, Paperback no. 5, February 1968), p. 86.

136. William A. Gamson, "Rancorous Conflict in Community Politics," *in* Terry N. Clark, ed., *Community Structure and Decision-making: Comparative Analyses* (San Francisco: Chandler Publishing Co., 1968), pp. 197–214. Nine communities with strong dispositions toward rancorous conflict are compared with nine that are low in susceptibility to rancorous conflict. Materials were gained through interviews with 426 informants, plus document research.

137. Richard H. Hall, J. Eugene Haas, and Norman J. Johnson, "Organizational Size, Complexity, and Formalization," *American Sociological Review*, 32 (December 1967): 903–912.

138. Amos H. Hawley, "Community Power and Urban Renewal Success," *American Journal of Sociology*, 68 (January 1963): 422–431.

139. *Ibid.*, p. 429.

140. Herman Turk, "Interorganizational Networks in Urban Society: Initial Perspectives and Comparative Research," *American Sociological Review*, 35 (February 1970): 1–19.

the following variables: extralocal integration, interorganizational activity level, interorganizational complexity, and extent of demand for interorganizational networks. Turk emphasizes throughout an organizational level of analysis, as well as the principle of working with units that belong to the same class of structures.[141] His data on the extent of extralocal integration characterizing cities proved capable of predicting the "activity level of a new interorganizational network having both local and nonlocal elements." [142] Moreover, "a complex portion of such a network tended to occur where a high organizational level of local integration had been indicated by the pre-existence of community-wide associations. *Demand*—i.e., the practical or normative pressures posed by deprivation rates within the population—was important to these interorganizational outcomes only where organizational integration had been high." [143] He states the major conclusion of his article in these words:

> *Definition of the urban setting in terms of multi- and interorganizational variables has proven fruitful. These variables were capable of predicting one another's values over time, it appears, without the intervention of nonorganizational sources of variation.*[144]

Both Hawley's study and that of Turk indicate the ways in which various kinds of available data are being used to construct imaginative and fruitful measures of structural variables for large numbers of similar subsocietal units.

3. A third type of research design that is beginning to take hold in the comparative study of structural variables in many units is the cross-national, intra-societal field study. Unlike many of the studies that have been mentioned, this design focuses on similar subsocietal units in several national settings. In addition, priority is given to informant interviews, multiple levels of collective life, and historical patterns in regional development. Our research on structural change in the Roman Catholic Church, initiated in 1966, and involving the study of four dioceses in each of three countries—France, Chile, and the United States—represents a modest beginning. As noted earlier in the essay,[145] we chose dioceses that were led by bishops with contrasting leadership styles, that were situated in different regions of each country, and that possessed different kinds of demographic and economic bases. The twelve dioceses selected were these: France—Toulouse, Lille, Rennes, and Grenoble; Chile—Santiago, Temuco, Concep-

141. *Ibid.*, p. 2.
142. *Ibid.*, p. 15.
143. *Ibid.*
144. *Ibid.*, p. 16, italics in original.
145. See above, p. 214.

ción, and La Serena; United States—Seattle, St. Louis, Worcester (Massachusetts), and Philadelphia. Informant interviews with national-level informants were followed by field work in each diocese involving interviews with diocesan leaders, officials, and elites in several types of lay organizations, and rank-and-file active members. We have followed a three-fold procedure in analyzing the qualitative field materials: (1) descriptive profiles of each diocese's collective properties, the main foci of structural strain, and patterns of the laity's demands and dissatisfactions for change; (2) a ranking of the dioceses on three dimensions of structural change; distribution of decision-making power, extent of communal developments within the diocese, and extent of structural integration between the Church's lay sphere and the wider society; and (3) an explanatory section in which variations in the structural features of the lay sphere in the twelve dioceses are related to demographic, ecological, economic, and national-cultural factors.

Although we cannot claim that the study is anything more than a preliminary entry into an extremely complex field of structural research, the design does allow us to formulate tentative conclusions about the differential importance of national-cultural patterns, regional-contextual variables, and intra-Church variables for the structural development of dioceses' lay spheres. Although the dioceses *in each country* share certain structural problems and problem-solving styles (thus suggesting an important role of national culture and societal-wide trends), within-nation variations are striking with regard to other patterns, such as episcopal-lay relations, the strength of the parish system, the role of conservative pastors, and the overall capacity of dioceses to initiate and sustain change programs. This suggests that national-cultural variables are critical for explaining variations in certain structural and collective patterns, but not for others. Instead, attention needs to be given to the local situation—the strength of the secular left in politiics, the class composition of the population, the economic base of the region within which a diocese is situated, the level of economic growth (or decline), and so on.

It will be clear to the reader that the kinds of structural studies I consider indicators of the new trend are still largely intra-societal. For certain sociologists, this means that the term "comparative" is not appropriate; comparative sociology, for Marsh, consists of studies that undertake *"the systematic and explicit comparison of data from two or more societies."* [146]

146. Robert M. Marsh, *Comparative Sociology. A Codification of Cross-Societal Analysis* (New York: Harcourt, Brace & World, 1967), p. 11. Marsh clarifies his position in a later publication: "On 'The Comparative Study of National Societies': A Reply to Hopkins and Wallerstein," *Social Science Information,* 7 (February 1968): 99–104.

This strikes me as somewhat restrictive, particularly if we assume that one of the main reasons for getting mixed up with the difficulties of comparative work is to achieve strong inferences about the sources of structural variation. Other aims of comparative work, including the validation of empirical generalizations and the test of general hypotheses, can also be served by intra-societal studies—at least in the first stages of work. From intra-societal studies focused on structural variables in many units representing a single class or species, it will be possible to work out to cross-national studies. In fact, it appears that we are now ready to actually combine the procedures which are being developed in intra-societal studies with cross-national designs. The study of the relationships between division of labor, professionalization, hierarchy, and administrative arrangements carried out by Blau and his colleagues on more than 150 small bureaucracies in North American could be extended to several industrial societies.[147] Clark's comparative study of community structure and decision-making in 51 American cities could be used as a departure point for carrying out a major cross-national project.[148] Our study on Catholic dioceses has stimulated me to develop a proposal for a long-range program of research involving 120 dioceses in 15 countries.[149] In short, I believe the intra-societal studies that are being done on high numbers of structural units provide a methodological base for moving into cross-national research. Although difficult problems of comparability, measurement, and data collection are to be expected, these are not insurmountable.

Taking account of the methodological developments I have sketched, it may be worthwhile to draw certain implications for research planning and graduate training. With regard to the formulation and implementation of new research, two things may be helpful: (1) The collaboration of specialists in developing long-term comparative programs (10-year calendar) that have a focused, analytical core but which will allow a number of autonomous, individual projects of an intra-national or cross-national nature to emerge within it. Programs on elite structures and decision-making, professionalism and bureaucracy, local stratification structures and economic change, economic and political interdependencies, technology and corpo-

147. Peter M. Blau, Wolf V. Heydebrand, and Robert E. Stauffer, "The Structure of Small Bureaucracies," *American Sociological Review*, 31 (April 1966): 179–191.

148. Terry N. Clark, "Community Structure, Decision-Making, Budget Expenditures and Urban Renewal in 51 American Communities," *American Sociological Review*, 33 (August 1968): 576–593.

149. Ivan Vallier, "Comparative Studies of Roman Catholicism: Dioceses as Strategic Units," *Social Compass*, 16 (1969): 147–184.

rate organization could be written up by individuals or collaborating specialists and then published for purposes of critical review. Research would be open to anyone interested in the program, so long as commitments were made to concentrate on the key variables built into the program and to relate the findings directly to the broad goals of the program in order that gains be consolidated as a part of a cumulative, collaborative effort. These procedures would allow for decentralized funding (each investigator finding his own sources of support), for open choice as to countries and regions, and for projects of varying time lengths. Yet shared commitments to a central analytical problem (or problems)—allowing for a variety of theoretical positions—and a limited number of variables, would facilitate cross-project communication, an exchange of findings, and an emergent body of comparatively based knowledge. (2) A second priority is to build up or to identify or to develop populations or universes of structural units from which systematic samples (purposive, probability, or random) could be drawn for comparative study. Turk speaks of the need for censuses of organizations;[150] Hall and others complain, in the course of presenting their methodological procedures in a study of 75 organizations, "that there is no clearly defined organizational universe from which . . . a sample could have been drawn." [151] LaPalombara feels that "if the interest group is to be made the institutional focus for comparative political science, we must be concerned with the designation of criteria that will permit us to abstract from a potentially infinite number of groups those that are of particular interest . . . and that meet the minimal definitional requirements for inclusion in a sample." [152] Many possibilities are open along these lines, e.g., the preparation of reference lists on local administrative units in countries within distinct geo-cultural regions—communes in France, municipios in Latin American countries, counties in the United States, and so on. There should also be working censuses of business organizations of different types and sizes, of hospitals and schools, of the location of the regional or urban offices of federal and national agencies, and a census of banks and other financial centers. Most, if not all, of these materials are hidden away in specialized reference works, and with some digging they can be found and used. What remains to be done is the putting together of these materials for purposes of cross-national research. University libraries should be urged to develop specialists who would be respon-

150. Herman Turk, *op. cit.*, p. 2.
151. Richard H. Hall and others, *op. cit.*, p. 907.
152. Joseph LaPalombara, "Macrotheories and Microapplications in Comparative Politics: A Widening Chasm," *Comparative Politics*, 1 (October 1968): 52–78.

sible for bringing materials together and making them available in an efficient format.

COMPARATIVE STUDIES AND THE POLICY IMPERATIVE

"Policy studies" is now one of the most fashionable phrases in the social sciences. Both domestic problems and continuing setbacks in nation-building overseas have led sociologists and others to define policy studies as an imperative: "If social scientists do not turn directly to policy studies, there is, first, no excuse for having them around and, second, they will die for lack of relevance." There are strong reasons for supporting this argument; there are equally strong reasons for another view, which, though not anti-policy, holds that the most certain way into effective policy roles is through basic, disinterested research that is concerned with isolating causal relationships and constructing models of structural change that incorporate such linkages.

It is not my intention to dwell on this debate or to provide a survey of other arguments, pro and con. Instead, I want to raise the question as to whether or not comparative studies have a place in policy research and, if so, what kinds of comparative studies seem to hold the most promise. From what I have heard about policy studies over the past few years, there seems to be a growing consensus that an unbridgeable gap exists between comparative studies and policy studies; that the former, while illuminating and ambitious in scope, do not provide either models or findings that are applicable to deep social problems or governmental dilemmas, and that the latter, i.e., policy studies, require a different style, a different perspective, and a different conception of the social scientist's role. As one well-placed social scientist put it: "You comparativists have had your chance; now let us do our thing."

I think that this is a false dichotomy. If this division is allowed, we are doomed to lose both our sources of vigor in comparative work and to weaken our possibilities for relating social science to policy issues. Policy research involves an identification of either the conditions under which certain outcomes occur, or of underlying "causal systems" that, in being described and refined as models, can be applied as frameworks for control sequences. Consequently, if policy research is to become an effective basis for relating social science knowledge to collective problems, it must be research that (1) identifies crucial sets of independent variables vis-à-vis some proposed or desired outcome, or (2) identifies and clarifies the nature of basic causal sequences in collective life, with attention to variables that are tractable or otherwise controllable and manipulable, or (3) gauges the contextual, i.e., socio-cultural, features of typical situations to the degree that a range of probable responses, reactions, or inclinations on the part of key social groups can be specified. Each of these goals is effectively served by studies of social structure that, by being comparative and rigorous, allow for the testing of hypotheses.

As a final point, I want to draw some implications from this essay for graduate training. If my observations on emerging developments in macro-comparative work are at all valid, then certain priorities emerge concerning the training of students who choose to work in this broad field. Six activities hold a high priority:

1. The organization of initial courses around theoretically important sets of structural-level dependent variables, e.g., courses focused on system performance, social cleavages, local-national integration, power relations, political-religious interdependencies, etc.;

2. Courses focused on the development of *research designs* that are capable of producing tests of hypotheses and identification of new independent variables;

3. Specialized seminars in basic types of *measurement* and scaling for structural variables (intra-societal and cross-national);

4. Field work involvement having to do with the *collection of data* on two or more units that are intersected by structural, systemic, and collective variables;

5. Instruction in the techniques of correlational and causal models, with supplementary attention to the use of negative evidence, the role of "controlled" comparisons, and the like; and

6. More attention to the relationships between comparative studies and policy-related research.

PART THREE
SYSTEMATIC PROCEDURES AND APPLICATIONS

INTELLIGIBLE COMPARISONS*

MORRIS ZELDITCH, JR.

The design of comparative research is conditioned largely by four rules:

(1) (Comparability). Two or more instances of a phenomenon may be compared if and only if there exists some variable, say V, common to each instance.

rule of agreement

(2) (Mill's 1st Canon). No second variable, say U, is the cause or effect of V, if it is not found when V is found.

rule of difference

(3) (Mill's 2nd Canon). No second variable U is the cause or effect of V if it is found when V is not.

(4) (Rule of One Variable). No second variable U is definitely the cause or effect of V if there exists a third variable, say W, that is present or absent in the same circumstances as U.

I will regard these four rules as the logical foundation of comparative analysis, although they are neither general nor complete.[1] Many other rules exist, but almost all occupy a logically inferior status to rules 1-4. Many are derivable from these rules: For example, "causes should be as general as their effects,"[2] which follows from rule 2, or "units should be constant and uniform,"[3] which can be shown to follow from rule 1. Of those that are not

* I would like to thank the Center for Advanced Studies in the Behavioral Sciences for the fellowship which made it possible for me to write this paper; and Frank and Ruth Young for their particularly penetrating comments on an earlier draft of it.

1. They are not general because they speak of cause and effect and are qualitatively expressed. The same rules apply to *any* invariant connections whatever, whether causally ordered, functional in the mathematical sense, or functional in the sociological sense. They apply equally to quantitative and qualitative variables. But to express them in such a way that this property is revealed would be to make them both complex and formal, neither of which is desirable in the present context. The rules are not complete because they omit the important idea that no variable is the cause of V if not antecedent to V. This rule has had little impact so far on the actual design of comparative research.

2. M. Bloch, *Land and Work in Medieval Europe* (Berkeley and Los Angeles: University of California Press, 1967), ch. 2.

3. S. Kuznets, "The State as a Unit of Study in Economic Growth," *Journal of Economic History*, 11 (1951): 25–41.

derivable, it is sometimes the case that their contradictories are. Thus, many ethnologists believe that our understanding of a society is violated if "native meanings" are not preserved in comparison.[4] This clearly conflicts with the implications of rule 1. It may therefore be regarded as "unsound"; and nothing more clearly reveals the central importance of rules 1-4 than the role they are able to play in ruling out unsound rules.

Of the many remaining rules, i.e., those that are neither derivative nor in conflict with rules 1-4, most [5] are not relevant, not general, or not method-ological. Many are rules such as "samples should be random," which clearly have an important bearing on how inferences are made from comparison, but which are irrelevant in the sense that they are not themselves about comparison. Many are rules of thumb that derive not from rules 1-4 but from special techniques of measurement and analysis, such as linear regres-sion, multivariate analysis, or scaling. For example, scales are more informa-tive, and permit more powerful analysis, than dichotomous classifications.[6] For the most part such rules are useful and sound, but they are not as gen-eral as rules 1-4. Finally, some of the remaining rules, such as Durkheim's "Social facts require social explanations," are of the sort that have an impor-tant bearing on the design of comparative sociological research but are not methodological in character. They are rules that belong to subject-matter paradigms, in Kuhn's sense.[7]

The purpose of the present paper is to study rules 1-4 keeping three objectives in mind. First, to what degree are these rules *adequate* guides to inference? We might question rule 3, for example, because there is always the possibility that two variables are related to V in equal degrees but opposite directions, each cancelling the other's effect. Recognizing this fact, some investigators will not give up an hypothesis even though a cause is found when the effect is not. Rule 3 does not formulate this situation quite adequately.

Second, to what degree are some of the rules derived from rules 1-4 *validly* deduced? From rule 1, for example, some sociologists deduce that we must construct "universals," which is valid, but they require of univer-sals that they occur in every known society, which is not. The difficulty lies in the misleading use of the word "universal," on which we will comment. Other sociologists deduce that only wholes are comparable, which in no way follows from rule 1.

4. Cf. R. Needham, *Structure and Sentiment* (Chicago: University of Chi-cago Press, 1962), ch. 4.

5. Some derive from the precedence rule mentioned in note 1.

6. P. Cutright, "National Political Development: Measurement and Analy-sis," *American Sociological Review*, 28 (1963): 253–264.

7. T. Kuhn, *The Structure of Scientific Revolutions* (Chicago: University of Chicago Press, 1962).

Third, to what degree are rules 1-4 _sufficient_ guides to inference? For with respect to these rules two views are possible: one regards the rules as sufficient to permit inference from comparisons. They provide a mechanical procedure that cranks out inductive inferences much in the way an assembly line cranks out automobiles. The other view regards the rules as insufficient. However scrupulously followed, supplementary knowledge is required if acceptable inferences are to be made. This somewhat vague description can be made more precise, for in fact both views insist on supplementary knowledge; what distinguishes them is really the character of the supplementary knowledge on which they insist. In the first view, the rules are supplemented by just those rules I have claimed are either special or irrelevant, such as "samples should be random." What distinguishes the first view, therefore, is that all the additional knowledge required is methodological. In the second view, the additional knowledge required is substantive in character; the rules are insufficient in the sense that subject-matter knowledge is required before intelligible inferences are possible from comparisons. In this chapter, we will find for the second view: the rules are not sufficient and subject-matter assumptions are required if comparisons are to be intelligible. It follows that there is no mechanical procedure that assures any fool of making correct inferences if only the rules are obeyed.

The third objective is the most important, and to many it will seem the most trite. Raw empiricism is a dead horse, and no useful purpose is served by another paper on the subject. But the objections to raw empiricism are mostly of two kinds: either they claim that hypotheses are necessary if data are to be selected, or they claim theory is necessary if research is to accumulate. Except for Cohen and Nagel's penetrating critique of Mill's canons, still brilliant and lively but somewhat out of date,[8] the objections are not usually extended to the process of warranting inferences from data. What the present paper undertakes to do is to emphasize the importance of subject-matter paradigms in making inferences from comparisons.

SCOPE OF INVESTIGATION

No effort is made in this paper to generalize the argument beyond a narrowly restricted scope. What is said applies in particular to systematic comparisons of societies, the purpose of which is explanatory.

(i) Not all comparisons are for explanatory purposes. Comparison is also important in descriptive investigations. For example, comparison provides a frame of reference in terms of which quantities may be interpreted. The present U.S. divorce rate looks quite high; but compared to pre-

8. M. Cohen and E. Nagel, _An Introduction to Logic and Scientific Method_ (New York: Harcourt, Brace, 1934), ch. 13.

industrial Japan, or contemporary Egypt, or to any matrilineal society, it is a relatively modest rate.[9] This is a common and important use to which comparison may be put, but for this sort of use what we have to say in this paper is mostly beside the point.

An investigation has an explanatory purpose if it yields or tests one or more general explanatory sentences. A sentence is *general* if all its terms are general. Its terms are general if they are not proper names and do not imply proper names. Thus,

(1)   Great Britain is a democracy.

is not a general sentence, but

(2)   A democracy is stable if its wealth is equally distributed.

is a general sentence. A sentence is *explanatory* if it asserts a relation between two or more variables. Therefore (2) is not only general, it is also explanatory, whereas

(3)   There are democracies.

contains only general terms but is not explanatory. A sentence such as

(4)   The nuclear family is universal.

is in the same class as (3) because, like (3), it contains general terms but is not about a relation between variables. Empirical generalizations, such as (4), are therefore not explanatory sentences in the present sense. Of course, sentences like (1), (3), or (4) could be important for the present purpose if they were implied by or implied, and might therefore serve to test, a general explanatory sentence.

(ii) Not every comparative study is explanatory and generalizing, but every explanatory generalizing study is comparative. However, in the present state of the social sciences there are investigations that pass as comparative that in fact are not in any useful sense comparative. Much of area research is called "comparative" by sociologists, political scientists, or economists, even when nothing is being compared. "Comparative government" is another case in point, for a political investigation is often said to be comparative if the political scientist is American but his subject is France or Russia.

A study is not comparative if there are not at least two units being compared: but more than this is required. For such symposia as *African Political Systems* [10] or *African Systems of Kinship and Marriage* [11] have

9. W. J. Goode, "Family Disorganization," *in* R. K. Merton and R. A. Nisbet, eds., *Contemporary Social Problems* (New York: Harcourt, Brace & World, 1961), pp. 390–458.

10. M. Fortes and E. E. Evans-Pritchard, eds., *African Political Systems* (London: Oxford University Press, 1940).

11. A. R. Radcliffe-Brown and D. Forde, eds., *African Systems of Kinship and Marriage* (New York: Oxford University Press, 1950).

been called comparative, though in them nothing is compared. No comparison is made between the cases; indeed no comparison is possible when each contribution to the symposium addresses different questions, collects data by different procedures, and organizes its results in terms of different concepts. A study will therefore be of interest to us only if comparative, and comparative only if two or more units are compared with respect to the same concepts.

(iii) A study is sometimes called comparative when all that it does is illustrate a concept by describing an example that is in some sense foreign. Even the most important pioneers of comparative investigation in the social sciences, such as Radcliffe-Brown, were often comparative only in the sense that specific examples of non-literate societies were used to illustrate general theoretical notions. There is of course no possibility of basing generalizing explanatory propositions on one or two arbitrarily chosen illustrations, and we therefore confine our attention only to cases of systematic comparison. To be systematic there must be some non-arbitrary procedure in virtue of which cases are selected that are equally likely to be favorable or unfavorable to the investigator's hypothesis. In particular, if he asserts that u causes v he must not only look at the instances of u and v but also of not-u and v. It was once said, and not so facetiously, that comic books caused delinquency because delinquents were observed to read comic books. A systematic investigation would need also to examine the rate at which non-delinquents read comic books.

(iv) All explanatory, generalizing research involves comparison, and almost every known research design in sociology is therefore comparative, whether experimental, survey, or macro-sociological. A convention has nevertheless developed that limits "comparative" sociology to just those comparisons the units of which are "societies." We will abide by this convention, even though it is an unreasonable one. The distinction is arbitrary, and without real methodological significance, even though the *technical* difficulties of, say, *The Civic Culture* [12] are quite different from those of, say, *The American Soldier*.[13]

But we shall not distinguish among various subtypes of comparative investigation, even though at least three very different kinds of study are therefore treated as similar. For example, we deal only with those general methodological problems that are common to the cross-national and to the

12. G. Almond and S. Verba, *The Civic Culture* (Princeton: Princeton University Press, 1963).

13. S. Stouffer and others, *The American Soldier*, vols. 1 and 2 (Princeton: Princeton University Press, 1949).

cross-national vs. cross-cultural research

cross-cultural investigation, not distinguishing between them, though it would be hard to find two more different kinds of investigation.[14] The units of the first kind are national states while the second is typically a comparison of "primitive" tribes; in addition, the first typically uses all the available techniques of modern data analysis to make quantitative statements about the people *within* nations while the second uses quantitative methods only to make statements true *between* tribes. The first therefore deals with problems arising from internal heterogeneity of units which the second ignores. Both investigations are very different from the controlled comparison, in which a small number of very similar societies, usually of the same cultural origin or in the same ecological region, are matched with respect to a large number of variables for the purpose of reasoning about some small number of differences between them.

unit of analysis: individuals vs. society

Furthermore, there are two quite different purposes that might be served by *any* of these three types of investigation, and we do not distinguish between these purposes either. One of the classic justifications of "comparative" research is that generalizations made about individuals in Western societies may be ethnocentric; therefore, quite different cultures are used to test them further, to assure us of their generality. In this sort of research the "society" is usually a unit only in the sense that it is the context in which observations are made; individuals are more typically the real units of the investigation. But comparative investigations have also been designed for the purpose of making general statements about *societies*, and, in these, "societies" are the unit in a more nearly theoretical sense. Again there are great differences between the two in detail, but we propose to treat only their common methodological problems.

The fact that its units are societies creates three special difficulties for comparative sociology. First, there is no way to manipulate the variables in which it is interested. Investigators must instead take what advantage they can of the varying circumstances discovered in existing social arrangements. But certain combinations of states simply do not exist to be taken advantage of: which means that for comparative sociology there is only a limited opportunity to separate variables in the manner required by the rule of one variable (rule 4). Second, there is no way to randomly allocate states of an independent variable to societal units. Randomization is the only known method of exercising control over variables that disturb a relation but are not known to the investigator. The degree of control possible in comparative investigations is therefore severely restricted. Third, there are relatively few societies in the world (even if counted in the thousands). This fact, for example, distinguishes comparative sociology from more conventional sur-

14. See T. K. Hopkins and I. Wallerstein, "The Comparative Study of National Societies," *Social Science Information,* 6 (1967): 25–58.

vey research, in which the first two difficulties are also found. Because the number of societies is limited, comparative sociology is limited in its capacity to exercise control even over confounding variables that are *known* to exist. These three properties are important conditions of the argument we make in the next two sections.

COMPARABILITY

Let 1, 2, 3, . . . n be units in each of which the process ϕ takes place. Then 1 is comparable to 2, 3, . . . n if and only if (*a*) there exists a variable V common to each of them and (*b*) the meaning of V is the same for all of them.[15]

Satisfying the first requirement is a relatively trivial problem. For example, if the economic development of France is to be compared with the economic development of the United Kingdom, one way to accomplish the comparison is to assign market values to all goods and services produced in each of the two nations, express these values in some common currency and divide by the population size. The exchange rates will pose some problems, but one will be able to find for each of the two countries a Gross National Product per Capita, as required by (*a*). In 1957 U.S. dollars, for instance, GNP per Capita was $943 in France, $1,189 in the United Kingdom.[16]

But satisfying the second requirement is not at all a trivial problem. For example, France is more agrarian than the United Kingdom, and its agricultural sector is more subsistence-oriented. The less market-oriented an economy, the fewer of its goods and services that get counted as Gross National Product and the more arbitrary the assignment of a market value to those products that do get counted. Food directly consumed, unpaid family labor, or, in general, any economic product consumed outside the money economy will be underestimated.[17] Hence, the meaning of French Gross National Product per Capita is not the same as the meaning of Gross National Product per Capita in the United Kingdom; and (*b*) is not satisfied. A good deal of the most difficult labor in comparative investigations is devoted to dealing with this particular kind of difficulty.

Requirements (*a*) and (*b*) give rise to many others that, taken to-

15. Cf. A. L. Kalleberg, "The Logic of Comparison: A Methodological Note on the Comparative Study of Political Systems," *World Politics*, 19 (1966): 69–82; H. Scarrow, "The Scope of Comparative Analysis," *The Journal of Politics*, 25 (1963): 565–577; E. A. Suchman, "The Comparative Method in Social Research," *Rural Sociology*, 29 (1964): 123–137; and H. Teune, "Measurement in Comparative Research," *Comparative Political Studies*, 1 (1968): 123–138.

16. B. M. Russett and others, *World Handbook of Political and Social Indicators* (New Haven: Yale University Press, 1964), p. 155.

17. Kuznets, *Six Lectures on Economic Growth* (Glencoe, Ill.: Free Press, 1959), pp. 13–41; O. Morgenstern, *On the Accuracy of Economic Observations* (Princeton: Princeton University Press, 1950); and Russett and others.

gether, are supposed to assure comparability. For example, units should be constant, procedures uniform, and points of reference invariant. The list of inferences from *(a)* and *(b)* is very long, and I do not propose to exhaust either myself or the reader by making an exhaustive study of them. But a few are important and their study instructive. My first concern will be with whether the inferences are valid, in the sense that they are logically deducible from *(a)* or *(b)*. In the final sections, however, I turn to a second important concern, namely, to the sort of supplementary information required to determine comparability, particularly to the role of the investigator's purpose, his knowledge of the subject, and theoretical analysis.

(i) From the fact that a common framework of concepts is required by comparison it is sometimes inferred that we must search for empirical universals as the foundation of comparative analysis. There may be such universals, but they are neither a solution to the problem of comparison nor necessary to the discovery of such a solution. For purposes of comparison it is sufficient that every unit in the domain of a given comparison, say *D*, possess some value of *V*. This condition is satisfied by any unit of which not-*V* is true. For example, even a society with no differentiated status system possesses some value of the variable *stratification*. Hence there is no reason to make empirically universal structures the basis of comparison. In any case, empirical universals are not sufficient for purposes of intelligible comparison: body hair is probably a universal, but surely the fact is of no particular theoretical importance. What matters for comparisons are variables in theories, not the prevalence of this or that particular state of affairs.[18]

It is of course true that in some sense "universals" are required for comparison, but what is required are *logical* universals, not empirical universals. The two are quite distinct kinds of propositions; the empirical universal is not universal, but existential.

It is useful to distinguish three classes of sentences: *Singular* sentences assert something true of a particular instance. Example (1) of the previous section, which it will be recalled was

(1)   Great Britain is a democracy.

is a singular sentence. Existential sentences assert something true of a finite *class* of instances, and in traditional logic the instances are supposed actually to exist. Example (3) of the previous section,

(3)   There are democracies.

is an existential sentence. *Universal* sentences assert something true of an

18. Cf. G. Sjoberg, "The Comparative Method in the Social Sciences," *Philosophy of Science*, 22 (1955): 106–117.

infinite set of instances of a particular kind (as opposed, for example, to referring only to a finite number of instances). Example (2) of the previous section

(2)   A democracy is stable if its
                           wealth is equally distributed.

is a universal sentence. To make its structure more clear, it should actually be written

(2')   For every democracy, if wealth is
                           equally distributed democracy is stable.

The prefix "for every . . ." is the peculiar mark of the universal sentence. But it is not necessary that *democracy* be universal for the *sentence* to be a universal, and furthermore sentences that do assert that something is universal are not logical universals. Thus, example (4) of the previous section,

(4)   The nuclear family is universal.

is not a logical universal. In fact, (4) is existential in import. It says really

(4')   There was a nuclear family in all the
                           250 societies in which Murdock[19] looked for one.

Sentence (4) is false, since we have discovered several counter-examples, though (4') is not. But the more important point is that (4') is not a universal sentence in the logical sense required by comparisons.

Instead of empirical universals, some sociologists infer that what comparison requires is *invariant points of reference* true of every society. Such points of reference have been provided by Aberle and others,[20] Levy,[21] Parsons,[22] and Kluckhohn,[23] among others. Levy's list is a typical example: according to Levy, every society must somehow provide for an adequate physiological relation to the setting and for sexual recruitment; for role differentiation and role assignment; communication; shared cognitive orientations; shared, articulated sets of goals; regulation of choice of means; regulation of affect; adequate socialization; effective control of disruptive forms of behavior; and adequate institutionalization.[24]

Because they are variables, invariant points of references serve comparison better than empirical universals. But they often suffer the defect that they are meant to be *all-purpose* categories, and as a consequence

19. G. P. Murdock, *Social Structure* (New York: Macmillan, 1949).

20. D. F. Aberle and others, "The Functional Prerequisites of a Society," *Ethics*, 60 (1950): 100–111.

21. M. J. Levy, *The Structure of Society* (Princeton: Princeton University Press, 1952).

22. T. Parsons, *The Social System* (Glencoe, Ill.: Free Press, 1951).

23. F. Kluckhohn, "Dominant and Substitute Profiles of Cultural Orientations," *Social Forces*, 28 (1950): 376–394.

24. Levy, *op. cit.*, ch. 4.

serve no purpose very well. In the first place, there is no reason why they must be true of *all* societies, unless the domain of comparison includes all societies—which is not required by the rule of comparibility. In the second place, there is every reason why they should not attempt to work for all *theories*; for there are no concepts that work in all theories, and those that claim to do so are as a matter of fact typically *a*theoretic. Invariant points of reference are components not of objects in the world but of theories;[25] as theories differ, so do the invariant points of reference of comparisons. The only real consequence of making invariant points of reference all-purpose is to make them vacuous. In any case, nothing in the rule of comparability requires such all-purpose categories.

(ii) From the fact that invariance of meaning is required by comparison, it is sometimes inferred that only wholes may be compared. This is deduced from the following argument: (1) Traits have different meanings in different contexts. For example, "matriliny" may in one society imply a dispersed, unorganized clan that provides hospitality and regulates marriage while in another it means a corporate group that regulates inheritance, land tenure, recruitment of warriors, and succession to the priesthood.[26] (2) If traits have different meanings in different contexts and meaning is to be preserved in comparison, contexts must be embodied in the traits used in comparisons. For example, comparisons must involve, not "matriliny," but dispersed matri-clans and corporate land-holding matrilineages. (3) But the context of any trait is the *whole* of the culture of any society, for every total configuration of traits makes a difference to any trait in the configuration.[27] For example, one should not compare the Eskimo with the American kinship system, even though the two kinship systems are very similar, because the two are at different levels of economic development.[28]

But wholes are unique. There is nothing else on earth quite like the United States (or the Navaho, or the Eskimo, . . .) taken as a whole. Therefore the rule of holism yields a clear and straightforward contradiction: only incomparables are comparable.

Because it leads to self-contradiction, we obviously ought to reject as unsound the rule that only wholes may be compared. But if the rule is unsound, how does it manage to survive? How, in fact, can two such different traditions as that reflected in Boas, Lowie, and Kroeber, on the one hand, or

25. Cf. Sjoberg, *op. cit.*
26. Cf. Aberle, "Matrilineal Descent in Cross-Cultural Perspective," *in* D. M. Schneider and K. Gough, eds., *Matrilineal Kinship* (Berkeley and Los Angeles: University of California Press, 1961), pp. 655–727.
27. Cf. R. Benedict, *Patterns of Culture* (Boston: Houghton Mifflin, 1946).
28. Cf. M. Harris, *The Rise of Anthropological Theory* (New York: Thomas Y. Crowell, 1968), p. 629.

that reflected in Evans-Pritchard, and more subtly in Leach and Needham, on the other, come to share a belief in holism?[29]

One answer is that in both cases the contradictory nature of the rule proves precisely what both traditions want to prove, that comparison, and with it generalization, is not possible. They may all be called *historicists* (despite Leach)[30] and the body of aims and assumptions they share, *historicism*.[31] Historicism is in Kuhn's sense of the term a particular *paradigm* of how to go about social science. A paradigm is a body not only of concepts and laws, but also and more importantly of methodological principles and strategies, definitions of problems to be solved and criteria of their acceptable solution, instrumentation and applications, standards of relevance, and an ordering of aims.[32] The historicist paradigm consists, among other things, of holism, particularism, and subjectivism—all of which lead to the conclusion that comparison is not possible, laws are not possible, and general knowledge of human behavior is not possible. Therefore, every investigation is a historical one: its purpose is to appreciate and understand each historical tradition in its own right and in its own terms. Here the investigation stops, and indeed historicists do not admit the possibility of going further. There is no desire to be general and abstraction is *ipso facto* a violation of the aim and purpose of the investigation.

What the self-contradiction in holism reveals, therefore, is not a logical fallacy but a clash between paradigms. And paradigm clashes are not resolved either by appeal to fact or appeal to reason. No appeal to fact is possible because paradigms view the relevance of facts differently, and view differently the significance of the facts that are relevant. No appeal to reason is possible because the purposes and principles from which the paradigms start are different. And no reasoning is possible if no common assumptions can be agreed on at the outset. When paradigms clash, the typical result is a joust, in which much heat is generated but no light.[33]

There is no possibility of rebutting historicism on its own ground. All that one can do is show that *if* one accepts as the aim of social science the explanation of events, *then* one requires generalization. And *if* one accepts

29. See, for example, E. E. Evans-Pritchard, "The Comparative Method in Social Anthropology," *in* E. E. Evans-Pritchard, *The Position of Women in Primitive Society and Other Essays* (New York: Free Press, 1965), pp. 13–36, and the discussion of historical particularism in Harris, ch. 9.

30. E. R. Leach, "Rethinking Anthropology," *in* E. R. Leach, *Rethinking Anthropology* (London: Athlone Press, University of London, 1961), pp. 1–27.

31. Cf. K. Popper, *The Poverty of Historicism* (New York: Basic Books, 1957).

32. See particularly Kuhn, *The Structure of Scientific Revolutions*, chs. 2 and 5, and also Kuhn, *The Copernican Revolution* (Cambridge: Harvard University Press, 1957).

33. A good example is Leach, "Review of S. Udy, *Organization of Work*," *American Sociological Review*, 25 (1960): 136–138.

generalization as the purpose of investigations, *then* it must be abstract. Therefore, *if* one commits oneself to an explanatory-generalizing paradigm of social science, *then* one must reject as unsound a rule of holism.

The importance of generalization follows from the way in which we use the word "explanation": An explanation establishes a connection between one or more initial conditions and some consequence. That is, an effect E is "explained" if

(5) C,

an initial condition, and

(6)   if C, then E,

a connection between the condition C and its consequence E, are both true.[34] It is sometimes held that (6) may be a singular sentence, as in (7).

(7)   If John eats ¼ lb. of sugar,

                                      he falls into a coma.[35]

A singular hypothetical such as (7) permits one to predict that if John eats ¼ lb. or more of sugar he will fall into a coma; and if he has fallen into a coma, it permits one to explain his condition by the fact that he ate ¼ lb. of sugar. In other words, (7) permits one to do anything required of (6)— anything, that is, except the most important thing: for it fails actually to establish the required connection. No singular hypothetical is sufficient to establish a connection between C and E. A sentence like (7) is either true also of Tom, Dick, and Harry or it is not. If it is true of Tom, Dick, and Harry, it is not singular; if it is not, then John's coma is due not only to the sugar he ate, but also to some other condition true of John that makes him different from Tom, Dick, and Harry, such as diabetes.[36] Furthermore, to discover what this other condition is it is never sufficient to study only John. For the difficulty we are in with (7) remains true of every additional connection we claim to discover. Suppose we claim that C causes E if C' is true; then this amended expression, (7′) is either true also of Tom, Dick, and Harry, or it is not. If it is not, there remains an undiscovered condition that is important in explaining John's coma. From which it follows that expression (6) is either general or it does not explain.[37]

That generalization requires abstraction follows simply from the

34. C. G. Hempel, "The Function of General Laws in History," *Journal of Philosophy*, 39 (1942): 35–48; and C. G. Hempel and P. Oppenheim, "Studies in the Logic of Explanation," *Philosophy of Science*, 15 (1948): 135–175.

35. See, for example, W. Dray, *Laws and Explanation in History* (Oxford: Oxford University Press, 1957). The sentence itself comes from A. Donagan, "The Popper-Hempel Theory Reconsidered," *History and Theory*, 4 (1964): 3–26.

36. Donagan, "The Popper-Hempel Theory Reconsidered."

37. The literature on the subject of explanation is extensive. A recent reformulation by Hempel will be found in Hempel, *Aspects of Scientific Explanation* (New York: Free Press, 1965). A review of the subject from an historicist's point

uniqueness of wholes. One cannot construct a general theory that says *everything* that is true of a particular instance: the more one intends to say about any one thing, the less general is the theory that results. The University of California at Berkeley is like no other university, much less like any other organization. A "theory" of that university that is *general* does not exist and cannot exist, though one might have a theory of economics that applies to it, a theory of organizations that applies to it, a theory of science that applies to it, a theory of politics that applies to it, a theory of student unrest that applies to it, and so on *ad infinitum*—quite literally *ad infinitum*, since an infinite number of properties are true of any particular whole. To have a theory that is general of even something so concrete as student unrest, one must abstract from the situation at Berkeley or one will never make the theory also apply to the University of Paris. It is not only that the particular facts of the two situations differ; not only that in one case the quarters are cramped and overcrowded and the university examination situation one in which 50 percent or more of the students are certain to fail—facts not true of Berkeley. Even the *theories* that apply in each situation, though general, combine in unique ways. In one case the theories of multi-party systems and of rapid modernization are relevant, whereas in the other they are not. While unquestionably general in themselves, the way these theories are related in the particular instance is unique, or at least not repeated in all instances of student unrest. Therefore, to construct a general theory one must abstract not only from the particular conditions, but even from other processes going on in particular instances. Of course, one will not explain all the variance in any particular concrete situation, or even in all cases of student unrest, but this objection is crippling only from an historicist viewpoint and may be counted irrelevant from an explanatory-generalizing viewpoint.

Holism in the historicist sense must be sharply distinguished from *structuralism*, a claim that parts of a structure cannot be isolated from the structure as a whole. The objection to holism cannot be made to structuralism. The difference in the two lies in what they mean by the term "whole." A well-known example of a structuralist argument is Lévi-Strauss's complaint about Radcliffe-Brown's analysis of the mother's brother.[38] Radcliffe-Brown's analysis depends on two social relations: the mother-son relation and the brother-sister relation. The mother-son relation, he claims, in-

---

of view will be found in Donagan, "Explanation in History," *Mind*, 66 (1957): 145–164.

38. C. Lévi-Strauss, "Structural Analysis in Linguistics and in Anthropology," in C. Lévi-Strauss, *Structural Anthropology* (New York: Basic Books, 1963), pp. 31–54.

volves always the indulgence of the son by the mother. In patrilineal kinship systems, furthermore, the unity of siblings reflects itself in the extension of the "mother" role to the mother's brother. Hence the widespread observation that the nephew is allowed a privileged familiarity in his relation to his uncle. But, Lévi-Strauss complains, "Radcliffe-Brown isolates particular elements of a global structure that must be treated as a whole." [39] Lévi-Strauss is not complaining that Radcliffe-Brown omits the level of economic development, the structure of the political system, the existence of ancestor cults; his own analysis treats only two further relations, the relation of brother to brother-in-law, and the relation of father to son. Four instead of two relations are the "whole structure." This is in no sense the whole society, and is from an historicist point of view quite as abstract as trait atomism. Even such entities as "the social system," or "the kinship system," are abstract, constructed entities rather than concrete wholes, and one is free to compare them, generalize about them, or treat them in any manner required by an explanatory-generalizing paradigm, without self-contradiction.

(iii) The rule of comparability yields another inference: that units must be of the same level to be compared. This rule differs from the first two we have studied: it is a sound rule.

The argument is as follows: first, define a *unit* as an independent occurrence of the process ϕ; where, of course, ϕ is the subject of our investigation. Typically comparative sociology uses nations, or cultures, or other things that are supposed to be societies, as units in this sense. A *member* is the smallest indivisible part of a unit. Typically it is individuals that count as members. A *subunit* is a proper subset of members; that is, a group of individuals, say, that is smaller than the whole unit. Often it is communities that count as subunits, sometimes clans or lineages, but of course many other possibilities exist.

Second, define the *level* of a property V as *collective* if it is a property of a unit and as *individual* if it is a property of a member. This follows the Lazarsfeld and Menzel analysis,[40] which does not provide a conventional term for the remaining class; we might simply call them *subunit* properties. (From the point of view of members, subunit properties are of course collective too.) The terminology of these properties sometimes occasions confusion, because individual properties are often social, as in the case of social class, and collective properties are often aggregate individual properties, as

39. *Ibid.*, p. 41.
40. P. F. Lazarsfeld and H. Menzel, "On the Relation between Individual and Collective Properties," *in* A. Etzioni, ed., *Complex Organizations: A Sociological Reader* (New York: Holt, Rinehart, and Winston, 1961), pp. 422–440.

in the case of mean income; but we will not attempt to deal with such confusions here.[41]

Third, note that invariance of meaning is not preserved as V shifts level. Take first the relation of subunit properties to collective properties. Would I attribute to Italy the characteristics found in South Italian villages? Montegrano, for example, is supposed to have minimal community organization because Montegranese peasants are concerned primarily with the interests of their families.[42] I would not attribute the same property to "Italy" (which happens to be a highly bureaucratized and centralized polity), because Montegrano is neither a microcosm of the society nor a representative of it. It is not a microcosm because Italy is a complex system of which Montegrano is a part. It is not representative because the culture of a South Italian village is very different from the culture of a North Italian village.[43] Nor would I attribute the characteristics of Italy to Montegrano. Italy is one of the most rapidly expanding economies of Europe while Montegrano is economically stagnant.

What is true for the relation of collective properties to subunit properties is true, a fortiori, for collective and individual properties.[44] Individual French enterpreneurs typically take few delights in expansion,[45] but the economy of France expands at a rate exceeded in Europe only by Italy and West Germany. It might be supposed that this is evidence to refute the hypothesis that family firms are stagnant.[46] But all it proves is that the properties of individual entrepreneurs are not to be confused with the properties of a national economy. There are, it is true, occasions when individuals and societies are said to have the same properties. Prothro and Melikian, for example, claim both that individual Egyptians are authori-

41. See Lazarsfeld and Menzel; Hopkins and Wallerstein; and E. K. Scheuch, "Cross-National Comparisons Using Aggregate Data," in R. Merritt and S. Rokkan, eds., Comparing Nations (New Haven: Yale University Press, 1966), pp. 131–167.

42. E. C. Banfield, The Moral Basis of a Backward Society (Glencoe, Ill.: Free Press, 1958).

43. See, for example, S. F. Silverman, "Agricultural Organization, Social Structure, and Values in Italy: Amoral Familism Reconsidered," American Anthropologist, 70 (1968): 1–20.

44. O. D. Duncan and B. Davis, "An Alternative to Ecological Correlation," American Sociological Review, 18 (1953): 665–666; L. A. Goodman, "Ecological Regressions and the Behavior of Individuals," American Sociological Review, 18 (1953): 663–664; W. S. Robinson, "Ecological Correlations and the Behavior of Individuals," American Sociological Review, 15 (1950): 351–357.

45. D. Landes, "French Business and the Businessman: A Social and Cultural Analysis," in E. M. Earle, Modern France (Princeton: Princeton University Press, 1951), pp. 334–353.

46. Cf. C. P. Kindleberger, "The Postwar Resurgence of the French Economy," in S. Hoffman and others, eds., In Search of France (Cambridge, Mass.: Harvard University Press, 1963).

tarian and that the Egyptian polity is authoritarian.[47] But this is the exception rather than the rule, and should be regarded as fortuitous.

Because variables can have different meanings at different levels, only units at the same level are comparable.[48] Yankee City, a subunit of a larger system, is not comparable to Tikopia, which is a society. It also follows, incidentally, that units at one level are not readily substituted for units at another: one would not compare Yankee City with Montegrano if the purpose were to compare the United States with Italy.

(iv) Because uniformity of units is essential to comparability, the criteria which units must satisfy are a matter of some importance. They cannot be treated cavalierly, as if the choice were arbitrary, or what amounts to the same thing, as if there were one unit satisfactory for all purposes. The most commonly used criteria seem to be criteria of convenience, such as ease of sampling or identification. But there are more stringent criteria than these, the most important of which are: (a) theoretical relevance, (b) independence, and (c) indivisibility.

(a) A unit is a replicate of the process ϕ. It is just that entity possessing the properties attributed to ϕ by some theory, say T. It is for this reason that one cannot assume that units are somehow out there in the real world, independent of our conceptualization of them. Why is the state the unit of economic development? Not, as might be supposed, because the state happens to be the unit which collects the sort of data our theories of economic development happen to use. Nor, what is even more plausible, because the state is the unit we use for every purpose, regardless of our problem. The state is the unit in investigations of economic development because it is the largest permanent source of the kinds of decisions that determine the conditions of economic growth.[49] One of the benefits of viewing the matter this way is that it makes it possible to ask whether particular states satisfy this theoretical requirement: Is Monaco a state for this purpose? [50]

(b) To be a replicate of the process ϕ, a unit must be independent of other instances of ϕ. If a unit is not independent, no new information about

47. E. T. Prothro and L. Melikian, "The California Public Opinion Scale in an Authoritarian Culture," *Public Opinion Quarterly*, 17 (1953): 353–362.

48. Under certain special circumstances a variable will not shift meaning at different levels. If the variable is an aggregate collective property, that is, if it is obtained by some mathematical operation in individual properties; and if the operation performed is linear, so that the collective property is some *linear function* of the individual property, such as a mean; and if the individual property is *homogeneous*, having no variance in the statistician's sense; then the meaning of the variable will be the same at any level. But in most investigations these are hardly circumstances to count on.

49. Kuznets, "The State as a Unit of Study in Economic Growth," see note 3, above.

50. Cf. *ibid.*, pp. 29–32.

ϕ is obtained by studying it twice, and no additional confirmation of T is obtained by counting it twice.

Doubts about independence are likely where two or more units have a common historical origin, a long history of contact, or are divided by vague, ill-defined, and hence arbitrary, boundaries. For example, the Navaho and Apache were historically one tribe, perhaps a thousand years ago. The Navaho and Zuni have been borrowing traits from each other for centuries. The Jicarilla and Chiricahua Apache, although politically autonomous bands, have a culture common to all Apache bands and might be regarded simply as subunits of the "Apache tribe." One might therefore argue that all four (Navaho, Zuni, Jicarilla Apache, Chiricahua Apache) are just one independent unit.[51]

If in fact they are just one independent unit, the effect is to cast doubt on any hypothesis of necessary connection between the traits they possess. For the traits might occur together simply by historical accident. (A necessary connection between U and V is called a *functional correlation;* pure historical accident is *hyperdiffusion.*) [52] For example, in the wake of the Reformation a large number of millenarian cults were founded in Germany, Switzerland, and the Lowlands. Almost all of them were totalitarian, insular, and antagonistic to established society and the church. These might simply be the properties of any emerging movement that reconstructs cognitive orientations, normative standards, and social identities (as Young claims).[53] On the other hand, they might occur together simply because so many of them were founded by just a few wandering prophets, such as John of Leyden.[54]

For variables sufficiently abstract, hyperdiffusion is not a plausible alternative to functional correlation.[55] For example, according to Young, millenarian cults are *solidarity movements,* movements constructing or re-

51. Cf. F. Galton and others, "Discussion" of E. B. Tylor, "On a Method of Investigating the Development of Institutions: Applied to Laws of Marriage and Descent," *Journal of the Royal Anthropological Institute,* 18 (1889): 270–272; L. T. Hobhouse, G. C. Wheeler, and M. Ginsberg, *The Material Culture and Social Institutions of the Simpler Peoples* (Series of Studies in Economics and Political Science, Sociology Monograph no. 3, London School of Economics, 1930), ch. 1; and Leach, "The Frontiers of Burma," *Comparative Studies in Society and History,* 3 (1960): 49–68.

52. See R. Naroll, "Two Solutions to Galton's Problem," *Philosophy of Science,* 28 (1961): 16–39.

53. F. W. Young, "Reactive Subsystems," *American Sociological Review,* 35 (1970): 297–307.

54. N. Cohen, *The Pursuit of the Millenium* (New York: Oxford University Press, 1957), ch. 12.

55. Cf. Young, "Macrostructural Research Methods," unpublished manuscript, Center for Advanced Study in the Behavioral Sciences, 1969.

constructing identities and orientations.[56] But solidarity movements include not only medieval millenarian cults; they include also cargo cults [57] and black power. If all of these movements make their own identity more distinct at the expense of their enemies, one can hardly argue that this is due to John of Leyden. History transmits only concrete similarities; abstract concepts should and do imply traits that are concretely dissimiliar; therefore, no common history explains their properties. (This follows from rule 2, which implies that no variable explains a constant.)

Even for relatively concrete variables, hyperdiffusion is not plausible if U or V varies within region—that is, within an area having a common history. For example, according to Young [58] solidarity movements emerge in those subsystems of larger systems that come to be internally differentiated but relatively unimportant in the symbolic world of the larger system. They might occur either because an older subsystem comes to be symbolically displaced or a newer one increasingly differentiated. In either case, the behavior of the solidarity movement differs from the behavior of other subsystems of the same larger system. But presumably they all share a common history and culture: if Young's hypothesis is true, it cannot be true because of hyperdiffusion. (This follows from rule 3, which implies that no constant explains a variable.)

If hyperdiffusion is implausible where U and V are abstract, and equally where U and V are concrete but vary within region, it follows that hyperdiffusion is plausible only in the case of hypotheses that are concrete and imply similarities within region. But there are a great many such hypotheses in comparative investigations; for example, most hypotheses about the isolated nuclear family, patrilateral cross-cousin marriage, patrilineal divorce rates, or matrilocal residence rules are of this sort. And for this sort of hypothesis, some safeguards are necessary if independence of cases is to be assured. The safeguards usually employed are: first, sample in such a way that historically dependent units are sifted out, as in Murdock's sample for the "Ethnographic Atlas." [59] Second, test, directly for hyperdiffusion and show that it can be ruled out. Naroll has developed the methods necessary for such tests.[60] Or, third, match historically dependent

56. Young, "Reactive Subsystems."

57. A. F. C. Wallace, "Revitalization Movements: Some Theoretical Considerations for Their Comparative Study," *American Anthropologist*, 58 (1956): 264–281.

58. Young, "Reactive Subsystems."

59. Murdock, "Ethnographic Atlas: A Summary," *Ethnography*, 6 (1967): 109–236.

60. See Naroll, "Two Solutions to Galton's Problem"; and R. Naroll and R. D'Andrade, "Two Further Solutions to Galton's Problem," *American Anthropologist*, 65 (1963): 1053–1067.

and independent societies in such a way that correlations between U and V can be contrasted in comparable dependent and independent cases; which permits one to test both for a necessary connection and hyperdiffusion at the same time.[61]

(c) If a unit is in fact a supra-unit, made up of two or more independent replicates of ∅, clearly we would divide it. In the first place we would want the information provided by each replicate. In the second place, for reasons already given, the supra-unit would not be comparable to other units in the same investigation.

But indivisible units are not that easily found. Take nations: Sometimes nations are used as units in comparative sociology because nations are the entities required by theory; for example, this would be so in studies of national polities. Sometimes nations are used as units because the nation is assumed to be a society, a politically autonomous and functionally self-sufficient social group. But nations are not always societies, nor do their boundaries neatly mark off natural social systems.[62] Did Italy in 1861 become one society where in 1860 it was many? Is it even now one society, when the North is literate, industrial, urban, sophisticated, scientific, market-oriented, while the South is illiterate, agrarian, traditional, aristocratic, and in many subregions subsistence-oriented? The two regions do not share a common culture: the North is rooted in the Renaissance and the cultures of Northern Europe, the South is rooted in Greece and in Spain's worst centuries. They do not speak a common language: most learn Italian in school the way Americans learn French, or Spanish, or German. They do not share the same national heroes, for Cavour is not the South's favorite hero nor Garibaldi the North's. On the other hand, there is a common lingua franca, Italian; a common currency, the lira; a common rail system; and a good deal of internal trade and immigration. All Italians vote in the same elections, if perhaps the same parties are not found everywhere in the nation. There is one school system, a highly centralized polity, and all Italians hear the same popular music over their radios. Because there is no satisfactory definition of what a society is, there is no clear criterion that would allow us to say whether Italy is a society or not. In any case, probably the only sensible answer to such a question is that for some purposes it is and for some not. No study of family structures would want to treat Italy as a society, for no more different family structures could be found than the family structure of urban Tuscany and the family structure of rural Calabria. They arise neither from common traditions nor common contem-

---

61. The necessary methods have been worked out by D'Andrade; see Naroll and D'Andrade, *op. cit.*

62. Cf. Leach, "The Frontiers of Burma." See note 51, above.

porary circumstances. On the other hand, a study of dual economies, of economies in which modernized and traditional sectors are mixed, would clearly count Italy as one unit. To treat it as two units would be to destroy the phenomenon it was the purpose of the study to investigate.

(v) Many other rules follow from the requirements of comparability, but I have no intention of exhaustively listing them. I simply mention two others very briefly; rules of uniform procedures and uniform stages.

(1) There is little point in comparing data from two or more units if they were not collected, recorded, classified, and otherwise treated according to uniform procedures. For example, one would certainly not compare data on personal incomes obtained by the U.S. government with data on personal incomes reported by the French. The former asks citizens about actual income and often verifies what it is told, while the latter regards both these procedures as an invasion of privacy and uses only very indirect methods of estimating incomes even for purposes of taxation.

(2) Given two instances of the process ϕ, it is reasonable to compare data on the process as a whole, or the steady states of the process, or the same stages of development of the process. Cross-sectional comparisons tend tacitly to assume that what are compared are steady states. But often no evidence is provided to support this assumption, and if it is false comparisons are very misleading. For example, from 1890 to 1950 the Japanese divorce rate decreased from 335 divorces per 1,000 marriages to 100; in the same period the U.S. rate increased from 55.6 to 231.7.[63] Now compare the two rates for 1950: if it is assumed that the Japanese rate is the rate associated with a less industrialized and more familistic social structure, one might be tempted to say that industrialization, by causing either family loss of functions or isolation of the nuclear family, increases divorce. Not only is the hypothesis false, the comparison itself is quite arbitrary. It is meaningless to compare an arbitrarily chosen point from a still increasing trend to an arbitrarily chosen point from a predominantly decreasing trend.

(vi) Comparability is not decided simply by consulting the evidence of our senses: it depends on the purpose of comparison and on theoretical analysis. This is particularly evident whenever it is decided that two values of the variable V "do not arise in the same manner." The following three instances, taken from comparisons of economic growth, are fairly typical:

(1) The Gross National Product (GNP) of mainland China was $46,256 million in 1957. That of West Germany was $49,906 million.[64] The two values are very close, and in a rank order of 122 nations West Germany

63. Goode, *op. cit.*, p. 406. See note 9, above.
64. Russett and others, p. 152. See note 16, above.

is 4th, mainland China 5th. But obviously the two values do not arise in the same manner. In the case of mainland China GNP reflects mostly population size, in the case of West Germany mostly a modernized economy. This is suggested, for example, by their GNP per capita (GNP/cap): West Germany is 14th, mainland China roughly 101st among 122 nations.[65] Now the purpose of comparing the two is to say something about their economic development. Furthermore, by economic development we mean something about changes in the structure of the economy that increases its productive capacity, population aside. Therefore, we would not compare the GNP of West Germany with that of mainland China.

(2) What this argument suggests is that we use GNP/cap as the basis for comparisons of economic development. But the GNP/cap of Kuwait is greater than that for the United States.[66] Is Kuwait the more developed nation? Or is it more nearly the case that Kuwait has a large income from oil, that, because it is concentrated in a few hands, is not reflected in increasing productive capacity in the economy. The two values of GNP/cap obviously do not arise in the same manner, and we would probably feel comfortable comparing the two only if some means were found to take inequality of income into account in measuring GNP/cap.

(3) The GNP/cap of the Massif Central is greater than that of Calabria, although it is doubtful that the Massif Central is the more developed economy. Both are traditional and subsistence-oriented, particularly by comparison with agriculture either in Northern Italy or Northeastern France. But GNP/cap may be high either because productive capacity is high or because population pressure is slight. A century of population stagnation has maintained the GNP/cap of the Massif Central despite its traditional economic organization. Calabria, on the other hand, is overpopulated. In establishing the comparability of economic development, therefore, we take into account not only GNP/cap, but also population changes taking place in the two regions.[67]

In each of the three cases, comparability is decided by three considerations: first, by subject-matter knowledge. It is because we know that the value of the GNP for China and West Germany arose in different ways that we question their comparability. Second, by the purpose of comparison. It is because our interest is in economic development that we choose the structure of the economy rather than population size as the variable we

65. *Ibid.*, p. 155.
66. *Ibid.*
67. Kuznets, "Problems in Comparisons of Economic Trends," *in* S. Kuznets, W. Moore, and J. J. Spengler, *Economic Growth: Brazil, India, Japan* (Durham, N. C.: Duke University Press, 1955), pp. 3–28; and Kuznets, *Six Lectures on Economic Growth.*

want reflected in GNP. Third, by theoretical analysis. It is because we define economic development as a change in the structure of the economy that increases its productive capacity, independent of change in population, that makes us insist on comparing Calabria only with other overpopulated regions.

Without a clear purpose, definite theory, and some knowledge of the instances to be compared, the making of comparisons is often a very dubious adventure. Consider the formidable difficulties in the way of making intelligible comparisons of, say, the size of industrial organizations in France and the United States. For the sake of comparability, it would be useful to compare specific industries, because size of organization is in part a function of industry and the distribution of firms by industry differs in the two economies. But what is an industry? How am I to classify General Motors, which makes not only autos but airplane engines, not only transport equipment but heating equipment? [68] To this question there are three possible answers. First, abandon industry classification; but this will threaten the comparability of my data. Second, invent arbitrary rules; this will settle any issue for all practical purposes, but will certainly not guarantee that my comparisons make any sense. Third, make a theoretical analysis of industrial organization, guided by the purpose of my comparison. The last is certainly the only guarantee of intelligible comparison; but it is also very difficult, and some people will think the game not worth the candle. If the comparison is worth making, however, the game *is* worth the candle; any other comparison is likely to give results that make no sense.

INTERPRETABILITY

A comparison is *interpretable* if it is possible to infer from it something about the relationship of two or more variables. The reason that case studies are of no use for explanatory purposes is that they are not interpretable in this sense. For given [69]

$$(1) \qquad\qquad\qquad uvwx\bar{y}$$

it cannot be held that u, say, is the cause of v; the rival hypotheses that w or x or $\bar{y}$ cause v are equally plausible, and no one of the hypotheses can be ruled either in or out from the evidence of (1) alone. For example, it could not be said from a study of the family in the United States that industrialization is a cause of the isolated nuclear family. Urbanization, the frontier, or

68. Cf. Morgenstern, *op. cit.*, pp. 36–37. See note 17, above.
69. The notation adopted here uses capitals for variables and lower-case letters for their values. As only dichotomous variables will be used, to ease the exposition, the variable V takes only the values v and $\bar{v}$. The sign $\bar{v}$ should be read "not-v."

a puritan heritage might equally well have caused it. It will be the purpose of any well-designed research on this subject to so arrange its comparisons that one or more of these rival hypotheses may be ruled out.

The rules for interpreting comparisons were codified as early as the 17th century, but achieved their most popular and influential expression in Mill's *Logic*.[70] It was Mill's purpose to provide scientists with canons of induction sufficiently complete and certain that any scientist, even a fool, could by following them discover and demonstrate causal relations. Even in Mill's day there were objections to this view of the rules,[71] and we shall see that they are neither perfectly *adequate* guides to inference nor completely *sufficient*, for they must be supplemented by additional knowledge, and furthermore knowledge of a substantive character. Nevertheless, although they have been slightly reformulated [72] and elaborated,[73] they have never actually been replaced. They still guide all well-designed comparative research, and in any case any imaginable substitutes would suffer from the same difficulties, since the real problem is that no methodological rules are by themselves complete.

Keep in mind that throughout we assume non-experimental data; varying circumstances are therefore discovered rather than manipulated by the investigator.

(i) If *u* is a cause of *v*, we anticipate that other things being equal whenever *u* occurs *v* will occur. Therefore, *uv* ought regularly to occur. This suggests a simple way to find the causes of *v*: examine several instances of *v* and look for the factor that is common to all these instances. Thus

(2) $uvwx \qquad uv\bar{w}\bar{x}$

permits the inference that *u* causes *v* or *v* causes *u*, because *u* and *v* occur together and no other factor that we regard as relevant also occurs with *v*. Mill called this method the *method of agreement*, and formulated it as his first canon of induction:

70. J. S. Mill, *A System of Logic* (London: Longmans, Green, 1843). Abridged by Ernest Nagel in *John Stuart Mill's Philosophy of Scientific Method* (New York: Hafner, 1950).

71. Cf. W. Whewell, *On the Philosophy of Discovery* (London: J. W. Parker and Son, 1860).

72. As in Cohen and Nagel, *op. cit.*, ch. 13. See note 8, above.

73. As in D. T. Campbell, "Factors Relevant to the Validity of Experiments in Social Settings," *Psychological Bulletin*, 54 (1957): 297–312; P. F. Lazarsfeld and P. L. Kendall, "Problems of Survey Analysis," *in* R. K. Merton and P. F. Lazarsfeld, eds., *Continuities in Social Research: Studies in the Scope and Method of "The American Soldier"* (Glencoe, Ill.: Free Press, 1950), pp. 133–196; H. Simon, "Spurious Correlation: A Causal Interpretation," *Journal of the American Statistical Association*, 49 (1954): 467–479; and S. Stouffer, "Some Observations on Study Design," *American Journal of Sociology*, 55 (1950): 355–361.

(3)   If two or more instances of the phenomenon under
             investigation have only one circumstance in common,
             the circumstance in which alone all the instances agree
             is the cause (or effect) of the given phenomenon.[74]

An unusually careful use of the method of agreement is Inkeles and
Rossi's study of comparative occupational prestige.[75] They wished to show
that the industrial factory system everywhere gives rise to the same set of
occupations, the same allocation of authority and responsibility, and the
same allocation of material and social rewards, without regard to the historical traditions of the society into which the industrial system is introduced. Comparing the occupational prestige ratings of the United States,
Russia, Great Britain, New Zealand, Japan, and Germany they show very
high correlations between the prestige ratings of comparable occupations of
any pair of countries in this set. As the traditions of these nations are in at
least some instances quite different, the agreement in their prestige ratings
must be attributed to the industrial system which they have in common,
rather than historical traditions which they do not.

Mill's first canon is open to the objection that the hypothesis it seeks to
establish is universal, for it takes u and v to be invariably connected; but
universals can never be verified, they can only be falsified.[76] For example,
the assertion

(4)   For every x, if x is a raven, x is black

is not verified even if every raven I have ever seen is black. For tomorrow I
may yet see a white raven. On the other hand, one white raven falsifies it.
Cohen and Nagel have made this argument a basis for reformulating Mill's
first canon negatively, thus:

(3')   Nothing can be the cause of a phenomenon which is
             not a common circumstance in all the instances of the
             phenomenon.[77]

This deals with the problem of verification, but even so is open to objections.
We shall postpone considering further objections, however, until a firmer
foundation has been established.

(ii) Mill regarded the method of agreement as only a weak demonstration of the connection between u and v, for if u causes v not only do we
expect that u will be found when v is found, we also expect that if v does

74. Mill, *op. cit.*, p. 214.
75. A. Inkeles and P. Rossi, "National Comparisons of Occupational Prestige," *American Journal of Sociology,* 61 (1956): 329–339.
76. Popper, *The Logic of Scientific Discovery* (New York: Basic Books,
1959).
77. Cohen and Nagel, *op. cit.*, p. 255.

not occur, then *u* does not. This suggests contrasting two kinds of instance, one in which *v* is found and one in which *v* is not, thus

(5) $uvwx \quad \bar{u}\bar{v}wx$

(5) permits the inference that *u* causes *v* or *v* causes *u*, because when *v* is found *u* is found and when *v* is not found *u* is not, though *w* and *x* are found in either case. Mill called this the *method of difference,* and he formulated it in his second canon:

(6)   If an instance in which the phenomenon under in-
         vestigation occurs and an instance in which it does not
         occur have every circumstance in common save one,
         that one occurring only in the former, the circumstance
         in which alone the two instances differ is the effect, or
         the cause, or an indispensable part of the cause, of the
         phenomenon.[78]

Like his first canon, Mill's second canon is open to the objection that no universal may be verified, it may only be falsified; we are therefore required to make a negative rather than a positive use of the canon. Restating it negatively, we have

(6')   Nothing can be the cause of a phenomenon if the
          phenomenon does not take place when the supposed
          cause does.[79]

It is in this form, for example, that we find the method playing its part in Thomas's objection to Inkeles and Rossi:[80] Thomas objects that if it is industrialization that accounts for the prestige hierarchies of the United States, Germany, Russia, and so forth, then there ought to be a *low* correlation between the prestige hierarchies found in these countries and those of an underdeveloped nation. But Tiryakian has shown that there is a high correlation between the prestige ratings of the Philippines and the United States, even where the ratings come from very rural parts of the Philippines;[81] and Thomas has shown that the prestige ratings of Indonesia have a high correlation with all those used by Inkeles and Rossi.[82] Thomas is therefore willing to rule out industrialization as the factor which gives rise to the Inkeles-Rossi prestige ratings, which follows from (6').

78. Mill, *op. cit.,* pp. 215–216.
79. Cohen and Nagel, *op. cit.,* p. 259.
80. R. M. Thomas, "Reinspecting a Structural Position on Occupational Prestige," *American Journal of Sociology,* 67 (1962): 561–565.
81. E. Tiryakian, "The Prestige Evaluation of Occupations in an Underdeveloped Country: The Philippines," *American Journal of Sociology,* 63 (1958): 390–399.
82. Thomas, *op. cit.*

(iii) Neither Mill's first nor his second canon assure that u is related to v unless one and only one factor agrees, in the first, or differs in the second canon. Thus, a comparison is interpretable if and only if the investigator varies one circumstance at a time—a rule usually known as the *rule of one variable*. It follows from the fact that given

(7) $uvwx$ $uvw\bar{x}$

either u or w might be the cause (or effect) of v. The variables U and W are said to be *confounded*. If the hypothesis $r(U,V)$, that there is a correlation between variables U and V, is preferred to $r(W,V)$, then a comparison must be so designed that $r(W,V)$ can be ruled out.

For example, it has been noticed that societies with complex and extensive bride-price have no, or almost no, divorce. But such societies almost always also have strong corporate patrilineages.[83] Therefore bride-price is confounded with descent rule. Bride-price and descent rule are confounded because they are correlated: Whenever one is found the other is found.[84] Patrilineal descent groups make possible the stability of lineage relations over a long period of time, permitting the development of the very elaborate system of debts and obligations that goes with complex bride-price. According to Gluckman, the patrilineal descent group also creates the conditions required for family stability, with the result that whenever patrilineal corporate descent groups are found, low divorce rates are found. The fact that both divorce rates and bride-price are correlated with the existence of patrilineal descent groups accounts for their apparent associations with each other. For the presence of the descent group will make for the presence of both family stability and bride-price, hence they will always appear together.

This effect is widely known as *spurious correlation*: a causal system such as

(8) $U \leftarrow W \rightarrow V$

will always produce spurious correlation between U and V, because the correlation of any two variables is a function in part of their direct association and in part of their associations with any *other* variables common to both of them.[85] Thus, even if $r(U,V)=0$, if $r(W,U)$ and $r(W,V)$ are positive, $r(U,V)$ will be positive.

Spurious correlation is obviously a handy and perennial rival to any

83. M. Gluckman, "Kinship and Marriage among the Lozi of Northern Rhodesia and the Zulu of Natal," *in* Radcliffe-Brown and Forde; and "Bridewealth and the Stability of Marriage." *Man*, 53 (1953), no. 223.

84. Gluckman, "Kinship and Marriage among The Lozi of Northern Rhodesia and The Zulu of Natal," and "Bridewealth and the Stability of Marriage."

85. G. U. Yule and M. Kendall, *An Introduction of the Theory of Statistics*, 11th ed. (London: Griffin, 1937), ch. 4; and Lazarsfeld and Kendall.

investigator's hypothesis, and a substantial part of any research effort goes to ruling it out. Whenever it is suspected, a comparison may be designed that contrasts $r(U,V)$ when w is present with $r(U,V)$ when w is absent, as in

(9) uvw $uv\bar{w}$

If the value of $r(U,V)$ is independent of W, as it is in (9), then it is not W that accounts for the correlation and it is not spurious; or more exactly, if it is spurious some variable other than W is the causal factor. Comparisons such as (9) are said to be *controlled* for W; the control is accomplished by *holding W constant*.

Udy, for example, has shown that the number of authority levels in primitive production organizations depends in part on the technical complexity of their tasks. More interesting is the fact that it also depends on the degree to which membership in the organization is ascribed. If the structure of the organization depends on the external status system, as it would if status were ascribed, then the number of status levels within the organization depends on the number of status levels in the society, and in general is greater than the number required by technical complexity. To establish the latter correlation, Udy controls for technical complexity, showing that the relation of ascription and the number of levels of authority is independent of any relation either might have to technical complexity.[86]

An alternative to holding W constant is to *match* for W. That is, two instances are compared that are alike in W instead of their differing in W. What they differ in is the value of V: in one instance V must be present and in one absent, as in

(10) uvw $\bar{u}\bar{v}w$

which should be compared closely with (9). Because w is common to both instances, the correlation of U with V cannot be attributed to W. This is the method relied on by Leach, for example, in comparing the divorce rates

---

86. S. Udy, "Technical and Institutional Factors in Production Organization," *American Journal of Sociology*, 67 (1961): 247–254. Much less commonly, it is U that is held constant in order to show that with the effect of U removed the correlation $r(V,W)$ vanishes. This is sufficient to rule out spurious correlation because for W to explain $r(U,V)$ both $r(U,W)$ and $r(V,W)$ must exist. For example: Swanson, *Birth of the Gods* (Ann Arbor: University of Michigan Press, 1960), shows that monotheism is correlated with the number of levels of sovereign organization in a society; that is, with the number of levels of social unit exercising original and independent jurisdiction over some aspect of social life, such as family, clan, village, and tribe. A plausible alternative explanation is to suppose that societal complexity, which is probably correlated with number of levels of sovereign organization, is the true cause of monotheism. To rule this alternative out, Swanson shows that with complexity held constant, the correlation between number of sovereign levels and monotheism remains; but also, that with number of sovereign levels of organization held constant, the correlation between complexity and monotheism vanishes (Swanson, ch. 3).

of the Gumsa Kachin with the Lakher.[87] Leach suspected that Gluckman [88] was wrong about the divorce rates of patrilineages, that some patrilineages had high divorce rates while others had low divorce rates. He therefore compared two very similar tribes, the Gumsa Kachin and the Lakher,[89] one of which had no divorce and one of which had high divorce rates, in order to find the factor that differentiated the two. Both tribes had matrilateral cross-cousin marriage, hypogamous marriages (in which males marry females of higher status than their own), complex and elaborate bride-price, the levirate; in both tribes a son-in-law was not only a son-in-law, he was also a vassal, in the political sense, of his father-in-law; and in both tribes there were strong patrilineal corporate descent groups. As both tribes had these factors in common, none of them could account for the difference in their divorce rates. What did account for the difference in divorce rates was the lineage-status of women after marriage. Among the Lakher a woman remained a member of her father's (and therefore her own) lineage after marriage; among the Gumsa Kachin she became a member of her husband's. Leach therefore concludes that it is the very different kinds of social bonds and legal rights created by the two kinds of lineage relations that probably accounts for the divorce rate.

It is a little surprising that the differences between (9) and (10) should assume the proportions of a paradigm clash, but often they do. Of course there are some differences. For example, where (10) typically owes its success to being able to take advantage of within-region correlations,[90] (9) will have failed if its correlations hold only within regions.[91] But such differ-

87. Leach, "Aspects of Bridewealth and Marriage Stability among the Kachin and Kakher," *Man*, 57 (1957), no. 59.

88. Gluckman, "Bridewealth and the Stability of Marriage."

89. A third case was also used, but adds nothing to the present argument.

90. This same success is found in within-nations comparisons, and for the same reasons (E. Allardt, "Social Resources of Finnish Communism: Traditional and Emerging Radicalism," *International Journal of Comparative Sociology*, 5 [1964]: 49–72; J. Linz and A. de Miguel, "Within-Nation Differences and Comparisons: The Eight Spains," *in* R. L. Merritt and S. Rokkan, eds., *Comparing Nations* [New Haven: Yale University Press, 1966], pp. 267–319). Linz and de Miguel, for example, point out that it is easier to interpret Catalan separatism by comparing it to Spanish Galicia than to separatism in other nations; Catalonia and Galicia both speak distinct languages and have distinct traditions, and they both have the same political framework. What differs between them is their economic development, which is great in Catalonia but slight in Galicia. The fact that they share a common government is better assurance that the character of the government can be ruled out as an hypothesis than if separatism in several different nations were compared.

91. Wilson has criticized Murdock's sample because some regions are more highly represented than others. The geographical distribution of its traits, therefore, is not random (T. R. Wilson, "Randomness of the Distribution of Social Organizational Forms: A Note on Murdock's *Social Structure*," *American Anthropologist*, 54 [1952]: 134–138). Furthermore, it can be shown that this affects Murdock's

ences are hardly enough to account for the gulf that divides the two in practice. The matched comparison is the favored method of a tradition that descends from Durkheim.[92] Typically its investigations are qualitative, intensive, and emphasize criticism of sources, reliability, validity, and elegance. Its proponents quite typically also scorn what they call the statistical comparison, in which (9) is the favored method of control.[93] The statistical comparison is the favored method of a tradition that descends from Tylor.[94] Typically its investigations are quantitative, extensive, depend on large samples, are very systematic in the analysis of data, if not very critical about the data themselves. It is clear that (9) requires numbers, because there must be enough cases in both the w class and the $\bar{w}$ class to permit further analysis, but the conflicts between the two traditions are nevertheless puzzling,[95] and certainly make no scientific sense. The two are better regarded as alternatives, suitable or not depending on the investigator's problem and the conditions of his investigation.

(iv) The relationships of two variables, U and V, is often *conditional* on the behavior of a third, say W. For example, Russett has tried to show that inequality of land tenure causes political instability.[96] But, he finds this to be true only when a substantial proportion of a nation's population depends on agriculture for its income. Australia and Venezuela, for instance, both have considerable inequality in land tenure, but in the former only a third as many people are engaged in agricultural occupations. Australia, therefore, is found to be more stable than Venezuela.

Finding such conditions is widely known as *specification* of a relation-

---

correlations. For example, patrilineal descent and divorce are strongly correlated in the World Ethnographic Sample (.41), but this is due to the over-representation of the circum-Mediterranean region in which the two are highly correlated (.60). In North America the correlation vanishes (.03) and in South America it is reversed (−.12) (H. E. Driver and K. F. Schuessler, "Correlational Analysis of Murdock's 1957 Ethnographic Sample," *American Anthropologist*, 69 [1967]: 332–352).

92. Particularly E. Durkheim, *Les formes élémentaires de la vie religieuse* (Paris: Alcan, 1912).

93. See, for example, A. J. Köbben, "New Ways of Presenting an Old Idea: The Statistical Method in Social Anthropology," *Journal of the Royal Anthropological Institute*, 82 (1952): 129–146.

94. E. B. Tylor, "On a Method of Investigating the Development of Institutions: Applied to Laws of Marriage and Descent," *Journal of the Royal Anthropological Institute*, 18 (1889): 245–269.

95. In any case, this is not the factor that accounts for the differences in the traditions since in point of fact the statistical comparison often makes little or no use of the opportunities for control provided by its sample size. It is remarkable how difficult it is to discover an illustration of a control for spurious correlation in the cross-cultural literature. Swanson, who makes liberal use of such controls, is the exception rather than the rule.

96. Russett, "Inequality and Instability: The Relation of Land Tenure to Politics," *World Politics*, 16 (1964): 442–454.

ship.[97] If W is regarded as a possible relevant condition of the relation between U and V, in a specification W is held constant and the correlation of U and V is examined for each value of W, as in (11).

(11) $wuv;$ $w\bar{u}\bar{v}$ $\bar{w}uv;$ $\bar{w}\bar{u}v$

What (11) shows is that U and V are correlated when W is present, but they are uncorrelated when W is absent.

Specification is particularly useful when more than one process is reflected in V. Mill always assumed that V was a unitary process; that is, there was one and only one process underlying it. But this is a scientific ideal, a product of progressive and increasing understanding of V, often not found in everyday practice. For example, one of the more interesting hypotheses about Communist Party strength is that it is correlated with rapid and early economic development.[98] Allardt has found for Finland that indeed there is a correlation between rapid, early development and party strength.[99] But he also finds the party strong in some urban, already industrialized areas. Furthermore, in developing regions of Finland, party strength correlates with degree of job intensity, brought about by social change; it is alienation that increases party strength. In urban areas, on the other hand, where industrialization in Finland is well advanced, prosperity is high, aspirations are therefore high—but in Finland these aspirations are unfulfilled because of rigid class barriers; it is frustrated expectations that are reflected in Communist Party strength. What Allardt shows, then, is that the higher the job security in developing areas, the higher the party strength; whereas in industrialized areas, the higher the prosperity the higher the party strength. Two quite different processes underlie the same observable effect, each one showing itself under a different set of conditions.

(v) The relationship between two variables may be either *direct* or *indirect*. For example, in (12)

(12) $U \rightarrow W \rightarrow V$

the relationship of U to W is direct, but the relationship of U to V is indirect. W is said to be the *intervening variable*. In purely formal terms, causal systems such as (12) have exactly the same properties as (8), though in a substantive sense their meaning is very different; and in particular, if $r(U,W)$ and $r(W,V)$ are positive, then $r(U,V)$ will be positive. For if u is present, so is w; and if w is present, so is v.

The similarity between (12) and (8) extends to the methods by which one tests that a causal ordering such as (12) exists. If, having found $r(U,V)$,

---

97. Following Lazarsfeld and Kendall. See note 73, above.
98. See, among others, the discussion in S. M. Lipset, "The Changing Class Structure and Contemporary European Politics," *Daedalus*, 93 (1964): 271–303.
99. Allardt, *op. cit.*, pp. 49–72.

one entertains the hypothesis that this is an expression of some more elaborate causal ordering; and if, in particular, one hopes to discover whether or not W is the intervening variable that accounts for $r(U,V)$; then one holds W constant, and the hypothesis is confirmed if the partial correlation $r(U,V;W)$ [100] vanishes. For it is evident from (12) that the whole of the correlation between U and V is due to W, and no effect should remain if the effect of W is removed.[101]

For example, Homans and Schneider devote a substantial part of *Marriage, Authority and Final Causes* to the variables that intervene between an observed correlation between descent rules and the form taken by cross-cousin marriage. If they have cross-cousin marriage at all, patrilineal societies typically have matrilateral cross-cousin marriage where matrilineal societies have patrilateral cross-cousin marriage. That is, male ego in a patrilineal society will be required to marry his mother's brother's daughter (MoBrDa), while male ego in a matrilineal society will be required to marry his father's sister's daughter (FaSiDa). According to Homans and Schneider, this is because in patrilineal societies jural authority is vested in fathers, the distance and respect associated with authority is extended to their sisters, and therefore marriage with FaSiDa is not "sentimentally appropriate." The sentimentally appropriate match is with MoBrDa, because mothers are close and affectionate and this sentiment is extended to their brothers. In matrilineal societies jural authority is vested in mother's brothers; the relationship between the mother's brother and sister's son is distant; the MoBrDa is not a sentimentally appropriate match. But because he has no authority over ego, father is affectionate and close; so is his sister; and FaSiDa is therefore the sentimentally appropriate match.[102] Now to demonstrate the plausibility of this chain of intervening variables, Homans and Schneider study each of their 35 cases of cross-cousin marriage to show that descent does determine the locus of jural authority, and that jural authority does determine the form of cross-cousin marriage. More important, where descent fails to determine the locus of jural authority, they attempt to show that it is jural authority,

100. Read "the correlation of U with V, with W held constant."

101. Many sociologists claim to *explain* $r(U,V)$ by this method, in the sense that W accounts for $r(U,V)$. Lazarsfeld and Kendall employ a different terminology, in my view correctly, since explanation is a term both more general and more strict (Cf. Hempel and Oppenheim). But they chose to call this procedure interpretation, which in my view is a more appropriate term for the whole process of drawing *any* conclusion from comparison. The matter is not very important; it is only worth noting that there is no established usage, and I do not propose to try to invent one.

102. G. Homans and D. Schneider, *Marriage, Authority, and Final Causes* (Glencoe, Ill.: Free Press, 1955).

not descent, that determines the form of cross-cousin marriage. Thus, there is a whole class of matrilineal societies that, like the Kaska and Gara, vest jural authority in the father until ego marries; in these, marriage is dependent not on descent but on jural authority, and cross-cousin marriage is matrilateral. There are also some societies, such as the Sherente, that do not vest authority in the father even though they are patrilineal. Instead, authority is more nearly exercised by members of the mother's moiety. In these, marriage depends on jural authority, not descent, and is patrilateral.[103]

(vi) The positive formulations of Mill's canons [as in (3) and (6) above] are imperfect largely because no logical universal is verifiable. One cannot conclusively demonstrate that u is the cause of v on the grounds that u has always been found when v is found, or even because v has not been found where u is not found. There is always the possibility that tomorrow someone will find evidence against the hypothesis. But any such hypothesis is falsifiable, so that a negative as opposed to a positive formulation of the canons ought to be acceptable. It should certainly be true that if u is *not* present when v is, then u is not the cause of v; and similarly, if u is present when v is not, surely u is not the cause of v. This negative formulation, due mostly to Cohen and Nagel,[104] is now the formulation accepted by most investigators, and there is no question that it improves on Mill.

But even in this negative form, Mill's canons are imperfect under certain conditions; and they are very common conditions. What (3′) tells us is that if we find the effect v but not the supposed cause, u then u is not the cause of v. But any causal system of the form (13) will often produce

(13) $$U \to V \leftarrow W$$

situations in which v is present though u is not. For example, it is probable that the existence of dispersed, unorganized matrilineal clans arose in at least three ways: through the decay of corporate matrilineal descent groups through the existence of double descent systems in which matrilineal descent regulates preferential marriage; or through earlier contact with a matrilineal society, where the mode of articulation of the two societies was through kinship.[105] If, now, I test the first of these hypotheses, I will sometimes find that the effect occurs when the cause does not. But this is no reason to reject the hypothesis, for it is true that decay of matrilineages is one cause of dispersed matri-clans. What the evidence shows is simply that

103. *Ibid.*, pp. 37–51.
104. Cohen and Nagel, *op. cit.*, ch. 13.
105. Aberle, "Matrilineal Descent in Cross-Cultural Perspective," pp. 660–661.

it is not the *only* cause. Or, put another way, only if plural causation is ruled out is the formulation in (3') an adequate guide to the conclusion we must draw from the evidence.

Similarly, what (6') tells us is that if u is found but v is not, then u cannot be the cause of v. But any causal system of the form (14) will often

(14) $$U \stackrel{+}{\rightarrow} V \stackrel{-}{\leftarrow} W$$

produce situations in which u is present but v is not. (The variable W may be regarded as a *cancelling* factor.) For example, it is probable that a society where the subsistence base makes the coordination of female work groups important to the economy, matrilocal residence will emerge; and where matrilocal residence emerges, matrilineal corporate descent groups will typically emerge. But once having emerged, there are many factors that will maintain matrilineal descent groups after the "causal" factors have ceased to be of any importance. Although subsistence activities may change so as to increase the importance of male coordination of work, as a result of which matrilocal residence may cease to be important, yet other factors will make for the survival of the matrilineage.[106] If I test the hypothesis that matrilocal residence "causes" matriliny, I will find that often the "cause" is absent though the "effect" is present. This will certainly force me to modify and complicate my causal hypothesis; but the fact that the effect is present when the cause is not is no proof against causation.

Not only multiple causation, but also conditional causation will sufficiently obscure a correlation that it will sometimes not be found when in fact it exists. For if $r(U,V)$ is conditional on W, it is perfectly possible to find $r(U,V)$ close to 0 if there is no control for W. Köbben [107] describes the following example: in one of the earliest cross-cultural surveys the Dutch anthropologist Nieboer argued that slavery would be found where resources were sufficiently abundant that people would not work for others unless forced to do so.[108] Baks and others found no correlation at all between the two variables when retesting this hypothesis on data from Africa, Indonesia, and Oceania.[109] But Köbben reasons that slavery is possible only where sufficient stratification exists to make it technically feasible; and, on reanalyzing the same data, he finds no correlation between resources and slavery in egalitarian societies, but a strong correlation in stratified societies.

106. *Ibid.*, pp. 656–662.
107. Köbben, "Why Exceptions? The Logic of Cross-Cultural Analysis," *Current Anthropology,* 8 (1967): 3–19.
108. H. J. Nieboer, *Slavery as an Industrial System* (The Hague: Nijhoff, 1910), pt. 2.
109. C. Baks, J. C. Breeman, and A. T. J. Nooy, "Slavernij," *Bijdragen Taal-land-, en Volkenkunde,* 122 (1961): 90–109.

Thus, just as the existence of a correlation is no proof of causation, nor even of genuine correlation, so absence of a correlation is no proof *against* causation or the existence of genuine correlation. It is possible for u to be present and v not, or for v to be present and u not, and still for u to be a cause of v. If plural or multiple causation can be ruled out, or if our knowledge of and control over the relevant variables is perfect, then Mill's two canons, in Cohen and Nagel's negative formulation, are adequate guides both to what we do in fact and what we ought to do. In any other case, if we strictly obey the rules we will too readily abandon good ideas.

(vii) But even if the foundations of comparative method were adequate, they would not be sufficient without supplementary knowledge, and furthermore, supplementary knowledge of a substantive, as opposed to methodological, character. There are four reasons for this:

(1) Every comparative investigation begins with an analysis of the factors that are relevant, and the successful outcome of the investigation depends on this analysis. For example, consider Cohen and Nagel's famous headache:

> Suppose a professor of hygiene finds that he had a splitting headache on three successive nights. He recollects that on Monday he read for ten hours and then took a walk; on Tuesday, he found the dinner delicacies irresistible, ate too much, and then sought repentance by taking a walk; on Wednesday, he slept during the day and then sought refreshment in a walk. If he were to employ the method of agreement, he might conclude that walking was the cause of his headache. But this is quite contrary to fact, since the walks he took (we happen to know on other grounds) have nothing to do with the bringing on of headaches.[110]

The error in the conclusion is not due to an improper use of the rules of method. It is due, rather, to an improper analysis into circumstances. But circumstances do not come to us neatly separated into recognizable factors that immediately suggest what should be looked at and how. This is true not only of possible "causes" but even of the "problem" itself. Is a headache a unitary phenomenon? That is, is it one simple "problem" for which we should expect to find one cause, or at least one system of causal factors? Often we look for the "causes" of some "thing" that is in fact many things, with many distinct causal processes. This may be true, for example, of the search for the causes of "democracy." For the problem is in part one of accounting for political consciousness and in part one of accounting for the *form* taken by a politically conscious society. It may be that political consciousness and political democracy are separate problems, developing

110. Cohen and Nagel, *op. cit.*, p. 254.

at different times, at different rates, for different reasons.

Not that there is necessarily one right analysis into factors. For example, compare Lipset's analysis of democracy with Cutright's analysis of political development.[111] Cutright claims to analyze political development, rather than the stability of democracy, but his measure of development is in terms of parliaments, elections, and oppositions, so we may regard his analysis as comparable to Lipset's. Lipset chooses *wealth, education, urbanization,* and *industrialization* as variables relevant to the stability of democracy. To Lipset, *wealth* means income per capita, persons per doctor, persons per motor vehicle, telephones, radios and newspapers per 1,000 population. Now Cutright chooses as variables relevant to political development *wealth, education, urbanization, industrialization,* and *communication;* and of these the greatest emphasis is given to *communication.* But *communication* means newspapers, telephones, and domestic mail. Thus, Cutright does not simply add a new factor. He reconceptualizes the way in which the *same* circumstances may be analyzed into factors.

The results of comparison depend on the way the problem is analyzed. But this analysis precedes rather than follows comparison. Therefore the investigator's theoretical formulation plays an essential part not only in the choice of facts but also in the kind of conclusions that will be drawn from comparison.

(2) Prior conceptualization determines not only how the factors are to be analyzed into "circumstances," but also, of course, just what factors are relevant. Suppose my problem is to explain inequalities in educational demand in emerging African nations. Using the method of difference, a good design would be to compare a village with low school enrollments to one or more similar neighbors with high enrollments.[112] For following the rule of one variable, if some one factor is to be called the cause of low enrollments, *all other factors* must be alike save one. What are the relevant factors? We might take into account: supply of school facilities, character of curriculum, cost to parents of children in school (both directly and in terms of opportunity costs), character of the local economy (particularly the amount of market exchange), geographical mobility of the inhabitants, the character of the local social structure (particularly the place occupied by ascriptive criteria of status), the diffusion of authority within the community, the homogeneity of the population, the degree of occupational differentiation and the extent to which wealth plays a part in determining

---

111. Lipset, "Some Social Requisites of Democracy," *American Political Science Review,* 53 (1959): 69–105; and Cutright.

112. As Foster does; see P. F. Foster, "Status, Power, and Education in a Traditional Community," *School Review,* 72 (1964): 158–182.

status.[113] This appears to be a fairly long list, but it is by no means exhaustive. It certainly is not demonstrated that *all* other factors are alike save one; nor *can* it be demonstrated, for the simple reason that the number of factors is infinite. What is meant, in practice, is that all the *relevant* factors are alike save one. We neglect those factors that are irrelevant. Studying educational enrollments, we do not ask if "the feet of the natives are large." [114] But if not, there must be some standard of relevance. And this standard is supplied not by the rules of method but by whatever substantive knowledge we possess at the moment.

Of course, we may as a result of a faulty standard omit a factor that is relevant. Banfield, for example, has interpreted his data from a South Italian village as showing that "amoral familism," the pursuit of short-run family interests as opposed to the interests of the community, accounts for the low degree of organization and cooperation in South Italian villages.[115] Cancian finds the explanation not in amoral familism, but in the view South Italians take of stratification and hierarchy: peasants, who constitute the bulk of the village population, know their place; and their place is not the making of decisions about nor the organizing of activities in the village. It is officials and large landowners who traditionally play this part. But the views of Italian peasants about hierarchial structure were not taken into account by Banfield in his analysis.[116]

If it were possible randomly to allocate the values of independent variables to societal units, objections of this sort would pose no serious difficulty. Randomization is useful precisely because of its effects on relevant but unknown factors. Failing randomization, our reliance is heavily on subject-matter knowledge.[117] For, given $r(U,V)$, if W is to be taken seriously as a rival causal hypothesis there must be some accepted knowledge that makes $r(U,W)$ and $r(V,W)$ plausible. If not, we would be at the mercy of an infinite number of trivial objections and no result of comparison would ever become acceptable. Thus, whether a result of comparison is acceptable or not depends not only on the rules of comparative method, but also on the state of our substantive knowledge at the moment. If what we know suggests a plausible, that is, a relevant, rival hypothesis, a given result is not acceptable until that hypothesis is ruled out; but if

113. Cf. Foster, *op. cit.*

114. The question comes from J. S. Berliner, "The Feet of the Natives Are Large," *Current Anthropology*, 3 (1962): 47–61.

115. Banfield, *op. cit.*, See note 42, above.

116. F. Cancian, "The South Italian Peasant: World View and Political Behavior," *Anthropological Quarterly*, 34 (1961): 1–18.

117. Cf. H. Wold, "Causal Inference from Observational Data," *Journal of the Royal Statistical Society*, Series A, 119 (1956): 28–50.

what we know suggests no good reasons to entertain the rival hypothesis, or if it suggests no rivals, then we for the moment accept the result.

(3) Given an analysis into circumstances and a standard of relevance, to test some hypothesis about the relations between circumstances we typically deduce some implication that will be true if our hypothesis is true. Sometimes this can be very straightforward but often it is not. And if it requires more than one step to go from conjecture to test implication, the chain of reasoning will often contain premises that are independent of the hypothesis H itself. These additional premises are *auxiliary* hypotheses, say A, and what we actually test is the composite hypothesis H *and* A. If the hypothesis fails a test, therefore it is possible that A and not H is at fault. Only if A is known, on other grounds, to be true, must we accept the conclusion that H itself is false.

For example, Young [118] has suggested that initiation rituals are dramatizations of change of status in groups which are solidary. Among males, he finds the relevant sort of solidarity in the presence of community-wide male work groups, clubs, or similar associations. A very satisfactory correlation is found between solidarity and male dramatization of change in status. Young reasons, however, that what is true for males should be true for females as well; there is no reason to suppose the initiation rituals of females obey different laws. But there is no correlation between community-wide solidarity of females and dramatization of female change in status.[119] From this result one could conclude either that the solidarity hypothesis is in trouble or that community-wide work groups and associations are not the place to look for female solidarity. Further tests show that it is the auxiliary, not the main hypothesis that is wrong: Female solidarity is found less in community-wide work groups than in the institutionalized unity of corporate households.[120]

In composite tests of this sort a good deal depends on the empirical status of the auxiliary hypotheses. If they are known for other reasons to be true, the fact that H *and* A is false is informative for H. If nothing is known about A, something has to be done to determine what it is that is wrong. But in any case, wherever the actual implication we test depends at least partly on auxiliary hypotheses, acceptance of the result of comparison depends not only on the rules of method, but also on the state of our empirical knowledge at the moment.

(4) What we conventionally think of as the "analysis" of the result of

118. Young, *Initiation Ceremonies: A Cross-Cultural Study of Status Dramatization* (New York: Bobbs-Merrill, 1965).
119. *Ibid.*, ch. 6.
120. *Ibid.*

a comparison requires us, among other things, to distinguish spurious from
genuine correlation and direct from indirect correlation. Simon has given
a formal proof that analysis in this sense depends on *a priori* assumptions
that do not arise from the data, although they are essential if the data are
to be interpreted. This proof depends on the fact that no body of data will
provide information about enough equations to estimate all the quantities
required by an interpretation. We do, of course, make interpretations; but
what we do is "estimate" the remaining quantities by use either of prior
substantive knowledge or what we think of as common sense—the sort
of common sense that tells us rain causes people to wear raincoats but not
that raincoats cause it to rain.[121]

A good example is provided by the formal properties of causal systems
(8) and (12), which I repeat here for easy comparison:

(8) $U \leftarrow W \rightarrow V$ (12) $U \rightarrow W \rightarrow V$

We typically feel very different about these two causal systems; as Lazarsfeld put it, we feel that in (8) we have explained something *away*, while
in (12) we have really explained something.[122] But the formal statistical
properties of (8) and (12) are identical, and it is *not* operations performed
on the data that cause us to believe we are dealing with (12) rather than
(8). In both cases, what the evidence shows is that the partial correlation
$r(U,V;W)$ vanishes. We decide that we have indirect correlation rather
than spurious correlation if we believe that U is antecedent to W, and
spurious rather than indirect correlation if we believe W is antecedent to
U. These beliefs are typically based on empirical knowledge of some sort,
but not on the data used in determining $r(U,V;W)$. Thus, Homans and
Schneider thought that the sentiments formed by nephew and uncle pre-
ceded the emergence of preferential marriage rules because it was unreasonable to suppose otherwise, not because the data proved it. It was for
much the same sort of *a priori* reason that they supposed descent rules
caused the allocation of jural authority.[123]

I am not simply repeating the well-known fact that time order determines what is cause and what effect, though the problem looks the same.
The problem lies deeper: the fact is that even when dealing simply with
the interpretation of correlations, no interpretation is possible without at
least some *a priori* assumptions, that, though they may be empirical, are
not derived from the data being interpreted. They are derived, therefore,
from other empirical knowledge. The interpretation of comparison depends
not only on obedience to rules of method but on what we know.

121. See Simon, or the discussion in H. M. Blalock, *Causal Inferences in
Nonexperimental Research* (Chapel Hill: University of North Carolina Press, 1961).
    122. Lazarsfeld and Kendall, *op. cit.*
    123. Homans and Schneider, *op. cit.*

Thus, we cannot view the rules of comparative method as sufficient to provide a mechanical procedure, analogous to multiplication, that will always lead to a correct and indisputable conclusion provided only that no "mistakes" are made in following the rules. The rules are not in themselves sufficient because theoretical formulation is required to analyze a problem into the appropriate circumstances, substantive knowledge is required to assure us of what factors are irrelevant, auxiliary hypotheses are often necessary—the truth of which depends on empirical knowledge that is independent of the particular investigation we are interpreting—and, finally, to interpret an observed result requires assumptions that, though they may be empirical in nature are not derivable from the data being interpreted, depending instead on other subject-matter knowledge.

SUMMARY

At the foundation of comparative method are four rules: a rule of comparability, Mill's rule of agreement, Mill's rule of difference, and a rule of one variable. They are "foundations" in the sense that the many other rules of comparison either derive from them, can be regarded as unsound in the light of them, or else are less general, irrelevant to comparison *per se,* or not methodological in character. The only independent and general methodological rule not included is the rule that causes precede effects, which has not as yet played much part in the comparison of societies. "Comparative method" is here treated in the special sense of a systematic comparison of two or more societies the purpose of which is to generalize about the relations among variables.

In this paper the rules of comparative method are studied in the light of three criteria: (1) their *adequacy,* in the sense that on some intuitive basis we agree that they counsel us to reject false hypotheses and accept true ones; (2) the *validity* of various rules inferred from them, in the sense of following from them logically; and (3) their *sufficiency,* in the sense of permitting sound interpretation of the results of comparison from a knowledge of the rules alone.

The rule of comparability may be treated separately from Mill's canons and the rule of one variable. What is of special interest is not so much the rule itself as the large number of rules of comparison derivable from it. Many of the rules that derive from it, however, are not valid inferences. Neither the search for empirical universals nor the emphasis given to all-purpose invariant points of reference are justified by the rule of comparability—though of course there may be other justifications for them, not treated here. What comparability requires is a logical universal common to every unit in a given domain of comparison. The state *not-V* will satisfy this requirement, and in any case empirical universals are not logically universal. Furthermore, although logical universals are invariant points of reference from the point of view of some one comparison, or some one theory T that guides that comparison, they are not *all-purpose* points of reference, independent of T. Indeed, all-purpose points of reference are essentially atheoretic as well as often vacuous. A second invalid inference from the rule of comparability is the deduction that only wholes may be compared. In fact, the holistic rule yields a self-contradiction, that only incomparables are comparable, so that if it is accepted, what is implied is that no comparison is possible. From the point of view of an explanatory-generalizing paradigm of social science, therefore, it must be accepted that abstraction is necessary to and does not violate the conditions of comparative inquiry. The self-contradiction in holism is not, however, true of structuralism, which like holism often gives rise to claims that some part of the "whole" has been neglected; but structuralism means by a "whole" an abstractly conceptualized entity having some given property or properties, not a concrete whole society.

On the other hand, the inference that only uniform units are comparable is a valid inference, following from the fact that the meaning of some state v is not constant at every level for which it is defined. Furthermore, it is valid to infer that procedures must be uniform and that only similar stages of a process may be compared, though this chapter devotes very little attention to the last two rules.

Even with all the guidance that is provided by its valid corollaries, the rule of comparability proves to be insufficient to decide comparability. Whether two things, or more correctly two values of a variable, say V, are comparable or not depends not only on the rule but on the purpose of comparison, a knowledge of the subject, and theoretical analysis of the meaning of the concept V. One might say that the rule of comparability tells you what to look for, but not how to find it.

Concerning the three remaining rules, which may be regarded as a single group, one issue is their adequacy. They are imperfect, in the sense that they sometimes counsel us to reject a true hypothesis. It is because of rules 2 and 3 that we treat absence of a correlation rather differently than presence of a correlation. If we find that $r(U,V) \neq 0$, we are suspicious; we test for spurious correlation, we subject the correlation to careful and endless scrutiny, we regard the issue of the relationship as always open to question. If we find that $r(U,V)=0$, we tend to take the correlation at face value, we accept it as evidence of no relationship, and often cease our investigations of the relation of U to V. But failure to pursue zero correlations further is poor practice, and we ought to discourage it as vigorously as possible. For in fact, it is only if we have ruled out multiple and plural causation, or only if we have perfect knowledge of and control over all the factors in the relevant causal system, that we can regard the absence of correlation is definitive evidence that no relationship between U and V exists.

The other main issue is the sufficiency of rules 2–4. As guides to the interpretation of comparisons they are insufficient unless supplemented by subject-matter knowledge and theoretical formulation because: first, a proper analysis into circumstances must be made before comparison. Second, without a standard of relevance the number of factors to be taken into account is (in the technical sense) infinite. Third, without prior or independent empirical knowledge, it is not clear whether disproof of an hypothesis H is evidence against H itself or against the auxiliary hypotheses very often required in order to deduce a test-implication from H. And fourth, without *a priori* assumptions, or empirical evidence from some source other than the data to be interpreted, no causal system is identifiable; that is, it is not possible to decide whether correlation is genuine or spurious, direct or indirect, or in general what the exact form of a system of relations is, without additional assumptions that, though certainly empirical in character, are justified only by evidence independent of data to be interpreted. The source of these assumptions is either subject-matter knowledge or what is often called "common sense," the sort of substantive knowledge too trivial or commonly known to be dignified by the term "scientific" knowledge. For these four reasons, it must be concluded that there is no royal road to intelligible comparisons that, if only the map is obediently read, can be followed by the foolish or ignorant investigator to certain and valuable results. Not only a sound knowledge of the foundations of the rules, but also trained judgment and knowledge of the subject are required to design and interpret intelligible comparisons.

CROSS-NATIONAL SURVEY RESEARCH: THE PROBLEM OF CREDIBILITY

SIDNEY VERBA

This paper will deal with the question of the credibility of cross-cultural survey research. The focus will be on survey research in relation to comparative political studies, though much of what will be said is relevant for comparative studies using methods other than the systematic survey and in relation to other substantive fields. And the focus will be on comparing nations, a type of comparison particularly important in political science because of the importance of the nation-state as a political unit. Comparative research has traditionally been linked to comparison across national borders, and we will follow the same convention though two points should be made clear. Within-nation studies are comparative research and face the same kinds of problems faced in cross-national research. And, as we shall discuss later, cross-national comparison may be most fruitful when based upon within-nation comparison.

If survey research is to be useful in understanding nations it must be cross-national. This does not limit our concern to those few cases where systematic and parallel studies are conducted in several countries at once. Fruitful comparisons can often be made among studies originally gathered for single country purposes. Though most of our examples will come from the former kind of study—where parallel research in different countries was conducted as part of the same research program—the strategies for comparison will in most part be relevant for the analyst interested in comparing two independent studies. Fortunately for the latter type of analyst (and unfortunately for the organizer of the former type of study) the problems faced in the parallel and coordinated study are not *that* different from the ones the secondary analyst faces. That a study is coordinated by no means indicates that the problems of comparability have been solved. The strategies for increasing comparability, to be discussed below, should be relevant for the design of comparative research, but relevant to the secondary analyst as well who is faced with data already gathered and over which he has no control in terms of research procedures. Furthermore, it is hoped that the discussion of strategies to increase comparability will be relevant to the scholar conducting survey research within a single nation in terms of the potential comparability of that research with research conducted elsewhere.

Multi-national surveys are useful for understanding political processes because of their multi-contextual nature—i.e., because the nation varies. But it is just this multi-contextual nature that makes such surveys difficult, and that poses the question of how comparable they really are. The sources of non-comparability have been discussed by various authors and do not need repetition here.[1] These critiques may be taken to indicate that the results of comparative survey research are always subject to challenges to their validity and that the challenges are never fully answerable. We may find a "similarity" or a "difference" between two societies. These similarities or differences may be in the proportions of a sample responding in particular ways, in the relations among variables in the two societies, in group differences within societies. Thus, if we are studying political participation, we may find differences or similarities between two societies in the proportions who vote, in the relationship between media exposure and voting, or in male-female differences in voting turnout. Or we might find more complicated differences or similarities in the patterning among measures—different factors emerging in a factor analysis, different multivariate relations between independent and dependent variables.

Such similarities and differences are always subject to challenge that they are not "real"; that that which seems similar is not really similar, that that which seems different is not really different. Assume for a moment that one has a satisfactory sample in two societies and that some difference between the societies in the response to an item or a pattern of relationships is clearly statistically significant. The finding is still subject to the challenge that the difference is invalid because the measurements in the two societal contexts are not comparable. And this in turn may be because of some systematic difference in measurement technique between the two contexts or because one is measuring something different in each society. Since cross-

---

1. See Sidney Verba, "The Uses of Survey Research in the Study of Comparative Politics: Issues and Strategies," *in* Stein Rokkan and others, eds., *Comparative Survey Analysis* (The Hague: Mouton, 1969), pp. 56–106. Small portions of this paper appear in the above. See also Erwin K. Scheuch, "The Cross-Cultural Use of Sample Surveys: Problems of Comparability," pp. 176–209 *in* S. Rokkan, ed., *Comparative Research Across Cultures and Nations* (Paris, The Hague: Mouton, 1968), and Adam Przeworski and Henry Teune, *The Logic of Comparative Inquiry* (New York: Wiley-Interscience, 1970).

cultural survey research is non-experimental, any difference between the two societies is subject to the challenge of an alternative hypothesis: that the "treatment" of the two societies was different and that the differences found are artifacts of the research design.[2] And these alternative hypotheses can apply not only to the relations among variables within nations, but (even more so) to simple findings of differences in responses between nations. The survey finding that organizational membership rates are greater in one country than another [3] is immediately subject to the challenge that the difference found between the two nations is not a difference in organizational membership rates at all. Rather it may be merely a difference in the way the question was asked in the two countries due to translation differences perhaps, or to any one of a hundred differences in the administration of the question. Or the argument can be made that organizational systems are so different between the two societies that one has not successfully measured the same thing in each society. The statement that the rates are different, therefore, has no meaning.

At the outset, it ought to be clear that such challenges are not limited to cross-cultural research. Survey research always studies different groups —different localities, different classes, different ethnic groups, men and women. As long as the criteria for experimental design are not met—and they never are—any group difference is subject to challenges of the sort described above. But survey research carried on in different social settings, and in particular when those settings are societies or nations, is a useful type of research to examine from the point of view of these problems. For one thing, such problems become more explicit in cross-cultural research. One more easily ignores dialect differences within a single language area and assumes, perhaps without validity, that one is dealing with the same interview across the entire sample. One cannot ignore the language problem in cross-cultural research. More important, the fact that the study is carried on in different contexts increases the number of plausible alternative hypotheses and, in particular, increases the number of alternative hypotheses that we might call methodological—that is, those alternative hypotheses that explain a difference or similarity as a by-product of the research design. Systematic differences in research instruments and processes between societies and cultures are inevitable and severe—language being the foremost. (And one can add a further reason why alternative

2. On the variety of errors possible when true experimental designs are not available, see Donald T. Campbell and Julian C. Stanley, "Experimental and Quasi-Experimental Designs for Research," paper prepared for the American Psychological Association Meetings, Washington, D.C., 1967.

3. Gabriel A. Almond and Sidney Verba, *The Civic Culture* (Princeton: Princeton University Press, 1963), ch. 12.

hypotheses are more likely to require consideration in cross-cultural research: There are usually a number of specialists in one society or the other uneasy about too facile comparison and ready to suggest such plausible alternatives.)

Let us consider a result of our comparative studies in political participation.[4] We were interested in frequencies of contacting some governmental office by citizens. In India, we found 18 percent of our sample who report having contacted some official in relation to some need or problem. In the United States the parallel figure is 30 percent.[5] Let us ignore, for the time being, questions of sampling. And, for the time being, let us not be concerned with the significance or interpretation of this finding. Let us simply ask whether the difference is real or perhaps merely the result of our research technique. To be sure that the difference between the two nations is not a by-product of the research techniques, we would have to be sure that individuals in both countries received the same "treatment"—that they were asked the same question in the same way. But since there were different interviewers interviewing in different languages this criterion is not met. And the most powerful technique for eliminating these contaminating effects—random assignment to the alternative treatments—is not possible. If Indians and Americans could be randomly given Hindi or English interviews, assigned randomly to situations where caste relations between interviewer and respondent were relevant and others where they were not, and so forth, one would have greater confidence that the difference in reported frequency of contact was not an outcome of the research

4. The data to be reported are from a cross-national study of political participation and social change conducted in four countries—India, Japan, Nigeria, and the United States. The field work in the first three countries was supported by the Ford Foundation, and that in the United States by the Carnegie Corporation. The data that will be reported come from the studies in India and the United States. The former study was conducted by the Centre for the Study of Developing Societies, New Delhi, under the direction of Rajni Kothari and Bashiruddin Ahmed; and the latter under the auspices of the Institute of Political Studies, Stanford University and the Institute of International Studies and the Survey Research Center, University of California, Berkeley, under the direction of Sidney Verba, Robert Somers, and Norman Nie. Analyses of the data will be reported in future publications, some of which are cited below.

5. The relevant questions were similar in the two countries. They followed upon extended questioning about the respondent's needs and problems and his perception of the needs and problems in the community. We asked respondents, in relation to any of these problems, "Have you ever personally gone to see or spoken to or written to (some member of the local government . . . specific examples were given) in the community about some need or problem?" The question was asked about several levels. Full details on questionnaires and sampling will be in future publications of the cross-national research program on participation. One point should be noted here: the Indian sample is not of all India, but rather of four states: West Bengal, U.P., Andhra Pradesh, and Gujarat. In the United States there were 2,549 interviews; in India, 2,637.

design but a "real" difference across the two countries. But, of course, the situation is just the contrary—the treatments differ and they differ systematically across the line one is trying to make the basis of the comparison. Caste is important in India, not the United States. Interviews in the United States are in one language, Indian interviews in other languages. Perhaps the words used to ask about contact in English are evaluatively neutral, while in Hindi the nearest approximation connotes something reprehensible. The lower rate reported in India might reflect this.

And even if one were to accept the difference as "real"—that indeed there is more contacting of officials among Americans than among Indians —questions remain as to the meaning of the difference. Are "contacts" equivalent in meaning in the two countries? The subject matter of the contacts, the officials contacted, the channels used, and so forth, all differ. And to go one step further, the social processes that lead to contacting may differ.

The situation might lead either to despair or encouragement. Despair would arise from the realization that powerful experimental techniques such as random assignment to treatment situations are in real world comparative studies beyond our reach. Encouragement of a sort might derive from the realization that such techniques are usually beyond the reach of the "within-culture" social scientist as well. Except for the laboratory, the attainment of true experimental design is difficult, if not impossible. And social scientists—warned of the pitfalls—must settle for approximations.

In the next sections of the paper I will suggest some ways to make comparisons more valid. In some sense, all the literature on survey design and analysis is relevant here—for the procedures of design and administration, of scaling, of data manipulation and analysis that apply to studies in a single country apply to cross-cultural studies. I would like to focus, rather, on some aspects of the problem that seem to be heightened by the cross-cultural character of comparative surveys. But the prefatory reminder should be repeated: the problems of design for within-nation studies apply to across-nation studies and vice versa. If the above sentence seems to say that there is nothing unique about cross-cultural studies, it is intended. The difference is that the problems are more severe but also more easily recognizable. In the discussion, I will refer to some general ways of dealing with the problem of comparability and illustrate them with some data from the cross-cultural survey studies on participation. One example I will carry along is the example of "contacting the government," and the different rates of such contact in India and the United States. In the examples given, I will be less interested in the substantive problem of contacting as a means of participation and what the difference in contacting rates means for the two political systems or for the citizens in the two countries. Rather my simple concern will be with the question: How much credence should one give to statements comparing the two nations? And how can one make statements that are more rather than less credible?

The general theme of the discussion is as follows: The problem of comparability of measures taken from two different social systems derives from the fact that the measures are embedded in different structural and cultural contexts. Methodologically this means that the measurements must be made in different languages and under different research conditions that are affected by the social structure and culture within which they are made. Substantively it means that the equivalence of measures will be affected by the various other aspects of the context from which the measure is abstracted. Under the circumstances the best way to increase comparability is to maintain the contextual grounding of the measures when making comparisons. Insofar as possible, comparisons should take into account the structural and cultural context of the measure before comparisons are made of the measures across systemic boundaries.

We shall consider the problem of contextual grounding of comparison in relation to: (1) the selection, measurement, and processing of the items for comparison; (2) the comparative analysis of the data; and (3) the structure of the survey design itself.

THE COMPARABILITY OF THAT WHICH WE COMPARE

If the meaning of that which we compare depends upon the context out of which it is measured, the context ought to be taken into account in making the comparison. One major problem is that these contextual characteristics—what cultural meanings are associated with a political act one wants to compare, what functional role particular acts play in those social structures that relate citizens to government, etc.—are often unknown before we have conducted comparative research. The knowledge to make our research comparable requires prior research that has often not been done. Thus, much of what follows will refer to a number of "bootstrap" techniques whereby the information to put a particular measure into context is gathered along with that measure. "Putting an item into context" is a rather vague notion. The next few sections will, I hope, make it a bit clearer.

1. *Functional equivalents.*—It is often argued that the face similarity of items for comparison is trivial and potentially misleading. What is important is the functional equivalence of items. There is more reference in the literature to the importance of functional equivalence than there are

clear definitions of what exactly a functional equivalent is or how you know one when you see it. In functional analysis, the term refers to the fact that the same function may be performed by alternative institutions or in alternative ways.[6] In the looser sense in which it is used in relation to comparative research it refers to the fact that the same variable may be indexed by a variety of items, and different items may be the most appropriate indicators in different settings. Wealth in one society may be best indexed by monetary income, in another by ownership of cattle; aggression, by verbal behavior among some groups and by physical violence in others. What this means is that one must begin with fairly general dimensions (and, better, fairly general hypotheses or theories) before one searches for equivalent measures. Before one compares voting rates, one ought to consider the underlying dimensions for which voting is relevant. This in turn means considering the underlying theory of politics (or some aspect of politics) for which the study of voting is relevant.

Several points follow from this. The fact that we are searching for functional equivalents makes clear that we are not looking for measures that are equivalent in all respects. What is important is that the measures be equivalent in those respects that are relevant to the problem at hand. As we shall indicate below, there are differences across societies in the "meaning" of the vote to individuals. In that sense votes are not equivalent across societies (or among individuals within societies). But the structure of political competition in a party system—particularly in a system with relatively few parties—can convert the vast variety of individual motives into a choice among two, three, or four alternatives. For certain problems having to do with election outcomes and the stability of party systems, the equivalence of the effect of the vote—despite variations in the meaning to the individual—may suffice to make votes comparable.

The above example is one in which the individual motivations for performing a particular act differ, but the substantive content of the act in terms of its impact on the system is equivalent. It is possible to find situations where the converse is true—the substantive political content of an attitude or act may differ, but on the level of the individual there may be important equivalences. Much contemporary work in attitude formation and change has dealt not with the content of attitudes but with their structure. Thus there has been concern with whether a set of attitudes are congruent one with another, whether a set of attitudes is rigidly held or flexibly held, whether an individual adheres to a closed and all-encompass-

6. See, among others, Robert Merton, *Social Theory and Social Structure* (Glencoe, Ill.: Free Press, 1957).

ing ideology or has, instead, a looser set of political orientations.[7] It may be possible, using measures of attitude structure, to compare political systems in terms of the frequencies of types of attitude structuring. In one system there may be more individuals with flexible political attitudes than in another. On this level it may not matter that individuals in one system are flexible on one aspect of politics, while individuals in another are flexible on another aspect.

In order to find functional equivalents, it may be necessary at times to change the level of generality. An example of this is given above, where the shift in emphasis is from the content of the belief to the structure of the belief. Such a shift in level may enable us to find comparable problems where comparability does not exist at a lower level.

For the frequencies of certain political attitudes or behaviors to be useful as explanatory factors on the system level, it is necessary that the attitudes or behaviors be defined in such a way that they have general relevance to the set of systems for which explanation is sought. One may not be able to look at political attitudes or behaviors which may be specific to a system. For instance, since specific political issues differ from system to system, propositions in terms of attitudes on these issues will have little general relevance. If, however, attitudes on political issues can be conceptualized in more general terms—say, in terms of broad tendencies in favor of or opposed to more government activity, or in terms of the rigidity of attitudes on specific issues, or in terms perhaps simply of whether or not many people have attitudes on issues—broad generalizations may be easier. One still studies this in terms of attitudes on specific matters, but the specifics can vary from one setting to another.

This can be illustrated if we consider the problem of whether or not respondents have opinions. One objection to carrying on studies of attitudes on public issues in some of the newer nations is that one will discover few attitudes on public issues—that the individuals interviewed will have little information on the subject and will have thought very little, if at all, about

7. On this general subject, see the growing literature on cognitive balance or dissonance, including Leon Festinger, *A Theory of Cognitive Dissonance* (Stanford: Stanford University Press, 1962); F. Heider, *The Psychology of Interpersonal Relations* (New York: John Wiley and Sons, 1958); C. E. Osgood, C. J. Suci and P. H. Tannenbaum, *The Measurement of Meaning* (Urbana: University of Illinois Press, 1957); M. J. Rosenberg and others, *Attitude Organization and Change* (New Haven: Yale University Press, 1960); and the special issue of *The Public Opinion Quarterly* on "Attitude Change," 24 (Summer 1960), especially the articles by Zajonc, Cohen, Rosenberg, and Osgood. For some studies of the structure of attitudes with more direct political implication, see Milton Rokeach, *The Open and the Closed Mind* (New York: Basic Books, 1960); and Ulf Himmelstrand, *Social Pressures, Attitudes and Democratic Processes* (Stockholm: Almquist and Wiksell, 1960).

what the interviewer is asking. And since one is studying opinions on different topics in different systems and since there is so little to be discovered about attitudes on these topics, it might suggest that such study is of little use. But if the problem is redefined so that what is of interest is simply whether or not respondents in various nations have opinions on various subjects, not what opinions they have, the comparative study of even the uninformed and inarticulate masses may become important.

By raising the level of generality of the problem to that of having opinions or not, it is possible to learn a lot about the relative politicization of the populations in various systems. Opinion-holding was suggested by Daniel Lerner to be a key variable in explaining the involvement of individuals in the modern aspects of their societies. In this way the inability or unwillingness of a respondent to answer a question does not involve the loss of data, but is itself an important datum.[8]

Another way in which variables may be made more equivalent is by breaking them down into the component parts. This again is related to the search for underlying theoretical dimensions. Such attributes as education, occupation, and the like are in fact bundles of variables. The occupation of an individual is important for his political or social attitudes for a number of reasons: It places him in a particular income; it relates him to the market in a variety of ways; it places him in a particular interpersonal set of relations within the plant; it requires of him that he have certain skills and think about problems in a certain way; it leads others to react to him in particular ways, and so on. A single occupation found in two nations—say lathe operator—may put two individuals in the same category on some of these dimensions but not on others. They may have the same skill, but not the same prestige.[9]

8. D. Lerner, *The Passing of Traditional Society: Modernizing the Middle East* (Glencoe, Ill.: Free Press, 1958). The search for new dimensions of political attitude may enable us to break down the barrier to survey studies that appears to be erected by the limited content of the attitudes that are found in survey research. Much of what scholars consider to be a paucity of important political attitudes may rather be an inability of the respondent to structure his political world the way the scholar does. The scholar asks questions about political dimensions that he considers important, with the result that the respondents often have difficulty in answering. If one were to use interview techniques that give the respondent more room to express his own views in his own terms, it might turn out that a richer set of political attitudes exists than we had heretofore expected. This suggests a research strategy involving longer and less structured interviews as a preliminary to the conduct of more highly structured survey research. An example of the richness of popular political ideology that can be gleaned from long and intensive interviews is found in Robert E. Lane, *Political Ideology* (New York: Free Press of Glencoe, 1962).

9. Early work by Inkeles and Rossi suggested that there were similar occupational prestige hierarchies in different countries, a finding that would make this problem less severe. A. Inkeles and P. H. Rossi, "National Comparisons of Occupa-

Thus, in dealing with occupational categories, these various dimensions may be taken into account—depending, of course, on which dimensions are most relevant to the problem at hand. If one is studying the strains associated with incongruent or uncrystallized status positions,[10] it may be most useful to measure the prestige ratings of occupations directly. Individuals could be asked to rate their own occupations in terms of prestige as well as to rate occupations in general in these terms. In this way one could develop occupational ratings for the system as a whole (by summing the results of a sample) as well as the individual's rating of his own and other occupations. And this—combined with other data that place the individual subjectively and objectively on various hierarchies—would allow testing of hypotheses about the strains associated with incongruities among various hierarchies.

Similarly, one might be interested in occupational variables as they relate to such variables as beliefs or non-occupational behavior. Thus modernization has been defined (in one of its myriad definitions) as the growth of the use of complex machinery and the substitution of inanimate for animate power.[11] The usual occupational categories would not allow us to place an individual on a "modernity" scale using this definition because

tional Prestige," *American Journal of Sociology*, 61 (January 1956): 329–339. Further studies have in general confirmed the finding, but suggested qualifications particularly when one is dealing with fairly precisely defined occupational categories and with less industrialized sectors. See V. S. D'Souza, "Social Grading of Occupations in India," *Sociological Review*, 10 (1962): 145–159; B. Hutchinson, "The Social Grading of Occupations in Brazil," *British Journal of Sociology*, 8 (June 1957): 176–189; J. C. Mitchell, "Occupational Prestige and the Social System: A Problem in Comparative Sociology," *International Journal of Comparative Sociology*, 5 (March 1964): 78–90; C. E. Ramsey and R. J. Smith, "Japanese and American Perceptions of Occupations," *American Journal of Sociology*, 65 (March 1960): 475–482; E. M. Thomas, "Re-inspecting a Structural Position on Occupational Prestige," *American Journal of Sociology*, 67 (March 1962): 561–656; and E. A. Tiryakian, "The Prestige Evaluation of Occupations in an Underdeveloped Country: The Philippines," *American Journal of Sociology*, 63 (1958): 390–399.

10. See B. Anderson and M. Zelditch, "Rank Equilibration and Political Behavior," *Archives Européenes de Sociologie*, 5 (1964): 112–125; I. W. Goffman, "Status Consistency and Preference for Change in Power Distribution," *American Sociological Review*, 22 (June 1957): 275–281; G. W. Lenski, "Status Crystallization: A Non-Vertical Dimension of Social Status," *American Sociological Review*, 19 (August 1954): 405–413, and "Social Participation and Status Crystallization," *American Sociological Review*, 21 (August 1956): 458–464; K. D. Kelly, "Status Consistency and Political Attitudes," *American Sociological Review*, 31 (June 1966): 375–381; G. B. Rush, "Status Consistency and Right Wing Extremism," *American Sociological Review*, 32 (February 1967): 86–92; and J. Galtung, "Rank and Social Integration: A Multidimensional Approach," pp. 145–198 *in* J. Berger and others, *Sociological Theories in Progress* (Boston: Houghton Mifflin, 1968).

11. See Marion J. Levy, Jr., *Modernization and the Structure of Societies* (Princeton: Princeton University Press, 1966) (esp. pp. 35–38).

certain occupations may vary in the complexity of the machinery used. This may have to be measured directly—through job descriptions, questions about technical training needed for one's occupation, questions about equipment used, and the like.

The point is that the equivalence of items may be marred by their multi-dimensionality. And the relation among the dimensions will differ from system to system. Thus, it may be necessary to define the theoretical purpose for which we want the item and to measure the item in terms of its subdimensions.

To return to our example of the comparison of rates of contacting officials in India and the United States, that comparison is interesting only if in some way contacting in India and the United States are equivalent. The first cut at answering the question of their equivalence is to point out that they are equivalent acts in each country from the point of view of our *a priori* notions of the alternative modes of political participation open to individuals. In our model of participation, acts of participation differ most significantly in terms of the types of governmental policy which they can affect and the types of gratifications that they offer to the individual participant. These considerations led us to consider four types of participation: voting, campaign participation beyond the vote, cooperative group activity, and contacting officials. Contacts, we assumed, were the only mode of participation in relation to which the individual participant could "choose the agenda"—that is, choose the subject matter of the participatory act—and it was the only mode of participation from which individuals might expect beneficial outcomes particularized to themselves.

My purpose here is not to explicate our framework for the study of participation.[12] I am merely using the comparison of contacting in India with contacting in the United States as an illustration of the problem of comparing items across cultures. The point being made here is that contacts were compared across two countries because they were assumed to perform similar political functions in terms of the gratifications they made available to participators and in terms of the kind of governmental output they could affect.[13] In other respects, contacting in the two countries may be different. The means for contacting may differ; in the United States we have many more examples of contacting by mail. Or the official contacted may differ;

---

12. For a fuller discussion see Sidney Verba and Norman Nie, *Participation in American Political Life* (tentative title), forthcoming, ch. 3.

13. In connection with contacting the government, the type of gratification available to the individual and the type of governmental activity affected by the act tend to be the same. In relation to other types of participation they are not; the individual receives gratification not from the governmental response to his act but from some side effect of the act. On this general topic, see *ibid.*, ch. 4.

in the United States we have more examples of contacts with distant officials. But our interest was in equivalence in terms of our other dimensions. And lastly, that contacts in India and the United States were equivalent in the sense we considered relevant was just an hypothesis. The study was designed so that the hypothesized equivalence in outcome and gratification could also be tested.

2. *Multiple measures.*—Multiple measures relevant to the same dimension are preferable to single measures. The reasons are familiar from the general literature on research design and scaling and need not be repeated here. Multiple items allow one to test whether the alternative items cluster together and can be assumed to be indeed measuring the same thing. The problem is compounded, however, across cultures. Suppose one uses a different set of items in each nation because the different items seem the best measures of the same dimension. If the items in each country cluster together, this indicates that the set of items in each country measures some dimension. But what is the warrant for considering the dimension to be the same in each country? A useful—though partial—solution is suggested by Przeworski and Teune, whereby cross-culturally equivalent scales are constructed out of sets of items some of which are "identical" while others are country-specific.[14] In a sense, the equivalence of the scale depends on the fact that there are in each nation items that are, on the face, identical; the internal consistency of the scale depends on the interrelation among the items in each country; and the relevance of the scale to each country depends on the adjustment of the items that derive from the country-specific measures.

Our work in participation used a similar approach (independently arrived at). In each country a wide range of questions was asked about specific acts of participation; the acts were assumed to be specific examples of the four types of participation listed above. In each country there were similar items of participation presumed to tap each type of participation and some different ones as well—since each nation provides its citizens with a different available repertory of participatory acts. The questionnaire items were then subjected to a factor analysis—an analysis that produced in each of the four countries a fairly close match to the structure we expected among the participatory items: Four factors associated with the four modes of participation were produced. The four factors are the "same" in each country in that the identical items pattern the same way in each country,

---

14. Adam Przeworski and Henry Teune, "Establishing Equivalence in Cross-National Research," *Public Opinion Quarterly,* 30 (1966); and Henry Teune, "Measurements in Comparative Research," *Comparative Political Studies,* 1 (1968).

and the additional country-specific items load in what is clearly the most appropriate factor given their face meaning.[15]

One of the four factors in India and the United States is a "contact" factor. This makes us more confident that when we compare contacting rates in the two countries, we are comparing similar variables. Since we have several measures of contacting—on different government levels—the factor loadings mean that an individual who engages in one contacting activity is more likely to engage in another contact than he is to engage in some other type of activity. And this is the case in each country.

3. *Open questions and associated meanings.*—One challenge to the comparability of similar sounding items cross-culturally is that the cultural meaning of an item may be quite different from one society to another. This makes the use of open questions without rigidly fixed response categories somewhat more attractive than they might be in single-culture research. The openness of the responses provides the researcher with a body of material out of which one can more easily locate lack of equivalence than one can in the response to a fixed choice question. The open responses more easily reveal linguistic differences than fixed responses, and by reading responses one can gain (or lose) confidence that the question was about the same subject. To return to our example of contacting the government: We asked not only a set of questions about contacts on several governmental levels—whether the respondent had ever contacted a governmental official on some problem—but also what position was held by the official, and what was the subject matter (the problem) of the contact. Thus, for each contact, we have not merely an affirmative answer that a contact was made, but a richly textured set of responses describing the details of the contact. The latter material is useful for two purposes. It increases our confidence that the contacts mentioned in fact took place and that we are recording more than a random selection among fixed alternatives. (It is, however, less certain on this basis that the contacts *not* mentioned *did not* take place. But we also asked a follow-up question on reasons for not contacting, the answers to which give us some sense of the extent to which those who report no contacts did, indeed, not contact.) And the open material about the contacts tells us something of the extent to which these acts are indeed equivalent across countries as we expect them to be—that is, that they are used in relation to certain types of problems and in relation to certain kinds of gratifications. The types of problems mentioned are the personally defined salient problems for which we hypothesized contacts to be useful. The

15. Further specification will be given in forthcoming publications of the research program.

answers are detailed and clear, indicating that the respondent is talking probably about real events, not some imagined political involvement, and that the events are of a similar type. Thus, the third answer as to the comparability of our results on contacting (the first answer being an *a priori* assumption of functional equivalence in our model of participation and the second the fact that the items cluster similarly) derives from the open-ended material surrounding the answers that, on the face of it, suggests that we are measuring a real phenomenon and a similar one in the two countries.

The need to embed cross-national survey research in different cultural contexts may lead to alternative decisions in the design of survey instruments from those that might be made for within-nation analysis. For instance, for survey answers to be equivalent the frame of reference of the various respondents must be the same. "Bad" survey questions are those that allow for more than one frame of reference (one respondent answers a question about "interest in politics" with reference to a current election, another with reference to politics in general; one respondent thinks of politics as referring only to domestic politics, another includes international politics). In cross-national survey work, the differences in culture and social structure mean that for many types of questions the frame of reference of the respondent will be unknown and may vary systematically from society to society. Under these circumstances, it may be difficult, if not impossible, for the researcher to be sure that the frame of reference is the same for different respondents.

One solution to this problem is to attempt to define the frame of reference as precisely as possible, which is simply to say that the questions should be precise and unambiguous. An alternative technique, often useful in cross-national research where the possible frames of reference are uncertain, would be to allow the respondent to set his own. In exploratory research, as most cross-national research must be, this is a particularly useful way to avoid placing the respondent into categories designed by social scientists that do violence to the respondent's beliefs. Allowing the respondent to set his own frame of reference may involve a two-stage process: The respondent makes clear his frame of reference and then is questioned further. An example of this is Hadley Cantril's cross-national study of the "pattern of human concerns." Cantril is interested, among other things, in the extent to which people perceive improvement in their lives. But there are many ways in which one can improve one's life, and a major improvement for one person might be quite minor for another. To measure the perception of improvement, Cantril first has each respondent set his own frame of reference—by telling what he considers the best and worst of all possible worlds. He then places himself on a scale that runs from his self-defined worst world to his self-defined best world—the scale being "self-anchored" by his own definitions of these two situations.[16]

Our work on participation involved a similar type of problem. We were interested in the extent to which individuals hold the government responsible for the solution of the major problems facing themselves or facing their communities. This was related to several concerns: measuring the "load" on the government in terms of the range and number of problems for which it was held responsible; studying the extent to which different types of problems are considered the responsibility of the government among different people or in different social settings, and so forth. The problem, though, was in the delineation of problems: We could present the respondent with a set of problems and ask if the government or the individual were responsible for solving them. The danger here is that the problems may not be those that are important or salient to the individual respondent. Our alternative approach was to ask respondents what problems *they* considered most important—first for their families and then for their communities. In relation to these problems, we then asked questions about responsibilities for solution. There are disadvantages to this approach, of course. Complicated problems of analysis are introduced by the fact that the questions on responsibility for problem solution follow upon a vast array of individually chosen problems. But we are at least following up something of interest to the respondent.

The above discussion is related to a point made by Smelser on the need for a combination of objective and subjective definitions of terms in comparative research.[17] Measures are embedded in different cultural contexts. Thus, it may be useful and necessary to measure not only the attributes of individuals, but the subjective meaning of these attributes. And one of the advantages of survey research—unlike many other research techniques—is that it can be used to measure both subjective and objective aspects of action or social structure. An example was given above in relation to functional equivalents: the simultaneous measurement of both the objective occupational position held by individuals and such subjective aspects as the prestige rating assigned that position by the respondent. Or consider measures of political activity—votes, campaign participation, or demands sent to political elites. These have, as suggested earlier, different

16. H. Cantril, *The Pattern of Human Concerns* (New Brunswick: Rutgers University Press, 1965); H. Cantril, "A Study of Aspirations," *Scientific American*, 208 (1963): 41; and H. Cantril and L. A. Free, "Hopes and Fears for Self and Country," *American Behavioral Scientist*, 6 Suppl. (October 1962).

17. See N. J. Smelser, "Notes on the Methodology of Comparative Analysis of Economic Activity," *Social Science Information*, 6 (1967).

implications in different political systems. One way both to assess and improve the comparability of measures of such activities would be to tap at
the same time the interpretations of the meaning of these activities by those
engaged in them. We know the rate of voting in various societies, and we
can estimate the objective impact of the vote in terms of its effect on electoral outcome. But we can also gather information on the meaning of
elections to those who engage in them, both voters and political elites. The
discovery of similarities or differences across populations in the meaning
of the vote would help us to evaluate the extent to which such acts can be
considered equivalent measures in different populations. In *The Civic Culture,* for instance, Almond and I report significant differences across the five
countries in the "meaning" of the vote—in the sense of reported feelings
about voting—to citizens.[18]

One way of dealing with possible alternative meanings of the same
act is to consider the other attitudes or orientations that accompany the act.
In our comparative work on participation, we have tried to enrich the comparative description of participation by adding information on what might
be called the "quality" of the participation. All acts of voting or all campaign activities are not the same. Some are accompanied by high levels of
information and some are not; some are accompanied by a general concern
with political and social matters and others are not. In comparing the distributions of political activities we attempt to distinguish between similar
acts in terms of the political orientations—information, involvement, and
so on—that accompany them. This is particularly interesting in relation to
the alternative modes of participation mentioned above. Some political acts
tend more than others to be accompanied by high levels of information or
political involvement; for other acts one finds a weaker relationship between
information or involvement and the activity and, therefore, more activists
who are uninformed or uninvolved in politics. By comparing the "quality"
of different political acts across the nations we shall be able to estimate the
extent to which similar acts are indeed equivalent, or whether they appear
to represent in one country an act initiated by the individual out of his
concern with political matters, while in other contexts the same act has no
relationship to the general political interest of the individual.

We can illustrate this in Table 1. This table reports the associations
between the four modes of political activity and political involvement for
the United States and India—the latter being a scale measuring the subjective involvement of the individual in general political matters (how much

18. Almond and Verba, *op. cit.,* ch. 4.

he reports he is interested in local and national politics, how much he discusses these topics). The data reveal a clear difference between voting and the other political acts. In India, if we know whether or not an individual votes, we still know very little additional about the likelihood that he is involved in politics. On the other hand, if we know that he is active in some other way, we know a lot about the likelihood that he is subjectively involved in politics. To put it another way, 42 percent of our Indian sample can be considered "regular" voters, 33 percent of these voters report no involvement in politics, a percentage not much different from the 38 percent of the total population that is uninvolved. A much smaller proportion —9 percent—are active in campaign activity. But of that smaller group, only 9 percent report no political involvement. The comparison with the United States is interesting. In both countries the associations of involvement with the three non-voting activities is higher than is the association of involvement with voting. Indeed, for the three non-voting activities, the situation is roughly the same in the two countries—there is a fairly close association between involvement and the activity. In relation to voting, there is a similarity across the countries in that voting is less closely associated with involvement than is any of the three activities, but there is a substantial difference between the United States and India in the strength of association.

Table 1

Association Between Various Activities and Political Involvement,
India and the United States

Country	Activity			
	Voting	Campaign	Cooperative	Contact
United States	.32	.58	.47	.51 ($N=2549$)
India	.10	.49	.62	.58 ($N=2637$)

(The measure of association is gamma.)

These data, of course, call for further close consideration in terms of the causal patterns involved. But the descriptive point to be made does not depend on the causal analysis. In both countries the population active in voting is more representative of the population as a whole, in terms of political involvement, than is the population of those active in other ways; but this is much more the case in India where the degree of involvement has little or no association with likelihood of voting. Thus, when we consider the three non-voting acts we find that in both countries—because of the similar association between level of involvement and activity—the activists tend to be involved in politics to roughly the same degree. On the other hand, when it comes to voting, the activists in the United States differ more substantially from those in India in terms of their degree of involvement. Thus, 9 percent of Indian campaign activists and 6 percent of American campaign activists are uninvolved. But 33 percent of Indian voters contrasted with 15 percent of American voters are uninvolved.

This example is relevant to the general question of whether what we compare is indeed comparable. From the point of view of involvement, voting in India and the United States are not as similar as contacting, campaigning, or cooperative activity. And similar results could be presented if one were concerned with political information rather than political involvement. The data illustrate why simple descriptive comparisons across diverse countries in terms of rates of participation should take into account the differences in the association of various acts of participation with such subjective measures as political involvement, information, and partisanship, and not merely the differences in absolute frequencies of activity. It is just in relation to voting that the rates of participation across the two nations are most similar. On the other activities the rates differ more. But just where the absolute rates are similar, the "meaning" of the political act may be most different—as evidenced by the differing associations of the voting act with political involvement. Thus, for instance, Indians vote roughly as frequently as do Americans, but engage in the other three forms of activity much less frequently. But the associations between the other three forms of activity and subjective involvement are similar for both national groups, while in relation to voting the association between activity and involvement is greater for Americans than Indians. Thus, similar proportions of Indians and Americans vote, but the two voting populations differ substantially in their level of involvement and information. Different proportions of the two groups take part in other activities, but the activists in the two countries are quite similar in their levels of information and political involvement.

In sum, similar seeming items—political acts, positions in a status hierarchy, and the like—may not be equivalent across nations because they are given different subjective meanings by those involved. Survey research has the advantage of giving one access to these alternative subjective meanings. The linking of these subjective states to the objective items measured is both substantively interesting and methodologically useful in increasing the credibility of claims that we are comparing equivalent items—or in making clear how items lack equivalence.

ACHIEVING EQUIVALENCE THROUGH DATA ANALYSIS

Most critiques of comparative survey research deal with the validity of direct comparison across national borders of the response pattern to a particular question. We have given an example of such a comparison—that of the rates of contacting between the United States and India. Such comparisons may be more or less credible, depending on the type of question. But of all types of comparison, such direct comparisons are most prone to challenges to validity because of non-equivalence in language, interviewing situation, and the like. They are also most prone to lack of equivalence because one is comparing a single phenomenon out of its context.

However, the simple comparison of rates of activity or attitudes across societies, though it may have some descriptive interest, is the least interesting comparison from the point of view of social science. Much more interesting is the comparison of processes or of the pattern of relationship among variables. The greater substantive interest of such comparisons coincides with the greater methodological validity of such comparisons. Comparisons are made not of the response to any single question across societies, nor of the response rates to any set of questions, but of the pattern of relations among variables. This increases the credibility of comparisons by allowing comparisons that are contextually grounded and by allowing one to test the extent to which alternative explanations of differences based on methodological weaknesses in the research design are plausible. Thus, I shall argue, the very process of data analysis can be considered a "bootstrap" operation. In the process of examining the data from a substantive point of view, one can also increase the credibility of the results. Such an approach to increasing credibility of comparison has a particular advantage from the point of view of the scholar conducting secondary analysis of survey data. Where the scholar has no control over the data-gathering process, he can still exercise some "data quality control" over the results.

1. *Contextual Comparisons.*—Stein Rokkan has argued for the greater validity of what he calls "second-order" comparisons.[19] What is compared

19. H. C. J. Duijker and S. Rokkan, "Organizational Aspects of Cross-National Social Research," *Journal of Social Issues,* 10 (1964): 8–24; S. Rokkan, "The Comparative Study of Political Participation. Notes Toward a Perspective on Current Research," *in* A. Ranney, ed., *Essays on the Behavioral Study of Politics* (Urbana, Ill.: University of Illinois Press, 1962), pp. 47–90; and S. Rokkan and A. Campbell, "Norway and the United States," *International Social Science Journal,* (Special issue: "Citizen Participation in Political Life,") 12 (1960): 69–99.

is not the absolute frequency of, say, voting between two systems, nor even the absolute frequencies of voting within comparable subgroups in two systems. Rather, one compares systems in terms of the ways in which voting rates *differ* among subgroups within the several systems. Does voting turnout increase as one moves up the status hierarchy in all systems under study, or are there differences among systems in the relationship between class and voting turnout? Thus, the comparative question one asks is not whether Americans participate more actively in politics than Frenchmen; nor if American workers participate more actively than French workers, but how workers in each nation differ from other occupational groups.

There are several ways in which such comparisons of patterns of distribution place survey results in a more comparable contextual frame. From the point of view of the achievement of equivalence in measures, this type of comparison controls for many of the contextual differences discussed earlier. Thus, for instance, the frequency of a specific measure of participation is not directly compared among systems, but rather, participation rates for various groups are compared within individual systems—with the differences among groups forming the focus of cross-system comparison. The results are comparable even if the specific participation measures differ. Consider an example. In *The Civic Culture,* Almond and I found sharp differences, among the five nations studied, in the frequency with which respondents reported that they believed they could influence the government. But the interpretation of such a direct comparison of frequencies across systems is difficult. The differences may reflect differences in socialization practices or differences in governmental structure. On the other hand, the finding that, in each of the five systems studied, the sense of ability to influence the government varies in a similar way with educational level and social class represents a more validly comparable finding. The differences in governmental structure are, to a large extent, controlled by the fact the relationships between education and sense of political competence are made in the first instance within individual nations. Though there may be differences from system to system in the meaning of the measures we use to estimate the sense of competence to influence the government, the measures are roughly comparable. And their comparability is ensured because they are, in the first instance, related to other variables within the system. We can, thus, conclude with some certainty that education has a similar relationship to this attitude in each of the nations studied.[20]

20. G. A. Almond and S. Verba, *op. cit.,* chs. 7, 9, and 13. See also A. Inkeles, "Industrial Man: The Relation of Status to Experience, Perception, and Value," *American Journal of Sociology,* 66 (July 1960): 1–31.

This kind of comparative analysis also simplifies the problem of finding equivalent social categories for cross-national comparison. As pointed out above, demographic measures may have different meanings because of their different contexts. If we concentrate upon second order comparisons, much of this problem fades. It is difficult to determine whether a university education in Burma is equivalent to a university education in Germany, but we are quite sure that a university education in each of these systems represents a higher level of education than does secondary education in each system. Though it is difficult to find equivalent absolute measures of social class or education in different political contexts, it is quite easy to find ordinal measures such that we can be sure that within each individual system we have people who are arrayed on similar hierarchies. And for second order comparisons, this is all that is needed.[21]

Let us return to our "contacting" example. Table 2 reports the data on the relationship between contacting and education in India and the United States. The results provide a striking similarity between the two countries. Whether or not contacting represents an identical type of activity in the two countries and whether or not equivalent levels of education are obtainable in the two countries, there is clearly a strong positive relationship between education and contacting in each country.

Table 2

Proportion "Contacting" by Level of Education,
India and United States

India			
Total	No Education	Some Primary	Above Primary
18%	11%	29%	46%
(2637)	(1354)	(592)	(680)

United States				
Total	Less Than 9 Years	Some High School	High School Graduate	Some College
30%	20%	25%	32%	47%
(2549)	(682)	(529)	(722)	(564)

(Numbers in parentheses are base on which percentage was calculated.)

21. In some cases, however, even an assumption of similar ordinality may not be warranted. The status hierarchy of occupations, for instance, may differ.

Furthermore, it appears that the difference in rate of contacting between the samples in the two countries is a function of the difference in the educational levels of the two samples, not a "cultural" difference. Indeed, at comparable educational levels, Indians contact more frequently. Furthermore, the credibility of this uniform relationship between education and contacting across the two nations is increased by the finding that education does not always have a strong and positive relationship to activity. In relation to the vote, for instance, we find that there is no relationship between education and voting in India and a weaker relationship between voting and education in the United States than between contact and education. (We shall return in a moment to indicate why this type of finding increases the credibility of the former finding.)

The substance of the argument in relation to education and modes of political participation is not of prime concern for this paper. What is important is the example of the way in which the mode of analysis of the survey material can both increase the comparability of the survey findings and relate the survey material to attributes of the system. Before comparisons are made, the particular variables are related to other aspects of the social context; political participation is placed in the context of the local educational system before one attempts to compare modes or rates of participation. In this way one increases the comparability of the measures by embedding them in their context as part of the process of comparison.

It is, of course, a bit presumptuous to consider the bivariate comparison described above as a solution to the contextual problem. To relate modes of political activity to level of education is not to put the political activity variable very deeply into the context. The social context is much more complicated than the single variable of levels of education. But it is a beginning, and one can go further. Comparisons across nations can be made after a two-step internal patterning of relationships. Is the relationship between education and political participation stronger in more industrialized segments of society than in less? Stronger among men than among women? And is the pattern the same in different nations? Recent work has illustrated the value of subnational comparisons among regions.[22] The next stage would be to compare the patterning of regional differences among nations. Or, to refer back to an earlier example, if one adds to the analysis information about the community context of the individual, one can test rather elaborate hypotheses about the interrelationship between individual and community characteristics in affecting political behavior. In this way

22. Linz and de Miguel, "Within Nation Differences and Comparisons," pp. 267–320 *in* Merritt and Rokkan, eds., *op. cit.*

comparison is not made until relatively elaborate internal analyses have taken place within each relevant political unit—in this case the nation-state.

The developing techniques of multivariate analysis—in particular the various modes of causal modelling—are particularly relevant here. What may be most interesting to compare are the complex causal paths by which individuals come to participate in politics. Preliminary analysis of our participation data suggests that the "path" to participation differs in relation to different acts and for different national groups and subgroups within nations. That is, from the statistical point of view, the path model that best fits the data for one group or kind of activity (say the voting behavior of Americans) is quite different from the path model that fits the data for some other kind of group or activity (say voting for Indians). From the substantive point of view, this suggests that the process of political mobilization—that process that brings the individual to participate—may differ from nation to nation or among groups within nations.[23]

My purpose is not to expound the substance of this argument here. Rather, the point is that the comparison of complex patterns of relations among variables—of causal paths—may reduce some of the dangers of bias in the comparison of the responses to individual questions. One is comparing across nations within context—that is, the complex intertwinings of measures within societies are the bases of comparison. The various methodological inequivalences that can affect individual measures are less likely to affect such patternings.

On the other hand, one cannot always be sure that the rosy picture painted in the last paragraph is accurate. It is possible that cumulative systematic bias might be built into these comparisons, leading to even greater distortion. This possibility cannot be completely eliminated. But let us turn in the next section to the ways in which internal analyses of the data can be directly applied to the question of the credibility of the findings one has—and particularly to some questions of systematic bias.

2. *Eliminating Plausible Alternative Hypotheses.*—Donald T. Campbell has pointed out that in comparative research one can always suggest plausible alternative hypotheses to the ones offered by the researcher. To prevent this would require a full experimental design.[24] He has suggested the tactic of the gradual elimination of plausible rival hypotheses. In this section I would like to apply this tactic, not to the substantive hypotheses that might be used to explain patterning in the data, but in relation to the

---

23. See Sidney Verba, Bashir Ahmed, and Anil Bhatt, *Blacks and Harijans: A Comparative Study of the Political Behavior of Two Deprived Groups,* forthcoming, for examples of such analyses.
24. See the references in note 2, above.

variety of alternative methodological hypotheses that could be offered to explain a particular finding or pattern of findings.

Let us return to the finding we have been using as an illustration in the present paper—the finding that 18 percent of our Indian respondents report contacting the government in comparison with 30 percent of those in the United States. We are, to repeat, not interested in explaining why that is the case (data in Table 2 suggest it is perhaps a function of the different levels of educational development in the two countries), but simply in examining the credibility of that comparison. Thus far we have argued for the credibility of that comparison in terms of the interrelationship among several contacting measures and because the questions are followed up by open questions that give us some ability to compare the meanings of the contact questions across the two populations.

But such findings are always subject to alternative explanations based on differences in the stimulus presented to the respondent—the most obvious being that the interviews were in different languages. But others involving different interviewer-respondent relations, different attitudes toward interviewing in the two societies, and other factors would also challenge the validity of the findings. As pointed out above, it would never be possible to answer all such challenges, because plausible additional ones could always be raised. And furthermore, data may not be available to test the plausibility of all alternatives. But it may often be possible to test some.

An example would be the linguistic hypothesis to explain the difference in the reported contacting rate in the United States and India. Perhaps in English the question seems to connote a less threatening mode of activity. But in this case we can take advantage of the further complexity of our study within India. Our study in India was conducted in a variety of languages. This methodological complexity within India is also the opportunity for testing the plausible alternative hypothesis of linguistic distortion. Table 3 reports the proportions who report contacting the government in four language areas represented by the states we studied. As can be seen, a similar proportion report contacting in each state. If there is some linguistic distortion that depresses the contacting rate in India, it would have to be one that runs across four different language areas.[25]

We do not have parallel data within the United States since all our interviewing was in English. But it is interesting to compare the rates of contacting across regions of the United States (also in Table 3). The range of variation is quite similar to the range across the Indian states. That is,

25. The states are not completely coterminous with language areas. But they represent a good approximation, the bulk of interviews in the areas being in languages which differ from state to state.

Table 3

Proportions Reporting Contacting in Four Indian States
and Four United States Regions

India				
Total	Andhra Pradesh	Gujarat	Uttar Pradesh	West Bengal
19% (2637)	18% (538)	19% (512)	19% (1078)	19% (509)

United States				
Total	Northeast	South	North Central	West
30% (2549)	30% (612)	27% (800)	33% (711)	34% (421)

(Numbers in parentheses are base on which percentage was calculated.)

the proportions contacting in each of the regions of the United States is much closer to the mean for the nation as a whole than it is to the figures for any of the Indian states.

Other plausible hypotheses as to the source of the difference in rate might conceivably be tested in a similar manner. One hypothesis might be that interviewing in India is not equivalent to that in the United States because of the reluctance of Indian respondents to communicate information about their political attitudes or behavior across caste lines—and many interviews are conducted by interviewers of one caste interviewing respondents of another. Such an hypothesis is testable if one has data on the caste affiliations of interviewer and respondent. One can use the comparison of within-caste and cross-caste interviews to locate those items of information that are more or less sensitive to such interviewer effects.[26]

To repeat, the above testing of alternative hypotheses is not yet an explanation of the differences between the two countries. If the differences disappear, it suggests that the alternative methodological hypothesis may explain the difference. If not, it does not mean that the difference is now explained as a result of "Indian culture versus American culture." Such explanations are indeed not explanations at all. Rather, the results of the

26. Raoul Naroll's *Data Quality Control* (New York: Free Press, 1962) is relevant here and contains a number of suggestions relevant to this type of problem.

elimination of a plausible alternative hypothesis simply increases one's confidence that one has a "real" phenomenon, not a by-product of the research method. At that point one can begin to explain the difference, using probably the same logic, but testing alternative substantive hypotheses. Furthermore, in testing substantive hypotheses, the procedure of increasing confidence in these hypotheses by eliminating rival methodological ones can be continued.

Let us continue with an example related to rates of contacting. In our research we have been concerned with the role of political parties in the political mobilization of the citizenry. Parties are often mentioned as the instrumentalities that mobilize citizens to political involvement and that provide channels for citizen participation. In relation to this we have been concerned with the extent to which partisan affiliation is a key variable leading one to participate. We have also been concerned with the extent of the influence of partisanship—that is, is partisanship related to all modes of participation, only to those closely associated with the electoral process, or is partisanship unrelated to any types of activity? Our hypothesis is that that the "reach" of partisanship would be greater in India than in the United States, that in the United States partisanship would be related to electoral activity, but that other activities such as cooperative activity or contacting would be relatively non-partisan. In India, on the other hand, partisanship would permeate all modes of political activity.

We can begin our consideration with Figure 1. That figure compares India with the United States in terms of the relationship between intensity of party affiliation and frequency of contacting the government. On the horizontal axis is a measure of intensity of party identification—does the respondent identify with a party and if so, does he do so strongly or relatively mildly? [27] The vertical axis shows the frequency of reported contacts among those with various intensities of party affiliations. The data in Figure 1 support our hypothesis as to the different role of partisanship in the two countries insofar as it relates to contacting government officials. In India, there is a clear relationship between intensity of party affiliation and likelihood of the reporting subject having contacted the government. In the United States there is little relationship, or, if anything, those with strong party affiliation are less likely to contact the government. The relationship, furthermore, is not reduced when one controls for education and other such variables. In the United States, no matter what the educational level, the partisan is no more likely to contact than the non-partisan. In India, no

27. For a fuller description of these measures see Verba and Nie, op. cit., and Verba, Ahmed, and Bhatt, op. cit.

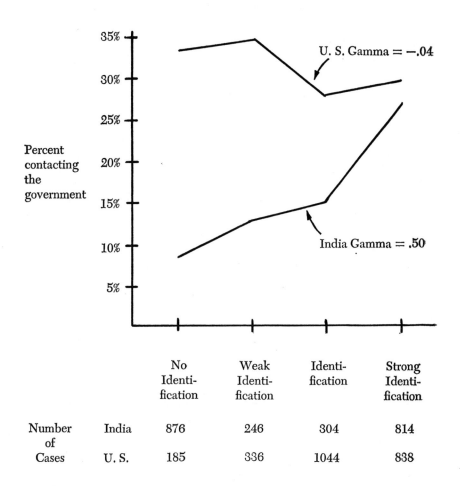

Figure 1
Percent Reporting Contacting the Government by Degree
of Party Identification: India and United States

matter what the level of education, the partisan is more likely to contact.[28]

Again, we are not interested in the substantive meaning of this difference in relationship between partisanship and contacting, but simply in the question of whether the difference is believable. Might such a difference be due to methodological difficulties? The number of alternative hypotheses that could be suggested to explain either the relationship within India or the lack of one within the United States is vast. Figure 2 presents a simplified schema for several types of errors that could challenge the validity of the relationship. Errors can be either random or systematic, and they can be specific to a particular question, or they can be found across a number of (or all) variables:

(a) Random error in relation to a particular variable would involve cases where characteristics of a particular variable were such that there was a large amount of random error introduced. A particular question may be difficult to understand, leading respondents to choose answers at random; they may guess on yes-no or other fixed alternative information items; interviewers may miss a particular question and fill in the information later at random, and so forth.

(b) Systematic error within a particular item: These are cases in which the indicator is measuring something else over and above that which the researcher thinks it is measuring. And the additional dimension skews the results in some unanticipated and unrecognized way. A question may be perceived as embarrassing or dangerous to answer in a particular way; a particular word in one language may have additional connotations that affect the responses; respondents may believe a particular answer is the proper one to give; and so forth.

(c) Random error across a large number or all items would exist if respondents did not understand many questions and were just choosing answers from fixed alternatives at random, or if there was a lot of interviewer cheating, or random key-punch errors, and the like.

(d) Systematic error across a large number of items would exist when there was systematic respondent error—a systematic "courtesy bias" leading the respondent to choose answers he expects the interviewer to want; systematic "yea-saying"; systematic exaggeration of certain attributes such as status and activity.

---

28. Since contacting in both countries is closely related to education, whereas partisanship is more closely related to education in India than the United States, there was some possibility that the difference in the patterns between the countries might simply reflect these alternative relations between partisanship and contacting on the one hand and education on the other. But this does not appear to be the case. The partial relationship of contacting and partisanship is zero in India, positive and significant in the United States. See Verba, Ahmed, and Bhatt, *op. cit.*

	Question Specific	General Across Questions
Random	a. Specific questions difficult and not understood.	c. Interview in general not understood. Interviewer cheating. Keypunch errors.
Systematic	b. Specific question asked in such a way that answers skewed in unanticipated ways: embarrassing questions, questions with unexpected and unrecognized connotations.	d. Various kinds of systematic respondent errors: "courtesy bias"; "yea-saying"; exaggeration of activity; systematic understatement.

Figure 2
Some Types of Errors

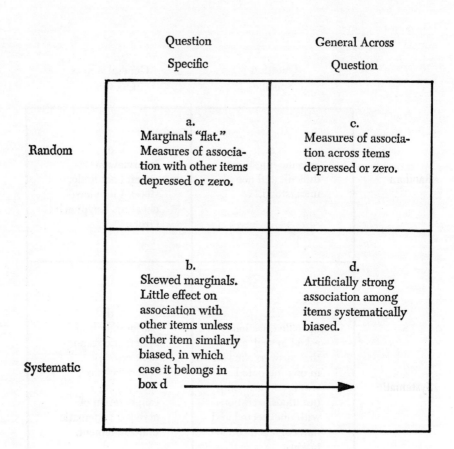

Figure 3
Consequences of the Types of Error

These alternative error forms underlie the alternative hypotheses that can be offered. Any difference between the results of a particular question in one nation and another can be explained in terms of systematic bias in one country; a difference in relations among variables in two countries can be explained by the working of random error or systematic error in one or both countries or random error in one and systematic error in the other. A summary of the consequences of each type of error in terms of the "shape" of the data is contained in Figure 3.

Since we can never be certain that our procedures are the same in two different cultures—indeed, we can always be certain that they are not the same—comparative findings can always be challenged. And any finding can be challenged. Thus, to return to the data in Figure 1, one could argue that the difference in the relationships between partisanship and contacting in the United States and India is due to:

(*a*) Question-specific error of a random sort depressing the relationship between partisanship and contact in the United States. Perhaps for some reason questions about party affiliation were often omitted (due to questionnaire format), and interviewers or key-punchers merely made up answers. (This is not terribly plausible on the face of it. The following errors are more so.) Thus, if partisanship had been more competently measured one would find a similar relationship to that in India.

(*b*) Systematic bias in one of the questions in India creating a relationship between the two variables where one does not really exist. Perhaps partisanship in India is really measuring level of support for the government in power, and the relationship one is observing is really between supportiveness of the government and contacting. If one had used a "support of government" measure in the United States, one would have found the same relationship. Or perhaps active Indians perceive the interviewers as representatives of the local dominant political party, and therefore contactors are more likely to report party affiliation because they believe that is what the interviewers want to hear. And so forth, and so forth.

(*c*) Or the absence of a relationship in the United States could be explained by a general randomness in the data—resulting from large amounts of random error somewhere in the research process: random responses by respondents, cheating by interviewers, key-punch errors, and so on. If not for this, one would have found a close relationship as in India.

(*d*) Or the stronger relationship in India could be explained by a general response set in the Indian interviews. A large proportion of the respondents might be trying to impress the interviewer with their activity level and political sophistication, and therefore report affiliation and contact. Perhaps the Indian sample is really divided into two groups: nervous and deferential peasants who deny everything (they say they never contact and they say they have no party attachment) and showy sophisticates (who attempt to impress the interviewer with their level of involvement and activity). Such a distribution (plus a few intermediary groups) would easily explain the data on Figure 1 for India.

How might one deal with this kind of plausible alternative hypothesis? The main technique is to see what they would predict for other relations within the data and then test these against the data. Table 4 provides some data for these tests. It contains the measure of association between partisanship and the four types of activity—contacting, cooperative activity, campaign activity, and voting—as well as the measures of association between these four types of acts and two other political orientations—a measure of

Table 4

Measures of Association Between Various Orientations and Activities:
India and the United States

Association	India	United States
Association between partisanship and:		
Voting	.31	.25
Campaign activity	.49	.16
Cooperative activity	.48	.02
Contacting	.50	−.04
Association between involvement and:		
Voting	.10	.32
Campaign activity	.49	.58
Cooperative activity	.62	.47
Contacting	.58	.51
Association between information and:		
Voting	.13	.50
Campaign activity	.54	.37
Cooperative activity	.55	.38
Contacting	.58	.44

(Measure of association is gamma. Measures of association less sensitive to marginal distribution—such as Somers' D—produce the same pattern.)

general involvement in politics and a measure of political information. The original relationship, illustrated on Figure 1—positive between partisanship and contacting in India, zero in the U.S.—is shown in bold-face numbers.

Consider the alternative hypotheses:

1. *The Hypothesis of Randomness in the United States Data.*—If there was a high degree of randomness on either the contacting or the partisanship question it would lead to a prediction that the relationship between those measures and other measures would tend to be zero. But we see that contacting is closely related to political involvement and information (gammas of .51 and .44 respectively in contrast with the −.04 for partisanship and contacting). Certainly contacting is closely related to other political orientations (with which one would expect it to be closely related). Conversely, partisanship has a positive (though weaker than those illustrated above) relationship with voting and campaign activity (.25 and .16 compared with the −.04 for contacting). (The fact that it is not related to cooperative activity, while being related to the two modes of activity where one would expect such a relationship, does reinforce our substantive interpretation that there is a wider range for non-partisan activity in the United States than in India. Where party plays a role in political activity it plays a weaker role than in India; and for some activities it plays no role.)

2. The argument against randomness in one of the items in the United States data also applies against an hypothesis of *general randomness in the data.* Furthermore, an inspection of column two of Table 4 would lead one to reject the hypothesis of general randomness. Indeed, the strong association of contacting and cooperative activity with involvement and information lends weight to the absence of relationship between those activities and partisanship.

3. The hypothesis of response set in India requires the opposite argument to refute it. The strong association between partisanship and contact is matched by associations between partisanship and the other political acts. This indeed could be evidence for response set or some other methodological problem. But if we consider the variables of involvement and information we find a more differentiated pattern. Voting has little association with involvement and information. It would be hard to imagine a general response set hypothesis that would explain these two deviations. Furthermore, and this is important, there are good reasons, given what we know from our data and other studies about voting in India, to expect the deviations from the high pattern of associations to come just in these relationships between voting on the one hand and involvement and information on the other. Indeed, if one controls for educational level, the associations between involvement and information, on the one hand, and the three non-

voting modes of activity, on the other, remain as strong, but the associations between voting and involvement and information become zero.

4. It is hardest of all to deal with counter-hypotheses that argue for a systematic bias in a single item—or different biases in different items. They can predict any pattern of relations. But the overall pattern of relationships in Table 4 becomes a partial refutation of such alternative explanations— the more so the more the pattern of relations is itself plausible. Thus the pattern of relations between partisanship and activity in the United States whereby the positive relations are with those modes of activity for which partisanship might be expected to be most relevant makes alternative hypotheses of a methodological sort less compelling. And similarly in India, the lack of association between voting and the involvement and information on measures lends weight to the other findings.

One could go on. The same logic could be used to deal with more specific alternative hypotheses. If one wanted to test out the alternative hypothesis that partisanship really measures another dimension in India —support for the current system, for instance—one might further refine the measure of partisanship by taking into account the specific party involved, distinguishing between support for Congress and other parties or distinguishing between support for the locally dominant party and support for other parties. Note that this is not as clear-cut an example of the test of an alternative methodological hypothesis. Unlike the situation in relation to language or response set, we are not merely trying to eliminate alternative explanations based on assumed weaknesses in the research design. We are in this case dealing with a substantive problem of the interpretation of the findings in India—which is, in turn, related to the comparative problem of the meaning of the difference between the United States and India. Indeed, the line between the plausible alternative substantive hypothesis and the plausible alternative methodological hypothesis is by no means clear, and the logic by which one deals with either is the same. The major difference is in the conclusion to be drawn from the testing of the hypothesis. If it is a methodological one that one is testing, the failure to disconfirm the alternative hypothesis may lead one to conclude that one has no "finding"—that the pattern of results is but a by-product of the research design—whereas a disconfirmation of the alternative hypothesis gives one greater confidence that one has a real phenomenon. If it is a substantive hypothesis that one is testing, confirmation or disconfirmation increases one's understanding of the relationship among variables without destroying one's confidence in the findings. And in a comparative context, it informs the comparison. If one were to find that party affiliation had a different substantive meaning in the United States and India, one would not have shown that the difference between the two countries in the relationship between partisanship and activity was meaningless; rather, one would understand the meaning of that difference more fully.

In sum, the analysis of survey data corroborates the believability of comparative survey results in the following manner:

1. Second-order comparisons or higher-order comparisons that compare the relationship among variables rather than absolute values in terms of a single variable increase the comparability of the data because they depend on the ordinal nature of the variables and not upon absolute equivalence.

2. Analysis allows the direct testing of alternative methodological hypotheses, the rejection of which increases the credibility of the data.

3. The comparison of patterns of relationships increase one's confidence in any part of the comparison. The differing role of partisanship between the United States and India is more convincing when one sees it as part of a more general pattern of the relationship among various orientations and various acts, as in Table 4. Indeed, Table 4 is but a beginning. Causal modelling applied to the problem indicates that the processes of political mobilization in India are somewhat different from those in the United States, and are particularly different in relation to voting and in the role of partisanship. The analysis of these data is far from complete but the comparison of the alternative role of partisanship in a multivariate analysis of the paths to participation gives one greater confidence that one is dealing with something comparable.[29]

4. And, it should be repeated, this is a bootstrap operation: The comparative analysis of the data across societies not only gives us the ordinary benefits of such analyses—a deeper understanding of the social processes in which we are interested—it also firms up our conviction that we are, indeed, dealing with comparable phenomena and not by-products of our research design.

Thus far we have suggested two broad ways in which comparative survey research can be made more comparable and more closely related to the context out of which the research grows. In relation to both approaches —selecting items for measurement that are more embedded in their context, and analyzing the data within context before comparing across nations —there was a happy coincidence between two goals. As we increase the degree to which we compare variables or relations among variables that are embedded in a context, we increase the credibility of our findings as well as their substantive interest.

29. See Verba, Ahmed, and Bhatt, *op cit.*

Most of the examples thus far, however, do not represent research designs or analyses different from those of ordinary survey research; we are essentially concerned with the relations among characteristics of individuals. We were led to comparative survey research by a concern with larger collectivities—nations or societies or other political entities—as the object of study. The analyses described above differ from standard single-nation survey analyses in one important respect that makes them more relevant for that kind of concern. Though the major data analysis is on the individual level—what are the correlates of or the causal paths to political activity? for instance—the analyses take place in different social systems. Thus we can ask whether the same process of political mobilization takes place in various countries—that is, whether variables relate to each other in the same way in different settings. This inevitably tells us something about the larger social unit. More specifically, it tells us of the boundary conditions for our individual level generalizations: Do they hold in all societies or only some? And if we can then begin to specify what is the nature of the boundary conditions that make one process of politicization take place in one country while a different process seems to take place in other countries, we will have learned much about the impact of social structure on political behavior. If the process by which Indians come to vote is different from that in the United States—as our data suggest—is this because of the different party structure, the different level of affluence, or what? No easy answer is possible, but comparison among a number of nations (and parallel comparisons among units within a nation) can increase our confidence in one explanation rather than another.

To see the potentialities of that type of analysis, let us turn to another set of research strategies relevant to increasing the comparability and contextual grounding of our data: strategies that build structure into the research design.

CONTEXTUAL SURVEY DESIGN

Traditional survey research has been conducted and analyzed on a "one-man one-vote" basis. The individual is the unit of analysis and he is selected as an individual in such a way as to obtain a representative sample of the entire population. Such an approach completely—and, indeed, deliberately—avoids assumptions about the internal structure of the social unit from which the sample is drawn. But internal structure can be taken into account. Two approaches may be suggested: movement beyond the simple random sample in order to consider social structure, and movement beyond the individual as the unit to be sampled.

1. *Weighted samples.*—Within the framework of the one-man one-vote

approach of random sampling, the preferences of the members of a collectivity or their political behavior is assumed to be the simple sum of the preferences of a random sample. This may conform to populistic ideology, but if one is concerned with a macro-political problem such as the impact on government policy of these patterns of preference or behavior, it is a highly inadequate perspective.[30] The sum of policy preferences of individuals tells us little unless we know something about the stratification of the population in terms of intensity and stability of preference. Erwin Scheuch has labeled the attempt to derive characteristics of a political system from the simple sum of the responses from a sample of individuals the "individualistic fallacy."[31] In contrast with the "ecological fallacy" which involves statements about patterns of individual behavior on the basis of measurements on the level of social units, the individualistic fallacy involves statements about a social unit on the basis of measurements based on individuals. Scheuch rightly points out that one cannot infer the extent of "democracy" in a nation on the basis of the proportion of respondents who give "democratic" answers to opinion questions. The political structure and the way in which it channels these responses will mediate between the response pattern and the way in which political decisions are made. Much evidence exists, for instance, to suggest that a system of civil liberties is not incompatible with the rejection of such liberties by majorities interviewed in cross-section population samples. The reason is that those who have anti-libertarian beliefs are also those least likely to act on their beliefs. On the other hand, those in more elite positions tend to have more libertarian outlooks.[32] What is needed thus are composition laws that incorporate assumptions about the social structure when one sums survey responses.

If we want to estimate the consequences of various patterns of preference in the mass public, we would want to know about the resources (wealth, information, access) available to different preference groups. Or

30. P. E. Converse, "New Dimensions of Meaning for Cross-Section Sample Surveys in Politics," *International Social Science Journal*, 16 (1964): 19–34; S. Rokkan, "The Use of Sample Surveys in Comparative Research," (Introduction to a special issue on "Data in Comparative Research"), *International Social Science Journal*, 16 (1964): 7–18; and E. K. Scheuch, "The Cross-Cultural Use of Sample Surveys: Problems of Comparability," pp. 176–209 *in* S. Rokkan, ed., *Comparative Research Across Cultures and Nations* (Paris, The Hague: Mouton, 1968). On the general subject, see also Wilhelm Hennis, *Meinungsforschung und reprasentativ Demokratie* (Tübingen: Mohr, 1957), and Robert A. Dahl, *A Preface to Democratic Theory* (Chicago: University of Chicago Press, 1956).

31. E. K. Scheuch, *op. cit.*

32. S. Stouffer, *Communism, Conformity and Civil Liberties* (Garden City: Doubleday, 1955); J. Prothro and C. Grigg, "Fundamental Principles of Democracy: Bases of Agreement and Disagreement," *Journal of Politics*, 22 (May 1960): 276–294; and H. McClosky, "Consensus and Ideology in American Politics," *American Political Science Review*, 58 (June 1964): pp. 361–382.

we might want to know how active different preference groups are. In other words, if one wants to use survey results based on a sample of individuals to make some interesting statements about the collectivity from which they are selected, one will have to make some assumptions as to how best to sum the characteristics of the individual respondents. What assumptions one wants to build into the summation process, of course, depend on the particular problem in which one is interested. Consider two examples:

(1) Much survey research is aimed at describing the policy preferences of a population on some burning issue of the day. The purpose of such research—a type usually carried on outside of academic auspices—is often to inform the public and the government of the state of public preferences on a particular issue. But the raw distribution of preferences conveys little information; one would want to consider the level of information of those with various preferences, the intensity of their beliefs, and so forth. Some weighting scheme that took these variables into account would give a better indication of the distribution of preferences. The use of filter questions to eliminate those who have not considered the problem or who have no information is one technique that has come into common use.

(2) If, on the other hand, one's concern were not with the mere distribution of preferences but with the likelihood that public preferences would affect the decisions of governing elites, one might want to weigh the preferences in terms of the likelihood that a preference will be converted into a demand on the government and in terms of the resources available to the preference holder to enforce his demand. The preference of an individual with a history of political activity who controlled such resources as money, access to influential people, skills, and the like would be weighted more heavily.

The weighting procedure can take place at one of two points: as part of a sample design or as part of the analysis of the survey results. At the sampling stage, one can increase the number of respondents from particularly relevant groups. If one is interested in political mobilization, one might oversample those most likely to have just been mobilized or more likely to become mobilized in the near future. Or, if one is interested in conflict and consensus among political groups within a nation, the sample might best be one drawn from the major conflicting groups, rather than from the population as an undifferentiated whole. The advantages of a sample design that reflects structural aspects is that it allows for more flexible data analysis. One is, for instance, more likely to have sufficient cases of the particular kinds of groups with which one is concerned.

The advantages and costs of such a sampling strategy are spelled out by Frank Bonilla and Jose A. Silva Michelena. Given the heterogeneity of Venezuela, the country they were studying, they note the unreality of a "poll plebiscite" as a guide to policy. The weight of diverse social groups in the process plainly had little relation to their numbers in the general population. A cross-section of the nation would not have yielded more than a few individuals in such key positions as parish priests, student or union leaders, university officials, or government officials. Increasing the sample size to ensure reaching enough such individuals for independent analysis, particularly if any attention was to be paid to within-group variations, would have pushed the number to be sampled far beyond the resources at hand or what seemed justifiable in view of the limited usefulness of the global figures.

> The selection of groups to be sampled was thus carried out with a number of priority development issues and an intuitive vision of the political structure in mind. The clear focus of policy makers on issues such as industrialization, agrarian reform, education, and community development in itself pointed to certain groups as indispensable to the survey.
> While this approach seems best suited to the aims of the study, it raised a great many difficulties that are not common to more conventional national surveys: Problems of field administration are multiplied by the need to deal with some three dozen independent sampling frames. . . . Cross-national checks or comparisons . . . become extremely difficult.[33]

One problem with this approach is that one may not know what assumptions to make about the structure of a population. In much research, one does not know the relevant distributions nor the implications of structural position. If the purpose of the research is to locate points of conflict within a society, one cannot design a sample around the conflicting groups. Under circumstances where empirical survey work is just beginning, an assumptionless random procedure may be preferable. But as data accumulate and as studies become more purposive and less exploratory, the argument for the simple random cross-section of the population may become less persuasive. And even at our present level of knowledge, we know enough about educational differences, rural-urban differences, and the like to justify violating principles of equal probability for all members of the population if the research problem warrants it. In many cases, the preferred strategy may be one of unbiased but weighted sampling.[34] In this way, the sample is weighted to reflect the assumed importance of each subgroup in relation to the research problem. If the research problem has to do with

33. F. Bonilla and S. Michelena, *Studying the Venezuelan Polity,* (Center of International Studies, MIT and Centro de Estudios del Desarrollo, Universidad Central de Venezuela, May 1966), pp. 8–9.

34. See P. Rossi, "Four Landmarks in Voting Research," pp. 5–54, in Eugene Burdick and Arthur J. Brodbeck, eds., *American Voting Behavior,* (Glencoe, Ill.: Free Press, 1959).

influence over the national government one can oversample those presumed to have more influence—such as those living in the capital, those with organizational affiliations, higher education, and the like. But others, not assumed to be in this favored position, are sampled as well. The latter allows one to check the assumptions built into the sample design.

In cases in which one has opted for the cross-section assumptionless strategy, it is still possible to build structural assumptions into the analysis stage. Here, a two-stage "bootstrap" procedure might be most appropriate. The data that are gathered can be used to test various assumptions about the nature of the political or social structure—one can test empirically whether or not particular subgroups are likely to attempt influence disproportionate to their numbers. These assumptions thus tested can then be built into the next analysis stage of the data, and into sample designs for further research.

An example of the difference between the characteristics one might find in a population where the summation of individual scores makes no assumptions about stratification patterns in the population, and the characistic one might find if one makes assumptions about stratification, is found in Figure 4. This figure compares, for the United States, the reported most salient problems that one finds in the population as a whole and in the more activist segments of the population. Let us assume that an observer—perhaps a governmental leader—wants to know what problems are most salient for the population in his society. One can imagine him using a variety of strategies to find out: One such strategy would be to conduct a random sample survey; another strategy would be to observe just the most visible parts of the population—that part that is active. Figure 4 is set up so that the width of the bars is proportional to the segment of the population it represents; the height represents the proportion reporting a particular problem as salient. As one moves from left to right, one is dealing with different "populations," the far left representing the most inactive 6 percent of the population on a general measure of participation; the center bar represents the entire population, activist and inactivist; and the far right bar represents that 3 percent of the population that is most active.[35] One can imagine an observer learning about public preferences by viewing these bars from the side without clear awareness of depth. Thus if participation mechanisms are at work and the leader observes only those messages brought to him by participants, while the inactives are ignored because not seen, he will see a different distribution of problems than would the leader who used the ran-

35. For an extended discussion of the problem and the measures used, as well as more examples, see Verba and Nie, *op. cit.*, ch. 8.

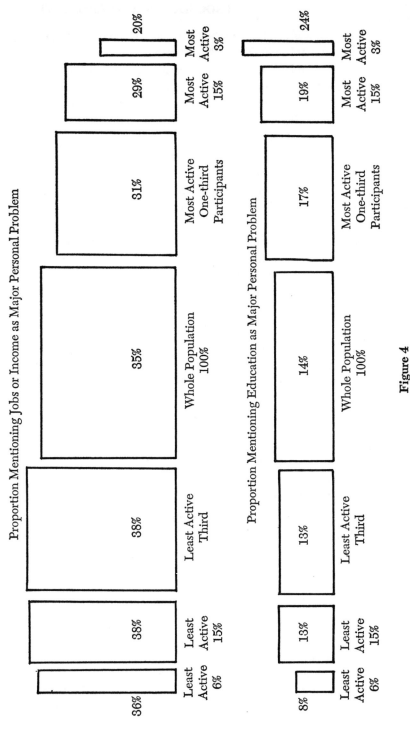

Figure 4

Types of Personal Problems Salient to Various Activist and Non-activist Populations, United States

dom technique. Thus if he observed the entire population (the wide bars in the center of Figure 4) he would find 35 percent interested in job or income as a major problem and 14 percent interested in education. If he observed the small, most activist group in the population, he would find 20 percent interested in jobs and income and 24 percent interested in education. In other words, the population as a whole may have a different preference distribution than the activist segment.

The point of this example is not to praise the random sample as a technique of obtaining information about the public in contrast with the strategy often used by leaders who observe the participant few. It is indeed quite unclear which is reality and which is distortion: Is reality the result of the random sample that represents the whole population but that also contains much information from those who care little about a particular issue, or is reality the result of voluntary participation, highly unrepresentative but containing only those who care enough to speak up? This is an issue for political theory. Here the point is merely that a summation of opinions that takes into account the rate of activity of the opinion holders gives a quite different picture from what one would obtain from an assumptionless random sample.

However, when we stratify the sample by degre of activity and report the responses contained in the far right columns of Figure 4, we are making the assumption that this population is more important because it has more impact on policy-making. This remains, however, an assumption. To go beyond this, one would have to study not only the individual respondents but those leaders whom we expect to be monitoring the opinions of the participants. Let us turn to those designs that make this feasible.

2. *Sampling units.*—Thus far we have discussed sample designs that reflect structural aspects of the social unit under study. Another approach would be to sample social units. If one samples units, one can, in principle at least, deal with them in the same way that one deals with individual respondents. Survey research becomes relevant for the macro-unit by being a survey of such units.

The difference between a sampling of social units and multi-contextual studies in which samples are drawn from a small number of political systems is that in the former the characteristics of the social unit may be systematically varied in order to study their interaction with individual characteristics. To take a concrete example: James A. Davis drew a sample of 172 groups containing 1,909 participants from groups in the University of Chicago's Great Books Program. Thus, he had a sample both of individuals and of groups. Propositions could be tested that related individual to group characteristics and vice versa. For instance, a good deal of the analysis focuses on what the author calls composition effects—i.e., the independent effect on an individual possessing certain characteristics of the proportion having that characteristic in his group. Thus, one studies not merely individual attitudes that are related to withdrawal from the group, but the effect of the culture of the group on withdrawal. Two individuals with the same *attitudes* toward their groups may differ in their *behavior*, depending on the attitudes of others in their respective groups.[36] It is clear that the study of composition effects is closely related to the subject of the aggregation of individual attitudes in terms of their systemic effects.

The use of a multiplicity of social units helps avoid the "individualistic fallacy" by developing rules as to the ways in which the relationship among individual attributes is affected by the context in which they exist. To take some examples: We may find in survey studies that hostility to the government is related to active involvement in revolutionary movements, or that level of need-achievement is related to involvement in entrepreneurial activity. But the study of composition effects would indicate the way in which the *rates* of hostile attitudes or need-achievement orientations affect activity. Thus, one might hypothesize that in a society in which many are hostile, hostility is more likely to lead to action, and even those not personally antagonistic toward the government may get caught up in revolutionary movements. In general, one can argue that the likelihood that an individual will act on the basis of a particular preference is related to the proportion of those around him who share that preference.[37] This argues for knowledge of individual preferences as well as knowledge of the distribution of preferences within the relevant social unit—be this small group, community, or nation. But this might not be sufficient to place the individual opinion in its context. Individual beliefs as to the distribution of preferences among others is also relevant. Though perceptions of what others prefer may be inaccurate, it may be more controlling over behavior than the actual distribution of preferences.[38]

36. J. Davis, *Great Books and Small Groups* (New York: Free Press of Glencoe, 1961), see ch. 1; see also P. M. Blau, "Structural Effects," *American Sociological Review*, 25 (April 1960): 178–193.

37. See B. Berelson and G. Steiner, *Human Behavior: An Inventory of Scientific Findings* (New York: Harcourt, Brace & World, 1964), p. 567.

38. An interesting example is found in some studies of Japanese attitudes on particularistic versus universalistic obligations. A large sample in Japan was asked how they would act if faced with the following dilemma: They have been asked to recommend an individual for a job. They know him to be disqualified for it but they have some personal obligation to the father of the applicant. Twice as many (48%) give the "universalistic" answer that they would tell the truth about him as say they would recommend him anyway (23%). On the other hand, when asked how they thought others would evaluate their acts, those who gave the more popular universalistic response were more likely to believe that others would disapprove, than

In our work on participation, the availability of data on the communities within which individuals live is most useful for a variety of explanatory purposes. For example, the rates of participation of an individual can be related not only to his own orientations to participation but to the community norms on such subjects. Or the rate of participation can be related to the institutional structure of the community. Preliminary analysis of our data in the United States suggests that the rate of participation of an individual is closely related to his own membership in voluntary associations. But over and above this relationship between the individual's membership pattern and his participation in politics, we find that the density of organizational structure in the community is related to political activity—and most closely related for those who are *not* themselves members of organizations. That is, the more organizations in a community, the more *non-members* participate in politics. The substantive finding is most intriguing from the point of view of the interaction between individual and community characteristics. It suggests an important "spillover" effect from organizations that particularly affects those who might not otherwise participate—i.e., those who themselves do not belong to organizations. But we cannot pursue that issue here. The point to be made is that such comparisons across nations—of the interrelationships between individual and community characteristics—represent a significant type of substantive comparison; and from our point of view of the problem of the credibility of cross-cultural research, represent an important way in which comparisons can be of contextually embedded relationships.[39]

The combination of these various types of data allow us, for instance, to increase the comparability of rates of political behavior in the same way that adding subjective meanings to comparisons of behavior rates increased comparability. As mentioned above, comparison of attitudes or behavior rates must be carried on with caution as to the meaning of the comparisons because the structure of the situation for the individual differs from system to system. If one population reports less exposure to communications than another this may be because of differential interest in receiving communi-

---

were those who gave the less popular particularistic response. See C. Hayashi and others, "A Study of Japanese National Character," *Annals of the Institute of Statistical Mathematics*, Tokyo, 11 (1960), Supplement. Here might be an interesting example of a situation in which a social norm (in the statistical sense of the numbers who hold a particular position) has changed in a universalistic direction from the more traditional norms, but the perception of the change has lagged behind. In such a case, the largest group might approve of a particular kind of behavior but the frequency of that behavior might be somewhat lowered by the absence of perception of this change. This is an example where knowledge of the context of the individual preference (in this case both the preferences of others as well as the perceptions of the preferences of others) places the individual preference in a more comprehensive social context.

39. See Teune, *op. cit.*, on comparability of community level measures.

cations or simply the lack of availability of communications media. Or if one group is less active in organizations than another it may be a reflection of different attitudes toward joining organizations or the different availability of organizations. But if one has data on the availability of communications media or of organizations within the environment of the individual, one can control for the "opportunity structure" presented to the individual and relate his behavior to his predispositions more reliably. In this way, the individual is "placed in context" and his attitudes and behavior are related to the environment in which they exist before they are compared with those of others who may live in different environments.

In the foregoing examples characteristics of the social unit are used to help explain individual attitudes or behavior. The systematic selection of groups as well as individuals as units of analysis also permits the development and testing of a type of proposition very rare in studies that utilize survey data—propositions in which the dependent variable is an attribute of the system. A sample of 172 groups, for instance, allows one to test propositions as to why some groups dissolve while others survive.

There are a few explicitly political studies that approximate the multi-level design. All are studies that use subnational political systems as the political unit. Thus there are studies of the way in which voting laws affect electoral behavior in which the political unit is the state,[40] of the way in which local party activities affect the outcome of elections in which the political unit is the precinct,[41] and of the ways in which the nature of the campaign, or the size of the town, or the distribution of the votes affect electoral behavior in which the community is the political system studied.[42]

Perhaps the most ambitious study of this sort is that being conducted by Miller and Stokes of congressional districts—in which one has data on the attitudes of voters in a sample of districts as well as system characteristics such as the attitudes and behavior of the incumbent Congressman and his opponents.[43] This study represents two important additions to the stan-

40. See Campbell and others, *The American Voter* (New York: Wiley, 1963) ch. 11: "Election Laws, Political System and the Voter," pp. 266–289, and A. Campbell and W. Miller, "The Motivational Basis of Straight and Split Ticket Voting," *American Political Science Review*, 51 (June 1957): 293–312.

41. D. Katz and S. Eldersveld, "The Impact of Local Party Activity Upon the Electorate," *Public Opinion Quarterly*, 25 (Spring 1961): 1–24; and P. Cutright and P. Rossi, "Grass Roots, Politicians and the Vote," *American Sociological Review*, 23 (April 1958): 171–179.

42. P. Ennis, "The Contextual Dimension in Voting," pp. 18–112, *in* W. N. McPhee and W. A. Glaser, eds., *Public Opinion and Congressional Elections* (New York: Free Press, 1962), pp. 18–211.

43. D. Stokes and W. Miller, "Party Government and the Saliency of Congress," *Public Opinion Quarterly*, 26 (Winter 1962): 531–546; and W. Miller and D. Stokes, "Constituency Influence on Congress," *American Political Science Review*, 57 (March 1963): 45–56.

dard techniques of survey research. One addition involves the systematic selection of units at more than one level—individuals and congressional districts. The second technique involves the coordinated interviewing of both ordinary voters and political elites. Since so much of the problem of integrating studies of mass attitudes with the operation of political systems is related to the way in which these mass attitudes interact with elite attitudes and behavior, this represents a step forward in the application of surveys to problems of macro-political analysis. Similarly, we hope to use our data on community leaders to test some hypotheses about the effects of various rates or types of communal activism on leader perceptions of behavior.

The above examples illustrate the variety of kinds of measures one can generate in a study that samples both individuals as well as social systems. It also points to an asymmetry between the individualistic and ecological fallacies: Individualistic data can be aggregated more easily than ecological data can be disaggregated. One type of variable that can be used to characterize a social unit is the aggregate of responses in a survey of individual attributes—assuming of course that one has an adequate sample or a full census. One can characterize a unit as having a high average income or one can use measures of distribution to characterize a unit on the relative equality or inequality of income, and so forth.[44] In addition, one can often add to the analysis "found" data that characterize the social unit—e.g., census data, voting data, and other forms usually considered to be ecological measures. This is, of course, facilitated if the social unit sampled is also a unit of measure for governmental statistics. And one can add to the research design explicit measures of "global" or unit-level characteristics, for which information may already exist, or that can be gathered as part of the research design. These can include such items as political structural characteristics,[45] beliefs and acts of leaders,[46] physical facilities of the social unit,[47] or aspects of the social organization of the unit used in the sample.[48] And, as Lazarsfeld has pointed out, any of these measures on the level of

44. See P. Lazarsfeld, "Evidence and Inference in Social Research," pp. 107–138, in Daniel Lerner, ed., *Evidence and Inference* (Glencoe, Ill.: Free Press, 1959); see also H. R. Alker and B. Russett, "Indices for Comparing Inequality," pp. 349–372 in R. L. Merritt and S. Rokkan, eds., *Comparing Nations: The Use of Quantitative Data in Cross-National Research* (New Haven: Yale University Press, 1966).

45. As in the Michigan Survey Research Center studies of voting, in which local laws can be added as an independent variable affecting voting turnout. See Campbell and others, *op. cit.*

46. W. Miller and D. Stokes, "Constituency Influence on Congress," *American Political Science Review*, 57 (March 1963): 45–56.

47. As in the forthcoming MIT studies of Turkish villages; see F. W. Frey, "Surveying Peasant Attitudes in Turkey," *Public Opinion Quarterly*, (Fall 1963): 335–355.

48. *Ibid.*

the social unit can be used, in turn, for micro-analyses because each individual respondent can be characterized by the nature of the social unit of which he is a member—e.g., he can be considered a resident of a high income community (over and above his own income); or a resident in a state with restrictive voting laws, and so forth. And these unit characteristics, in addition to what we might call individual specific characteristics such as his own beliefs or attitudes, help explain the individual's behavior.[49]

One shortcoming in the above examples of the systematic selection of political units will be immediately apparent to the student of comparative politics. In all cases, the political units selected are subnational units—congressional districts, communities, electoral precincts—rather than nation-states. The latter has been the traditional unit of analysis for comparative political science and is indeed the most general focus of political integration and political development in the modern world. The use of subnational units has, however, certain advantages. For one thing it is feasible; it takes fewer resources to sample a series of local units than to sample a series of nations. The complex organizational and technical problems that accompany cross-national research can be avoided.[50] Furthermore, it is easier to get a fairly reliable sample. Though there are over one hundred autonomous nations from which a sample could be drawn, not all are available for research, and the thought of drawing a sample of, say, thirty nations and conducting surveys in each staggers the imagination. On the other hand, there are many local political units much more amenable to systematic sampling. In fact, the value of such locally based comparative studies may be that they will alert the student of comparative politics to the fact that useful systematic comparisons may be pursued on many different levels. One problem in comparative analysis of political systems—unlike analysis of micro-politics—is that one soon runs out of cases. The systematic comparative study of local political units is one way of increasing the number of cases. A problem remains, though, and needs further consideration, and that is the comparability of national and subnational units. Lastly, the comparative study of local political units has the methodological advantage of controlling for many of the contextual variations that were cited in the beginning of this paper as complicating multi-contextual research. By dealing with communities within a nation, one holds constant a large number of political factors

49. See the way in which individual motivation is combined with restrictiveness of state laws to help explain voting behavior in Campbell and others, *op. cit* (ch. 11: "Election Laws, Political System and the Voter," pp. 266–289).

50. H. C. J. Duijker and S. Rokkan, "Organizational Aspects of Cross-National Social Research," *Journal of Social Issues*, 10 (1964): 8–24; G. A. Almond and S. Verba, *op. cit.*; and S. Rokkan, "The Development of Cross-National Comparative Research: A Review of Current Problems and Possibilities," *Social Science Information*, 1 (October 1962), 21–38.

and, therefore, can isolate somewhat more unambiguously the relevant differences among the systems.[51]

On the cross-national level, it may be possible to approximate some of the benefits that would be forthcoming if one could systematically select a sample of nations. Coordinated cross-national studies are rare, and coordinated cross-national studies in which the nations are systematically selected on the basis of their characteristics as systems are even rarer, perhaps nonexistent. Though such coordinated study is greatly to be desired, it may be possible to approximate some of its benefits in several ways. There have been a number of recent attempts to gather aggregate data about nations and to relate these data to the political characteristics of these systems.[52] Such work ought to provide some standard criteria for the description of the macro-characteristics of systems in which survey research is carried on.[53] This will facilitate the development of a cumulative body of survey material which, though carried on by different researchers is, nevertheless, similar enough to allow comparison. For this purpose, the survey method particularly recommends itself, for it makes possible the replication of survey instruments or parts of survey instruments by different scholars in different contexts. Thus without the development of centrally directed and coordinated programs of multi-national survey research, it may still be possible to develop a body of survey data from many nations that can be coordinated with data on the macro-characteristics of the system and that will allow systematic comparative treatment.

Many of the suggestions in this paper on increasing the comparability (and credibility) of comparative survey data are applicable to data already collected. The process of analysis itself can increase one's confidence that one is comparing truly comparable data even if the collection was done by others and even if the data from various societies were collected at different times or even for different purposes.

51. J. J. Linz and A. de Miguel, "Within Nation Differences and Comparisons," pp. 267–320, in Merritt and Rokkan, eds., op. cit.

52. K. Deutsch and others, "The Yale Political Data Program," in R. L. Merritt and S. Rokkan, eds., op. cit., pp. 81–94; K. W. Deutsch, "The Theoretical Basis of Data Programs," in R. L. Merritt and S. Rokkan, eds., op. cit., pp. 27–56; A. S. Banks and R. B. Textor, A Cross-Polity Survey (Cambridge, Mass.: MIT Press, 1965); B. Russet and others, World Handbook of Political and Social Indicators (New Haven: Yale University Press, 1964); B. Russett, "The Yale Political Data Program: Experience and Prospects," in R. L. Merritt and S. Rokkan, eds., op. cit., pp. 95–107; R. M. Retzlaff, "The Use of Aggregate Data in Comparative Political Analysis," Journal of Politics, 27 (November 1965): 797–817; and E. K. Scheuch, "Cross-National Comparisons Using Aggregate Data: Some Substantive and Methodological Problems," in R. L. Merritt and S. Rokkan, eds., op. cit., pp. 131–168.

53. Phillip M. Gregg and Arthur S. Banks, "Dimensions of Political Systems: A Factor Analysis of a Cross-Polity Survey," American Political Science Review, 59 (September 1965): 602–614.

APPLICATIONS OF AN EXPANDED SURVEY RESEARCH MODEL TO COMPARATIVE INSTITUTIONAL STUDIES

ROBERT H. SOMERS

In this essay I review some aspects of the methodology of comparative macro-sociology from the vantage point of training and experience in quantitative analysis and a strong statistical orientation. It has long been my belief that there is a need for more intermingling between qualitative historical-comparative scholarship and statistical analysis to supplement and perhaps to counter two undesirable tendencies—the natural burgeoning of statistical research in areas where statistical analysis is easily accomplished, and the continuing tendency of macro-sociologists to posit intellectual creations that are sometimes far removed from a firm evidential basis. Rather than attempting to assay the range of problems addressed by macro-sociologists and to assume the distasteful posture of presuming to pronounce methodological prescriptions that should be followed as canons of scientific method, I have chosen to address my remarks primarily—though not exclusively—to a particular study, Barrington Moore's recent comprehensive study of the historical origins of certain contemporary political institutions.[1] By thus focusing on the work of one author, I hope to remain within the boundaries of the realistically possible in considering alternative methodological strategies. An analysis of this one study provides an appropriate vehicle for considering general strategies of methodology in a useful way, and in my analysis I hope to make suggestions that will have merit for other scholars. At the same time, this is not simply commentary on Moore's study. When appropriate, I go far from Moore's domain in discussing methodological strategies. To show the range of possibilities and types of obstacles that can arise at various points in a research study carried out

---

1. Barrington Moore, Jr., *Social Origins of Dictatorship and Democracy: Lord and Peasant in the Making of the Modern World* (Boston: Beacon Press, 1967), paperback edition.

within the framework introduced below, various illustrations are presented, not infrequently those that reflect my own research experience. In particular, I shall make occasional reference to a collaborative, comparative study of political and social development in four countries with which I have been associated in recent years: the Cross-National Study of Political and Social Change.

There are a number of reasons why I have singled out Moore's work for special attention. Systematic methodology in the social sciences has advanced the most in recent years in the areas of survey research and in particular related areas of multivariate analysis, such as path analysis.[2] These methods attempt to test explanatory or theoretical hypotheses with data that are gathered at one point in time in spite of the fact that hypotheses of causation require observations at more than one point in time. It has long been my belief that, in contrast, more pertinent data for the explanation of social system behavior are longitudinal or historical. Moore's study is obviously of this nature. Moore is primarily a historian, and an analysis of his work offers a great challenge for one who views it from the relatively distant perspective of statistical and quantitative analysis. An assessment of the larger methodological issues that Moore's study raises, in terms of strategies normally employed in quantitative analysis, leads to problems that are not easily solved by the conventional canons of quantitative methodology—problems that, indeed, raise questions about the very meaning of scientific work in this domain to a person with a background such as mine. It is quite possible that some of these problems have no solution. A work such as Moore's remains, in many respects, art rather than science. While I have nothing against art, I believe there is merit in considering whether historical analysis, especially when it is intended to help man make more rational choices in the pursuit of desirable goals, cannot be made a basis for the development of knowledge that is more reliable, consensual, and systematic than artistic insights ordinarily are. At least it is useful to at-

2. Path analysis has been discussed by various writers. For example, C. C. Li, *Population Genetics* (Chicago: University of Chicago Press, 1955), chs. 12–14, discusses Sewell Wright's work. J. Tukey, "Causation, Regression and Path Analysis," *in* O. Kempthorne, ed., *Statistics and Mathematics in Biology* (Ames, Iowa: Iowa State College, 1954), criticizes aspects of Wright's approach and makes alternative suggestions. See also M. Turner and C. Stevens, "The Regression of Causal Paths," in Biometrics, 15 (June 1959): 236–258. A recent addition is two chapters on this topic in S. Wright, *Evolution and the Genetics of Populations,* (University of Chicago, 1968), vol. 1. H. M. Blalock, *Casual Inferences in Nonexperimental Research* (Chapel Hill, N.C.: University of North Carolina Press, 1964) presents social science applications of the method, as does O. D. Duncan, "Path Analysis: Sociological Examples," *American Journal of Sociology,* 72 (July 1966): 1–16. E. Borgatta and G. Bohrnstedt, eds., *Sociological Methodology 1969* (San Francisco: Jossey-Bass, 1968) contains some useful discussions of the method.

tempt to articulate the limitations of a scientific approach. It is also pertinent that in his historical-comparative study Moore hopes to have learned
something relevant to contemporary public policy decisions in India (one
of his cases) and other countries. As will be seen, this active element in
Moore's intellectual effort is important both to Moore and to me, and one
that needs to have an explicit place in social science method; I try to provide such a place in the following. Finally, I am considering Moore's study
because, although he makes no overt claim to being a sociologist, he is
heavily sociological in orientation and intent. His work is comprehensive
in its analysis of several divergent societies, and for this very reason Moore,
whose style of analysis is idiographic with its emphasis on the unique developments in particular societies, is forced to deal with nomothetic problems of comparability—problems that are fundamental to the development
of comparative sociology.

It is impossible to consider methodological aspects of research activity
without employing some kind of framework or model of that activity.
Within such a framework, it is possible to give focused attention to each of
the several steps that constitute the process of social research. In suggesting
the following framework, I hope not to imply the necessity for a rigid
paradigm of scientific activity or to impose any particular theoretical viewpoint. On the contrary, an appropriate research framework should be sufficiently flexible to incorporate the range of research styles and activities
acceptable to contemporary social science. It may even extend that range.
Rather than connoting the imposition of a specific research style, the explication of an appropriate framework can increase flexibility of research
procedure, for the framework articulates what are essentially decision-
points for the investigator, reflecting the fact that research activity is largely
a decision-making process. As in other types of social activity, the articulation of areas of decision-making can reduce rigidity by making the actor
more conscious of the range of choices that are open to him at that particular decision point and more aware of the meager logical basis upon which
the conventional wisdom is based. Methodology is useful not only in clari-
fying the consequences of particular decisions that are made, but also in
bringing to deliberate consideration areas of decision-making that may
remain largely unconscious or may become routine for inappropriate reasons. The articulation of a model of the research process may, therefore, be
an encouragement to flexibility and innovation.

The following research framework is, in part, a traditional one that
has been the organizing framework for many a textbook discussion of methodology as well as for discussions of the methodology of particular research
studies. A recent outline of this model and application of it to many diverse

types of social science research, both qualitative and quantitative, is presented by Riley.[3] The traditional model of research includes the elements listed below and discussed in detail in the body of the essay. (i) A *model* of the theoretical framework believed appropriate to the processes that are being studied is formulated; (ii) a systematic statement is made about the *scope* of the study and the entities (persons, organizations, etc.) that will form the "units of analysis" since they are to be described in the research; (iii) a set of criteria is presented according to which the units outlined in (ii) are described; (iv) observations are made in specific ways; (v) explicit consideration is given to the manner in which observations of the variables are to be *manipulated and analyzed* in order to obtain desired conclusions; (vi) observations are *interpreted* in particular ways as relevant to particular concepts or variables;[4] and (vii) a *conceptualization* phase may be distinguished from the interpretation phase.

These elements of the traditional research model are most explicitly developed in contemporary *survey* research for a variety of reasons. However, this general model of activity is increasingly being adopted in historical and institutional research. Particular investigations may emphasize particular aspects of the model, such as the conceptualization phase or the exploration of different methods of analyzing the data for particular purposes. A division of labor in which different investigators focus on different elements of the process is, of course, not inappropriate. Listing the elements in the model of research activity in the above order does not imply a natural serial ordering to the activities of an investigator who undertakes the full range of activities in his study. On the contrary, he will ordinarily begin his research with certain conceptual assumptions in mind and may modify these through empirical analysis. This reconceptualization may, in turn, reshape the kind of theoretical model that he thinks appropriate. In general, there is a constant interaction between theoretical suppositions and empirical analysis that conditions the ultimate research conclusions. In a similar way, there is an interaction between the model of research activity outlined above and the research contexts within which it is applied. As the model is increasingly employed outside of survey research it is likely that it will be modified by these new applications, modifications that may, in turn, be reflected in innovations in survey methodology. In such ways social science methodology grows.

3. Matilda W. Riley, *Sociological Research* (New York: Harcourt, Brace & World, 1963).

4. The term "interpretation" is used here in the sense of Richard Bevan Braithwaite, *Scientific Explanation* (New York: Harper Torchbooks, 1960). See also William Hays, *Statistics for Sociologists* (New York: Henry Holt, 1963), p. 8.

I have found it useful, not only in the following analysis but more generally, to augment the above traditional model of research activity by making explicit certain additional intellectual activities that are frequently a part of social research but only occasionally viewed as essential aspects of methodology. For one, much social research has implicit or explicit value premises. In part as a consequence of those value premises, an investigator must cope in some way with the fact that social research is a part of, rather than isolated and divorced from, ongoing social action. It is partly because of Moore's explicit consideration of social values that I have chosen to emphasize his study in the following. It appears to me that it is useful to augment the traditional research model, outlined above, by adding some of these other elements to make a model of what I have referred to elsewhere as "active" social science methodology.[5] Because these additional elements are not often given explicit methodological consideration, the following formulation should be taken as tentative and my remarks on them in the subsequent analysis will be brief, but I believe it is important not to omit them entirely. Thus, an active social science, as I conceive it, would include the following elements in addition to the traditional ones just mentioned:

(viii) The goals or *values* toward which the research is directed are made explicit. In some cases the values will need justification; in others, they will be viewed as having sufficient consensus so that they may simply be asserted. In nearly all cases they will need some definition, clarification, and elaboration. It is surprising that traditional social science methodology provides no explicit locus for such activities as a part of the social research process.

(ix) In addition to the necessity to articulate values, one must engage in a process similar to the conceptualization and interpretation phases of traditional social research (described in paragraphs (vi) and (vii) above), namely, of *elaborating* the valued concepts and *linking* them with empirical observations or "indicators." [6] Here, as in the preceding phases of research, abstract concepts need to be linked to reality, and it is often only in their empirical interpretation that the meaning of concepts of value becomes clear.

(x) A social science actively enmeshed in questions of social policy must give consideration to the forms of *communication* and *utilization* of

5. Robert Somers, "On Problem-Finding in the Social Sciences: A Concept of Active Social Science," (April 1969), submitted for publication.
6. See Bertram Gross, "The State of the Nation: Social System Accounting," in Raymond Bauer, ed., *Social Indicators* (Cambridge, Mass.: MIT Press, 1966), pp. 265–267, also cited at length below. Selections reprinted by permission of the American Academy of Arts and Sciences, Boston, Mass.

research results. Research directed to influencing social processes must give consideration to the intended audience for the conclusions drawn from a study and the manner in which the recommendations will be implemented. Indeed, research on the process of implementation may become an important part of a more active and involved social science.

Such an expanded model provides an explicit place for consideration of the utilization of obtained knowledge and of the values toward which the research is directed. It thus clarifies the actual linkages between social science and human action and also facilitates the utilization of that knowledge—and an understanding of the process of utilization—for desired social goals.

In sum, the general emphasis of this essay is to consider the methodological strategies for comparative historical and institutional macro-sociology that are suggested by the above research framework and, in order to maintain a coherent discipline on the remarks, to place special emphasis on the manner in which the framework might be adapted to a work of scholarship such as Moore's. In thus commenting critically on Moore's work, I repeat (a) it is far easier to criticize than to construct the original theoretical-empirical structure, and (b) my analysis should not be construed as a depreciation of the importance of Moore's work. On the contrary, it was selected because of its significance in the areas noted earlier. The analysis should be viewed as the answers of one methodologist to the question: Having Moore's monumental effort before us, how might a future study —or program of studies—be conceived and organized to enhance the reliability and usefulness of the results?

ILLUSTRATIVE APPLICATIONS OF THE
RESEARCH FRAMEWORK

In the following pages I illustrate the research framework outlined above, discuss some of the many choices that are available at each point, and describe what I consider to be an appropriate choice for Moore's historical-comparative study. In illustrating and applying the research framework in this way, I do not mean to imply that decisions, once made, must be rigidly adhered to. While it is true that decisions at one point generally influence the possible choices at later points in the research, approaches to research in the social sciences, particularly where new ground is being explored, frequently are selected in a tentative and experimental way, and one frequently expects that choices may have to be revised as work progresses.

Since Moore's *Social Origins* is a recurring illustrative case study for the following methodological analysis, it is appropriate to give a brief summary of the intent and scope of his work. The reader should, however, be forewarned that the subsequent analysis will in no way attempt to present a comprehensive critique of the major theoretical and substantive arguments offered by Moore. I will suggest in passing that these arguments and the evidence for and against them could perhaps be more clearly discerned had the author attempted to pursue the analysis in the somewhat more "behavioral" methodological style that underlies the research framework with which I am working.[7]

For an overview, it seems best to rely heavily on the author's own words:

> This book endeavors to explain the varied political roles played by the landed upper classes and the peasantry in the transformation from agrarian societies (defined simply as states where a large majority of the population lives off the land) to modern industrial ones. Somewhat more specifically, it is an attempt to discover the range of historical conditions under which either or both of these rural groups have become important forces behind the emergence of Western parliamentary versions of democracy, and dictatorships of the right and the left, that is, fascist and communist regimes.[8]

Moore makes detailed studies of the beginning stages of industrialism in England, France, the United States (taken as relatively democratic regimes), in Japan (where fascism emerged), in China (where communism emerged), and in India (where parliamentary democracy is perhaps emerging). Comparable materials on Germany (fascist) and Russia (communist) are freely employed, although Moore deleted chapters that focused on developments in those two countries. Three theoretical chapters conclude the book.

In explaining the different types of political structures that have provided the framework within which a nation has entered the modern world, Moore emphasizes the importance, for democracy, of a "bourgeois revolution, . . . a necessary designation for certain violent changes that took place in English, French and American societies on the way to becoming modern industrial democracies. . . . A key feature in such revolutions is the development of a group in society with an independent economic base, which attacks obstacles to a democratic version of capitalism that have been inherited from the past."[9] The progress of modernization in Germany

---

7. Connotations of the term "behavioral" will become clear in the sequel and may also be discerned from A. Kaplan, *The Conduct of Inquiry: Methodology for Behavioral Sciences* (San Francisco: Chandler, 1964).

8. Moore, *op. cit.*, p. xi.

9. *Ibid.*, p. xv.

and Japan culminated in fascism, Moore argues, because in these countries the

> bourgeois impulse was much weaker. If it took a revolutionary form at all, the revolution was defeated. Afterward sections of a relatively weak commercial and industrial class relied on dissident elements in the older and still dominant ruling classes, mainly recruited from the land, to put through the political and economic changes required for a modern industrial society, under the auspices of a semi-parliamentary regime. Industrial development may proceed rapidly under such auspices. But the outcome, after a brief and unstable period of democracy, has been fascism.[10]

> The third route (to modernization) is of course communism, as exemplified in Russia and in China. The great agrarian bureaucracies of these countries served to inhibit the commercial and later industrial impulses even more than in the preceding instances (of Germany and Japan). The results were twofold. In the first place these urban classes were too weak to constitute even a junior partner in the form of modernization taken in Germany and Japan, though there were attempts in this direction. And in the absence of more than the most feeble steps toward modernization a huge peasantry remained. This stratum, subject to new strains and stresses as the modern world encroached upon it, provided the main destructive revolutionary force that overthrew the old order and propelled these countries into the modern era under communist leadership that made the peasants its primary victims.[11]

Such, then, are the main themes of Moore's study. In the following pages I discuss generally the possible choices that might be made in selecting a theoretical model within which to pursue such comparative macrosociological research and then suggest the kinds of choices that seem appropriate to Moore's study.

(i) *The Theoretical Model.*—Among the many possible choices of a representation and explication of the theoretical model for a particular study, it is difficult to say that one is more appropriate than another. The one that is chosen doubtless reflects both the style and background of the author who makes the choice and the topic being studied. A model selected should reflect the meta-theoretical framework within which the study is undertaken and should help provide intellectual links between the study being presented and previous and subsequent research activity.

Deutsch [12] has pointed out the manner in which the originating im-

10. *Ibid.*, pp. xv–xvi.
11. *Ibid.*, p. xv.
12. K. Deutsch, *The Nerves of Government* (New York: Free Press, 1963), ch. 2.

agery of theoretical models reflects general intellectual fashions. It is not surprising that in this present era of electronic computation many research models are presented in a form that bears a striking resemblance to the "flow-chart" form in which a computer program is outlined. Such a flow-chart model was developed in planning conferences of the Cross-National Study in Political and Social Change [13] with which I have been associated and has served as a touchstone for organizing and presenting the data. One current working version of this model is presented in Figure 1. Since that model pertains to data that are largely (although not entirely) survey in nature, since it is discussed elsewhere, and since it was derived, for purposes of the project, from more general theoretical statements by Almond, Easton and others, it will not be discussed here.

This general form of a model of "boxes and arrows" is a useful way of presenting the structure and dynamics of a modeled process without making heavy requirements on the measurement properties of variables that are introduced for study. March and Simon [14] have compiled a collection of useful examples of "flow-chart" models, formulating existing theories in this more systematic and explicit form. McPhee [15] and others have argued that this form of model is particularly appropriate for the representation of social theories. They propose that computer programs based on them be employed for simulations of those theories, but they do not make clear how one links empirical data to the simulation. More restrictive, in terms of measurement requirements, are models presented in the form of mathematical equations, such as those proposed by Coleman.[16] "Flow-chart" models also permit more qualitative complexity, often appropriate to social models, than the complex geometrical schemes presented by Stinchcombe,[17] although the latter schemes may permit a more parsimonious and graphic portrayal of dynamic aspects of theories.

It would seem that a study such as Moore's, in which *historical change*

13. The Cross-National Study in Political and Social Change is a collaborative, comparative research project with which I have been associated for several years. It is directed by a team of participating social scientists from four (and at times, more) countries studying, with data collected through interviews with a cross-section of the population and with elites in small communities and from documents describing those communities, the processes of social and political development and change. The overall coordinator is Professor Sidney Verba, Department of Political Science, University of Chicago.

14. J. March and H. Simon, *Organizations* (New York Wiley, 1958).

15. W. McPhee, *Formal Theories of Mass Behavior* (New York: Free Press, 1963), especially Introduction, chs. 1, 3, 4.

16. J. Coleman, *Introduction to Mathematical Sociology* (New York: Free Press, 1964).

17. A. Stinchcombe, *Constructing Social Theories* (New York: Harcourt, Brace & World, 1968).

Figure 1

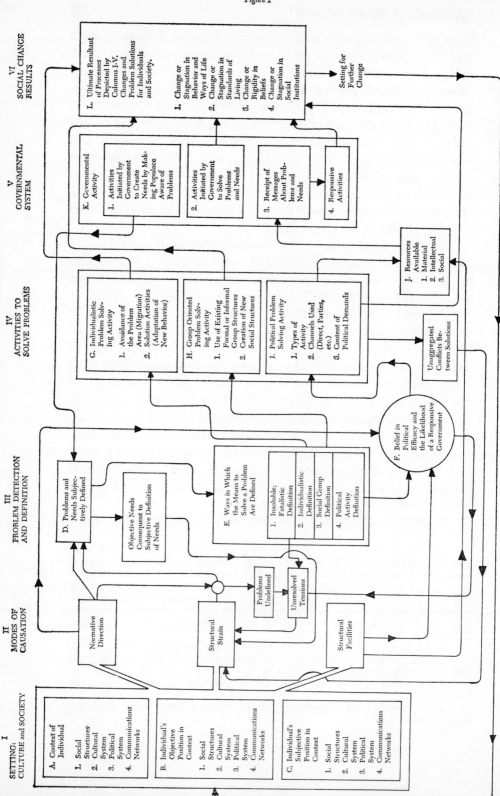

Time Period, Country X

1   2   3   4   .   .   .   .

Variables

  I. Groups (exist, not exist)

      Landed aristocracy
      Peasantry
      Urban bourgeoisie
      Central government

 II. Structures (exist, not exist

      Strong central government
      Bureaucratic administration
      Exploitative paternalism
      Commercial agriculture
      Cohesive society
      Balance of power between
          nobility and crown

III. Environmental factors
          (inhibiting, not inhibiting)

      External relations
      Resources

 IV. Past events and experience

      (have taken place,
          have not taken place)
      Wars between nobility and crown
      Peasant uprisings
      Feudal landholdings pattern

  V. Cultural values (exist, not exist)

      Climate of opinion unfavorable
          to human freedom
      Aristocratic values

Figure 2

A Partial Model Appropriate to Moore's
Social Origins of Dictatorship and Democracy
(To record observations for a particular country)

is the major theme would benefit from being presented in this form of a dynamic model. Such is not always the case. The behavior that is modeled in Figure 1 is being studied at one point in time. Dynamic elements are brought into the model empirically, by comparing individuals who are located at different points in the social structure and who have different backgrounds of experience and knowledge. It is not intended for studying major historical-structural changes in society. On the other hand, Moore's *Social Origins* does focus on major structural changes. Among the many types of models appropriate for a systematization of this study, I have chosen a simpler model that is almost no more than a listing of the pertinent variables.[18] The reason for selecting this type of model, illustrated in Figure 2 and discussed below, is that the appearance or disappearance of various structures within a society is the major theme of Moore's work, and that these structural characteristics of historical development are most easily presented by employing a simple "matrix" form. It is not the model itself but the manner in which it is used to draw conclusions that is most useful in a study of this nature. In spite of the fact that he obviously is endeavoring to explain the reasons for the development of particular types of political institutions, Moore's work may be viewed as largely a descriptive study, intent on describing sequences of historical patterns ("routes to modernization") in different societies. This form of "model" suggested as most appropriate to Moore's study has an advantage over more mathematically structured models of historical change of avoiding the sometimes pretentious epistemological and perhaps ontological assumptions required by more rigorous models.

The research model, presented in Figure 2, also has the advantage of maintaining a focus on the descriptive questions that arise in determining where the various societies stand in relation to each of the variables. The "model" consists simply of a listing of the pertinent variables,[19] together with a listing of the time periods during which observations will be made on the selected societies for each of the variables. The matrix of observations is filled out by recording an observation for each variable in each time period. Each country entering into the analysis would be represented by its own matrix.

The variables are grouped into general categories that seem best to structure their substantive content. The list of variables may be redundant. For instance, listed among the groups that may or may not be present in

18. There is precedent in designating a list of pertinent variables, intended for empirical or theoretical applications, as a model. See R. Mach and R. Snyder, "The Analysis of Social Conflict: Toward an Overview and Synthesis," *Journal of Conflict Resolution*, 1 (1957): 245.

19. Surely the listing in Figure 2 is far more an exhaustive rendering of concepts and variables employed by Moore. Figure 2 is intended to be suggestive only.

the society is "central government." Listed among the structures that may or may not be present is a "strong central government." Of course, if there is no central government, the "value" of the second "variable" is determined. This seems to be no particular problem at this stage, where inclusiveness should be the aim. In addition, the variables, as listed, will vary considerably in their degree of abstractness. Thus, one of the structures listed below is "exploitative paternalism." This pertains, in Moore's study, to the relation between peasant and overlord and deals with a facet of that relationship that may be found to occur together with other aspects, and those other aspects might or might not be listed as pertinent variables. Some more abstract characterization of the relationship between peasant and overlord that includes many such dimensions might also be listed as a "structural" variable. There is no particular reason why it is necessary to be concerned with these logical details at this point.

In the course of research, it is likely that the original scheme of variables will be greatly modified. One will find that certain observations have been made about a society that suggest new variables to be brought into the scheme. Case studies often suggest these new kinds of observations. Or, in the course of study, the logical status of an observation may change. When, for instance, one thought it sufficient at the outset of a study to distinguish only four groups in the society, it might later be deemed appropriate to separate one of those groups into two or more subclasses.

In the model presented in Figure 2 it is assumed for convenience that a "dichotomous" coding at each of the variables will suffice. Thus, simply the presence or absence of each variable is recorded (with the exception of "external factors," where the dichotomous coding requires more substantive judgments). No matter how complex the nature of the variable, a dichotomous coding scheme, probably most convenient, is always possible. Thus, if one had several religious groupings and wished to record which grouping was dominant at a particular time, it would be possible to construct several variables that could be coded in dichotomous fashion ("Was group A dominant?" "Was group B dominant?" and so on). At the same time, there is no reason why, in subsequent analysis, one could not deal with variables having more than two values.

It is also clear that the model permits a kind of conclusion that is more common in historical writing than in other spheres of thought. The *absence*, rather than presence, of a particular factor (feudal patterns in the U.S.) is an important part of some historical explanations. By listing this variable (existence of feudal pattern) such an explanation becomes possible.

This form of model, simple though it is, permits a clear yet flexible exposition of other aspects of historical explanation. One might ask why a feudal landholding pattern or the development of commercial agriculture is so important to the development of subsequent institutions. Moore and others have offered a variety of causal explanations, and these explanations generally involve the addition of new variables. Thus, the absence of a feudal past in the United States is used to explain the relative openness of American society by suggesting that the United States has avoided the rigid class distinctions which are persisting consequences of feudalism. In this way the new variable—"rigid class distinctions"—is added to the model. The matrix formulation makes more apparent than does the usual prose analysis the fact that, having added this consideration in one society, it is necessary to consider its relevance to *all* the societies that are being compared. If functional alternatives are considered, the matrix model can also make this explicit.

It should be evident that the model applied to historical explanation serves more or less as a bookkeeping device. The manner in which it suggests a particular kind of empirical analysis will be considered in a later section. But note its convenience as a record of empirical observation and logical argument. A common form of criticism of a complex causal hypothesis is to argue that a particular factor or item of information has been overlooked; the use of a matrix model makes this much less likely since it forces a systematic handling of concepts and variables. Again, a common mode of thinking is to focus on particular kinds of phenomena to the exclusion of others: the human mind has a limited capacity. A systematic framework such as a matrix is an aid that is intended to enlarge that capacity. One of the most common modes of thinking to be found among theoretically oriented social scientists is one that makes only "illustrative" use of data. A theoretical argument is set forth, and empirical material is presented to illustrate the validity of the theory. The theoretical argument is then extended, and more observations are offered in support of it. But in the second illustration, the events or case studies that were used to illustrate the first point have been left behind, in spite of the fact that, at least in the eyes of other investigators, they may be as relevant to the second line of reasoning as to the first. If not, the matrix formulation calls for a justification of their exclusion. The model described in Figure 2 is filled out by providing information for all countries on all variables and leads immediately to a systematic use of empirical data. The illustrative use of empirical data is that which would occur if certain parts of the matrix were omitted without warrant at various stages in the analysis.[20]

There is a different sense in which omission of elements of the matrix

20. For a detailed consideration of the application of a data matrix to qualitative studies, see J. Galtung, *Theory and Methods of Social Research* (New York: Columbia University Press, 1967).

detracts from comparative work. Verba [21] has considered the manner in which those studies that emphasize complex idiographic configurations of particular cases can be made to contribute more directly to the development of comparative political theory. In reviewing an effort in systematic comparisons of case studies by Dahl and others, Verba suggests that increased comparability would result from a more disciplined use of an explicit multivariate model of the political process in the explanatory phases of the studies. Acknowledging that the configurative-idiographic emphasis of case studies has its special virtues, Verba suggests that to some extent the " 'uniqueness' of the explanation for any particular case arises from the fact that the combination of relevant factors that accounts for a nation's pattern of politics will be different from the combination in other cases, and the relative importance of various factors will differ from case to case." To overcome this problem, Verba advocates an explicit formulation of the relationship of the particular case being examined to the general model that provides a place for a large number of cases. What is needed, of course, is an explicit, general frame of reference, such as a theoretical model of sufficient complexity to incorporate social patterns in divergent contexts, that will serve the purpose of organizing the empirical observations in each case or unit of analysis.[22] Verba refers to the examination of case studies within such a larger framework as a "disciplined configurative approach," and he provides a tentative formulation of multivariate analysis procedures for such a method. He suggests that factors relevant to an explanation of one case should have general relevance to all the cases under consideration, and that all factors in the general model be taken into account even if they are not relevant to the particular case under study. In a word, he is advocating the use of a matrix model such as Figure 2 by *different* investigators, each of whom will fill in some parts of the matrix for the *particular* cases they study. Of course Verba is also making reference to the manner in which data are manipulated in the analysis; further remarks on that topic are included in section (v) below.

Verba illustrates the usefulness of a matrix model by suggesting that there is a logical fallacy in omitting from consideration variables that have been found pertinent in other circumstances but that are not deemed per-

21. S. Verba, "Some Dilemmas in Comparative Research," *World Politics,* 20 (October 1967): 111–127.

22. The plea for a common framework is similar to that made by Apter in the field of comparative politics, D. Apter, "A Comparative Methodology for the Study of Politics," *American Journal of Sociology,* 64 (1958): 221–238, and by many others before and since that time. A study to ascertain why such pleas so often go unheeded, except perhaps by schools that develop around particular scholars, would be a useful contribution to the sociology of social science.

tinent and are ignored in the case under study. For instance, in some nations geographical factors have an impact on politics, while in others they do not. The student of a nation where these factors do not play a role should, suggests Verba, recognize this and be sensitized to such a recognition by having at hand, at the inception of his research, a general model in which geographical factors are among the theoretically appropriate conceptual variables.

There have been countless calls for the employment of a general model or framework of concepts by students of nearly all persuasions. In much the same way that Lazarsfeld has suggested that a mathematical model serves to order and organize the observational materials, Parsons has advocated a general conceptual framework that may be employed in various types of social studies. One may adopt such a scheme without assuming specific relations among the variables involved. A first task is to have a set of concepts that can be generally employed in developing comparable analyses by diverse investigators of different materials, such as different historical periods and different historical settings. There is no need, at the inception of such a research program, to have a fully developed theory, but merely a common set of conceptual categories (which of course imply, in and of themselves, certain theoretical presuppositions). If different investigators approach their materials with the same concepts, then a fruitful ground has been prepared for the development of propositions relating those concepts in diverse contexts. This will not be the case if different investigators, starting from different orientations, investigate their materials with concepts of their own devising or with concepts that have meaning only within a particular subdisciplinary orientation.

At times it appears that there is an unwritten norm operating in the discipline of sociology that militates against the provisional acceptance of an existing theoretical scheme on the grounds that an important quality of advanced scholarship is the development of one's own theory. I would argue that the cumulative development of social science is enhanced by a greater measure of tolerance of incompleteness in available theoretical schemes and by a gradualist rather than a revolutionary posture toward their modification. The social sciences have not reached the point where prevailing theories are overthrown by the insights gained from crucial observations in the manner of the revolutions in science described by Kuhn.[23] It would come closer to this point if disciplined empirical testing of existing theories and careful replication of previously established conclu-

23. T. Kuhn, *The Structure of Scientific Revolutions* (Chicago: University of Chicago Press, 1962).

sions were as important a source of prestige in the discipline as the announcement of a new "theory of. . . ." In this respect perhaps sociology has yet to outgrow its philosophical origins.[24]

(ii) *Scope of the Observations.*—It is unnecessary to discuss this topic at length since elsewhere in this volume Verba presents a number of appropriate comments. To his remarks I would add the importance for comparative studies of having samples of units of analysis that are defined according to *conventional boundaries.* For research to be truly comparative, a study must be replicable at a later time by a different investigator; this is possible only if that later investigator is able to replicate the *scope* of the study.

In a recent experience with surveys of the student protest movement at the University of California, I realized the advantages of using sampling methods that were representative of clearly defined populations. In the course of these studies, I became interested in comparing my data with previous surveys of students. In some cases, such comparisons were possible. In others, the data were not comparable, since the surveys had not defined a target population that could be easily reproduced or even approximated from a representative sample. Consequently, comparisons with these other surveys were always subject to an unknown amount of error.

A concrete example is useful. I do not mean to imply that a survey should represent an entire population of an administratively defined community in order to lend itself to future comparisons, but rather that the basis for selection of the target population, from which the sample is, in turn, selected, should be information that is readily available, such as that from administrative records. For instance, if an earlier investigator had selected a sample consisting only of graduate students, or only male students, it would be very simple to make comparisons with future samples by excluding all students from a new sample who do not fall in the category "graduate student" or "male." On the other hand, in the event that one

24. The emphasis on originality appears in various guises in various places. As noted earlier, survey research is not immune to criticisms regarding the level of explicitness of the assumptions that are made, particularly in regard to the variables that are included or excluded in an analysis and in regard to the decisions that are made regarding the relative importance of particular relationships observed. See, for example, the problems that arose when Scheuch and others attempted to make a systematic record of the manner in which survey analysts operationalized certain concepts: "Quite often, the concepts used in an article seemed to have no obvious connection with the questions [that were asked in the survey]. It appears that some researchers do not seem to use the usual meaning of a concept. The emphasis on 'originality' also appeared as a troublesome factor as represented in the temptation to use mere verbal ingenuity" E. Scheuch and others, "Experiments in Retrieval from Survey Research Questionnaires by Man and Machine," *Social Science Information,* 6 (April-June 1967): 139.

investigator draws his sample from a particular class of students or from those living in particular housing arrangements, the possibilities of direct comparisons are lessened. The reason is that replication of the population of students in a particular class or with a particular living arrangement is unlikely, since curricula change and information is generally not on record about students' housing in the university administration.

It would still be possible, although more difficult, to make comparisons with a sample based on information about living arrangements of students or other information not a matter of public record. The next investigator can obtain that information from sampled respondents. Yet in order that this be done, it is necessary that the previous investigator give a clear and explicit statement describing how his sample was drawn. (This is simply another point at which explicit formulation of procedure improves comparability.) Although this illustration is based on survey experience, it is applicable to any type of comparative study where systematic observation methods are used.

Consider, for example, the obvious ease with which Moore's study can be related with previous and future comparisons since the units he selected for comparison study are conventionally defined nation-states. In other respects the scope of Moore's study is well designed. (Precisely because of this scope, of course, it is beyond the reach of scholars who find it impossible to immerse themselves in such a diversity of materials. One of the aims of a cumulatively developing program of comparative studies should be to provide the conditions whereby a study such as Moore's could be undertaken by several scholars, each within his own geographical area of specialization.) In order to assure himself that the patterns of development he discerned were not due to particular aspects of the religious or secular culture of Western Europe, or of the Far East, Moore included countries representing both areas. Thus he acknowledged the possible diversity of causal hypotheses and avoided a facile assumption of homogeneity. A major factor in the selection of cases for analysis by Moore was in the extent to which those countries occupied a clear status on the "dependent variable" of interest to him—the democratic or dictatorial character of their political institutions at a particular stage of development. It is not at all unusual in scientific investigation to select particularly outstanding examples for comparison. Moore went beyond this, however, to make his study of more than simply historical interest. By including India, a country where the historical developments he observed in other countries are still in flux, his study became pertinent to contemporary policy and ideology.

Of course a primary consideration in the selection of cases for analysis by Moore was the availability to him of relevant historical and contemporary materials. In some parts of his analysis he makes occasional reference to various countries other than those to which he gives focused attention. These references are unsystematic and it is not clear that they contribute more than suggestively to his analysis. Had all of his analysis been carried out in this "illustrative" fashion, developing and illustrating a particular theory of development with sporadic references to particular countries in particular periods, the work would obviously be much closer to speculation and much less well based in empirical fact. On the other hand, Moore could well have singled out one or two countries for focused analysis and would have left the reader wondering whether his conclusions had any generality at all. Considering the nature and magnitude of the task he set himself, Moore made sensible if ambitious decisions that seem to have weighed well the conflict between generality and intensive empirical investigation.

Are there those who would argue that Moore's results may be meaningless (due only to "chance variation") until they are tested for statistical significance? Such tests would be nearly impossible to perform without more quantification than Moore achieved, but even if he had presented summary tables such as that shown in Figure 4 (see below), it is hard to see how the logic of statistical inference would be justified in this case. Arguments have been made for and against statistical testing with little resolution,[25] but it does seem clear that they should be used only where a probability model to justify the inferences can be made to seem plausible. Although there are those who would argue that inferences could be made to a "hypothetical population" of countries from which Moore has randomly selected a sample, the possible misinterpretations of such tests (e.g., assuming that a statistically significant result is evidence against spuriousness, or confusing statistical with theoretical significance) are so many that it seems well to avoid such magic numbers in this case.

(iii) *Variable Lists.*—One procedure used in survey analysis for making explicit certain vital aspects of research methodology unfortunately is not often publicized since it is only rarely included in the published report of the survey. This is a listing of the conceptual variables on which the research is based and the questions that are asked of respondents to obtain

25. See chapter 13, "Statistical Inference," *in* Travis Hirschi and Hanan Selvin, *Delinquency Research: An Appraisal of Analytic Methods* (New York: Free Press, 1967) and the references cited therein, especially Leslie Kish, "Some Statistical Problems in Research Design," *American Sociological Review*, 24 (June 1959): 328–338. See also Leslie Kish, *Survey Sampling* (New York: Wiley, 1965), especially sec. 14.4. Although these arguments are stated in relation to survey research, in most respects they may be applied to the present example.

information relevant to those variables. This "conceptual inventory" of the data collection instrument is a way of making explicit (a) the very important link between theoretical variables and empirical data and (b) the entire range of data gathered and of theoretical concepts employed.

Of course, it is common for certain questions to be used repeatedly in successive surveys by different investigators, since those questions form the basis for a scale that has become a commonly accepted method for obtaining information about that particular topic. The concept of authoritarian personality, for instance, has been the basis of much empirical research using survey questions developed by the initial investigators. "Alienation" is another variable that has benefited from cumulative and comparative survey research.[26] But all surveys obtain information about a variety of other variables that are neither the focus of special attention in that particular survey nor the outgrowth of a history of consistent and cumulative usage. For such other variables, survey researchers often have to devise *ad hoc* and special procedures that they hope will provide them with pertinent information. Availability of "biographical" material from previous surveys, such as a list of concepts to be measured and the questions intended as pertinent to those concepts, is an aid in the planning of the survey and in the development of standardized, cumulative, and comparable procedures. The common practice in survey work at the present time is to present a finished report mentioning the questions useful for special analyses, together with a copy of the questionnaire. Only infrequently are reasons given for the failure to analyze questions that were indeed asked. It is not common to provide the intended meaning of the many questions that were asked but not singled out for analysis. The inclusion of a conceptual inventory as an appendix to the final report is helpful in this regard.

A conceptual inventory is an appropriate place to start the type of systematic reference system described by Scheuch.[27] Much of the labor of the task he proposes—making explicit the conceptual variables for which particular survey questions are intended—is already disposed of by such an inventory. It is obvious that such systematization makes cumulative work more likely. Of course, a conceptual inventory is tentative, especially one that is constructed at the time the survey interview is planned, prior to analysis of the data. This does not diminish its value. In addition, it will typically contain a kind of ambiguity in that one question might be assumed to be pertinent to more than one conceptual variable. Possibly subsequent

26. See, for example, Charles J. Bonjean and others, *Sociological Measurement: An Inventory of Scales and Indices* (San Francisco: Chandler, 1967).
27. E. Scheuch and others, *op. cit.*

analysis will resolve such ambiguities; with records of these decisions sub-sequent investigators will perhaps not have to repeat them. The converse situation—one concept and many indicators—is common in survey research, and the conceptual inventory will not make clear the manner in which the indicators are to be combined. Yet this is not such crucial information, as often various possible methods of combination yield essentially the same substantive conclusions.

As one considers the possibility of broadening the traditional survey design to include information about units other than individual respondents and from sources other than personal interviews, a conceptual inventory will perhaps be an even more useful scheme for maintaining a coherent picture of the mass of accumulating data. For each conceptual variable, in an expanded survey design, an investigator will list not simply the ques-tions asked of respondents, but also the information derived from other sources. This kind of organization leads automatically to procedures for combining survey information with other kinds of information relevant to the same conceptual variables in the manner called for by Webb and others, among other commentators.[28] Such organization will, in fact, represent an advance over their introductory remarks, since it will make clear the *manner* in which information from such diverse sources is to be combined, a topic that they leave open for future investigations.

Thus there is obvious merit in the explicit designation of variables that are to be conceptualized and analyzed in traditional survey research. This procedure has special merit when the conventional survey model is being expanded to include data from sources other than direct interviews with respondents. Historical-comparative research would also greatly benefit, in my opinion, from a more explicit consideration of the variables that are being used to organize and explicate descriptions and observations drawn from sources other than survey interviews; yet little systematic considera-tion is ordinarily given to this aspect of historical-comparative research. In fact, my earlier proposal for a "model" for Moore's study, represented above in Figure 2, is little different from a conceptual inventory of the variables Moore is attempting to characterize for the various different cases and time periods that enter into his study. In a study such as Moore's it is perhaps premature to employ a research framework that makes a clear distinction between the model and a conceptual inventory. As research progresses—as it has in some areas of political science—to the point where more sophisti-cated models are postulated, then a clearer distinction may emerge between

28. E. Webb and others, *Unobtrusive Measures: Nonreactive Research in the Social Sciences* (Chicago: Rand McNally, 1966).

the model of the process being studied and a conceptual inventory of the variables that are to be included in that model.

(iv) *Observations.*—A conceptual inventory, or listing of variables, as it is employed in survey research, is ordinarily different from an explicit statement of the manner in which the observations are made that are combined in various ways to construct those variables. In conventional surveys observations are made in terms of single questions to the respondent, or occasionally observations about the respondent or the interview setting made by the interviewer. Each of these separate "items" constitutes the raw observations. Thus to learn how the observations are made, one may ordinarily inspect the actual questionnaire employed in the research, although some qualities of this manner of observation, such as the tone used by the interviewer and his appearance to the respondent, remain hidden from view. Interviewers are ordinarily trained to adhere closely to the phrasing of the given questions so that the precise manner in which the observations are made may be a matter of record.

In historical-comparative studies a model or a conceptual inventory constitutes a listing of the variables that are to be observed but does not give a detailed statement of the manner in which the observations pertinent to those variables are made—the "questions asked of the data." Such a full description of observations is, of course, a large order for a historical-comparative study that encompasses many diverse variables, but perhaps no larger than the conventional survey that may include questionnaires of twenty or more pages in length. There is merit in thus making explicit the precise types of observations that are noted even though in many cases the source materials are drawn from observations and summaries made by others. Thus Table 1 lists some of the variables included in Moore's study but gives no indication of the precise types of observations that would be made in order to ascertain the values of particular variables for particular cases. It would enhance the systematic nature of the research if Moore had listed explicitly the kinds of questions he asked of the historical materials in order to obtain information pertinent to such concepts. How, for example, did he ascertain whether or not an urban bourgeoisie existed in France in 1750? Having made the manner of observation clear, he would have enhanced the prospects for future cumulative comparative work based on the conceptual categories that he has chosen.

Since much historical-comparative work is based on secondary sources, it becomes necessary to devise some system for classifying the reports of primary observations, but this is not so different as it may at first appear from procedures that are commonly employed in surveys. In surveys, after all, an interviewer frequently is asking a respondent for reports about matters to which he alone is privy, or which could be more effectively ascertained by clinical interviews and more extended and professional observations. Swanson,[29] among others, has developed procedures for making systematic uses of secondary ethnographic material contained in the Human Relations Area Files, involving coding procedures for classifying the reports of ethnographers. In similar fashion a historian, and particularly a comparative historian, could evaluate and classify historical observations. Naroll [30] has, in turn, developed methods for including evaluations of the authenticity of the original observations in the analysis of secondary materials—again, illustrating his work with ethnographic materials. It would be instructive to consider the relation between these procedures and the internal and external analyses commonly used by historians to evaluate their sources, but I have not done so here. Instead, I now turn to the manipulation of data, once gathered.

(v) *Data Manipulations.*—The most common research procedure to follow when one is presented with a set of systematic observations is a kind of statistical procedure based in some way on correlation analysis. In the usual survey application of the research framework being discussed here, one makes observations on each variable of a statistical sample of persons or, in some recent studies, communities or organizations. In effect, one thus obtains a data matrix showing the observations on each variable for a set of units of analysis at one point in time. By studying trends across individuals, taking into account two or more variables simultaneously, one summarizes the relationships among variables, obtaining information about clusters of conceptually related variables, possible causal patterns, and various other conclusions. In sum, the usual survey can be characterized as (1) having many variables (2) observed on many units of analysis (ordinarily persons) (3) at one point in time. Unlike many macro-sociological comparative studies, and unlike Moore's comparative history, surveys are unlikely to deal with structural variables such as the "groups present or absent" record in Figure 2. Frequently, however, they approximate this by (4) subdividing groups contained in the survey, but analyzing in such a way that the presence or absence of a particular group is a constant rather than, with Moore, a variable.

Since structural variables are of considerable interest to the field of macro-sociology, it is pertinent to ask why surveys that make structural analyses are so rare. One reason for this is that surveys, being close to

29. Guy E. Swanson, *The Birth of the Gods: The Origin of Primitive Beliefs* (Ann Arbor: University of Michigan Press, 1962).
30. Raoul Naroll, *Data Quality Control: A New Research Technique* (New York: Free Press, 1962).

empirical reality, rarely present "all or none" results; one would instead be likely to find, on detailed analysis, that a group was more or less present, not completely absent. But there are more fundamental reasons. Consider an example where the presence of a particular group, commercial entrepreneurs, for instance, is of interest and how this might appear in a survey. Suppose that a procedure is devised whereby it becomes possible to determine by survey interviews, with small margin of error, whether a person belongs to this class (surely this is not difficult). We may then suppose that a series of interviews is obtained with a sample of respondents in several countries. Within each national sample, it becomes possible to identify the commercial entrepreneurs. A comparison of national samples—where the whole national sample is taken as a single case—would then permit a comparison of structures in which the size of this class was variable. In this way, the use of a structural variable could become possible in a survey, and the example suggests that the rarity of this kind of analysis is due to (a) the dearth of multi-national survey studies and (b) the tentativeness of conclusions that can be drawn from the necessarily small sample of countries that will be surveyed and compared.

This is not the whole answer, however. Consider the above example so changed that only a sample of adults in one country, the United States, for example, was drawn. In this case no cross-national comparisons could be made, yet it would still be possible to make regional comparisons within the United States in regard to the existence and relative size of a class of commercial entrepreneurs. But one would be likely to compare no more than four or five regions; the problem of tentativeness of conclusions remains. If we now return to the condition where we have several national samples, a basis for extending the analysis appears: several regions in several countries provide perhaps twenty or more units of analysis for this type of structural variable.

These examples make clear that this kind of structural analysis is not impossible with survey data. But it takes major segments of the sample, rather than individual respondents, as units of analysis for purposes of comparison. In this sense, the use of survey data for this purpose leads to a form of analysis identical to that which would be carried out in a series of case studies undertaken in a disciplined, coordinated fashion not unlike the "disciplined configurative" approach advocated by Verba. Moreover, when this rather small number of comparisons is made at one point in time, it is likely to be of more *descriptive* than *explanatory* interest. That is to say, the causes and consequences of the observed structural differences are not likely to lie in other information that has been collected in this survey, but rather in other sources of information, particularly historical information.

One glaring exception to the rule that surveys are not well suited to structural analysis is in the study of intergenerational mobility and, more generally, structural analysis based on information about the past that can be recalled with considerable accuracy by living respondents. By asking a living respondent to give information about his own occupation and the occupation of his father at the same age, survey data can effectively study occupational mobility and generalize this in order to study the changing occupational structure. Yet when national or regional structure is to be used as the unit of analysis, even the historical information obtained in this way is not the most appropriate because, of course, the typical family is not geographically stationary. We can learn, for instance, of the occupational distribution of fathers of sons now living in Region A, but not the occupational distribution of men living in that Region 25 years ago. Thus, even in this way surveys are not ideally suited to structural analysis although they may be the best available source for such purposes.

To establish that a variable can appropriately play the role of a structural variable is a descriptive problem from the viewpoint of data manipulation, a conceptual problem from a theoretical standpoint. Descriptive problems are common in the manipulation of data, but should not be confused with questions of causal explanation that are frequently the essential questions in analysis. For either purpose, some kind of multivariate analysis is likely to be employed.

Sometimes writers are reluctant to use the term multivariate analysis when variables are not easily quantified or amenable to statistical treatment. Verba, for instance, takes this view.[31] In my opinion it is mistaken to assume that a multivariate analysis needs to be quantitative and statistical; Figure 2 represents the inception of a multivariate analysis even though nearly all observations are qualitative. The logical essentials of a qualitative analysis of many variables are no different from the logical essentials of a quantitative analysis. The latter, to be sure, has achieved a more sophisticated level of development. Contrast, for example, the material contained in a modern statistical treatment of multivariate analysis, such as Anderson's work,[32] with the section on multivariate analysis in the reader on social research methodology edited by Lazarsfeld and Rosenberg.[33] Yet the logical essentials, as described in the earlier chapters of Yule and Kendall's introductory statistics text [34] or in a more modern treatment in the

31. S. Verba, *op. cit.*, p. 114.
32. T. Anderson, *Introduction to Multivariate Statistical Analysis* (New York: Wiley, 1958).
33. P. Lazardfeld and M. Rosenberg, *The Language of Social Research* (New York: Free Press, 1953), Section II.
34. G. Yule and M. Kendall, *Introduction to the Theory of Statistics* (New York: Hafner, 1950), chs. 1–3.

Kemeny and others, elementary mathematics textbook [35] are the same. The special quality of the kind of multivariate analysis described by Verba is not that many of the relationships are qualitative, which is true, but that empirical data for the description of a variety of relationships that necessarily enter into the general model are absent. Such deficits will gradually be overcome as increasingly appropriate data become available through the work of individual scholars, collaborative research projects, and administrative agencies. But there is no reason to eschew systematic handling of observations even though they remain qualitative and impressionistic in nature.

A similar plea for a more explicit kind of multivariate analysis has recently been made by a historian and pursued by means of a critique and reanalysis of the classic study of the social origins of the American constitution by Charles Beard. Benson, adopting the language and approach of Lazarsfeld's type of multivariate analysis,[36] quotes Beard's major hypothesis:

> If men in the same economic group were equally divided on the matter of adoption or rejection—it would then become apparent that the Constitution had no ascertainable relation to economic groups or classes, but was the product of some abstract cause remote from the chief business of life—gaining a livelihood. But if substantially all support came from members of groups of personal property interest and substantially all or the major portion of the opposition came from the non-slave-holding farmers and the debtors—would it not be pretty conclusively demonstrated that our fundamental law was not the product of an abstraction known as the whole people, but of a group of economic interests which must have expected beneficial results from its adoption? [37]

Since only two variables (membership in certain economic classes and manifest support for the Constitution) are considered, Benson argues that the implied statistical relationship may be spurious: "Stated in somewhat formal terms, Beard's design of proof is logically fallacious because it assumes that the relationship between two variables can be discovered without considering the possible influence of other variables." [38] Thus he accuses Beard of failing to consider whether or not the manifest statistical relationship might not have been due to other factors such as ethnic status. In a later study of voting behavior in New York State in the 1840's,[39] Benson

35. J. Kemeny and others, *Introduction to Finite Mathematics* (Englewood Cliffs, N. J.: Prentice-Hall, 1956), chs. 1–4.

36. L. Benson, *Turner and Beard: American Historical Writing Reconsidered* (New York: Free Press, 1960).

37. *Ibid.*, p. 152.

38. *Ibid.*, p. 154.

39. L. Benson, *The Concept of Jacksonian Democracy* (Princeton: Princeton University Press, 1961).

marshals statistical evidence suggesting that Beard's hypothesis cannot be supported.

The multivariate analysis that Benson advocates for dealing with the question posed by Beard is the same as the kind of multivariate procedure advocated by Verba for dealing with case studies. However, there is a difference in application that is worth recognizing. Verba is advocating the explicit consideration of variables that enter into a general model for the analysis of social systems, whether or not these variables are pertinent to a particular case. Thus Verba is making reference to an analysis in which the nation that is studied in what he calls a "disciplined configurative approach" is the unit of analysis. Benson, on the other hand, refers to a mode of statistical analysis in which the *individual citizen* (or his representative) is the unit of analysis and the multivariate analysis is used to draw conclusons about the one nation in which all those units of analysis are citizens. In this sense, Benson did not face another difficult problem discussed by Verba and reviewed below—the lack of sufficient numbers of units of analysis to permit the desired conclusions to be drawn.

An aside on assumptions of "developmental equivalence." One additional form of manipulation of survey data that is relevant to this kind of structural analysis should be noted. Given the fact that survey data are almost always collected at one point in time, a type of "equivalence" assumption is often made, an assumption logically identical to one that demographers must employ to draw certain kinds of inferences from cohort analysis, and indeed one that is necessary whenever statistical (other than experimental or time-trend) procedures are used to infer a causal connection. Although the assumption is widely employed, it seems to have no name; for purposes of identification, I shall refer to it as the "developmental equivalence" assumption.[40] If one wishes to analyze survey data gathered at a particular point in time, yet make *causal* inferences, one must apparently always make this assumption. For instance, suppose a survey finds urban regions to have a lower birthrate than rural regions or industrial workers to be more politically radical than agricultural workers. From these findings it is tempting to infer that as a region becomes urbanized its birthrate will decline or that workers who move from agricultural to industrial employment will become more politically radical. These projections may be made—provided that "developmental equivalence" holds. That is, it must be true that the cross-sectional comparisons (between rural and urban regions or industrial and agricultural workers) replicate the developmental

40. Brief remarks very similar to the following appear in Cohen and Nagel's critique of the "comparative method" of Spencer and Morgan. See M. Cohen and E. Nagel, *Introduction to Logic and the Scientific Method* (New York: Harcourt, Brace, 1934), p. 346.

changes that would occur if the one (rural region, agricultural worker) were to be transformed into the other (urban region, industrial worker).

In order that the nature of this assumption of developmental equivalence be made perfectly clear, a diagram is useful. In Figure 3, I present, on the left, a portion of a conventional data matrix as it appears when *cross-sectional* data are being analyzed. At the top are two (of many) units of analysis. To show that the logic is independent of the unit of analysis, it is illustrated twice: In the first illustration the units are respondents in a survey (Smith and Jones, by name) and in the second illustration they are regions (Region A and Region B). In the body of the matrix are observed values of two (of many) variables: X, employment sector, and Y, political views in the first illustration. In the second illustration X is urbanism and Y is birthrate. Each of the variables has two possible values in these illustrations, denoted by subscripts and identified in the illustrations below the matrix. The logic would be no different if we instead employed variables having more than two, even an infinity, of values.

On the right of Figure 3 is presented a data matrix appropriate when *sequential* data are being analyzed—identical in form to the matrix presented in Table 1, above. It is necessary in this case to have a separate matrix for each unit of analysis, so information is presented here about only one (Smith, Region A) of the two units shown in the cross-sectional matrix on the left.

Under the cross-sectional matrix, the two illustrations present the basis of all correlation analysis: a *comparison* of *two different* units of analysis.[41] In the first illustration on the left, we note that Jones, an industrial worker, is more politically radical than Smith, an agricultural worker. In the second illustration on the left we find, similarly, that Region B, an urban region, has a lower birthrate than Region A, a rural region. From these facts (taking other correlated variables into account in actual practice) we infer from the survey data on the left, with the aid of the assumption of developmental equivalence, what is *actually observed* in the *sequential* data matrix on the right. In the first and second illustration on the right, Smith, the agricultural worker, is observed to become more politically radical as he becomes an industrial worker, and Region A, the rural region, is observed to undergo a decrease in the birthrate as it is transformed from a rural to an urban region.

Only longitudinal data, recording actual changes that have occurred over time, can be used as a basis for conclusions of causation, and even this is necessarily subject to the many problems of concomitant variation in

41. This basis for correlation analysis is most clearly presented in M. Kendall, *Rank Correlation Methods* (London: Griffin, 1955), ch. 2.

Cross-Sectional Data Matrix				Sequential Data Matrix		

	Units of Analysis			Time Periods	
	Smith or Region A	Jones or Region B		Smith or Region A Time 1	Smith or Region A Time 2
Variables			Variables		
X Employment or Urbanism	x_1	x_2	X Employment or Urbanism	x_1	x_2
Y Politics or Birthrate	y_1	y_2	Y Politics or Birthrate	y_1	y_2

Illustration 1

Smith   Smith, Time 1

  Employment: agricultural (x_1)   Employment: agricultural (x_1)
  Politics: conservative (y_1)   Politics: conservative (y_1)

Jones   Smith, Time 2

  Employment: industrial (x_2)   Employment: industrial (x_2)
  Politics: radical (y_2)   Politics: radical (y_2)

Conclusion: industrial employment leads to
political radicalism.

Illustration 2

Region A   Region A, Time 1

  Urbanism: rural (x_1)   Urbanism: rural (x_1)
  Birthrate: high (y_1)   Birthrate: high (y_1)

Region B   Region A, Time 2

  Urbanism: urban (x_2)   Urbanism: urban (x_2)
  Birthrate: low (y_2)   Birthrate: low (y_2)

Conclusion: Urbanism leads to a decline in the birthrate.

Figure 3
An Illustration of Conclusions Drawn From Two Types of Data Matrices

correlated variables. Without the assumption of developmental equivalence, then, cross-section data seem completely irrelevant to questions of cause-and-effect.

It does not seem to be recognized generally that this assumption of developmental equivalence is not only at the basis of inferences from survey data to temporal trends, but, indeed, at the basis of all correlation analysis (i.e., non-experimental procedures) from which causation is to be inferred, except for that in which actual temporal sequences are observed. Nearly all correlation analysis is based on simultaneous observation of several variables at one point in time. Yet nearly all causal theories assume that there must be some *temporal ordering* of variables that stand in a causal relation one to another, with the cause preceding the effect. When correlations form the basis for a causal analysis, the logic they follow is that of a simulated experiment, but the simulation is valid only if (among other things) developmental equivalence is assumed. For example, Lieberson and Silverman [42] made a comparative study of urban riots in U.S. cities and found that riots were more likely in cities where Negroes appeared to have competed more successfully with whites for better paying and more secure jobs. Their analysis suggested that this was a causal relationship. In fact, they established the following: Cities with a lower proportion of Negroes in traditional unskilled occupations have experienced more riots. Stated differently, if Negroes succeed in moving out of their traditional occupations, race riots are more likely. In this last statement of the conclusions developmental equivalence has been assumed since the authors have not based their conclusion on an observation of the *actual temporal* change in riot-predisposition in one or more cities as the comparative occupational structure of whites and Negroes has changed. Rather, they have drawn their conclusions from a *comparison* of a number of cities, this comparison being the essential ingredient in all correlation analysis.

In view of the widespread use of the assumption of developmental equivalence, and even the increasing frequency of inferences from correlations to rather refined conclusions about the relative importance of one among a set of interconnected causal variables,[43] it is surprising that this

42. S. Lieberson and A. Silverman, "The Precipitants and Underlying Conditions of Race Riots," *American Sociological Review*, 30 (December 1965): 887–898.

43. See the references in note 2 to path analysis and the many applications of this in recent political science publications, especially W. Miller and D. Stokes, "Constituency Influence in Congress," *American Political Science Review*, 57 (March 1963): 46–56; C. Cnudde and D. McCrone, "The Linkage between Constituency Attitudes and Congressional Voting Behavior: A Causal Model," *American Political Science Review*, 60 (March 1966): pp. 66–72; D. McCrone and C. Cnudde, "Toward a Communications Theory of Democratic Political Develop-

assumption has neither been more widely discussed (or at least given a name) nor subjected to empirical test. Such testing, once the difficult problem of obtaining appropriate data has been solved, is relatively straightforward. To my knowledge, Kuznets is one of the few to have commented on this problem with empirical data to support his conclusions, and his findings are not auspicious. In examining the trend patterns of certain consumption variables in an economic analysis, he found "a number of disagreements" between the expectations based on cross-section analysis and the actual growth trends revealed by time series data; the results are sufficiently incompatible for him to warn against the easy acceptance of this assumption.[44] In a related discussion, the facile assumption of homogeneity (which may be interpreted as a parsimonious rationale for assuming developmental equivalence) has also been criticized in the analysis of psychological materials.[45]

This lengthy aside on the assumption of developmental equivalence may seem digressive. But it is relevant to the present topic in several ways: (1) It pertains to the manner in which data are to be manipulated to bring them into correspondence with the verbal, theoretical conclusions to be drawn from the analysis; (2) it is pertinent to the manner in which survey

---

ment: A Causal Model," *American Political Science Review*, 61 (March 1967): 72–79; A. Goldberg, "Discerning a Causal Pattern Among Data on Voting Behavior," *American Political Science Review*, 60 (December 1966): 913–922; and H. Alker, Jr., *Statistics and Politics: The Need for Causal Data Analysis*, prepared for delivery at the Annual Meeting of the American Political Science Association, Chicago, September 5–8, 1967. For an early methodological statement, see H. Blalock, "Evaluating the Relative Importance of Variables," *American Sociological Review*, 26 (December 1961): 866–874.

44. S. Kuznets, *Modern Economic Growth: Rate, Structure and Spread* (New Haven: Yale University Press, 1966), p. 506.

45. "The behavioral sciences have attempted to erect a superstructure without paying sufficient attention to its foundation. A uniformity of expression over individuals, and even across species, has too often been assumed for behaviors under study" J. Kirsch, "Behavior Genetics and Individuality Understood," *Science*, 142 (13 December 1963): 1436. The contrasting views of a natural scientist and a sociologist nicely pose the issue: "So, if I follow this box of 32 molecules for 10,000 collisions, it's true that I have only 32 molecules, but I will get an enormous number of samples of the ways in which they might behave. In physics, we're always interchanging a time average and a population average, exploiting this to the hilt" E. Purcell, "Discussion," *in* D. Lerner, *Parts and Wholes* (New York: Free Press, 1963), p. 26. On the other hand, "It is true . . . that a study of the total class requires much greater effort and time than an investigation of its representative samples. But despite some progress in sampling techniques, there is an absence of a precise definition of what sort of sample is an adequate or truly representative sample in a study of numerous, many-dimensional, complex, abstract and discrete sociocultural phenomena," P. Sorokin, "Reply to My Critics," *in* P. Allen, ed., *Pitrin A. Sorokin in Review* (Durham, N.C.: Duke Univ. Press, 1963), p. 433. Further comments on this topic can be found in A. Rose, *Theory and Method in the Social Sciences* (Minneapolis: University of Minnesota, 1954), p. 259, and M. Cohen and E. Nagel, *op. cit.*, pp. 267–269.

data lend themselves to a cause-and-effect analysis of structural variables; and (3) it suggests some of the reasons why one may think of trading, so to speak, a large sample size for a gain in historical depth (to be noted below). In sum, conclusions about causation based with apparent confidence on a large-sample multivariate analysis are of little value if developmental equivalence cannot be assumed; it is only on surface appearance that they are of greater validity than the conclusions of a study that traces, for a small sample of countries, the actual developmental trends in those countries over time. "How large was the sample?" is sometimes a misleading question.

A form of "sequence analysis" for historical studies. Of course, neither cross-sectional inference to causal patterns nor time series analysis of trends provides conclusions about causation that are as plausible as conclusions obtained from experimental manipulation, but experimentation is beyond the reach of most macro-sociological hypotheses. In view of the fact that trend analysis is more to the point than inference from cross-sections, macro-sociological knowledge will grow to the extent that time series data become available. Time series data will, in turn, become available largely through the data collection efforts of administrative agencies by means of censuses and descriptive sample surveys. Only a minor contribution to actual bodies of relevant data can be expected from the increasingly and deliberately cumulative efforts of scholars through activities such as data libraries, although these developments are important for other reasons; hence this essay emphasizes throughout an active social science that views itself as a part, rather than a detached observer, of contemporary history and that sees itself as taking part in attempts to make increasingly rational decisions based upon systematically collected information.

For all of these reasons, it is appropriate to consider compensating for the small size of sample when structural analysis of national or regional units are analyzed by adding historical depth to the studied materials. Even in a conventional statistical framework, there is a gain in efficiency when overtime observations are made. It has the effect of using a much larger sample size, since one source of "random variation," a source that may be seen as coming from unsystematic ("random") violation of the assumption of developmental equivalence, is eliminated.[46] One may think of trading large sample size for historical depth. Yet this suggests a mode of analysis of the data different from the conventional correlation analysis, and one such alternative mode, especially appropriate to the type of study Moore has undertaken, is discussed here.

Among the many methods that are available for analyzing time series

46. Cf., W. Wallis and H. Roberts, *Statistics: A New Approach* (Glencoe, Ill.: Free Press, 1956), sec. 13.2.2.2, especially p. 422.

data, the procedure that is suggested here seems most appropriate for extracting relevant information from a rich body of historical data pertaining to a few complex organizations such as the societies studied by Moore. There is nothing particularly complex or technical about this method, and I would not identify it by name except that such identification sometimes makes more likely the focused development of methodological procedures. I shall refer to the kind of analysis described below as "sequence analysis"; it is little different from stochastic process analysis except that probability assumptions are not essential; they are invoked—if at all—only with proper justification. The term sequence is emphasized since the method suggests another solution to the "Verba problem" of many variables and few cases. Each case may give rise to a number of sequences that can be placed in the same conceptual category, so that the evidential basis for conclusions is enhanced by observing replications within a single case.

The essence of many of the arguments of Moore, and of much historical writing, is that certain combinations of factors make certain subsequent events more likely. This type of information follows the pattern that Nagel [47] has identified as "genetic explanation." One wants to know: what are the antecedents or consequences of structure X? Weber has referred to the notion that once certain structures appear, the "die is cast," making it more likely that certain events will occur on the next roll of the dice. Such arguments are very familiar in application to current events as well as historical writing. It is argued, for instance, that the assertion of new rights by an underprivileged group is likely to result in a "backlash" by more established groups in society. Many judgments about current events are made in terms of an assessment of the likelihood of such sequences. A memoir of the late Senator Robert Kennedy pointed out the manner in which military advisors to his brother during the Cuban missile crisis seemed unrealistically optimistic about the Soviet response to the U.S. action.[48] In a great variety of situations, both policy-maker and citizen, as well as scholar, are interested in conclusions of this sort: Given this combination of events, what is the likely change (if any) in that variable? Sequence analysis is a systematic method for the study of such questions.

In essence, sequence analysis is simply the systematic exposition of the kinds of sequences of historical or institutional events or structures that are of interest and the recording of the number of times these sequences are observed in the studied materials. To return to the set of variables consid-

47. E. Nagel, *The Structure of Science* (New York: Harcourt, Brace, 1961), p. 25.

48. R. Kennedy, "Lessons of the Cuban Missile Crisis," *Saturday Review* (26 October 1968), p. 24.

ered in Figure 2, taken from Moore: Across how many of his sequential matrices (one for each studied country) do we find, for instance, that democratic institutions appear in a country that previously had a commercial non-labor-repressive agrarian system? How many times was there some other outcome? Having brought us to the point of making such assertions, although heavily qualified, and suggesting that they are relevant to the contemporary development of democracy in India, Moore surprisingly feels unable to present an unambiguous summary of his conclusions in some form such as that shown in Figure 4.

Admittedly Figure 4 oversimplifies Moore's conclusions in many ways even if we confine ourselves momentarily to these two variables.[49] In writing about France, he notes that France's failure to develop the English agrarian pattern suggests an alternative route to democratic institutions; the summary table, on the other hand, implies a kind of homogeneous development of the eight societies presented in it. Yet a systematic summary of this kind need not make such an assumption of homogeneity. The "alternative route" model employed by Moore could be pictorially represented by using an adaptation of the kind of tree diagram discussed by Kemeny,[50] adapted by biologists in presenting evolutionary theories,[51] and by Barton on social science classification.[52] But summary tables of some sort, dealing not only with the agrarian systems of the societies he studies, but also with the many other variables he discusses, including the existence at some point in the history of the society of a revolutionary or violent conflict between essentially different political orders, are implicit in Moore; summary tables, heavily qualified where necessary, would be a great aid in the communication of his conclusions about classifications that are now scattered unsystematically throughout different chapters that alternatively focus on (a) a detailed history of particular societies, but contain many comparative references or (b) general thematic conclusions that contain, in some instances, a great deal of idiographic detail.

49. For ease of interpretation I follow a procedure that is convenient—when sample size is small and units of analysis are publicly known—of placing the names of the units (societies in this case) in the proper cells rather than inserting simply a frequency count. In addition, a page reference is included as there are many places where material relevant to the classification can be found (and some discussions may, on balance, contradict others). In spite of the fact that this argument is one of Moore's major conclusions (see one verbal statement of it appended to Table 2), it is not obvious from a rereading of his book how each society should be classified in this scheme.

50. J. Kemeny and others, *Introduction to Finite Mathematics*, p. 25.

51. G. Simpson, *Life* (New York: Harcourt, Brace, 1957), pp. 459–474.

52. Cf. A. Barton, "The Concept of Property-Space in Social Research," in P. Lazarsfeld and M. Rosenberg, eds., *The Language of Social Research* (Glencoe, Ill.: Free Press, 1955), esp. pp. 49–50 on "functional reduction."

Time 1

Commercial, non-labor-repressive
agrarian system[*]

	Quite developed	Only slightly developed	Not developed

Time 2

Democratic Political Institutions	Yes	England (pp. 30-32) U. S. (p. 111)	France (pp. 106-7)	
	Outcome yet unknown			India (p. 430)
	No		Japan (pp. 286-7)	China (p. 180) Russia (p. 422) Germany (p. 465)

[*]"The taming of the agrarian sector has been a decisive feature of the whole historical process that produced such a society (as modern Western democracy)" p. 429,
Moore, *op. cit.*

Figure 4
Evidence for a Sequence Conclusion from Moore

If progress is to be made in objectifying conclusions about historical sequences, it is necessary to make a concerted effort to reach agreement on the classification of historical events that constitute those sequences. If Moore and others would present their conclusions about classification—and, indeed, about the very language they deem appropriate to those conclusions —in a less ambiguous way, subsequent investigators might more readily build upon their efforts and increase the reliability with which such classifications may be made. Eisenstadt [53] has recently presented a number of summary classification tables of historical social structures similar in nature to those examined by Moore. Eisenstadt's commendable procedures quite properly raise the next questions: What evidence do we have that his classification is correct and by what logical device do we make those classifications, given that evidence? By presenting a summary table, Eisenstadt has performed the very important task of making clear the *conceptual language* that is relevant to the classification. This is an important building block. It provides a touchstone, so to speak, for subsequent work on classification that is lacking when material is presented in the fashion chosen by Moore, without explicitly defined and consistently used variables.

Sequence analysis can be viewed as the systematic study of particular kinds of sequences of events that are assumed to have some kind of causal connection. As the Moore example illustrates, they need not be derived from the examination of different units of analysis in the same chronological time period. Moore examines England largely in the 17th century and Japan largely in the 19th and early 20th centuries. Sequence analysis thus studies more abstract units of historical or temporal patterns and does so in a comparative way by suggesting that there is merit in juxtaposing the behavior of one unit of analysis at a particular time (e.g., England in the 17th century) with the behavior of one or more units of analysis at some point in its development (e.g., Japan in the 19th and early 20th centuries). The units of analysis that are studied in sequence analysis need not be total societies or even collectivities. When a social psychologist argues that certain child-rearing practices have predictable consequences in adult behavior, a form of sequence analysis is being applied to the individual as a unit. When a student of conflict processes asserts that one consequence of the development of a conflict around a particular issue, such as water fluoridation in an American community, is that other issues are brought into contention, as the conflict escalates,[54] he is making an assertion about the sequences to be observed in units of analysis that are conflict processes.

53. S. Eisenstadt, *The Political Systems of Empires* (New York: Free Press, 1963), esp. pp. 375–471.
54. J. Coleman, *Community Conflict* (Glencoe, Ill.: Free Press, 1957).

Such a conflict process may or may not be defined so as to include only those persons within the boundary of a conventional political unit.

The role of probabilistic reasoning in sequence analysis is somewhat ambiguous. In a sense, my notion is simply a formalization of remarks contained in Weber's critique of Eduard Meyer.[55] Weber argues that Meyer's reasoning on the causes of war is misleading and that one can argue that certain events "tip the scales" or "load the dice" in favor of definite historical outcomes. Yet it is not true, suggests Weber (and with this I concur), that in the realm of historical events one can attach a precise numerical value to the chances that are thus influenced. One can attach exact numerical values only in the sphere Weber refers to as "absolute chance (in the logical sense), i.e., in cases where—for example, as in the throwing of dice or in drawing balls of various colors from an urn, unaffected in composition by the drawings therefrom—given a very large number of cases, certain simple and unambiguous conditions remain absolutely the same." [56] On the other hand, Weber remarks, despite the inability to assign a precise numerical measure of chance to historical sequences, we can "render generally valid judgments . . . that as a result of certain situations the occurrence of a type of reaction . . . is 'favored' to a more or less high degree." In other words, one can make a judgment that the occurrence of a specific condition (the appearance of commercial agriculture) makes a certain outcome (the rise of democratic institutions) more likely than would be the case if that condition were not present, although it would be foolish to try to attach a precise numerical probability to this judgment. As in sequence analysis, Weber goes on to say that this judgment can be made by comparing it with other circumstances where the event in question was not present. The major difference between Weber's formulation and that which I present here is that Weber relies on the "imagination" for such comparisons and I am suggesting that one rely largely on *empirically observed* comparisons such as those presented by Moore and summarized in Figure 4.

This interpretation of Weber's remarks suggests that there is nothing particularly new in my suggestion that sequence analysis be applied to historical materials. There may be some value in considering more recent thinking on "subjective probability," which would be the basis of the imaginative consideration of alternative possibilities Weber had in mind.[57] Also appropriate, perhaps, are the very careful and thoughtful procedures de-

55. M. Weber, *The Methodology of the Social Sciences* (Glencoe, Ill.: Free Press, 1949), esp. p. 183.

56. Cohen and Nagel, *op. cit.*, p. 182.

57. See, for example, Bruno de Finetti, "Probability: Interpretations," *International Encyclopedia of the Social Sciences*, (New York: Free Press, 1968), 12: 496–504.

scribed by Komarovsky for "discerning" a causal influence when examining case histories.[58] My inclination would be to remain closer to empirical observations and to avoid probability calculations altogether, either subjective or objective. After a sufficiently large body of sequences was accumulated and judged to be essentially similar in nature, then I would deem it appropriate to apply objective probability calculations. Kendall, for example, has applied probability methods to historical events in an appropriate fashion,[59] but it is very rare that events of the macro-sociological type considered by Moore (and Weber) are found susceptible to actual probability calculations of this sort. Aside from the weighty task of assembling the appropriate information, one would always be troubled by the *ceteris paribus* assumption that is a necessary part of any comparative analysis. In addition, when using sequential analysis to predict the outcome of a contemporary event, as Moore effectively is doing for India, one faces the same questions of comparability with regard to the sequence that is being predicted. Will future developments in India, for instance, duplicate past developments in other countries, or at least depart from them in systematic ways? In this sense, a "firm" knowledge (even on a probabilistic basis) of historical developments will probably remain forever elusive, in spite of pretentious theoretical and methodological arguments one sometimes hears in support of the eventual development of rigorous social theory. Nevertheless, a focus on particular types of sequences that can be classed together (at least provisionally) may eventuate in the development of a reasonable estimate of probabilities of the outcomes of those sequences. In such probability estimates, it is likely that the degree of similarity of one sequence and another would become a part of the estimate in somewhat the same way that Naroll [60] suggests that the reliability of ethnographic information can be systematically incorporated into conclusions drawn about those data. In other words, one would present several estimated values distinguished by the plausibility of the reasoning (often analogical) underlying them.

It might be noted that Weber's discussion of this kind of causal judgment makes reference to the impact of events on individual "persons who confront these situations." It is at this point that survey analysis, which had hardly begun to be developed in Weber's time, can be built into sequence analysis by comparing the subjective impressions of those who have confronted particular situations with those who have not. Consider how

58. Mira Komarovsky, *The Unemployed Man and His Family* (New York: Dryden, 1940), pp. 134–146.

59. M. Kendall, "Natural Law in the Social Sciences," *Journal of Royal Statistical Society*, A (pt. 1, 1961): 1–16.

60. Naroll, *op. cit.*

Moore's analysis would be enhanced, for instance, if one had survey data permitting a comparison of the political attitudes of landowners in early 17th-century England with those of landowners in wine-growing areas of pre-revolutionary France with attitudes of landowners in other regions of that country. Future historians will find these types of survey data available to the extent that contemporary data archives and survey researchers emphasize descriptive as well as explanatory designs and collection procedures.[61]

For the present, many conclusions in both scholarly and practical affairs will have to be made without a strong evidential basis. In such circumstances, how can one improve understanding of a sequence? One procedure is to introduce new variables. A previous example suggested that in order to enhance the plausibility of the sequence "absence of feudalism leads to an open class structure," one should examine the consequences of feudalism in relation to class attitudes. It might be that some rather hard evidence could be obtained for the sequence "feudalism leads to rigid class attitudes," as well as the sequence that "the absence of rigid class attitudes leads to an open class structure." When the two sequences are considered simultaneously, the first sequence becomes much more plausible than when the variable "class attitudes" is omitted. Another way in which sequences are made more plausible is by inserting more complex variables within them. If one considers not a single variable but a combination of variables, the sequence "successful war of independence from a monarchy together with absence of feudalism leads to open class structure," seems more plausible than the simpler one, in part because of the plausibility of causal assumptions about the effects on attitudes of a successful war against a monarchy.

The chief advantage of the sequence matrix formulation and systematic summary of it is that it brings into focus the conclusions that have been reached about particular types of sequences, and at the same time it clarifies some aspects of the limited evidential basis for that conclusion. Scholarly knowledge is always partial and qualified; if used in policy and action, there is a point at which one must decide whether any useful information has been obtained or whether the qualifications and partial nature

61. I have incorporated survey questions of a nature particularly appropriate to this aspect of sequence analysis (in that the respondent was asked to estimate the likelihood of different outcomes of contemporary public political events) in a series of comparative surveys made of students on the Berkeley campus of the University of California since 1964. Details may be obtained from International Data Library, Survey Research Center, University of California, Berkeley, 1964, "Mainsprings of the Rebellion—Two Wave Panel," Questions 38 and 39, and 1968, "Students at UC Berkeley, Winter-Spring, 1968," Questions 4, 6, 33, 34, and 35.

of the evidence make the conclusions too unreliable. To bridge the gap between scholar and policy-maker, it is necessary to develop systematic procedures that will aid in making this decision. Sequence analysis is intended as a step in the direction of the development of appropriate procedures.

(vi) *Interpretations.*—The task of linking empirical observations to theoretical concepts is fundamentally a question of weighing evidence for or against particular types of descriptive conclusions about the nature of the "real world." As these conclusions come to pertain more to macro-sociological types of structures and events than to micro-sociological descriptions, and particularly where value-laden concepts are employed, the weighing of evidence is often controversial. In part, this is because macro-sociological conclusions are likely to be subjected to independent replications to a greater degree than are micro-sociological conclusions. The classification of a social system relationship between elite and mass as "democratic" or "paternalistic," for example, may be more subject to public scrutiny than a conclusion that particular sampled respondents in a survey are "alienated" or "anti-Semitic." The latter conclusion might be as controversial as the former if the result were to be publicly announced, especially to the respondent himself.

Judgments of this nature, making assessments of the empirical world in terms of abstract conceptions, can be made in a variety of ways. A common procedure in the social sciences is to employ the notion of "indicators," asserting that particular kinds of evidence serve to indicate the presence or absence of a general tendency or predisposition. In the natural sciences, as well as in the social, and indeed in the world of non-scientific discourse about social affairs, indicators are often the only clues on which the judgments of this nature are made. All such judgments are necessarily approximate; some are based on more evidence than others. An individual may be known to his friends as prejudiced against Jews because of general remarks in his conversations; a well-written interview should be able to probe beliefs and opinions so that the inference of prejudice can be detected with a relatively small margin of error. If the individual himself were asked directly about anti-Semitism, he would probably deny that he had feelings of that kind. If a study were published in which a public figure were identified as an anti-Semite, it would certainly be controversial, and almost as certainly some scientific opinion would come forth to support the man's denial even though most scientific opinion supported the assessment. Clearly, such assessments are rarely made public except those of particular elites (Eichmann, Hitler, etc.) about whom opinion is likely to be established.

Classifying collectivities instead of individuals involves logic no different from that described earlier. But for reasons noted above, judgments of this nature are likely to be more controversial. Very often such judgments are a matter of public, as well as scholarly, discussion. Value controversies are often involved. And different scholars, bringing different viewpoints to bear, are in a position to make independent judgments about the same events and structures, much as if clinical psychologists were in a position to make public their evaluations of particular patients who were available for assessment and diagnosis by many clinicians. It is not surprising that there are controversies about such judgments. As macro-sociological assessments are made about more distant events, in terms of historical time or accessibility on other grounds, reliance is placed on the evaluations of particular investigators whose conclusions are employed without independent assessment, and we approach the more "normal," but less scientific, condition of one clinician assessing a particular patient. In such circumstances, it is necessary to rely heavily on the competence of the single evaluator. Sociologists engaged in comparative studies who rely largely on the assessments of historians or ethnologists only infrequently have opportunity to consider, with systematic deliberation, the manner in which specific interpretations of data have been made.

Nevertheless, it is at this level that scientific procedures are most important. To the extent that assessments are the work of a single individual, scientific judgments are essentially precluded and the ensuing consensus is likely to rest, in the words of Cohen and Nagel,[62] on the "method of authority" rather than "the method of science or reflective inquiry." Obviously much reliance on experts is necessary, but equally obvious is the conclusion that assessment methods for macro-sociological structures and events will have to become more complex and subtle if they are to take account adequately of the quantities of significant information that may be obtained about macro-sociological structures in the contemporary world.

In a recent discussion of "social indicators," Gross has eloquently stated both the role played in human affairs by abstract macro-sociological descriptions and the process by which these concepts are operationally defined. It is significant that although Gross, in the excerpt below, is discussing concepts that have strong evaluative connotations, the procedures by which he suggests they are given scientific status in no way differ from the procedures employed for the value-neutral concepts more common to conventional social science.

62. Cohen and Nagel, *op. cit.*, p. 193.

For centuries the "grand abstractions" have been the ideas that have stirred men's souls. They have become the symbol and inspiration of mass movements, wars and revolutions and the creation of new states. In declarations of independence and national purpose, in constitutions, charters, and solemn covenants, they have become enshrined as national and international goals. Similarly, the "intermediate abstractions" are those which are the lifeblood of controversy, planning negotiations and maneuver in bureaucracies, legislatures, and courts.

At times both the grand and the intermediate abstractions become empty shells, devoid of meaning and content or else a shoddy facade to disguise tyranny, slavery, prejudice, exploitation, stagnation or intellectual or moral bankruptcy. The continuing strength of the grand abstractions lies in their recurring use to refer to specific interests in specific aspects of system performance. They are most powerful when rooted in the intermediate abstractions and, through them and along with them, in the keenly felt interests of people and well-organized groups. These intermediate abstractions may themselves be meaningless or fraudulent. They become more meaningful only when supported by more specific indicators at lower levels on the ladder.

When we come down to earth and spell out just what we mean by a grand abstraction like "abundance," we can now attain much greater precision. This has the great value of providing data that give a better understanding of relations and interrelationships, make it easier to verify or disprove conclusions, and facilitate communications among different people and groups. Such data may also be of considerable symbolic value, sounding more "objective" and "scientific." At the same time, greater precision may eliminate the possibilities for consensus and coalition that stem from vagueness and ambiguity.

At the same time, as we come near the bottom of the ladder, we encounter the phenomenon of the decreasing relevance of any indicator. Thus the monetary value of a certain type of output may give an extremely one-sided or distorted view of events. One-sidedness or distortion may occur when an increase in output quantity is used without considering marginal increments; or when one type of index number is used without seeing what happens when other types are used. All these, and many other, possibilities illustrate the danger of focussing on a *single* precise indicator. This danger may be avoided only by using a *set* of indicators.

To avoid the danger of irrelevance at the bottom of the ladder, we must recognize the necessity of multiple dimensions, even for such a presumably concrete and homogeneous phenomenon as output. How we select the components of any particular set depends, of course, on the nature of the available data, the cost of obtaining it or improving it, and the particular purpose at hand.

This "horizontal multiplicity," in turn, must be combined with "vertical multiplicity," if the specific indicators are to be linked with the intermediate and grand abstractions. Any rich understanding of a past or present system state or any rich portrayal of future purpose requires one to run up and down the abstraction-specificity ladder. This is the only way to escape the "slippage" resulting from decreased precision as one goes up, and of increasing multiplicity and decreasing relevance as one moves downward.

But a multiplicity of concepts and measures, it must be recognized, always creates new difficulties. The most obvious one is the problem of working them into some manageable pattern rather than allowing them to create confusion by unordered proliferation. The less obvious difficulty is that multiplicity creates excellent opportunities for the manipulation of data to vindicate or indict. Indeed, unless one is prepared to handle a multiplicity of concepts and measures at various levels of the abstraction-specificity ladder, one may be readily misled by those who are more proficient in the arts of data interpretation and presentation.[63]

Further remarks on the topic of empirical interpretation of *evaluative* concepts will be presented in section (ix) below, but they may be brief because, as is suggested by a comparison of Gross's remarks with those of Lazarsfeld and Rosenberg [64] (for example) in discussing non-evaluative concepts, the logic is the same. It is useful at this point to view the matter of interpretation from a more psychological viewpoint, and to see if it is possible to outline a simple and provisional reconstruction of the manner in which descriptive interpretations are carried out in the mind of a single investigator and consider whether this reconstruction bears any resemblance to statistical methods of measurement that are current in social science.

A verbal model of "qualitative measurement."—The perceptive and cognitive apparatus of the human mind engages in assessments every day. Rarely are these scientific in nature; for various reasons of efficiency and emotion, the human mind engages in shortcuts and distortions in making such assessments. The process of making such judgments on a scientific basis may be viewed as (1) making public the deliberations upon which such assessments are based so that, in the words of Goodenough,[65] the conclusions may be "subject to public scrutiny," and (2) taking precautions against the making of distortions and the taking of unnecessary shortcuts. A working procedure for a human mind engaged in "reflective inquiry"— Cohen and Nagel's term for science—about the "nature of the real world," a procedure that attempts to correct for distortions and avoid biasing shortcuts, may be described as the following sequence of three interrelated steps:

(*a*) The inquiring mind entertains an initial hypothesis. In common

63. B. Gross, "The State of the Nation: Social Systems Accounting," *in* R. Bauer, ed., *Social Indicators* (Cambridge, Mass.: MIT Press, 1966), pp. 265–267. Quotation marks indicating the author's citations to his earlier discussion of this same topic in B. Gross, *The Managing of Organizations* (New York: Free Press, 1964, 2 vols.) have been deleted in order to make the passage more readable.

64. Lazarsfeld and Rosenberg, *op. cit.*, sec. II, Introduction.

65. Ward Goodenough, "Componential Analysis," *Science,* 156 (2 June 1967): 1204.

experience, this frequently derives from some institutionalized authority. In scientific work, the very usefulness of the category system, as well as the expertise of the authority, are questioned. Not only are the social sciences subject to distortions on this level. Training procedures in the natural science of physics have, surprisingly, been accused of encouraging attitudes of credulity toward the fundamental assumptions upon which physical theory rests.[66] In the social sciences, individuals who have an impressive command of a body of literature, a personal conviction that they have special insight into the workings of society, and an energetic capacity to articulate that insight may become figures with special authority in spite of their failure to make explicit the detailed deliberations on which particular judgments rest. As a reliance on empirical data and systematic methodology for descriptive assessments and judgments grows, these problems should decline. "If we wish clarity and accuracy, order and consistency, security and cogency, in our actions and intellectual allegiances, we shall have to resort to some method of fixing beliefs whose efficacy in resolving problems is *independent of our desires and wills.* Such a method, which takes advantage of the objective connections in the world around us, should be found reasonable not because of its appeal to the idiosyncrasies of a selected few individuals, but because it can be tested repeatedly and by all men." [67]

(*b*) As a second step in the assessment process, the hypothetical "inquiring mind" determines a new piece of evidence to be relevant to the initial hypothesis. This determination has no firm basis when clinical procedures are being followed. Usually, a judgment has to be made of the fact that either (1) the new indication is an observation that occurs with differential frequency according to the truth or falsity of the initial hypothesis when it is examined over many units of analysis, or (2) the new indication is a cause or an effect of the hypothesized condition, or (3) that the new indication appears, over time within the same unit, with differential frequency according to the truth or falsity of the initial hypothesis. In qualitative analysis, these three types of judgment are commonly used but generally implicit. Their explication would be a boon to the development of scientific consensus in comparative historical and institutional studies. Creativity can play a great role here; note the ingenuity in interpretations suggested by Webb and others,[68] for various descriptive indicators. In statistical analysis, each of the three types of judgment is the basis of a measurement technique. The first type of judgment, being the basis for

66. M. Hubbert, "Are We Retrogressing in Science?" *Science,* 139 (8 March 1963): 884–890.

67. Cohen and Nagel, *op. cit.,* p. 195 (emphasis added).

68. E. Webb and others, *Unobtrusive Measures, op. cit.*

factor analysis, Guttman scaling, latent structure analysis, and other measurement methods, is by far the most common. For pragmatic reasons, the second type of judgment, that emphasizes cause-or-effect relations, is not often a convenient solution to the measurement problem although it has recently been cogently argued by Duncan.[69] The third is the basis for the construction of index numbers in economics.[70]

In survey work, as in other endeavors, non-empirical judgments also enter into such interpretations. In developing an index of socio-economic status of individuals, for example, income is an obvious indicator. Education, always positively correlated with income, is frequently used in combination with the former. Occupational status can also be added to the index. But the extent of social involvement in informal organizations or in the mass media, while correlated with status, is not ordinarily included in an index of status, since those observations are deemed to have separate *conceptual status* and meaning.

(c) Having judged an observation relevant to the initial hypothesis, the problem is then to consider whether the new piece of information contributes to or detracts from the tentative initial hypothesis entertained at the outset. This is done by making a judgment similar to that made in *(b)*, but different in intent. Here the *substantive* meaning rather than the *conceptual* meaning of the new observation is determined. Taking an example from material considered by Moore, if the new item of information is that a landlord shows a certain enterprise in encouraging his peasants to improve the grain yield on his lands, one has to judge whether this *enhances* or *detracts from* the initial hypothesis that the landlord was repressive in his behavior. Such judgments are not always easy, although many times they are so obvious as not to require any deliberation. In survey work, for instance, it is hardly arguable to assert that the information that a respondent voted in the most recent presidential election is indicative of his having participated, to some degree, in the political process. This is both relevant to and confirming of an initial hypothesis that he is a "political participant." When the judgment is more difficult, as in the example of a landlord initially thought to be "repressive," who is found to have encouraged greater crop yields, the observation is likely to suggest a typology of landlord-peasant relationships more differentiated than that initially conceived. Landlords who are otherwise repressive, but who differ in the extent to which they make constructive improvements in agriculture, might be distinguished from the more general class of repressive landlords. In statistical and survey analysis, this "deviant"

69. O. Duncan, "Discrimination Among Negroes," *Annals of the American Academy of Political and Social Science*, 371 (May 1967): 86–87.
70. See, for example, Yule and Kendall, *op. cit.* (note 34), ch. 25.

type might be ascribed to error if it occurred infrequently.

Where substantive meaning is clear and the new indication confirms the initial hypothesis, the hypothesis is enhanced;[71] it is jeopardized if the new evidence contradicts it. When sufficient contrary indications are obtained, the initial hypothesis is discarded. The procedure is identical to the procedures employed in statistical analysis except that it is common to employ an initial hypothesis only in certain special statistical techniques. Most commonly, the evidential indications are simultaneously juxtaposed and summarized in some way. Sometimes they are given differential weights, although the choice of weights is often problematic. Some investigators perform experiments to learn whether differential weights affect the conclusions they wish to draw; more such experimentation is needed.

A procedure to enhance objectivity: In much historical and institutional analysis, the types of judgments described above that are required in the course of the analysis remain implicit, or are taken over from established authorities in the particular fields. Even if the investigator himself makes such judgments from time to time, his objectivity is generally suspect because the judgments he makes about one set of observations are almost never made *independently* of the judgments he makes about other observations. Rather, evidence is accumulated by an investigator against *known outcomes*. It is of little scientific value to rely on the judgment of a single scholar poring over material on particular structural relations in the 19th century in various countries to account for the structure of political institutions in those countries in the 20th century when it is clear that the scholar has been reviewing that historical material with full knowledge of the outcome that indeed occurred. As the illustration suggests, this criticism is especially cogent when applied to materials for which "sequence analysis," described above, is appropriate. Consider, for example, Moore's discussion of the relationship between the landlord and peasant in late 19th-century Japan. He wishes to account for the fact that Japanese political institutions eventually became fascistic. It would obviously be inappropriate to find that the Japanese landlord resembled the "enterprising landlord who so impressed foreign visitors to eighteenth-century England."[72] But his conclusion would be much more convincing and consequently more scientific if the evidence were weighed *independently* of the known outcome. For such purpose, an objective assessment procedure would be required. One such procedure is suggested.

71. A descriptive hypothesis, like any other, is unlikely to be "confirmed"; I use the word "enhanced" to refer to the fact that additional supporting evidence has accumulated.

72. Moore, *op. cit.* (note 1), p. 286.

(1) Suppose that a paragraph description of different *hypothetical* "*landlord behaviors*" were to be compiled in which neutral language were used so that the national origin of the illustrative example could not be detected, but with sufficient detail in the examples so that the richness of historical reality could be captured. In keeping with Moore's observations, this description should include the relation of the landlord to the peasant through indirect channels such as the state and other "more informal levers," as well as the extent of landlord involvement with improvement of agricultural practices, involvement in commercial aspects of agriculture, amount of crop exaction, and other matters. One can conceive of a number of hypothetical—but potentially real—descriptions of landlord behaviors being compiled in this way, that would reflect the range of possible behaviors that might be observed.

(2) Second, the *empirical materials* obtained from each of the countries being studied would be cast into descriptions in the same way—descriptions that were faithful to the empirical reality, but written in a neutral language so that the country of origin could not be detected from terms alone. Substantive differences might, of course, contain strong clues as to the nature of the country of origin, and this fact presents fundamental but not insurmountable problems.

In coding qualitative material in survey research, just such procedures as this are employed. A set of *coding categories*, essentially identical to the hypothetical "landlord behaviors" in (1), is developed. These are obtained both on the basis of common sense, and also by examining a sample of obtained responses. They will ultimately be used as "values" of the "variable" that is being coded. In the Moore example, the variable is "relation of landlord to peasant." In survey work, similarly complex and qualitative variables are sometimes employed.

Also in survey work, the actual *empirical response*, as in (2), is identified and, often without undue deliberation, effectively isolated from the values of other variables. That is to say, it is effectively examined independently of what in the Moore case would be the *outcome* of the historical developments in a particular country. In survey work, this is relatively easy to achieve, in part because one investigator does not do the actual classification of empirical cases; it is frequently made into a clerical operation. Yet it does sometimes transpire in a survey that the investigator himself classifies, let us say, a respondent as "anti-Semitic" (supposing that is a major observed variable), while holding before him a questionnaire in which it is obvious that the respondent is politically conservative. If the investigator performs this for many of his sampled respondents, then under certain conditions the results of subsequent analysis would be suspect. That is, suppose a major hypothesis of his study is that there is a positive correlation between anti-Semitism and political conservatism. This relation would be suspect under a condition that is frequently present when historical and macro-sociological qualitative institutional data are being examined; that is, if the material given by the respondent is *qualitative* and requires impression-istic judgment for proper classification. Frequently in survey work this is not the case; the respondent is classified by himself or by an interviewer in one or another objective category. Under these latter conditions, the rela-tionship between such an objective response and a judgment that the respondent is anti-Semitic is made explicit in subsequent analysis.

The similar isolation of *classification* procedures from *analysis*—the avoidance of "contamination" in Hyman's terms [73]—is more difficult in work-ing with historical materials. So far as I know, no one has suggested that historians construct routine procedures permitting clerks ignorant of the investigator's hypotheses to perform the classification. This has, however, been done by Swanson,[74] and others working with the empirical materials in the Human Relations Area Files. Such research procedures could be developed for dealing with historical materials more generally. Recognizing the fact that historical and institutional studies will often have to rely on impressionistic, qualitative judgments, the task of making them more scien-tific would generally benefit by the development of such a program. It could well begin by expanding current "data banks," which contain mostly survey information, to include descriptive qualitative information about larger units of analysis—institutional and national—for certain blocks of time—decades in recent times, and larger time periods for the more distant past.

Alternative Degrees of Precision Required. It surely is true, but infre-quently stated and occasionally forgotten, that precision is not an end in itself. Economists are sometimes critical of the fact that in social survey work "personal income" is treated as a set of crude categories when infor-mation appropriate to it can be obtained to the nearest dollar. For most surveys, all that is needed is a gross distinction between income groups, and greater precision is not used even if it is collected. The common tendency of some social researchers to perform analyses of many variables with those variables crudely grouped or "collapsed" into two categories (dichotomies) is sometimes looked upon as a procedure that introduces unwarranted error into the analysis. For much (but not all) analysis, this view is mis-taken. When studying relationships between variables, it is likely that *general* conclusions about relationships will be *unaffected* by such lack of

73. H. Hyman, *Survey Design and Analysis* (Glencoe, Ill.: Free Press, 1955), p. 180.
    74. Swanson, *op. cit.*

precision in measurement and classification procedures. This remark deserves additional comment.

In referring to the fact that general conclusions are not substantially affected by lack of precision in measuring procedures, great care has to be taken that the statement is not misinterpreted. Suppose that an investigator hypothesizes that there is a positive relationship between two variables—social position and conservative ideology. This is a "general" conclusion that he wishes to draw from the data since it deals only with the sign of the relationship rather than its precise magnitude. This conclusion is sufficient for a great deal of social theory and almost certainly it can be obtained with accuracy from even a crude analysis in which both variables are dichotomized. It would not be a worthy investment of resources, if this is the desired conclusion, to seek to measure social position and political ideology with a great deal of refinement; having done so there would be little or no gain in the validity of that conclusion.

A lack of precision, which introduces random or self-cancelling errors into the data, is not to be confused with the incorporation of systematic error or *bias* into the analysis. Error of a particularly pernicious sort, which produces a consistent bias, would arise if the observations of social position are not made *independently* of the observations of political ideology. It is much more worthwhile to invest resources in some procedure such as that described above to avoid "contamination" of variables, so as not to bias the conclusions, than to invest resources in a more refined measure of the variables being related, so as to increase their precision.

Consider again the above analysis. What is an appropriate next step? It is possible to argue, now that we know the general nature of the relationship between social position and ideology, that it is appropriate to seek more refined information about the *magnitude* of the relationship. This information is not often especially pertinent. A more appropriate question to raise is whether the relationship is not perhaps "spurious"—an outgrowth of concomitant variation between social position and ideology and having some third and causally prior variable that can be brought into the analysis, such as social position of family of orientation. This is precisely the question raised by Benson about Beard's hypothesis, noted above. Again, this kind of question can be answered with considerable validity by employing only a rather crude measure of family position. Most frequently, then, a wise investment of resources would seek to expand the analysis by the inclusion of more variables, independently observed, rather than a refinement of measurement procedures.

It seems likely that a significant gain could be achieved in comparative and historical studies of institutions if there were a more systematic treatment of variables being related to one another, even if the procedures employed in the measurement of those variables are rather imprecise— provided that they are not biased. In most such studies, the kinds of conclusions to be drawn from data deal with rather general matters, such as the existence and direction of a relationship. And imprecise measurement methods are sufficient to draw such conclusions.

There is another sense in which imprecise but unbiased measurement procedures are advantageous. As noted at some length in Section I, scientific progress is measured by the extent to which competent investigators achieve consensus. One important area in which consensus may arise is in the measurement process, and it is readily apparent that consensus about imprecise measurement is much more likely than consensus about fine details of classification or measurement. For example, to differentiate social positions and investigate the relationship between position and ideology, with both variables taken as dichotomous, it is only necessary to obtain agreement that the one position is higher than the other position, and the one ideological grouping more conservative than the other. If, on the other hand, one were to seek to establish more precise measurements of position in the social hierarchy so that, for example, there is a greater discrepancy between the upper class and the middle class than between the middle and the lower class, consensus is much less likely.

It seems, in other words, that even rather crude measurements may suffice for many of the conclusions that are to be drawn from data examined in comparative and historical perspective, and that it often may not be difficult to establish consensus regarding the necessary level of measurement for precisely the reason that it is crude. For both of these reasons, the elimination of unintended bias in the making of the observations is a task of greater urgency than the refinement of measurement techniques.

In addition, I have noted that "multivariate analyses" are in most instances more appropriate than further refinement of measurement techniques. One of the contemporary reasons for the eagerness found in some quarters to seek more refined measurements of variables is the fact that many multivariate techniques require observations on an "interval scale" of measurement, which means data in numerically measured form.[75] In view of the fact that many powerful statistical techniques presuppose numerical measurements, it is not surprising that considerable energy has been invested in the development of more precise measurement techniques.

75. In particular, this assumption is necessary for any methods that are based on regression or correlation analysis, including factor analysis and the variants of path analysis cited in notes 2 and 43, above.

But by the same reasoning as presented above, where it was suggested that the development of consensus about relatively imprecise but unbiased measures is more likely than the development of consensus about more refined measures, it seems that attempts to measure according to an interval or numerical scale are likely to be controversial. This should not detract from such efforts, unless there are alternative possibilities that appear to circumvent such controversy. One such possibility is the wider use of *rank-correlation* methods, since ranked variables occupy a position, in terms of precision, that is intermediate between numerically scored data and simply dichotomous variables. Further, it appears that recent developments have provided some useful multivariate statistical procedures for dichotomies and rank-orderings, and progress in this realm is continuing.[76]

(vii) *Conceptualization.*—Implicit in many of the preceding discussions is the notion that there exist various theoretical concepts that are to be empirically observed. At some point in many research studies it is useful to make explicit the grounds on which these conceptual distinctions rest and the manner in which concepts are defined. As Merton [77] noted in his classical essays on the relations between empirical and theoretical analyses, there is an interplay between conceptions that are shaped on theoretical grounds and the empirical materials that are used to observe and describe the real world in relation to those conceptions. In the previous section I noted, for instance, that in developing a notion of socio-economic status it is customary to include some measure of educational attainment but not to include some measure of involvement in voluntary organizations or media exposure. These decisions, and other similar ones, are made on theoretical-conceptual grounds. In the case of a concept like socio-economic status the decisions have become more or less conventional while in other areas they are less so.

In a criticism of the general approach to social empirical-theoretical research that frames research questions in terms of explicity designated

76. See, in particular, J. Davis, "A Partial Coefficient for Goodman and Kruskal's Gamma," *Journal of the American Statistical Association*, 62 (March 1967): 189–193; M. Rosenberg, "Test Factor Standardization as a Method of Interpretation," *Social Forces*, 41 (October 1962): 53–61; R. Somers, "Simple Measures of Association for the Triple Dichotomy," *Journal of the Royal Statistical Society*, A 127 (pt. 3, 1964): 409–415; R. Somers, "An Approach to Multivariate Analysis of Ordinal Data," *American Sociological Review*, 33 (December 1968): 971–977; R. Somers, "A Partitioning of Ordinal Information in a Three-Way Cross-Classification," to appear in *Multivariate Behavioral Research*, April 1970. Also pertinent for sampling theory is L. Goodman, "Partial Tests for Partial Taus," *Biometrika*, 46 (1959): 525–532.

77. Robert K. Merton, *Social Theory and Social Structure* (Glencoe, Ill.: Free Press, 1949), chs. 2 and 3.

variables to be empirically described and analyzed, Blumer [78] has commented on the lack of consensus among investigators in the selection of variables and implies that it is pretentious to impose such a framework of variables without having more agreement regarding the theoretical concepts that should suggest variables to be observed. It is my view, on the contrary, that there is merit in at least provisionally outlining in deliberately systematic form the variables that are to be observed in a particular research study in order that subsequent observers may have an explicit framework to build upon or modify. Without such explication, there is less likelihood of consensus developing since without explicitly defined concepts that are operationalized in deliberate ways, there is less opportunity for clarity and intellectual focus in the analysis and subsequent critical work.

Moore's study is primarily empirical rather than theoretical; it suffers from a lack of coherently defined concepts which would have given order to the observations that he has gleaned from the diverse source materials. But this surely is not meant to imply that Moore has achieved the impossible of accomplishing an investigation without employing conceptual language. Rather, he has, for the most part, employed concepts that are not too abstract or technical and that generally are a part of the common language, a level of conceptualization that is much more common in qualitative and descriptive studies than in studies that create more abstract variables from quantitative analyses. Many of the concepts that are focal points in Moore's analysis are listed in the index: royal absolutism, peasant and plebeian anticapitalism, anti-intellectualism, bourgeoisie, agrarian bureaucracy, capitalism, caste and caste system, and so on. A differentiation may be made among these concepts, particularly between those that are simply descriptive and those that, like democracy and fascism, bear a special relation to ideological goals and have an evaluative status, but it is not especially pertinent to consider such distinctions at this point. Nor is it necessary here to consider how Moore makes observations that are deemed relevant to the particular conceptions. The making of observations is discussed above in (iv), and the linkage between concept and observation, a question of interpretation, is discussed in (vi). Here the theoretical grounds for the selection of particular concepts and the theoretical considerations that give rise to a particular definition and reject other definitions, considerations that are often indistinguishable from questions of interpretation, are at issue. This theoretical dicussion is absent from Moore because the study is mostly empirical and because he, perhaps quite properly, eschews the employment of an abstract theoretical scheme utilizing concepts that are more abstract

78. Herbert Blumer, "Sociological Analysis and the 'Variable,'" *American Sociological Review,* 21 (December 1956): 683–690.

than is common in historical narratives of the periods under consideration.

A historical study of particular periods in the development of different societies such as Moore has undertaken requires that certain theoretical points be established very early in the design of the investigations. It is impossible to designate the different societies he has chosen for study as comparable units unless there are some grounds for determining that each of the societies has moved from a particular stage to another stage in its development. Discussions of the basis for separation and classification of historical periods and epochs are of a theoretical and conceptual nature and of considerable significance to historical studies. There is relatively little of this in Moore—no real justification, for instance, of his inclusion of the United States Civil War as an event comparable to the Puritan Revolution in England, except for a note [79] that historians have come to accept this comparison. In this sense, an introductory chapter that summarizes the consensus among historians about the comparability of at least some of the cases Moore has selected is missing from his study.

In another sense, a theoretical statement is implicit in Moore's analysis. He works within a general theoretical framework that places heavy emphasis on demographic and structural changes, that considers [80] but rejects the importance of cultural variations among the cases studied, and that focuses in particular on the relations between different societal groups (landed gentry, monarchy, peasantry, and urban bourgeoisie), the manner in which marketing needs are satisfied, and the character of response, particularly among the peasantry, to injustice and exploitation. A more abstract, summarizing, model could be developed from the remarks contained in Moore that would convey the dynamic qualities of the historical processes he suggests, but Moore has not attempted to move to this level of abstraction. The closest he comes to it is to delineate the different routes to modernization [81] on a relatively low level of abstraction in a fashion that he deems most appropriate to the historical materials and to his handling of them. A somewhat more explicit theoretical model would ease the adaptation of Moore's scheme of analysis to other cases that have not been included in his analysis.

(viii) *The Explication of Values.*—Unlike much writing in the contemporary social sciences, it is not hard to discern the values that Moore upholds and the evaluative and ideological aims of his investigation. Although a chief motivating impulse in the inception of the research could be taken as theoretical—to understand better the role of agrarian social structures as opposed to industrial developments in shaping the nature of modernization

79. Moore, *op. cit.*, p. xv.
80. *Ibid.*, p. 421.
81. *Ibid.*, pp. 413–432.

in society—it is quite clear that Moore is, throughout his analysis, seeking to understand the circumstances that give rise to democratic political institutions and that prevent the appearance of fascist and communistic totalitarian regimes.

Moreover, Moore quite properly deems it necessary to define democracy or, more particularly, Western democracy, which he sees as oriented to the "long and certainly incomplete struggle" to attain certain specific aims.[82] Similarly, a lengthy discussion of the nature of fascism and its different geographical variants is included.[83] In addition, he has recognized the need for introducing the notion of "semi-parliamentary regimes," [84] recognizing, with other empirical analysts, that neat theoretical classifications are generally insufficient to represent reality in a valid way. Thus Moore's analysis may be seen as one in which particular valued and dis-valued forms of political and social organization are the dependent variable; he has adequately defined several empirically relevant categories of this variable.

The inclusion of the present section, like one earlier (iii) that points out the virtues of listing variables to be examined in the analysis, is simply a reminder that scientific procedures benefit from this explication. There are, of course, other concepts employed by Moore that have evaluative connotations. One of the more interesting of these pertains to the justice of the relation between peasant and overlord in feudal societies. Problems of conceptualization and interpretation of this concept are discussed in the following section. It is worth noting here, however, that this and other concepts of value employed by Moore play a different role in his analysis than do concepts of democracy and fascism. Moore is trying to contribute, through his research, to the development of "that long and certainly incomplete struggle" for democracy in the modern world. One cannot say that he is in the same sense trying to contribute to the minimization of injustice in the feudal relations that still remain around the world except insofar as these detract from the development of democracy. Justice in feudal relationships is not, for Moore, an ultimate goal but rather a circumstance that, in his theory, has to be destroyed, sometimes through violent means, in order to contribute to the ultimate goals of democratic political organizations. In this sense, justice or injustice in a feudal relationship is a concept that enters in an active way into Moore's theoretical understanding of the process of development rather than a valued concept posited *a priori* as are democracy and fascism. While the former may be dealt with as any other theoretical term without special consideration of its evaluative connotations

82. *Ibid.*, p. 414.
83. *Ibid.*, pp. 447–452.
84. *Ibid.*, p. 438.

(except, perhaps, for the reasons given below), the latter designate the values underlying the purposes of the research and are of special relevance to the present section.

(ix) *The Interpretation and Conceptualization of Value Concepts.*— There is no need here to repeat remarks that were included in the earlier discussion of interpretation and conceptualization of non-evaluative terms. It should be emphasized that there is no logical difference between the intellectual activities that relate terms with evaluative content to empirical reality and the establishment of a relation between non-evaluative terms and empirical reality. Indeed, this logical unity has already been emphasized by incorporating a lengthy discussion of the empirical interpretation and clarification of evaluative terms in an earlier section.

As noted above, it is not easy to distinguish between conceptualization and interpretation. The former process refers, in the present section, to the analysis of the theoretical meaning of evaluative concepts. Some of the political and social organizational aspects of democracy that are connoted by the term "Western democracy" might be elucidated in this type of analysis and distinguished from the political and organizational aspects of other types of regimes. Conceptualization, in my usage, is carried out purely on a theoretical level, but then, this kind of analysis is rarely done without some reference to existent empirical cases. Hence, interpretation of these abstractions is generally a part of conceptualization. This is as true of evaluative concepts as of other types.

Moore has devoted little of his analysis either to an examination of the concepts of democracy and fascism or to a justification of the interpretations that he makes whereby the United States and England are viewed as having developed relatively stable democratic institutions, Japan and Germany having gone through a fascist phase, and so on. He has, instead, taken the defensible but not completely satisfactory route of accepting the conventional wisdom of those who view the world from those Western democracies, just as Lipset,[85] who has devoted a good part of his career to an understanding of the prerequisite and supporting structural conditions for democracy, has chosen to work with a simple and conventional notion of democratic institutions—(at least) two competing parties. It is likely that world and domestic events are forcing a re-examination of the concept of democracy and that future investigators will have to devote more systematic effort to a clarification and analysis of the valued social organizational states toward which their work is oriented than has either of these scholars. However, no one investigator can accomplish all of the tasks outlined here

85. Seymour M. Lipset, *Political Man* (Garden City: Doubleday, 1960).

in a satisfactory way. One of the advantages of having a research framework like the one outlined in this essay is to provide for a clearer division of labor in the work of scholars who should be contributing, in their individual efforts, to a larger scheme. In the present instance, a conceptual critique of democracy such as is contained in Bachrach's analysis of theories of democracy[86] can provide a clearer theoretical basis for future empirical work on democratic social organization.

There are other evaluative concepts that play a role in Moore's theory. One is of special interest because of the remarks he makes about the possibility of objectifying value and the manner in which he uses these remarks as a basis for a critique of conventional social science. This concept is not given a simple, consistent label by Moore but generally pertains to the relation between peasant and overlord—hence runs through much of the discussion—and in particular refers to the kind of obligation that lord and peasant feel toward the other party to the relationship. But, as Moore suggests, difficulties arise from the notion of

> . . . rewards and privileges commensurate with the services rendered by the upper class. In a feudal society just how many hens and eggs at stated times in the year, how many days of work on the lord's field, would be a "fair" repayment for the lord's protection and justice? Is the matter not wholly arbitrary, one that can only be decided by a test of strength? More generally, is not the concept of "exploitation" a purely subjective one, no more than a political epithet, that cannot receive any objective pinning down or measurement? Very likely a majority of social scientists today would answer these questions with an affirmative.[87]

If it is not possible to objectify the notion of exploitation, then, Moore suggests, his theoretical statement that (to paraphrase) serfs will revolt when they feel exploited, becomes a tautology.

As Moore indicates, this is a complex topic that is subject to lively debate. It also is a debate on several issues at once. One of these issues is whether or not there are *absolute* (Moore uses the term "objective") standards that can be invoked to argue that more is being exacted from the peasant by the overlord than is "just." Here I would agree with Moore that certain minimum absolute standards could be established but disagree if by this he means that such standards are not heavily dependent upon both culture and personality. Partly perhaps for reasons of genetic constitution and partly because of cultural conditioning there is an amazing variety of ways

86. Peter Bachrach, *The Theory of Democratic Elitism: A Critique* (Boston: Little, Brown, 1967).
87. Moore, *op. cit.*, p. 470.

an individual can respond to an authority structure. One man accepts as legitimate what another rejects as exploitative; there is no possibility of gainsaying this fact. It also seems apparent that the more exploitative a relationship becomes, the more likely all men are to reject its legitimacy. Pursuing this variation in exploitativeness to its logical conclusion, we arrive at the image of a prison or concentration camp, but even here it is now well established that, albeit with accompanying personality distortions, some men can come to accept even this level of exploitation as somehow "legitimate." I do not intend to settle this matter here; rather, I include these remarks to illustrate one of the issues involved in this essentially conceptual analysis of exploitation. In sum, one can, I suppose, argue with Moore that at some point objective standards may be applied, but one may add the qualification that it is extremely difficult to achieve consensus on what the precise standards should be. The more exploitative the relationship, the greater the likelihood of consensus; the role of consensus, rather than "objectivity" or absoluteness, is what I think should be most emphasized.

Another issue in this debate pertains to the possibility, noted in passing by Moore, *of measuring* the extent of exploitativeness of a relationship. This raises questions that are somewhat different from the conceptual questions discussed above, for they are questions of the empirical interpretation of the concept of exploitativeness. Moore fails properly to distinguish these two problems. There is no reason that the concept must be objectified by reference to absolute (even if culturally conditioned) standards in order that the degree of exploitativeness of the relationship be measured. Various possibilities of the measurement of subjective properties now exist in the social sciences, and among the most interesting are those that impose on the measurement process some criterion of consensus among appropriate segments of the population.[88] By and large, these procedures rest on the assumption that where there is sufficient consensus, it seems appropriate to consider as objective reality the concept measured regardless of the level of subjectivity of the actual content of the observations. Of course, it would have been impossible for Moore or anyone else working with historical materials to go very far with these procedures since they rely heavily on the collection of special kinds of attitude surveys or similar data. Regardless of whether they could have been used by Moore, it is clear that the question he raises regarding the possibility of measuring the exploitativeness of

88. See, for example, Thorstein Sellin and Marvin Wolfgang, *The Measurement of Delinquency* (New York: Wiley, 1964), and the more general discussion in Robert H. Somers, ch. 4, "Psychophysics, Occupational Prestige and Exploitation: Notes Toward a Natural History of Social Measurement," *Problems and Issues in Comparative Analysis* (December 1967, unpublished).

a relationship may in principle be answered affirmatively: it can be measured in various possible ways, probably with varying degrees of consensus among competent observers as to whether it has been validly measured.

Yet measurement of a concept like exploitativeness is likely to lead to extensive controversy for the simple reason that the term has strong evaluative connotations. Critics are likely to assess the measurement of actual empirical cases according to their own evaluative standards and disagree that a particular instance represents "exploitation." Such criticism can be avoided by choosing more evaluatively neutral terminology, and this is perhaps one reason many social scientists prefer to avoid strongly evaluative terminology. However, such critics misunderstand the general intent of such measurement. Given several different instances of feudal relationships, a measuring procedure would provide explicit grounds for the conclusion that, for example, in a particular region in France in 1750 the relation between peasant and overlord was more (or less) exploitative than the similar relation in India in 1950. By yielding a rank ordering of exploitativeness, such a measuring procedure precludes the necessity for a conclusion that in this case there is "exploitation" while in that case there is not. Instead, the conclusion is that exploitativeness is higher in the one case than the other. This is a sufficiently difficult conclusion on which to agree, but not so difficult as obtaining agreement that a particular absolute standard has been achieved.

By thus accepting the measurement process that yields only rank orderings, one can in fact make the kinds of assertions that Moore would like to make without having any objective and absolute standard for defining what exploitation is. Degrees of exploitation can be measured while at the same time arguments of "objective" exploitation can be avoided. If one accepts the methodology of contemporary scaling procedures, at least in dealing with contemporary rather than historical materials, comparable cases of landlord-peasant relations can be ranked regarding their exploitativeness *independently* of the rebelliousness of the peasants involved in the relations. Consequently, the tautology to which Moore refers is avoided. Rather than having to assert that when peasants are sufficiently rebellious exploitation is present and the peasants will rebel, it is possible to conclude that the likelihood of rebellion increases as the degree of exploitativeness (measured independently) increases. Thus, both logical problems can be avoided without recourse to objective absolute standards.

By such approaches as this, it is possible to clarify the conceptual standing and the empirical linkages of theoretical terms that have strong value connotations. Although most of the discussion in this section has dealt with special problems of objective measurement of a term that has theoretical importance for Moore, in fact the principal purpose of this section is to emphasize that some clarity is essential in the values toward which the investigations are directed. It is insufficient for scholarship to have ostensible but vague, unclear and implicitly anticipatory involvement in human goals and actions. Scholarship is, in fact, at the core of rational action and its place there should be based on articulate foundations.

(x) *The Communication and Utilization of Social Research.*—It would be advisable for social scientists to work within a framework or model of the relationship between scholarship and human action, but this is difficult at the present time since only inadequate models exist. Of importance to the development of such a model are the various audiences who are attuned to social science and the manner in which the results of such studies can be put into practice. It is neither my intention nor my desire at this point to introduce such a model, but I would like to make a few comments here about elements to be contained in a model.

The most common image of the communication process in the social sciences is one that assumes that a professional community is the intended audience for social research. This image has been derived from assumptions and practices in the natural and physical science community, where cumulative theoretical work is accomplished within a kind of paradigmatic framework in the manner elucidated by Kuhn.[89] Precisely because, as Kuhn suggests, the social sciences do not have professional consensus regarding a paradigm forming the basis for cumulation of knowledge, this popular image leaves something to be desired. In particular, it does not seem appropriate to a field of study in which historical-comparative methodology is pursued. In physical and natural sciences, where such paradigmatic development prevails, not only is there a consensus that is the basis for accepting, criticizing, and building upon communications of scientific knowledge directed to the profession, but there is also a set of ancillary social groups that make use in various applied ways of the cumulating professional knowledge—schools of engineering, medicine, and the like. It is the task of such applied fields to take abstract knowledge from the theoretical professors and employ it in various ways that have relevance to human activities.

In developing a model of the manner of utilization of knowledge in the social sciences, where paradigmatic development is unusual if not unknown, one needs to specify the kinds of social groups that play a role analogous to the applied fields of engineering and medicine, taking into account the fact that these applied professionals may find it impossible to

89. Kuhn, *op. cit.*

translate abstract theoretical knowledge into "practical arts" in the absence of professional consensus in relation to a scientific paradigm.

A second image of the communication and utilization process that seems more appropriate to historical-comparative research and that seems most appropriate to the kind of study undertaken by Moore is a model of human action that distinguishes a stratum of society often referred to as an "intelligentsia." Such a stratum of educated persons can become, in this second image, an intended audience for the research, and the process of acceptance, criticism and cumulation of knowledge, to the extent that they occur, take place within this stratum of society in a fashion that is roughly analogous to the way in which they occur within a scientific profession.

Clearly, such a stratum of intelligentsia is not characterized by consensus, at least in societies where divergent ideologies and philosophies are tolerated. Yet one may map various subgroups within such a stratum where large areas of consensus exist. Such, for example, would be the consensus, first stated by Marx and taken as problematic by Moore, regarding the development of socialism from industrial societies. Although it would be inappropriate from an epistemological point of view to refer to such areas of consensus as paradigms in the sense of Kuhn, there are many similarities. One of the essential characteristics of a scientific paradigm, according to Kuhn, is that it is subject to radical modification from time to time, by a "scientific revolution" that occurs when new empirical observations cannot be justified within the prevailing scientific outlook. Illustrating this development in the natural science of chemistry, Kuhn has discussed at length the theoretical and conceptual implications of the "discovery of oxygen" or, more appropriately, the "oxygen theory of combustion. That theory was the keystone for a reformulation of chemistry so vast that it is usually called the chemical revolution." [90] It is suggestive of this intellectual process to consider the way in which the new "empirical observation" of a successful communist revolution in non-industrialized China (especially when considered in conjunction with the earlier one in Russia) overthrew an earlier consensus among many intellectuals about the development of socialism or communism in industrial societies. These events provoked Moore, among others, to recognize that altogether new theoretical approaches are needed to subsume the new observations.

Thus, although in this second image there are intellectual frameworks in human action that play a role quite similar to the paradigms of Kuhn in the natural sciences, it must also be recognized that it is impossible to draw sharp boundaries around the social groups that accept, reject, or criticize

90. *Ibid.*, p. 56.

and build upon these frameworks—boundaries that are essential to the first image. Stated differently, there is no social science profession that is competent to make definitive statements about the validity of political ideological frameworks underlying much historical-comparative social science in the way that chemistry as a profession is in a unique position to make definitive statements about the validity of the oxygen theory of combustion. Secondly, it is impossible to put sharp or, perhaps, any boundaries around the human action implications of these social-intellectual frameworks and their "revolutionary" overthrow. University students and others who are now in rebellion in many parts of the world base their political actions in part on a framework of historical interpretations and perceived choices that are conditioned by various "revolutionary observations": the horrendous distortions of industrialized society into a fascist totalitarianism in Germany, of capitalist industrial democracy into counter-revolutionary imperialism in the United States, and of classless communism into Stalinist terror in the Soviet Union. Although these public events may be forgotten in time (events of this nature always have their greatest impact on the "political generations" that experience them first hand), and although some of the more constant elements in human nature, those that are psychological, and social-psychological, may move most men when they act in the political sphere, still the consequences of these intellectual and ideological revolutions differ sharply from those that followed the discovery of oxygen.

A third image of the knowledge cumulation and utilization process is perhaps germane to much present work in the social sciences. In this situation, we find a combination of the first and second images in the following sense. For the most part, the second image is the *correct* one, insofar as audiences and communication and utilization patterns are actually structured, but many social scientists *believe* the first image to be true and act accordingly. In this third image, we find social scientists writing as though there is a theoretically and empirically grounded consensus based in a professional group that will receive, evaluate, and build upon their work, while related applied professions will translate (contemporaneously or, more likely, in some future generation) their theoretical work in ways that are appropriate for ongoing human action and the furtherance of human value. But, in reality, there is no such theoretically grounded consensus, and the applied professions frequently feel they must do necessary theoretical work of their own in order to have material that can be translated for practical application.

A second implication of this third image is that if social science material is directed to an assumed professional audience that in actuality cannot be identified as a meaningful and consensually based scientific community, then it is likely that it will be written in a form unsuitable for general evaluation by a wider group of intelligentsia, i.e., phrased in a technical language appropriate only to professional publications. For this and other reasons, such writing is most often scrutinized by a subgroup of the intelligentsia or of the social science profession that accepts the intellectual presuppositions of the author—who agree with his paradigm—and ignored by those who would not agree. In this circumstance, it would not be surprising to find self-serving subgroups of persons on occasion giving evaluations of others in their coterie on grounds that are not generally accepted bases for critical evaluation in science. At the same time, members of the intelligentsia and others who maintain an interest in the understanding of political and social events and their interpretation with respect to political and social action and ideology will be confused and frustrated by the fact that social science offers so little help in this regard. It is my view that the prevalence of this third image accounts for some of the strains currently within social science professions as well as for some of the irrationalities of policy-making in the larger society.

I implied earlier that where the second image is applicable, there are potential political implications to much contemporary work in the social sciences and that a work such as Moore's is in part directed to an understanding of these political implications. (I might add that Moore's recent essay on the prospects for revolution in the contemporary United States,[91] which in a rather distant sense is an outgrowth of his *Social Origins*, is an example of his continuing interest in understanding and communicating these political implications.) The recognition of political implications suggests that the stratum of intelligentsia mentioned above can be roughly subdivided into (a) those whose position in the stratum has some formal institutional basis, such as administrators, elected politicians, and the like, and (b) others who have no such formal basis of power. Having made this distinction one can, in turn, consider that some social science writings directed to this wider audience are intended for intelligentsia with formal power, some for those without formal power, and some to both. For example, the Cross-National Study of Political and Social Change, on which I am collaborating, is directed in large part to the social science profession, but ostensibly has as its ultimate destination some parts of this wider audience, and perhaps most clearly the formally based elites who are immersed in the development process of industrializing countries—development administrators, planners and policy-makers. Yet precisely because institutional links

91. Barrington Moore, Jr., "Revolution in America?" *New York Review of Books*, 12, no. 2 (30 January 1969): 6–12.

are not well established between these applied professions and the theoretical social sciences, little systematic effort has been made in this study to ensure satisfaction of the needs and concerns of this potential audience. The Cross-National Study was undertaken largely within the confines of the first image, oriented primarily to a theoretical social science that is somewhat suspicious of the practical concerns of policy-making. A future task of such research efforts should be to explore and establish appropriate kinds of institutional linkages so that the usefulness of theoretical studies for contemporary problems of policy can be more clearly seen.

These remarks, as well as criticisms of work with which I have been intimately associated, suggest to me that a fourth and fifth image of the communication and utilization process should be noted briefly in closing. A fourth image, one formulated recently by Etzioni,[92] is one in which social science works closely with established centers of power and policy formulation, undertaking studies of areas that are viewed as problematic to those who formulate and execute policy. It would be appropriate to call this applied science if the term could stand independently of its counterpart, pure science, which does not seem to have any validity in the absence of some reality to the first image described above. At any rate, an image of social science working closely with the established centers of power and policy-making is one that immediately brings to mind both advantages and disadvantages. By having research activities linked to centers of action, there is clearly a greater likelihood of relevant application of the fruits of scientific research to human problems; yet at the same time there is a danger that the aims of research will be distorted to become too closely tied to the preservation of the power and privilege of the Establishment and insufficiently directed to the necessary and proper human values.

In turn, then, this fourth image suggests the necessity for a fifth image of social science communication and utilization. In this fifth image, as in the fourth, little faith is placed in the ultimate and presently unforeseeable human benefits of a pure social science that may never be established, yet a proper degree of autonomy is maintained from centers of political power that at times run the risk of being self-serving. According to the fifth image, the interests that serve to further human values of democracy and individual fulfillment of persons and groups throughout the world who may lack access to power and privilege are placed uppermost in the aims of applied social research. The appropriate institutional locus for such social science generally seems to be the University and related institutions of higher learning, yet the present turmoil about the lack of both indepen-

92. Amatai Etzioni, *The Active Society* (New York: Free Press, 1968).

dence from a self-serving establishment and relevance to human values of such institutions suggests that proper models cannot now be clearly identified. Indeed, it may be that for a time, at least in the United States, research of this nature is more likely to take place in *ad hoc* institutes and research centers on the periphery and formally outside the University until more lasting institutions that play the necessary social role can be established; it is not coincidental that I am now associated with the Wright Institute in Berkeley, an institute attempting to play just such a role.

To the extent that there is validity in these images, it is clear that macro-sociologically oriented social science should give focused attention to these aspects of methodology. If the first image described above is the appropriate one for the social sciences, convincing evidence of its validity should be brought forward. The manner in which research studies carried out under the second image accept, even perhaps implicitly, an intellectual and ideological consensus that works ultimately as a disservice to democratic values by crystallizing and exacerbating international and intercultural ideological conflicts should be examined. Further consideration should be given to the manner in which patterns of research, communication and utilization briefly noted in the fifth image can become more of a reality if that is the proper road to the furtherance of appropriate human values. By considering the manner in which the scientific study of human institutions bears upon and enters into the mainstream of human action, it may be possible to suggest new and different images, if necessary, that are more appropriate to this goal.

BIBLIOGRAPHY

COMPARATIVE STUDIES: A SELECTIVE, ANNOTATED BIBLIOGRAPHY

COMPILED BY

SUSAN BETTELHEIM GARFIN

The following bibliography has been divided into two major parts: (1) monographs and articles which treat theoretical, methodological, and technical problems of comparative research; (2) comparative studies. These sections have been further subdivided into what it is hoped will be analytically useful categories. A full outline of the classifications employed follows this introduction. Many items in the bibliography can be located in several of the categories. An attempt has been made to classify each according to its major contribution to comparative research. Items were selected for the bibliography on the basis of their quality, general sociological interest, and unique contribution to the comparative field. Due to space limitations many other items of better than average quality have had to be omitted. All items included in the bibliography are available in English and cover the period from 1950 to 1970.

OUTLINE

Part One: Theoretical, Methodological, and Technical Works

I. Methodological Reviews of Comparative Studies or Fields of Comparative Research

II. Models, Typologies, and Other Conceptual Frameworks for Comparative Research

Part Two: Comparative Studies

V. Paired Comparisons (2 Cases)
  A. *Using Historical Data*
    (1) Cross-societal
    (2) Intra-societal

III. Methodology of Comparative Research
  A. *General*
  B. *Selection of Units for Comparative Analysis*
  C. *Data Collection, Measurement, and Analysis*

IV. Collections of Methodological and Technical Essays

  B. *Using Observation, Survey, and Aggregate Data*
    (1) Cross-societal
    (2) Intra-societal

PART ONE: THEORETICAL, METHODOLOGICAL, AND TECHNICAL WORKS

I. METHODOLOGICAL REVIEWS OF COMPARATIVE STUDIES OR OF FIELDS OF COMPARATIVE RESEARCH

Apter, D. E., and Andrain, C. "Comparative Government: Developing New Nations," *Journal of Politics* 30 (1968): 372–416.

Apter and Andrain examine recent tendencies in the comparative study of new nations. They identify major analytic problems and conceptual frameworks as well as techniques of data collection and analysis that underlie the normative, structural, and behavioral approaches. They argue for a combined structural-behavioral approach as the analytic basis for future comparative studies of developing nations.

Dodge, P. "Comparative Racial Systems in the Greater Caribbean," *Social Economic Studies* 15 (1967): 249–261.

A thoughtful, critical review of Hermannus Hoetink's *Two Variants in Caribbean Race Relations* (1967) which examines New World race relations in light of contrasting Iberian and other Western European attitudes about physical appearance—especially color. Dodge also summarizes the main theses of earlier books on New World race relations and stresses the need for a multi-causal approach to the problem.

Flint, J. T. "A Handbook for Historical Sociologists," *Comparative Studies in Society and History* 10 (1968): 492–509.

Flint focuses on Guy Swanson's use of comparative historical inquiry in *Religion and Regime: A Sociological Account of the Reformation* (1967). He includes in the critique an outline of Swanson's major propositions, the conceptual basis of the dependent and independent variables, a tabular summary of findings, and an examination of interpretations of the findings. Flint finds Swanson's approach very desirable.

Grew, R., and Thrupp, S. L. "Horizontal History in Search of Vertical Dimensions," *Comparative Studies in Society and History* 8 (1966): 258–264. Also in Taylor, C. L., ed. *Aggregate Data Analysis: Political and Social Indicators in Cross-National Research*. Paris: Mouton, 1968, 107–113.

Grew and Thrupp review Bruce M. Russett and others, *World Handbook of Political and Social Indicators* (1964). They view the volume as a landmark in the internationalization of social science along the lines of worldwide comparative study. The main focus of the review is the *Handbook's* interpretative synthesis of quantitative historical data, an advancement over past compartmentalized, quantitative historical work. Grew and Thrupp also discuss the shortcomings of the *Handbook's* use of available historical data.

Haas, M. "Aggregate Analysis," *World Politics* 19 (1966): 106–121.
Haas reviews Arthur S. Banks and Robert Textor, *A Cross-Polity Survey* (1963); Norton Ginsburg, *Atlas of Economic Development* (1961); and Bruce M. Russett and others, *World Handbook of Political and Social Indicators* (1964). He analyzes these three volumes of aggregate data in terms of their success in operationalizing concepts; the sensitivity, comparability, and reliability of indicators; substantive results; the use of cross-sectional data to test process theory; and the generalizability of findings.

Heydebrand, W. V. "The Study of Organizations," *Social Science Information* 6 (1967): 59–86.
Heydebrand examines recent developments in studies of organizations. He identifies contending positions in organization theory, outlines the methodological contributions to the field made by key studies, and formulates a methodological basis for quantitative comparisons of structural patterns in large samples of organizations. He concludes with a description of the Comparative Organization Research Program (CORP), the projects in process, and a statement of priorities for future organizational research.

Hill, R. "Cross-National Family Research: Attempts and Prospects," *International Social Science Journal* 14 (1962): 425–451.
Hill develops a typology of comparative family research and discusses studies which exemplify each of the four types. Problems of comparative research on the family are noted, e.g., the securing of local collaborators, gaining cooperation from families, and response error. Hill concludes with an overview of the methodological and theoretical emphases in the field. The article includes a bibliography of family studies.

Lewis, O. "Comparisons in Cultural Anthropology," *in* Moore, F. W., ed. *Readings in Cross-Cultural Methodology.* New Haven: HRAF Press, 1961, pp. 50–85.
Lewis seeks to show how comparative studies in anthropology (1950–1954) differ in methodological approaches. Two hundred forty-eight recent studies are classified in terms of research objectives, location in space, substantive focus, research design and methods of data collection. Patterned relationships among the resulting data are discussed and six major types of comparative studies identified.

Richter, M. "Comparative Political Analysis in Montesquieu and Tocqueville," *Comparative Politics* 1 (1969): 129–160.
The comparative methods of Montesquieu and Tocqueville are examined in depth and shown to be of first-order significance for current work. The in-

tellectual antecedents of Montesquieu and Tocqueville are discussed and each man is assessed as a comparativist. In this context, Richter identifies four major approaches in comparative studies: to show differences, to show similarities, to reveal ranges of variation subsumed under generalizations, and to establish universal laws. Contemporary social scientists are urged to become better acquainted with the comparative principles that are contained in classic works.

Verba, S. "Some Dilemmas in Comparative Research," *World Politics* 20 (1967): 111–127.

Verba reviews Robert A. Dahl, *Political Oppositions in Western Democracies* (1965) and W. Arthur Lewis, *Politics in West Africa* (1965) against the background of new trends in comparative politics, e.g., a concern with macrotheory, an emphasis on processes and functions, and the problem of variations in the Third World. Verba analyzes Dahl's underlying model in detail and evaluates its applicability to the African situation as described by Lewis.

II. MODELS, TYPOLOGIES, AND OTHER CONCEPTUAL FRAMEWORKS FOR
COMPARATIVE RESEARCH

Allardt, E. " 'Basic' Dimensions in the Comparative Study of Social Structures," in *Transactions of the Sixth World Congress of Sociology*. Geneva: International Sociological Association, 1966, vol. 1, 173–186.

Allardt discusses the problems related to the use of fundamental, structural dimensions in comparative research, both cross- and intra-national. He constructs a model of basic structural dimensions and sets forth a procedure for determining and using them. He applies the model to data from 548 Finnish communes to illustrate its use.

Apter, D. E. "A Comparative Method for the Study of Politics," *American Journal of Sociology* 64 (1958): 221–237.

Within the framework of a general theory of politics, Apter delineates variables of comparative scope for each of three major societal subsystems—social stratification, politics, and government. He advocates the development of an open-ended political theory based on the types of variables contained in his research model.

Burns, T. "The Comparative Study of Organizations," in Vroom, V. ed. *Methods of Organizational Research*. Pittsburgh: University of Pittsburgh Press, 1967, pp. 113–170.

After assessing the purposes of comparative studies and their importance for explanation, Burns formulates a taxonomic framework for the study of organizations. Seven sets of variables are defined and illustrated. Specific methodological attention is given to the problems of studying organizational change comparatively, the measurement of structural variables, and inferences from cross-cultural studies. Examples are drawn from leading comparative studies of organizations.

Clark, T. N. "Community Structure, Power and Decision-Making," in Clark, T. N., ed. *Community Structure and Decision-Making: Comparative*

Analyses. San Francisco: Chandler, 1968, pp. 15–126.

Clark develops a general framework for the comparative study of community power and decision-making that builds on a synthesis of past work and charts directions for future studies. Basic analytical variables are introduced and combined into typologies of social stratification and power. Systematic propositions for comparative research are formulated.

Cornblit, O.; Di Tella, T.; and Gallo, E. "A Model for Political Change in Latin America," *Social Science Information* 7 (1968): 13–48.

Cornblit, Di Tella, and Gallo develop a general model for the cross-national and longitudinal study of political change in Latin American countries. This model centers on the "behavior" of social actors (status groups, corporate organizations, etc.) and the effects of this behavior for political variables, especially the structure of government. Several categories of measurable variables are presented and equations for predictive purposes introduced. The authors refer to the data bank that is being developed for testing hypotheses derived from the model.

Davis, K., and Blake, J. "Social Structure and Fertility: An Analytic Framework," *Economic Development and Cultural Change* 4 (1956): 211–235.

Davis and Blake develop a general, analytical framework for the comparative study of fertility with special attention to variables that may determine methods of controlling fertility. Social organization and fertility patterns are shown to be closely related, drawing attention to the kinds of intervening variables that operate under given conditions and in different types of societies.

Deutsch, K. W. "Social Mobilization and Political Development," *American Political Science Review* 55 (1961): 493–514.

Deutsch introduces a general definition of social mobilization and proceeds to develop a methodological procedure for its quantitative measurement. Several types of indicators are combined into a general index. The main thrust of the article is to illustrate how aggregate data may be transformed into theoretically relevant measures of social and political processes.

Deutsch, K. W. "Toward an Inventory of Basic Trends and Patterns in Comparative and International Politics," *American Political Science Review* 54 (1960): 34–57. Also in Taylor, C. L., ed. *Aggregate Data Analysis: Political and Social Indicators in Cross-National Research.* Paris: Mouton, 1968, pp. 29–45.

Deutsch argues for a combination of historical insight and quantitative analysis in comparative research. Focusing on governmental stability and capabilities, he proposes a quantitative country profile system in which each country would be ranked on each of several variables. Rankings could then be combined for purposes of typological development and comparative analysis.

Eisenstadt, S. N. "Primitive Political Systems: A Preliminary Comparative Analysis," *American Anthropologist* 61 (1959): 200–220.

Eisenstadt presents a general scheme for the comparative analysis of primitive political systems that is based on the concepts of functional problems and differentiated structures. This scheme is then used as a classificatory device for grouping a wide range of concrete tribes and polities. Eisenstadt concludes with tentative hypotheses about the relationship between social structure and political organization.

Etzioni, A. *A Comparative Analysis of Complex Organizations.* New York: Free Press, 1961.
Etzioni develops a model centering on compliance relations. He distinguishes three main types of compliance relations: predominantly coercive, predominantly utilitarian, and predominantly normative. Each type is related to organizational goals, elites, communications, socialization, recruitment, and the like.

Goldschmidt, W. *Comparative Functionalism.* Berkeley and Los Angeles: University of California Press, 1966.
Goldschmidt develops a model for the comparative functional analysis of society based on the notion that functions are universal and institutions are responses to these universal functions. This point of view supplants that in which the primary concern is with the institutions themselves. Goldschmidt does not advocate the study of isolated phenomena but assumes that functional analysis must include the full social context (environmental, personal, and cultural) of the subject of study.

Hester, J. J. "A Comparative Typology of New World Cultures," *American Anthropologist* 64, Part 1 (1962): 1001–1015.
Hester develops a classification of New World archaeological cultures into a system of stages based on a summary analysis of 88 cultures. He describes the rationale behind his typology, defines terms used in it, and formulates hypotheses about the relationship between the stages and the environment in which they occur. He illustrates how specific cultures can be coded into the typology.

Hillery, G. A., Jr. *Communal Organizations: A Study of Local Societies.* Chicago: University of Chicago Press, 1968.
Hillery emphasizes model-building as a basis for achieving a theory of communal organization. He develops models of four community types—the folk village, the city, the vill and the total institution. The data from which the models are constructed are contained in appendices.

Levy, M. J., Jr. *Modernization and the Structure of Societies: A Setting for International Affairs.* Princeton: Princeton University Press, 1966. 2 volumes.
Levy gives attention to the relationships between the structure of societies and international affairs. His analytical framework guides attention to variations in the interdependencies among total societies and the implications for the international system. Comparative materials are used to support his theoretical propositions, with attention both to relatively modernized and relatively unmodernized societies.

Macridis, R. C. *The Study of Comparative Government*. Garden City: Doubleday, 1955.

Macridis presents an overview of the field of comparative government in which he surveys and criticizes the major characteristics of the traditional approach to the subject. He develops a detailed schema for future comparative analysis centered upon four basic analytical categories: decision-making, power, ideology, and institutions in the political system.

Marsh, R. M. *Comparative Sociology*. New York: Harcourt, Brace & World, 1967.

Marsh's central task in this volume is the codification of cross-societal research in major substantive fields and determination of the degree to which the findings of comparative research can be explained by levels of structural differentiation. Marsh develops a very useful classification of the scientific yields of comparative studies: replication, universal generalization, contingency generalization, and specification. His volume also provides a brief, analytic history of comparative research, an index of societal differentiation for 581 societies, and an excellent annotated bibliography of comparative studies published in the period 1950–1963 which explicitly compare data from two or more societies. Selected theoretical and methodological items are also included in it.

Nye, J. S. "Comparative Regional Integration: Concept and Measurement," *International Organization* 22 (1968): 855–880.

Nye presents a set of concepts and measurements for the study of inter-nation integration. He focuses on economic, social, and political integration, and their subtypes. Nye's procedures are intended to show the benefits of studying types of integration, as against the focus on levels of integration. Major concept-indicator problems are clarified as a basis for further research.

Parsons, T. *Societies: Evolutionary and Comparative Perspectives*. Englewood Cliffs, N. J., Prentice-Hall, 1966.

Parsons moves from his earlier analytical models of systems and functional problems to a general evolutionary theory of social change. Major types of societies are classified in terms of level of structural complexity and overall adaptive capacities. Within each of the major typological groupings (primitive, archaic, historic intermediate empires, and seedbed societies) particular societies are examined.

Perrow, C. "A Framework for the Comparative Analysis of Organizations," *American Sociological Review* 32 (1967): 194–208.

Perrow develops a framework for the comparative analysis of entire organizations based on their technology. Perrow sees technology as the defining characteristic of organizations. It is the independent variable. Goals are dependent. Perrow develops four types of organizations from the dichotomizing of two aspects of technology relevant to organizational structure: the number of exceptional cases encountered in the work and the nature of the search process undertaken when exceptions occur.

Rogers, D. "A Framework and Hypothesis for Comparative Studies," *in* Swanson, B. E., ed., *Current Trends in Comparative Community Studies.* Kansas City: Community Studies, 1962, 31–48.

Rogers reviews reputational, positional, and decision-making methods used in the study of community power structure. He proposes a typology of communities in which community power structure—from monolithic to pluralistic —is the dependent variable. Rogers' typology is based on existing comparative studies and theories.

Rokkan, S. "The Structuring of Mass Politics in the Smaller European Democracies: A Developmental Typology," *Comparative Studies in Society and History* 10 (1968): 173–210.

Rokkan attempts to develop a model for the study of comparative politics based on the critical steps in the development and structuring of mass politics. One of his main goals is to identify the historico-political determinants of party systems; another is to translate these concrete patterns into variables and typologies capable of facilitating comparative research. Rokkan generates his typology from historical data about 11 small European democracies in the period from the sixteenth century through the 1920's.

Slesinger, J. A. *A Model for the Comparative Study of Public Bureaucracies.* Ann Arbor: University of Michigan Bureau of Government, Institute of Public Administration Papers in Public Administration no. 23, 1957.

Slesinger cites the need for a framework for the comparative analysis of public administration. He outlines a model of bureaucratic structures, functions, goals, operations, and relation to the environment. He develops a classification system for bureaucracies in terms of the dimensions: organizational goals versus general interests of the electorate and special interest groups versus general needs of the encompassing social structure.

Symmons-Symonolewicz, K. "Nationalist Movements: An Attempt at a Comparative Typology," *Comparative Studies in Society and History*: 7 (1965): 221–230.

Symmons-Symonolewicz reviews classifications of nationalism presented by historians, students of developing countries, and sociologists. He proposes a typology of nationalism of which the major categories are minority movements and liberation movements.

III. METHODOLOGY OF COMPARATIVE RESEARCH

A. *General*

Bendix, R. "Concepts and Generalizations in Comparative Sociological Studies," *American Sociological Review* 28 (1963): 532–539.

Bendix argues against the use of universal, abstract concepts for comparative research in favor of more limited, or middle-range concepts which take account of history and context. He then shows how comparative studies reduce the gap between concepts and empirical findings, e.g., comparative studies illuminate the meaning of societal universals, they check implicit generalizations that are contained in composite sociological concepts and they help characterize the limits of applicability of concepts. Some specific strategies of comparison are presented.

Blau, P. M. "The Comparative Study of Organizations," *Industrial and Labor Relations Review* 18 (1965): 323–338.
Blau discusses the problems, foci, and requirements of three areas of organizational analysis: (1) the individual in his role as member of an organization, (2) the structure of social relations among individuals or groups in organizations, and (3) the system of interrelationships of elements which characterize organizations. He points to systematic comparative analysis as the only method which will establish the relationship between characteristics of organizations and state the conditions under which these hold. He indicates the importance of this for theory building.

Bock, K. "The Comparative Method of Anthropology," *Comparative Studies in Society and History* 8 (1966): 269–280.
Bock argues that the comparative method should be revived because no fruitful alternative to it has appeared. The comparative method should however be understood as a series of assumptions about social and cultural processes rather than as a specific set of investigative procedures. The uses of the comparative method by functionalists and social evolutionists are examined.

Eggan, F. "Social Anthropology and the Method of Controlled Comparison," *American Anthropologist* 56 (1954): 743–763. Also in Moore, F. W., ed. *Readings in Cross-Cultural Methodology*. New Haven: HRAF Press, 1961, pp. 109–129.
Eggan advocates the use of the comparative method on a small scale with as much control over the framework of comparison as is possible. To achieve this, Eggan advocates comparing regions of a relatively homogeneous culture with ecological and historical factors controlled. The results of such a comparison can be matched to results of other similar studies to develop broader generalizations.

Eisenstadt, S. N. "Problems in the Comparative Analysis of Total Societies," in *Transactions of the Sixth World Congress of Sociology*. Geneva: International Sociological Association, 1966, vol. 1, pp. 187–201.
Eisenstadt points to analytical focus, not method, as the distinctive feature of comparative analysis. He also indicates that there is a close relationship between selection of problems for comparison and typology construction, the central meeting point of theory and method. Eisenstadt identifies methodological, theoretical, and analytic problems that attend type construction as well as those which arise in the study of transformations of total institutions.

Evans-Pritchard, E. E. *The Comparative Method in Social Anthropology*. London: University of London Athlone Press, 1963.
Evans-Pritchard provides a historical account of the comparative method. Comparisons are viewed as both essential scientific procedure and an elemen-

tary human thought process. Intensive comparative investigations on a limited scale are advocated because they allow for greater control over possible sources of variation. Some shortcomings of the comparative method are discussed.

Fallers, L. A. "Societal Analysis," *in* Sills, D. L., ed. *International Encyclopedia of the Social Sciences*. New York: The Macmillan Company and The Free Press, 1968, vol. 14, pp. 562–572.
Fallers examines the comparative macro-sociological perspective as both an intellectual tradition and as a strategy for the study of societies. He gives particular attention to the differences between investigators who work intensively on particular societies and those who seek universal, general laws. Three periods of development are identified with illustrative discussions. Proposals are made for improving the strength of macro-sociological studies.

Frijda, N., and Jahoda, G. "On the Scope and Methods of Cross-Cultural Research," *International Journal of Psychology* 1 (1966): 109–127.
The meaning of "cross-cultural" research and types of studies are discussed. Extant conceptual frameworks are assessed and the methodological problems of comparative research identified. Although the specific focus is personality studies, the article is relevant to comparative works in general.

Harsanyi, J. C. "Explanation and Comparative Dynamics in Social Science," *Behavioral Science* 5 (1960): 136–145.
Harsanyi sees the fundamental problem of social science to be the explanation of social facts in terms of a comparative, dynamic theory of social development. Social scientists are urged to abandon static analyses in favor of dynamic explanations. Harsanyi classifies and assesses variables in terms of their explanatory power.

Hopkins, T., and Wallerstein, I. "The Comparative Study of National Societies," *Social Science Information* 6 (1967): 25–58.
Hopkins and Wallerstein argue against the general conception of comparative sociology, holding that the most fruitul focus for cross-national research is the modernization of national societies. They develop a typology of plurinational studies and demonstrate how properties at five different societal levels can be measured as bases for the comparison of national societies.

Kalleberg, A. L. "The Logic of Comparison: A Methodological Note on the Comparative Study of Political Systems," *World Politics* 19 (1966): 69–82.
Kalleberg attempts to clarify the logical requirements of classification and comparison in the light of recent developments in comparative political analysis. He gives specific attention to the differences between classification and comparison, the need for properly defined concepts, and the need for the specification of operational measures of dimensions used in comparisons.

Köbben, A. J. F. "The Logic of Cross Cultural Analysis: Why Exceptions?" *in* Rokkan, S., ed. *Comparative Research Across Cultures and Nations*. Paris: Mouton, 1968, pp. 17–53.
Köbben examines the reasons for exceptions in cross-cultural research, with

close attention to defective classification, multi-causality, pluri-causality, functional equivalents, intervening variables, diffusion, cultural and social lags, coincidence, personality, or a combination of these.

LaPalombara, J. "Macrotheories and Microapplications in Comparative Politics: A Widening Chasm," *Comparative Politics* 1 (1968): 52–78.
LaPalombara argues for reducing the proliferation of macro-theories. He holds that gains in the field of comparative politics are dependent on rigorous methodologies applied to problems of partial segments of polities conceptualized at the middle range level. He describes research on segments of political systems and discusses problems of such research.

Lasswell, H. D. "The Future of the Comparative Method," *Comparative Politics* 1 (1968): 3–18.
Laswell predicts that the present emphasis on comparative data will become the core of the discipline of comparative politics in the future. He suggests ways to understand and apply the comparative method. He argues for an increasingly contextual, problem-oriented comparative approach with less restrictive research techniques. He further suggests a continuing seminar arrangement for planned, large-scale studies of the future.

Leach, E. R. "The Comparative Method in Anthropology," *in Sills*, D. L., ed. *International Encyclopedia of the Social Sciences.* New York: The Macmillan Company and the Free Press, 1968, vol. 1, pp. 339–345.
Leach views cross-cultural comparison as essential to inductive reconstruction of long-term cultural histories and for the development of general propositions about culturally regulated human behavior. He identifies and assesses main approaches to comparative work. Encouragement is given to comparative studies that emphasize differences, rather than similarities, and that add contextual understanding.

Levy, M. J., Jr. "Comparative Analysis of Societies in Terms of Structural Functional Requisites," *Civilizations* 4 (1954): 191–197.
Levy provides a general structural-functional schema for explicit comparative analysis and suggests how to generate basic theorems. Particular stress is placed on the problems of dealing with analytic and concrete structures.

Linz, J. J. "Ecological Analysis and Survey Research," *in* Dogan, M., and Rokkan, S., eds. *Quantitative Ecological Analysis in the Social Sciences.* Cambridge, Mass.: MIT Press, 1969, pp. 91–131.
Linz assesses the merits of ecological and survey analysis and shows the advantages that accrue from using them in combination. He also points out the problems involved in combining the two methods. Future gains depend significantly on the delineation of types of societies with comparisons directed to inter- and intra-societal variables within a given type.

Macridis, R. C. "Comparative Politics and the Study of Government: The Search for Focus," *Comparative Politics* 1 (1968): 79–90.
Macridis evaluates the effects of the behavioralist revolution in comparative

politics, holding that it tends toward either one or another of two extremes: creating grand theory or studying political trivia. Behaviorism has failed to pay adequate attention to middle-range phenomena, such as the structures of government, decision-making processes, and civic cultures. It has not given adequate attention to the state, the strategic level for linking macro and micro emphases.

Marsh, R. M. "On 'The Comparative Study of National Societies': A Reply to Hopkins and Wallerstein," *Social Science Information* 7 (1968): 99–104.
Marsh questions Hopkins and Wallerstein's selection of the nation as opposed to all other collectivities as the basic unit for comparison. He questions this choice especially in terms of the limitedness of the concept of the nation for the study of modernization. He also criticizes Hopkins and Wallerstein for seeing the subject matter of comparative sociology as different from that of all of sociology. He answers Hopkins and Wallerstein's critique of his view presented in his article, "Making Comparative Research Cumulative."

Murdock, G. P. "Anthropology as a Comparative Science," *Behavioral Science* 2 (1957): 249–254.
Murdock views the cross-cultural approach as indispensable to the comprehension of the range of variation of human social behavior and generalizing about it. He discusses methods and problems of comparative research including controlled comparison, worldwide statistical comparison, his own *Social Structure* (1949), and the development of the World Ethnographic Sample.

Nadel, S. F. "Experimental Anthropology," *in* Nadel, S. F. *The Foundations of Social Anthropology.* London: Cohen and West, 1951, pp. 222–288.
Nadel views the comparative method as equivalent to the experimental method, although the comparative method needs refinement to gain the accuracy of the experimental approach. Using the work of John Stuart Mill and Emile Durkheim as departure points, Nadel identifies the major types of comparative studies, assesses their powers, and lays down general procedural guidelines for developing research designs.

Naroll, R. "Some Thoughts on Comparative Method in Cultural Anthropology," *in* Blalock, H. M., Jr., and Blalock, A. B., eds. *Methodology in Social Research.* New York: McGraw-Hill, 1968, pp. 236–277.
Naroll cites the development of an adequate comparative method as the dominant problem of modern, scientific, cultural anthropology. He reviews the leading methods of cross-cultural study and points to the cross-cultural survey as the most effective means of theory testing. Six fundamental problems of cross-cultural survey are discussed: (1) causal inferences from correlations; (2) societal unit definition; (3) sampling bias; (4) Galton's problem (interdependence of cases); (5) data quality control; (6) categorization (concept definition suitable for any cultural context).

Osgood, C. E. "On the Strategy of Cross-National Research into Subjective Culture," *Social Science Information* 6 (1967): 5–37.

Osgood discusses general issues of cross-cultural analysis on the basis of three past comparative studies. One central focus of his article is the language barrier in the cross-cultural study of subjective culture. Osgood also covers areas such as research design, sampling, and interpretation of data.

Przeworski, A., and Teune, H. *The Logic of Comparative Social Inquiry.* New York: John Wiley and Sons, 1970.
The primary objective of this book is to show how the comparative study of social systems promotes the growth of general theory. It provides a fundamental assessment of current assumptions about the mutual relations between theory and comparative studies and develops general procedural principles for resolving methodological issues. Special consideration is given to problems of comparability, explanation, and measurement as they bear on the task of developing general theories. More specific attention is given to types of research designs, levels of analysis and inference, theory construction, indicator equivalence, and replication.

Radcliffe-Brown, A. R. "The Comparative Method in Social Anthropology," *The Journal of the Royal Anthropological Institute of Great Britain and Ireland* 81 (1951): 15–22.
Radcliffe-Brown distinguishes between ethnology, which has the task of historical reconstruction, and social anthropology, which formulates and tests hypotheses about social systems. He provides examples of the systematic use of comparison on ethnographic data from Australia.

Scarrow, H. A. "The Scope of Comparative Analysis," *Journal of Politics* 25 (1963): 565–577.
Scarrow enumerates various functions of comparative analysis and identifies and distinguishes uses of the term as a means of research. He covers the attribute survey, trend analysis, attribute uniformities and sequential regularities, cross-unit testing of behavioral hypotheses, variable analysis, and the creation of analytic schemes. He concludes with a discussion of comparative description.

Schapera, I. "Some Comments on Comparative Method in Social Anthropology," *American Anthropologist* 55 (1953): 353–362. Also in Ford, C. S., ed. *Cross-Cultural Approaches: Readings in Comparative Research.* New Haven: HRAF Press, 1967, pp. 55–64.
Schapera suggests that intensive comparative studies within a region, followed by generalizations about traits and their interrelationships, will help resolve some of the problems anthropologists face. He then undertakes critical reviews of G. P. Murdock's *Social Structure* (1949) and Radcliffe-Brown and Forde (eds.), *African Systems of Kinship and Marriage* (1950), applying the principles he has formulated.

Scheuch, E. K. "The Cross-Cultural Use of Sample Surveys: Problems of Comparability," in Rokkan, S., ed. *Comparative Research Across Cultures and Nations.* Paris: Mouton, 1968, pp. 176–209.
Scheuch identifies the gains that have resulted from the use of cross-cultural

surveys, but notes that there is now an awareness that their basic methodological problems are not as simple as earlier supposed. This thesis is carried forward in his discussions of question meaning and verbal communication, equivalence of indicators, the respondent as a unit in study design and analysis, the usage of "culture" in research, and administrative and diplomatic problems of cross-cultural study.

Sjoberg, G. "The Comparative Method in the Social Sciences," *Philosophy of Science* 22 (1955): 106–117.
Sjoberg's aims are to clarify the meaning of the comparative method, to show its significance for the social sciences, and to identify the chief procedural issues that have to be addressed if valid, empirical generalizations are to be achieved. He deals more specifically with the problem of universal categories, with references to the works of F. Kluckhohn and Talcott Parsons. Unit selection, operational definitions, and data collection needs are among the other problems discussed.

Smelser, N. J. "The Methodology of Comparative Analysis of Economic Activity," *in* Smelser, N. J. *Essays in Sociological Explanation.* Englewood Cliffs, N. J.: Prentice-Hall, 1968, pp. 62–75.
A basic essay on the problem of comparability and concept-indicator relationships, with special reference to economic activity. The adoption of quantitative indicators of economic activity that are "culturally-biased" is criticized, leading to the proposal that comparisons to be valid must take account of cultural values and meanings. Specific substantive problems and theoretic concepts are analyzed to explicate the problems of comparability and the dilemma of universalism and relativity. Strategies of comparative research are proposed that resolve this dilemma.

Strodtbeck, F. L. "Considerations of Meta-Method in Cross-Cultural Studies," *American Anthropologist* 66 (1964): 223–229.
Strodtbeck identifies the basic rationales for cross-cultural study. Study in more than one culture can shed light on the range of variation of a trait. It can also explain the differences in the manifestations of that trait in different cultures. Strodtbeck sees the ability of comparative research to generate new hypotheses—in addition to testing existing ones—as one of its particular strengths.

Suchman, E. A. "The Comparative Method in Social Research," *Rural Sociology* 29 (1964): 123–137.
Suchman covers several issues related to the development of a systematic comparative methodology. Among other points he suggests that time and space factors are best included in the stating of comparative generalizations. Theoretical and methodological issues must be clarified before frameworks for comparative research can be developed.

Vallier, I. A. "Macro-Methods," in Smith, R. B., ed. *Social Science Methods: A New Introduction.* New York: Free Press, forthcoming.

This essay identifies the main features of macro-structural analysis, including points of theoretical controversy and underlying methodological assumptions. Variations within macro-structural studies are explicated by reference to ten prominent works in terms of their research objectives, modes of choosing units, measurement strategies, and the scientific status of conclusions. Section three sets forth decision-making guidelines for beginning students in macro-structural studies. An extensive bibliography is included.

Whiting, J. W. M. "The Cross-Cultural Method," in Moore, F. W., ed. *Readings in Cross-Cultural Methodology*. New Haven: HRAF Press, 1961, pp. 287–300. Also in Lindzey, G., ed. *Handbook of Social Psychology*. Cambridge, Mass.: Addison-Wesley, 1954, vol. 1, pp. 523–531.

This is one of the earliest systematic discussions of the cross-cultural method as a specialized comparative approach. The development of cross-cultural studies is described beginning with E. B. Tylor's study of 1889 ("On a Method of Investigating the Development of Institutions; Applied to Laws of Marriage and Descent,"). The advantages of the cross-cultural method are illustrated, followed by an examination of its basic assumptions and units of analysis. The steps involved in carrying out a cross-cultural study are noted with attention to technical problems and the implications of specific designs.

B. Selection of Units for Comparative Analysis

Allardt, E. "Implications of Within-Nation Variations and Regional Imbalances for Cross-National Research," in Merritt, R. L., and Rokkan, S., eds. *Comparing Nations: The Use of Quantitative Data in Cross-National Research*. New Haven: Yale University Press, 1966, pp. 337–348.

Allardt finds the study of regional imbalances important for cross-national research because of the similarity of methodological problems in the two kinds of study and because of the difficulties countries with regional imbalances present for cross-national research. Allardt enumerates these difficulties and uses Finnish data to illustrate how they can be treated.

Eberhard, W. "Problems of Historical Sociology," in Eberhard, W. *Conquerors and Rulers: Social Forces in Medieval China*. Leiden: E. J. Brill, 1965, pp. 1–17.

Eberhard discusses the limitations of the use of the "social system" as a unit on which to base the comparative study of historical societies. He focuses his critique on the assumption of functional interdependence of subsystems in a social system and on the idea that the social system is a political-geographical area with clear-cut boundaries. He says neither assumption can be made about many historical societies. He advocates the use of a layer model of society instead. He argues further that false analogies are made in the comparison of events without taking account of the different time periods in which they occurred.

Linz, J. J., and Miguel, A. de. "Within-Nation Differences and Comparisons: The Eight Spains," in Merritt, R. L., and Rokkan, S., eds. *Comparing*

Nations: The Use of Quantitative Data in Cross-National Research. New Haven: Yale University Press, 1966, pp. 267–319.

Linz and Miguel argue that comparisons of sectors of two societies with a great degree of common characteristics but which differ on some crucial ones may be more fruitful than overall national comparisons. The comparison of regions increases the previously limited number of cases available for comparison. Linz and Miguel make a typology of eight regions into which Spain's 50 provinces can be classified as an example of regional comparison.

Murdock, G. P. "Cross-Cultural Sampling," *Ethnology* 5 (1966): 97–114.

Murdock discusses sampling problems in cross-cultural research and provides some solutions for them. Among the problems covered are independence of units, selection without bias, and equality of chance for all cultures to be sampled. Murdock suggests a random number method to solve the last problem and presents cultural clusters from Africa, the Near East, and Europe as part of the solution. He indicates that he plans to extend his cluster development to other areas of the world.

Oliver, D. and Miller, W. P. "Suggestions for a More Systematic Method of Comparing Political Units," *American Anthropologist* 57 (1955): 118–121.

Oliver and Miller propose the use of a common set of questions to produce sharper comparisons. As an example they suggest ten questions to designate the political unit as a subject of comparison and four questions to outline the concept of power centralization. Because of the complexity of this approach, the authors suggest starting with a few variables in a few societies and conducting in-depth comparative research.

Scheuch, E. K. "Society as Context in Cross-Cultural Comparisons," *Social Science Information* 6 (1967): 7–23.

Scheuch criticizes the implicit ethnocentricity of cross-cultural research. He traces this inherent bias historically and illustrates the ways in which research procedures have strengthened it, especially by using culture as explanatory— an aggravation of the ecological fallacy. To counter this ethnocentric tendency Scheuch advocates cooperative research in carefully selected societies with nation-states treated as a set of internally differentiated conditions. He recommends collecting data on more than one level (e.g., combining ecological and survey data).

Vallier, I. A. "Comparative Studies of Roman Catholicism: Dioceses as Strategic Units," *Social Compass* 16 (1969): 147–184.

Comparative studies in the sociology of religion have been weakened by insufficient attention to basic methodological problems, particularly a casualness in the definition, selection, and systematic observation of structural units. The diocese is proposed as a basic unit. Vallier describes the diocese, identifies its relationships to local, regional, national, and international levels, and conceptualizes a number of analytical variables for comparative research. As the basis for a ten-year collaborative program, Vallier selects 15 western countries and a sampling plan for a study of 120 dioceses.

C. Data Collection, Measurement, and Analysis

Alker, H. R., Jr., and Russett, B. M. "Indices for Comparing Inequality," *in* Merritt, R. L., and Rokkan, S., eds. *Comparing Nations: The Use of Quantitative Data in Cross-National Research.* New Haven: Yale University Press, 1966, pp. 349–372.

Alker and Russett examine over twenty indices of inequality which attempt to make non-comparable distributions comparable. They classify indices of inequality into three major categories: (1) measures of extremeness; (2) measures of average tendencies; and (3) cumulative value distributions. They conclude that there is no general index of inequality because of the existence of several possible definitions of inequality. In each analysis the index most appropriate to the data under examination must be selected.

Davis, K. "Problems and Solutions in International Comparison for Social Science Purposes." Berkeley: University of California, Center for International Population and Urban Research, Population Reprint Series, no. 273, 1966.

Cross-national, quantitative studies are considered essential for growth in the social sciences, and their improvement depends largely on better data and procedures that collect data in terms of theoretically significant variables. Davis proposes that a Commission on Social and Economic Information be established in each country. Each Commission would have responsibilities for advising on all plans for collecting, organizing, and publishing information relevant to social science. Representatives from the social science specialties would be members of the Commission.

Ervin. S., and Bower, R. T. "Translation Problems in International Surveys," *Public Opinion Quarterly* 16 (1952–53): 595–604.

Ervin and Bower systematize problems encountered by representatives of several research agencies in the carrying out of surveys in more than one language. They conclude their report with a discussion of problems of reliability and validity in cross-cultural research.

Gregg, P. M., and Banks, A. S. "Dimensions of Political Systems: Factor Analysis of *A Cross-Polity Survey*," *American Political Science Review* 59 (1965): 602–614.

Gregg and Banks undertake a factor analysis of the political data presented in Banks and Textor, *A Cross-Polity Survey* (1963). The data are found to be highly correlated along a relatively limited number of factors which provide evidence for inferring seven basic political dimensions: access, differentiation, consensus, sectionalism, legitimation, interest, and leadership. These dimensions are relevant for theory, research, comparison, and typology construction. The findings also suggest seven propositions about conflict in political systems.

Hyman, H. N.; Levine, G. N.; and Wright, C. W. "Studying Expert Informants by Survey Methods: A Cross-National Inquiry," *Public Opinion Quarterly* 31 (1967): 9–26.

An attempt is made to determine whether survey techniques can be used successfully to gather specialized data from skilled informants. Four hundred and forty-five informants, selected to meet certain criteria of knowledge about planned social change, were surveyed in 13 countries and in three languages to evaluate this specialized use of survey techniques. Generally the reports of informants were found to be informed by their knowledge and only rarely distorted by error.

Jacobson, E. "Methods Used for Producing Comparable Data in the OCSR-Seven-Nation Attitude Study." *Journal of Social Issues* 10 (1954): 40–51.
Jacobson describes the steps taken to insure collection of equivalent, comparable data in the seven nations of the OCSR study. He describes meetings of researchers, sampling, gathering interviews, content analysis, and the preparation of the data for comparative analysis.

Janson, C. "Some Problems of Sociological Factor Analysis," *in* Dogan, M., and Rokkan, S., eds. *Quantitative Ecological Analysis in the Social Sciences.* Cambridge, Mass.: MIT Pess, 1969, 301–341.
Janson discusses the general principles of factor analysis and then presents examples of two categories of factor analysis: analysis of intra-community variations and analysis of inter-community variations. He outlines the basic assumptions of factor analysis and discusses related technical assumptions and problems.

Lindzey, G. *Projective Techniques and Cross-Cultural Research.* New York: Appleton-Century-Crofts, 1961.
Lindzey discusses the uses and problems of projective techniques in cross-cultural research. He provides a general description and lists the varieties of projective techniques, their theoretical foundations, problems involved in their use, and their cross-cultural applicabilities.

Naroll, R. "Two Solutions to Galton's Problem," *Philosophy of Science* 28 (1961): 15–39. Also in Moore, F. W., ed. *Readings in Cross-Cultural Methodology.* New Haven: HRAF Press, 1961, pp. 221–245.
Naroll offers two solutions to Galton's problem of distinguishing historical from functional associations in cross-cultural research. The two methods presented are the bimodal sift method and the cluster method. They are applied to the relationship of social stratification and political complexity—which is found to be a semi-diffusional, or mixed, historical-functional association.

Naroll, R., and D'Andrade, R. G. "Two Further Solutions to Galton's Problem," *American Anthropologist* 65 (1963): 1053–1067.
Naroll and D'Andrade offer the interval sift method and the matched pair method to solve Galton's problem. The first of these methods is the most economical, yielding the greatest statistical significance for the smallest sample. The matched pair method provides a direct measure of the relative importance of historical and functional factors in producing cross-cultural correlations.

Naroll, R. "A Fifth Solution to Galton's Problem," *American Anthropologist* 66, Part 1 (1964): 863–867.

Naroll reviews Galton's problem, the four earlier solutions to it, and presents a fifth—the linked pair method—as a possible solution. This method was developed as part of the War, Stress, and Culture Project, a cross-cultural survey of 58 societies selected from two probability samples.

Ohlin, G. "Aggregate Comparisons: Problems and Prospects of Quantitative Analysis Based on National Accounts," *in* Rokkan, S., ed. *Comparative Research Across Cultures and Nations.* Paris: Mouton, 1968, 163–170. Also in Taylor, C. L., ed. *Aggregate Data Analysis: Political and Social Indicators in Cross-National Research.* Paris: Mouton, 1968, pp. 79–86.

The problems of cross-national comparisons based on aggregate economic data are critically examined. Included are the referents of economic activity and the validity of inferences when data are drawn from countries with different economies and different price systems. Skepticism is shown toward mechanical statistical techniques that treat each nation as an observation of equal weight. The merits of disaggregation, as opposed to procedures of making higher combinations among indicators (factor analysis and multiple regression), are discussed.

Pool, I. de S. "Use of Available Sample Surveys in Comparative Research," *Social Science Information* 2 (1963): 16–35.

Pool spells out a methodology for using data banks that have been built up from many different surveys as the basis of comparative research. Computer simulation provides the basis for this technique. Pool discusses problems of this computer methodology including issues such as the establishment of the equivalence of questions and how to deal with correlated issues.

Przeworski, A., and Teune, H. "Equivalence in Cross-National Research." *Public Opinion Quarterly* 30 (1966–67): 551–568.

Przeworski and Teune view equivalence of indicators as a major problem of cross-national research. They suggest that a concept can be measured cross-nationally by using equivalent indicators. Or, relationships can be analyzed within countries and compared across countries. Examples of the development and use of equivalent indicators are presented. The special problem of intervening variables in relationships to be measured is also discussed.

Retzlaff, R. "The Use of Aggregate Data in Comparative Political Analysis," *Journal of Politics* 27 (1965): 797–817. Also in Taylor, C. L., ed. *Aggregate Data Analysis: Political and Social Indicators in Cross-National Research.* Paris; Mouton, 1968, pp. 63–78.

Retzlaff discusses the use of aggregate data in the study of comparative politics. He outlines four models developed from aggregate data (two by Karl Deutsch, one by Lipset, and one by Cutright) to show the level of sophistication of those working with aggregate data. He argues for the comparison of intranation regions as well as of nations.

Rommetveit, R., and Israel, J. "Notes on the Standardization of Experimental

Manipulations and Measurements in Cross-National Research," *Journal of Social Issues* 10 (1954): 61–68.

Rommetveit and Israel focus on problems of testing non-operationally phrased hypotheses in different cultural settings. They show that experimental manipulations deviating from traditional standardization procedures may sometimes produce conceptually identical experimental conditions better than traditional methods do.

Scheuch, E. K. "Cross-National Comparison Using Aggregate Data: Some Substantive and Methodological Problems," *in* Merritt, R. L., and Rokkan, S., eds. *Comparing Nations: The Use of Quantitative Data in Cross-National Research.* New Haven: Yale University Press, 1966, pp. 131–167.

Scheuch discusses problems in the use of aggregate data in cross-cultural comparisons. The main problems discussed are those arising in the combined use of aggregate and individual data: data accuracy, comparability of measurements, representativeness of aggregate data for properties of a collectivity, and types of inference which can be made from such data.

Schmitter, P. C. "New Strategies for the Comparative Analysis of Latin American Politics," *Latin American Research Review* 4 (1969): 83–110.

Schmitter views aggregate data analysis as a powerful tool for the study of Latin American politics. Although major problems concerning data reliability and completeness cannot be avoided at present, sufficient bases do exist for many types of studies. The possibilities of aggregate data analysis are illustrated from a Latin American data bank that he is developing.

Sears, R. "Transcultural Variables and Conceptual Equivalence," *in* Kaplan, B., ed. *Studying Personality Cross-Culturally.* New York: Harper and Row, 1961, pp. 445–455.

Sears argues that universal properties of man or his environment are transcultural variables measurable in all cultures. The value of such variables is that they allow for tests of variation across a wider population range than do case studies, and they serve as the basis for showing systematic variations by culture. Sears suggests three trans-cultural motivational variables as the basis for comparative research: aggression, dependency, and competition. He also presents criteria for their analysis.

Smith, D. H., and Inkeles, A. "The OM Scale: A Comparative Socio-Psychological Measure of Individual Modernity." *Sociometry* 29 (1966), 353–377.

Smith and Inkeles derive an overall measure of individual modernity from 150 interview items administered to 5,500 men in six different countries—Argentina, Chile, India, Pakistan, Israel, and Nigeria. The resulting OM scale is evaluated methodologically.

Teune, H. "Measurement in Comparative Research." *Comparative Political Studies* 1 (1968): 123–138.

Teune argues for the development of measurement techniques which have cross-national validity. He focuses on this problem at both the level of the individual and at the level of the collectivity. He illustrates his approach to the problem with data from India and the United States.

IV.   COLLECTIONS OF METHODOLOGICAL AND TECHNICAL ESSAYS

Clark, T. N., ed. *Community Structure and Decision-Making: Comparative Analyses*. San Francisco: Chandler, 1968.
This volume draws together recent comparative work that makes explicit methodological contributions to the comparative study of communities. Clark's introduction formulates an analytical framework for the comparative analysis of community structure and decision-making, with specific attention to types of stratification systems and to structural variables. The concluding chapter of the volume reviews recent major comparative studies, discusses areas of data comparability, and outlines recent developments and future trends in the field. The main body of the book contains six sections of new and reprinted comparative community studies.

Dogan, M., and Rokkan, S., eds. *Quantitative Ecological Analysis in the Social Sciences*. Cambridge, Mass.: M.I.T. Press, 1969.
An edited collection of 24 essays dealing with the merits, problems, and trends in ecological studies, as well as with their growing linkages with other forms of data analysis, e.g., the sample survey. The volume includes a general essay on the methodological problems of comparative research by Karl Deutsch, sections on multivariate and factor analysis, and discussions of the organization of ecological data archives. Studies using the quantitative ecological approach are also included.

Ford, C. S., ed. *Cross-Cultural Approaches: Readings in Comparative Research*. New Haven: HRAF Press, 1967.
This edited collection of essays provides a general background to and report of cross-cultural studies. Essays in it are classified into five sections: (1) those constituting a general framework; (2) comparative studies of reproduction; (3) comparisons of projective systems; (4) studies of the interrelationships of social life and culture; and (5) data codings and ratings. This volume is seen as a supplement to Moore's edited *Readings in Cross-Cultural Methodology*. It draws heavily on HRAF materials.

International Social Science Bulletin 7 (1955): 553–641.
This special issue of the *International Social Science Bulletin* is devoted to comparative cross-national research. It includes articles on issues of comparative research and an excellent classified bibliography of substantive comparative studies as well as items on theory, methodology, and research techniques.

Kaplan, B., ed. *Studying Personality Cross-Culturally*. New York: Harper and Row, 1961.
A volume of collected articles dealing with the cross-cultural study of per-

sonality. The second half of the book is especially useful as it covers methodological and other problems of cross-cultural personality research and presents various approaches to the field.

Merritt, R. L., and Rokkan, S., eds. *Comparing Nations: The Use of Quantitative Data in Cross-National Research.* New Haven: Yale University Press, 1966.
An early and important collection of 25 papers presented at the Yale Political Data Conference in 1963. The main theme is methodological, with secondary attention to data-bank development and the organizational problems of cross-national research.

Moore, F. W., ed. *Readings in Cross-Cultural Methodology.* New Haven: HRAF Press, 1961.
An edited collection of basic essays on cross-cultural research. The volume is divided into four headings—development, theory, sampling, and methods. This book provides an excellent introduction to the field.

Rokkan, S., ed. *Comparative Research Across Cultures and Nations.* Paris: Mouton, 1968.
An edited collection of the papers presented at the April, 1965, Round Table Conference on Comparative Research, Paris, dealing with approaches to and problems of cross-societal research. The volume is divided into three sections of essays on cross-cultural comparisons, comparative histories of processes of development, and quantitative approaches to cross-national comparisons.

Rokkan, S.; Verba, S.; Viet, J.; and Almasy, E. *Comparative Survey Analysis: A Trend Report and Bibliography.* The Hague: Mouton, 1969.
This is the first in a series of volumes to be published reviewing developments in cross-national, cross-societal, and cross-cultural research. The volume's main substantive section consists of an essay by Stein Rokkan on cross-national survey research and one by Sidney Verba on the uses of survey research in the study of comparative politics. The greater portion of the volume is an annotated bibliography of theoretical works, methodological articles, and substantive comparative studies.

Taylor, C. L., ed. *Aggregate Data Analysis: Political and Social Indicators in Cross-National Research.* Paris: Mouton, 1968.
A compilation of articles on aggregate data in cross-national research. The articles included fall into three classifications—those on the intellectual context, those on problems of aggregate data analysis, and selected analyses of *World Handbook* data.

PART TWO: COMPARATIVE STUDIES

V. PAIRED COMPARISONS (2 CASES)

A. *Using Historical Data*

(1) Cross-societal

Bellah, R. N. "Religious Aspects of Modernization in Turkey and Japan,"

American Journal of Sociology 64 (1958): 1–5.

Bellah examines the change from a prescriptive to a principial value system as a key condition of modernization and as a problem of religious change. Transformations carried forward by the Ataturk movement in Turkey and the Meiji Restoration in Japan are examined as instances of religiously based value change. Secularization is viewed not as a decline of religion but as a change in its functional relationships to society.

Bendix, R. "Preconditions of Development: A Comparison of Japan and Germany," in Bendix, R. *Nation-Building and Citizenship: Studies of Our Changing Social Order.* New York: John Wiley and Sons, 1964, pp. 177–213. Also in Dore, R. P., ed. *Aspects of Social Change in Modern Japan.* Princeton: Princeton Universty Press, 1967, pp. 27–68.

Bendix focuses on the problem of non-indigenous, "transplanted" change in the form of development (modernization and industrialization). He uses historical data in the comparison of the Japanese and German experiences to show that the nature of a country's traditional structure and the way in which it enters the political management of a country can help (Japanese case) or hinder (German case) development.

Briggs, A. "Social Structure and Politics in Birmingham and Lyons (1825–1848)," *British Journal of Sociology* 1 (1950): 67–80.

Briggs undertakes a controlled comparison of Birmingham and Lyons in the nineteenth century to indicate the way in which differing social structures of leadership affected social integration in the two cities, leading to harmony in Birmingham and conflict in Lyons.

Brzezinski, Z. "Deviation Control: A Study in the Dynamics of Doctrinal Conflict," *American Political Science Review* 56 (1962): 5–22.

Brzezinski uses the historical analysis of deviation control in the clashes between the Roman Catholic Romanists and Jansenists and the Jesuit missionary dispute with Franciscan and Dominican critics as a background setting against which to view developments in contemporary international communism. Explicit comparisons are made between these Roman Catholic historical experiences and those of the Communist International.

Brzezinski, Z., and Huntington, S. P. *Political Power: USA/USSR.* New York: Viking Press, 1964.

Brzezinski and Huntington compare the U.S. and Soviet political systems with regard to their principal similarities and differences, their strengths and weaknesses, and the question of whether the two systems are becoming more alike or increasingly dissimilar over time. Given the different philosophies on which each system was established and the unique historical experience of each, the authors conclude that continued evolution, not convergence, will characterize the future course of each.

Elkins, S. M. *Slavery: A Problem in American Institutional and Intellectual Life.* Chicago: University of Chicago Press, 1959.

Elkins traces the development of historical scholarship on American slavery and points to the necessity of examining slavery as an institutional and intellectual problem. He gives special attention to the ways in which the absence of strong, institutional centers in the U.S. influenced how slavery was defined and approached. He makes comparisons between the United States and Brazil to show the significance of culture and context on the institutional development of slavery. The effects of slavery on the slave's personality are compared with the psychological effects of the German concentration camps.

Geertz, C. *Islam Observed: Religious Development in Morocco and Indonesia.* New Haven: Yale University Press, 1968.
Geertz undertakes a systematic comparison of Islam's features and developmental patterns in Indonesia and Morocco. For each of the variants, he constructs an ideal type of the classical religious style—the mystical-aesthetic configuration in Indonesia and the moral-warrior configuration in Morocco. Each of these types is examined as an indicator of the respective cultures and of problems Islam faces in religious development. General issues in the relationship of beliefs to social change, identity, and meaning are studied in the concluding chapter.

Hoetink, H. *The Two Variants in Caribbean Race Relations: A Contribution to the Sociology of Segmented Societies.* New York: Oxford University Press, 1967.
Hoetink compares race relations in Brazil and the U.S. on the basis of historical data. He singles out differing attitudes toward color and physique as crucial variables in the development of dissimilar patterns of race relations in the two countries. This study draws upon the analyses of earlier comparative studies of U.S. and Latin American race relations and finds them inadequate because they fail to attribute enough significance to somatic variables.

Klein, H. S. *Slavery in the Americas: A Comparative Study of Virginia and Cuba.* Chicago: University of Chicago Press, 1967.
Klein makes a detailed comparison of Cuba and Virginia to show how institutional context and relations with the colonial centers affected the characteristics of the two systems of slavery. Particular stress is laid on the role of the Roman Catholic and Anglican churches. Klein's study provides a basis for expanding the scope of explanatory studies of slavery.

Levy, M. J., Jr. "Contrasting Factors in the Modernization of China and Japan," *Economic Development and Cultural Change* 2 (1953): 161–197.
Levy undertakes a sociological explanation of Japan's rapid industrialization. China is selected as a control case for two reasons: lack of rapid industrialization, a marked contrast to Japan on the dependent variable; second, many broad similarities with Japan on other variables. This "quasi-experimental" design facilitates the identification of the crucial independent variables, and thus the beginnings of a causal theory.

Wolf, E. R., and Mintz, S. W. "Haciendas and Plantations in Middle America and the Antilles," *Social and Economic Studies* 6 (1957): 380–412.

Wolf and Mintz combine historical materials and field data from Puerto Rico, Jamaica, and Mexico to create a comparative typology of the hacienda and the plantation as social systems. Included in the typology are general conditions, initiating conditions, operational conditions, and derived cultural conditions.

(2) Intra-societal

Vallier, I. A. "Church, Society, and Labor Resources: An Intra-Denominational Comparison," *American Journal of Sociology* 68 (1962): 21–33.

This is an explanatory study of variation in religious organization. Vallier selects two denominations that share basic beliefs, goals, and values (Mormons and Reorganites) yet differ markedly with regard to the size, structure, and economic basis of their missionary programs. Differing geo-cultural contexts and differing relationships between church and society are identified as the main sources of variation.

B. Using Observation, Survey, and Aggregate Data

(1) Cross-societal

Blood, R. O., Jr. *Love Match and Arranged Marriage: A Tokyo-Detroit Comparison.* New York: Free Press, 1967.

Blood compares patterns of courtship and marriage in Tokyo and Detroit on the basis of interview data collected in the United States in 1955 and in Tokyo in 1958–1959. He focuses on the consequences of old and new patterns of mate selection in Japan and compares internal and external forces on marriage in Tokyo and Detroit.

Campbell, A., and Valen, H. "Party Identification in Norway and the United States," *Public Opinion Quarterly* 25 (1961): 505–525.

This is a study of variations within western-type democracy: the United States and Norway are two democratic countries yet each has a different party system. On the basis of survey data, Campbell and Valen attempt to locate differences in party identification. They conclude that identification with Norwegian parties is associated with greater demographic and political distinctiveness than is party identification in the United States.

Clignet, R. P., and Foster, P. "Potential Elites in Ghana and the Ivory Coast: A Preliminary Comparison," *American Journal of Sociology* 70 (1964): 349–362.

Two samples of male secondary students in Africa (Ghana and the Ivory Coast) are studied to determine variations in the relationship between school systems and elite recruitment. Although the members of the two samples differed importantly on background items, they shared aspirations. The two school systems are viewed as having similar roles in the national society.

Clinard, M. B. "A Cross-Cultural Replication of the Relation of Urbanism to Criminal Behavior," *American Sociological Review* 25 (1960): 253–257.

A sample of Swedish prisoners is used in a cross-cultural replication of Clinard's original study, "The Process of Urbanization and Criminal Behavior"

(1942). Five hypotheses are tested with the Swedish data providing confirmation of the earlier U.S. study. Replicative studies of a cross-cultural nature are encouraged.

Converse, P. E., and Dupeux, G. "Politicization of the Electorate in France and the United States," *Public Opinion Quarterly* 26 (1962): 1–23.

Converse and Dupeux find that the most notable differences in politicization between the United States and France occur at the elite level, not within the electorate at large. Data for the study were gathered in France during the 1958 constitutional referendum using national cross-section sampling techniques. U.S. data were collected over six elections.

Deutsch, K. W.; Edinger, L. J.; Macridis, R. C.; and Merritt, R. L. *France, Germany and the Western Alliance: A Study of Elite Attitudes on European Integration and World Politics*, New York: Charles Scribner's Sons, 1967.

Interviews were conducted with 147 members of the French elite and 173 members of the German elite in an analysis of four aspects of Western European politics: domestic affairs; foreign politics and international relations; European integration and alliances; and arms, arms control, and disarmament. The volume includes the plan of study, a recounting of French and German elite attitudes, and a comparison of these two elites.

Form, W. H., and D'Antonio, W. V. "Integration and Cleavage among Community Influentials in Two Border Cities," *American Sociological Review* 24 (1959): 804–14.

This research was designed to determine the degree of social integration among top influentials in economic and political spheres in Ciudad Juarez, Mexico, and El Paso, Texas. Data were collected from interviews. Based on four measures of integration, the El Paso elite was found to be more highly integrated than the Ciudad Juarez elite although neither city had a single power system.

Goldrich, D. *Sons of the Establishment: Elite Youth in Panama and Costa Rica. Chicagos* Rand McNally, 1966.

Goldrich compares the political orientations and their relationship to future problems of change of elite youth in Panama and Costa Rica. He uses data collected in Panama in 1961 and in 1963 and in Costa Rica in fall, 1962, from a questionnnaire given to students in the last two of five years of Roman Catholic high schools, to assess the morale of their social strata in relation to theoretical formulations on revolution.

Miller, D. C. "Decision-Making Cliques in Community Power Structures: A Comparative Study of an American and an English City," *American Journal of Sociology* 64 (1958): 299–310.

The hypothesis that key community leaders influence policy-making by acting in concert through cliques is tested on the basis of data gained from top influentials in a city in northwest U.S. and a city in southwestern England. Miller finds that different structural models of influence relationships operate in each place.

Miller, D. C. "Industry and Community Power Structure: A Comparative Study of an American and an English City," *American Sociological Review* 23 (1958): 9–15.

Using the same cities and nearly the same data sources as in the above study, Miller tests the hypothesis that businessmen exert a predominant influence in community decision-making. Like Hunter in his study of Southern Regional City, Miller finds that in the U.S. Pacific community businessmen do exert a predominant influence in community decision-making. In England, where occupational prestige follows dissimilar patterns, this does not hold.

Richardson, S. A. "Organizational Contrasts on British and American Ships," *Administrative Science Quarterly* 1 (1956): 189–207.

Richardson compares crews of British and American merchant ships to show cultural differences in organizations that have similar purposes and environments. He collected data while spending nine years on British and U. S. ships and also interviewed 72 British and American deck crews and officers and U.S. union officials.

Rogoff, Natalie. "Social Stratification in France and in the United States," *American Journal of Sociology* 58 (1953): 347–357.

Rogoff tests the hypothesis that certain classes in France can be traced to the old, pre-revolutionary order, while other French classes and those in the United States are rooted in the modern, post-revolutionary stratification system. Data from a 1950 French survey and similar 1940 and 1949 U.S. surveys indicate that the French classify themselves into four classes, two of which are based on ascription, while Americans classify themselves in only two classes, both based on achievement. Rogoff points out the need for uniform, cross-national data collection to further comparative research.

Rokkan, S., and Campbell, A. "Citizen Participation in Political Life: Norway and the United States of America," *International Social Science Journal* 12 (1960): 69–99.

Rokkan and Campbell use similar survey data collected on elections in Norway and the U.S. within a one-year period to analyze the similarities and differences of recruitment of active participants in electoral contests in each country. They attempt to relate individual reactions and choices (micro-level) to differences in the structures in which they occur (macro-level).

Seeman, M. "Alienation, Membership, and Political Knowledge: A Comparative Study," *Public Opinion Quarterly* 30 (1966): 353–367.

Seeman conducted 558 interviews in Malmö, Sweden, to replicate U.S. studies about the relationship between powerlessness, organizational membership, and political knowledge. The Swedish findings substantiated the conclusions of the American studies.

Turner, R. H. "Acceptance of Irregular Mobility in Britain and the United States," *Sociometry* 29 (1966): 334–352.

Turner compares U.S. and British attitudes toward mobility on the basis of interview data. He concludes that adherents of sponsored mobility are less approving of irregular mobility than are adherents of contest mobility. Both groups support standard mobility.

Valsan, E. H. *Community Development Programs and Rural Local Government: Comparative Case Studies of India and the Philippines.* New York: Praeger, 1970.

Valsan undertakes an in-depth comparison o two developmental programs in India and two in the Philippines. He provides a general comparison of the two countries as well as of the cases studied. He proposes hypotheses and topics for future research.

(2) Intra-societal

Blankenship, L. V. "Community Power and Decision-Making: A Comparative Evaluation of Measurement Techniques," *Social Forces* 43 (1964): 207–216.

Blakenship studies five decisions in two New York towns by restructuring decisions. Decision-makers and influentials are interviewed using a snowball technique to determine the relationship between those reputed to have power and those who make decisions. Blankenship finds the relationship to be weak in general and to vary in each case.

Blau, P. M. *The Dynamics of Bureaucracy: A Study of Interpersonal Relations in Two Government Agencies.* Chicago: University of Chicago Press, rev. ed. 1963.

A federal agency and a state agency are studied in depth to ascertain the relationships between work goals, work procedures, role-relations, and bureaucratic structure. Data were collected by observation and interviews. Variations in bureaucratic organization and structural change are related to the two contexts. General implications are drawn for bureaucratic theory. Blau includes a detailed discussion of the study's methodology.

Booth, D. A., and Adrian, C. R. "Power Structure and Community Change: A Replication Study of Community A." *Midwest Journal of Political Science* 6 (1962): 277–296.

Booth and Adrian replicate George Belknap and Ralph Smuckler's 1954 study of Community A, a midwestern city of 50,000 people, to show changes in leadership and participation there. They follow V. O. Key in arguing that isolated community studies should be replaced by studies of numerous, comparative cases carried out within a single framework.

Clelland, D. A., and Form, W. H. "Economic Dominants and Community Power: A Comparative Analysis," *American Journal of Sociology* 69 (1964): 511–521.

Clelland and Form replicate a study of economic dominants in community power relations originally conducted in 1958. The original site of the study was an independent city, now a satellite of a larger city. It was replicated in an independent city following the data techniques of the original study. Findings indicate that there has been increasing differentiation of economic and political spheres in both cities, but economic dominants are influential more often in the independent city than in the satellite city.

Coser, R. L. "Authority and Decision-Making in a Hospital: A Comparative Analysis," *American Sociological Review* 23 (1958): 56–63.
Coser studies the relationship between behavior and social structure in the medical and surgical wards of an East Coast, U.S. hospital, thus gaining control over many important sociological variables. Her analysis is based on three months of observation. She explains differences in the nurse-doctor relations in the two wards in terms of the networks of social relations in each ward.

Crozier, M. *The Bureaucratic Phenomenon*. Chicago: University of Chicago Press, 1964.
This is a systematic comparative study first of bureaucratic systems in France (a clerical agency and an industrial monopoly). Crozier uses interview, questionnaire, observational, and institutional data to describe variations in intergroup relations, authority patterns, and decision-making processes. These findings are used as a basis for assessing models of bureaucracy and for formulating a new theory of bureaucratic change. Bureaucratic patterns in France are shown to be intimately linked to the national culture. The French bureaucratic system is compared with those in the U.S. and the Soviet Union. Additional French administrative subsystems are described.

Elder, J. W. "Fatalism in India: A Comparison Between Hindus and Muslims," *Anthropological Quarterly* 39 (1966): 227–243.
Based on data from 2,500 interviews in Lucknow and Madurai, Elder compares Hindus, Muslims, Sikhs, and Christians on fatalism. He finds that the Hindus are low on theological fatalism but high on empirical and social fatalism.

Gouldner, A. W. *Patterns of Industrial Bureaucracy*. Glencoe, Ill.: Free Press, 1954.
Gouldner compares bureaucratic patterns in two sectors of the General Gypsum Company: the subsurface mine and the surface factory. These field data are used to identify types of bureaucracy and the conditions that give rise to one or another type. Specific attention is given to the relationship between leadership succession and bureaucratic growth. Weber's model of bureaucracy is assessed and qualified.

Grusky, O. "The Effects of Succession: A Comparative Study of Military and Business Organizations," *in* Janowitz, M., ed. *The New Military: Changing Patterns of Organization*. New York: The Russell Sage Foundation, 1964, pp. 83–111.
Grusky studies succession in a military organization and in a business firm. Particular attention is given to the structural context in which succession occurs, the consequences of succession for organizational commitment, and the adjustment of the organization to community life. Data were collected by interviews, observation, and the use of official documents and questionnaires.

Nadel, S. F. "Two Nuba Religions: An Essay in Comparison," *American Anthropologist* 57 (1955): 661-679.

Nadel compares the differences in the Heiban and Otoro Nuba religions. Heiban religion is more magically oriented, aggressive, and emotionally tense. Otoro religion is calmer, more dispassionate and optimistic. Nadel looks for the sources of this religious variation in the differences in size and political integration, regulations of adolescence, jural status of wives, and sexual morality between the two groups. He identifies the second and third factors as the bases on which variations must be explained.

Stinchcombe, A. L. "Bureaucratic and Craft Administration of Production: A Comparative Study," *Administrative Science Quarterly* 4 (1959): 168-187.

Stinchcombe re-examines Weber's theory of bureaucracy on the basis of the analysis of published economic and demographic data (including the 1950 U.S. census) about administration in mass production and construction industries. He finds that craft administration (the construction industry) differs from bureaucratic adminstration (mass production) because it replaces detailed centralized planning of work with professional training of manual workers.

Thompson, J. D. "Authority and Power in 'Identical' Organizations," *American Journal of Sociology* 62 (1956): 290-301.

Direct observation, semi-stuctured interviews, and work-contact questionnaires were among the types of data in this study of authorized and real power in two "identical" Air Force wings. Technical requirements of operations, not personal relations, were found to be the source of deviations of real from authorized authority structures.

Vallier, I. A. "Social Change in the Kibbutz Economy," *Economic Development and Cultural Change* 10 (1962): 337-352.

Using Parsons' AGIL framework as a research model, Vallier compares the effects of two types of auxiliary labor groups on kibbutz life. Observations are made on 11 variables for each labor group to show the kinds of consequences structural change holds for a functioning system.

Vogt, E. Z., and O'Dea, T. F. "A Comparative Study of the Role of Values in Social Action in Two Southwestern Communities," *American Sociological Review* 18 (1953): 645-654.

Vogt and O'Dea compare the behavioral and social patterns of Mormons in Rimrock and members of the Homestead Community (Texans) in terms of how technological, economic, and community problems are handled. Differences in basic values are proposed as the main explanation for the contrasting patterns of collective life.

Weintraub, D., and Bernstein, F. "Social Structure and Modernization: A Comparative Study of Two Villages," *American Journal of Sociology* 71 (1966): 509-521.

Weintraub and Bernstein seek to explain contrasting patterns of modernization in two neighboring Israeli villages. Inter-village variations are related to differences in kinship structure. The processes that led to the crystallization of the different kinship structures are identified. Data used were collected from observation and surveys.

VI. MIDDLE N COMPARISONS (3–12 CASES)

A. Using Historical Data

(1) Cross-societal

Ben-David, J. "Scientific Productivity and Academic Organization in Nineteenth Century Medicine," *American Sociological Review* 25 (1960): 828–843.

Ben-David explains differences and fluctuations of productivity in the medical sciences in Germany, France, Britain, and the United States from 1800 to World War I. Indexes are constructed for the dependent variables. Among the many sets of factors that are examined as possible sources of variation, Ben-David finds that academic decentralization and competition are crucial. This article is an especially good example of how to proceed with an explanatory study.

Bendix, R. *Work and Authority in Industry: Ideologies of Management in the Course of Industrialization.* New York: John Wiley and Sons, 1956.

Bendfix focuses on the relationship between managerial ideologies, action, and social context, with particular attention to the early phases of industrialization in England and Russia and the recent industrial histories of the United States and East Germany. Changes in ideology, and the ways in which ideology is related to patterns of social control, are studied with reference to religious and political variables and to bureaucratic growth.

Coulborn, R., ed. *Feudalism in History.* Princeton: Princeton University Press, 1956.

This volume is concerned primarily with non-western feudalism. Coulborn begins with a description of feudalism. This is followed by eight specialized studies of feudalism in different geographical areas by different authors. Coulborn concludes the volume with a comparative analysis of feudalism.

Etzioni, A. *Political Unification: A Comparative Study of Leaders and Forces.* New York: Holt, Rinehart, and Winston, 1965.

Etzioni presents a paradigm for the study of political unification. He examines four contemporary unification efforts in terms of their types of leadership and power, indicating the conditions that account for variations in outcome. Etzioni's study illustrates the significance of a comparative sociological approach to the field of international relations.

Goode, W. J. *World Revolution and Family Patterns.* New York: Free Press, 1963.

Goode uses demographic and other social scientific accounts as the basis for his comparative study of changing family patterns in six major areas of the world undergoing rapid change. The descriptive focus is on the degree to which these family systems, starting from different points, are moving toward the conjugal family. The main theoretical argument is that actors other than industrialization must be assessed to explain the trend toward the nuclear family.

Greenfield, S. M. "Industrialization and the Family in Sociological Theory," *American Journal of Sociology* 67 (1921): 312–322.
Greenfield uses historical and comparative data from the United States, Europe, Japan, and the Barbados to indicate that modernization and industrialization may exist without the small nuclear family and that the nuclear family has been found without urbanization and industrialization.

Huntington, S. P. "Political Modernization: America vs. Europe," *World Politics* 18 (1966): 378–414.
Huntington compares three distinct patterns of political modernization in the United States, England, and on the European continent. He defines political modernization as including rationalization of authority; the replacement of traditional authorities by one secular, national, political authority; and increased participation by social groups in public life. He concludes that the first two of these three processes has occurred more slowly and less completely in the United States than in Europe.

Lipset, S. M. *The First New Nation: The United States in Historical and Comparative Perspective.* New York: Basic Books, 1963.
Lipset examines the institutional and cultural features of the United States historically as a prototypical case of political development. The values and institutions of the United States are compared with those of select European and English-speaking democracies to highlight the United States case.

Moore. B., Jr. *Social Origins of Dictatorship and Democracy.* Boston: Beacon Press, 1966.
Moore examines the political roles of the landed upper classes and the peasantry in the transformation from agrarian to industrial societies in Great Britain, France, the United States, China, Japan, and India. He gives secondary attention to Germany and Russia. The main explanatory problem is to identify the structural conditions that historically determine variations in political development giving rise to parliamentary democracy, fascism, and communism. Historical generalizations from the several cases are translated into analytic hypotheses which are then used as a basis for assessing the political future of India.

Patai, R. "Religion in Middle Eastern, Far Eastern, and Western Culture," *Southwestern Journal of Anthropology* 10 (1954): 233–254.
Patai makes a general comparison between the role of religion and its cultural position in Middle Eastern, Far Eastern, and Western religion. He concludes, among other things, that Far Eastern and Middle Eastern religions are the dominant normative forces in each of these geographical areas while this is no longer true in the West.

Spiro, M. E., and D'Andrade, R. G. "A Cross-Cultural Study of Some Supernatural Beliefs," *American Anthropologist* 60 (1958): 456–466. Also in

Ford, C. S., ed. *Cross-Cultural Approaches: Readings in Comparative Research.* New Haven: HRAF Press, 1967, pp. 196–206.

Spiro and D'Andrade assume that religious beliefs and practices can be explained to the same degree and in the same naturalistic framework as other aspects of culture. A preliminary test of ethnographic data for eleven societies indicated that dependence is the most important behavior system for prediction of nurturance. The oral and anal systems are the most important for predictions of punitiveness, and sex and aggression have little predictive value. Data for the study were coded by raters using a seven-point scale based on the Schedule for Religious World Views.

Vallier, I. A. "Church 'Development' in Latin America: A Five Country Comparison," *Journal of Developing Areas* 1 (1967): 461–476.

This is an explanatory study of structural variations in five national Catholic churches in Latin America (Argentina, Chile, Colombia, Mexico, and Brazil). A general index of "church development" is constructed from four ordinal variables. The Chilean church emerges as especially highly developed relative to the other four, and is made the focus of an explanation that relates demographic, institutional, and cultural variables.

Van den Berghe, P. L. *Race and Racism: A Comparative Perspective.* New York: John Wiley and Sons, 1967.

Van den Berghe focuses on two questions: (1) why some people become racially prejudiced and others don't, and (2) how an internalizing of prejudice at the personality level is related to the social morphology of racism. He develops a typology of paternalistic and competitive race relations, then compares race relations in Mexico, Brazil, the United States, and South Africa.

B. Using Observation, Survey and Aggregate Data

(1) Cross-societal

Alford, R. R. *Party and Society: The Anglo-American Democracies.* Chicago: Rand McNally, 1963.

Alford focuses on the social factors related to party preference in the United States, Great Britain, Canada, and Australia. He uses data gathered from 50 public opinion surveys in the four countries which asked questions about occupation, religious membership, and party preference. The volume includes methodological and explanatory appendices.

Almond, G. A., and Verba, S. *The Civic Culture: Political Attitudes and Democracy in Five Nations.* Princeton: Princeton University Press, 1963.

Almond and Verba survey political culture in five Western democracies: the United States, Great Britain, Germany, Italy, and Mexico. They conducted 1,000 interviews in each country, and the results of the interviews are compared with respect to patterns of political cognition, civic competence, and political socialization. These data are aggregated to delineate types of political cultures which in turn are viewed as significant for the functioning and change of political institutions.

Fox, T. G., and Miller, S. M. "Economic, Political and Social Determinants of Mobility: An International Cross-Sectional Analysis," *Acta Sociologica* 9 (1966): 76–93.

Fox and Miller find that five mobility determinants—GNP per capita, education, political stability, urbanization, and achievement motivation—account for 80 percent of the variance in manual and non-manual outflow in the form of inter-generational occupational change. The study was carried out in 12 nations for which roughly comparable data for the 1949–1957 period were available.

Hsu, F. L. K. *Clan, Caste, and Club.* Princeton: D. Van Nostrand, 1963.

Hsu uses familial relationships as a starting point for explaining differences between three world views: the supernaturally centered Hindu view, the individually centered view in the United States, and the situation-centered world view of the Chinese. From his analysis of the family Hsu moves into a comparison of the important secondary groupings characteristic of each society—the Hindu caste, the American club, and the Chinese clan. The volume is based on Hsu's field work in each of these countries.

Inkeles, A. "Making Men Modern: On the Causes and Consequences of Individual Change in Six Developing Countries," *American Journal of Sociology* 75 (1969): 208–225.

Inkeles' focus is on the problems of the impact of modernization on the individual. A questionnaire was administered to 6,000 men designated by systematic sampling methods in Argentina, Chile, India, Nigeria, and East Pakistan. Among the issues addressed are the degree to which an empirically identifiable modern man exists, the influences that make man modern, the behavioral consequences of modernization at the level of individual attitudes, and the question of whether or not men can go through modernization without deleterious consequences.

Inkeles, A., and Rossi, P. H. "National Comparisons of Occupational Prestige," *American Journal of Sociology* 61 (1956): 329–339.

Inkeles and Rossi use both primary and secondary data for the United States, Great Britain, Japan, New Zealand, Germany, and the Soviet Union to compare occupational prestige hierarchies in these countries. They find that prestige hierarchies are basically similar in these industrial societies.

Kerr, C., and Siegel, A. "The Interindustry Propensity to Strike: An International Comparison," *in* Kornhauser, A. W. and others, *Industrial Conflict.* New York: McGraw-Hill, 1954, pp. 189–212.

Kerr and Siegel compare the propensity to strike of sixteen industrial groupings in 11 industrialized countries. Their comparison suggests that the nature of the industrial environment is an important factor in determining inter-industry propensity to strike. Data for the study came from statistical handbooks about the 11 countries.

Lenski, G. E. "Status Inconsistency and the Vote: A Four Nation Test," *American Sociological Review* 32 (1967): 298–301.

Lenski uses available data from the United States, Britain, Canada, and

Australia to analyze status inconsistency as illustrated by Roman Catholic and Protestant voting patterns. Twenty-one out of 25 sets of data tested supported Lenski's hypothesis that inconsistency produces stress which generates political discontent resulting in support for liberal parties.

Lipset, S. M., and Rogoff, N. "Class and Opportunity in Europe and the U.S.," *Commentary* 18 (1954): 526–568.
Lipset and Rogoff use data from social mobility studies carried out in Germany, France, Great Britain, Finland, Italy, the Netherlands, and Sweden to compare social mobility in farm, manual, and non-manual categories. They conclude that there are no significant differences in social mobility rates in the United States and industrially advanced European countries.

Nadel, S. F. "Witchcraft in Four African Societies: An Essay in Comparison," *American Anthropologist* 54 (1952): 18–29. Also in Ford, C. S., ed. *Cross-Cultural Approaches: Readings in Comparative Research*. New Haven: HRAF Press, 1967, pp. 207–218.
Nadel compares two pairs of African societies: Nupe and Gwari, Korongo and Mesakin. Though these societies share many features, they vary in terms of beliefs about witchcraft and types of witchcraft. Through comparative analysis of each of the two pairs of societies, Nadel identifies explanatory variables and explores the intervening processes that link structural and psychological levels.

Rokkan, S. "Party Preferences and Opinion Patterns in Western Europe: A Comparative Analysis," *International Social Science Bulletin* 7 (1955): 575–596.
Interviews were conducted with 400 primary and secondary school teachers in each of seven Western European countries to study the (1) socio-economic contexts of party preference; (2) cross-national regularities in patterns of policy perception, and (3) general ideological orientations. Rokkan proposes that this research framework be extended to other occupational groups and to additional countries.

Ross, A. M., and Irwin, D. "Strike Experience in Five Countries, 1927–1947: An Interpretation," *Industrial and Labor Relations Review* 4 (1951): 323–342.
Ross and Irwin measure and compare the volume of strike activity in Australia, the United States, Great Britain, Sweden, and Canada on the basis of existing statistics about the length of strikes, the number of men involved in them, and the number of strikes in each country. The data indicate that the general trend is to greater union size, strength, and strike participation but to shorter strikes with less work time and salary lost. The reasons for this trend are analyzed.

Schapera, I. *Government and Politics in Tribal Societies*. London: C. A. Watts and Company, 1956.
Schapera examines political organization in African tribal societies. He systematically compares the government and politics of the Bushman, Bergdama,

Hottentots, and Southern Bantu. He uses data from his own field work and from other ethnographic sources.

Shanas, E.; Townsend, P.; Wedderburn, D.; Friis, H.; Milhøj, P.; and Stehouwer, J. *Old People in Three Industrial Societies*. New York: Atherton Press, 1968.

This volume is a cross-national survey of living conditions and the behavior of the elderly in Denmark, Britain, and the United States. The focus of the study is on the capacity of the elderly for self-care, the role of the elderly in the family, and the ability of the elderly to provide for themselves. The authors see this as a pilot study setting forth hypotheses on which to base future work.

Zinnes, D. A. "A Comparison of Hostile Behavior of Decision-Makers in Simulated and Historical Data," *World Politics* 18 (1966): 474–502.

Zinnes tests 13 hypotheses about the determinants and consequences of a decision-maker's perceptual framework with simulated and historical data. The units studied are ordered pairs of nations involved in the six-week crisis preceding the outbreak of World War I.

(2) Intra-societal

Alford, R., and Scoble, H. M. *Bureaucracy and Participation: Political Culture in Four Wisconsin Cities*. Chicago: Rand-McNally, 1969.

Alford and Scoble undertake a comparative analysis of four Wisconsin cities to ascertain their levels of governmental bureaucratization and political participation. Interview data from respondents in each of the cities are used to test the hypothesis that greater size is associated with greater bureaucratization and participation. As predicted, Madison is the most bureaucratized and exhibits the most political participation; Green Bay is least bureaucratized and active; Kenosha and Racine fall in the middle.

Dean, L. *Five Towns: A Comparative Community Study*. New York: Random House, 1967.

Dean tests the hypothesis that social systems which differ on socio-economic characteristics vary also in belief systems, especially those that concern political and economic goals, policies, and institutions. Dean bases her study on data from 133 interviews and observations in five U.S. towns.

Kluckhohn, F. R., and Strodtbeck, F. *Variations in Value Orientations*. Evanston: Row, Peterson, 1961.

This volume is an exposition and test of Florence Kluckhohn's theory of variations in value orientations carried out in five communities of the southwestern United States in the so-called "Rimrock" area: a Texan homestead community, a Mormon village, a Spanish-American village, a decentralized Navaho Indian band, and a highly centralized Zuni pueblo. The value orientations studied are four: relation of man to nature, time orientation, activity orientation, and relational orientation. Interview data and ethnographic data are analyzed statistically and graphically to show patterns of variation and to test a general theory of culture.

Lenski, G. *The Religious Factor: A Sociological Study of Religion's Impact on Politics, Economics, and Family Life.*

Lenski develops a theoretical framework for the study of religious associations and behavior, and then analyzes data from interviews with more than 650 Protestants, Catholics, and Jews in Detroit to show the significance of religion for economic, political, and family behavior. The main empirical conclusions are used to assess and qualify the Weber thesis on religious ethics and social action.

Luckmann, T. "Four Protestant Parishes in Germany," *Social Research* 26 (1959): 423–448.

Luckmann uses data from participant observation, interviews, content analysis of conversations, and questionnaires to measure attributes of congregational life in four Protestant parishes in Germany. Luckmann finds inter-parish variations in the process of secularization as well as differences in counter trends to it.

Street, D.; Vinter, R. D.; and Perrow, C. *Organization for Treatment. A Comparative Study of Institutions for Delinquents.* New York: Free Press, 1966.

This study is concerned with the consequences of different goals (traditional custodial vs. modern rehabilitative) for organizational structure, staff perspective and behavior, and inmate behavior. Six juvenile correction instiutions are surveyed in this study. A methodological appendix is included.

Williams. O. P., and Adrian, C. R. *Four Cities: A Study in Comparative Policy Making.* Philadelphia: University of Pennsylvania Press, 1963.

Williams and Adrian observe four cities of similar size, location, and economic base to determine the relationship between policy, the policy formation process, and general community character. They use data from interviews and newspapers in the study, and they develop a typology of local political values.

VII. LARGE *N* COMPARISONS (MORE THAN 12 CASES)

A. *Using Available Data*

(1) Cross-societal

Aberle, D. "Matrilineal Descent in Cross-cultural Perspective," *in* Schneider, D. M., and Gough, K., eds. *Matrilineal Kinship.* Berkeley and Los Angeles: University of California Press, 1961, pp. 655-727.

Aberle uses Murdock's World Ethnographic Sample (WES), supplemented by other ethnographic data, as the basis for a study of matriliny. He concludes after quantitative analysis of the data, including tests of hypotheses proposed by Schneider and Gough, that in general matriliny is associated with horticulture and disappears with plough cultivation. It is inimical to bureaucratization. Many matrilineal systems have transformed their matrilocal characteristics to meet changing conditions.

Abrahamson, M. "Correlates of Political Complexity," *American Sociological Review* 34 (1969): 690-701.

Abrahamson tests cross-cultural hypotheses of political complexity in 38 pre-industrial societies. He develops indices of political complexity and social differentiation, demographic complexity, pervasiveness of kinship organization, socio-economic development, and external threat for the data. He works out the inter-correlations among these factors and concludes that political complexity is most strongly related to degree of social differentiation.

Adelman, I., and Morris, C. T. *Society, Politics, and Economic Development: A Quantitative Approach.* Baltimore: Johns Hopkins Press, 1967.

Adelman and Morris undertake a systematic statistical analysis of aggregate data on social, political, and economic characteristics of 74 nations at different levels of economic development to gain precise empirical knowledge about the inter-relationship of economic and non-economic aspects of development. They use the method of factor analysis on available qualitative and quantitative data from the years 1957-1962.

Banks, A. S., and Textor, R. B. *A Cross-Polity Survey.* Cambridge, Mass.: MIT Press, 1963.

Banks and Textor have compiled a volume which surveys data, arranged by 57 major variables, for all of the 115 independent polities in the world (at the time of the compilation). Nominal and ordinal scales organize the data. The *Survey* is intended to be a research and reference tool.

Barry, H., III; Child, I. L.; and Bacon, M. K. "Relation of Child Training to Subsistence Economy," *American Anthropologist* 61 (1959): 51-63. Also in Ford, C. S., ed. *Cross-Cultural Approaches: Readings in Comparative Research.* New Haven: HRAF Press, 1967, pp. 246-258.

Barry, Child, and Bacon hypothesize that in subsistence societies based on agriculture child training will stress obedience and responsibility—the faithful performance of one's role. In hunting and fishing subsistence societies development of individual initiative and skill—achievement and self-reliance—will be stressed. They test this hypothesis on a sample of 104 societies selected from the World Ethnographic Sample and 110 societies in Bacon and Barry's ratings on socialization. The results substantiate the hypothesis.

Buck, G. L.; and Jacobson, A. L. "Social Evolution and Structural-Functional Analysis: An Empirical Test," *American Sociological Review* 33 (1968): 343-355.

Buck and Jacobson attempt to operationalize the main dimensions contained in the evolutionary model presented by Talcott Parsons in "Evolutionary Universals in Society" (*ASR*, 1964). Data from 50 contemporary societies are organized into Guttman scale rankings and analyzed to test Parsons' major hypotheses. A subsequent typology of the 50 countries is constructed as a basis for identifying the ways in which evolutionary universals are interrelated at varying levels of societal development.

Cutright, P. "National Political Development: Measurement and Analysis," *American Sociological Review* 28 (1963): 253–264.

Cutright constructs an index of political development for 77 countries based on measures of structural complexity, composition of legislative bodies, and form of political leadership. Using this index, he tests the hypothesis that political institutional development is interdependent with level of educational development, urbanization, labor force distribution, communication systems, and economic growth. He finds communication systems to be the variable most closely associated with political development. He gives several examples in the article of how the index can be used predicatively and to shed light on factors influencing political development.

Cutright, P. "Political Structure, Economic Development and National Social Security Programs," *American Journal of Sociology* 70 (1965): 537–550.

Cutright identifies five types of social security programs and makes a Guttman scale of these from available data for 76 nations. Viewing the level of social security development in a country as a direct consequence of government activity, he analyzes the relationship of his social security index to an index measuring political representativeness of the nations and to other indicators of social and economic development. His purpose is to assess the importance of representativeness in governmental organization to social security and welfare of national populations.

Davis, K.; and Golden, H. H. "Urbanization and the Development of Pre-Industrial Areas," *Economic Development and Cultural Change* 3 (1954): 6–26.

Davis and Golden present a historical and comparative overview of urbanization. They examine three underdeveloped countries as case studies in the light of the comparative framework they have established. They view urbanization as an index of economic development and social change, also as a stimulus to change in these areas. They include an appendix describing The World Urban Resources Index.

Driver, H. E.; and Schuessler, K. F. "Correlational Analysis of Murdock's 1957 Ethnographic Sample," *American Anthropologist* 69 (1967): 332–352.

Answering the need to make anthropological data more succinct, Driver and Schuessler apply correlational methods to data from societies included in the World Ethnographic Sample to show relationships among cultural traits. They try to determine whether a small number of factors is responsible for the inter-correlations, establish regional differences in inter-correlations, and consider the tenability of the hypothesis of functional necessity. The article concludes with a methodological note describing the techniques used in the analysis.

Eisenstadt, S. N. *From Generation to Generation: Age Groups and Social Structure.* Glencoe, Ill.: Free Press, 1956.

Eisenstadt presents and examines the thesis that age groups arise and exist only under specific social conditions. He uses comparative data from primitive, historical, and modern societies as a basis for identifying types of age-group systems and their corollaries.

Eisenstadt, S. N. *The Political Systems of Empires*. New York: Free Press, 1963.
Eisenstadt applies sociological concepts to historical data to discover structural and processual patterns in the development of historic bureaucratic empires. Thirty-two systems are examined in terms of institutional inter-dependencies, the relationship between political structure and bureaucratic growth, and the conditions that promote political rationalization. The historical data are transformed into nominal and ordinal scales in a comparative appendix.

Freeman, L. C.; and Winch, R. F. "Societal Complexity: An Empirical Test of a Typology of Societies," *American Journal of Sociology* 62 (1957): 461–466.
Freeman and Winch develop a Guttman scale composed of six traits—punishment, government, education, religion, economy, and written language—to measure societal complexity. The scale was successfully tested on a sample of 48 societies selected from the Human Relations Area Files (HRAF). Freeman and Winch suggest this technique for the empirical testing of polar ideal types.

Gouldner, A. W.; and Peterson, R. A. *Notes on Technology and the Moral Order*. Indianapolis: Bobbs-Merrill, 1962.
The central aim of this study is to explore the potential of factor analysis techniques for the comparative study of institutions. Data from 71 pre-industrial societies are factor analyzed, with four resulting factors. Level of technology and "Apollonianism" account for the highest amount of variation.

Gurr, T. *New Error-Compensated Measures for Comparing Nations: Some Correlates of Civil Violence*. Princeton: Center for International Studies, 1966.
Gurr, T.; and Ruttenberg, C. *The Conditions of Civil Violence: First Tests of a Causal Model*. Princeton: Center for International Studies, 1967.
Gurr, T., and Ruttenberg, C. *Cross-National Studies of Civil Violence*. Washington, D.C.: American University Center for Research in Social Systems, 1969.
These three volumes report various stages of Gurr and Ruttenberg's comparative study of civil violence using aggregate data. The first volume reports on the data and methods developed in the study, especially the optimum-interval concept. The second summarizes initial attempts to evaluate the multivariate theory of causes of civil violence for a large number of polities using aggregate data. The third tests the model developed on all reported outbreaks of civil violence in the world's 119 polities for the 1961–1963 period.

Lipset, S. M. "Some Social Requisites of Democracy: Economic Development and Political Legitimacy," *American Political Science Review* 53 (1959): 69–105.

Lipset examines the relationship between democracy and the state of economic development for four sets of countries: stable democracies and unstable democracies and dictatorships in European and English-speaking nations and in Latin America. Indices of economic development are developed from data on wealth, industrialization, education, and urbanization. Lipset concludes that economic development and democracy are positively correlated. A methodological appendix is included in the article.

Murdock, G. P. "World Ethnographic Sample," *American Anthropologist* 59 (1957): 664–687. Also in Moore, F. W., ed. *Readings in Cross-Cultural Methodology.* New Haven: HRAF Press, 1961, pp. 195–220.

Murdock has compiled and systematically ranked data on major cultural variables for a sample of 565 world societies in six world regions, each of which is subdivided into ten subregions. This systematic sample is intended to be as representative as possible of the entire known range of cultural variation and to function as a source of ethnographic data for comparative research.

Olsen, M. E. "Multivariate Analysis of National Political Development," *American Sociological Review* 33 (1968): 699–712.

Olsen takes a sample of 115 independent nations from Banks and Textor's *A Cross-Polity Survey* (1963) as the basis for this study of the relationship between processes of political and socio-economic development, both of which are viewed as multi-dimensional. He constructs seven indices of political development and multiple regression coefficients for 14 socio-economic variables from the data. Among other things he concludes that the two variables are closely interrelated.

Russett, B. M. *International Regions and the International System: A Study in Political Ecology.* Chicago: Rand McNally, 1967.

Russett uses a wide variety of types of social scientific data and methods to address questions regarding (1) the number of regions needed to describe similarities and differences among nations, (2) the countries found in each grouping, (3) how his constructed groupings compare with conventional classifications, (4) variables for discriminating groupings, and (5) the relevance of the groupings to theories of comparative and international politics.

Russett, B. M.; Alker, H. R., Jr.; Deutsch, K. W.; and Lasswell, H. D. *World Handbook of Political and Social Indicators.* New Haven: Yale University Press, 1964.

This volume was produced out of the Yale Political Data Program to assist in testing hypotheses concerning variables relevant to policy-making. One hundred thirty-three nations are ranked on 75 sets of statistical data, 1958–1963, in the two-part volume. Among the variables for which rankings can be found in the first part are population size and distribution, government and politics, and distribution of wealth and income. The second part of the book is an attempt at the preliminary analysis of the data presented. Data sources include United Nations and government statistics.

Sawyer, J.; and Levine, R. A. "Cultural Dimensions: A Factor Analysis of the World Ethnographic Sample," *American Anthropologist* 68 (1966): 708–731.

Sawyer and Levine attempt to consolidate data from the World Ethnographic Sample into a more concise, but useful form. They scale 30 cultural characteristics of societies in the sample and then show inter-correlations for the worldwide and regional levels. They suggest that characteristics are inter-related on the basis of functional necessity, rather than as a result of historical diffusion.

Swanson, G. *The Birth of the Gods: The Origin of Primitive Beliefs*. Ann Arbor: University of Michigan Press, 1960.

Swanson specifies Durkheim's theory of religion on the relationship between social structure and belief systems as a basis for an empirical study of society and the supernatural in 50 systematically selected societies. The study is focused principally on the ways in which sovereign groups are associated with beliefs in high gods, ancestral spirits, and reincarnated souls. Theories of religion are assessed on the basis of these findings.

Udy, S. H., Jr. *Organization of Work: A Comparative Analysis of Production Among Nonindustrial People*. New Haven: HRAF Press, 1959.

Based on HRAF data on 426 production organizations in 150 nonindustrial societies, Udy establishes seven types of production organization and constructs an index of technological complexity for ranking organizational types. He then tests 64 propositions about the relationship of technology to the organizational structure of work.

Whiting, B. "A Cross-Cultural Study of Sorcery and Social Control," *in* Whiting, B. *Paiute Sorcery*. New York: Viking Fund Publications in Anthropology, No. 15 (1950), pp. 82–91.

Whiting uses data from the Cross-Cultural Survey for 50 societies. She dichotomizes the societies along two sets of two variables: presence of superordinate justice and importance of sorcery, and superordinate punishment and importance of sorcery, in an attempt to determine the nature of the relationship between sorcery and social control.

Whiting, J. W. M.; and Child, I. L. *Child Training and Personality*. New Haven: Yale University Press, 1953.

Whiting and Child examine personality as an intervening variable between two aspects of culture—child training and responses to illness. They use the comparative method to test general hypotheses about five systems of behavior—oral, anal, sexual, dependence, and aggression—all assumed to be universal and subject to socialization. They use three judges to rank the HRAF cultures in terms of initial indulgences and later discipline. They find, ultimately, that variations in the response to illness of individuals in a society are products of personality differences among the individuals, which in turn stem from patterns of childhood socialization.

Young, F. W. *Initiation Ceremonies: A Cross-Cultural Study of Status Dramatization.* Indianapolis: Bobbs-Merrill, 1965.
Young tests the hypothesis that the degree of solidarity of a given social system determines the degree to which status transitions will be dramatized in it. He undertakes multivariate analysis of ethnographic data to test this proposition in a non-random sample of societies.

Zelditch, M., Jr. "Role Differentiation in the Nuclear Family: A Comparative Study," *in* Parsons, T.; and Bales, R. and others. *Family, Socialization and Interaction Process.* New York: Free Press, 1955, pp. 307–352.
Based on Parsons and Bales' theory, Zelditch begins with the assumption that the nuclear family is discernible in all societies. He tests two hypotheses about differentiation in the nuclear family in a carefully specified sample of 56 societies. He concludes (with noted exceptions) that when the nuclear family can be distinguished from its incorporating solidarities, differentiation and role allocation occur as would be expected from his hypotheses and the Parsons-Bales theory.

(2) Intra-societal

Anderson, T. R.; and Warkov, S. "Organizational Size and Functional Complexity: A Study of Administration in Hospitals." *American Sociological Review* 26 (1961): 23–28.
Anderson and Warkov study a sample of 51 Veterans Administration hospitals divided into two categories: general medical and surgical hospitals and tuberculosis hospitals. Contrary to earlier results, their findings indicate that relative size of the administrative component decreases as size increases. But, it increases with an increase in the number of tasks performed in a place or as the number of places where work is performed increases. Data for the study were taken from the monthly Veterans Administration reports of the number of hospital personnel in various structural capacities.

Blau, P. M.; Heydebrand, W. V.; and Stauffer, R. E. "The Structure of Small Bureaucracies," *American Sociological Review* 31 (1966): 179–191.
Based on available data about 156 American personnel agencies, this study analyzes relations among four dichotomous structural variables of bureaucracies and their implications for operations. Among the conclusions reached is that centralized authority increases with an increase in bureaucratic size only within a less professionalized bureaucratic structure.

Hawley, A. H. "Community Power and Urban Renewal Success," *American Journal of Sociology* 68 (1963): 422–431.
Hawley tests the hypothesis that ratios of managers, proprietors, and operators to employed labor force are lowest in urban renewal cities at the stage of executing their programs and highest in cities which have not attempted urban

renewal. He uses available data to test this hypothesis in cities of 50,000 or more. His focus is on power as a feature of social systems, not an individual attribute.

B. Using Survey Data

(1) Cross-societal

Haire, M.; Ghiselli, E. E.; and Porter, L. W. *Managerial Thinking: An International Study*. New York: John Wiley and Sons, 1966.

This study surveys 3,641 managers in 14 countries to determine variations in attitudes toward management by country and by clusters of countries. Findings indicate that although a high degree of similarity exists in managers' attitudes, about 25 percent of the variation that was found was related to national differences.

McClelland, D. C. *The Achieving Society*. Princeton: D. Van Nostrand, 1961.

McClelland attempts to isolate and show the importance of psychological factors in economic development and decline. Data on achievement motivation, drawn from respondent samples and the content analysis of historical and cultural materials are correlated with indices of economic development for a wide range of past and present societies. McClelland's evidence underlies the importance of psychological variables and provides him with a basis for exploring policy implications.

(2) Intra-societal

Clark, T. N. "Community Structure, Decision-Making, Budget Expenditures, and Urban Renewal in 51 American Communities," *American Sociological Review* 33 (1968): 576–593.

Clark compares 51 cities in 22 states with regard to four issue areas: urban renewal, mayoral elections, air pollution, and poverty programs, using data from informant interviews, censuses, and other demographic sources. He uses the data to test a series of propositions relating community structure to decision-making, budgetary, and urban renewal patterns.

Hall, R. H.; Haas, J. E.; and Johnson, N. J. "Organizational Size, Complexity, and Formalization," *American Sociological Review* 32 (1967): 903–912.

For this study data from tape-recorded interviews were collected from informants in 75 organizations ranging from six to 9,000 members in size. When organizations were grouped by size and in terms of four variables of complexity and five of formalization, there was a slight tendency for larger organizations to be the more complex and more formal. The authors conclude that size may be a more important variable for the study of morale and inter-organizational relations than it is for formality or complexity.

Smith, C. G., and Tannenbaum, A. S. "Organizational Control Structure: A Comparative Analysis," *Human Relations* 16 (1963): 299–316.

Smith and Tannenbaum compare 200 geographically separate organizational units to study organizational control processes and their implications. They use this survey method of data collection and a control graph method for data analysis.

Turk, H. "Interorganizational Networks in Urban Society: Initial Perspectives and Comparative Research," *American Sociological Review* 35 (1970): 1–19.

Turk undertakes a controlled, longitudinal study of inter-organizational networks in 130 U.S. cities. Data analysis in the study indicates that extra-local integration of a city can be used to predict the activity level of a new inter-organizational network with both local and non-local elements. The success of this study points to inter-organizational systems as a useful variable for comparative macro-sociological research.

Woodward, J. *Industrial Organization: Theory and Practice.* London: Oxford University Press, 1965.

Woodward surveys 100 small firms in England followed by case studies of 20 firms. Her findings indicate that the technology of production is a greater determinant of the hierarchical and administrative structure of an organization than was previously recognized. Woodward's volume provides a chronological account of the research and developments it made in the direction of revamping classical management theory.

INDEX